THE PAPERS OF

James Madison

SPONSORED BY

The University of Virginia

"The Old Capitol," Richmond, built in 1780 and used by the General Assembly until 1788 as its meeting place. From a woodcut in the Richmond *Dispatch*, 21 May 1885. (Courtesy of the Valentine Museum, Richmond.)

THE PAPERS OF

James Madison

VOLUME 8

10 MARCH 1784—28 MARCH 1786

EDITED BY

ROBERT A. RUTLAND   WILLIAM M. E. RACHAL

BARBARA D. RIPEL   FREDRIKA J. TEUTE

THE UNIVERSITY OF CHICAGO PRESS

CHICAGO AND LONDON

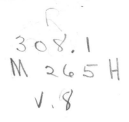
The Papers of James Madison have been edited with financial aid from the Ford and Rockefeller Foundations, the National Archives Trust Fund, and the General Assembly of the Commonwealth of Virginia. From 1956 until 1970 the editorial staff was maintained jointly by the University of Chicago and the University of Virginia.

The University of Chicago Press, Chicago 60637
The University of Chicago Press, Ltd., London

International Standard Book Number: 0-226-50104-3
Library of Congress Catalog Card Number: 62-9114

To
ADRIENNE KOCH
1912–1971

CONTENTS

CONTENTS

CONTENTS

CONTENTS

CONTENTS

1786

CONTENTS

ILLUSTRATIONS

INTRODUCTION

When James Madison returned to Montpelier after over three years in the Continental Congress, he faced a delicate decision. The orange-brown acres of the Piedmont estate needed overseeing, but Madison's father and brothers had that business well in hand. There was no seat of higher learning closer than William and Mary, and another James Madison already presided at that academic cloister. Neither farming nor scholarship beckoned Madison as a means of livelihood, so he had to think about his future place in society. He still considered (not too seriously) the idea of reading for a career in law. The spring elections of 1784 made the choice for Madison, however; or rather his neighbors, the Orange County electors, eliminated the sources of doubt. Political life came naturally to Madison and there was much work left before the unsettling question deep-rooted in his consciousness would find a solution. To some extent the remainder of Madison's life would be pledged to a positive answer to the query: Could the American Revolution fulfill its promise to better mankind? By 1784 some evidence indicated that the Revolutionary ardor was only a flare soon to be extinguished, leaving Americans to struggle unguided in the darkness.

The tragic implications of a failure were never far from Madison's mind. Thus when he returned from Philadelphia in the late fall of 1783, the path he took at the crossroads of his life—he was thirty-two years old—was predetermined. Had Madison loved land the way that most Virginians did, he might have joined many of his Orange County neighbors who were heading west to the cheap and fertile acres of the Kentucky district. Many of the brightest minds were attracted to the banks of the Ohio, so that Virginia was all the poorer for the migration of the Barbours, Breckinridges, Marshalls, Nicholases, and others who would soon cast their lot across the Cumberland Mountains. Madison believed, as Benjamin Rush and others did, that the Revolution was only partly accomplished and that the remaining job was to realize the full promise of the Revolution. "This is the most difficult part of the business of the patriots and legislators of our country," Rush told an Englishman, and Madison knew the truth of this opinion from his own experience.[1]

Let it be remembered that in 1784 the Virginia legislature was one of the most powerful political bodies in the United States. The Virginia Constitution of 1776 left most of the power in the legislative hands, and more particularly in the House of Delegates, so that in this largest and most populous state of the Union the roll call, extending from Accomack through York counties, brought decisions affecting the lives of some 600,000 citizens and slaves. In terms of power, Madison was in a position to be more effective as an Orange County delegate than as a Virginia representative in Congress. Congressmen talked a lot but they were frustrated by a lack of authority that hampered vigorous, dynamic government. In 1784 the states had no intention of loosening their grip on the reins of power and it was readily argued that the Confederation, however loose and weak it appeared, had sustained a war effort so well its Articles needed only mending and patching to become "a venerable fabrick."

Madison knew better, of course, and as an influential delegate in the state legislature he was not bothered by some of the concerns diluting the abilities of other Virginians. For one thing, he was not trying to make a killing in land speculation; for another, he was not eager to perpetuate the one-crop system that was strangling the state's cash economy. Above all, Madison's commitment was to give the revolutionary ideal of republican government practical embodiment in both state and national governments. With long experience in state and congressional politics he had learned that a powerful opponent such as Patrick Henry should be outmaneuvered, not publicly whipped. For a time Madison nursed his favored ideas and avoided a head-on collision with certain reactionary forces in Virginia akin to her rivers—numerous, divergent, and shallow. After a year, Madison helped move Henry out of the way by "kicking him upstairs" into the largely ceremonial job of governor. The tactic weakened the core of localistic opposition. The years 1784–1785 became one of the most exciting times in the state's legislative history, in part because Madison persisted on behalf of measures dealing with the much-needed revision of the Virginia legal code, the Mississippi and Kentucky problems, the nation's financial distress, and efforts to shore up the decaying edifice of a state-supported religion.

Madison was operating independently. His good friend Jefferson was

[1] Rush to Richard Price, 25 May 1786, Butterfield, *Letters of Benjamin Rush,* I, 388.

no longer at Monticello or sitting at the next desk. His great and good colleague was assigned to foreign service, and for five years they would consult each other only through correspondence. But what a correspondence—rich in political discourses and candid in part because of their own private coding device that permitted words which were not meant for the prying eyes of a postmaster or an adversary. The beginnings of what became a lifelong trail of exemplary letters fall in this period when Madison was keeping his own counsel and then relaying the panorama of Virginia life to Paris.

Routine matters took time, but in the Virginia of the 1780s there was no particular premium on days or months. From March, when the fresh-plowed earth spread an aroma of spring, until fall rains clogged the muddy roads, there was time at Montpelier to read and reflect; and when the frosts came Madison was back in Richmond working for his Orange County neighbors in the best way he could—as a devoted friend to the Union. There was time for a trip up the Hudson, and a summer swing through the North when the weather at home—as his father recorded—was "hot, very humid." If there were parties and gaiety at Montpelier, we hear little of it, for Madison was a serious-minded correspondent who even amid congenial company avoided family chitchat and probably made a better spectator than player in the card games that occupied after-dinner hours on winter nights. The surviving records tell us nothing of Madison's interest in the belles of Orange or Richmond and allow only speculation on his innermost thoughts as his friend Monroe took a wife and the bachelor ranks thinned.

This phase of Madison's life had many rewards and few setbacks. One accomplishment in particular during the period between March 1784 and February 1786 has left its mark on history—his Memorial and Remonstrance against a bill to subsidize religious instruction. Although further research on this petition, which Madison wrote in the spring of 1785, indicates that it was not the sole protest or main reason the bill (patronized by Henry) failed, still the Memorial and Remonstrance summarized the thinking of a majority of the enlightened citizens of Virginia and left its impression in other parts of the new nation. On the heels of a rejection of the subsidy bill, Madison was able to marshal support for Jefferson's 1779 statute for religious freedom which passed at the same session of the General Assembly. Taken in tandem, the two documents signaled a fresh approach to religious freedom which would not be lost on other men in other places.

In writing Jefferson about the accomplishments of the October 1785 legislative session, Madison recorded some disappointments, but on the whole it was clear that he was an effective legislator trusted by Washington, envied by Henry, and much admired by Edmund Randolph and other young men poised for public service. Curiously, he was not an early supporter for the proposed national conference at Annapolis, but as Volume VIII concludes we will see that Madison's thought turned expectantly to the forthcoming meeting. Apathy seemed to be the nation's chief problem, and any effort to strengthen the Confederation deserved attention. Busy days lay ahead.

EDITORIAL NOTE

William T. Hutchinson retired on 31 December 1970 after over fourteen years of distinguished service as senior editor of the *Papers of James Madison*, and Robert L. Scribner left the project in September 1971 after thirteen years as an editorial associate. Both gentlemen left their scholarly imprint on the first seven volumes in an indelible fashion. The present editors, more perhaps than any other historians of this generation interested in Madison's career, came to know of the prodigious effort these gentlemen made and to admire their fortitude and dedication. Miss Jean Schneider, also a diligent scholar who from the beginning of the project presided over the office insuring both accuracy and order, supervised the moving of materials from the University of Chicago to Charlottesville. She remained there until the new staff was familiar with her systematic arrangement of over 21,000 documents.

During 1971 the profession generally, and this project in particular, lost a giant in the death of Adrienne Koch. Miss Koch, to whom this volume is dedicated, served briefly on the Advisory Board but had always been busy with scholarly concerns that related to Madison's life. Her death was a grievous loss for all historians, but for those who had come to know and love her as a warm, singular human being, it was indeed tragic.

In addition to the Advisory Board members who assisted the project with helpful advice and suggestions, the editors are also indebted to Mr. Sol Feinstone of Washington Crossing, Pennsylvania, for generous permission to use documents in his collection deposited at the American Philosophical Society Library; and to Mr. Irby B. Cauthen, Jr., Charles Cullen, Atcheson L. Hench, Donald Jackson, Virginia Moore, George H. Reese, Dorothy Twohig, and Patricia Watlington for their scholarly assistance. The staff's gratitude to these scholars and friends is incalculable.

EDITORIAL METHOD

The editors have sought to follow the original texts of documents with scrupulous fidelity, but several exceptions should be noted. Superior letters have been brought down, thorns ("ye," "yt," "yn,") as well as words with a tilde ("comissrs" and "comitee.") have been expanded, and confusing punctuation has been eliminated. The first letter of a sentence is invariably capitalized, regardless of the writer's eccentricities. Inconsequential decoding errors made by Madison, Jefferson, or Monroe in their ciphered correspondence have been ignored, but substantial mistakes have been corrected (with brackets) or annotated. Obvious slips of the pen, usually repeated words, are silently corrected. Long dashes or gaps have been interpreted to indicate a new paragraph. Beyond these exceptions, alterations are noted in textual footnotes. The dateline has been placed at the head of a document, regardless of its position in the original manuscript. Missing manuscripts for which some clue as to their contents exists have been calendared, but those lost items for which there is no hint of their purpose are recognized in a footnote. Legislative matters that were not of particular concern to Madison but which he handled in perfunctory fashion are calendared in Appendix A of this volume.

Several changes in format appear in this volume which are deviations from the practice followed in Volumes I through VII. The note dealing with provenance, cover, docket, and other markings, formerly at the head of each document, is now at the end of each document, preceding the annotations. The abbreviated method of citing major libraries, as set forth in *Symbols of American Libraries* (Washington, 1969) is used, and DLC—standing alone—is employed throughout to cite the Madison Papers in the Library of Congress. Otherwise, collections in the Library of Congress are cited as they are specifically designated. The location symbols most frequently used in this volume are:

Vi   Virginia State Library, Richmond

ViHi   Virginia Historical Society, Richmond

ViU   University of Virginia Library, Charlottesville

ViW   College of William and Mary Library, Williamsburg

DNA   National Archives, Washington

NN   New York Public Library, New York City

PPAmP American Philosophical Society, Philadelphia

CSmH Henry E. Huntington Library, San Marino, California

ABBREVIATIONS

FC   File copy. Any version of a letter or other document retained by the sender for his own files and differing little if at all from the completed version. A draft, on the other hand, is a preliminary sketch, often incomplete and varying frequently in expression from the finished version.

JM   James Madison.

Ms   Manuscript. A catchall term describing numerous reports and other papers written by Madison, as well as items sent to him which were not letters.

PCC Papers of the Continental Congress, a collection in the National Archives.

RC   Recipient's copy. The copy of a letter intended to be read by the addressee. If the handwriting is not that of the sender, this fact is mentioned.

Tr   Transcript. A copy of a manuscript, or a copy of a copy, customarily handwritten, made considerably later than the date of the manuscript and ordinarily not by its author or by the person to whom the original was addressed.

SHORT TITLES FOR BOOKS AND OTHER FREQUENTLY CITED MATERIALS

In addition to these short titles, bibliographical entries are abbreviated if a work has been cited in the previous volumes.

AHR. American Historical Review.

Boyd, *Papers of Jefferson.* Julian P. Boyd et al., eds., *The Papers of Thomas Jefferson* (18 vols. to date; Princeton, N. J., 1950——).

Brant, *Madison.* Irving Brant, *James Madison* (6 vols.; Indianapolis and New York, 1941–61).

Burnett, *Letters.* Edmund C. Burnett, ed., *Letters of Members of the Continental Congress* (8 vols.; Washington, 1921–36).

Cal. of Va. State Papers. William P. Palmer et al., eds., *Calendar of Virginia State Papers and Other Manuscripts* (11 vols.; Richmond, 1875–93).

Evans. Charles Evans, ed., *American Bibliography* ... *1639* ... *1820* (12 vols.; Chicago, 1903–34).

Executive Letter Book. Executive Letter Book, 1783–1786, manuscript in Virginia State Library.

Fitzpatrick, *Writings of Washington*. John C. Fitzpatrick, ed., *The Writings of George Washington, from the Original Sources, 1745–1799* (39 vols.; Washington, 1931–44).

Gwathmey, *Historical Register of Virginians*. John H. Gwathmey, *Historical Register of Virginians in the Revolution: Soldiers, Sailors, Marines, 1775–1783* (Richmond, 1938).

Heitman, *Historical Register Continental*. F. B. Heitman, *Historical Register of Officers of the Continental Army during the War of the Revolution* (Washington, 1914).

Hening, *Statutes*. William Waller Hening, ed., *The Statutes at Large; Being a Collection of All the Laws of Virginia, from the First Session of the Legislature, in the Year 1619* (13 vols.; Richmond and Philadelphia, 1819–23).

JCC. Worthington Chauncey Ford et al., eds., *Journals of the Continental Congress, 1774–1789* (34 vols.; Washington, 1904–37).

JCSV. H. R. McIlwaine et al., eds., *Journals of the Council of the State of Virginia* (4 vols. to date; Richmond, 1931——).

JHDV. *Journal of the House of Delegates of the Commonwealth of Virginia; Begun and Held at the Capitol, in the City of Williamsburg*. Beginning in 1780, the portion after the semicolon reads, *Begun and Held in the Town of Richmond. In the County of Henrico*. The journal for each session has its own title page and is individually paginated. The edition used is the one in which the journals for 1777–1786 are brought together in two volumes, with each journal published in Richmond in either 1827 or 1828 and often called the "Thomas W. White reprint."

Madison, *Letters* (Cong. ed.). [William C. Rives and Philip R. Fendall, eds.], *Letters and Other Writings of James Madison* (published by order of Congress; 4 vols.; Philadelphia, 1865).

Madison, *Papers* (Gilpin ed.). Henry D. Gilpin, ed., *The Papers of James Madison* (3 vols.; Washington, 1840).

Madison, *Writings* (Hunt ed.). Gaillard Hunt, ed., *The Writings of James Madison* (9 vols.; New York, 1900–1910).

Papers of Madison. William T. Hutchinson et al., eds., *The Papers of James Madison* (8 vols. to date; Chicago, 1962——).

Sabin. Joseph Sabin et al., eds., *Bibliotheca Americana* . . . (29 vols.; New York and Portland, Me., 1868–1936).

Swem and Williams, *Register*. Earl G. Swem and John W. Williams, eds., *A Register of the General Assembly of Virginia, 1776–1918, and of the Constitutional Conventions* (Richmond, 1918).

Syrett and Cooke, *Papers of Hamilton*. Harold C. Syrett and Jacob E. Cooke, eds., *The Papers of Alexander Hamilton* (15 vols. to date; New York, 1961——).

Va. Gazette. Virginia Gazette, or, the American Advertiser (Richmond, James Hayes 1781–86).

VMHB. Virginia Magazine of History and Biography.

Wharton, *Revol. Dipl. Corr.* Francis Wharton, ed., *The Revolutionary Diplomatic Correspondence of the United States* (6 vols.; Washington, 1889).

WMQ. William and Mary Quarterly.

MADISON CHRONOLOGY

1784

March	At home in Orange County.
1 April	Begins making entries in meteorological journal in Orange County.
ca. 4–13 May	Arrives in Richmond and takes seat in House of Delegates.
1 July	May 1784 session of General Assembly ends.
1–5 July	In Richmond on private business.
ca. 5–8 July	Returns home to Orange County.
ca. 25–28 August	Departs Orange for Baltimore.
ca. 1–2 September	Arrives in Baltimore.
3 September	Departs Baltimore with Lafayette for Philadelphia.
4 September	Arrives in Philadelphia.
9 September	Departs Philadelphia for Trenton.
10 September	In Trenton.
11 September	In New York.
15 September	Departs New York with Lafayette's party for Albany.
23 September	In Albany.
28 September	Departs Albany for Fort Schuyler to witness Indian treaty.
29 September	At Fort Schuyler.
30 September– 1 October	Visits Oneida reservation with Lafayette.
2 October	At Fort Schuyler.
7 October	Descends Mohawk Valley with Lafayette's party.
8 October	In Albany; parts with Lafayette to return to New York.
11 October	Departs New York for Philadelphia.

17 October	In Philadelphia.
1 November	In Richmond; takes seat in House of Delegates.

1785

7 January	October 1784 session of General Assembly ends.
ca. 7–22 January	Reads law in the library of Attorney-General Edmund Randolph.
21 January	Elected member of American Philosophical Society.
ca. 23 January– 8 February	Returns to Montpelier in Orange County.
March–August	At home in Orange County.
ca. 20 June	Writes Memorial and Remonstrance.
ca. 31 August	Departs Orange to travel north.
3–5 September	Visits at Mount Vernon.
ca. 7 September	Arrives in Philadelphia.
ca. 21–22 September	Departs Philadelphia for New York.
ca. 22 September– 1 October	In New York.
2 October	Arrives in Philadelphia.
ca. 5 October	Departs Philadelphia for Virginia.
12–14 October	Visits at Mount Vernon.
25 October	Takes seat in House of Delegates.

1786

21 January	1785 session of General Assembly ends.
30 January	Returns to Orange County.
February–March	At home in Orange County.

THE PAPERS OF

James Madison

To Edmund Randolph

Orange March 10th. 1784

My dear friend

Your favor of the 27th. Jany. was safely delivered to me about a fourtnight ago, and was recd. with the greater pleasure, as it promises a continuance of your friendly attention. I am sorry that my situation enables me to stipulate no other return than sincere & thankful acknowledgments. On my arrival here which happened early in Decr. I entered as soon as the necessary attentions to my friends admitted, on the course of reading which I have long meditated. Co: Litt: in consequence & a few others from the same shelf have been my chief society during the Winter.[1] My progress, which in so short a period, could not have been great under the most favorable circumstances, has been much retarded by the want of some important books, and still more by that of some living oracle for occasional consultation. But what will be most noxious to my project, I am to incur the interruptions wch. will result from attendance in the legislature, if the suffrage of my County should destine me for that service, which I am made to expect will be the case.[2] Among the circumstances which reconcile me to this destination, you need not be assured that the opportunity of being in your neighbourhood has its full influence.

I have perused with both pleasure and edification your observations on the demand made by the Executive of S. C. of a citizen of this State.[3] If I were to hazard an opinion after yours, it would be that the respect due to the chief magistracy of a confederate State, enforced as it is by the articles of Union, requires an admission of the fact as it has been represented. If the representation be judged incomplete or ambiguous, explanations may certainly be called for; and if on a final view of the charge, Virginia should hold it to be not a casus fœderis, she will be at liberty to withold her citizen, (at least upon that ground) as S. C. will be to appeal to the Tribunal provided for all controversies among the States. Should the Law of S. C. happen to vary from the British Law, the most difficult point of discussion I apprehend will be, whether the terms "Treason &c." are to be referred to those determinate offences so denominated in the latter Code, or to all those to which the policy of the several States may annex the same titles and penalties. Much may be urged I think both in favor of and agst. each of these expositions. The two first of those terms coupled with "breach of the peace" are used in the 5 art: of the Confederation, but in a way that does not clear

3

the ambiguity. The truth perhaps in this as in many other instances, is, that if the Compilers of the text had severally declared their meanings, these would have been as diverse as the comments which will be made upon it.

Wa[i]ving the doctrine of the confederation, my present view of the subject would admit few exceptions to the propriety of surrendering fugitive offenders. My reasons are these: 1. By the express terms of the Union the Citizens of every State are naturalized within all the others, and being entitled to the same privileges, may with the more justice be Subjected to the same penalties.[4] This circumstance materially distinguishes the Citizens of the U. S. from the subjects of other nations not so incorporated. 2. The analogy of the laws throughout the States, and particularly the uniformity of trial by Juries of the vicinage, seem to obviate the capital objections agst. removal to the State where the offence is charged. In the instance of contiguous States a removal of the party accused from one to the other must often be a less grievance, than what happens within the same State when the place of residence & the place where the offence is laid are at distant extremities. The transportation to G. B. seems to have been reprobated on very different grounds: it would have deprived the accused of the privilege of trial by jury *of the vicinage* as well as of the use of his witnesses, and have exposed him to trial in a place where he was not even alledged to have ever made himself obnoxious to it; not to mention the danger of unfairness arising from the circumstances which produced the regulation.[5] 3. Unless Citizens of one State transgressing within the pale of another be given up to be punished by the latter, they cannot be punished at all; and it seems to be a common interest of the States that a few hours or at most a few days should not be sufficient to gain a sanctuary for the authors of the numerous offences below "high misdemeanors." In a word, experience will shew if I mistake not that the relative situation of the U. S. calls for a "Droit Public" much more minute than that comprised in the fœderal articles, and which presupposes much greater mutual confidence and amity among the Societies which are to obey it, than the law which has grown out of the transactions & intercourse of jealous & hostile Nations.[6]

Present my respectful compliments to your amiable lady & accept the sincerest wishes for your joint happinesses

Yr. affe. friend & Obt. Servt

J. MADISON JR.

4

P. S. By my brother who is charged with this I send Chattelleux's work de la Felicetè public which you may perhaps find leisure to run through before May—also a notable work of one of the Representatives of the U. S. in Europe.[7]

RC (DLC). Addressed. Docketed by Randolph.

[1] An allusion to Sir Edward Coke's *The First Part Of The Institutes of the Lawes of England, Or, A Commentarie upon Littleton,* a standard legal treatise for JM's generation (*Papers of Madison,* I, 108, 110 n. 4).

[2] The voters of Orange County on 22 Apr. chose JM and Charles Porter to be their representatives in the session of the Virginia House of Delegates, scheduled to convene 3 May (Vi: Certificate of Election, 26 Apr. 1784; *JHDV,* May 1784, p. 3).

[3] For the alleged assault in South Carolina upon a public official of that state by George Hancock, a citizen of Virginia, for the provisions of Article IV of the Articles of Confederation to which JM referred near the opening of his paragraph, and for Randolph's view of the issue, see *Papers of Madison,* VII, 415–18 n. 2. JM agreed with Randolph that Governor Benjamin Harrison of Virginia should await further information from Governor Benjamin Guerard of South Carolina before deciding whether Hancock should be extradited to South Carolina. However, unlike Randolph, JM centered the matter at issue upon the meaning of "high misdemeanor" as used in the Articles of Confederation (casus fœderis) rather than upon the possible divergence between the laws of South Carolina and Virginia in defining that offense.

In his letter of 27 Jan., Randolph had posed a hypothetical case involving a British subject who broke a French law and then fled "to his own country." Randolph also expressed doubt whether Harrison needed to extradite Hancock if his alleged offense, even though a "high misdemeanor" by the law of South Carolina, was not within that category as defined by the law of Virginia. On this point JM held that in extradition proceedings the governor of the state to which the offender had fled should accept upon proof the designation given to his offense by the governor of the state in which the alleged crime had been committed. If, however, Harrison refused to extradite Hancock, the matter would become a controversy between two sovereign states, within the purview of Article IX of the Articles of Confederation.

[4] In using the term "naturalized," JM somewhat overstated the intent of Article IV of the Articles of Confederation. He referred to the passage: "The better to secure and perpetuate mutual friendship and intercourse among the people of the different states in this union, the free inhabitants of each of these states, paupers, vagabonds and fugitives from justice excepted, shall be entitled to all privileges and immunities of free citizens in the several states" (*JCC,* XIX, 214–15). A Virginia statute, enacted on 26 June 1779 and entitled "An act declaring who shall be deemed citizens of this commonwealth," included provisions for the extradition of "Fugitives from Justice, in other states" (*JHDV,* May 1779, p. 70; Hening, *Statutes,* X, 129–30). The statute of Dec. 1783, which specifically repealed the one of 1779 and defined anew those persons who were or who were not eligible to become citizens of Virginia omitted any reference to extradition (*JHDV,* Oct. 1783, pp. 69, 70, 81; Hening, *Statutes,* XI, 322–24).

[5] JM referred to the Transportation Act of May 1774, which empowered the royal governor or lieutenant governor, "with the Advice and Consent of the Council," to have any person who was charged with "Murther, or other capital Crime" in resisting the revenue acts of Parliament removed from Massachusetts for trial

in "some other of his Majesty's Colonies, or in *Great Britain*" (*Statutes at Large* [1776 ed.], XII, 75–77).

6 JM used "Droit Public" in contrast to "droit des gens" (international law).

7 The brother was probably William Madison, then twenty-two years of age. JM sent François Jean, Chevalier de Chastellux, *De la félicité publique, ou, Considérations sur le sort des hommes dans les différentes époques de l'histoire* (2 vols.; Amsterdam, 1772; 2d ed.; 2 vols., corrected and augmented; Bouillon, 1776); Henry Laurens, *Mr. Lauren's True State of the Case. By Which His Candor to Mr. Edmund Jenings is Manifested, and the Tricks of Mr. Jenings are Detected* (privately printed; London, 1783). This notable "work" was a rejoinder to a published attack on Laurens by Jenings in a pamphlet of "about forty pages of misrepresentation and falsehood" (Wharton, *Revol. Dipl. Corr.,* VI, 694).

To Thomas Jefferson

ORANGE March 16. 1784

DEAR SIR

Your favour of the 20. Ult. came duly to hand a few days ago. I can not apprehend that any difficulties can ensue in Europe from the involuntary & immaterial delay of the ratification of the peace, or if there should that any imputations can be devised which will not be repelled by the collective force of the reasons in the intended protest; some of which singly taken are unanswerable. As you no doubt had recourse to authorities which I have no opportunity of consulting, I probably err, in supposing the right of the Sovereign to reject the act of his Plenipotentiary to be more circumscribed than you lay it down.[1] I recollect well that an implied condition is annexed by the usage of Nations to a Plenipotentiary commission, but should not have extended the implication beyond cases where some palpable & material default in the minister could be alledged by the Sovereign. Wa[i]ving some such plea the language both of the Commission and of reason seems to fix on the latter as clear an engagement to fulfil his *promise* to ratify a treaty, as to fulfil the *promises* of a treaty which he has ratified.[2] In both cases one would pronounce the obligation equally personal to the Sovereign, and a failure on his part without some absolving circumstance, equally a breach of faith. The project of affixing the Seal of the U. S. by 7 States to an Act *which had been just admitted to require nine,*[3] must have stood self-condemned; and tho' it might have produced a temporary deception abroad, must have been immediately detected at home, and have finally dishonored the fœderal Councils everywhere. The competency of 7 States to a Treaty of Peace has often been a subject of debate in Congress and has sometimes been admitted into their practice,

6

at least so far as to issue fresh instructions. The reasoning employed in defence of the doctrine has been "that the cases which require 9 States, being exceptions to the general authority of 7 States, ought to be taken strictly; that in the enumeration of the powers of Congress in the first clause of art: 9. of the Confederation, the power of entering into treaties and alliances is contradistinguished from that of determining on peace & war & even separated by the intervening power of sending & receiving ambassadors; that the excepting clause therefore in which "Treaties & alliances" ought to be taken in the same confined sense, and in which the power of determining on peace is omitted, cannot be extended by construction to the latter power; that under such a construction 5 States might continue a war which it required nine to commence, though where the object of the war has been obtained, a continuance must in every view be equipollent to a commencement of it; and that the very means provided for preserving a state of peace might thus become the means of preventing its restoration." The answer to these arguments has been that the construction of the fœderal articles which they maintain is a nicety which reason disclaims, and that if it be dangerous on one side to leave it in the breast of 5 States to protract a war, it is equally necessary on the other to restrain 7 States from saddling the Union with any stipulations which they may please to interweave with a Treaty of peace. I was once led by this question to search the files of Congs. for such lights as the history of the Confederation might furnish, and on a review now of my papers I find the evidence from that source to consist of the following circumstances: In Doctr. F.s. "Sketch of Articles of Confederation" laid before Congs. on 21 day of July 1775. no number beyond a majority is required in any cases.[4] In the plan reported to Congress by the Committee appointed 11. June 1776. the general enumeration of the powers of Congs. in Art: 18. is expressed in a similar manner with the first clause in the present 9th art:, as are the exceptions in a subsequent clause of the 18 art: of the report, with the excepting clause as it now stands: and yet in the Margin of the Report and I believe in the same hand writing, there is a "Qu: If so large a majority is necessary in concluding a Treaty of peace." There are sundry other marginal queries in the report from the same pen. Hence it would seem that notwithstanding the preceding discrimination between the powers of "determining on peace" and "entering into Treaties," the latter was meant by the Come. to comprise the former. The next form in which the articles appear, is a printed copy of the Report as it had been previously amended, with sundry amendments, erasures & notes on the printed copy itself in the hand of Mr. Thomson. In the printed text of this paper art: 14. the phraseology which defines the general powers of Congress is the same with that in art: 18 of the manuscript report. In the subsequent clause requiring nine States, the text as printed ran thus: "The United States in Congs. assembled shall never engage in a war nor grant letters of marque & reprisal in time of peace, nor enter into any Treaties or alliances except for peace," the words *except for peace* being erased, but sufficiently legible through the erasure. The fair inference from this passage seems to be 1. that without those words 9 States were held to be required for concluding peace. 2. that an attempt had been made to render 7 States competent to such an act, which attempt must have succeeded either on a preceding discussion in Congress or in a Come. of the whole, or a special Come. 3. that on fuller deliberation the power of making Treaties of peace was meant to be left on the same footing with that of making all other Treaties. The remaining papers on the files have no reference to this question. Another question which several times during my service in Congs. exercised their deliberations was whether 7 States could revoke a Commission for a Treaty issued by nine States, at any time before the faith of the Confederacy should be pledged under it.[5] In the instance of a proposition in 1781 to revoke a Commission which had been granted under peculiar circumstances in 1779 to *J. Adams* to form *a treaty of Commerce with G. B.* the competency of 7 States, was resolved on (by 7 States indeed) and a revocation took place accordingly. It was however effected with much difficulty, and some members of the minority even contested the validity of the proceeding. My own opinion then was and still is that the proceeding was equally valid & expedient.[6] The circumstances which had given birth to the commission had given place to others totally different; not a single step had been taken under the commission which could affect the honour or faith of the U. S. and it surely can never be said that either the Letter or spirit of the Confederation, requires the same majority to decline as to engage in foreign treaties. The safest method of guarding agst. the execution of those great powers after the circumstances which dictated them have changed, is to limit their duration, trusting to renewals as they expire, if the original reasons continue. My experience of the uncertainty of getting an affirmative vote even of 7 States had determined me before I left Congress, always to contend for such limitations.

I thought the sense of the term "appropriation" had been settled by the latter practice of Congs. to be the same as you take it to be. I always understood that to be the true, the parliamentary and the only rational sense. If no distinction be admitted between the "appropriation of money to general uses" and "expenditures in detail" the Secretary of Congs. could not buy quills or wafers without a vote of nine States entered on record, and the Secretary to the Committee of the States could not do it at all. In short unless one vote of appropriation can extend to a *class*[7] of objects, there must be a physical impossibility of providing for them, & the extent & generality of such classes can only be determined by discretion & conveniency. It is observable that in the specification of the powers which require 9 States, the single technical word "appropriate" is retained. In the general recital which precedes, the word "apply" as well as "appropriate" is used. You were not mistaken in supposing I had in conversation restrained the authority of the fœderal Court to territorial disputes, but I was egregiously so in the opinion I had formed. Whence I got it I am utterly at a loss to account. It could not be from the Confederation itself, for words could not be more explicit. I detected the error a few days ago in consulting the articles on another subject, & had noted it for my next letter to you. I am not sure that I comprehend your idea of a cession of the territory beyond, the Kanhaway and, on this side the Ohio. As all the *soil* of value has been granted out to individuals a Cession in that view would be improper, and a cession of the *jurisdiction* to Congs. can be proper only where the Country is vacant of settlers.[8] I presume your meaning therefore to be no more than a separation of that country from this, and an incorporation of it into the Union; a work to which all three must be parties. I have no reason to believe there will be any repugnance on the part of Virga. The effort of Pena. for the Western commerce does credit to her public Councils. The commercial genius of this State is too much in its infancy I fear to rival the example. Were this less the case, the confusion of its affairs must stifle all enterprise. I shall be better able however to judge of the practicability of your hint when I know more of them. The declension of George Town does not surprise me tho' it gives me regret.[9] If the competition should lie between Trenton & Philada. & depend on the vote of *New York* it is not difficult to foresee into which scale it will be thrown, nor the probable effect of such decision on our Southern hopes. I have long regarded the Council as a grave of useful talents, as well as objectionable in point of expense, yet I see not how such a reform as you suggest can be brought about.[10] The Constitution, tho' readily overleaped by the Legislature on the spur of an occasion, would probably be made a bar to such an innovation. It directs that 8 members be kept up, and requires the sanction of 4 to almost every act of the Governor. Is it not to be feared too, that these little meliorations of the Government may turn the edge of some of the arguments which ought to be laid to its root? I grow every day more & more solicitous to see this essential work begun. Every days delay settles the Govt. deeper into the habits of the people, and strengthens the prop which their acquiescence gives it. My field of observation is too small to warrant any conjecture of the public disposition towards the measure; but all with whom I converse lend a ready ear to it. Much will depend on the politics of Mr. H.; wch. are wholly unknown to me. Should they be adverse, and G. M.[11] not in the Assembly hazardous as delay is, the experiment must be put off to a more auspicious conjuncture.

The Charter granted in 1732 to Lord Baltimore makes, if I mistake not, the *Southern Shore* of the Potowmac, the boundary of Maryland on that side.[12] The constitution of Virginia cedes to that State "all the territories contained within its charter with all the rights of property, *jurisdiction and Government and all other rights whatsoever,* which might at any time have been claimed by Virginia, excepting *only the free navigation & use* of the Rivers Potowmac & Pokomoque &c."[13] Is it not to be apprehended that this language will be construed into an entire relinquishment of the Jurisdiction of these rivers, and will not such a construction be fatal to our own port regulations on that side & otherwise highly inconvenient? I was told on my journey along the Potowmac of several flagrant evasions which had been practised with impunity & success, by foreign vessels which had loaded at Alexandria. The jurisdiction of half of the rivers ought to have been expressly reserved. The terms of the surrender are the more extraordinary, as the patents of the N. neck place the whole river potowmac within the Government of Virginia, so that we were armed with a title both of prior & posterior date, to that of Maryland. What will be the best course to repair the error?—to extend our laws upon the River, making Maryland the plaintiff if she chooses to contest their authority—to state the case to her at once and propose a settlement by negociation—or to propose a mutual appointment of Commissioners for the general purpose of preserving a harmony, and efficacy in the regulations on both sides. The last mode squares best with my present ideas. It can give no irritation to Maryld.; it can weaken no plea of Virga., it will give Maryland an opportunity of stirring the question if she chooses, and will not be fruitless if Maryland should admit our jurisdiction. If I see the sub-

ject in its true light no time should be lost in fixing the interest of
Virginia. The good humour into which the Cession of the back lands
must have put Maryland, forms an apt crisis for any negociations which
may be necessary.[14] You will be able probably to look into her charter
& other laws, and to collect the leading sentiments relative to the matter.

The winter has been so severe that I have never renewed my call on
the library of Monticello, and the time is now drawing so near when I
may pass for a while into a different scene, that I shall await at least the
return, to my studies. Mr. L. Grymes told me a few days ago that a few
of your Books which had been borrowed by Mr. W. Maury, and ordered by him to be sent to his brother's the clergyman, on their way
to Monticello, were still at the place which Mr. M. removed from.[15]
I desired Mr. Grymes to send them to me instead of the Parson, supposing as the distance is less, the books will probably be sooner out of
danger from accidents, and that a conveyance from hence will not be
less convenient. I calculated also on the use of such of them as may
fall within my plan. I lately got home the Trunk which contained my
Buffon, but have barely entered upon him. My time begins already to
be much less my own than during the winter blockade. I must leave to
your discretion the occasional purchase of rare & valuable books, dis-
regarding the risk of duplicates. You know tolerably well the objects
of my curiosity. I will only particularise my wish of whatever may
throw light on the general Constitution & droit public of the several
confederacies which have existed. I observe in Boinaud's Catalogue several pieces on the Du[t]ch, the German & the Helvetic. The operations
of our own must render all such lights of consequence. Books on the
Law of N. & N. fall within a similar remark.[16] The tracts of Bynker-
shock which you mention I must trouble you to get for me & in french
if to be had rather than latin. Should the body of his works come nearly
as cheap, as these select publications, perhaps it may [be] worth considering Whether the whole would not be preferable. Is not Wolfius also
worth having? I recollect to have seen at Pritchards a copy of Hawkin's
abridgt: of Co: Litt: I would willingly take it if it be still there & you
have an opportunity. A copy of Deane's letters which were printed in
New York & which I failed to get before I left Philada. I should also
be glad of.[17] I use this freedom in confidence that you will be equally
free in consulting your own conveniency whenever I encroach upon it;
I hope you will be so particularly in the request I have to add. One of
my parents would be considerably gratified with a pair of good Spectacles which can not be got here. The particular readiness of Dudley

to serve you inclines me to think that an order from you would be well executed.[18] Will You therefore be so good as to get from him one of his best pebble & double jointed pair, for the age of fifty five or thereabouts with a good case; and forward them by the first safe conveyance to me at orange or at Richmond as the case may be. If I had thought of this matter before Mr. Maury set out, I might have lessened your trouble. It is not material whether I be repayed at the bank of Philada: or the Treasy of Virginia, but I beg it may be at neither till you are made secure by public remittances. It will be necessary at any rate for £20 or 30 be left in your hands or in the bank for little expenditures which your kindness is likely to bring upon you.

The Executive of S. Carolina, as I am informed by the Attorney have demanded of Virginia the surrender of a citizen of Virga: charged on the affidavit of Jonas Beard Esqr. whom the Executive of S. C. represent to be "a Justice of the peace, a member of the Legislature, and a valuable good man" as follows: that "three days before the 25th. day of Octr. 1783 he (Mr. Beard) was violently assaulted by G. H. during the sitting of the Court of General Sessions, without any provocation thereto given, who beat him (Mr. B) with his fist & switch over the face head and mouth, from which beating he was obliged to keep his room until the said 25th. day of Octr. 1783. and call in the assistance of a physician." Such is the case as collected by Mr. Randolph from the letter of the Executive of S. C. The questions which arise upon it are 1. whether it be a charge of high misdemesnor within the meaning of the 4 art: of Confederation. 2. whether in expounding the terms high misdemesnor the Law of S. Carolina, or the British law as in force in the U S before the Revolution, ought to be the Standard. 3. if it be not a casus fœderis what the law of Nations exacts of Virginia? 4. if the law of Nations contains no adequate provision for such occurrences, Whether the intimacy of the Union among the States, the relative position of some, and the common interest of all of them in guarding against impunity for offences which can be punished only by the jurisdiction within which they are committed, do not call for some supplemental regulations on this subject? Mr. R. thinks Virginia not bound to surrender the fugitive untill she be convinced of the fact, by more substantial information, & of its amounting to a high misdemesnor, by inspection of the law of S. C. which & not the British law ought to be the criterion. His reasons are too long to be rehearsed.

I know not my dear Sir what to reply to the affectionate invitation which closes your letter.[19] I subscribe to the justness of your general reflections. I feel the attractions of the particular situation you point out to me; I can not altogether renounce the prospect; still less can I as yet embrace it. It is far from being improbable that a few years more may prepare me for giving such a destiny to my future life; in which case the same or some equally convenient spot may be commanded by a little augmentation of price. But wherever my final lot may fix me be assured that I shall ever remain with the sincerest affection & esteem Yr. friend and servant

J. MADISON JR.

RC (DLC). Cover missing. Docketed by JM. Upon recovering the letter many years later, JM added the docket, "to Mr. Jefferson Mar. 16. 1784." The italicized words, unless otherwise noted, are those encoded by JM in the code first used by Jefferson on 14 Apr. 1783. Indicated below are a few words and several brief passages which JM may have altered or excised in his old age. At the same time, he almost certainly interlineated the words symbolized by the ciphers of the code.

[1] Jefferson never presented to Congress his protest against the validity of having only seven, rather than nine, state delegations ratify the definitive treaty of peace. The protest reads: "Because by the usage of modern nations it is now established that the ratification of a treaty by the sovereign power is the essential act which gives it validity; the signature of the ministers, notwithstanding their plenipotentiary commission, being understood as placing it, according to the phrase of the writers on this subject, sub spe rati, only, and as leaving to each sovereign an acknoleged right of rejection" (Boyd, *Papers of Jefferson*, VI, 424). The Latin phrase may be translated as, "in a state of hoped-for ratification."

[2] Words italicized in this sentence were not in code but underlined by JM. For the "language" of the commission bestowed by King George III upon Alleyne Fitzherbert, his plenipotentiary for making a general peace, see JM's "skeleton" of the document in *Papers of Madison*, V, 212–13; 214–15 nn. 3–9.

[3] Italicized words not coded by JM.

[4] *JCC*, II, 195–201. "Franklin's" is interlineated above "F's" in JM's hand, but he probably inserted it many years later. He copied the title of the plan from the docket of the manuscript (PCC). JM referred especially to Article V, which begins, "That the Power and Duty of the Congress shall extend to the Determining on War and Peace, to sending and receiving ambassadors, and entring into Alliances." The "Sketch" provided that decisions should be reached by "a Majority" of the individual delegates rather than by each state delegation having one vote, as stipulated by the Articles of Confederation which became effective in Mar. 1781.

[5] Between "at any time" and "before the faith," JM so completely deleted about ten words as to make them illegible.

[6] Subsequent to the ratification of the Articles of Confederation, JM held that actions taken prior thereto by a bare majority of the states represented in Congress continued to be binding, even though the ninth of those articles obliged actions of the same nature to have the sanction of at least nine states before becoming effective. In his judgment, however, Article IX did not exclude seven states from issuing, altering, or revoking commissions or instructions, even if they authorized "making peace," or changed instructions relating to a commercial convention or commercial treaty (*Papers of Madison*, IV, 437 and n. 1, 438 n. 7, 445 and n. 2; VI, 15–16). On 12 July 1781 Congress adopted JM's motion to revoke the commission of 29 Sept. 1779 empowering John Adams to conclude a commercial treaty with Great Britain

(*JCC*, XX, 746–77). On 30 May 1783, when only eight states were effectively represented, Congress adopted additional instructions to its commissioners negotiating
a definitive treaty of peace (*JCC*, XXIV, 374–76; *Papers of Madison*, VII, 95, 96 n. 3).
On 12 June 1783 eight states, each with two or more delegates in Congress, were
considered sufficient to adopt JM's committee report concerning the League of
Armed Neutrality and including instructions to the peace commissioners of the
United States (*JCC*, XXIV, 392–94,; *Papers of Madison*, VII, 137–38, 140 and n. 2,
141 n. 3).

⁷ Italics used by JM.

⁸ Between "can be proper" and "only," JM wrote about eight words and later
deleted them so completely as to render them illegible. The allusion to the *soil*
is, of course, to the fact that only the poor acres remaining for cession would
scarcely provide Congress with a large source of future income. But if *jurisdiction*
over the whole should be granted, in what legislative body would the settlers be
represented? Certainly it would not be in the Virginia General Assembly, for it
had relinquished control. Nor would it be in Congress itself, for as a body politic,
the settlers would not yet constitute a state. For Jefferson's explanation of his "proposition to bound our country to the Westward," see his letter to JM, 25 Apr. 1784.

⁹ JM used "declension" in the now obsolete sense of a diminution of status. His
reference is to Jefferson's statement that as a site on which congressional attention
had been focused as a possibility for a permanent confederation capital, "Georgetown languishes" (*Papers of Madison*, VII, 424).

¹⁰ JM's oft-quoted condemnation of the Virginia Council of State "as a grave
of useful talents" was prompted by a continuing discussion with Jefferson regarding
a revision of the 1776 state constitution (ibid., VII, 401). JM had sounded out
George Mason, the drafter of that document, and reported to Jefferson on 10 Dec.
1783 that Mason was "*sound and ripe*" for a revision. Jefferson's drastic revision
was enclosed in his letter to JM of 17 June 1783 (ibid., VII, 156–57). Lethargy and
conservatism would deny the reformers their opportunity, however, and JM
waited until 1829 before constitutional revision became acceptable. Then seventy-
seven, JM attended the 1829 Constitutional Convention as a patriarch rather than
an activist.

¹¹ Interlined above the H and M are JM's additions of a later date to spell out
Henry and Mason.

¹² The phrase "Southern Shore" is italicized because JM underlined it. The charter
of 1632 (not 1732) granted by Charles I to Cecilius Calvert, second Lord Baltimore,
defined a part of Maryland's boundary as from "the first Fountain of the River of
Pattowmack, thence verging towards the South, unto the further Bank of the said
River, and following the same on the West and South, unto a certain Place called
Cincquack, situated near the Mouth of the said River, where it disembogues into
the aforesaid Bay of *Chesopeake*" (William MacDonald, ed., *Select Charters and
Other Documents Illustrative of American History, 1606–1775* [New York, 1906],
p. 54).

¹³ JM's italics and a loose quotation from the opening sentence of Article XXI of
the 1776 Virginia Constitution (Hening, *Statutes*, IX, 118). The lower reaches of
the Pokomoque (Pocomoke) River form part of the boundary between southern
Maryland and the Eastern Shore of Virginia.

¹⁴ Although influential Marylanders were speculators in the lands ceded by
Virginia in 1783 and accepted by Congress on 1 Mar. 1784, the terms of the cession
tacitly excluded the pretensions of private land companies to title to the soil (Abernethy, *Western Lands and the American Revolution*, pp. 171, 239; *JCC*, XXVI,
110–17). Certainly Marylanders as a whole had reason to be in a "good humor" with
the triumph of a demand first presented to Congress on 15 Oct. 1777 (*JCC*, IX, 806–

8). For the background, see Marshall Smelser, *The Winning of Independence* (Chicago, 1972), particularly the chapter "Of Real Estate and Nationalism, 1780–1781" (pp. 297–316).

15 Ludwell Grymes (d. ca. 1795) had engaged in land transactions with James Madison, Sr., and his wife, and with Walker Maury (Vi: Orange County Court Records, Will Book 3, 1778–1801, pp. 334–37; Minute Book 1, 1764–1774, pp. 321, 337; Minute Book 2, 1774–1789, p. 198, microfilm). Grymes, who lived outside the senior Madison's tax district, was a farmer of modest means. When he died intestate, his estate was appraised at £170 9s. (Vi: Orange County Land-Tax Books, 1782, 1794–1795; Orange County Personal-Property Tax Books, 1782–1784, 1794–1795). For Walker Maury, see *Papers of Madison*, VII, 408 n. 8, 418. His brother, the "Parson," was the Reverend Matthew Maury (1744–1808), rector of Fredericksville Parish in Hanover and Louisa counties from 1770 until his death (Malcolm H. Harris, *History of Louisa County, Virginia* [Richmond, 1936], pp. 163, 165, 389–90).

16 A thin vertical line of ink, probably drawn by Jefferson to emphasize JM's preferred book purchases, parallels most of the left edge of the text from "to your discretion" to "Helvetic." For "droit public," see JM to Randolph, 10 Mar. 1784, and n. 6. "N. & N." signifies "Nature and Nations." JM's reading about "the several confederacies" is illustrated by his undated manuscript (DLC), thirty-nine pages in length, entitled "Ancient & Modern *Confederacies*" and by nine of his *Federalist* essays (Jacob E. Cooke, ed., *The Federalist* [Middletown, Conn., 1961], Nos. 18, 19, 20, 37, 38, 42, 43, 45, and 54).

17 *Paris Papers; or, Mr. Silas Deane's late intercepted Letters, to His Brothers, and other intimate Friends, in America . . .* [New York, 1782], reprinted by James Rivington from his New York *Royal Gazette*, 24 Oct.–12 Dec. 1781.

18 Benjamin Dudley, a British subject and an artisan of "most uncommon extensive Genius," had arrived in Boston, probably in 1780, after fleeing from his native country. Among his diverse skills were the assaying and smelting of ore, the fashioning of dies and machinery for minting coins, and the making of spectacles (PCC).

19 JM and Jefferson were separated by about twenty-five miles between Montpelier and Monticello. In his old age, JM inserted an asterisk after "invitation" and wrote at the foot of the letter, following a matching asterisk, "To establish himself near Mr. Jefe."

From Thomas Jefferson

Annapolis Mar. 16. 1784.

Dear Sir

I received yesterday by mr. Maury your favor of Feb. 17. That which you mention to have written by post a few days before is not yet come to hand. I am induced to this quick reply to the former by an alarming paragraph in it, which is that *Mazzei* is coming to Annapolis. I tremble at the idea. I know he will be worse to me than a return of my double quotidian head-ach. There is a resolution reported to Congress by a Committee that they will never appoint to the office of minister, chargé des affairs, consul, agent &c (describing the foreign emploiments) any but natives. To this I think there will not be a dissenting vote: and it will be taken up among the first things. Could you not, by making him acquainted with this divert him from coming here? A *consulate* is his object, in which he will assuredly fail. But his coming will be attended with evil. He is the violent enemy of *Franklin* having been some time at *Paris*, from my knolege of the man I am sure he will have emploied himself in collecting on the spot facts true or false to *impeach* him. You know there are people here who, on the first idea of this, will take him to their bosom & turn all Congress topsy turvy. For god's sake then save us from this confusion if you can.[1]

We have eight states only & 7. of these represented by two members. Delaware & S. Carolina we lost within these two days by the expiration of their powers. The other absent states are N. York, *Maryland* & Georgia.[2] We have done nothing & can do nothing in this condition but waste our time, temper, & spirits in debating things for days or weeks & then losing them by the negative of one or two individuals.

We have letters from Franklin & the Marq. Fayette of the 24th. & 25th. of Dec.[3] They inform us that North & Fox are out, Pitt & Temple coming in, that whole nation extremely indisposed towards us, & as having not lost the idea of reannexing us, the Turks & Russians likely to be kept quiet another year, the Marquis coming to America this spring, mr Laurence then about sailing for America, mr Adams leaving England for the Hague, mr Jay at Bath but about returning to Paris. Our ratification tho' on board two different vessels at N. York in the hands of officers as early as the 20th. of Jan. did not sail thence till the 17th of Feb. on account of the ice. I will attend to your desire about the booksellers. I am considerably mended in my health & hope a favourable change in the weather which seems to be taking place will reestablish me.

I wish you would keep a diary under the following heads or columns: 1. *day of the month.*[4] 2. thermometer at sunrise. 3. barometer at sunrise. 6.[5] thermom. at 4. P. M. 7. barometer at 4. P. M. 4 direction of wind at sunrise. 8. direction of wind at 4. P. M. 5. the weather viz rain, snow, fair at sunrise &c. 9. weather at 4. P. M. 10. shooting or falling of the leaves of trees, of flours, & other remarkable plants. 11. appearance or disappearance of birds, their emigrations &c. 12. Miscellanea. It will be an amusement to you & may become useful. I do not know whether you have a thermom. or barom. If you have not, those columns will be unfilled till you can supply yourself. In the miscellaneous column I have generally inserted Aurorae boreales, &, other unclassed rare things. Adieu Adieu Yours affectionately

the above columns to be arranged according to the order of the numbers as corrected.[6]

RC (DLC). Unsigned, but cover addressed and franked by Jefferson and committed "to the care of mr Maury Fredsbgh." Docketed by JM. Italicized words, unless otherwise noted, are decoded by JM using the code first used by Jefferson on 14 Apr. 1783.

[1] The stay of Philip Mazzei "some time at Paris" was from Feb. 1780 until about 1 July in that year, and from 1 Feb. 1783 until late in May of that year. There John Adams befriended him, but Franklin discouraged his mission to Italy and neglected him in other ways. The partisans of each man had often been at odds in Congress over Franklin's conduct as minister to the court of France. The Massachusetts delegation and Arthur Lee were leaders of the pro-Adams group in Congress. The Pennsylvania delegation, Robert Morris, and JM were among Franklin's defenders. Although in the spring of 1784 factionalism on this score was quiescent, Jefferson obviously feared that if his voluble friend Mazzei came to Annapolis he would revive the discord by supplying Lee with new "facts true or false" to injure Franklin (Richard Cecil Garlick, Jr., *Philip Mazzei, Friend of Jefferson: His Life and Letters* [Baltimore, 1933], p. 83; Howard R. Marraro, ed., "Philip Mazzei, Virginia's Agent in Europe: The Story of His Mission as Related in His Own Dispatches and Other Documents," *Bulletin of the New York Public Library*, XXXVIII [1934], 546; Boyd, *Papers of Jefferson*, VII, 30, 32).

[2] Jefferson probably underlined "Maryland" because although Congress was meeting in Annapolis, the state was unrepresented. The absence of the Maryland delegation was the more conspicuous because its members in Oct. 1783 had worked hard to have Congress move from Princeton to Annapolis.

[3] Contrary to Jefferson's statement, two of Franklin's letters are dated 25 Dec. and two, 26 Dec. Lafayette's letter is dated 26 Dec. 1783 (Wharton, *Revol. Dipl. Corr.*, VI, 740–48). Congress, upon receiving them on 5 Mar. 1784, referred them, along with other dispatches from overseas, to the committee (chairman, Elbridge Gerry) that included Jefferson (PCC; *JCC*, XXVI, 143–45).

[4] Jefferson underlined rather than encoded this phrase.

[5] Jefferson wrote over this and the following numbers, explaining the alteration in his postscript.

[6] Lacking both a barometer and a thermometer, JM was handicapped when he undertook the business of keeping a weather log and never was able to procure a barometer. JM began the entries on 1 Apr. 1784 and depended on his father and possibly other members of the family to keep records when he was away from Montpelier. The entries in JM's hand through 31 Mar. 1786 are found in Appendix B of this volume. So many entries were made by James Madison, Sr., that JM regarded the journal as his "father's meteorological diaries" when loaning them to Jefferson in 1817 (Jefferson to JM, 22 June 1817 [DLC: Jefferson Papers]). The records to 13 Apr. 1793 are owned by the American Philosophical Society. The Ms journal from 13 Apr. 1793 to 4 July 1796 is owned by the Presbyterian Historical Society of Philadelphia (William B. Miller, "The Weather Log of James Madison," *Journal of Presbyterian History*, XL [1962], 209–12).

From Eliza House Trist

Letter not found.

ca. 13 April 1784. Mrs. Trist was at Fort Pitt awaiting transportation down the Ohio for a reunion with her husband. She wrote Jefferson regarding a misunderstood report that Virginia had "reward[ed] merit by making our friend Madison Governor. . . . I have wrote to him, but before I got your letter, which I beg you to forward" (Boyd, *Papers of Jefferson*, VII, 97–98). This letter was probably that forwarded by Jefferson with his 1 July 1784 letter to JM.

From Patrick Henry

LEATHERWOOD Apl. 17th. 1784

DEAR SIR.

After so long Time had passed without hearing from you, Mr. Mazzei did me great pleasure in telling me you were well, & not averse to render stil further Services to our Country.[1] Altho' from the Length & Importance of those you have so happily accomplished some Respite might be demanded for the present, yet I must tell you I think several Matters of the greatest Moment forbid it. Is not the federal Goverment on a bad Footing? If I am not mistaken you must have seen & felt that it is. This is not the only Matter that wants Correction & Improvement. How mortifying is it to see a rich Harvest of Happiness, & Labourers wanting to gather it in?

I take my leave of you only 'til next month when I confide in seeing you at Richmond. Adeiu my dear Sir, I am yr. affectionate

P. HENRY

RC (NjMoW: Lloyd C. Smith Collection). Addressed and marked "favr. Mr. Mazzie." Docketed by JM. The probable docket page no longer accompanies the letter but is in DLC. It includes two additional endorsements, one by JM, "Jefferson Ths. (to Presdt. W.) June 4. 1793," and a second in an unknown hand, "Ths. Jefferson Jan. 4. 1793." No letter from Jefferson to JM on either of those dates is known to exist. JM probably used the page to docket a copy of Jefferson's letter of 4 June 1793 to Washington (Jefferson to JM, 9 June 1793 [DLC]), and the unknown inscriber misread the date. An addendum to the original docket suggests a further correspondence, for JM later added a question mark after the date and his comment, "intimation from him thro' Wm. Madison with answer of J. M."

[1] Mazzei later reported his conversation with both Henry and JM in a letter to John Adams. A notorious flatterer, Mazzei spoke of JM as "One of the most noble, most sensible, and virtuous men on the Globe" (Boyd, *Papers of Jefferson*, VII, 124 n.).

18

From Alexander Hamilton

18 April [1784?]

I take the liberty to introduce him to you, as to one who will be disposed, as far as your situation will permit and the circumstances of the State may render practicable, to patronise any just or equitable claims which he may have upon the State. What those claims are he will himself explain to you,[1] I have assured him that he will find in you a friend to justice and an able advocate for whatever ought and is possible to be done for him, . . .

Extract (Frederick B. McGuire Catalogue of "President Madison's Correspondence" [Philadelphia, 26 Feb. 1917], item 52). The catalogue states that the letter consists of one page with an incomplete date, and was directed to JM.

[1] The excerpt in the catalogue is introduced with the explanation that it "Relates to claims against the state of Virginia by a Mr. Perrault." Obviously this was Canadian-born Joseph François Perrault (1753–1844), who in 1778 was an established western fur trader (Louise Phelps Kellogg, ed., *Frontier Retreat on the Upper Ohio, 1779–1781* [Madison, Wis., 1917], p. 86 n. 3). Possibly it was JM who submitted Perrault's petition, which was presented to the Virginia House of Delegates on 17 May, but this is not hinted in the journal. Perrault asked reimbursement for supplies and money furnished to Colonel John Todd for Virginia troops in the Illinois country in 1778–1779. Captured by the Shawnee Indians in 1779 while en route to Virginia to press his claims, Perrault asserted that he "had been robbed of his Vouchers," treated with inhuman cruelty, marched to Detroit, and given over to the British (*Cal. of Va. State Papers*, III, 583). On 25 May the House of Delegates suspended consideration of Perrault's petition and two days later referred it to Governor Harrison in Council. At the Council meeting on 5 June 1784, it was decided that Perrault's claims "appear to be inadmissible" on the ground that "several of the Bills presented by him have been already carried to the Credit of Mr. Oliver Pollock, and that there is good reason to suppose that the rest of the Bills have been negociated at New Orleans, and are now in possession of some other claimant" (*JHDV*, May 1784, pp. 19, 23; *JCSV*, III, 352).

To Thomas Jefferson

ORANGE April 25th. 1784

DEAR SIR

Your favor of the 16th. of March came to hand a few days *before Mazzei called on me. His plan was to have proceeded hence directly to Annapolis. My conversation led him to pr[o]mise a visit to Mr. Henry from whence he proposed to repair to Richmond & close his affair with the executive.*[1] Contrary to my expectation he returned hither on

Thursday last proposing to continue *his* circuit *thro Glo[u]cester, York & Williamburg* recommended *by Mr. Henry for obtaining from* the *former members of the Council* certain *facts relating* to *his appointment* of which the *vouchers have been lost.* This *delay* with the expectation of *your ad[j]ournment* will probably *prevent his visit to Congress.* Your letter gave me the first information both of *his view toward a consulate* and of *his enmity toward Franklin.* The first was not betrayed to *me by any conversation* either before or after *I made known to him* the determination *of Congress to confine such appointment[s] to natives of America.*[2] As to the second *he* [was] *unreserved* alledging at the same time that the *exquisite cunning of the old fox* has so [e]*nveloped his iniquity* that its reality cannot be *proved by those who are th[o]roly satisfied of it.* It is evident from several circumstances stated *by himself that his enmity has been embittere[d] if not wholly occasioned by incident[s] of a personal nature. Adams is* the *only public man in* whom *he thinks favorably of* or seems to *have associated with, a circumstance which* their mutual *characters may perhaps account for.* Notwithstanding these sentiments *toward F & A his hatred* [of] *England* remains *unabate[d]* & does not *exceed his partiality for France* which with many other considerations, which need not be pointed out, persuade me that however dreadful an actual *visit from him* might be to *you in a per-*[son]*al view* it would not produce the *public mischiefs you apprehend from it.* By *his interview with Mr Henry I learn* that the present *politics of* the *latter* comprehend very friendly *view[s] toward the confederacy, a* wish tempered with much caution for *an amendment of our own constitution, a* patronage *of* the *payment of British debts* and *of* [a] *scheme of a general assessment.*[3]

The want of both a Thermometer & Baromr: had determined me to defer a meteorological diary till I could procure these instruments. Since the rect. of your letter I have attended to the other columns.

I hope the letter which had not reached you at the date of your last, did not altogether miscarry. On the 16 of March I wrote you fully on sundry points. Among others I suggested to your attention the case of the Potowmac, having in my eye the river below the head of navigation. It will be well I think to *sound* the *ideas of Maryland* also as to the upper parts of the N. branch of it. The *policy of Ba[l]timore* will probably thwart as far as possible, the *opening of* [it]; & without a very favorable construction of the *right of Virginia* and even the privilege of using the *Maryland bank* it would seem that the *necessary works could not be* accomplished.[4]

Will it not be good policy to suspend further Treaties of Commerce, till measures shall have been taken place in America which may correct the idea in Europe of impotency in the fœderal Govt. in matters of Commerce? Has Virginia been seconded by any other State in her proposition for arming Congress with power to frustrate the unfriendly regulations of G. B. with regard to her W. India islands? It is reported here that the late change of her Ministers has revived the former liberality which seemed to prevail on that subject. Is the Impost gaining or losing ground among the States? Do any considerable payments come into the Continl. Treasury? Does the settlement of the public accts. make any comfortable progress? Has any resolution been taken by Congress touching the old Contl: currency? Has Maryland foreborne to take any step in favor of George Town? Can you tell me whether any question in the Court of Appeals, has yet determined whether the war ceased on our coast on the 3d of March or the 3d. of April? The books which I was told were still at place left by Mr. W. Maury, had been sent away at the time Mr. L. Grymes informed of them.

Mr. Mazzei tells me that a subterraneous city has been discovered in Siberia, which appears to have been once populous & magnificent. Among other curiosities it contains an equestrian Statue around the neck of which was a golden chain 200 feet in length, so exquisitely wrought that Buffon inferred from a specimen of 6 feet sent him by the Empress of Russia, that no artist in Paris could equal the workmanship. Mr. Mazzei saw the specimen in the hands of Buffon & heard him give this opinion of it. He heard read at the same time a letter from the Empress to Buffon in which she desired the present to be considered as a tribute to the man to whom Nat: Hist: was so much indebted. Monsr. Faujas de St. Fond thought the City was between 72 & 74.° N. L. The son of Buffon between 62 & 64.° Mr. M. being on the point of departure had no opportunity of ascertaing the fact. If you should have had no better account of the discovery this will not be unacceptable to you & will lead you to obtain one.[5]

I propose to set off for Richmond towards the end of this week. The election in this County was on thursday last.[6] My colleague is Mr. Charles Porter. I am your affecte. friend

J. MADISON JR

RC (DLC). Cover missing. Docketed. The italicized words, unless otherwise noted, are those encoded by JM in the code first used by Jefferson on 14 Apr. 1783. Accompanying the manuscript is a page on which Jefferson deciphered the coded words. Many years later, upon the return of the letter, JM interlined his own decoding.

¹ The first of Philip Mazzei's two visits to Montpelier in 1784 was from 27 to 31 Mar. (Garlick, *Philip Mazzei*, pp. 85–86).

² In a letter of 4 Apr. to Jefferson, Mazzei denounced "the narrow-minded resolution to exclude from certain posts those not born in America" (Boyd, *Papers of Jefferson*, VII, 64 n.).

³ Garlick, *Philip Mazzei*, pp. 21, 64, 67, 81; Howard R. Marraro, trans., *Memoirs of the Life and Peregrinations of the Florentine Philip Mazzei 1730–1816* (New York, 1942), pp. 276–77.

⁴ The "head of navigation" on the Potomac River was near Georgetown. Any scheme to open the Potomac and extend the navigation of that stream by use of canals would likely arouse the hostility of Baltimore merchants, who were geographically positioned to hold a practical monopoly on the trade routes into western Maryland as well as northern and northwestern Virginia.

⁵ Upon receiving the present letter on 7 May, Jefferson at once wrote about the buried city to Francis Hopkinson, a fellow member of the American Philosophical Society (Boyd, *Papers of Jefferson*, VII, 124 n., 227). Buffon was Georges Louis Leclerc, Comte de Buffon; the Empress of Russia, Catherine II (the Great); Barthélemy Faujas de Saint-Fond (1741–1819), a French geologist best known as a student of volcanoes; and the son of Buffon, Georges Louis Marie Leclerc (1764–1793), himself later Comte de Buffon.

⁶ Randolph wrote to Jefferson on 24 Apr.: "I have not heard since the election, but I am confident from what reached me before, that our friend Madison will certainly be a member. His aid will be necessary to correct the extravagencies of some plausible men, who have many schemes of romance much at heart" (Boyd, *Papers of Jefferson*, VII, 117; Vi: Certificate of Election, 26 Apr. 1784).

Endorsement of Philip Mazzei's Petition

April 25th. 1783[4].

I have perused a paper entitled "A representation of Mr. Mazzeis conduct from the time of his appointment to be Agent of the State in Europe untill his return to Virginia"; and believe the proceedings of the Executive Board whilst I was a member of it to be therein correctly stated.¹ Not having been present at the conversation between Governor Henry and Mr. Mazzei relative to an allowance of £1000 Sterlg per annum for his expences, I can say nothing as to that fact. I recollect only that that sum was mentioned at the Board as a Salary not exceeding the dignity of the business on which he was to be sent; and that the prevailing idea was that the salary should be left unfixed till his return to Virginia when he ought to receive a decent reward over and above the sum which he should have necessarily expended in supporting the rank and promoting the object of his Commission.²

J. MADISON JR.

RC (PHi). Misdated 1783 by JM. The page bearing JM's endorsement also has a briefer one by John Page, and an accompanying sheet has similar testimonials from Dudley Digges and David Jameson.

[1] See Mazzei's "narrative," *Bulletin of the New York Public Library*, XXXVIII (1934), 541–62. JM was a member of the Virginia Council of State from 14 Jan. 1778 until shortly after 14 Dec. 1779. JM, Digges, and Page were among the members of the Council of State who were present on 8 Jan. 1779, when Mazzei was commissioned by Governor Henry as the Virginia agent empowered to procure a loan and military supplies in Europe. His mission failed. In his old age Mazzei recalled that Governor Henry had asked him, in the presence of JM and other members of the Council, whether £1,000 would be an adequate sum to cover his expenses (Marraro, trans., *Memoirs of Philip Mazzei*, pp. 224–25, 267–68, 275 81).

[2] On 12 June 1784 Governor Harrison in Council directed the state Board of Auditors "to issue Warrants on the Contingent Fund" in Mazzei's favor for £2,133 6s. 8d., "being the balance due him for his services & expences." Prior to 10 June 1784, he had received some payment, on account, for his services (*JCSV*, III, 354–55, 319, 351). See also Harrison to Mazzei, 23 Dec. 1783; Harrison to Leighton Wood, 10 June 1784, Executive Letter Book, pp. 250, 337; Giovanni E. Schiavo, *Philip Mazzei, One of America's Founding Fathers* (New York, 1951), pp. 151 55. Prior to Mazzei's departure for Europe he had received £7,000 Virginia currency. On 6 Apr. 1780 in Paris he was advanced 300 louis d'or by a banker acting on behalf of Virginia. Harrison in Council considered all these sums to total 600 louis d'or a year, the remuneration set for Mazzei from 8 Jan. 1779 to 8 Apr. 1783 (*JCSV*, III, 354). Governor Harrison in Council on 24 Jan. 1782 terminated Mazzei's appointment, and in a letter of 31 May 1783, Harrison told Mazzei that his commission had expired three months after the notice of his recall reached him—that is, 30 Nov. 1782. Evidently the governor in Council later decided to pay Mazzei for an additional period of about four months (ibid., pp. 34, 425).

From Thomas Jefferson

ANNAPOLIS Apr. 25. 1784.

DEAR SIR

My last to you was of the 16th. of March, as was the latest I have received from you. By the proposition to bound our country to the Westward, I meant no more than the passing an act declaring that that should be our boundary from the moment the people of the Western country & Congress should agree to it. The act of Congress now inclosed to you will shew you that they have agreed to it, because it extends not only to the territory ceded, but *to be ceded;* and shews how and when they shall be taken into the union. There is no body then to consult but the people to be severed. If you will make your act final as to yourselves so soon as those people shall have declared their assent in a certain manner to be pointed out by the act, the whole business is settled. For their assent will follow immediately. One of the conditions

is that they pay their quota of the debts contracted. Of course no difficulty need arise: on this head: as no quota has been fixed on us unalterably.[1] The minuter circumstances of selling the ungranted lands
will be provided in an ordinance already prepared but not reported.
You will observe two clauses struck out of the report, the 1st. respecting hereditary honours, the 2d. slavery. The 1st. was done not from an
approbation of such honours, but because it was thought an improper
place to encounter them. The 2d. was lost by an individual vote only.
Ten states were present. The 4. Eastern states, N. York, [&] Pennsva.
were for the clause. [Je]rsey would have been for it, but there were
but two members, one of whom was sick in his chambers. South Carolina Maryland, & ! Virginia ! voted against it. N. Carolina was divided
as would have been Virginia had not one of its delegates been sick in
bed.[2]

The place at which Congress should meet in Nov. has been the subject of discussion lately. Alexandria, Philada & Trenton were proposed.
The first was negatived easily. Trenton had the 4. East. states. N. Y. N. J.
& Pennsylva. We expect Georgia & Delaware shortly, in which case it
will become possible that Philada may be determined on. The question
is put off to be considered with the establishment of a commee of the
states, which to my astonishment would have been negatived when
first proposed had not the question been staved off. Some of the states
who were against the measure, I believe because they had never reflected on the consequences of leaving a government without a head,
seem to be come over.[3] Dr. Lee is appointed an Indian Commr. He is
not present, but is known to have sought it, & of course will accept.
This vacates his seat here. I wish Short could be sent in his room. It is a
good school for our young statesmen. It gives them impressions friendly
to the federal government instead of those adverse which too often
take place in persons confined to the politics of their state.[4]

I like the method you propose of settling at once with Maryland all
matters relative to Patowmac. To introduce this the more easily I have
conversed with mr Stone (one of their delegates) on the subject & finding him of the same opinion have told him I would by letters bring the
subject forward on our part. They will consider it therefore as originated by this conversation.

Mercer is acting a very *extraordin*[ary] *part. He is a candidate for*
the *secretaryship* of *foreign affairs*[s] *and tho' he will not* get the *vote
of one state* I beleive he *expect*[s] the *appointment. He* has been *en-
deavoring to defeat* all *foreign treaty* to force the *nations* of *Europe* to

sen[d] *ministers* to *treat here* that *he* may have the *honor* of *fabricat-in*[g] this *whole business.* Tho' *he could* not *change* the *vote* of *his state,* he *intrigued* with a *young fool* from *North Carolina* & an *old* one from *New York, go*[t] them to *decide* their *states* by *voting* in the *negative,* & there being but *eleven states present one* of *which* was *know*[n] before to be *divid*[e]*d* the *whole set* of *instructions* were *re*[j]*ected,* tho *approve*[d] by *twenty one* out of *twenty five members present.*[5] The *whole business* has been in *the dust* for a *month* & whether it can be *resumed* & *past depends* on the incertainty of *Delaware* or *Georgia coming* on. *Vanity* & *ambition seem* to be the *ruling passions* of this *young man* and as *his objects* are *impure* so also are *his means. Intrigu*[e] is a *principal one* on *particular occasions* as *party attachment* is in the *general. He takes* now about *one half of* the *time of Congress* to *himself,* & in *conjunction* with *Read* [and] *Spaight obstruct business inconcievably.* The *last* is of *North Carolina* & no otherwise of *consequence than* as by *his vote according*[ly] can *divide his state.*

The more I have reflected on your proposition for printing the Revisal the more I have like it. I am convinced too from late experiments it cannot be passed in the detail. One of the Eastern states had their laws revised and then attempted to pass them thro' their legislature, but they got so mangled that all consistence was destroyed & I beleived they dropped them altogether. Should this be printed I will ask you to send me half a dozen copies wherever I shall be.

Would it not be well for Virginia to empower persons privately to buy up her quota of old Continental money. I would certainly advise this were I not afraid that the possession of her quota on such easy terms would tempt her to refuse justice to the other states on this matter. For surely there would be no justice in wiping off her part of this debt by so much smaller a contribution than the others.[6] If she would avail herself of it only to sheild herself against injustice and to enable her from an high ground to declare & do what is right, I should much wish to see her adopt secret measures for the purchase. I think some other states will do this, & I fear with unjust views. You know that many gentlemen of this state had money in the hands of merchants in England. I am well informed that these merchants have uniformly refused to pay them interest, saying the money was always ready if they would have called for it. This adds another to the many good reasons we had before against paying interest during the war.

I inclose herewith the spectacles you desired, price 13 2/3 Dollars. I have as yet done nothing on your commission either general or particular for books, because I am in constant expectation of a short trip to Philadelphia & can so much better execute it on the spot. The money hitherto remitted us amounts to about 4. Dollars a day. The predicament in which this places us is well known to you. It is inconceivably mortifying. I expect daily to hear from the Treasurer. As soon as I do it will enable me to give some directions on the subject of your money. I have not heard lately from mrs House. Mrs Trist got safely to Fort Pitt through much distress.[7] Congress hope to adjourn by the last of May. The estimate & requisitions for the year, the arrangements for the land office, & Foreign treaties are subjects they will endeavor to complete. Vermont is pressed on them by N. York & a day declared beyond which they will await no interposition but assert their right of government. The Chevalr. Luzerne has taken his leave of us. He makes a tour to the lakes before he leaves the continent. Marbois acts as Chargé des affaires till the arrival of a successor.

As it is certain that Congress will shortly adjourn, to meet again in Nov. it is desireable that the assembly should at as early a day as convenient appoint their delegation for the ensuing year, in order that such gentlemen as shall be continued, may receive notice of it while here, as this will enable them to take measures for their accomodation at the next meeting, determine them whether to send their baggage Northwardly or Southwardly &c.

Apr. 30. a London ship is arrived here which left that port the 25th: of March. Pitt was still in place, supported by the King, Lords, & nation in general, the city of London enthusiastically in his favor. Still there was a majority of 12 in favor of Fox who was supported by the Prince of Wales. It was thought the parliament would be dissolved. Congress has determined to adjourn on the 3d of June to meet in November at Trenton. Adieu Yours affectionately

Th: Jefferson

RC (DLC). Cover missing. The italicized words, unless otherwise noted, are those encoded by Jefferson in the code he first used on 14 Apr. 1783.

[1] Jefferson underlined "to be ceded." On 3 Feb. 1784 Congress appointed Jefferson chairman of a committee including Jeremiah T. Chase and David Howell "to prepare a plan for temporary governmt. of western territory" (PCC). Although on 15 Oct. 1783 Congress had named James Duane, chairman, JM, and Samuel Huntington as a committee with that directive as an important part of its duties, the committee had not submitted a report and no one on it was a member of Congress by 1784. The report drafted by Jefferson and approved by Chase and Howell was submitted to Congress on 1 Mar. 1784. After being debated and amended it was recommitted on 17 Mar., redelivered five days later, debated both by a grand

committee and Congress, amended and finally adopted on 23 Apr. 1784. By "no quota has been fixed on us unalterably," Jefferson meant that the plan including a quota provision for restoring public credit, mainly drafted by JM and adopted by Congress about a year earlier, had not yet been sanctioned by all the states and that Congress had not yet allocated financial quotas for 1784 among the states. When Jefferson wrote this letter Congress was considering his report on the national debt "and a requisition of money on the states for discharging the same." After amending the report Congress adopted it on 27 Apr. By adopting the report Congress resolved to requisition no additional quotas but to call on each state to send money to an amount sufficient, when added to any money the state had already paid of its quota for 1782, to equal 50 percent of that quota (*JCC*, XXVI, 185–98, 211, 297–309, and esp. 304–6, 308–9). Thus, as Jefferson implied, any temporary or permanent government which Congress might sanction in the West during 1784 would not be called upon for money during that year. The copy "now inclosed" has not been found. It was probably a broadside of the committee's revised report of 22 Mar., perhaps with marginalia by Jefferson to make it conform with the ordinance adopted by Congress on 23 Apr. 1784 (*JCC*, XXVII, 719; Boyd, *Papers of Jefferson*, VI, 581–617). The Richmond *Va. Gazette*, 15 May 1784, includes an unaltered copy of the committee's revised report.

² On the day before the antislavery proviso was eliminated by a sectional vote of six states to three (Maryland, Virginia, South Carolina), North Carolina's vote was lost owing to a deadlock between its two delegates. Delaware and Georgia were unrepresented in Congress. Of the Virginia delegation Samuel Hardy and John Francis Mercer voted to excise and Jefferson to retain. The illness of Dr. John Beatty, a delegate of New Jersey, was decisive in the outcome of the poll. If illness had not kept him from Congress, he would have concurred with his New Jersey colleagues, thus assuring the retention of the proviso by the required vote of 7 to 3 (*JCC*, XXVI, 247; Boyd, *Papers of Jefferson*, VI, 611 n. 21; VII, 121 n.; Burnett, *Letters*, VII, xxxviii–xl; Burnett, *The Continental Congress*, pp. 599–600, 630).

³ For the background of the Committee of the States issue prior to the 26 Apr. 1784 decision see *JCC*, XIX, 219, 220, 221. For the doubt until about 17 Apr. whether Congress would appoint such a committee before adjourning, and the subsequent regret of some delegates, including David Howell, that the committee would be created, see Burnett, *Letters*, VII, 463, 480 and passim. See also Edmund C. Burnett, "The Committee of the States, 1784," *Annual Report of the American Historical Association for the Year 1913* (2 vols.; Washington, 1915), I, 141–52.

⁴ William Short was then a member of the Virginia Council of State.

⁵ A review of the journal of Congress makes evident the fact that Mercer's voting record was often duplicated by Richard Dobbs Spaight, a twenty-six-year-old "*young fool* from *North Carolina*," and by Ephraim Paine, at fifty-four an "*old* one from *New York*" (*JCC*, XXVI, 177, 355). Jacob Read represented South Carolina.

⁶ The concern of eighteenth-century public men over both state and the continental debt was nearly uniform. "Most people then regarded a public debt much as they regarded a private one—something that should be paid in full within a reasonably short time. They did not as yet accept the idea that the principal of a public debt might conveniently be permanent" (Curtis Nettels, *The Emergence of a National Economy, 1775–1815* [New York, 1962], pp. 76–77). Jefferson's dismay over the unrealistic 1780 quota came during congressional deliberations on a fair solution to the problem of debt retirement (*JCC*, XVI, 262–67; XXIV, 39–42, 357–58; XXVII, 394–96, 472–74, 540–46). Williamson of North Carolina had thoughts parallel to Jefferson's, a likely circumstance, since both states had huge land reserves and a scarcity of old continental dollars (Burnett, *Letters*, VII, 597–98). As E. James Ferguson notes, "All the southern states cherished the notion . . . that they had contributed more than their share to the prosecution of the war and that they

would emerge from the final settlement of accounts with large balances in their favor" (*Power of the Purse*, p. 212).

7 Eliza House Trist was then bound for the Louisiana country, where she hoped to join her husband, Nicholas Trist. She reported to Jefferson her "tedious journey [was] allmost compleated . . . when I received the dreadfull account of his being no more" (25 Dec. 1784, Boyd, *Papers of Jefferson*, VII, 583).

From Thomas Jefferson

ANNAPOLIS May 7. 1784.

DEAR SIR

The inclosed resolutions on the subject of commerce are the only things of consequence passed since my last.[1] You will be surprised to receive another pair of spectacles. The paper with them will explain the error. If you can dispose of the supernumerary pair do so, & I will remit the money to Dudley: if you cannot, return them by the next post & I will return them to him.

Congress is now *on foreign treaties*. *Mercer* has *devised* new expedients for *baf[f]ling* the measure. *He has* put it into *Reads head to think* of being *appointed* a *foreign minister* and has by *his intrigues defeated* every proposition which did not proceed on that *ground. He is very mischievous. He is under no moral restrain[t]*. If *he* avoids *shame* he *avoids* wrong according to *his system*. His fondness for *Machiavel* is *genuine* & founded on a true *harmony* of *principle*.

RC (DLC: Rives Collection, Madison Papers). In Jefferson's hand but not signed. Cover missing. Italicized words were encoded by Jefferson in the code he first used on 14 Apr. 1783. Enclosure not found.

[1] The missing enclosure must have been a copy of the resolutions passed by Congress on 30 Apr. 1784, a day when Jefferson appears to have been absent although he served on the committee which submitted them. The resolutions recommended to the states that they vest in Congress, for a period of fifteen years, power to prohibit importations or exportations "in vessels belonging to or navigated by the subjects of any power with whom these states shall not have formed treaties of Commerce," and to prohibit foreigners from importing goods "not the produce or manufacture of the dominions of the sovereign whose subjects they are" (JCC, XXVI, 320 n. 1, 322). For JM's probable use of this measure see Resolutions to Strengthen Powers of Congress, 19 May 1784, and Bill Granting Congress Limited Power to Regulate Commerce, 5 June 1784.

To Thomas Jefferson

Letter not found.

8 May 1784. In his "Summary Journal of Letters," Jefferson recorded that he received in Philadelphia on 24 May a letter from JM written in Richmond on 8 May (Boyd, *Papers of Jefferson,* VII, 235; Jefferson to JM, 25 May 1784). There is no clue concerning the subjects treated by JM in this missing letter. If JM adhered to his plan of leaving Montpelier for Richmond about 30 April, he would have been there for four or five days before writing to Jefferson (JM to Jefferson, 25 Apr. 1784). It is probably this letter which was offered in the Stan. V. Henkels Catalogue No. 686 (11–12 May 1892), item no. 182.

As a delegate from Orange County to the Virginia General Assembly, JM may have appeared before a member of the Council of State on 3 May to take the required oath, but the House of Delegates failed to muster a quorum until nine days later (*JHDV,* May 1784, pp. 3, 4).

From Thomas Jefferson

ANNAPOLIS May 8. 1784.

DEAR SIR

I will now take up the several enquiries contained in your letter of Apr. 25. which came to hand yesterday.

'Will it not be good policy to suspend further treaties of commerce till measures shall have taken place in America, which may correct the idea in Europe of impotency in the federal government in matters of commerce?' Congress think such measures requisite, and have accordingly recommended them as you will perceive by my last. In the mean time they seem to think that our commerce is got & getting into vital agonies by our exclusion from the West Indies, by late embarrasments in Spain & Portugal, and by the dangers of the Mediterranean trade. These you observe form the aggregate of our valuable markets. They think that the presumption of one or two countries should not be a reason for suspending treaties with all countries: and that the prospect of effect from their recommendations on commerce will perhaps drive on the treaties. The present favourable disposition of the piratical states on the Barbary coast has been repeatedly urged by our ministers as a circumstance which may be transient & should therefore be seised to open the Mediterranean to us.

'Has Virginia been seconded &c. in her proposition for arming Congress with powers to frustrate the unfriendly regulations of Great Britain?' Pennsylvania & Maryland offered much larger powers. Those of Virginia might have been defeated by the British king repealing his proclamation one day & renewing it the next. Yet the powers & plans from all these states were different: and it was visible they would authorize no single measure. Therefore Congress recommended a uniform measure.

'Is the impost gaining or losing ground?' Gaining, most certainly. Georgia, North Carolina, New York, Connecticut & Rhode island are yet to pass it. The three first are supposed to be willing to do it. Connecticut has held off merely to try whether Congress would not rescind the commutation. Finding a firmness on this point it is said & beleived that at their next session they will come into it. Howell has often told me that R. I. will not accede to it as long as any other state holds off: but when every other shall have adopted it, she will.

'Does the settlement of the public accounts make any comfortable progress'? They are going on, but slowly I believe. However they go on, and of course approach their term.

'Has any resolution been taken by Congress touching the old Continental currency'? That question has been debated by a grand **Commee** upwards of a month. They yesterday came to the inclosed resolution. It was decided by only 6. votes against 5. I think it will gain strength in the House. The Southern and middle states I beleive are for it, & I think one or two of the Eastern may perhaps come over. Yet there is far from being a certainty of this.[1]

'Has — forborne to take any step in favor of —?' Their object was certainly not the same with ours. Yet they have not openly set their faces against us, they have one delegate, honest & disinterested, who certainly will in no case do it?[2]

'Whether the war ceased in March or April?' I think no decision has taken place on that subject in our court of Appeals. Our ministers write that it is no question on that side the water but that it ended in March.

The produce of our slave tax being nearly equal to the Continental requisitions, can you not get it appropriated to that purpose, & have it all paid in money?[3] Virginia must do something more than she has done to maintain any degree of respect in the Union & to make it bearable to any man of feeling to represent her in Congress. The public necessities call distressingly for aid, and very ruinous circumstances proceed from the inattention of the states to furnish supplies in money. S. Carolina is the foremost state in supplies notwithstanding her distresses.[4]

Whence does this proceed? from a difference of spirit solely; from a pride of character; from a rejection of the unmanly supineness which permits personal inconveniency to absorb every other sentiment. There is no man who has not some vice or folly the atoning of which would not pay his taxes.

I am now to take my leave of the justlings of states and to repair a feild where the divisions will be fewer but on a larger scale. Congress yesterday joined me to mr Adams & Dr Franklin on the foreign commercial negotiations. I shall pursue there the line I have pursued here, convinced that it can never be the interest of any party to do what is unjust, or to ask what is unequal. Mr. Jay was to sail for America this month. His health has obliged him to return to try his native air. He is appointed Secy. for Foreign affairs. I pray you to continue to favor me with your correspondence. At the close of every session of assembly a state of the general measures & dispositions, as well as of the subordinate politics of parties or individuals will be entertaining and useful. During recesses other objects will furnish matter sufficient for communication. On my part I shall certainly maintain the correspondence. If moreover you can at any time enable me to serve you by the execution of any particular commission I shall agree that my sincerity may be judged by the readiness with which I shall execute it. In the purchase of books, pamphlets &c. old & curious, or new & useful, I shall ever keep you in my eye. Whether I shall procure for you the books you have before desired at Philadelphia or Paris shall be decided according to circumstances when I get to Philadelphia, from which place I will write to you.

I have a tender legacy to leave you on my departure. I will not say it is the son of my sister, tho her worth would justify my resting it on that ground; but it is the son of my friend, the dearest friend I knew, who, had fate reversed our lots would have been a father to my children.[5] He is a boy of fine dispositions, and sound masculine talents. I was his preceptor myself as long as I staid at home, & when I came away I placed him with mr Maury. On his breaking up his school I desired mr Short to dispose of him, but mr Short I expect will go with me to Europe. I have no body then but you to whose direction I could consign him with unlimited confidence. He is nearly master of the Latin, and has read some Greek. I beleive he is about 14. years of age. I would wish him to be employed till 16. in completing himself in latin, Greek, French, Italian & Anglosaxon. At that age I mean him to go to the college. I have written to my sister of the application I make to you

31

& she will be very happy to have your advice executed. My steward Mr Key will furnish money to his tutors &c on your order. There is a younger one, just now in his Latin rudiments.[6] If I did not fear to overcharge you I would request you to recommend the best school for him. He is about 10. years old, and of course ceteris paribus, of any two schools that nearest his mother would be most agreeable. You will readily understand I am speaking of the sons of mr Carr. I think Colo Monroe will be of the Committee of the states. *He wishes a correspondence with you;* and I suppose his situation will render him an useful one to you.[7] The scrupulousness of his honor will make you safe in the most confidential communications. A better man [there] cannot be. I think your two loans to me amounted to 503 1/3 Dollars. I paid for the first pair of spectacles 13 2/3 Doll. & shall pay the same for the 2d. unless they should be returned. I now inclose you an order on the Treasurer for 407 1/3 Dollars which will leave in my hand a balance of 68 2/3 Dollars due to you which was about the sum you desired.

May 11. Many considerations have determined me to go on to Boston & take shipping from thence. This was a conclusion of yesterday. All my letters dated previous to that will state me as purposing to sail from N. York. I leave this place to-day; expect to stay in Philadelphia till the 25th. and to be at Boston about the 3d. of June. I am with the sincerest esteem Dr. Sir Your affectionate friend & servt.

TH. JEFFERSON

RC (DLC: Rives Collection, Madison Papers). Franked by Jefferson and addressed by him to "James Madison junr. esq. of Orange now in Richmond." A six-page Ms of which the first four pages are in DLC: Rives Collection, and the last two in DLC: Madison Papers.

[1] The enclosure, in Jefferson's hand and dated "[1784, May 7]," was a report on "continental Bills of Credit" designed to liquidate and, according to equitable scales of depreciation, eventually to discharge the indebtedness arising from the issuance of such bills (Boyd, *Papers of Jefferson*, VII, 221–24).

[2] The blanks should be filled respectively with "Maryland" and "George Town" (JM to Jefferson, 25 Apr. 1784). The "honest & disinterested" delegate from Maryland was probably Thomas Stone.

[3] By an act of the Virginia General Assembly at its session of Oct. 1782, an owner paid annually a tax of 10 s. for each of his slaves except those exempted "through age or infirmity" by a county court (Hening, *Statutes*, XI, 113). The annual income from the tax was potentially £225,635. This may have been over twice as much as was actually realized in 1784 from the slave tax, for in that year the net revenue received from "lands and lots, slaves, free male titheables and taxable property" was approximately £242,678. In that year the "State's quota of the interest on the debts due by the United States" was £120,000 (ca. $400,000) (*JHDV*, Oct. 1784, p. 85).

4 Although suffering heavily from the war in 1780 and 1781, South Carolina by the close of 1783 had paid most of its quota of a congressional requisition totaling $8 million; she had paid a far greater proportion than any other state. Virginia had paid less than 10 percent (*JCC*, XXVI, 194; Ferguson, *Power of the Purse*, pp. 181–83).

5 Jefferson meant that if he rather than Dabney Carr, Peter's father, had died in 1773, then Carr would have been the guardian of Jefferson's children (Boyd, *Papers of Jefferson*, I, 98 n.; Malone, *Jefferson the Virginian*, p. 431).

6 The "younger one," Dabney Carr, Jr. (1773–1837), was nearly eleven years of age. JM also undertook to advise about this boy's education (JM to Jefferson, 3 July, 20 Aug. 1784).

7 Unless an earlier interchange of letters has been lost, the voluminous correspondence between JM and Monroe began with a brief note from the latter to JM on 7 Nov. 1784.

To James Madison, Sr.

RICHMOND May 13. 1784.

HOND. SIR

The Spectacles herewith inclosed came to my hands yesterday with information that the pr. first sent were forwarded by mistake. It will however give my mother a double chance of suiting herself. I wish the pr. which may not be preferred, to be sent down to me by the earliest opportunity, unless they should suit yourself & you chuse to keep them, as I am desired by the Maker to return them in case they sd. not be wanted. We did not make a House till wednesday & of course are but just beginning the business of the Session. Mr. Jefferson has been appd. an Associate with Dr. F. & Mr. Adams in forming commercial Treaties and will proceed immediately to Europe. He takes the place of Mr. Jay who is returning to America & who is to be the Secretary of F. Affairs if he will accept the office. I do not find that S. Jones[1] is as yet here, & I suspend the sale of the Tobo. with a hope of its further rise. 38/. I believe may now be got, but 40/. is generally expected. I am your dutiful son.

J. MADISON JR.

RC (DLC). Cover missing. Docketed by James Madison, Sr., and by JM at a later date.

1 Probably Captain Samuel Jones, Henrico County businessman, frequently employed by the state in settlement of accounts (*JCSV*, III, 212, 266; *JHDV*, May 1783, p. 77; Oct. 1783, pp. 47–48). If his absence was not owing to death, he certainly died within a month after the writing of the present letter (Vi: Henrico County Court Records, Will Book 1, 1781–1787, microfilm, pp. 138–39).

To Thomas Jefferson

Letter not found.

14 May 1784. In his "Summary Journal of Letters," Jefferson recorded that he received on 19 June a letter written by JM in Richmond on 14 May, "inclosing on account B. Harrison John Pirkman's draught on John J. Rogert [Bogert] Phila. for 333 1/3 D." (Boyd, *Papers of Jefferson,* VII, 251). Writing to Jefferson from Richmond on 22 May, William Short appears to have enclosed JM's now missing letter with his own (ibid., VII, 284–85 n.). B. Harrison was in all likelihood Benjamin Harrison, Jr.; John Pirkman (d. ca. 1786) was a Richmond merchant.

To Thomas Jefferson

RICHMOND May 15. 1784

DEAR SIR

Your favor of the 7th. inst: with another pr. of spectacles inclosed came safe to hand on thursday last. I shall leave the person for whose use they were intended to take choice of the most suitable & will return the other pr. to Mr. Dudley by the first conveyance, unless I meet with a purchaser which I do not expect. The arrangement which is to carry you to Europe has been made known to me by Mr. Short who tells me he means to accompany or follow you. With the many reasons which make this event agreeable, I can not but mix some regret that your aid towards a revisal of our State Constitution will be removed. I hope however for your licence to make use of the ideas you were so good as to confide to me, so far as they may be necessary to forward the object. Whether any experiment will be made this Session is uncertain.[1] Several members with whom I have casually conversed give me more encouragemt. than I had indulged. As Col: Mason remains in private life, the expediency of starting the idea will depend much on the part to be expected from R. H. L. & P. H. The former is not yet come to this place, nor can I determine any thing as to his politics on this point. The latter arrived yesterday & from a short conversation I find him strenuous for invigorating the federal Govt. though without any precise plan, but have got no explanations from him as to our internal Govt. The general train of his thoughts seemed to suggest favorable expectations. We did not make a House till wednesday last, & have done nothing yet but arrange the Committees & receive petitions. The former Speaker was re-elected without opposition. If you will either before or after your leaving America point out the channel of communication with you in Europe, I will take the pleasure of supplying you from time to time with our internal transac[tions] as far as they may deserve your attention, & expect that you will freely command every other service during yr. absence which it may be in my power to render. Wishing you every success & happiness I am Dr Sir Your affecte. friend

J. MADISON JR.

RC (DLC). Cover missing. Docketed by JM many years later.

1 While JM and Jefferson had toyed with the idea of a drastic revision of the 1776 Virginia Constitution, most public men in Virginia were in no mood to tinker with the machinery of state government. A far more pressing matter was the distinct possibility that debts owed by Virginians to British merchants would have to be paid in full, as provided by the 1783 peace treaty. James Monroe believed the sum involved to be a staggering £2,800,000 (Boyd, *Papers of Jefferson*, VII, 48). Speaker John Tyler was seeking allies who knew "how unjust it was to consent to the payment of the debts after such an unusual manner of Warfare had been carryed on" (ibid., p. 277). But whatever the focus of legislative strife, Edmund Randolph predicted to Jefferson, "our friend of Orange will step earlier into the heat of battle, than his modesty would otherwise permit, For he is already resorted to, as a general, of whom much has been preconceived to his advantage" (ibid., p. 260).

From Samuel House

Letter not found.

18 May 1784. Mentioned in JM's letter to House, 29 May 1784. Probably related the news of Nicholas Trist's death.

The General Assembly Session of May 1784

EDITORIAL NOTE

The sword had been sheathed, so the problems faced by the Commonwealth of Virginia and her sister states in 1784 were no longer a life-and-death matter. As James Madison rode down to Richmond in May his thoughts must have been on the still-unsolved dilemma that had confronted Congress from almost the outset: finance. The cost of running the small bureaucracy that kept the Confederation operating was not great, but the debt accumulated through seven years of war was by 1784 standards staggering, totaling some £40 million, while the interest kept piling up with unpaid creditors both at home and abroad. Americans in Madison's time regarded that national debt in the same manner as English politicians had looked upon theirs—a high-priority matter of both national honor and fiscal solvency. Most of the difficulties Madison and his fellow legislators faced came down to a single concern—money, or the lack of it.

Thus there had been little cheering when the end of the war was formally proclaimed, and if a German traveler's observations are to be credited, the delegates were more concerned with talking about "horse-races, runaway negroes, yesterday's play, [or] politics," than with carrying on legislative business. Johann Schoepf's view of Patrick Henry certainly rang true. "Among the orators here is a certain Mr. Henry who appears to have the greatest influence over the House" (Johann David Schoepf, *Travels in the Confederation, 1783–1784*, trans. Alfred J. Morrison [2 vols.; Philadelphia, 1911], II, 55, 56). Indeed, Henry was as powerful in 1784 as he had been in 1774—still a man to be reckoned with before any substantial changes could be wrought. From early conversations, JM was led to believe that one of his favored schemes—a revision of the Articles of Confederation "giving greater Powers to the fœderal government"—would have Henry's support during this May session (Boyd, *Papers of Jefferson*, VII, 257). But if Henry made such a promise, he quickly forgot it.

What JM soon learned was that the peacetime power structure in Virginia was as jealous and static as in earlier days. Peace brought a shifting of attention to the lingering problems of prewar debts owed to British merchants which many Virginians were not eager to settle. Then there was the need to repeal wartime legislation. The revised code of Virginia's statutes, which a committee headed by Jefferson had undertaken back in 1777–1779, was gathering dust. Great Britain had taken steps to choke the lucrative trade with her West Indian colonies. The states' accounts with the Confederation desperately needed settlement.

On the other hand, there was some good news. Prices for corn and tobacco were rising, which meant that farmers could pay their taxes (at least part of them) without undue strain. Some of the northern states were quibbling over boundaries and resented the rapacity of their neighbors, but Virginia had no quarrels with North Carolina, and the Maryland legislature appeared disposed toward a settlement of grievances related to the maritime use of Chesapeake Bay. There was a small surplus in the state treasury, but state contributions to the federal government were not possible unless taxes were forthcoming. Various kinds of paper currency (including tobacco warehouse receipts) kept the economy from stagnating. Nobody was starving, and if tobacco prices kept rising, there were prospects for an unusually prosperous year ahead.

JM saw signs of coming trouble, however, and hoped to forestall some of it at the May 1784 session of the General Assembly. The Virginia cession of its vast western territory above the Ohio had given the entire Union a stake in its development. For the moment, Congress looked on the enormous wilderness as the solution for the debt problem, a majority of the delegates being disposed to sell the Northwest Territory to pay off wartime debts. Left unsettled were the irritating Spanish presence in the Mississippi Valley and the British garrisons still (because of unfinished business from the Treaty of Paris) holding western posts. The Spanish were inclined to block western expansion by closing the great central river to American shippers. The two European powers thought they were maintaining valid interests, but in asserting their power they also aided the cause of American nationality by demonstrating the weaknesses of a decentralized Confederation.

A weak Congress was powerless to force concessions from haughty diplomats from Madrid or London, but at Richmond the talk was tough. Patrick Henry said more than once that Virginia ought to make no concessions to British creditors until the frontier posts were properly in American hands. Between the British and Henry's followers there stretched a tightrope on which JM, at the 1784 legislative sessions, was forced to dance.

Fortunately JM was never one to seek a showdown in a fight he was sure to lose. He wanted to answer Congress in the most positive terms when a flexibility in the Articles of Confederation was sought that would have given the national government a certain source of revenue. JM took to the hustings, he later recalled, because in the forum of the House of Delegates he would have an opportunity to bring about "a rescue of the Union, and the blessings of liberty staked on it, from an impending catastrophe." He could also help restore public confidence in the fiscal soundness of the new nation (Madison, *Papers* [Gilpin ed.], II, 693–94). Unquestionably the younger men in Virginia politics expected him to furnish leadership. "The Assembly . . . have formed great Hopes of Mr. Madison, and those who know him best think he will not disappoint their most sanguine Expectations," William Short informed Jefferson (Boyd, *Papers of Jefferson*, VII, 257).

At the outset of the session, the prospects were not bleak. Henry told JM and others, during a coffee-house conversation, that he would work for a strengthening of the Confederation because "a bold Example set by Virginia would have Influence on the other States" (ibid., p. 257). As JM learned, Henry was capable of saying one thing and doing another. The battle grew hotter as the session progressed, with JM in the thick of it because of numerous assignments, including the chairmanship of the Commerce committee. But JM had learned a deftness that gave him a great advantage over intractable men. He knew the heat of battle, but JM was never burned badly because he knew when to let go of an overheated issue. By fending off measures to subsidize the Protestant Episcopal church, by keeping Kentuckians from feeling totally neglected, and by holding out hope that Congress and the British creditors might all get their money some day, he demonstrated remarkable skills as a legislator.

JM's role during this session is readily apparent from the legislation preserved in his handwriting and printed in this volume. It is not a complete record, however, because the General Assembly files in the Virginia State Library are fragmentary. JM's holographs need no justification, but probably many bills are missing which carried his ideas if not his whole construction. A clue to his unrecorded work is furnished by a ceremonial courtesy of that day: the House of Delegates expected a bill's author to carry the passed measure forward to the Senate. Nevertheless the journal entry "Mr. Madison was ordered to carry the bill to the Senate" is not an infallible guide, for on

37

a given occasion the drafter of legislation could be absent on other business or ill—in which case a designated committee member may simply have performed an assigned errand. Sometimes, committee chairmen filled this role. This was doubtless the case with some of the bills for which there exists no evidence of JM's interest other than the fact that he took it to the Senate. Appendix A of this volume carries a full listing of legislation which JM introduced or carried to the Senate but did not draft.

Resolutions to Strengthen Powers of Congress

EDITORIAL NOTE

On 19 May a special Committee of the Whole House heard Henry Tazewell introduce seven resolutions, the first and last of which are those printed below. All seven dealt with subjects of confederation or state finance and lay within an area to which JM had devoted much attention as a delegate in Congress. Designed to strengthen the powers of Congress, they were closely attuned to his political philosophy, and each may have been in whole or in part the product of his mind. Of Tazewell's resolutions, only the "3d:" has been found in Ms (Vi), and this is not in JM's hand.

[19 May 1784]

Resolved, that it is the opinion of this committee, That the alteration of the eighth of the articles of the confederation and perpetual union, proposed by the United States in Congress assembled, on the 18th of April 1783, ought to be acceded to by this State.[1]

Resolved, that it is the opinion of this committee, That the United States in Congress assembled, ought to be invested with power for the term of fifteen years, to prohibit any goods, wares or merchandize from being imported into or exported from any of the States, in vessels belonging to or navigated by the subjects of any power with whom these States shall not have formed treaties of commerce, and with a further power for the like term of fifteen years of prohibiting the subjects of any foreign State, Kingdom or Empire, unless authorised by treaty, from importing into the United States, any goods, wares or merchandize which are not the produce or manufacture of the dominions of the sovereign whose subjects they are: *Provided,* that to all acts of the United States in Congress assembled, in pursuance of the above powers, the assent of nine States be necessary.[2]

Printed text (*JHDV*, May 1784, pp. 11, 12).

[1] The proposed amendment was designed to replace land valuations by a triennial census of state populations as a means of determining congressional requisitions. Set forth in JM's Report on Public Credit, 6 Mar. 1783 (*Papers of Madison*, VI, 313–14), the amendment had been adopted by Congress on 18 Apr. 1783 (*JCC*, XXIV, 260–61), and its acceptance by the states strongly urged in his Address to the States, 25 Apr. 1783 (*Papers of Madison*, VI, 491–92). Passed on 19 May, the present resolution was approved by the Senate on 8 June. There the matter rested for nearly two weeks until on 21 June a delegate offered a resolution "That leave be given to bring in a bill 'to authorise the delegates representing this State in Congress, to subscribe and ratify an alteration in the 8th of the articles of confederation and perpetual union between the thirteen States of America.' " The resolution was passed and JM appointed the chairman of a three-member committee to prepare such a bill, which suggests that it was JM who moved the issue. He conferred with his colleagues and introduced the bill later in the same day. See Bill Authorizing an Amendment in the Articles of Confederation, 21 June 1784.

[2] In Jefferson's letter of 7 May, JM had received a copy of the congressional resolution on which the seventh committee resolution was based. This resolution follows almost verbatim that of Congress (*JCC*, XXVI, 320, 322). That the copy forwarded by Jefferson served as the model seems likely since the official transcript of the resolution was not received by the House of Delegates until the following day—that is, 20 May (Executive Letter Book, p. 325; *JHDV*, May 1784, p. 13).

JM was on a committee appointed to prepare a bill of implementation that became law on 30 June (*JHDV*, May 1784, pp. 12, 37, 81, 86, 89). He may well have drafted the bill himself, but so closely did the bill follow the wording of the congressional resolution that to all practical effect it had already been drafted by Congress in session at Annapolis (Hening, *Statutes*, XI, 388–89). The legislation was in further retaliation to British trading restrictions imposed in July 1783 which prevented the resumption of the lucrative trade with the British West Indies. An act passed at the Oct. 1783 session had authorized Congress to prohibit West Indian imports "so long as the said restriction shall be continued on the part of Great Britain" (ibid., pp. 313–14). Fortunately, American exports to the French West Indies rose steadily during the 1780s to offset some of the loss (John H. Coatsworth, "American Trade with European Colonies in the Caribbean and South America, 1790–1812," *WMQ*, 3d ser., XXIV [1967], 246–47; Albert Anthony Giesecke, *American Commercial Legislation before 1789* [New York, 1910], pp. 126–27).

Bill for Regulating the Appointment of Delegates to Congress

[22 May 1784]

Whereas Congress by their Act of November in the Year of our Lord one thousand seven hundred and eighty three have recommended to the Respective States in the Union to pass Laws for the purpose of keeping up a full Representation in Congress from each State, and it is expedient to reduce the several Acts of Assembly now in force in this CommonWealth respecting the appointment of Delegates to Congress into one Act.[1]

Be it therefore enacted that all and every Act or Acts which now are in force concerning the Mode of appointing & the manner of supporting Delegates to Congress from this State shall be and the same are hereby repealed. And be it enacted that   Delegates shall be annually chosen to represent this CommonWealth in Congress by joint ballot of both Houses of Assembly for one Year to commence from the first Monday in November next ensuing the date of their Appointments. [that so soon] as such election [shall be made]² the Speakers of each House of General Assembly shall notify the same to his Excellency the Governor who thereupon shall cause a credential to be made Out, the Seal of the CommonWealth affixed thereto, signed by him, & delivered to each Delegate so as aforesaid chosen—which credential shall be in the Words following to wit—Virginia Sci: The General Assembly of this CommonWealth on the   day of   17 by joint ballot of both Houses elected   Esquire a Delegate to serve this CommonWealth, in Congress for one Year to commence from the first Monday in November next ensuing the date of his appointment. Given under my hand and the Seal of the CommonWealth this   day of   17 And be it further enacted that in case of the death resignation or removal from office of any Delegate to Congress the person who shall be elected to supply the vacancy occasioned by such death resignation or removal from office shall serve only for the period which such Delegate would have served in case such death resignation or removal from office had not happened And the Credential to be given as aforesaid by the Governor shall be varied accordingly.

And for the better support of the Delegates so as aforesaid elected, Be it further enacted that the Treasurer of this CommonWealth shall pay to each of them or to their order the sum of   per day³ for every day they shall be attending or travelling to, or returning from Congress, together with their Carriages in going to and returning from Congress.

Nothing in this Act shall extend to the Delegates at present representing this State in Congress who shall continue to act and receive the same allowance as they would do, had this Act never been made, until the first Monday, in November, that shall be in the Year 1784. And in case any vacancy shall happen in the present representation of this State in Congress, before that period the same shall be supplied in the same manner as if this Act had never been made.⁴

Ms (Vi). Written in several hands and docketed as "A Bill For regulating the appointment of Delegates to Congress," by John Beckley, clerk of the House of

Delegates. Accompanying the Ms are two folios recording changes made in the bill after its introduction.

¹ Congress had adopted the "Act" on 1 Nov. 1783 (*JCC*, XXV, 790–91). For the "several Acts" in Virginia, see Hening, *Statutes*, IX, 73–74, 133–34 and passim; X, 74–75 and passim; XI, 31, 249.

² Several words in the original are illegible but have been restored from the printed text in Hening, *Statutes*, XI, 365. The House later inserted an important amendment preceding this phrase and after "Appointments": "three of whom at least shall be constantly attending to discharge the duties of their Office, when, and where that Honorable Body shall be sitting." For an effective vote to be cast in Congress by a state, at least two of its delegates had to agree on the question at issue. The requirement that three be present avoided the possibility of a deadlock in voting. This improved the 1779 law, which provided that "any one" of the delegates in Congress, "or a majority of those present, if more than one," could "give the vote of the commonwealth" (ibid., X, 163). This provision had virtually become obsolete on 1 Mar. 1781 with the adoption of the Articles of Confederation, since Article V stipulated that at least two state delegates should agree for the vote of that state to be effective (*JCC*, XIX, 215).

³ In its final form, the House fixed a delegate's pay at $8.00 per diem.

⁴ The bill was debated and amended on 28 May, passed the House on 31 May, and became law on 17 June 1784 (*JHDV*, May 1784, pp. 25–28 and passim). As enacted, it carries an amended section rephrasing that portion of this paragraph after the words "as they would . . ."

Motion on Settlement of National Accounts

[22 May 1784]

Ordered, That a committee of five members be appointed to inquire into the progress made by the commissioners employed in settling the accounts between this State and the United States, and into the difficulties which may impede the same, and make report thereupon to the House.[1]

Printed text (*JHDV*, May 1784, p. 16).

¹ Having long been concerned about this subject JM almost certainly offered this motion, a probability increased by his appointment as chairman of the committee. The other members were James Hubard (1743–ca. 1786), Wilson Cary Nicholas (1761–1820), William Norvell (ca. 1726–1802), and James Wood (1750–1813). JM delivered the report for the committee on 28 May.

From Thomas Jefferson

DEAR SIR

Your favors of the 8th. & 15th. came to hand yesterday. I have this morning revised your former letters to see what commissions it would be best for me to execute here for you. In that of Feb. 17, you desire a recommendation of a fit bookseller in Paris & London. This certainly I can better do from the spot. In the mean time address yourself to me as your bookseller for either place, because at whichever I shall be I can easily order books to be sent you from the other. In the letter of March 16. you wish for any good books on the Droit public or constitutions of the several existing confederacies & on the Law of Nature & Nations. There are some books at Boinod's on the first of these subjects but I have not time to examine them. I can do this so conveniently in Paris, get them on so much better terms, have them bound, & send them so speedily that I will refer the execution of this commission till I get there.[1] Bynkershoeck & Wolfius I will also examine there & send you such parts of their works as I think you will like. Boinod will receive very soon the following books which he wrote for for me. Should you chuse any of them you will write to him & he will send them to you.

Les troubles des pais bas de Grotius.

Wicquefort des ambassadeurs.

Memoires de l'Amerique.

Barrington's miscellanies.

Scheele's chemical observations on air & fire.

whatever has been written on air or fire by Fontana, Priestly, Ingenhouse, Black, Irvine, or Crawford.[2]

I have searched every book shop in town this morning for Deane's letters & Hawk' abr' Co. Lit. except Bell's. It is in none of them. Pritchard had sold Zane's copy. I shall examine Bell's also before I leave town & if I get them they shall come with Blair's lectures which I purchased for you of Aitken & have desired him to send to Richmond to the care of James Buchanan.

Mr Zane is probably with you.[3] Pray deliver my friendly compliments to him, tell him I have written three letters to him and find him unpunctual, having answered none of them. I am very anxious to receive the thermometrical trials I asked him to make in his cave. I wish they could be sent to me immediately to Paris. I could not get my notes

printed here & therefore refer it till I shall cross the water where I will
have a few copies struck off & send you one.[4] The assembly of N. York
have made Payne the author of Common sense a present of a farm.
Could you prevail on our assembly to do something for him. I think
their quota of what ought to be given him would be 2000 guineas, or
an inheritance worth 100 guineas a year. It would be peculiarly magnanimous in them to do it; because it would shew that no particular &
smaller passion has suppressed the grateful impressions which his services have made on our minds.[5] Did I ever inform you that Genl. Washington would accept the superintendance of the clearing the Patow'm'
& Ohio, if put on a hopeful footing? Two vessels are arrived here in
24 & 25 days passage from London. They say the elections are going
in favor of the ministry. Mrs House is well and her lodgings well accustomed.[6] Poor mrs Trist is in a situation which gives us much pain.
Her husband is dead, and she without knowing it is proceeding down
the Ohio & Missisipi in hopes of joining him. There is a possibility only
that letters sent from hence may overtake her at the Falls of Ohio &
recall her to this place. I am obliged to put a period here to my letter
being desired to assist in a consultation on a very disagreeable affair.
A Frenchman of obscure & worthless character having applied to mr
Marbois to give him the Consular attestations to a falsehood and being
refused, attacked him in the streets a day or two after and beat him
much with his cane.[7] The minister has taken up this daring insult & violation of the law of nations in the person of the Secretary to their
embassy & demands him to be given up (being a subject of France) to
be sent there for punishment. I doubt whether the laws of this state
have provided either to punish him sufficiently here or to surrender
him to be punished by his own sovereign: and the——of this state is
so indecisive that no defects of law will be supplied by any confidence
of his in the justification of his assembly when they shall meet.[8] They
have not yet declared what they can or will do, & the scoundrel is going
at large on bail, sending anonymous letters to the minister & Marbois
with threats of assassination &c if the prosecution be not discontinued.
The affair is represented to Congress who will have the will but not
the power to interpose. It will probably go next to France & bring on
serious consequences. For god's sake while this instance of the necessity
of providing for the enforcement of the law of nations is fresh on men's
minds, introduce a bill which shall be effectual & satisf[act]ory on this
subject.[9] Consuls you will always have. Ministers may pass occasionally
through our country. Members of Congress must pass through it.

Should Congress sit in or near the state, frequent instances of their members & public ministers entering the state may occur: I wish you every possible felicity & shall hope to hear from you frequently. I am with sincere esteem Dr. Sir your friend & sert

TH: JEFFERSON

RC (DLC). Cover missing. Docketed by JM and in an unkown hand.

[1] Jefferson used "refer" in the now obsolete sense of "postpone."

[2] The short titles of works alluded to: Cornelius van Bynkershoek, *Traité du juge competent des ambassadeurs;* Christianus Wolfius, *Principes du droit de la nature et des gens,* and *Jus gentium methodo scientifica pertractatum;* Hugo Grotius, *De rebus Belgicis; or, The Annals and History of the Low-Countrey-Wars;* Abraham van Wicquefort, *The Ambassador and His Functions, to Which Is Added, an Historical Discourse concerning the Election of the Emperor, and the Electors;* MM. de Silhouette, de la Galissonière, Abbé de la Ville, *Memoires des commissaires du roi et de ceux de Sa Majesté Britannique, sur les possessions & les droits respectifs des deux Couronnes en Amérique;* Daines Barrington, *Miscellanies;* Carl Wilhelm Scheele, *Chemical Observations and Experiments on Air and Fire;* Felice Fontana, *Recherches physiques sur la nature de l'air nitreux et de l'air déphlogistiqué;* Joseph Priestly, *Experiments and Observations on Different Kinds of Air;* and *Philosophical Empiricism;* Jan Ingenhousz, *Experiments upon Vegetables;* Joseph Black, *Experiments upon Magnesia Alba, Quick Lime and Other Alcaline Substances;* William Irvine (1743–1787), professor of chemistry at the University of Glasgow, was famed for the clarity and logic of his lectures, but none of his writings appeared in print until 1805; Adair Crawford, *Experiments and Observations on Animal Heat, and the Inflammation of Combustible Bodies.*

[3] Isaac Zane, Jr., was a delegate from Frederick County, 1776–1782, and thereafter from Shenandoah County until his death in 1795 (Swem and Williams, *Register,* p. 450; Roger W. Moss, Jr., "Isaac Zane, Jr., a 'Quaker for the Times,'" *VMHB,* LXXVII [1969], 291–306). Zane's presence in the current session before 11 June cannot be demonstrated (*JHDV,* May 1784, p. 51).

[4] Jefferson had 200 copies of his *Notes on the State of Virginia* printed in Paris in 1785 (Boyd, *Papers of Jefferson,* IV, 167 n.).

[5] Thomas Paine's personal distress aroused Jefferson's sympathy and moved other Virginians despite the "particular & smaller passion" that upset many in 1782. Then, Paine had written the pamphlet *Public Good* in support of a land speculating clique that challenged Virginia's title to the lands north and west of the Ohio River. A bill introduced by JM in the House of Delegates on Paine's behalf was defeated on 30 June 1784.

[6] "Well accustomed," i.e., well filled with lodgers.

[7] The "obscure & worthless character" was Charles Julien Longchamps (Alfred Rosenthal, "The Marbois-Longchamps Affair," *Pennsylvania Magazine of History and Biography,* LXIII [1939], 294–95). This episode created issues involving the "law of nations," extradition, the power and duty of Congress and of the sovereign commonwealth of Pennsylvania, respectively, which embarrassed Franco-American relations for over two years.

[8] Jefferson intended that JM should fill in the blank with "President John Dickinson" of Pennsylvania.

[9] Pennsylvania enacted a law providing further punishment of a "violation of the law of nations" in the fall of 1784. Then, at its Oct. 1784 session, the Virginia Gen-

eral Assembly became the only other state to enact a similar law up to that time by explicitly providing for the extradition, upon the request of Congress. Any inhabitant of Virginia who had returned after allegedly violating the "law of nations" or "any treaty between the United States and a foreign nation" had to be surrendered to the offended nation (*JHDV*, Oct. 1784, p. 110; Hening, *Statutes*, XI, 471–72). Thus after three years only these two states had heeded the congressional resolution of 23 Nov. 1781 urging each state to create or designate a court invested with power "to provide expeditious, exemplary and adequate punishment" of anyone found guilty of "offences against the law of nations" (*JCC*, XXI, 1136–37). See also J. Rives Childs, "French Consul Martin Oster Reports on Virginia, 1784–1796," *VMHB*, LXXVI (1968), 27–40. Oster was arrested in Norfolk on the complaint of a French national.

Report and Resolution on Accounts between Virginia and the United States

In the House of Delegates Friday the 28th of May 1784.

It appears from the enquiries of your Committee, that no progress has yet been made in the settlement of the said Accounts.

It appears from the representation of the said Commissioner that he arrived at this place in September last & has been since in readiness to receive & examine, both the Debits of the State & the demands of its Citizens against the United States, but that neither the former nor the latter have been presented to him for that purpose.[1]

It appears from the representation of the Solicitor, who was instructed to prepare a state of the Debits of this CommonWealth against the United States[2]—that he has executed the task, but has foreborne to present the Accounts for settlement—alledging principally as his reason therefor, that as the powers of the Commissioner were restrained to the Debits which are allowed by the existing Resolutions of Congress, he was apprehensive that a partial settlement disallowing so great a proportion of the expences for which Virginia expects reimbursement might detract from her future Claim of reimbursement.

It further appears to your Committee, that the non-settlement of the Accounts between the United States & individuals, within this State, so far as the Claims of the latter are authorized by Resolutions of Congress, has been owing to the provision made by Law for liquidating such Accounts in common with others, in a mode which makes the CommonWealth Debtor to such Individuals, and invests it with the Claims of the latter against the United States

Whereupon Resolved that it is the opinion of your Committee that the Solicitor be instructed to submit forthwith to the Commissioner aforesaid, all the Accounts & Claims whatever of this CommonWealth against the United States which he may be authorized by Resolutions of Congress to liquidate—that the said Solicitor support the same by the best proofs & Vouchers, which the cases may respectively admit, and that he prepare a statement under proper heads and descriptions, of all such Claims as are not yet allowed by Resolutions of Congress, and lay the same before the General Assembly at their next Session.[3]

Ms (Vi). In a clerk's hand. Docketed, "Mr. Madison." For the background of the report, see Motion on Settlement of National Accounts, 22 May 1784.

[1] The Confederation commissioner was Zephaniah Turner (1734–1794), the auditor general of Maryland from Feb. 1781 until his resignation in Aug. 1783 (Mrs. Willetta Baylis Blum et al., comps., *The Baylis Family of Virginia* [Washington, 1958], pp. 425–26; *Archives of Maryland*, XLV, 307; XLVIII, 449).

[2] The solicitor general was Leighton Wood. His instructions are in the Executive Letter Book, pp. 202, 206, 250, 289, and 319.

[3] Instead of the report requested, Wood sent the Oct. 1784 session of the General Assembly a message dwelling on "some of the obstacles" impeding his progress in disentangling the confusion of claims (Executive Letter Book, p. 437; *JHDV*, Oct. 1784, p. 72).

To Samuel House

RICHMOND May 29. 1784

DEAR SIR

I have just recd. your favor of the 18 inst: inclosing one from my amiable friend Mrs. Trist.[1] I feel pathetically for her in case she should have proceeded down the river before the news of Mr. Trist's death got to Fort Pitt. The situation in which she will find herself at the end of her voyage bereft of the object of her pursuit, and surrounded wholly by strangers whose very language will be unknown to her, must excite the deepest sympathy in all who are acquainted with her merit & sensibility. I make no doubt that the first advice of the melancholy event was forwarded by you to the place at which she was to embark, and therefore indulge some hope, that her voyage may have been prevented. Should it be otherwise my anxiety for her happiness & interest will excuse me in suggesting to your fraternal affection, the propriety of takeing an immediate passage for N. Orleans, not only for the purpose of soothing & supporting her under her misfortunes, but of securing to her the fruits of Mr. Trists labours and accompanying her return. The letter referred to in that of the 18th. has never come to hand.[2] Let me hear from you on the receipt of this, that I may know through what channel & to what place, I may direct an answer to Mrs. Trists letter & in case you should in the mean time have an opportunity, assure her of my unalterable friendship & esteem. Present my affect. respects also to your worthy Mamma.[3] I am Dear Sir Yrs. sincerely

J. MADISON JR.

RC (ViU). Addressed, "Mr. Samuel House Corner of Market & fifth streets Philadelphia" with a postal clerk's addition of "1/10" and "Market St." Docketed by House, "Richmond May 29 1784 Js Maddison."

[1] Neither the letter of 18 May nor its enclosure has been found.

[2] Apparently Samuel House had written a letter to JM prior to the 18 May letter, which has not been found.

[3] Mrs. Mary House, whose boardinghouse was JM's living quarters when he stayed in Philadelphia.

Resolution on the Revision of the Virginia Statutes

EDITORIAL NOTE

Among the many reforms introduced during the exciting 1776 session of the Virginia House of Delegates was Jefferson's plan for a thorough revision of the new state's statutory code "corrected, in all it's parts, with a single eye to reason, and the good of those for whose government it was framed" (Boyd, *Papers of Jefferson*, II, 307). JM was an Orange County delegate at that historic first meeting of the newly designated House of Delegates, but he was not involved in Jefferson's plan to create a Committee of Revisors charged with the arduous assignment of a reformation of the Commonwealth's laws. By an act of the General Assembly, the task was first assigned to Jefferson, Thomas Ludwell Lee, George Mason, Edmund Pendleton, and George Wythe (*JHDV*, Oct. 1776, p. 41). For a variety of reasons, the committee membership shrank and the work went slowly. Jefferson was impatient with the delays, but the committee which finally undertook the work consisted of the thirty-three-year-old lawyer and two other attorneys—Pendleton and Wythe. By 1779, the revisors had prepared at least 130 bills, although some had meanwhile become law because of wartime expediency. The bulk of the committee's report had been turned over to Speaker Benjamin Harrison on 18 June 1779, but consideration was postponed until the next meeting of the Assembly. It was not until 1785 that action was systematically taken upon the greater proportion of the bills (Mays, *Edmund Pendleton*, II, 138–43, 158–61, 373 n. 55; Boyd, *Papers of Jefferson*, II, 301–2, 306–665).

When JM returned to the General Assembly after an absence exceeding eight years he had pledged to Jefferson his personal exertions to end this inexcusable delay. Jefferson, the chief architect of the intended legal reform, was himself absent and soon would be in France. It remained for JM to construct the edifice as best he could. The present resolution represented the opening move. Disappointed that the Virginia Constitution of 1776 had never been submitted to the people for their acceptance or rejection, and that the movement for a new, popularly endorsed state constitution was finding only feeble support among the legislators, JM now proposed that the people might indirectly share in the process of bringing Virginia's legal code in line with her republican aspirations. With Jefferson abroad, it became JM's duty at the October 1785 session of the General Assembly to implement the revisors' work. Considering the importance of the work, the time involved was not unusual.

IN THE HOUSE OF DELEGATES Saturday the 29th. of May 1784.

WHEREAS in pursuance of an act entitled "An Act for the Revision of the Laws["]—a Revisal of the Laws of this Commonwealth has been executed with great Labour and Care and reported to the General Assembly by the Committee appointed for the said Purpose; and whereas it is highly expedient that the said Revisal should as early as possible undergo the Consideration and if approved receive the Sanction of the Legislature And whereas it is necessary for that Purpose and for the Purpose of affording to the Citizens at large an Opportunity of examining and considering a Work which proposes such various and material Changes in our legal Code that the same should be printed and Copies thereof diffused throughout the Community.

RESOLVED that the Clerk of this House be empowered and directed to make out a complete sett of the Bills contained in the said Revisal, as originally reported, and after the same shall have been inspected and approved by the members of the Committee of Revisal or any two of them, to cause five hundred Copies thereof to be forthwith printed: That of the Copies when printed, one shall be delivered to each member of the General Assembly, of the Executive, of the General Court, of the Courts of Chancery, & Admiralty, to the Attorney General, and to each of the Delegates representing this State in Congress, and that the Residue of the said Copies be distributed throughout the several Counties, by the Executive, in such manner as they shall judge most conducive to the end proposed.

RESOLVED that the money necessary for carrying the preceeding Resolution into Effect be advanced by the Treasurer in Warrant from the Auditors out of the first unappropriated Money which shall come into his Hands.[1]

Ms (Vi). In John Beckley's hand, with the exception of the endorsement by William Drew, clerk of the Senate. Docketed: "Reso respecting the Revision of the Laws. 29th. May *1784*"; "(Copied)"; and "Mr. Madison."

[1] As introduced on 29 May, the motion also included an additional resolution: "And whereas, no allowance hath hitherto been made to the committee of revisors aforesaid, for their labor and expenses in executing their important trust;

"*Resolved,* That the sum of   be allowed to each member who shall have actually participated in the work, to be paid by the treasurer on warrant from the auditors, out of any unappropriated money which may be in his hands" (*JHDV,* May 1784, p. 27). This resolution was tabled on 29 May and revived on 1 June.

State Property and Poll Assessments for 1782

EDITORIAL NOTE

It is not possible to state with precision when JM prepared this document. The source of JM's information is also uncertain. With minor variations the statistics in columns 3 through 7, and in columns 10 and 12 (counting from the left) are identical with those in Jefferson's *Notes on the State of Virginia* (ed. William Peden [Chapel Hill, N. C., 1955], p. 86). This would indicate that JM either was assembling data for his friend's use, or that they both used the same source in preparing reports. JM may have wanted to have the information on hand for the May 1784 session of the House of Delegates, when taxation rates were certain to be reviewed. He would have found the statistics useful when he served on the drafting committees charged with adjusting the continental account (28 May) and with reporting the census (5 June).

Much of the data required had already been accumulated under provisions of a Virginia act "for ascertaining certain taxes and duties, and for establishing a permanent revenue," which became effective on 5 January and was amended on 1 July 1782 (*JHDV,* Oct. 1781, p. 74; Hening, *Statutes,* X, 501–17; XI, 66–71). This was exactly the sort of information that a conscientious committeeman would have sought, and presumably it was available at the office of the state auditors of public accounts, since the law ordered county clerks to transmit the required information to the auditors.

Tazewell on 5 June introduced a bill "to ascertain the quantity of land, the improvements thereon, and the number of people within this Commonwealth." Thereafter it emerged from the legislative mill with "several amendments" and was signed into law on 30 June (*JHDV,* May 1784, pp. 37, 39, 46, 47, 60, 89; Hening, *Statutes,* XI, 415–17). If JM's prime motive in collecting the data was for guidance while serving on this committee, then it is improbable that he prepared the present document before 19 May or after 4 June 1784.

State of taxes under the Revenue law of Virginia from 68[1] of the Counties in 1782

Valuation of lands & lots	Amt. of taxes pd. on lands & lots	No. of Whites subject to poll tax[2]	No. of Blacks total	No. of Horses	No. of Cattle
£6042401..2s.5d	£57,077..17.1¼	53282	211698	195439	609734

No. of Wheels taxed	value of taxable property exclusive of land & lots	Sum collected & to be collected	Ordinaries licensed	Billiard Tables	No. of Whites & blacks not d[is]tinguished.[3]
5126	£173928..11s.6d	231,011.14.10¼	195	3	23,766

Ms (DLC: Madison Miscellany). A single, undated page in JM's handwriting.

1 That returns had not been made from all of Virginia's 75 counties, Governor Benjamin Harrison informed the General Assembly, was owing to the fact that the law in no way penalized delinquency (Executive Letter Book, pp. 312–13).

2 That is, free white males "of the age of sixteen years and upwards" (Hening, *Statutes*, VI, 40–41).

3 Jefferson in his *Notes* (p. 86) added to this caption "in the returns, but said to be titheable slaves."

Resolution Ordering the Election of a Northwest Claims Commissioner

IN THE HOUSE OF DELEGATES Tuesday the 1st: of June 1784.

WHEREAS it has been agreed by the United States in Congress assembled and the General Assembly of this Commonwealth that the necessary and reasonable expences incured by this Commonwealth in subduing any British Posts or in maintaining Forts or Garrisons within and for the defence, or in acquiring any part of the territory North Westward of the River Ohio, shall be reimbursed by the United States; and that one Commissioner shall be appointed by Congress, one by this Commonwealth, and another by those two, who, or a Majority of them shall be empow[er]ed to liquidate the said expences;

RESOLVED that this House will on Friday next proceed by joint ballot with the Senate to the choice of the Commissioner so agreed to be appointed on the part of this Commonwealth.[1]

Ms (Vi). In a clerk's hand. Endorsed and docketed: "Reso to ballot for a Commissioner to liquidate expences incured in defending Territory North-Westward the River Ohio." At the bottom of the docket a clerk added: "Mr. Madison."

1 Although no manuscript in JM's hand has been found, the entry of his name on the docket and the order of the House for JM to "acquaint the Senate" with the resolution are convincing evidence of his authorship. Usually the author of a resolution or bill was accorded that courtesy, and evidence abounds regarding JM's concern with the settlement of the continental accounts. While still in Congress, JM had helped pass the compromise embodied in the resolution. On 1 Mar. 1784 the United States took over most of the Northwest Territory previously claimed by Virginia and agreed to assume the state's wartime expense in reinforcing its claimed chartered limits. By joint ballot on 11 June, Edward Carrington was chosen as the state commissioner.

Resolution on Payment of Revisors

[1 June 1784]

WHEREAS no allowance hath hitherto been made to the Committee of Revisors ⟨appointed under an Act entitled "An Act for the revision of the laws"⟩ for their labour and expences in executing their important trust

RESOLVED that the sum of   each be allowed to the Honorable Edmund Pendleton, George Wythe and Thomas Jefferson Esquires, to be paid by the Treasurer on Warrant from the Auditors, out of any unappropriated Money in his hands.[1]

Ms (Vi). In a clerk's hand, with an additional phrase written by JM enclosed in angle brackets. Docketed with the notation: "Committed to the Courts of Justice June 1st: 1784" and "June 4th. 1784/Allowed £500 each." For the background of the resolution, see Resolution on the Revision of the Virginia Statutes, 29 May 1784.

[1] Following a second reading, the resolution was committed to the standing Committee for Courts of Justice, of which JM was a member. Three days later committee chairman Joseph Jones successfully proposed that the sum left blank in the resolution be filled with the words "five hundred pounds." The Senate announced its concurrence on 11 June (JHDV, May 1784, pp. 30, 35–36, 50).

From Thomas Jefferson

Letter not found.

ca. 1 June 1784. In his "Summary Journal of letters," Jefferson wrote under June, "Jas. Madison. Inclosed Deane's letters." In New York on 31 May, Jefferson noted in his account book a payment to James Rivington "for paper and books £3.4" (Boyd, *Papers of Jefferson,* VII, 299). In his letter to JM on 1 July, Jefferson wrote: "I inclosed you by Genl. Gates from N. York Deane's letters which I could not get in Philada." The missing letter must have been written in June no later than the fifth when Jefferson left New York. JM received the book and presumably the lost letter about 20 July 1784 (JM to Jefferson, 20 Aug. 1784).

Resolution for Schedule of Tax Rates on Documents

EDITORIAL NOTE

JM was appointed on 18 May to serve on a House of Delegates committee charged with amending "the several acts of Assembly, for ascertaining certain taxes and duties, and for establishing a permanent revenue" (*JHDV*, May 1784, p. 9). Before this committee reported, JM laid his suggestions before the whole house on 2 June, and after some amendments the Committee of the Whole adopted the schedule. In the final stage of passage the purpose of the bill became more explicit, so that it was retitled a bill "to levy certain taxes in aid of the public revenue, and to apply the same in payment of the debts due to foreign creditors" (ibid., pp. 82, 88). JM considered this bill in the nature of a stamp act, so worded as to avoid the obnoxious phrase; he calculated it would raise £15,000 to £20,000 annually (JM to Jefferson, 3 July 1784). In legislative parlance, this bill was a rider meant to accompany an act suspending portions of the permanent revenue measure passed at the October 1782 session. The bill and its "ryder" were passed by the House on 29 June and sent to the Senate, where the rider was approved while the main measure was not. Thus the rider became law, but the bill to which it was intended to be attached remained in legislative limbo. JM must have had this sort of thing in mind when he observed that bills "at present are drawn in manner that must soon bring our laws and our Legislature into contempt among all orders of Citizens" (JM to Jefferson, 3 July 1784).

[ca. 2 June 1784]

Resolved that it is the opinion of this Committee that in aid of the funds already established for supplying the Public exigences, the following duties ought to be imposed, viz.[1]

		£.	S.	D.
To be paid by the party obtaining such writ, attachment or appeal, If taxed in bill of Costs	On each original writ or subpœna issued from the General Court or H. C. Chancery.......		6	
	On each original citation from Court of Admiralty...............................		6	
	On each original writ, or subpœna in Chancery from any County Court[2].................		3	
	On each attachment issued by any Justice of the peace against effects of persons about to abscond...............................		3	
	On each appeal to the Court of appeals.......		12	
	On each writ of Error, of supersedeas, & of certiorari from Gen: Court or, H. C. Chany		6	
	On each appeal from any County Court[3].......		6	
To be paid by the obligor and taxed in the bill of Costs	On each appearance bond, recognizance of special entered bail or bail-piece returnable into the General Court....................	...	3	
	On each appearance-bond, and recognizance of special entered bail returnable into any County Court...........................	...	3	

£.   S.   D.

To be paid by the party prevailing and taxed in bill of Costs

On each final judgment or decree in any Court concerning lands, slaves, or vessels 12

On each final judgment or decree in any Court for a determinate sum of money . . . . 1/8 perCent

On each final judgment or decree concerning any other property 3

On each Deed recorded concerning any improved lot or lots in any City or incorporated town for each lot . . . . 12 . .

On each Deed recorded concerning any unimproved lot or lots in such City or town for each lot 6

On do. as to improved lots in any unincorporated town, for each lot. 6/-unimproved lots - 3/.

On each Deed recorded concerning other lands for each 100 acres 3

On each other Deed recorded 3

On each patent issued from the land office . . . .

On each probate of wills, or grant of administration where lands or slaves are concerned . . £1 . . . .

On each probate or grant where no lands nor slaves are concerned[4] . . . . 6 . .

On each exempli[fi]cation under the seal of any Court[5] 6

On each admission of Attorneys to practise in the superior Courts . . . . £15 . . . .

On each licence of attorneys to practise in County Courts . . . . £5 . . . .

On each admission of Clerks to their Clerkships in any Court . . . . £15 . . . .

On each licence for keeping a ferry on tide water over Elizabeth, James, York, Rappahan: or Potowmk. rivers . . . . £10 . . . .

On each licence for keeping a ferry above tide water on sd. rivers, or over any other rivers . . £2 . . . .

Ms (DLC). In JM's hand. Late in life, JM wrote above this report, "JM's project of tax, for House of Delegates Virga in 178 ."

1 Whether the rates in JM's hand were his recommendations, or were supplied by the drafting committee, is uncertain. The act as adopted follows this schedule except for the high rate on probates of wills, which was cut from £1 to 6 shillings, the omission of provisions for clerkships and ferries, and the addition of a 2/6 transfer tax on surveyor's certificates (Hening, *Statutes*, XI, 377–79).

2 As enacted, "or Court of Hustings"—a court of borough or city jurisdiction—was added.

³ Preceding this entry the House added, "on each writ of habeas corpus, cum causa, six shillings."

⁴ The House dropped this provision.

⁵ Deleted in the final draft.

From James Madison, Sr.

June 4th. 1784

I wrote to you two days since,¹ by Ralph Cowgill, since which I have got of Mr. Benjamin Winslow £144— & have sent it to Capt. S. Jones in Frederick by Mr. Hite—so that you must deduct that Sum in settling my Bond to him. & I desire you will pay the Treasurer out of the Money you sell my Tobo. for on Acct. of Mr. Winslow for the Taxes due from him as Collector £170 which will reimburse him the Money I got of him & will discharge the Ballance of my Taxes due for the last Payment.² This method Mr. Winslow takes for a safe, as well as speedy, method of conveying the Money into the Treasury. He has likewise some Interest Warrants which he will transmit to you the first opportunity, perhaps next Week, to pay to the Treasurer with the Money, if you do not pay it in before you receive them; & if you should, as soon as convenient afterwards. I am Your Affectionate Fathr.

JAMES MADISON

RC (DLC). Docketed. The salutation is missing owing to a tear in the Ms. Addressed to JM at Richmond, "Favor'd by Capt. Thos. Porter." Porter (d. 1824) served in the Continental Line and moved to Wilkes County, Georgia, no later than 1792 (Gwathmey, *Historical Register of Virginians*, p. 633; Grace G. Davidson [Mrs. John Lee], *Early Records of Georgia, Wilkes County* [2 vols.; Macon, Ga., 1932], II, 186).

¹ The letter from JM's father has not been found.

² Ralph Cowgill (d. 1795) was a planter in Loudoun County (Vi: Loudoun County Court Records, Will Book E, 1793–1797, microfilm, pp. 85–87). Benjamin Winslow (ca. 1737–1826) in 1784 was Orange County tax collector. Capt. Samuel Jones was a veteran of three years' service in the 11th and 15th Virginia regiments in the Continental Line (Heitman, *Historical Register Continental*, p. 246). Isaac Hite (1758–1836), of Belle Grove, Frederick County, had married JM's sister Nelly in 1783.

To James Madison, Sr.

Richmond June 5th. 1784.

Hond Sir

I have disposed of the tobacco entrusted to me for 40/. per Ct. but receive in hand no more than will be delivered by Mr. Craig. The residue will be paid before I leave this place. I inclose a draught on S. J. from Col: Harvey, for £200 for Which I have credited Mr. Anderson on his bond. Mr. Anderson could not pay the balance now, but expects to do it shortly. The draught & the remittance will I hope with such addition as you will be able to make, redeem your bond out of the hands of Mr. Jones. I have applied to Genl. Wood for Majr. Hite's warrant. He promises to get it if possible, before Mr. Craig sets out. If he does it will be forwarded. I have laid Majr. Lee's case before the House and it has been referred to the Committee of propositions. The mass of business before this Committee & my avocations from it to other Committees have delayed it hitherto. Having but a moment to write this I must refer to Mr. Craig for the news of the Session.[1] The House of Delegates have agreed to postpone the June tax till Jany. It is not improbable that the Senate may require 1/2 to be collected at an earlier period.[2] Mr. Winslow[3] will probably be glad to be apprized of these circumstances. Remember me affecty. to the family & accept of the dutiful respects of your Son

J. Madison Jr.

RC (DLC). Addressed to Colonel Madison at Orange. Docketed many years later by JM.

[1] "Mr. Craig" was probably the Reverend Elijah Craig (*Papers of Madison*, I, 183 n. 7). "S. J." was Captain Samuel Jones. Colonel John Harvie (ibid., I, 188–89, nn. 1, 2) was at this time register of the Virginia land office. "Mr. Anderson" was in all likelihood William Anderson, of Hanover County (ibid., I, 317 n. 13). James Wood represented Frederick County in the House of Delegates. "Majr." Isaac Hite was JM's brother-in-law. Maj. John Lee (1743–1802) was the brother of Mary Willis Lee, who about 1780 had married JM's brother Ambrose (J[unie] Estelle Stewart King, comp., *Abstract of Early Kentucky Wills and Inventories* [Baltimore, 1961], p. 249). Lee's petition for a 1,000-acre veteran's warrant was presented to the House of Delegates on 26 May, found "reasonable," and in time the warrant was issued (*JHDV*, May 1784, pp. 40, 46). By 1790, Lee had moved to Woodford County, Kentucky (Heinemann and Brumbaugh, *First Census of Kentucky, 1790*, p. 57).

[2] The postponement of taxes was a familiar legislative device in the General Assembly. A bill to suspend a 1782 tax measure was introduced in the House of Delegates on 24 May and was approved by the Senate on 8 June. It changed from 1 June 1784 to 31 Jan. 1785 the date when sheriffs and tax collectors could impose penalties on delinquent taxpayers (Hening, *Statutes*, XI, 368–69).

[3] Benjamin Winslow, Orange County tax collector.

Bill Granting Congress Limited
Power to Regulate Commerce

[5 June 1784]

WHEREAS the United States in Congress assembled, more effectually to preserve the Commercial Interests thereof, ought to be invested with power for a limitted time, to prohibit the importation and exportation of Goods, Wares & Merchandizes to and from any of the United States in Vessels, not the property of the States, or the Subjects of a power who shall have formed a Commercial Treaty with the same

BE IT ENACTED that the United States in Congress assembled, shall be and they are hereby authorized and empowered to prohibit in any manner they shall think proper, for any term not exceeding fifteen years, the importation & exportation of any Goods, Wares, or Merchandize to or from this State in Vessels belonging to or navigated by the Subjects of any power with whom the United States, shall not have formed Treaties of Commerce, and also for the like term to prohibit the Subjects of any foreign State, Kingdom or Empire, unless authorized by Treaty from importing into this State, Goods, Wares or Merchandize which are not the produce or manufacture of the Dominion of the Sovereign whose Subjects they are. PROVIDED that to all Acts passed by the United States in Congress assembled, in pursuance of the above powers, the assent of nine States shall be necessary.

THIS ACT shall commence and be in force so soon as each and every State in the Union shall pass similar Acts, and as soon as the Governor of this Commonwealth shall be notified that each and every State in the Union have passed similar Acts, he shall & he is hereby authorized to issue his proclamation declaring the Act in force.[1]

Ms (Vi). In Henry Tazewell's hand. Docketed: "A Bill To invest the united States in Congress assembled with additional powers for a limited time." The bill was first read on 5 June and passed on 28 June (*JHDV*, May 1784, pp. 37, 81). Though not in JM's hand he must have introduced the 19 May resolution which called for enactment of this bill (ibid., p. 12).

[1] For the background of this legislation see the Resolutions to Strengthen Powers of Congress of 19 May 1784. The approved bill was carried to the Senate by Thomas Mathews, a circumstance which renders JM's authorship tenuous. The act is printed in Hening, *Statutes*, XI, 388–89. Governor Harrison had already expressed skepticism about "divided measures" by individual states (Harrison to John Tyler, 3 May 1784, Executive Letter Book, pp. 317–18). His pessimism was warranted, for the matter was never acted upon by Congress after delegate Samuel Hardy presented it to the Committee of the States (*JCC*, XXVII, 589; Burnett, *The Continental Congress*, p. 634).

Resolutions on Private Debts
Owed to British Merchants

Among the leading public men of revolutionary Virginia JM's rising eminence is the more noticeable because of his youth and the advantages attending it. As a man in his mid-twenties when the war began, unmarried and under no obligation to provide for a family, he had not been upon the scene long enough to become encumbered with the prewar debts that were the constant fret of almost all Virginia planters. Thus, upon his return from Congress to Montpelier at the age of thirty-two, he could regard the haunting British debt problem with more detachment than could numerous legislators whose personal interests were heavily involved.

The tory James Parker may have overstated the case in 1774, when he equated a Virginian's radicalism with the extent of his indebtedness to British merchants, contending that " 'the more a man is in debit, the greater patriot he is' " (Thad W. Tate, "The Coming of the Revolution in Virginia: Britain's Challenge to Virginia's Ruling Class, 1763–1776," *WMQ*, 3d ser., XIX [1962], 336). Yet the £2 million Virginians owed to Scottish and English merchants certainly could have furnished a grievance and caused a portion of the resentment that pushed the colony from protests in 1769 to war in 1775. Actually, popular notions had inflated the size of the real debts, but still £2 million appeared to be a staggering load in 1775 "and represented approximately half of the total American private indebtedness" (Emory G. Evans, "Private Indebtedness and the Revolution in Virginia, 1776–1796," *WMQ*, XXVIII [1971], 349–50).

What debts JM's father owed to British creditors apparently were never of sufficient weight to cause a conflict of interest. Living in the Piedmont, the senior Madison seems to have been a man of such ample means and moderate tastes that his cash crops and extensive blacksmith shop carried him along without outlays for extremely expensive imports. Thus, his instilled concepts of honor aside, JM was enabled to be a fairly detached student of the British debt problem that remained an emotional issue in Virginia politics until after ratification of the federal Constitution.

The debt-collecting problem had been complicated by a number of legal roadblocks passed by the legislature that affected debts contracted prior to 1777. During the war the Assembly also had passed legislation which in effect legalized the repayment in depreciating paper currency of British debts contracted in terms of specie. An auxiliary problem was that of confiscated British property, which was seized under the same statute. The act also forbade recovery suits by British subjects (Hening, *Statutes*, IX, 377–80). Other acts suspended any postwar payment of accumulated interest, and all had the support of Patrick Henry (Jensen, *The New Nation*, pp. 279–80). There was an outside chance that the overhanging burden could somehow be relieved by further legislation; but much of that desideratum was dispelled when in 1783 the terms of the peace treaty with Great Britain, which recognized the validity of the claims of bona fide British creditors, became public knowledge. JM was serving in Congress when a resolution was passed in May 1783 calling "all demands for interest accruing during the war . . . highly inequitable and unjust" (*JCC*, XXIV, 375; *Papers of Madison*, VII, 95, 96 n. 3). JM was aware that withholding interest was one thing, but that liquidating the debt was neither manly nor fair.

Although the original state debt-repayment law had been repealed, Virginians were on unsteady ground as they contemplated the effect of the treaty, for the possibility of still owing £2 million sterling, plus interest for eight or more years, was a sword hanging by a frayed thread over the economic recovery of their state (Hening, *Statutes*, X, 227). The sentiment for settling the question as soon as possible was probably strongest in the trade centers and weakest in the rural areas (of which Virginia was mainly comprised), but resentment against Great Britain was potent everywhere, and to many Virginians it must have seemed common justice that the £272,588 (worth only about $15,000 in specie) paid into the state treasury under the law of 1777 be passed on to British rascals as all that they deserved.

With the approach of the session of the General Assembly of May 1784, it was clear to all observers that the problem of the British debts could be deferred no longer. It was well known that John Tyler, John Taylor of Caroline, and other spirited delegates wished to strike for outright repudiation (Boyd, *Papers of Jefferson*, VII, 260). Such a blow would have accorded little with the views of George Mason, who a year before had written a friend that "We are very much alarm'd, in this Part of the Country, least the Assembly shou'd pass some Laws infringing the Articles of Peace, and thereby involve us in a fresh Quarrel with Great Britain" (Rutland, *Papers of George Mason*, II, 769). Nor would it accord with those of JM, whose background, character, and experience in Congress dictated his position on the question. He had to oppose any plan that would negate the provisions of the treaty of peace. Accordingly, JM was fixed in his commitment and course, but prudence dictated that he move circumspectly, lest his political future in Virginia be jeopardized by an issue that, although already constitutionally settled, must be presented in forms acceptable to his constituents. How to force Virginia into line graciously was the real problem.

A quick, friendly compromise was out of the question as the legislative in-fighting soon indicated. The opponents of repayment, led by the redoubtable Patrick Henry, brought up their own set of grievances, including the loss of slaves owned by Virginians to British forces and the destruction of private property by enemy raiders. A resolution was passed on 7 June calling for an inquiry into the enforcement of that section of the peace treaty (Art. VII) which charged Great Britain with releasing all prisoners "without causing any Destruction or carrying away any Negroes, or other Property of the American Inhabitants." The tender point at issue was whether former slaves going under the British flag remained American property. General Washington had made a strong protest to Sir Guy Carleton in May 1783, whereafter, as JM informed Jefferson, Carleton "confessed that a number of Negroes had gone off with the Refugees since the arrival of the Treaty, and undertook to justify the permission by a palpable & scandalous misconstruction of the Treaty" (*Papers of Madison*, VII, 40). The British commander had added that a register of the blacks departing under British protection was being kept, so "that if the sending off the Negroes should hereafter be declared an Infraction of the Treaty, Compensation must be made by the Crown of Great Britain to the Owners" (Fitzpatrick, *Writings of Washington*, XXVI, 403–4).

Whether JM wrote the offsetting resolution (Resolution A) offered on 7 June, after the anti-debt faction had won the first round, is problematical. Since it bears on the later document (Resolution B) in JM's hand and the amendments that on 23 June he almost certainly offered to a third resolution (Resolution C), it is printed below in order to keep the whole controversy in perspective.

Resolution A

[7 June 1784]

Resolved, That so much of all and every act or acts of Assembly, now in force in this Commonwealth, as prevents a due compliance with the stipulations contained in the definitive treaty entered into between Great Britain and America, ought to be repealed.[1]

Printed copy (*JHDV*, May 1784, p. 41).

[1] The motion was offered immediately after a committee was appointed to inquire into "an infraction on the part of Great Britain, of the seventh article of the definitive treaty of peace between the United States of America and Great Britain, so far as the same respects the detention of slaves and other property, belonging to the citizens of this Commonwealth." Defeated, 57 to 37 (JM voted for passage), the motion would have thwarted the purpose for which the committee of inquiry had been set up.

Resolution B

[ca. 22–23 June 1784]

⟨J. M.'s propositions to the Gen. Assembly see Journal⟩[1]

Whereas by the 4th. article of the Definitive Treaty of Peace ratified and proclaimed by the United States in Congress assembled on the 14th. day of Jany. last "it is agreed that Creditors on either side shall meet with no lawful impediment to the recovery of the full value in sterling money, of all bona fide debts heretofore contracted:" And whereas it is the duty and determination of this Commonwealth, with a becoming reverence for the faith of Treaties, truly and honestly, to give to the said article, all the effect which circumstances, not within its controul, will possibly admit; And inasmuch as the debts due from the good people of this Commonwealth to the subjects of G. Britain were contracted

under the prospect of gradual payments, and are justly computed to
exceed the possibility of full payment at once, more especially, under
the diminution of their property resulting from the devastations of the
late war; and it is therefore conceived that the interest of the British
Creditors themselves will be favored by fixing certain reasonable periods, at which divided payments shall be made:

RESOLVED, that it is the opinion of this Committee, that the laws now
in force relative to British debts, ought to be so varied & amended as to
make the same recoverable in the proportions & at the periods following; that is to say, part thereof with interest of 5 Per Ct. from the date
of the definitive Treaty of peace, on the   day of   another   on
the   day of   another   on the   day of   and the remaining   on the   day of

And whereas it is further stipulated by art: 7th of the said Treaty,
among other things, that "his Britannic Majesty shall with all convenient speed, and without causing any destruction, or carrying away any
negroes or other property of the American inhabitants, withdraw all his
armies, garrisons and fleets from the said United States; and from every
post place and harbour within the same, leaving in all fortifications the
American artillery that may be therein, and shall also order and cause
all archives, records, deeds & papers, belonging to any of the said States,
or their Citizens, which in the course of the war, may have fallen into
the hands of his officers, to be forthwith restored and delivered to the
proper States and persons to whom they belong," which stipulation was
in the same words contained in the Provisional articles signed at Paris
on the 30th. day of November 1782 by the Commissioners empowered
on each part: and whereas posterior to the date of the said provisional
articles, sundry negroes the property of Citizens of this Commonwealth
were carried away from the City of New York whilst in possession of
the British forces, and no restitution or satisfaction on that head, has
been made,[2] either before or since the Definitive Treaty of peace: And
Whereas the good people of this Commonwealth have a clear right to
expect that whilst, on one side, they are called upon by the U. S. in Congress Assembled to whom by the fœderal Constitution the powers of
war & peace are exclusively delegated, to carry into effect the stipulations in favour of British Subjects, an equal observance of the stipulations in their own favour should, on the other side, be duly secured to
them under the authority of the Confederacy;

RESOLVED, that it is the opinion of this Committee, that the Delegates
representing this State in Congress ought to be instructed to urge in

Congress peremptory measures for obtaining from G. Britian satisfaction for the infringement of the article aforesaid; and in case of refusal or unreasonable delay of such satisfaction, to urge that the sanction of Congress be given to the just policy of retaining so much of the debts due from Citizens of this Commonwealth, to British subjects, as will fully repair the losses sustained from such infringement: and that to enable the said Delegates, to proceed herein with the greater precision & effect, the Executive ought to be requested to take immediate measures for obtaining & transmitting to them, all just claims of the Citizens of this Commonwealth under the said 7th. art: as aforesaid.[3]

Ms (DLC). The resolution is in JM's hand. Docketed "Resolves on Definitive Treaty" in an unidentified hand.

[1] JM added this heading some years later. He then wrote on the docket: "Proposition of J. M. regarding the fulfilment of stipulations of British treaty to Legislature of Virginia." Below this an unidentified writer added: "at May Sess. 1784. See Jour. p. 74."

[2] On 14 June the committee formed to investigate treaty infractions reported that there was good reason to suspect that Great Britain had permitted the removal of slaves and thus broken faith in respect to Article VII (*JHDV*, May 1784, p. 54). The Committee of the Whole House on 22 June debated, amended, and reported five resolutions respecting the payment of private debts to British creditors (ibid., pp. 72–73). These resolutions (1) accepted the findings of the committee of inquiry elected to investigate alleged British infractions of the seventh article of the treaty of peace; (2) found that there had "been an infraction" on the part of Great Britain; (3) instructed the state delegates in Congress according to the provisions set forth in unamended Resolution C; (4) declared that repeal of "such acts of the Legislature passed during the late war, as inhibit the recovery of British debts" should be conditioned upon the response of Great Britain to a remonstrance against her infraction; and (5) stated that "the further operation of all and every act or acts of Assembly concerning escheats and forfeitures from British subjects, ought to be prevented." The first and second resolutions were approved, while the other three were tabled until the following day.

[3] Delegates hostile to debt repayment moved ahead on 23 June by introducing a defiant resolution in which the delegates threatened "to withold their co-operation in the complete fulfillment of the said treaty, until the success of the aforesaid remonstrance [on slave losses and western posts] is known" (*JHDV*, May 1784, p. 74). JM tried to water down this effort by substituting milder language. He must have gone into the session prepared to bargain with the militants. From the silence of the journal it appears that JM never actually offered all of Resolution B as a whole compromise package. Specifically, he withheld the plan calling for staggered repayment over a period of time. He lost this skirmish but remembered the installment-plan features of this resolution when the issue was revived at the next legislative session. Meanwhile, two clauses from JM's second resolution were laid before the Committee of the Whole. These appear below as amendments to Resolution C.

Resolution C

Resolved, that it is the opinion of this committee, That the delegates representing this State in Congress, be instructed to lay before that body, the subject matter of the preceding report and resolution, and to request from them a remonstrance to the British court complaining of the aforesaid infraction of the treaty of peace, and desiring a proper reparation for the injuries consequent thereupon; *that the said delegates be instructed to inform Congress, that the General Assembly have no inclination to interfere with the power of making treaties with foreign nations, which the confederation hath wisely vested in Congress; but it is conceived that a just regard to the national honor and interest of the citizens of this Commonwealth, obliges the Assembly to withold their co-operation in the complete fulfilment of the said treaty, until the success of the aforesaid remonstrance is known, or Congress shall signify their sentiments touching the premises.*[1]

Printed copy (*JHDV*, May 1784, p. 74).

[1] As the House resumed discussion of the previously tabled motions, a delegate moved to strike the italicized portions of Resolution C. This apparently was JM's move, as the words to be substituted were his from Resolution B: "and that in case of refusal or unreasonable delay of due reparation, the said delegates be instructed to urge that the sanction of Congress be given to the just policy of retaining so much of the debts due from the citizens of this Commonwealth, to British subjects, as will fully repair the losses sustained by the infraction of the treaty aforesaid,— and that, to enable the said delegates to proceed herein, with greater precision and effect, the executive be requested to take immediate measures for obtaining and transmitting to them all just claims of the citizens of this Commonwealth, under the treaty aforesaid."

JM's substitution was rejected by a 33 to 50 vote. As finally approved, the resolutions declared that until Great Britain had paid reparations on Virginia claims nothing would be done regarding debt recovery, although it was conceded that Congress might regard the repeal of certain wartime stay laws as "indispensably necessary." In the latter case, repayment would proceed "in such time and manner as shall consist with the exhausted situation of this Commonwealth" (*JHDV*, May 1784, p. 74). The door for recovery of the debt was left only slightly ajar. JM would again face the problem at the next session, when Henry was no longer in the House.

Bill Restricting Foreign Vessels to
Certain Virginia Ports

EDITORIAL NOTE

Although in Tazewell's hand, Edmund Randolph told Jefferson this bill (along with the Resolution for Schedule of Tax Rates on Documents, 2 June 1784) "originated from Madison" (Boyd, *Papers of Jefferson*, VII, 260–61). Tazewell was chairman of the committee appointed 28 May to draft a bill that would restrict foreign commerce so that smuggling could be better controlled and duties more readily collected. As JM reported to Jefferson on 3 July, a hot legislative battle followed the attempt to confine foreign commerce to the ports of Norfolk and Alexandria. On the surface, it seemed an unfair advantage for the merchants located near those two harbors, and local interests had to be accommodated between the time of the first debate and 17 June, when three more port cities were added, so that enough votes for passage could be won over. Even so, it was a close vote (64 to 58), and those arrayed against JM included Wilson Cary Nicholas, John Marshall, and John Taylor of Caroline. The wonder is that the bill passed at all, and without Patrick Henry's support it would surely have lost. The House journal indicates JM carried the amended measure to the Senate. The act as passed is in Hening, *Statutes*, XI, 402–4. Passage touched off much controversy. Washington approved the bill and assured JM that with some slight changes the measure would "be productive of great good to this Country; without it, the Trade thereof I conceive will ever labor and languish" (Fitzpatrick, *Writings of Washington*, XXVIII, 336). But George Mason fumed when he read the act and wrote a protest which appeared as a broadside, probably late in 1786, when the General Assembly considered a revision of the law (DLC: printed broadside; Rutland, *Papers of George Mason*, II, 859–63). The act was revised by the General Assembly in both 1786 and 1787 and finally became a dead letter after the Federal Constitution went into effect and transferred control over foreign commerce to the national government.

[8 June 1784]

WHEREAS the Trade and Commerce carried on between the Citizens of this CommonWealth and forreign Merchants would be placed upon a more equal foundation, and expedition & dispatch thereby the better promoted if the Vessels of forreign Merchants trading to this State should be restricted to certain Ports and places within the same in lading and unlading—And the Revenue arising from Commerce would also thereby be more certainly collected.

Be it therefore enacted that the Ships and other Vessels trading from forreign parts to this CommonWealth which are the property of other than the Citizens of the same, shall enter, clear out, lade, and unlade at   [1] and at no other Ports or places therein. And all ships & other Vessels trading to this CommonWealth from forriegn Parts owned by a Citizen or Citizens jointly with a foreigner or foreigners shall also be restricted to enter, clear out, lade and unlade at the said Ports or places and at none other. All duties payable upon Tonnage—and upon Goods Wares and Merchandize imported, into this State in such Ship or other Vessels shall be paid & accounted for by the Master or owner thereof to the naval officer or Collector at such of the aforesd. ports or places where such Ship or other Vessel shall enter & break bulk. And if the Master or owner of any such Ship or other Vessell shall enter clear out, lade or unlade or break bulk at any port or place within this commonwealth other than those aforementioned, the Master or owner of such Ship or other Vessel shall forfeit and pay double that duty on Tonnage and the Goods Wares and Merchandize by him imported which by Law he would be compelable to pay at any of the aforesd. Ports, which said double duties shall be paid by such Master or owner in forty eight Hours after his arrival at any other port or place. & for failure thereof he shall be subject to the like penalty as by Law the Citizens of this CommonWealth are now subject in case of failure to pay the duties required from them upon the importation of Goods Wares & Merchandize which said penalty shall be recovered & applied in like manner as the Penalty from Citizens in the case aforesd. is directed to be recovered and applied.[2]

This Act shall commence and be in force from & after the   day of   and so much as all Acts of Assembly as comes within the perview of this Act shall be repealed.[3]

Ms (Vi). In the hand of Henry Tazewell. Dated and docketed, "A Bill To restrict forreign Vessels to certain ports within this Commonwealth." A further endorsement indicates the bill was on "June 8th. 1784 Read the first Time June 9th: 1784. read the second time & Committed to a Committee of the Whole House on Monday next."

[1] In the final version of the bill, the Committee of the Whole House inserted Norfolk, Portsmouth, Tappahannock, Yorktown, or Alexandria. When the Senate considered the measure, the port of Bermuda Hundred (which served Henrico County) was added and remained after a conference. In the bill as passed, Norfolk and Portsmouth, which are separated by the Elizabeth River, were to be considered "as one port." Another important addition from the Senate-House conference was a section insisted on by the western members that clearly stated the act would not "extend to the navigation of the rivers westward of the Allegany mountains." With navigation of the Mississippi such a touchy matter, the Westerners must have insisted that their lanes of commerce be exempted from the remotest encumbrance (*JHDV*, May 1784, p. 80).

2 At this point, the Committee of the Whole House on 15 June added:

"And whereas the navigating small country craft by slaves, the property of the owners of such craft, tends to discourage free white seamen, and to encrease the number of such free white seamen would produce public good:

"IV. *Be it therefore enacted*, That not more than one-third part of the persons employed in the navigation of any bay or river craft, shall consist of slaves. And if the owner of any bay or river craft shall presume to put on board any such craft as navigators, more slaves than the proportion aforesaid, such owner shall forfeit and pay the sum of one hundred pounds for each offence, to be recovered by action of debt or information, in any court of record" (Hening, *Statutes*, XI, 403–4).

3 The act was to go into effect 10 June 1786.

From James Madison, Sr.

June 10th. 1784—9 O'Clock P. M.

Mr. Mordicai Barbour, by whom you will receive this, is just from Kentucky[1] & informs us that one John Stanley & George Wilson has entered a Caveat against a Patent issuing for our 40 000 Acres of Land on Pant[h]er Creek & also part of Col. Mason's, for not being surveyed according to the entry & has entered them with the Surveyor.[2] Who is blameable for this piece of fatal misconduct I am not certain. I have not time to look into the Law, but am inform'd that all Caveats are to be tryed in the Western district & that there is no appeal allowed from that Court, if there is, perhaps it may be prudent to engage Mr. Randolph for the Company; but I expect you will receive fuller advice from some of the Partners.

I am inform'd there are many scandalous advantages taken by some persons who constantly attends the Offices to examine if the surveys are litterally made according to the entries, & that the entries are properly made. Mr. Harry Green inform'd me to day that my Surveys on Elk Horn are entered by two other persons & surveyed by one of them & a Caveat entered against it by another; their entries are later than mine which it seems was to begin at a S. E. corner of the adjacent entry which it seems had no corners but the cardinal Points, so that it is probable I may have a dispute abt. that, & perhaps lose the Land. I hope the legislators will take up the Matter this Session & put a Stop to such unreasonable practices.

I wish you would let me hear from you & inform me what you have done with my Tobo. & how many Hhds you have recd—some was lodged on the Road & I can't learn what is done with it. Have you recd. the Money from Messrs. Anderson's? If you have a safe hand send me the Money for Mr. Jones, or to Mr. Abram Maury at Fredg about £360. will be sufficient. I expect—he has recd. the £144 I got of Mr. Winslow, which you must make up £170 & pay it to the Treasurer for him. I observe in the Catalogue you left with me Burrows Reports[3] are mentioned 3 Vol. I am told there are 4 or 5 Vol. published. Would you have them all wrote for, or only 3 Volumes? The messenger is waiting so must conclude, Your Affectionate Father

                                                                    JAMES MADISON

Fanny is gone to Fredk. with her Sister[4]

RC (ViU). The salutation is made illegible by a tear in the Ms. Addressed to JM at Richmond and, "Favoured by Mr. Morda. Barbour."

[1] A Mordecai Barbour was a Revolutionary War pensioner in Orange County until the middle of the next century. In all likelihood Barbour was speculating in western lands where the family left its mark. Barboursville is the county seat of Knox County, Kentucky, and there is a Barbour County in West Virginia. James and Thomas Barbour were among the largest speculators in Kentucky lands, with extensive holdings on the Green River and Panther Creek (W. W. Scott, *History of Orange County*, p. 250; Gwathmey, *Historical Register of Virginians*, p. 39).

[2] After enactment of the 1779 Virginia land settlement law, many Virginians began exercising their land warrants in the Kentucky district. "Col. Mason" was George Mason of Gunston Hall, who sought to patent 53,000 acres in the vicinity of Panther Creek and the Green River. George Wilson was an official surveyor who had been accused of using his office to seek flaws in the surveys of others and then to file caveats against them (which prevented issuance of a clear title). A memorandum supporting Mason's right to the Panther Creek tract is in DLC: Madison Papers (Rutland, *Papers of George Mason*, III, 867–68).

[3] James Burrow, *Reports of Cases Adjudged in the Court of King's Bench, since the Death of Lord Raymond; in four parts* . . . (5 vols.; London, 1766–1780). The title page gives the incorrect impression that three earlier sections exist.

[4] "Fanny" was JM's sister Frances (1774–1823), and "her Sister," Mrs. Isaac (Nelly Conway Madison) Hite (1758–1836), lived at Belle Grove, Frederick County.

From George Washington

MOUNT VERNON June 12th 1784

DEAR SIR,

Can nothing be done in our Assembly for poor Paine? Mus[t] the merits, & Services of *Common Sense* continue to glide down the stream of time, unrewarded by this Country? His writings certainly have had a powerful effect on the public mind; ought they not then to meet an adequate return? He is poor! he is chagreened! and almost, if not altogether, in despair of relief.

New York it is true, not the least distressed, nor best able State in the Union, has done something for him. This kind of provision he prefers to an allowance from Congress—he has reasons for it, which to him are conclusive, and such I think, as would have weight with others. His view[s] are moderate—a decent independency is, I believe, all he aims at.[1] Should he not obtain this? If you think so, I am sure you will not only move the matter, but give it your support. For me, it only remains to feel for his Situation, and to assure you of the sincere esteem & regard with which I have the honor to be Dr. Sir, Yr Most Obedt Hble Serv[t].[2]

GO: WASHINGTON

RC (CSmH); FC (DLC: Washington Papers). Cover missing: In a clerk's hand. The FC contains slight variations in phraseology but no substantial differences from the RC.

[1] In Apr. 1784 the General Assembly of New York presented Paine with a confiscated tory estate at New Rochelle. Although Paine desired to be the historiographer of the Revolution, he found distasteful the proposition of depending on a salary appropriated annually by a political body such as Congress (Alfred Owen Aldridge, *Man of Reason: The Life of Thomas Paine* [Philadelphia and New York, 1959], pp. 101, 103).

[2] Washington wrote similar letters on 12 June to Patrick Henry and Richard Henry Lee (Fitzpatrick, *Writings of Washington*, XXVII, 421–23). The latter's brother, Arthur Lee, could not forget that Paine had written the pamphlet *Public Good* a few years earlier, which was meant to prejudice the western land claims of Virginians in the Ohio Valley. Lee therefore proceeded to wreck the whole plan. JM explained the circumstances of the unsuccessful effort in his letter to Washington, 2 July 1784. For an earlier commentary by a Virginian who considered *Public Good* a scandalous performance, see Mays, *Papers of Edmund Pendleton*, I, 328–38. Pendleton did not then know Paine was the author of the pamphlet but observed that "His fine Compliments upon Virginia remind me of the Robber of Mrs. Sutten, who paid many fine Compliments to her beauty, whilst he was dispoiling her of jewels."

Resolution to Expedite Settlement of Simon Nathan's Claims

IN THE HOUSE OF DELEGATES Monday 14th. of June 1784

It appearing from the information of the Attorney General, that accident hath hitherto prevented the settlement of the dispute between the Commonwealth and Mr Simon Nathan,[1] and that he agreed with the said Nathan to submit the same to arbitration, on a case to be stated and supported by Arguments on both sides in writing provided a due

Sanction should be obtained for his so doing:

RESOLVED that the General Assembly are desirous that the dispute aforesaid may be adjusted with expedition: and that the Atto[r]ney General be authorized to submit it in such manner and to such persons as he shall approve, to be determined on principles of Law and equity; and that he make report to the General Assembly of his proceedings therein

Ms (Vi). In a clerk's hand, docketed, "Reso respecting Simon Nathan." The docket indicates copies were ordered for Attorney General Randolph and Nathan. A clerk has written "Mr Madison" below the other endorsements.

[1] The story of Simon Nathan's effort to receive payment for money advanced to Gen. George Rogers Clark in the winter of 1779–1780 is a tangled skein. A Philadelphia speculator and money-lender, Nathan claimed that bills of exchange in state currency, which greatly depreciated later, were accepted at New Orleans and Havana for his account at par. He insisted that he had been victimized by the rapid depreciation and that Virginia owed him "a hard dollar for every one named in the bill" (Jefferson to Edmund Randolph, 18 July 1783, Boyd, *Papers of Jefferson*, VI, 320). Nathan's claim then was for 15,000 livres plus 10 percent interest and damages (*JHDV*, Oct. 1782, p. 57). An adjustment was attempted and arbitration sought, but after several efforts at a settlement the tedious business was still unfinished. JM had helped arrange a 1783 compromise, which was rejected by the General Assembly (*Papers of Madison*, VII, 216, 217 n. 5). After more meetings in Baltimore and Alexandria, the irritating business was no closer to a final arbitration. What "accident" caused further delays is not clear, but after this resolution passed the House, JM carried it to the Senate (*JHDV*, May 1784, p. 57). As a result of this action, Attorney General Edmund Randolph named John Marshall and Cyrus Griffin as the Virginia arbitrators. On 28 Dec. 1786, Marshall and Griffin reported their findings in Nathan's favor, but by 1791 the matter was still unsettled (*Cal. of Va. State Papers*, V, 259–60).

Resolution on the Pauly and Beaumarchais Claims

EDITORIAL NOTE

On 27 May there was laid before the House of Delegates a petition of Lewis Abraham Pauly (1743–1828) (ViHi: Pauly Family Bible Records) and a letter from Governor Benjamin Harrison enclosing a memorial from Pierre Augustin Caron de Beaumarchais. Both petition and memorial contained claims against Virginia for military supplies purchased in behalf of the state during the late war (*JHDV*, May 1784, p. 24). Pauly's claim rested on charges against the bankrupt J. Pierre Penet and associates. Beaumarchais's were complicated by the fact that his former agent had engaged in a speculation that decreased the market value of the supplies delivered. These papers were committed for investigation and report to the standing Committee of Commerce. JM, as chairman of the committee, offered this resolution.

[14 June 1784]

Resolved, that it is the opinion of this committee, That the claims of the said Lewis Abraham Pauley, and Mr. Beaumarchais against this State for military stores and clothing, furnished the same, ought to be referred to the executive for their settlement; and that they make report to the Legislature of such balances as shall appear to be due the said claimants.[1]

Printed copy (*JHDV*, May 1784, p. 56). Ms copy of the resolution has not been found.

[1] The immediate outcome of the resolution was that Governor Harrison directed Solicitor General Leighton Wood to audit the claims and subsequently informed Beaumarchais's current agent in Baltimore that it would be necessary for him or a representative to come to Richmond to explain his retainer's "several demands" (Executive Letter Book, p. 347). On 23 June the governor forwarded to the delegates Wood's statement of Pauly's accounts, rendered "in so perfect a manner that Nothing is left for me to say on the subject, except that I suppose the State may with Safety pay to Mr. Pauly the balance due Penet da Costa Freres & Company." Harrison cautioned, however, that payment in full would probably open the floodgates for other claims by those hoodwinked by "that adventurer" Penet (ibid., pp. 350–51). Under pressure of other business, and with only a week of the current session left, Speaker John Tyler apparently never presented these papers to the House.

Amendments to Bill for Regulating Elections

[ca. 14 June 1784][1]

If any *Sheriff or* Deputy Sheriff shall directly or indirectly *so* interfere in the election of *Senators or* Delegates *as to show partiality for any of the Candidates* he shall forfeit and pay the sum of   [2] to be recovered on bill, plaint or information in any Court of Record, one *moiety* to the use of the Informer and the other for the use of the Commonwealth, and more over be deprived of his right of voting for   [3] years at any *such* Election thereafter.[4]

Ms (Vi). Docketed with notations on the dates of the several readings. The text may be in Thomas Mathews's handwriting. A separate half-page contains emendations by JM printed here in italics. Most of the original bill was deleted by the final reading.

[1] A committee was appointed on 20 May in the House of Delegates to repeal and supersede the ordinance of the convention of July 1775 "for regulating the election of delegates." Henry Tazewell was chairman and JM one of five other committeemen. Tazewell introduced a bill on 8 June which was titled "A bill to repeal an

ordinance of Convention, and to regulate elections, and enforce the attendance of the members of the General Assembly." This measure passed its first reading, and was read again on 9 June, when it was committed to a Committee of the Whole House. Heavily amended by that committee on 14 June, the bill passed its third reading on 15 June, under the title "an act, for altering the time of the annual meeting of the General Assembly, and for other purposes" (*JHDV*, May 1784, p. 57; Hening, *Statutes*, XI, 387–88). Thomas Mathews was ordered to carry the approved bill forward to the Senate and was probably the principal author of the legislation, but JM, who well knew how influential county officials could be at election time, made a bid for impartiality with emendations in the section on sheriffs' duties.

² In the approved bill "two hundred pounds" was inserted here.

³ Before final passage, "two" was inserted.

⁴ The Senate announced concurrence on 17 June, and the speaker signed the bill into law on 30 June (*JHDV*, May 1784, pp. 61, 89).

Rules of the Constitutional Society of Virginia

EDITORIAL NOTE

Philip Mazzei appears to have been instrumental in the formation of the short-lived organization known as the Constitutional Society of Virginia. Allegedly conceived when "some members of the Assembly proposed to revise the Constitution" of Virginia, the society was born during the session of the General Assembly in Richmond in June 1784. In his memoirs Mazzei asserted that he had organized the society, which included the state's leading public men, and claimed that he was urged by his fellow members to become its president, but because of his impending return to Europe, he "nominated Mr. John Blair, who was unanimously elected by a voice vote" (Marraro, *Memoirs of Philip Mazzei*, p. 285 n. 6).

[ca. 14 June 1784]

We, the underwritten, having associated for the purpose of preserving and handing down to posterity, those pure and sacred principles of Liberty, which have been derived to us, from the happy event of the late glorious revolution, and being convinced, that the surest mode to secure republican systems of government from lapsing into tyranny, is by giving free and frequent information to the mass of people, both of the nature of them, and of the measures which may be adopted by their several component parts, have determined, and do hereby most solemnly pledge ourselves to each other, by every holy tie and obligation, which freemen ought to hold inestimably dear, that every one in his respective station, will keep a watchful eye over the great fundamental rights of the people.

That we will without reserve, communicate our thoughts to each

·other, and to the people, on every subject which may either tend to amend our government, or to preserve it from the innovations of ambition, and the designs of faction.

To accomplish this desirable object, we do agree to commit to paper our sentiments, in plain and intelligible language, on every subject which concerns the general weal; and transmit the same to the Honorable John Blair, Esq; whom we hereby constitute President of the said Society, with powers to congregate the members thereof, either at Richmond, or Williamsburg, whenever he may suppose that he has a sufficient quantity of materials collected for publication. It is farther agreed, that it shall be a rule of the said Society, that no publications shall be made till after mature deliberation in the convocation, it shall have been so determined, by at least two thirds of the present members.[1]

John Blair,	B. Randolph,
James Madison,	James Marshall,
Robert Andrews,	Richard Henry Lee,
James M'Clurg,	William Lee,
John Page,	Ludwell Lee,
James Innes,	William Grayson,
Mann Page,	Francis Corbin,
James Madison, jun.	Philip Mazzei,
Patrick Henry,	Wilson C. Nicholas,
Thomas Lomax,	John Nicholas,
Edmund Randolph,	John Taylor,
William Short,	J. Brown,
William Fleming,	Richard B. Lee,
John Breckenridge,	Spencer Roane,
Archibald Steuart,	Alexander White,
Joseph Jones,	James Monroe,
William Nelson, jun.	Arthur Lee.

At a meeting held on the 15th of June, 1784.

Resolved, that the following declaration be added to the paper originally signed by the members, viz.

"The Society being persuaded, that the liberty of a people is most secure, when the extent of their rights, and the measures of government concerning them are known, do declare that the purpose of this institution is to communicate by fit publications such facts and sentiments, as tend to unfold and explain the one or the other."[2]

Printed copy (DLC: Rare Book Room). Evans 18756. From an undated pamphlet, *Minutes of the Meeting of the Constitutional Society*, which may have been prepared under the direction of Philip Mazzei. A broadside copy (NCU) is reproduced in Schiavo, *Philip Mazzei*, p. 159.

[1] For sketches of most of these signers, see the brief biographies in *Papers of Madison*, vols. I–VII. Archibald Steuart was of course Archibald Stuart of Botetourt County. The first-mentioned James Madison was undoubtedly the president of the College of William and Mary, JM's second cousin. The newer faces in Virginia politics belonged to John Breckinridge (1760–1806), a graduate of William and Mary College who served in the House of Delegates, first as a Botetourt County representative and later from Montgomery County. Admitted to the bar in 1785, he moved to Kentucky in 1792 and became the attorney general and a state legislator. He was involved in the resolutions of 1798 passed in protest to the Alien and Sedition Acts. He was elected to the U.S. Senate in 1805, but resigned to become Jefferson's attorney general (Lowell H. Harrison, *John Breckinridge: Jeffersonian Republican* [Louisville, 1969], pp. 72–88; Swem and Williams, *Register*, pp. 13, 17, 20). James Marshall must have been a misprint for John Marshall, then a Fauquier County delegate and a close friend of the society's organizers. Ludwell Lee (1760–1836), a son of Richard Henry Lee, was educated in England, returned to Virginia in 1780, and served on Lafayette's staff during the Peninsular campaign against Cornwallis. He attended William and Mary College, where he studied law under Chancellor George Wythe, and may have been in Richmond in 1784 as a spectator rather than a participant in public business. Lee later served in the House of Delegates as a representative from Prince William and Fairfax counties, 1787–1790, and Fairfax County senator, 1792–1800 (Cazenove Gardner Lee, Jr., *Lee Chronicle*, ed. Dorothy Mills Parker [New York, 1957], pp. 280–81). The John Nicholas who signed the rules was probably the John Nicholas, Jr., of Buckingham County who served in the May 1784 session of the House of Delegates. However, Wilson Cary Nicholas had an older brother, John Nicholas (1757–1819), who probably was not politically active at this time. Wilson Cary Nicholas (1761–1820) left William and Mary College to serve in the Continental army, where he rose to command of Washington's Life Guard. He later settled in Albemarle County, which he represented in the House of Delegates from 1784 to 1789 and from 1794 to 1800. In 1788 he was a member of the state convention that ratified the federal Constitution, and became an important supporter of the Virginia and Kentucky resolutions in 1798–1799. Nicholas was elected to the U.S. Senate in 1799 but resigned in 1804 to become customs collector at the port of Norfolk. In 1807 he helped organize JM's bid for the presidency, then retired from public life because of ill health. Nicholas became active again in public affairs in 1814, when he was elected governor of Virginia, and during three terms as the chief executive he was instrumental in helping Jefferson establish the University of Virginia (Swem and Williams, *Register*, p. 412; Edgar Woods, *Albemarle County in Virginia*, pp. 90, 290–91). John Brown (1757–1837) was an Augusta County senator from 1784 to 1787 who had attended the College of New Jersey (Princeton) and later William and Mary College. Brown, a commissioned officer in the Revolution, studied law and moved to Kentucky ca. 1786. He served as a Virginia delegate in the Continental Congress, 1787–1788, and in the House of Representatives until 1792, when Kentucky was made a state (a movement in which Brown was a key figure). Kentucky sent him to the U.S. Senate (1792–1805) and thereafter he practiced law in his adopted state. Brown shared with JM a particular interest in navigation rights on western waters and the adoption of the federal Constitution (Swem and Williams, *Register*, pp. 21, 22, 25, 27; Abernethy, *Western Lands and the American Revolution*, pp. 250, 347–48, 350). Richard Bland Lee (1761–1827) was a newly elected delegate from Loudoun Coun-

ty to the House, where he served intermittently until 1800, except for his three terms in Congress (1789–1795). JM appointed Lee as a claims adjuster after the War of 1812, and from 1820 until his death he was judge of the Orphans' Court of the District of Columbia (Lee, *Lee Chronicle*, pp. 86, 174, 314; Swem and Williams, *Register*, p. 20, and passim). Spencer Roane (1762–1822) of Essex County studied law at William and Mary College and was admitted to the bar in 1782. After serving in the House of Delegates (1783–1784), Roane was a state senator and member of the Council of State but is principally remembered as a judge of the General Court (1789–1794) and the state Supreme Court of Appeals (1794–1822). Roane opposed JM in the Richmond convention of 1788 over adoption of the federal Constitution, but they later agreed on the propriety of the Virginia resolutions. Roane is noteworthy for his later advocacy of the states' rights doctrine (*JCSV*, III, 165, 448–579; JM to Jefferson, 4 Dec. 1788 [DLC]; Tyler, *Encyclopedia of Virginia Biography*, II, 61–62). Alexander White (1738–1804) was a graduate of Edinburgh University and a former student of law at the Inner Temple (1762) and Gray's Inn (1763). He returned to Virginia in 1765 and launched a career that eventually made him a leading lawyer in the northern valley counties. In 1772 he represented Hampshire County in the House of Burgesses. His patriotism was suspected during the Revolution, but he nonetheless was returned as representative of Frederick County to the House of Delegates (1782–1786, 1788, 1799–1801). One of JM's ablest allies, he worked for the adoption of the federal Constitution; but the political views of the two men came to differ, and it was as a Federalist that White served in Congress (1789–1793). From 1795 to 1802 he was one of three commissioners appointed to lay out the new capital at Washington, D.C. (Hugh Blair Grigsby, *The History of the Virginia Federal Convention of 1788* [2 vols.; Richmond, 1890–91], II, 71–73; *DAB*, XX, 85).

2 These rules were reprinted in the *Va. Gazette*, 23 Apr. 1785, and *Pa. Packet*, 25 May 1785, with an addition to the minutes omitted in the DLC pamphlet:

"As the intention of this society is to be useful to the community, and not merely to shew a desire of being so, *Resolved*, That it is expected that each member should send to the President, every six months, an essay or problem on some political thesis of importance, which it is hoped will be confined to the subject thereof; and that any one failing in this duty, be informed by the Secretary, that two essays or problems will be expected from him during the next six months; and that any member, on a second delinquency herein, shall not thereafter be considered as a member of this society.

"*Resolved*, That candidates to become members of the society shall be nominated by a member at a meeting preceding his election or rejection."

These resolutions were adopted on 15 June 1784. His memory dimmed by time, Mazzei recalled "several meetings, held at the president's home in Williamsburg." However, the minutes indicate that meetings were held on 11, 15, and 28 June, when Mazzei read a paper on sumptuary laws to the eight assembled members. At the 11 June meeting JM had been appointed to a six-member committee formed "to draw up rules for the organization of this Society." The rules were signed at the meeting on 15 June. On that date JM was appointed to another committee charged with drafting permanent rules, but with the society little was destined to be permanent. The well-intentioned committeeman who proposed the resolution calling for semiannual essays may have helped push the society toward its grave.

As long as Mazzei remained in the U. S. he continued to promote the society and to seek new members, even beyond the bounds of Virginia. There is no doubt that Mazzei was long on promises and short on delivery, but he continued to write political essays which he hoped would be published in Virginia newspapers (Mazzei to JM, 3 June, 15 June 1785). Blair in the *Va. Gazette*, 23 Apr. 1785, called for a meeting on 24 May at Anderson's tavern in Richmond. The supposition is warranted that the May meeting, if ever held, ended not in praising Mazzei's brainchild but in burying it.

Notes for a Speech Favoring Revision of the Virginia Constitution of 1776

EDITORIAL NOTE

Certainly by 1783 JM saw flaws in the 1776 Virginia Constitution that confirmed his early disappointment with it. As has been noted, he thought the Council of State, on which he served, was "a grave of useful talents," and the jealousy displayed by the House of Delegates toward the other branches of government could scarcely have escaped his attention. This constitution, essentially the work of George Mason, gave lip service to Montesquieu's doctrine of a separation of powers while really leaving the main powers of government in the hands of the speaker of the House of Delegates and its most influential members. Jefferson prepared a draft in 1776 which, unlike the constitution adopted by the convention, would have given the governor more extensive powers, clarified the duties and jurisdiction of the courts, liberalized the granting of public lands, ended primogeniture, and specified certain religious and civil rights which the state was bound to honor. Only Jefferson's preamble was grafted into the final version of the Constitution of 1776. After his trying experience as governor (1779–1781), Jefferson complained that the fundamental law of Virginia contained "very capital defects." JM agreed and was ready to launch a reform movement once the great issue of national survival had been settled.

By the fall of 1782 the subject was being privately discussed with the May session of the General Assembly in view. George Mason told close friends he understood "that the present Assembly intend to dissolve themselves, to make Way for a General Convention, to new-model the Constitution," but questioned whether or not it was prudent to delay such action "until the present Ferment . . . has subsided, and Mens Minds have had time to cool" (Rutland, *Papers of George Mason*, II, 768–70). The reform movement was not well developed, however, and it became apparent that most delegates had no enthusiasm for constitutional reform. Perhaps, as Philip Mazzei said, they "feared that by jumping out of the frying pan they would fall into the fire" (Marraro, *Memoirs*, p. 285 n. 6).

If any one person kept the idea of constitutional revision alive, it was Jefferson. In the summer of 1783 he reported to JM that a revising convention had "been much the topic of conversation for some time," and the day to act seemed at hand. Accordingly Jefferson sent JM his notions on a revision but cautioned him not to share them with fellow Virginians because of "prejudices frequently produced against propositions handed to the world without explanation or support" (*Papers of Madison*, VII, 156–57). Probably Jefferson expected to broach the subject to the House of Delegates that spring, but the illness of his wife drew him away from the session and back

75

to Monticello, with the result that he sent JM his propositions. It seems likely that Jefferson expected JM to take up the cudgel of constitutional reform and use the enclosures of 17 June (printed in Boyd, *Papers of Jefferson*, VI, 294–305) as the point of departure. At least the circumstances forced such a decision for Jefferson returned to the Congress that fall and thereafter remained only an observer of state politics. Jefferson's severe critique of the 1776 Constitution called for a strengthened governorship, with the tenure extended to five years, and his powers extended so as better "to carry into execution the laws."

Jefferson undoubtedly urged JM to stop by Gunston Hall early in the winter of 1783 en route from Philadelphia to Orange County. JM tested Mason on a proposed constitutional convention "for revising our form of government" and found Mason *"sound and ripe and I think would not decline a participation in the work"* (italicized words in code; *Papers of Madison*, VII, 401). Mason's political power could well limit the success of the reform yet Jefferson and JM apparently thought they could not move ahead without the elder statesman's help, or at least a promise that he would not interfere (Jefferson to JM, 11 Dec. 1783, ibid., p. 406). During the next few months, the subject was gingerly offered to another great man in Virginia politics, the redoubtable Patrick Henry. As Jefferson and JM viewed matters, Henry would not risk his reputation by favoring any measure not certain of success. Before the session of the General Assembly of May 1784 began, JM decided constitutional revision depended upon Richard Henry Lee and Henry, since Mason had refused to leave Gunston Hall (JM to Jefferson, 15 May 1784). JM tried to learn Henry's sentiments and was mildly encouraged by the great orator's guarded remarks. "The general train of his thoughts seemed to suggest favorable expectations," JM reported to Jefferson.

What then happened is clear from JM's post mortem on the session. As Edmund Randolph had correctly predicted a year earlier, the delegates "constantly profess a sacred regard to the constitution" (*Papers of Madison*, VI, 319). However, an Augusta County petition, with its casual reference to the state constitution, gave JM and his ally Richard Henry Lee an excuse to raise the whole question of revision. Carter Henry Harrison introduced a resolution which declared that the 1776 Constitution did "not rest upon an authentic basis, and was no more than a temporary organization of government for preventing anarchy." A companion resolution called for the convening of a general convention, "with powers to form a constitution of government to which all laws present and future should be subordinate" (*JHDV*, May 1784, p. 55). The line of reasoning used by JM in a speech which he made either on 14 June or a week later bears the heavy stamp of Jefferson's earlier writings. Comparing this and the resolutions, it is likely JM composed the reform propositions.

After 14 June, however, the revisionists' battle was all uphill. Richard Henry Lee, counted on as a stalwart friend of revision, became ill and left the session on 20 June. The next day, the Committee of the Whole upset the revisionists' applecart by rejecting a resolution for a constitutional convention, 42 ayes to 57 noes. The majority then went further and declared "such a measure not being within the province of the House of Delegates to assume; but on the contrary, it is the express duty of the representatives of the people at all times, and on all occasions, to preserve the same inviolable, until a majority of all the free people shall direct a reform thereof" (*JHDV*, May 1784, pp. 70-71). The vote was closer (41 to 47) on a resolution to leave the door to revision slightly ajar. A number of bright young men joined JM in voting for reform—among them Wilson Cary Nicholas, John Taylor, and John Marshall—but in the opposition there was a lone figure they could not circumvent—Patrick Henry. So with Jefferson bound for France and concerns in a different sphere, JM looked to another time when the climate of opinion would be favorable toward constitutional reform. Time went by, and the great expectations of 1783-1784 faded.

Eventually, what the reformers could not accomplish in a single state became easier to manage in a Union of thirteen states. Moreover, the great overhaul of the national machinery of government in 1787-1788 eased much of the pressure for local change. By October 1788, JM had already differed with Jefferson's ideas, as his commentary sent to the Kentuckians about to write a constitution indicates (DLC: Observations on Mr. Jefferson's draught of a Constitution for Virginia, Oct. 1788). The anxieties of 1784 had long since disappeared when JM was elected an Orange County delegate to the Convention of 1829. JM attended the Richmond gathering as a patriarch and spoke only in a whisper. As the only survivor of the Virginia Convention of 1776, JM then looked on the first constitution with some affection.

[14 or 21 June 1784]

Nature of a Constitution ⟨examd.⟩[1]

          See Mass p. 7, 8. 15, 16

          N. Y. p. 63.

          Penna. p. 85, 86.

          Delaw. p. 106

          N. C. p. 146, 150

          S. C. p. 158

          Georgia p. 175, 186.

Convention of 1776. without due power from
people.   1. passed ⟨the ordinance for Constn.⟩ on recommendation of Congs. May 15, 1776 prior to declaration of Independence[2] as ⟨was done⟩ in N. H. p. 1. & N. J. p. 78-84.

      2. ⟨passed it⟩ from impulse of Necessity—see last clause of Preamble to Constution.

      3. before independance declared by Congs.

      4. power from people no where pretended

      5. provision for ⟨case⟩ district of ⟨West⟩ Augusta[3] p: 140 ⟨in its nature temporary⟩

      6. other ordinances ⟨of same session⟩ passed by same authority

deemed alterable—as ⟨relative to⟩ Salt—Senators—Oaths

7. Convention make themselves branch of ⟨the⟩ legislature

Constitution if to be so called defective &c

1. ⟨in a⟩ Union of powers of Govt. ⟨which is⟩ tyranny. Montes-queu.
2. Executive dependant: ⟨on Legislature⟩ 1. for Salary—2. stigma ⟨for character in the triennial expulsion⟩ 3. expensive— 4 ⟨may be⟩ for life contrary to 5 art. D ⟨eclaration of⟩ R⟨ights⟩[4]
3. Judiciary dependent for ⟨amt. of⟩ salary.
4. Privileges & wages of ⟨members of Legislature unlimited & undefined⟩ H. D. & Senate neither limited and defd. & ⟨5⟩ Senate restrained ⟨badly constituted & improperly barred of the⟩ from originating ⟨of⟩ laws.
5. ⟨6⟩ equality of Representation not provided for Counties as for Cities & boroughs—See N. Y. p. 65
                    S. C. p. 165
6. ⟨7⟩ Impeachmts. of great moment & ⟨on bad footing.⟩ not on good footing
7. ⟨8⟩ County Courts seem to be fixed p. 143. 144.[5] ⟨also General Court.⟩
8. ⟨9⟩ Habeas Corpus omitted
9. ⟨10⟩ No mode of expounding Constitution—⟨& of course no check to Genl. Assembly⟩[6]
10. ⟨11⟩ Right of Suffrage, ⟨not well fixed, quere if popish re-cusants &c are not disenfranchised?⟩ exclusion of Papists recusants

Constitution rests on acquiescence, ⟨a bad⟩ dangerous basis

———

revision during the war improper

———

On peace decency requires surrender of power to people.

———

No danger in refer⟨r⟩ing to people ⟨who already exercise an equivalent power.⟩

———

if ⟨no change be made in the⟩ prest. Const. be ⟨it is advisable to have it⟩ ratified by them, more stable ⟨and secured agst. the doubts & imputations under which it now labours⟩.

———

without it, doubts render it unstable

78

Ms, Tr (DLC). Both the original notes on a half-sheet and the transcript are in JM's hand. Variations in the handwriting suggest that JM made additions at some later time, adding portions which are printed here within angle brackets. The docket of the original Ms is in several hands: "Notes June 1784 Speech in Va. Legislature on amendment of State Constitution at May Session 1784." Headings "II. Paper Money" and "III. Disposition to give Congress regulation of Taxe[s]" have been crossed through.

[1] JM's copy made some time later is headed: "Virga. Legislature For Amending Constitution of Va. 1784." The page citations were taken from *The Constitutions of the Several Independent States of America* (Philadelphia, 1781). Francis Bailey printed this compendium by order of the Continental Congress.

[2] The line beginning with "prior" and ending at this point appears to have been added to the original Ms by JM at a later day.

[3] The "district of Augusta," the westernmost settled region of Virginia in 1776, was singled out for treatment as a county with two representatives in the House of Delegates. By noting this, JM intended to call attention to the tentative nature of the Constitution of 1776, since there was by 1784 no longer a West Augusta district but rather eight separate western counties. This item was interchanged with item 6 in the later draft.

[4] The Constitution of 1776 prohibited the governor from serving "longer than three years successively" and he had to be out of office four years before eligible for reelection. It also provided that two of the eight members of the Council of State should every three years be removed by joint ballot "of both Houses of Assembly," but since those members most recently elected might be the very ones removed, six members could indeed serve for life. This was in conflict with Article V of the Declaration of Rights that stated legislators and members of the executive should "at fixed periods, be reduced to a private station" (Hening, *Statutes*, IX, 115, 116, 110).

[5] The pages noted from the edition of *The Constitutions* of 1781, pp. 143–44, are probably cited because the constitution speaks there of "the respective county courts" and court clerks as continuing bodies whose duties & jurisdiction are implicitly to be the same as when Virginia was a royal colony.

[6] But a mode of "expounding Constitution" had already been developed by the Court of Appeals in *Caton v. Commonwealth* (4 Call [Va.] 5; *Papers of Madison*, V, 217–19). JM more probably had in mind the chaos likely to result if the right of exposition should be claimed by other officials (ibid., VI, 346–47, 347 n. 5).

To James Madison, Sr.

RICHMOND June 15. 1784

HOND SIR

Yours by Mr. Barbour was duly handed to me as have been several others of late. Mine by Mr. Craig will have answered the enquiries in most of them. I am now at a loss what step to take with the certificates of Mr. Winslow, having sent you all the money arising from your Tobo. which is now payable. I shall wait till I hear from you on the subject. If payment into the Treasury be immediately wished by Mr.

Winslow as I suppose to be the case, it will be best for you to send back part of the money rcd. from Mr. Craig, to wit £170. I have not yet had time to present the claim last rcd. from Mr. Winslow, or to examine it critically. On a slight perusal of the papers I suspect he is mistaken in supposing it to be within the purview of the Contl: Commissr.[1] I shall obtain & forward as soon as I can the exact state of Tobo. sold by me. You will let Mr. Winslow know that the Senate have ratified the postponemt. of the taxes till the last day of Jany. It is thought by some that an intermediate tax of some kind or other will be essential, but whether any such will take place is uncertain & perhaps improbable, though we shall make a sharp figure, after our declarations with regard to Congs. & the Continental debt, if we wholly omit the means of fulfilling them.[2] I have got a resolution for Majr. Lee's Warrant & will get it for him & send it as soon as I can. I have been slightly indisposed for several days past, but feel myself better this morning. With my affect. regards to the family I am Yr. dutiful son

J. MADISON JR.

I mean that the whole of Burrow's Reports including any continuation supplemental to the 5 Vols: to be sent for.

I see not how any thing can be done by the Legislature with regard to Kentucky: nor would I have you rely on such expectation, but be prepared to maintain your rights as well as you can in the ordinary way.

RC (DLC). Cover missing. Written above the date: "Madison Jr. To his Father."

[1] Benjamin Winslow's claim, "for 23½ Bushells of Potatoes" delivered to the Albemarle Barracks on 19 Dec. 1780, was filed on 25 Mar. 1784 (Vi: Court Booklet, Orange County, p. 40).

[2] JM was foremost among those delegates who were concerned over "our declarations with regard to Congs. & the Continental debt," but his direct role in drafting two ad valorem levies to help the impoverished Continental treasury is vague. He doubtless was a strong proponent of a 1½ percent duty on imports and a 1 percent ad valorem land tax—the only tax measures meant to raise money earmarked for the national continental requisition (Hening, *Statutes*, XI, 374–75, 376–77).

From John Blair Smith

HAMPDEN SYDNEY, June 21. 1784.

DEAR SIR;

I am sorry to interrupt your attention to important business, by introducing a matter in this letter, which you are already tired of. However as it is of some importance, I presume upon your usual patience & candor.

Since my arrival at home,[1] I have seen a part of your Journals, & by them have learned the objects of the Petition from the Episcopal Clergy, which in one or two instances, appear to me very exceptionable. The first part of their prayer is necessary & proper; & the whole of it might pass without much animadversion to its disadvantage, 'till you hear them requesting that "they, the Clergy, may be incorporated by law;" & then an attentive mind must revolt against it as very unjustifiable, & very insulting to the members of their communion in general.[2] Had they requested that an incorporating act should pass, in favour of that Church as a party of Christians, whereby the *people* might have had a share in the direction of ecclesiastical regulations, & the appointment of Church officers for that purpose, it would have been extremely proper. But as the matter now stands, the Clergy seem desirous to exclud[e] *them* from any share in such a privilege & willing to oblige the members of their Churches to sit down patiently, under such regulations as an incorporated body of Clergymen, who wish to be peculiarly considered as ministers in the view of the law, shall chuse to make, without a legal right to interfere in any manner, but such as these spiritual leaders may think fit to allow. I should expect that such an Idea of spiritual domination, would be resented & opposed by every adherent to that Society. I should suppose that every one of them who felt the spirit of his station would regard the attempt as an indefensible remain of Star-chamber tyranny, & resist it accordingly. However, if the Gentlemen, of the communion are so used to Dictators, that they either have not observed the Jure divino pretension to domineer over them, or have not inclination or Spirit to oppose it, perhaps it may be thought proper for one so little interested in the matter as myself to be Silent. I confess that I have less reason to interfere than many others: but as a Citizen of a free State I am interested in the Spirit which my Countrymen discover, & am sorry that there is room to suppose them too insensible of their own importance in any instance whatever.

But that part of the petition, which concerns me most, as well as every Non-Episcopalian in the state, is, where these Clergymen pray for an act of the Assembly to *Enable*, them to regulate all the spiritual concerns of that Church &c. This is an express attempt to draw the State into an illicit connexion & commerce with them, which is already the ground of that uneasiness which at present prevails thro' a great part of the State. According to the spirit of that prayer, the Legislature is

81

to consider itself as the head of that Party, & consequently they as Members are to be fostered with particular care. This is unreasonable & highly improper, as well as dangerous. It ought therefore to [be] treated by the assembly as an ill-digested Scheme of policy in the present State of affairs. I am sorry that Christian Ministers should virtually declare their Church a mere political machine, which the State may regulate at pleasure; but I shall be surprized if the Assembly shall assume the improper office. The interference of the Legislature is always dangerous, where it is unnecessary. And I am sure it is plainly so in this case. It would be to decide upon a matter which a Superior power, I mean the Convention in the Bill of Rights, has already determined.[3] It would be to give leave to do what every class of Citizens has a natural, unalienable right to do without any such leave; for surely every religious society in the State possesses full power to regulate their internal police; without depending upon the Assembly for leave to do so. Surely we are not again to be irritated & harassed with the heavy weight of a State-Church, that is to sit as sovereign over the rest, by depending in a more particular manner for direction in Spirituals, upon that antiquated fountain head of influences, the secular power.

I have here hastily throw together the very first thoughts which occurred to me upon reading the Journals; & as you certainly have taken notice of the same improprieties in the petition which I have now done, I hope you will use your extensive influence to prevent the consequences intended to flow from it.[4] I am, Dr. Sir, with the greatest respect Yr. very hble Servt.

JOHN B: SMITH.

RC (DLC). Cover missing. Docketed by JM.

[1] The Reverend John Blair Smith (1756–1799) had been an undergraduate at the College of New Jersey when JM was in his final year of study. In the graduating class of 1773 with Henry Lee, Smith was a professor at Hampden-Sydney, 1775–1779, captain of the Hampden-Sydney volunteers, 1776–1777, and president of the college, 1779–1791 (Charles Grier Sellers, Jr., "John Blair Smith," *Journal of the Presbyterian Historical Society*, XXXIV [1956], 201–25). From 1795 to 1799 he was president of Union College, Schenectady, New York. Smith was more than usually interested in this session of the General Assembly, for Hampden-Sydney had petitioned the legislature for a gift of land on 1 June, and by 12 June had approval for "certain lands . . . in the County of Prince Edward" (*JHDV*, May 1784, pp. 30, 38, 48, 51). JM, along with other public men then serving in the General Assembly, was a member of the Hampden-Sydney board of trustees, though there is no evidence that he ever attended a meeting (Alfred J. Morrison, *The College of Hampden-Sydney: Calendar of Board Minutes, 1776–1876* [Richmond, 1912], p. 171; *General Catalogue of Princeton University, 1746–1906* [Princeton, 1908], pp. 96, 97).

2 The unexceptional "first part" of the Protestant Episcopal petition of 4 June sought repeal or amendment "of sundry laws now in force, which direct modes of worship and enjoin the observance of certain days." Smith objected to the request that the former Anglican church be incorporated and the clergy thereof permitted "to regulate all the spiritual concerns of that Church, alter its form of worship, and constitute such canons, by-laws and rules . . . as are suited to their religious principles . . ." (*JHDV*, May 1784, p. 36).

3 As principal author of Article XVI of the Virginia Declaration of Rights, JM had no need for instruction in its meaning. See Brant, *Madison*, I, 241–48; *Papers of Madison*, I, 170–79.

4 JM served on the Committee on Religion and knew all too well that this measure had few supporters but a single and powerful one—Patrick Henry. On 8 June the committee reported in favor of incorporating the Episcopal church, and a bill was introduced on 16 June. On 25 June the Committee of the Whole debated the bill and finally ordered it held over until the "second Monday in November next" (*JHDV*, May 1784, p. 79). "Extraordinary as such a project was, it was preserved from a dishonorable death by the talents of Mr. Henry," JM reported to Jefferson on 3 July 1784.

Bill Authorizing an Amendment in the Articles of Confederation

EDITORIAL NOTE

Whether JM introduced the resolution on 19 May calling for compliance with the act of Congress (17 Feb. 1783) that sought to apportion taxes amongst the states according "to the value of all land . . . & improvements thereon" is highly conjectural. JM thought a land tax scheme unreasonable and on 21 June he seized the opportunity to strike at the weakness, as he viewed it, of Article VIII of the Articles of Confederation. The point of JM's bill was to make the national treasury revenues proportionate to the state's population rather than its land wealth. JM had seen the old system founder, and on 14 January 1783 had discussed with other congressmen an alteration in the basis of Article VIII from land values to a census (*Papers of Madison*, VI, 35–37). He opposed the 17 February 1783 act of Congress that maintained land values as the basis for treasury requisitions as "ineffectual," but his population principle triumphed in the package approved by Congress on 18 April 1783. Indeed, most of this bill follows verbatim the congressional recommendation for a shift of the tax base to people rather than property. Convinced that population rather than land value was the only equitable solution to the nation's tax apportionment, JM admitted the three-fifths principle was hardly a perfect solution either. But JM hoped in April 1783 that "an equal spirit of accomodation among the several Legislatures, will prevail against little inequalities . . . on one side or on the other" (*Papers of Madison*, VI, 492). Fourteen months later, JM was still trying to solve the problems created by a rickety fiscal plan.

[21 June 1784]

For the purpose of introducing a more convenient and certain rule of ascertaining the proportions to be supplied to the common Treasury of the United States recommended by Congress in their act of the 18 of April 1783.[1] Be it enacted by the General Assembly that so much of the 8th. of the articles of Confederation & perpetual Union between the 13 States of America, as is contained in the words following, to wit, "all charges of war, and all other expences that shall be incurred for the common defence, or General welfare, and allowed by the U. S. in Congs. assembd. shall be defrayed out of a Common Treasury, which shall be supplied by the several States in proportion to the value of all land within each State granted to or surveyed for any person, as such land and the buildings & improvements thereon, shall be estimated according to such mode as the U. S. in Congress assembd. shall from time to time direct and appoint," shall be revoked & made void on the part of this Commonwealth; and in place thereof it is declared & concluded, the same having been agreed to in a Congress of the U. States, that all charges of war & all other expences that have been or shall be incurred for the common defence or general welfare, and allowed by the U. S. in Congress assembled, except so far as shall be otherwise provided for, shall be defrayed out of a Common Treasury, which shall be supplied by the several states in proportion to the whole number of white & other free Citizens & inhabitants of every age, sex and condition, including those bound to servitude for a term of years, and three fifths of all other persons not comprehended in the foregoing description,[2] except Indians not paying taxes, in each State; which number shall be biennially[3] taken & transmitted to the U. S. in Congress assembled, in such mode as they shall direct and appoint: And the Delegates representing this State in Congress, or any two of them, are hereby authorised & required to subscribe & ratify the said alteration of the Articles of Confederation & perpetual Union; and the same when subscribed & ratified by the said Delegates, and by the Delegates of each of the other Confœderated States[4] duly authorised therefor, shall be valid & binding as to this Commonwealth.

Ms (Vi). In JM's hand. His heading, "An Act authorising the Delegates representing this State in Congress to subscribe & ratify an alteration of the 8th of the Articles of Confederation and perpetual Union between the 13 States of America," was crossed through and placed on the docket by a clerk. For background of the act see Resolutions to Strengthen Powers of Congress, 19 May 1784.

[1] JM had been active in the debate which preceded the act of 18 Apr. 1783, an attempt by Congress to reform the entire financial structure of the Confederation. The plan called for liberal territorial concessions by the states to Congress, the granting to Congress for twenty-five years the power to collect duties on imports, payment of annual requisitions of state quotas for retirement of the continental debt, and a shift of the national taxation base from one proportioned on land values to a system based on a census. JM had voted for this measure and may have helped write the final section which he had long held to be the only fair basis for a continental tax program (*JCC*, XXIV, 257–61).

[2] The idea that slaves should not be counted as equals with freemen in a census for taxation purposes was first suggested by Virginian Benjamin Harrison during the preliminary debate on the Articles of Confederation (Burnett, *The Continental Congress*, p. 226).

[3] The congressional recommendation of 18 Apr. 1783 called for a triennial census.

[4] Because amendments to the Articles of Confederation needed to be ratified by thirteen states, the possibility that this drastic change would ever be enacted was remote. Over a year later, JM was still pondering the difficulties of this situation, and vented his anguished thoughts in a letter to Jefferson (3 Oct. 1785). The matter was still pending when the Federal Convention met in 1787 and drafted the Constitution which gave Congress the power to levy and collect taxes and set federal representation and direct taxation in proportion to this same census ratio.

Resolution for Procuring a Statue of General Washington

In the House of Delegates Tuesday the 22d. of June 1784

Resolved that the Executive be requested to take measures for procuring a Statue of General Washington to be of the finest marble and best Workmanship with the following inscription on its pedestal Viz:

The General Assembly of the Commonwealth of Virginia have caused this Statue to be erected as a monument of affection and Gratitude to George Washington who uniting to the endowments of the Hero the virtues of the Patriot and exerting both in establishing the Liberties of his Country has rendered his name dear to his fellow Citizens and given the world an immortal example of true Glory. Done in the year of Christh and in the year of the Commonwealth .[1]

Ms (Vi). In Beckley's hand, with exception of Drew's attestation. Docketed and dated, with separate notations, "C[opie]d." and "Mr Ronald." Printed in Hening, *Statutes*, XI, 552.

[1] William Ronald was chairman of a special committee instructed, on 15 May, "to consider and report" on a suitable means of demonstrating "the gratitude and veneration" of his native state for George Washington. This fact, coupled with Ronald's introduction of the present resolution and the order of the House that he bear the approved document to the Senate, ordinarily would stamp him as the

principal author. However, William Cabel Rives stated that the second paragraph of the resolution was "known to have been the composition of Mr. Madison" (*Life of Madison*, I, 572). If Rives was well informed, then it was tact that caused JM to conceal his authorship (JM to Jefferson, 12 May 1786, Boyd, *Papers of Jefferson*, IX, 518). When completed the inscription read: "Done in the year of Christ One thousand seven hundred and eighty-eight, and in the year of the Commonwealth the twelfth."

To James Madison, Sr.

RICHMOND June 24. 84.

HOND SIR

Your letter by Capt: Cowherd with that of my brother's[1] have been just put into my hand. I shall leave to him the sale of the Tobo. belonging to Capt: Conway[2] & Ambrose, not being at leisure myself to do it before he proposes to set out. I think it will be well to accept of Mr. Lawson's offer of the Madeira. I shall do the best I can towards satisfying the Treasury on acct. of Mr. Winslow. Majr Lee's warrant has been ordered by the assembly, but Mr. Harvey being a little puzzled by the peculiarity of the case, could not make it out immediately on my first application, & I have not time now to repeat it. I hope the delay will not be inconvenient to Majr. Lee. Much time has been lately spent by the Assembly in abortive efforts for amendment of the Constitution, and fulfilling the Treaty of peace in the article of British debts. The residue of the business will not be completed till next week. If my brother W. is at leisure as before, I beg him to bring down the Chair for me to be here by Wednesday next. I am your dutiful son

J. MADISON JR.

RC (DLC). Cover missing. Docketed by JM.

[1] Capt. Francis Cowherd (1757–1833), of Oak Hill, Orange County, formerly of the Continental Line, served as county deputy sheriff in 1785 and 1786. From the mid-1790s until 1802 he was a distinguished county public servant, being successively overseer of the poor, coroner, justice of the peace, and sheriff. In later years he was a federal military pensioner (ViHi: Martha Frances [Woodroof] Hiden Papers, ca. 1900–1958; Vi: Orange County Court Records, microfilm; Scott, *History of Orange County*, p. 61; Gwathmey, *Historical Register of Virginians*, p. 184). Neither the letter of James Madison, Sr., nor that of JM's undesignated brother, presumably Ambrose, has been found.

[2] Capt. Francis Conway (1749–1794), of Port Conway, King George County, erstwhile of the Continental Line, was JM's first cousin. The May 1784 session of the General Assembly passed an act authorizing the settlement on his lands of a town bearing the name of his estate (George Norbury Mackenzie, *Colonial Families of the United States of America* . . . [7 vols.; New York and elsewhere, 1907–20; reprint, Baltimore, 1966], V, 138; Hening, *Statutes*, XI, 363–64).

Opinion in Controversy between Joseph Jones and William Lee

RICHMOND June 26, 1784

A dispute between Mr. Joseph Jones of King George and Mr. William Lee[1] being mutually referred to us: We are of opinion that Mr. Jones never was an enemy to the payment of British or other debts: We are also of opinion that Mr. Lee's inference respecting the opposition of Mr. Jones to the payment of debts, was founded on Mr. Jones' support to the prohibitory laws[2] revived last session of Assembly against the recovery of British debts and admitting commutables into the payment of [do]mestic debts,[3] which inference altho' erronious appears not to have been confined to Mr. Lee alone. We therefore decide that Mr. Lee misconceived Mr. Jones' principles with respect to the payment of debts, and that he was led by this misconception, into a statement of them injurious to Mr. Jones, to remove which impressions, propriety requires that Mr. Lee should take the first opportunity of communicating to Mr. Fitzhugh of Marmion,[4] the misconception into which he was led relative to Mr. Jones' principle.

J. MADISON JR.
HENRY LEE JUN.[5]

Ms (Vi). In an unidentified hand, endorsed: "June 26. 1784 Jones & Lee."

[1] After fifteen years abroad, William Lee had returned to America on 25 Sept. 1783 and soon established himself at his plantation, Green Spring, in James City County. In the present session of Assembly he was serving in the Senate (Lee, *Lee Chronicle*, pp. 234–35; Swem and Williams, *Register*, p. 21).

[2] The practice of submitting a dispute to an agreeable third party seems to have been fairly common in JM's day (see Mays, *Papers of Edmund Pendleton*, II, 701). Acrimony over the British debt repayment had strained the bonds of friendship and even brought hapless John Warden before the House on 14 June, accused of saying the delegates who wished to ignore the British debts "had voted against paying for the coats on their backs" (*JHDV*, May 1784, p. 57). Jones had supported "the prohibitory laws" or the "lien law" at the October session of the General Assembly, but it was of limited duration (Hening, *Statutes*, XI, 349). Jones told Jefferson he had a plan for installment repayment of the debts but refrained from introducing it because some key members left the session early so that "the thinness of the House" made it inexpedient to offer "a proposition of such importance" (Boyd, *Papers of Jefferson*, VI, 566).

[3] Tobacco, hemp, flour, and deerskins had been declared "commutables" in lieu of cash payments on taxes at the Oct. 1782 session of the General Assembly (Hening, *Statutes*, XI, 118, 128). The controversial measure was repealed at the following session of the legislature (May 1783), but revived by the next (Oct. 1783).

[4] William Fitzhugh (1725–1791), of Marmion, King George County, was a fel-

low senator with William Lee (*VMHB*, VIII [1900–1901], 92–93; Swem and Williams, *Register*, p. 21).

⁵ Henry ("Light Horse Harry") Lee, Jr., a first cousin once removed of William Lee.

Bill to Aid Thomas Paine

EDITORIAL NOTE

Despite the concern expressed to JM by Jefferson and Washington over the penury afflicting Thomas Paine, all legislative attempts in Virginia to aid the author of *Common Sense* failed. On 28 June there was appointed a special committee, of which Patrick Henry was chairman and JM a member, to prepare a bill "vesting a certain tract of public land, in Thomas Payne and his heirs" (*JHDV*, May 1784, p. 82). As JM on 2 July reported to Washington, the "gift first proposed" offered Paine "a moiety of a tract . . . known by the name of 'the Secretary's land.' " This was true so far as the proposal was first made to the House of Delegates; but the present manuscript clearly indicates that within the committee itself there was a disposition to reward Paine with the entire tract. Evidently fearing (justifiably, as time would reveal) that a donation so liberal might cause the raising of more than eyebrows, JM persuaded the committee to halve the acreage.

[28 June 1784]

Whereas Thomas Paine author of the Pamphlet entitled common Sense printed at Philadelphia in the year 1776 has by the said and several other literary performances published in the Course of the late Revolution rendered distinguished Service to the United States and it is just and expedient that such patriotic exertions of Genius should be honorably and substantially rewarded Be it enacted that in Testimony of the Esteem entertained by this Commonwealth for the merits of the said Thomas Paine the tract of Public Land lying in the County of Northampton and known by the name of the Secretarys Land¹ ⟨shall be divided into two equal moieties in such manner as the Executive shall direct, and for such moiety as the said Thomas Paine shall prefer a patent shall issue vesting the same⟩ *be and the same is hereby vested* in him and his heirs forever; Saving to all persons other than those claiming under the Commonwealth any Interest which they may have therein.²

Ms (Vi). In hand of John Beckley, with amendment by JM within angle brackets, and canceled words indicated by italics.

1 The "Secretary's Land," 500 acres lying on King's Creek, was first tenanted in 1620. In 1633 the income from the leases thereon was made a perquisite of the office of the secretary of the colony (Ralph T. Whitelaw, *Virginia's Eastern Shore: A History of Northampton and Accomack Counties* [2 vols.; Richmond, 1951], I, 167–75).

2 On the same day that the committee was formed, Henry introduced the bill which promptly passed two readings. On the following day it was referred to the Committee of the Whole, which "made several amendments thereto," and was ordered engrossed. A second Ms of the bill, together with Beckley's notes on the amendments, is in the Virginia State Library. These documents verify JM's statement to Washington that the donation to Paine was augmented to include "the other moiety" (2 July 1784). The result justified JM's fear of attempting too much, for on its third reading the bill was "thrown out by a large majority" (*JHDV*, May 1784, pp. 82, 86, 87).

Time was pressing (30 June was the last day of session); so JM undertook a hurried salvage operation by moving that a new special committee be appointed to prepare a bill for selling the Secretary's Land "and applying part of the money arising therefrom, to the purchase of a tract to be vested in Thomas Payne, and his heirs." As chairman of the committee, JM later in the day introduced the second bill, no Ms of which is known to exist, but it "lost by a single vote" (*JHDV*, May 1784, pp. 87, 87–88; JM to Washington, 2 July, 12 Aug. 1784).

Resolutions Appointing Virginia Members
of a Potomac River Commission

Monday the 28th. of June 1784.

Whereas great inconveniences are found to result from the want of some concerted regulations, between this State, and the State of Maryland touching the jurisdiction & navigation of the River Potowmack:1

Resolved that George Mason, Edmund Randolph, James Madison jr & Alexander Henderson Esqrs. be appointed Commissioners & that they or any three of them do meet such Commissioners, as may be appointed on the part of Maryland, and in concert with them, frame such liberal & equitable regulations concerning the said River as may be mutually advantageous to the two States, and that they make report thereof to the General Assembly.

Resolved, that the Executive be requested to notify the above appointment with the object of it to the State of Maryland, and desire it's concurrence in the proposition.

Ms (Vi). In a copyist's hand and endorsed by clerks John Beckley and Will Drew. Dated and docketed: "Reso appointing Commissioners on the part of this State to concert with Commissioners from the State of Maryland respecting the Jurisdiction & Navigation of the River Potowmack 28th. June 1784   Cd. for Govr & 2 others."

¹ JM's anxiety regarding jurisdiction over the lower Potomac was explicit in his letter to Jefferson of 16 Mar. 1784. Jefferson followed through and in his reply of 25 Apr. expressed the belief that the best way to solve the problem was through appointment of a joint commission—JM's preferred plan. Possibly the seed for the conference originated in Jefferson's earlier remark to JM (20 Feb. 1784) that a scheme was afoot to annex the Northern Neck of Virginia to Maryland, and that Arthur Lee favored such a measure (*Papers of Madison*, VII, 424).

JM must have been the author of these resolutions (he was directed to carry them to the Senate [*JHDV*, May 1784, p. 84]), but through a circumstance of bureaucratic ineptness, he and Randolph were not notified that the meeting was scheduled for Mar. 1785. Thus JM was absent when the commissioners met at Mount Vernon and learned of the proceedings only from personal letters (Mason to JM, 9 Aug., 7 Dec. 1785).

From Thomas Jefferson

Boston July 1. 1784.

Dear Sir

After visiting the principal towns through Connecticut, Rhode-island, this state & N. Hampshire in order to acquire what knowlege I could of their commerce & other circumstances I am returned to this place & shall sail the day after tomorrow in the Ceres bound for London: but my purpose is to get on shore in some boat on the coast of France & proceed directly to Paris. My servant being to set off to-day, & much on hand to prepare for my journey I have no time for any particular communications. Indeed there are few I should have to make unless I were to enter into a detail which would be lengthy as to the country & people I have visited. The lower house of this state have passed a bill giving Congress the powers over their commerce which they had asked: it has had two readings with the Senate & meets with no opposition. I find the conviction growing strongly that nothing can preserve our Confederacy unless the band of Union, their common council be strengthened. I inclose you a letter from mrs. Trist & a new pamphlet.¹ Since I came here I have received from mr. Harrison a bill of John Pirkman on John J. Bogert Philadelphia for 333 1/3 Dollars. This being for part of the money included in my draught on the Treasurer in your favor, and which at the time of that draught I did not know had been forwarded for me, I now inclose the bill to mr. Saml. House in Philadelphia & desire him to receive & lodge the money in the bank in your name, and to give you advice of it that you may know when it may be safely drawn for. You shall hear from me as soon as I reach the other side the Atlantic. In the mean time I am with truth Dr. Sir Your affectionate friend & sert.

TH: JEFFERSON

P.S. I inclosed you by Genl. Gates from N. York Deane's letters which I could not get in Philada.[2]

RC (DLC). Cover missing. Docketed.

[1] Eliza House Trist's letter was written ca. 13 Apr. 1784. The "new pamphlet" Jefferson sent was Brian Edwards's *Thoughts on the late Proceedings of Government respecting the Trade of the West India Islands with the United States of North America* (London and Boston, 1784). JM acknowledged the arrival of this 32-page work on 20 Aug. 1784.

[2] Gates seems to have been in New York in a futile quest for the hand of the widow of Brig. Gen. Richard Montgomery. He was returning to Virginia to attend a meeting with former comrades of the Virginia Line (Samuel White Patterson, *Horatio Gates, Defender of American Liberties* [New York, 1941], pp. 348–51).

To George Washington

RICHMOND July 2d. 1784.

DEAR SIR

The sanction given by your favor of the 12th. inst: to my desire of remunerating the genius which produced *Common Sense*, led to a trial[1] for the purpose. The gift first proposed was a moiety of the tract on the Eastern Shore, known by the name of "the Secretary's land." The easy reception it found induced the friends of the measure to add the other moiety to the proposition which would have raised the Market value of the donation to about £4000 or upwards, though it would not probably have commanded a rent of more than £100 per annum. In this form the bill passed through two readings. The third reading proved that the tide had suddenly changed, for the bill was thrown out by a large majority.[2] An attempt was next made to sell the land in question and apply £2000 of the money to the purchase of a Farm for Mr. Paine. This was lost by a single voice. Whether a greater disposition to reward patriotic and distinguished exertions of genius will be found on any succeeding occasion is not for me to predetermine. Should it finally appear that the merits of the Man, whose writings have so much contributed to infuse & foster the Spirit of Independence in the people of America, are unable to inspire them with a just beneficence: the world, it is to be feared, will give us as little credit for our policy as for our gratitude, in this particular. The wish of Mr. Paine to be provided for by separate acts of the States, rather than by Congress, is I think a natural and just one. In the latter case it might be construed into the wages of a mercenary writer, in the former it would look like the returns of gratitude for voluntary services. Upon the same principle the mode wished by Mr. Paine, ought to be preferred by the States themselves. I beg the favor of you to present my respectful compliments to Mrs. Washington and to be assured that I am with the profoundest respect & sincerest regard your Obdt. & humble servant

J. MADISON JR.

RC (DLC: Washington Papers); Tr (DLC). Addressed by JM. The RC is badly faded, while the first page of the transcript is torn along the left margin. The RC was docketed by Washington.

[1] In his transcript JM here placed a caret and above it wrote, "[in the Legislature]." For the "trial," see Bill to Aid Thomas Paine, 28 June 1784.

[2] Richard Henry Lee added in a letter of 22 July to Washington that he understood the movement to compensate Paine "miscarried from its being observed that he had shewn enmity to this State by having written a pamphlet injurious to our claim of Western Territory" (DLC: Washington Papers). Thus in the Lee family's view Paine's *Public Good* more than offset *Common Sense*. JM's note on the transcript asserts "the Change was produced by prejudices against Mr. Paine, thrown into circulation by Arthur Lee."

To Thomas Jefferson

RICHMOND July 3d. 1784.

DEAR SIR

The Assembly adjourned the day before yesterday.[1] I have been obliged to remain here since on private business for my Countymen with the auditor's and other departments. I had allotted towards the close of the Session to undertake a narrative for you of the proceedings, but the hurry on which I did not sufficiently calculate, rendered it impossible, and I now find myself so abridged in time that I cannot fulfil my intentions. It will however be the less material, as Mr. Short by whom this goes, will be possessed of almost every thing I could say. I inclose you a list of the Acts passed excepting a few which had not received the last Solemnity when the list went to the press. Among the latter is an Act under which 1 per Ct. of the land tax will be collected this fall and will be for Congress. This with the 1 1/2 per Ct. added to the impost on trade, will be all that Congress will obtain on their last requisition for this year. It will be much short of what they need, & of what might be expected from the declarations with which we introduced the business of the Session. These declarations will be seen in the Journal, a copy of which I take for granted will be carried by Mr. Short. Another act not on the list lays duties on law proceedings, on alienations of land—on probat[e]s of Wills, administration & some other transactions which pass through official hands. This tax may be considered as the basis of a stamp-tax; it will probably yield £15 or 20,000 at present, which is set apart for the foreign Creditors of this State.

We made a warm struggle for the establishmt. of Norfolk & Alexandria as our only ports; but were obliged to add York, Tappahannock & Bermuda hundred, in order to gain any thing & to restrain to these ports foreigners only.[2] The footing on which British debts are put will appear from the Journal noting only that a law is now in force which forbids suits for them. The minority in the Senate have protested on the subject. Having not seen the protest I must refer to Mr. Short who will no doubt charge himself with it.

A trial was made for a[3] Convention, but in a form not the most lucky. The adverse temper of the House & particularly Mr. Henry had determined me to be silent on the subject. But a Petition from Augusta having among other things touched on a Reform of the Govt. and R. H: L. arriving with favorable sentiments, we thought it might not be amiss to stir the matter. Mr. Stuart from Augusta accordingly proposed to the Committee of Propositions, the Resolutions reported to the House as per Journal.[4] Unluckily R. H: L. was obliged by sickness to leave us the day before the question came on in Com[m]ittee of the Whole, and Mr. Henry shewed a more violent opposition than we expected. The consequence was that after two days Debate, the Report was negatived, and the majority not content with stopping the measure for the present availed themselves of their strength to put a supposed bar on the Journal against a future possibility of carrying it. The members for a Convention with full powers, was not considerable for number, but included most of the young men of education & talents. A great many would have concurred in a Convention for specified amendments, but they were not disposed to be active even for such a qualified plan.

Several Petitions came forward in behalf of a Genl. Assessmt which was reported by the Come. of Religion to be reasonable. The friends of the measure did not chuse to try their strength in the House. The Episcopal Clergy introduced a notable project for re-establishing their independence of the laity. The foundation of it was that the whole body should be legally incorporated, invested with the present property of the Church, made capable of acquiring indefinitely—empowered to make canons & by laws not contrary to the laws of the land, and incumbents when once chosen by Vestries to be immovable otherwise than by sentence of the Convocation. Extraordinary as such a project was, it was preserved from a dishonorable death by the talents of Mr. Henry. It lies over for another Session.

The public lands at Richmond not wanted for public use are ordered to be sold & the money, aided by subscriptions, to be applied to the erection of buildings on the Hill as formerly planned. This fixes the Govt. which was nearly being made as vagrant as that of the U. S. by a coalition between the friends of Williamsbg & Stau[n]ton. The point was carried by a small majority only.

The lands about Williamsbg are given to the University, and are worth Mr. H. Tazewell thinks £10,000 to it. For the encouragement of Mr. Maury's School, license is granted for a lottery to raise not more than £2000.[5]

The revisal is ordered to be printed. A frivolous œconomy restrained the no. of copies to 500. I shall secure the no. you want & forward them by the first opportunity. The three Revisors' labour was recollected on this occasion, and £500 voted for cash. I have taken out your warrant in five parts, that it may be the more easily converted to use. It is to be paid out of the first unappropriated money in the Treasury, which renders its value very precarious unless the Treasurer sd. be willing to endorse it "receivable-in-taxes" which he is not obliged to do. I shall await Your orders to the disposition of it.

An effort was made for Paine & the prospect once flattering. But a sudden opposition was brewed up which put a negative on every form which could be given to the proposed remuneration. Mr. Short will give you particulars.

Col: Mason the Attorney & Mr. Henderson & myself are to negociate with Maryland if she will appt. Comissrs. to establish regulations for the Potowmac.

Since the receipt of yours of May 8. I have made diligent enquiry concerning the several schools most likely to answer for the education of your Nephews. My information has determined me finally to prefer that of Mr. W. Maury as least exceptionable: and I have accordingly recommended it to Mrs. Carr. & on receiving her answer shall write to Mr. Maury pointing out your wishes as to the course of study proper

for Master Carr. I have not yet made up any opinion as to the disposition of your younger Nephew, but shall continue my enquiries till I
can do so. I find a greater deficiency of proper schools than I could
have supposed, low as my expectations were on the subject. All that I
can assure of is that I shall pursue your wishes with equal pleasure and
faithfulness.

Your hint for appropriating the slave-tax to Congress fell in precisely
with the opinion I had formed and suggested to those who are most
attentive to our finances. The existing appropriation of one half of it
however to the Military debt was deemed a bar to such a measure.[6] I
wished for it because the Slave holders are Tobo. makers, and will generally have hard money as alone will serve for Congress. Nothing can
exceed the confusion which reigns throughout our Revenue department. We attempted but in vain to ascertain the amount of our debts,
and of our resourses, as a basis for some thing like a system. Perhaps
by the next Session the information may be prepared. This confusion
indeed runs through all our public affairs, and must continue as long as
the present mode of legislating continues. If we cannot amend the constitution, we must at least call in the aid of accurate penmen for extending Resolutions into bills, which at present are drawn in manner that
must soon bring our laws & our Legislature into contempt among all
orders of Citizens.

I have communicated your request from Philada. May 25. to Mr.
Zane. He writes by Mr. Short & tells me he is possessed of the observations which he promised you. I found no opportunity of broaching a
scheme for opening the Navigation of the Potowmac under the auspices
of Genl. Washington, or of providing for such occurrences, as the case
of Marbois. With the aid of the Attorney perhaps something may be
done on the latter point next Session. Adieu My dear friend.

J. MADISON JR.

RC (DLC). Docketed by JM. Cover and enclosure missing.

[1] Actually two days "before yesterday," on 30 June.

[2] JM had been unable to beat back the last-minute additions forced by various
local interests. He concurred with Monroe in thinking that the objects of the bill
(ease of customs collections, prevention of smuggling, and the creation of a Virginia rival to Baltimore as a key Atlantic port) might be defeated by allowing
shipping from five ports. "Will it not be an exertion to promote their interest by
collecting the produce of the State to particular ports, and thereby throw it more
particularly into the vortex of Baltimore, since the operation of each town will be
confin[e]d to the river on which it is plac'd?" (Monroe to Jefferson, 20 July 1784,
Boyd, *Papers of Jefferson*, VII, 380).

3 Some time later the word "State" was placed within brackets here by an un-known hand.

4 Archibald Stuart was inclined to overreach himself. JM tried to save the occasion with a speech analyzing the old constitution's flaws. See Notes for a Speech Favoring Revision of the Virginia Constitution of 1776, 14 or 21 June 1784.

5 Hening, *Statutes*, XI, 406, 407.

6 The "slave tax" of 10s. on all slaves over sixteen had been applied toward arrearages due to soldiers and officers by an act of the May 1783 General Assembly (Hening, *Statutes*, XI, 247–48). On 8 May 1784 Jefferson had asked JM to seek an appropriation of this fund directly to the continental treasury.

From Noah Webster

HARTFORD 5th July 1784.

SIR

From the small acquaintance I had with you at Philadelphia & the recommendation of Mr Jefferson, I take the liberty to address you on the subject of Literary property & securing to authors the copyright of their productions in the State of Virginia. The *Grammatical Institute* of the English Language[1] is so much approved in the Northern States, that I wish to secure to myself the copy-right in all. General Laws for this purpose are passed in New England in New Jersey—& I believe also in New York and Pensylvania. In one of these States, the period mentioned is twenty years—in another twenty on[e], & in Connecticut, the right is secured to the author &c for the term of fourteen years & if the author should live beyond the first term, then the right returns to him & his heirs for another term of fourteen years; & all give the inhabitants of other States, the benefit of the laws, as soon as the States where the author is an inhabitant shall have passed a similar law.

It is my request Sir, that you would move for a law of this kind in your next Session of Assembly;[2] & if the Legislature shall not think proper to pass a general law; be pleased to present a petition in my name, for a particular law securing to me & my heirs & assigns the exclusive right of publishing & vending the above mentioned works in the State of Virginia for the term of twenty years—or for such other term as the Legislature shall think proper. I shall endeavour to publish the Works in Virginia as soon as circumstances will permit; I therefore beg your assistanc[e] in this matter & shall take the earliest opportunity to make a suitable acknowledgment for the favour.

I am, Sir, with the highest respect Your most obedient most humble Servant

NOAH WEBSTER JR

RC (DLC). Addressed to JM in Orange County, with cover endorsements that indicate it was forwarded from Fredericksburg by James Maury. Enclosed was Webster's advertisement for a copy of William Stith's *History of Virginia* "& some works containing the Charters, Constitutions, ancient Laws &c of the State— Also any Pamphlets or papers that throw light upon the Settlement & progress of the State to the Revolution. . . ."

[1] Noah Webster (1758–1843), the Connecticut lawyer lexicographer, first published his famous spelling book as *A Grammatical Institute, of the English Language,* . . . at Hartford in 1783. His quest for a copyright led to many contacts with leading public men and so hastened the enactment of legislation that by the summer of 1786 every state except Delaware had a law to encourage and protect the production of literary property (Thorvald Solberg, comp., *Copyright Enactments, 1783–1900,* . . . [Washington, 1900], pp. 9–29). On 16 Oct. 1829 Webster wrote JM to recall their early association and reported that his "little books" had "sold in forty six years" almost ten million copies (DLC).

[2] As Webster knew, JM had in May 1783 been a member of a committee successfully moving that Congress recommend to the states the enactment of copyright laws (Emily Ellsworth Fowler Ford, comp., *Notes on the Life of Noah Webster* [2 vols., New York, 1912], I, 57; *JCC,* XXIV, 180, 211 n. 1, 326–27). JM responded to Webster's request, but not until the session of Oct. 1785. See Act Securing the Copyright for Authors, 16 Nov. 1785.

From William Overton Callis

LOUISA 9th August 1784

SIR,

Mrs. Carr was informed by Mr Jefferson, previous to his departure to Europe, that he had requested the favor of you, to direct the Studies of her two sons Peter & Dabney in his absence. Should it be convenient for you to comply with Mr Jeffersons request, Mrs. Carr will be much obliged to you to inform her, when, and in what manner you would wish them disposed of. I am with great respect, Sir, Yr. Mo. Ob. & very Hum Sert.

W. O. CALLIS.[1]

RC (DLC). Cover missing. Docketed by JM.

[1] Militia Maj. Callis (1756–1814), once a subaltern in the Continental Line, eventually became master of the historic estate of Cuckoo, in Louisa County. He was a justice of the peace and sheriff of Louisa County, 1790–1810, and represented the county in the House of Delegates for most of the sessions between 1788 and 1800. In 1788 Callis was a member of the state ratifying convention. His later poli-

97

tics were Jeffersonian (Heitman, *Historical Register Continental,* p. 113; Harris, *History of Louisa County, Virginia,* pp. 23, 54, 63, 131, 442, 445). As JM made clear in a letter to Jefferson, 20 Aug. 1784, Callis had both of the Carr brothers in his custody.

To George Washington

ORANGE August. 12th 1784

DEAR SIR

I had the honor of receiving your favor of the 12th. of June during my attendance in the Legislature and of answering it a few days, before I left Richmond. Since my return home I have been informed that the gentleman into whose hands my answer was put has mislaid or lost it, and that I cannot rely on its ever finding its way to you.[1] I have therefore to repeat, Sir, that the sanction which your judgment gave to the propriety of rewarding the literary Services of Mr. Payne led to an attempt in the House of Delegates for that purpose. The proposition first made was that he should be invested with a moity of a tract of public land known by the name of the Secretary's lying on the Eastern Shore. The kind reception given to this proposition induced some gentlemen to urge that the whole tract containing about 500 acres might be included in the donation as more becoming the dignity of the State, and not exceeding the merits of the object. The proposition thus enlarged, passed through two readings without apprehension on the part of its friends. On the third a sudden attack grounded on considerations of economy and suggestions unfavorable to Mr. Payne, threw the bill out of the house. The next idea proposed was that the land in question should be sold and £2000 of the proceeds allotted to Mr. Payne to be laid out in the purchase of a Farm if he should think fit. This was lost by a single vote. Whether a succeeding Session may resume the matter and view it in a different light, is not for me to say. Should exertions of genius which have been every where admired, and in America unanimously acknowledged, not save the author from indigence and distress, the loss of national character will hardly be balanced by the savings at the Treasury. With the highest respect and sincere regard I am Dear Sir, Your most Obedient and humble servant

J. MADISON JR.

RC (DLC: Washington Papers); Tr (DLC). Addressed to Washington at Mount Vernon, and docketed by the general.

[1] Though JM's 2 July letter seemed lost or strayed, it had in fact reached Washington. JM had no way of knowing this, since Washington had not acknowledged the information sent him regarding the defeat (chiefly engineered by Arthur Lee) of the proposal to reward Paine for his wartime services to the nation.

Deed of Gift of Orange County Lands

[19 August 1784]

THIS INDENTURE made the nineteenth day of August One Thousand Seven hundred eighty four Between James Madison the Elder of the County of Orange of One Part And James Madison the Younger his Son of the sd. County of the Other Part Witnesseth that the Said James Madison the elder in Consideration of Paternal affection and of five Shillings the Receipt of which is hereby Acknowledged Doth by these Presents grant bargain and Sell unto the Said James Madison his Son a Tract of land Situated in the Said County containing by estimation five hundred & sixty Acres (Conveyed to the Said James Madison the Elder by James Edmundson[1] of the County of Essex by Deed dated the fifteenth day of September One Thousand Seven hundred Sixty Six Remaining of Record in the General Court) And Bounded by the lands of Johnny Scott, James Newman, Reubin Smith an infant, Prettyman Merry, And the Said James Madison the Elder To have And to hold the Said land unto the Said James Madison the Younger his heirs & Assigns to his And there own Use. In Witness Whereof the Parties have hereunto Set Their hands And Seals the day And Year Above Written

JAMES MADISON

JAMES MADISON JUR.

Sealed And Delivered in
the Presence of

JONATHAN COWHERD   THOMAS GILBERT
FRANCIS COWHERD   A. MADISON
JAMES COLEMAN

Ms (Vi: Orange County Court Records, Deed Book 18, microfilm, p. 316). James Taylor, clerk of the court, verified and recorded the deed on 26 Aug. 1784. A marginal note states that he made a transcript of the document and delivered it to JM in "Jany. 1789."

[1] JM's father purchased the land from James Edmondson (d. 1779), who served with JM in Virginia convention of May 1776 and in the first session of the newly created House of Delegates, Oct.–Dec. 1776 (Vi: Essex County Court Records, Will Book 13, microfilm, p. 262; Swem and Williams, *Register*, p. 371).

Bill of Sale for Orange County Lands

ABSTRACT

19 August 1784. A standard bill of sale conveying 281 acres in Orange County from JM's parents, James Madison, Sr., and Nelly Madison, to Francis Cowherd, for £400 "current money." Signed by five witnesses.

Ms (DLC). Entirely in JM's hand, except for the signatures of sellers, buyer, and witnesses.

To Thomas Jefferson

EDITORIAL NOTE

The decision to introduce the Mississippi question in the context of JM's experience is necessarily an arbitrary one because an open western waterway was among his concerns from the early days in Congress until the matter was settled by the Louisiana Purchase. The main point is that JM never looked upon the problem as a Virginia riddle. As a Virginia legislator he hoped to see citizens in the Kentucky district flourish through an easy access to ports via the Ohio and Mississippi rivers. But beyond that hope there was a greater realization that American nationality was involved, and thus JM's perspective of the Mississippi was that of a chess player who was not so much concerned with the next Spanish move as with the eventual American victory.

When Europe looked to America for silver and pelts, the Mississippi "as the key to control of the Middle West," was staked out early in the seventeenth century as a likely testing ground for national ambitions. The spilled blood of Spanish and French explorers solidified certain claims which English victories at sea and on land could not erase. Besides Hennepin and La Salle there were Cadillac and Pontchartrain, and even the memory of the "Mississippi Bubble" which haunted European finance. The direct line of JM's concern, however, began with the Treaty of Paris of 1763, which gave England jurisdiction to all the land east of the Great River previously claimed by France. The wily maneuvers of American diplomats in 1782 gave the United States those same rights to the Upper Mississippi, while Spain retained the Floridas (Samuel Flagg Bemis, *The Diplomacy of the American Revolution* [1967 reprint], pp. 235, 263). Before the Revolution had been won Virginia had entrenched its western claims (originally ocean to ocean) by dispatching George Rogers Clark into the Illinois country on an expedition raised by the Commonwealth of Virginia. Whatever the navigation of the Mississippi had been before 1778, thereafter it was to be a problem of consequence to any political figure in Virginia. Clark's so-called conquest by a handful of raw-boned Virginians and river-landing adventurers gave Virginia a heavy stake in the trans-Allegheny west which less kindly neighbors related to extensive western land speculation. While JM served on the Virginia

Council of State in 1779 he knew that the Articles of Confederation had not been ratified, and the western lands were part of the problem, since states with no vast tracts beyond the mountains were intensely jealous. Meanwhile, reports of Spanish harassment of Americans moving into the Mississippi territory caused the Virginia legislature to speed up its activity. A western land office was opened and at about the same time Virginia made gestures offering to surrender all claims to lands north of the Ohio (Allan Nevins, *The American States during and after the Revolution* [New York, 1924], pp. 223–24). A Virginia bloc in Congress also gained passage on 5 August 1779 of a resolution staking an American claim to navigational rights on the Mississippi to the Gulf of Mexico (*JCC*, XIV, 926). Reinforcing this action, the Virginia legislature at its October 1779 session instructed its delegates in Congress to stand firm in any diplomatic negotiations touching on American rights to travel the western waters. In October 1780 JM was appointed chairman of a committee that soon reported on the Mississippi navigation dispute. JM had studied the moods and maneuvers of Congress that fall and became actively involved in the Mississippi debate. Spain's jealousy and desire to close the river to American commerce were not secrets. Delegates from the West and South feared the Northerners might barter away the Westerners' river rights in exchange for a Spanish market for codfish. That did not happen, but JM knew why it had not. The instructions to John Jay on 4 October 1780, which were a legal treatise on American rights to use the Mississippi, were explained by JM on 17 October 1780 (*Papers of Madison*, II, 127–35). The game of diplomacy requires patience, JM learned, and sometimes concessions. He accepted the idea of conceding jurisdiction over part of the Mississippi to Spain early in 1781 and offered a motion withdrawing the previous insistence on complete navigational rights provided this move would remove an "obstacle to the speedy conclusion of an Alliance between his Catholic Majesty & these States" (ibid., II, 302). These gestures gained the young nation nothing, however. Spain threw restrictions on river traffic below the 31° parallel and "the Southwest stood in immediate danger of becoming commercially stagnant" (Frederic A. Ogg, *The Opening of the Mississippi* [New York, 1904], p. 418). Thereafter JM was on his guard against northern logrolling and the indifference of tidewater Virginians who thought the best way to tie the knot of union was with river routes from the Atlantic to the piedmont, leading to wagon roads through the great river gaps.

Washington and Jefferson were among JM's friends who were more indifferent to the Mississippi problem than prudence allowed. During 1784 Jefferson "had for some months been concentrating attention primarily on developing the Potomac route to tap northwestern trade and bring it to Virginia ports; he had been a primary if not the determining influence in persuading Washington to sponsor that cause" (Boyd, *Papers of Jefferson*, VII, 408 n.). JM obviously believed that Jefferson's new role at the French court would give his friend unusual opportunities to clarify the Mississippi situation to the French, and if possible gain support for the American position. After much study and many conversations, JM wrote Jefferson in his new capacity as the resident minister in Paris. In this significant letter JM tried to show Jefferson that, with or without the Potomac and James canals, legislation had been enacted which would channel much commerce to Virginia ports. At the same time, JM explained the great need to convince Europeans that a Spanish blockade of the Mississippi would hurt their pocketbooks as much as it would injure the Americans. In time, Jefferson came to share JM's concern when, as secretary of state, he realized that linked with the Mississippi question was the western problem, and "the maintenance of the Union depended on a successful solution of it" (Malone, *Jefferson*, II, 408–9). Perhaps this seedling idea was planted in Jefferson's mind when this letter reached Paris on 24 October 1784.

Aug: 20. 1784

DEAR SIR

Your favor of the 1st. of July written on the eve of your embarkation from Boston was safely brought by your servant Bob who got thus far about the 20 of the same month. Along with it I recd. the pamphlet on the West: India Trade, and a copy of Deane's letters. My last was written from Richmond on the adjournment of the Assembly and put into the hands of Mr. Short. It contained a cursory view of legislative proceedings, referring to the bearer for a more circumstancial one. Since the adjournment I have been so little abroad that I am unable to say with certainty how far those proceedings harmonize with the vox populi. I am led by the opinion of those who have better means of information, to suppose, that a large majority of the people either from a sense of private justice or of national faith, dislike the footing on which British debts are placed. The proceedings relative to an amendment of the Constitution seem to interest the public much less than a friend to the scheme would wish. The act which produces most discussion & agitation is that which restricts our foreign trade to the enumerated ports. Those who are devoted from either interest or prejudice, to the British trade and meditate a revival of the old plan of monopoly and credit, with those whose local situations give them or are thought to give them an advantage in large ships coming up and lying at their usual stations in the Rivers, are busy in decoying the people into a belief that trade ought in all cases to be left to regulate itself, that confining it to particular ports is renouncing the favour which nature intended in diffusing navigation throughout our country; and that if one sett of men are to be exporters and importers, another set to be carryers between the mouths & heads of the rivers, and a third retailers thro' the country; trade, as it must pass thro' so many hands all taking a profit from it, must in the end come dearer to the people, than if the simple plan sd. be continued which unites these several branches in the same hands. These and other objections, tho' unsound, are not altogether unplausible; and being propagated with more zeal & pains by those who have a particular interest to serve, than proper answers are by those who regard the general interest only, make it very possible that the measure may be reversed before it is to take effect. Should it escape such a fate, it will be owing to a few striking and undeniable facts; namely: that goods are much dearer in Virginia than in the States where the trade is drawn to a general mart, that even goods brought from B[altimore]. & P[hiladelphi]a. to Winchester & other W. & S. W. parts of Virga. are retailed cheaper than those imported directly from Europe are sold on tide water: that generous as the present price of our Tobo. appears, that the same article has currently sold from 15 to 20 per Ct. at least higher in Pa. where, being as far from the ultimate market, it can not be intrinsically worth more; that scarce a single vessel from any part of Europe, other than the British dominions, comes into our ports, whilst vessels from so many other parts of Europe resort to other ports of America, almost all of them too in pursuit of the Staple of Virga. The exemption of our own Citizens from the operation of this law is another circumstance that helps to parry attacks on the policy of it. The warmest friends to the law disliked much this discrimination which gives it an illiberal aspect to foreigners but it was found to be a necessary Concession to prevailing sentiments. I still fear that many of them may mistake the object of the law to be a sacrifice of their conveniency to the encouragement of our mercantile citizens, whereas in reality it was as far as foreigners were in question only meant to reduce the trade of G. B. to an equality with that of other nations. The like discrimination between our own Citizens & those of other States contrary to the Confederation was an erratum which will no doubt be rectified. Notwithstanding the languor of our direct trade with Europe, this country has indirectly tasted some of the fruits of independence. The price of our last crop of Tobo. has on James River been from 36 to 42/6 per Ct. & has brought more specie into the Country than it ever before contained at one time. Much of it however which has been drained from the Northern States will return in payment for goods which continue to be imported in considerable quantities thro' that channel. The price of hemp has been reduced as much by the peace as that of Tobo. has been raised, being sold in the back country as low as 18/ per Ct. Our crops of wheat have been rather

scanty, owing partly to the rigors of the winter, partly to an insect*
which in many places in the S. side of the J[ame]s. River has destroyed
whole fields of that grain. They have in a few instances only appeared
on this [side] of the river, crops of corn though injured in some places
by the same insect will be the most excuberant remembered, and will
spare plentiful supplies to the W. Indies if their European Masters will
no longer deny themselves the benefit of such a trade with us. The
crops of Tobo. will be much shortened by the want of early rains in
many places, and the excessive rains of late in others; and more than
either by a devouring multitudes of ground worms and grasshoppers
everywhere. All these enemies however will not prevent a tolerable
crop, if the seasonable weather which has latterly prevailed in most
places, and produced the present prospects should continue. It will be
politic I think for the people here to push the culture of this article
whilst the price keeps up; it becoming more apparent every day that
the richness of the soil & fitness of the climate on the Western waters
will in a few years both reduce the price and engross the culture of it.
This event begins already to be foreseen & to spread the demands for
land on the Ohio. What think you of a guinea per acre being allready
the price of choice tracts with sure titles? Nothing can delay such a
revolution with regd. to our staple, but an impolitic & perverse attempt
in Spain to shut the mouth of the Miss[issipp]i. agst. the trade of the
inhab[itan]ts. above. I say *delay*, because she can no more finally resist
the current of such a trade than she can stop that [of] the river itself.
The importance of this matter begins to awaken much curiosity & enquiry among those who have shifted or mean to shift their fortunes into
the W. country. I am frequently asked what progress has been made
towards a treaty with Spain, and what may be expected from her liberality as to the Missi. the querists generally counting on an early ability
to apply to less honorable motives, if that should be found inadequate.
My answers have been both from ignorance & prudence evasive: I have
not thought fit however to cherish unfavorable impressions,[1] being
more & more led, by revolving the subject to conclude that Spain will
never be so mad as to persist in the doctrine She seems hitherto to have
set up. For want of better materials for correspondence I will state the
grounds on which I build my expectations:

First, apt as the policy of nations is to disregard justice & the general
rights of humanity, I deem it as no small advantage to us that these
considerations are in our favor. The[ir] influence most corrupt councils

* the Chinch bug

must feel [to] some degree & on a question whether the interest of Millions shall be sacrificed to views relating to a distant & paltry settlemt.[2] They are every day deriving weight from the progress of Philosophy & civilization, and they must operate on those nations of Europe who have given us a title to their friendly offices, or who may wish to gain a title to ours.

Secondly. May not something be hoped from the respect which Spain may feel for consistency of character, on an appeal to the doctrine maintained by herself in 1609 agst. the U Provinces touching the navigation of the scheld; or at least from the use which may be made of this fact by the powers disposed to forward our views.

Thirdly.[3] Should none of these circumstances have influence her councils, she can not surely so far disregard the general usage of nations as to contend that her possessions at the mouth of the Mississippi, justify a total denial of the use of it to the inhabitants above, when much more important possessions on the lower parts of much smaller rivers, have been no farther urged or admitted than as a ground of right to a moderate toll. The case of the Rhine, the Maese & the Scheld as well as of the Elbe & oder are if I mistake not in point here. [Whether] the other rivers running through different dominions afford parallel cases, I cannot pretend to say. ⟨The Po runs thro' the Milanese & other States of Italy & terminates within the Jurisdiction of Venice, but whether it is navigable above her jurisdiction, or whether the upper States have even had an interest in claiming the use of the river below.⟩[4]   The case of the Mississippi is probably the strongest in the world.

Fourthly. The interest of Spain at least ought to claim her attention. 1. a free trade down the Missipi. would make N[ew]. O[rleans]. one of the richest and most flourishing Emporiums in the world; and deriving its happiness from the benevolence of Spain, would feel the firmest loyalty to [. . .] her Govermt. At present it is an expensive establishment, is settled chiefly by French who hate the Govt. which oppresses them, who already covet a trade with the Western States, will be made every day more sensible of the rigor which denies it to them, and will no doubt join the Americans in the first probable attemp[t] agst. the authority of their Masters. 2. a generous policy on the part of Spain towards the U. S. will be the cement of friendship & a lasting peace with them: a contrary one will produce immediate heart burnings: and sow the seeds of inevitable hostility. The U. S. are already a power not to be despised by Spain: the time cannot be distant when in spight of all her precautions, the safety of her possessions in this quarter of the

Globe must depend more on our peaceableness, than her own power. 3. In another view it is agst. the interest of Spain to throw obstacles in the way of our Western settlements. The part which she took during the late war shews that she apprehended less from the rising power in her neighbourhood, if under an independent Government, than if subject to that of G. B. If in this she calculated on the impotence of the U. S. under their dismemberment from the British Empire, she saw but little way into futurity: if on the pacific temper of republics, unjust irritations on her part will soon teach her that Republics have like passions with other Governts. Her *permanent* security rather lies in the Complexity of our fœderal Govt. and the diversity of interests among the members of it which render offensive measures, improbable in Council, and difficult in execution. If such be the case when 13 States compose the System, ought she not to wish to see the number enlarged to three & twenty? A source of *temporary* security to her, is our want of naval strength. Ought she not then to favor those emigrations to the Western lands, which as long as they continue will leave no supernumerary hands for the sea? Other nations as well as Spain may think themselves concerned in these considerations.

Fifthly. Must not the generall interest of Europe in all cases influence the determinations of any particular nation in Europe, and does not that interest in the present case clearly lie on our side. 1. All the principal powers have in a general view more to gain than to lose by denying the right of those who hold the mouths of great rivers to intercept agst. a communication with those above. France, G. B. (except indeed as to Canada) & Sweeden have no opportunity of exerting such a right, and must wish for a free passage for their merchandize into every Country. Spain herself has no such opportunity, & has besides three of her principal rivers, one of them the seat of her metropolis running thro' Portugal. Russia can have nothing to lose by denying this pretension, and is bound to deny it in favor of her great rivers the Neiper the Niester, & the Don which mouth in the black sea, and of the passage through the Dardanelles which she has extorted from the Turks. The Emperor in common with the inland States of Germany, and moreover by his possessions on the Maese & perhaps those on the Scheld has a similar interest. The possessions of the King of Prussia on the Rhine, the Elbe and the oder are pledges for his orthodoxy. The U. Provinces indeed hold the mouths of the Rhine, the Maese and in part of the Scheld, but a general freedom of trade is so much their policy and they now carry on so much of it through channels of rivers running thro' different States, that it is not probable, her influence will be thrown into the wrong scale. The only powers which can have an interest in opposing the American doctrine, are the Ottoman which has already given up the point to Russia, Denmark which is suffered to retain the entrance of Baltic, portugal whose principal rivers all head in Spain, Venice which possesses the mouth of the Po.[5] Dantzic which commands the mouth of the Vistula, if since the partition of Poland it has not ceased to be [a] free City. The prevailing disposition of Europe on this point I find defeated an Attempt once made by Denmark to exact a toll at the mouth of the Elbe by means of a Fort on the Holstein side which commands it. The fact is mentioned in Salmon's Gazateer under the head of "Gluckstat."[6] I have no opportunity of ascertaining the circumstances of the [case]. 2. In a more important view the settlement of the back country, which will be greatly promoted by a free use of the Missipi. will be beneficial to all the nations who either directly or indirectly trade with the U. S. By this expansion of our people, the establishmt. of internal manufactures will not only be for many years delayed, but the consumption of foreign manufactures will be continually increasing with the increase of our numbers: and at the same time all the productions of the American Soil required by the nations of Europe in return for their manufactures, will be proportionally augmented. The vacant land of the U. S. lying on the waters of the Mississippi is perhaps equal in extent to the land actually settled. If no check be given to emigrations from the latter to the former, they will probably keep pace at least with the increase of people, till the population of both become nearly equal. For 20 or 25 years we shall consequently have few internal manufactures in proportion to our numbers as at present, and at the end of that period our imported manufactures will be doubled. It may be [obse]rved too, that as the market for these manufactures will first increase, & the provision for supplying is to follow, the price of supplies will naturally rise in favor of those who manufactures them. On the other hand as the demand for the Tobo. indigo, rice, hemp, Indian Corn lumber &c produced by the U. S. for exportation will neither precede nor keep pace with their increase, the price of them must naturally sink in favor also of those who consume them. Reverse the case & suppose the use of the Miss: denied to us, and the consequence is that many of our supernumerary hands who in the former case would [be] husbandmen on the waters of the Missipi will on this other supposition be manufacturers on this [side] of the Atlantic: and even those who may not be discouraged from seating the vacant lands will be obliged by the want of vent for the produce of the soil & of the means of purchasing foreign manufactures, to manufacture in a great measure for themselves. ⟨The only point of view in which it can appear impolitic in the nations of Europe to open the channel of the Missi. to our western settlements is that the prospect may the more entice the emigration of their subjects. But this objection will never be listened too by those who consult experience, instead of ancient prejudices. The example of Engld. alone proves beyond a possibility of doubt, that vacancies produced by this cause in an industrious country, are not only Speedily filled but that population is ever increased by the demand of the emigrants & their descendants, on the industry of those left behind. America does not contain at this moment perhaps less than 2 million of inhabitants who have sprung from the loins of Englishmen: does England contain the fewer on this acct.? Is she not on the contrary more populous than she was before a single Englishman had set his foot on american ground, more populous upon this very acct.? This fact claims the particular attention of France. Her productions and manufactures are well suited to the climate of the U. S. and our ports are as open to them, as to those of G. B. yet we find that the predilections and habits of our people give to the latter a preference, amounting nearly to a monopoly. 10,000 French emigrants diffusing throughout the U. S. and diffusing a taste for French fashions & productions, would probably create employment for 20,000 hands in France, in other words wd. create 10,000 more than would fill the void left by them. It wd. be the like letting out money for an interest greater than the principal itself. In every 20 or 25 years these emigrants would double their number and far more than double their influence; and proportionably enhance the benefits to France. The only sufferers by the encouragement of the Western settlemts. will be those [who] remain in the Atlantic States. They may it's true be relieved from taxes in proportion to the price added to the vacant land by the freedom of the Missi. but this advantage will be greatly outweighed by the danger to the Confederacy from multiplying the parts of the Machine, by the depopulation of the country, by the depreciation of their lands and by the delay of that maritime strength which must be their only safety in case of war. N. Y. Pa. & Va. will also lose the advantage of being merchants for the Western States in proportion as their trade has a ready passage thro' the Missi. Va. will moreover suffer a loss of her Staple tho' she may be thought to have an equivalent for this in being disburdened of the slaves who will follow the culture of that plant.⟩

Should Spain yield us the point of the navigation of the Missi. but at the same time refuse us the use of her shores, the benefit will be ideal only. I conferred with several persons who have a practical knowledge of the subject, and am unanimously informed that not only the right of fastening to Spanish shores, but that of holding an entrepot of our own or using N. O. as a free port, is essential to our trade thro' that channel. It has been said that sea vessels get up as high as Lat: 32. to meet the river craft, but it will be with so much difficulty & disadvantage, as to amt. to a prohibition. I have heard the idea suggested also of large Magazines constructed for floating, but if this expedient were otherwise admissible, the hurricanes which in that quarter frequently demolish edifices on Land, forbid the least confidence in those which wd. have no foundation but water. Some territorial privileges therefore seem to be as indispensible to the use of the river as this is to the prosperity of the Western Country. I am told a place called the Englishman's turn on the Island of N. O. abt. six leagues below the town, wd. be the fittest for our purpose, and that the lower Side of the Peninsula is the best. Baton rouge is also mentioned as a convenient station; and point Coupe as the highest to which vessels can ascend with tolerable ease. Information however of this sort from men who judge from a general & superficial view only, can never be recd. as accurate. If Spain be disposed sincerely to gratify us, I hope she will be sensible that it can not be done effectually without allowing a previous survey & deliberate choice. Should it be impossible to obtain from her a portion of ground by other means, wd. it be unadvisable to attempt it by purchase. The price wch. might be demanded cd. not well exceed the benefit to be obtained; and a reimbursemt. of the public advance might easily be provided for by the sale to individuals & the conditions which might be annexed to their tenures. Such a spot could not fail in a little time to equal in value the same extent in London or Amsterdam. The most intellegt among those I have conversed with thinks, that on whatever footing our trade may be allowed by Spain, very judicious provision will be necessary for a fair adjustment of disputes between the Spaniards & Americans, disputes of wch. must be frequent, and will not only be noxious to trade, but tend to embroil to the two nations. Perhaps a joint tribunal under some modification or other, might answer the purpose. There is a precedent I see for such an establishment in the XXI art. of the Treaty at Munster in 1648 between Spain & the U. Provinces.

I am informed that after the Is: of N. O. fell into the hands of Spain, her Govr. forbid all British vessels navigating under the Treaty of Paris to fasten to the Shore, and caused such as did so to be cut loose. In consequence of this practice a British frigate, went up near the town, fastened to the Shore, and set out guards with orders to fire on such as might attempt to cut her loose. The Governor after trying in vain by menaces to remove the frigate, acquiesed, after which Brit: vessels were indiscriminately admitted to use the Shore; and even the residence of British Merchts. in the Town of N. O. Trading clandestinely with Spaniards as well as openly with their own people, connived at. The Treaty of 1763 stipulated to British subjects, as well as I recollect no more than the right of navigating the river, and if that of using the shore was admitted under that stipulation, the latter right must have been admitted to be involved in the former being incidental to the beneficial enjoyment of it.

In consequence of my letter to Mrs. Carr I have [been] called on by your elder Nephew, who is well satisfied with the choice made of Wmsbg. for his future studies.[7] I have furnished him with letters to my acquaintances there & with a draught on your Stewd. for the advances requisite for the first quarter. He will be down on the opening of Mr. Maury's School of the end of the vacation which will [be] on the first of Octr. I have the greater hopes the preference of this school will turn out a proper one, as it has re[c]d. the recommendation of the literary gentlemen in Wmsbg. & I understand will be attended to and periodically examnd. by Mr. Wythe & others. Your younger nephew is with Majr. Callis, who will keep [him] some little time longer. I am at a loss where it will be most proper to fix him. I shall decide however in time to prevent any idle interval.

When you were about leaving America for Europe as a Commisser. for peace you intimated to me that a report was in circulation of being concerned in jobbing for Kentucky lands, and authorized me to contradict the report as absolutely groundless & false. I have some reason to believe that the credit of your name has been lately made use of by some who are making purchases or locations in that quarter. If they have done it without any sanction from you, it may not be amiss to authorize me anew to correct misrepresentations.[8]

FC (DLC). Although the RC is ordinarily used by the editors, this letter has been chosen to illustrate the striking differences between JM's first ideas and the final letter. Moreover, the RC is printed in Boyd, *Papers of Jefferson*, VII, 401–8, is partly in code, and Boyd has indicated the additions. The text above was edited by JM and the portions within angle brackets were omitted when he made the RC.

1 JM crossed through the rest of his original sentence: "[fearing?] I should in future contradict all my opinions on the subject."

2 JM had difficulty phrasing this sentence. As written and emended it reads: "The influence most corrupt councils will feel by by [sic] must feel some degree."

3 When JM rewrote his draft he rearranged the order of the third and fourth paragraphs for Jefferson's RC.

4 JM did not finish this sentence.

5 The clause on Venice was transposed with the one on Danzig in the RC.

6 Thomas Salmon, *The Modern Gazetteer: or, A short view of the several nations of the world . . . with . . . maps . . .* (London, 1782).

7 JM's letter to Jefferson's sister, Mrs. Dabney Carr, has not been found. Her delayed reply of 18 Apr. 1785 commented on JM's efforts to enroll Jefferson's nephew in "Mr. Maury's School" in Williamsburg.

8 In the RC, this paragraph was transposed with the preceding one.

From Benjamin Hawkins

SWEET-SPRINGS IN BOTETORT 4th September. 1784

DEAR SIR,

I returned from Congress to Carolina in February was elected one of the representatives for the County I live in, and served in the spring session.[1] All the requisitions of Congress were fully complied with except the one for our proportion of one million five hundred thousand dollars in addition to the five Pcent: the act for this purpose establ[ished?] has the principle laid down by Congress but will fall short in the sum required as it will not raise more than twenty five thousand dollars.

The Cession of the Western territory was long debated and opposed by a party powerful in number in the house of Commons,[2] but was carried by fifty three against forty one. Some of those of the Minority have bee[n] very illiberal in attributing the conduct of some of the advocates for it to improper motives and representing them in their Counties as unfit for members of the legislature. A friend informs me that I was accused (as he calls it) at our election in August by a man of much influence tho' of infamous character of being sent from Congress to negociate the cession, that I was to recieve if I succeeded ample compensation by an agency for this disposal of it. This report had such an effect on the electors that I was not elected for the ensuing year.

I have been much indisposed this summer without knowing from what cause. I set out the last of July for this place to try what effect the waters would have on me, and I am either benefited by them or the air; I think of returning some time in this month and going to Georgia to spend the winter. I am with great and sincer[e] esteem Dear Sir Your Most obedient and most humble servant

BENJAMIN HAWKINS

RC (DLC). Cover missing. Docketed by JM.

[1] Hawkins had been JM's colleague in Congress as a North Carolina delegate (1781–1784) and they had recently worked together on the committee investigating relations with the southern Indian tribes. Hawkins served in the House of Commons of the North Carolina General Assembly as a delegate from Warren County.

[2] The "Cession of Western territory" of Apr. 1784 proved unpopular and a powerful opposition soon formed to repeal the "impolitick Act" in Oct. 1784 (Hugh T. Lefler and Albert Ray Newsome, *North Carolina the History of a Southern State* [Chapel Hill, 1954], p. 259; Boyd, *Papers of Jefferson*, VIII, 218–19; Nevins, *American States during and after the Revolution*, pp. 595–96).

To James Madison, Sr.

PHILADA. Sepr. 6. 1784.

HON'D SIR

I arrived at this place the night before last only, having declined starting from Fredg. at the time I proposed when I parted with you & having staid at Baltimore one day. At the latter place I fell in with the Marquis & had his company thus far. He is proceeding Northwd. as far as Boston from whence he goes to the Indian Treaty at Fort Stanwix & from thence returns to Virga. about the same time that I must be there. He presses me much to fall into his plan, and I am not sure that I shall decline it.[1] It will carry me farther than I had proposed, but I shall be rewarded by the pleasure of his company and the further opportunity of gratifying my curiosity. I have nothing to add at present but that I am your affec. Son

J. MADISON JR.

RC (DLC). Cover missing. Docketed by JM.

[1] By a chance encounter with the Marquis de Lafayette in Baltimore, JM changed his travel plans from a health-seeking "ramble into the Eastern States" into a rousing tour with the famous Frenchman (JM to Jefferson, 7 Sept., 15 Sept., 17 Oct., 1784; Brant, *Madison*, II, 325–35). The "Indian Treaty" negotiations JM witnessed led to some acrimony because some delegates in Congress believed New York commissioners had interfered in the business by trying to conduct their own separate treaty arrangements. A full account of the conference is found in Henry S. Manley, *The Treaty of Fort Stanwix* (Rome, N. Y., 1932).

To Thomas Jefferson

PHILADA. Sepr. 7th. 1784.

DEAR SIR

Some business, the need of exercise after a very sedentary period, and the view of extending my ramble into the Eastern States which I have long had a curiosity to see have brought me to this place. The letter herewith enclosed[1] was written before I left Virginia, & brought with me for the sake of a conveyance hence. Since the date of it I have learned that Mr. Short who was to be the bearer of the letter to which it refers has not yet left Richmond. The causes of his delay are unknown to me. At Baltimore I fell in with the Marquis de la Fayette returning from a visit to Mount Vernon. Wherever he passes he receives the most flattering tokens of sincere affection from all ranks. He did not propose to have left Virginia so soon but Genl. Washington was about setting out on a trip to the Ohio, and cod. not then accompany him on some visits as he wished to do. The present plan of the Marquis is to proceed immediately to New York, thence by Rhode Island to Boston, thence through Albany to Fort Stanwix where a treaty with the Indians is to be held the latter end of this month, thence to Virginia so as to meet the legislature at Richmond. I have some thoughts of making this tour with him, but suspend my final resolution till I get to N. Y. whither I shall follow him in a day or two.

The *relation in* which *the Marquis stands to France* and *America* has *induced me to enter into a fre*[e] *conversation* with *him on the* subject *of the Mississippi.* I have *endeavored emphatically to impres*[s] on *him* that the *ideas of America and Spain irreconciliably clash—that unless the mediation of France be effectually exerted* an *actual rupture is near at hand—that in such an event the connection between France and Spain* will *give the enemies of the former in America the fairest opportunity of involving her in our resentments against the latter* and *of intro*[duc]*ing Great Britain as a party with us against both—that America can not possibly be diverted* from *her object and therefore France is bound to set every engine at work to divert Spain from hers* and *that France has besides a great interest in a trade with the western country thro the Mississippi.* I thought *it not amiss also to suggest to him* some of the *considerations which seem to appeal to the prudence of Spain. He admit*[t]*ed the force of every thing I said* [and] *told me he would write in the most* [approving?] *terms to the Count de Vergen*[n]*es by the pac*[k]*et which will probably carry this and let me se*[e] *his letter*

113

at New York before he seals it. He thinks that Spain is bent on *excluding us from the Mississippi and mentioned* several *anecdotes* which *happened while he was at Madrid in proof of it.*

The Committee of the States have dispersed. Several of the Eastern members havg by quitting it reduced the number below a quorum, the impotent remnant thought it needless to keep together. It is not probable they will be reassembled before Novr. so that there will be an entire interregnum of the fœderal Government for some time, against the intention of Congs. I apprehend, as well as against every rule of decorum.

The *Marquis this moment stepped into my room and* se[e]*ing my cyphers before me drop*[p]*ed* some *questions* which *obliged me* in order *to avoid reserve to let him know* that *I was writing to you.* I *said nothing of the* subject, but *he will probably infer from our conversation that the Missisipi is most in my thoughts.*[2]

Mrs. House charges me with a thousand compliments & kind wishes for you & Miss Patsy. We hear nothing of Mrs. Trist since her arrival at the Falls of Ohio on her way to N. Orleans. There is no doubt that she proceeded down the river thence, unapprized of her loss. When & how she will be able to get back since the Spaniards have shut all their ports agst: the U. S. is uncertain & gives much anxiety to her friends. Browze has a wind fall from his grandmother of £1000 Sterling.[3] Present my regards to Miss Patsy and to Mr. Short if he should be with you, and accept yourself Dear Sir, the sincerest affection of your friend & servant

J. MADISON JR.

RC (DLC). Docketed by JM many years later. Headed, "No. 2." JM enclosed his letter of 20 Aug. 1784. The italicized words are those encoded by JM using the code first used by Jefferson on 14 Apr. 1783.

1 JM's letter of 20 Aug. 1784.
2 Obviously many of JM's tidewater acquaintances did not share his alarm over the Spanish blockade of the Mississippi. When Washington and other influential Virginians concerned themselves with river transportation their thoughts were on the nearby James or Potomac, and the hoped-for diversion of western trade toward the Chesapeake Bay rather than New Orleans. Jefferson believed the western trade was "under a competition between the Hudson, the Patomac and the Missisipi itself. Down the last will pass all heavy commodities. But the navigation through the gulf of Mexico is so dangerous, and that up the Missisipi so difficult and tedious, that it is not probable that European merchandize will return through that channel" (Boyd, *Papers of Jefferson*, VII, 26). After talking with Washington, Lafayette himself confirmed the apathy of "Many people [who] think the Navigation of the Mississipy is not an advantage" (Lafayette to JM, 15 Dec. 1784).

3 Hore Browse Trist, in 1784 about six years of age, was the grandson of Mrs. Mary House.

To Thomas Jefferson

NEW YORK. Sepr. 15: 1784.

DEAR SIR

In pursuance of my intentions as explained in my last dated in Philada. I came to this City on saturday last. The information I have here recd. convinces me that I can not accomplish the whole route I had planned within the time to which I am limited, nor go from this to Boston in the mode which I had reckoned upon. I shall therefore decline this part of my plan, at least for the present, & content myself with a trip to Fort Schuyler,[1] in which I shall gratify my curiosity in several respects, & have the pleasure of the Marquis's Company. We shall set off this afternoon in a Barge up the North River. The Marquis has recd. in this City a continuation of those marks of cordial esteem & affection which were hinted in my last. The gazettes herewith inclosed will give you samples of them.[2] Besides the personal homage he receives, his presence has furnished occasion for fresh manifestation of these sentiments towards France which have been so well merited by her, but which her Enemies pretended would soon give way to returning affection for G. Britain. In this view a republication of those passages in the Gazettes of France may be of advantage to us. They will at least give a pleasure to the friends of the Marquis.

We have an account from Canada, how far to be relied on I can not say, that the Indians have surprised & plunderd fort Michellimackinac where the English had a great amt. of stores & Merchandize; and that they have refused to treat with Sr. Jno. Johnson. Being in danger of losing the conveyance by the packet which is just sailing I subscribe in haste Yrs sincerely

J. MADISON JR

The M. has shewn me a passage in his letter to the Ct. de V. in which he Sketches the idea relative to the Miss: he says he has not had time to dilate upon it, but that his next letter will do it fully.[3]

RC (DLC). Cover missing. Docketed by JM many years later. Headed, "No. 3." The enclosures are missing.

[1] Fort Schuyler (on the site of present-day Rome, N. Y.) was often referred to by its prerevolutionary name, Fort Stanwix.

2 The newspapers JM alluded to were undoubtedly the *N. Y. Gazetteer* issues of 24 Aug. and 14 Sept. 1784. The 24 Aug. edition carried a full column on Lafayette's reception in Pennsylvania. The 14 Sept. issue tells of a dinner at Cape's Tavern honoring the French hero. If JM attended this feast he had to drink thirteen toasts while well-wishers fired thirteen cannon salutes, and then listen to an effusive poem dedicated to their guest, who

> "Dar'd ease and pleasures, friends and country fly,
> With us the rugged scenes of war to try,"

and finally drink a fourteenth toast to "THE MARQUIS."

3 JM's next sentence has been deleted. The first word appears to have been "His." It is likely that JM made the deletion some years later, when he was more charitable toward Lafayette than in the autumn of 1784.

To Thomas Jefferson

EDITORIAL NOTE

A colorful account of JM's journey with the Lafayette entourage is supplied by Brant, who reported that after JM's "chance encounter" with Lafayette in Baltimore the Virginian found the "northward trip . . . entirely too enjoyable to be cut off at New York" (*Madison*, II, 325, 328). Many of the incidents on this excursion were reported by Marbois for his superiors in Paris and are found in Eugene P. Chase, ed., *Our Revolutionary Forefathers: The Letters of François, Marquis de Barbé-Marbois* (New York, 1929). Louis Gottschalk devotes a whole chapter to the incident in his *Lafayette between the American and French Revolution*, pp. 96–107. Lafayette's own recollections of the Indian council ignore JM's presence and confirm JM's impression that the young Frenchman was not lacking in self-esteem (*Mémoires, correspondance et manuscrits du Général Lafayette* [6 vols.; Paris, 1838], II, 98–113). By his presence among the Iroquois chieftains at Fort Schuyler JM was able to observe one of the last enactments of a westering tradition. Perhaps he recalled these scenes twenty-one years later when, as secretary of state, JM watched the head tribesmen gather "in Dolley Madison's drawing room" on their diplomatic mission (Brant, *Madison*, IV, 307).

N. YORK OCT. 11. 1784

DEAR SIR

My last dated from this place on the 14. ult.[1] informed you of my projected trip to Fort Schuyler. I am this momemte arrived so far on my return to Virginia. My past delay requires so much hurry now that I can only drop a few lines for the packet which is to sail on the 15th. inst. The Marquis's & myself were overtaken at Albany by Mr. de Marbois[2] on the same errand with ourselves. We reached Fort S. on the 29. & on the next day paid a visit to the Oneida Nation 18 miles distant.

The Commissrs. did not get up till the Saturday following. We found a small portion only of the Six nations assembled: nor was the number much increased when we quitted the scene of business. Accts. however had come of deputies from more distant tribes being on the way. The Marquis was recd. by the Indians with equal proofs of attachment as have been shewn him elsewhere in America. This personal attachment with their supposed predilection for his nation, and the reports propagated among them that the Alliance between F. & U. S was transient only, led him with the sanction of the Commissrs. to delive[r] a Speech to the Indian cheifs coinciding with the object of the Treaty. The answers were very favorable in their general tenor. Copies of both will be sent to Mons. de Vergennes & the M. de Castres by Mr. Marbois & be within the reach of your curiosity.[3] The originals are so much appropriated to this use during my stay with the Marquis that I had no opportunity of providing copies for you. What the upshot of the Treaty will be is uncertain. The possession of the posts of Niagara &c. by the British is a very inauspicious circumstance.[4] Another is that we are not likely to make a figure otherwise that will impress a high idea of our power or opulence. These obstacles will be rendered much more embarrassing by the instructions to the Commissrs. which I am told leave no space for negociation or concession, & will consequently oblige them in case of refusal in the Indians to yield the ultimate hopes of Congress, to break up the Treaty. But what will be [the] consequence of such an emergency? Can they grant a peace with out cessions of territory—or if they do must not some other piece hereafter purchase them. A Truce has never I believe been introduced with the Savages, nor do I suppose that any provision has been made by Congress for such a contingency. The perseverance of the British in retaining the posts produces various conjectures. Some suppose it is meant to enforce a fulfilment of the Treaty of peace on our part. This interpretation is said to have been thrown out on the other side. Others that it is a salve for the wound given the Savages who are made to believe the posts will not be given up till good terms shall be granted them by Congress. Others that it is the effect merely of omission in the B. Govt. to send orders others that it is meant to fix the fur trade in the B. channel & it is even said that the Govr. of Canada has a personal interest in securing a monopoly of at least the Crop of this season. I am informed by a person just from Michi[lli]mackinac that this will be greater than it has been for several seasons past or perhaps any preceding season, & that no part of it is allowed by the British Commanders to be brought thro' the U. S. From the same quarter I learn that the posts have been lately well provisioned for the Winter, & that reliefs if not reinforcements of the Garrisons will take place. Col: Monroe had passed Oswega when last heard of & was likely to execute his plan.[5] If I have time & opportunity I will write again from Philada. for which I set out immediately; if not, from Richmond. The Marqs. proceeded from Albany to Boston from whence he will go via R. Island to Virga. & be at the Assembly. Thence he returns into the N. States to embark for Europe. I am Yrs. affecy.

J. MADISON JR.

RC (DLC). Docketed by JM many years later. Headed, "No. 4."

[1] JM erred, for his last letter from New York was dated 15 Sept. He corrected the date many years later.

[2] The French chargé d'affaires, François de Barbé-Marbois, joined Lafayette, JM, and the Chevalier de Caraman out of "curiosity and official interest" (Gottschalk, *Lafayette between the American and the French Revolution*, p. 97).

[3] Lafayette's oratory had upstaged the commissioners, but even more distressing was the subsequent publication of the marquis's speech and the chiefs' replies in Philadelphia newspapers before their official report to Congress (Boyd, *Papers of Jefferson*, VII, 447 n.). Lafayette's remarks are in the *Pa. Journal*, 24 and 27 Nov. 1784.

[4] British tenacity in holding the frontier forts was one of the grievances that led New York to announce its intention of occupying Forts Oswego and Niagara. A confrontation thus appeared to be in the offing, and to add to the woes of Congress, New York sent its own delegation into the Indian country ahead of the federal commissioners to negotiate an understanding (Burnett, *Letters*, VII, 587–88). The treaty party sent by Congress negotiated a pact which presented thorny problems later when reported to the delegates at Trenton (*JCC*, XXVIII, 423–24; Monroe to JM, 15 Nov. 1784). Meanwhile, the British refused to evacuate the forts and based their action, in part, on the failure of Virginia to solve the riddle of prewar debts to English and Scottish merchants.

[5] Monroe's "plan," originally conceived as a joint enterprise with Jefferson before the latter's commissioning as minister to France, was to acquire a personal knowledge of the West and, so far as his private interests were concerned, not to neglect opportunities for land speculation. Traveling part of his way with the New York commissioners, he resumed his seat in Congress on 19 Oct. 1784 (Harry Ammon, *James Monroe: The Quest for National Identity* [New York, 1971], pp. 45–48).

To Thomas Jefferson

PHILADA. Octr 17. 1784.

DEAR SIR

On my arrival here I found that Mr. Short had passed through on his way to N. York & was there at the date of my last. I regret much that I missed the pleasure of seeing him. The inclosed was put into my hands by Mrs. House who recd. it after he left Philada. My two last, neither of which were in cypher, were written as will be all future ones in the same situation, *in expectation of their being read by* the *post masters.* I am well assured that this is the *fate of all letters* at least to *and from public persons* not only in *France but all the other countries of Europe.* Having now the *use of my cypher I can write without restraint.* In my last I gave you a sketch of what past at Fort Schuyler during my stay there: mentioning in particular that the *Marquis had made a Speech to* the *Indians with the sanction of the Commissioners Wolcot*[t] *Le*[e] *Butler.* The question will probably occur how *a foreigner and a private one* could *appear on the theatre of a public treaty* between *United States and the Indian nations* and how *the Commissioners could lend a sanction to it.* Instead of offering *an opinion of the measure* I will state the *manner in which it* was *brought about.* It seems that most of the *Indian tribes* particularly *those of the Iroquois retain a strong predilection for the French* and most of *the lat*[t]*er an enthusiastic idea of the Marquis.* This idea has resulted from *his being a Frenchman, the* figure *he has made during the war* and the arrival of several important *events which he foretold to* them soon after *he came to this country.* Before *he went to Fort S.* it had been suggested either in *compliment or sincerity* that his *presence and influence* might be of *material service to the treaty.* At *Albany* the *same thing had been said to him by General Wolcot*[t]. On *his arrival at Fort S.* Mr. *Kirkland* recommended an exertion of *his influence as of essential consequence to the treaty* painting in the strongest colours the *attachment of the* Indians *to his person* which seemed indeed to be *verified by their caresses* and the artifices employed by the *British partizans to frustrate the objects of the treaty*[,] among which was a pretext that the *alliance between the United States and France* was *insincere and transitory* and consequently the respect of *the Indians for the lat*[t]*er ought to be no motive for their respecting the former.* Upon these *circumstances the M. grounded a written message to the Commissioners* before *they got up* intimating *his disposition to render the United States any services his small* influence *over the Indians* might *put in his power* and *desiring to know* what *the Commissioners would chuse him to say.* The *answer in Mr. Lee*[']*s hand* consisted of *polite acknowledgements* and information that the *Commissioners would be happy in affording him an opportunity of saying whatever he might* [wi]*sh* forbearing to *advise or suggest* [what] *it would be best for him to say. The M. perceived the caution but imputed it to* Le[e] *alone.* As *his stay however was to be* very *short* it was *necessary for him to take provisional measures* before *the arrival of the Commissioners* and particularly for *calling in the Oneida cheifs* who were *at their town.* It fell *to my lot to be consulted in his dilemma.* My *advice was* that *he should invite the* chief *in such a way as* would *give him an opportunity of* ad[dres]*sing* them *publicly,* if on a *personal interview with the Commissioners* it should be judged expedient; or *of satisfying their expectations* with a friendly *entertainment in return for the civilities his visit to their town* had met with. This *advice was approved* but the *Indians* brought with *them such ideas of his importance as* no *private reception* would *probably have been equal to.* When *the Commissioners* arriv[ed] *the M. consulted them in person.* They were *reserved, he was embarrassed.* Finally *they changed their plan* and *concurred* explicitly *in his making a speech in form.* He accordingly *prepared one, communicated it to the Commissioners* and *publicly pronounced it, the Commissioners* pr[o]*mising such an one as* was thought proper to *int*[ro]*duce his.* The *answer of the sachems* as well as the *circumstances of the audience* denoted the *highest reverence for the orator.* The cheif of *the Oneidas* said that the *word which he had spoken to them early in the war* had *prevented them from being misled to the wrong side of it.* During this *scene* and even during the *whole stay of the M. he* was *the only conspicuous figure.* The *Commissioners were eclipsed.* All of *them probably felt it.* Le[e] *complained to me of the im*moderate *stress laid on the* influence *of the M.* and evidently *promoted his departure.* The *M. was not insensible of it but consoled himself* with the *service which he thought the Indian speeches* would witness that *he had rendered to the United States.* I am persuaded that the *transaction* is also pl[eas]*ing to him in another view as* it will *form a bright column in the gazet*[te]*s of Europe,* ⟨and that he *will be impatient for its appearance there* without seeing *any mode in* which *it can happen of course.*⟩[1] As it is *blende*[d] *with the proceedings of the* Commissioners it will probably not be *publi*[sh]*ed in America very soon,* ⟨if at all.⟩ *The* time I have lately *passed with the M. has given me a* pretty thorough *insi*[gh]*t into his character.* With great *natural frankness of temper he unit*[e]*s much addres*[s] ⟨with very⟩ *considerable talents,* ⟨a strong *thirst of praise and popularity.*⟩ In *his politics he* says *his three hob*[b]*y horses* are the *alliance between France and the United States,* the *unio*[n] *of the lat*[t]*er* and the *manumission* of the *slaves.* The two former are the *dearer to him* as *they are connected* with *his personal glory.* The last *does him real honor* as it is a *proof of his humanity*. In a word I take *him to be as amiable a man as can be imagined*[2] and as *sincere an American as any Frenchman can be;* one *whose past services gratitude* obliges *us to acknowle*[d]*ge,* and *whose future friendship* prudence *requires us to cultivate.*

The Committee of the States have never reassembled. The case of Longchamps has been left both by the Legislature & Executive of this State to its Judiciary course. He is sentenced to a fine of 100 Crowns, to 2 years imprisonment, and Security for good behaviour for 7 years. On teusday morning I set off for Richmond, where I ought to be to-morrow, but some delays have put it out of my power.[3] The ramble I have taken has rather inflamed than extinguished my curiosity to see the Northern & N. W. Country. If circumstances be favorable I may possibly resume it next Summer. Present my compliments to Miss Patsy, for whom as well as for yourself Mrs. House charges me with hers. She has lately recd. a letter from poor Mrs. Trist, every syllable of which is the language of affliction itself. She had arrived safe at the habitation of her decd. husband, but will not be able to leave that Country till the Spring at the nearest. The only happiness she says she is capable of there is to receive proofs that her friends have not forgotten her. I do not learn what is likely to be the amount of the effects left by Mr. T. former accounts varied from 6 to 10,000 dollars. I am Dear Sir Yrs. very affecty.

J. MADISON JR.

RC (DLC). Addressed to Jefferson in Paris and docketed by JM many years later. Headed, "No. (5)." The words in italics, unless otherwise noted, are in the code first used by Jefferson on 14 Apr. 1783. Some important changes made later by JM are noted below.

[1] The editing of Julian P. Boyd in 1953 revealed that JM had taken liberties with this and the next two sentences by crossing through the words here restored within angle brackets. The purpose of JM's alterations, made many decades later when the letter came back into his possession, was to strike from the record his 1784 opinion of Lafayette as a vain, attention-seeking young man. There is a tinge of sarcasm in the first stricken lines, while the second alteration (crossing out "if at all") covered up JM's miscalculation of reports on Lafayette's speech, which drew great attention in America to the French nobleman (see JM to Jefferson, 11 Oct. 1784, and notes). Perhaps from personal pique or jealousy, JM was inclined to underrate Lafayette's abilities, hence his desire forty years later to destroy this 1784 allusion to the Frenchman's "thirst of praise and popularity."

[2] As JM struck out certain words in preceding sentences, in this one he tried to alter the record. Another comment about Lafayette's vanity distressed JM in his old age, so that the words "can be imagined" which JM interlined decades later falsifies the original wording, which Boyd properly read as: "his vanity will admit" (Boyd, *Papers of Jefferson*, VII, 451 n.). Boyd calls attention to JM's septuagenarian efforts to imitate Jefferson's handwriting while leaving the code readable

but altered so as to be nonsensical. Boyd surmised: "Madison had evidently hoped that no one would suspect his carefully covered traces" (ibid., 452 n.).

[3] The House of Delegates was scheduled to convene in Richmond on 18 Oct. 1784. However, JM did not attend until 1 Nov.

The General Assembly Session of October 1784

EDITORIAL NOTE

Wartime emergencies faded as peace returned and the pace of political life in Virginia slipped back into its earlier tempo. The May 1784 session was the last spring meeting held by the legislature, the members having determined that henceforth a single session would be adequate. JM had no quarrel with the slower pace—it was the power rather than the working habits of the older crowd that bothered him. The election of Patrick Henry as governor removed the chief obstacle to JM's legislative endeavors, but certain lieutenants were eager to serve the same interests patronizing Henry, so that in a real sense JM's chief contribution in the House of Delegates was not as an initiator of needed legislation but a brake on ill-advised measures.

Much routine business was carried on by JM in his role as chairman of the Committee for Courts of Justice. In this role he tried to solve the old riddle of revamping an outmoded court structure bogged down by crowded dockets, long trips to Richmond, and the entrenchment of courthouse cliques. Hoping for reform, JM introduced the Courts of Assize bill written by Edmund Pendleton early in the Revolution. Pendleton's plan provided for a circuit court system that would eliminate some of the delays of the prevailing county courts and also ease the burden of appeals. JM maneuvered the bill through the session despite "much secret repugnance" from a surly though nearly silent opposition. Ultimately the victory turned into an empty triumph, for the legislature kept postponing the day when the act went into force until it was ultimately repealed. But at the time it appeared that JM was strong enough to prevail in the House of Delegates against an opposition jealous of any lessening of the power lodged in local courthouses. The reason for JM's concern over the creaking court system probably related to the touchy British debt problem. The debts which Virginians owed British merchants when the war broke out had been left in limbo, and although the sum was great the issue was more emotional than economic. The law prevented a British creditor from going into the state courts to recover his money, and this point had not been overlooked at the treaty negotiations in Paris. By 1784 the treaty was operative only so far as the recognition of American independence by Great Britain, but the irritation of occupied frontier posts and unpaid debts kept relations between the former colonies and Great Britain embroiled. JM worked futilely with Joseph Jones to redeem the state's honor but avoided a clear break with the anti-payment faction that would have been public acknowledgment of the hopelessness of a forthright solution. The installment payment plan which JM supported was a compromise which more than anything else would have demonstrated the willingness of indebted

Virginians to meet their obligations. Moreover, the western counties were placed under great hardship by an appeal system which left litigants only one recourse—a long, expensive trip to Richmond.

Other concerns at the October 1784 session centered on internal improvements and taxes. Most public men favored canals and market roads or turnpikes as a means of maintaining life lines to the west. JM was anxious to sponsor legislation authorizing canal companies for the Potomac, James, and Elizabeth rivers for he was convinced that privately financed schemes of this sort would be self-supporting while fostering the markets farmers needed for their products. Washington's enthusiasm for the Potomac canal was a confirmation of JM's approach, and when his friend came forward with a model bill from Annapolis JM withdrew his own work to promote the general good expeditiously. His enthusiasm for the Dismal Swamp canal proved premature but was in the same intellectual channel as the plan he would support a generation later when the Erie waterway was proposed.

The other business was knottier—for Virginians believed the war had been fought in part over taxes, and they were not eager to pay them in altered circumstances. As the General Assembly had learned, a tax gatherer is never popular, yet certain expenses had to be met to keep the national and local machinery of government in operation. Interest on the national debt kept piling up, and JM was impatient with fellow legislators who sought excuses for postponed payments and displayed a niggardliness toward the state quota of Confederation costs. The 5 percent national impost, which would have solved part of the problem, was a favorite scheme of JM's which was generally unpopular in the legislature. Without some independent source of the revenue, there was no way the national government could ever meet its obligations, and at each session of the legislature as the matter was debated and then postponed it was clear to a logician of JM's caliber that a day of reckoning was due.

Finally, the submerged issue of support for the old established church was about to surface. The southside counties where Henry was strongest had petitioned for a tax-supported agency whereby Christians might be instructed in holy ways. With Henry's shadow in the foreground, a General Assessment bill for teachers of Christianity came close to passage and was only at the last moment postponed by a stratagem. JM joined with other lawmakers who, fearing an outright battle over the bill, sent it out as a public declaration of intent, with an invitation to the citizenry to comment upon its provisions for the future guidance of the legislature. The ploy worked, but when the October 1784 session adjourned, the conservative forces had much the upper hand. Indeed, their strength was greater than they knew, and as JM looked toward the autumn of 1785 and the next meeting he was obligated to bestir himself. The enthusiasm of 1776 was a distant memory and there was a danger that Virginians might slip back into their old ways, under a new flag but with the same old pseudo-aristocratic fabric that was—as JM viewed it—essentially counter-revolutionary in intent.

Appendix A of this volume carries a full listing of legislation which JM introduced or carried to the Senate but apparently did not draft.

Resolutions on Western Law Enforcement
and Mississippi Navigation

EDITORIAL NOTE

Indian unrest and rumors of Spanish intrigue on the western frontier cast a shadow over the General Assembly sessions late in 1784. Virginians were moving into areas roamed by peaceable tribes and committing depredations that could only lead to retaliation, while word drifted eastward of provocative moves in the Ohio Valley that might bring an open clash between Virginians and Spaniards. JM was acutely aware of this western ferment and reported that the lawmakers sought the "means of obviating these dangers" while the reckless talk of men living on the frontier led the delegates in Richmond to believe that "we are every day threatened by the eagourness of our disorderly Citizens for Spanish plunder & Spanish blood" (JM to Monroe, 14 and 27 Nov. 1784). The later circumstance was the direct cause of House debates concerning lawlessness in the Kentucky district, followed by passage of resolutions that recognized the dual nature of the problem. Fugitive Americans had to be punished, but Spain also had to understand that the sword of law cut both ways. Virginians had rights as well as responsibilities. Thus Virginia would surrender lawbreakers to Spain, but the subjects of Charles III needed to understand that American rights pertaining to navigation of the Mississippi would never be surrendered.

American rights to the Mississippi were involved in delicate negotiations with the Spanish court that dragged on for years, but the matter of turning Virginians who broke the law over to a foreign power was an immediate concern. JM served on a committee charged with implementing the euphemistically titled law-and-order resolution on western tranquillity, and on 12 November a draft was offered to the House which caused prolonged debate. The solution finally agreed upon by the slenderest of margins interposed the authority of Congress and shifted the ultimate decision on extradition of international lawbreakers from state to national officials. See JM's Preamble and Portion of an Extradition Bill (26 Nov. 1784).

[3 November 1784]

Resolved, that it is the opinion of this committee, That for preserving the tranquillity of our western inhabitants, speedy and exemplary punishment ought to be inflicted on every person doing injury to the subjects of Spain or the Indians in that quarter; and that proper laws for that purpose ought to be enacted.

Resolved, that it is the opinion of this committee, That it is essential to the prosperity and happiness of the western inhabitants of this Commonwealth, to enjoy the right of navigating the river Mississippi to the sea, and that the delegates representing this State in Congress, ought to be instructed to move that honorable body to give directions, (unless the same have already been given to the American ministers in Europe) to forward negotiations to obtain that end, without loss of time.[1]

Printed copy (*JHDV*, Oct. 1784, p. 9). The first resolution has not been found in Ms, while the second (Vi) is not in JM's hand.

[1] These resolutions followed discussions in the Committee of the Whole House on the State of the Commonwealth and were probably drafted by Joseph Jones with some assistance from JM. It is hardly possible that the author of the 20 Aug. letter to Jefferson played no important part in giving them final form. See also JM to Jefferson, 9 Jan. 1785. JM served on a special committee that prepared an extradition bill which was offered on 12 Nov. to implement the first resolution (*JHDV*, Oct. 1784, pp. 20, 22). The bill encountered considerable opposition and was salvaged by the legislative dexterity of JM and Joseph Jones (Preamble and Portion of an Extradition Bill, 26 Nov. 1784).

From James Monroe

TRENTON Novr. 7 1784.

DEAR SIR

I enclose you a cypher which will put some cover on our correspondence.[1] We have yet only 5. States, & not a man from the Eastward except Mr. Holton.[2] There is nothing new without doors, wh. I have not communicated to the Governor &, of those within I must defer writing you, untill the next post; the present is certainly an important crisis in our affairs, but as I shall write you very fully by the next post shall only add that I am with Great respect & esteem yr. friend & servant

JAS. MONROE

[Enclosure]

1. Spain	11. the Delegates
2. Ld. Shelburne	12. Maryland
3. Ct. Vergennes	13. Mr. Mercer
4. Dr. Franklin	14. Mr. Hardy
5. Mr. Grayson	15. Georgia
6. Pennsylvania	16. Mr. Jefferson
7. King of France	17. Mr. J. Adams
8. King of Sweden	18. Mr. Fox
9. France	19. the U. Netherlands
10. No. Carolina	20. of

21. the Governor
22. N. York
23. Mr. Gerry
24. Virginia
25. Mr. P. Henry
26. Arthur Lee
27. the Indian comrs.
28. Jersey
29. Great Britain
30. The minister
31. Ireland
32. Mr. Marbois
33. Governor Harrison
34. Canada
35. impost
36. commander in chief
37. resources
38. army
39. finances
40. N. Hamshire
41. confiscation
42. Delaware
43. Mr. Laurens
44. hostilities
45. R. Island
46. Mr. Dana
47. U. States
48. Mr. Read of So. Carolina
49. Connecticut
50. the President of Congress
51. R. H. Lee
52. Court
53. blame
54. Mr. Jay
55. So. Carolina
56. definitive treaty
57. Massachusetts
58. war
59. provisional treaty

60. peace
61. western posts
62. committee of the States
63. commerce
64. Laws of nations
65. attack
66. northern
67. variance
68. conduct
69. Indians
70. Southern
71. detention
72. ships
73. Carlton
74. treaty
75. negroes
76. Genl. Assembly
78. disposition
79. degrade
80. LaFayatte
81. Ld. North
82. unfriendly
83. publick expence
84. Mr. Burke
85. defence
86. prepare
87. Mr. Ellery
88. Robt. Morris
89. Baron Steuben
90. Mr. Howell
91. Trenton
92. Phila.
93. Genl. Washington
94. Mr. Tyler
95. consul
96. Congress
97. lose
98. gain
99. Mr. Jones

RC (DLC); enclosure (ViU). Cover missing. Docketed. This is the first known letter from a correspondent whom Jefferson had predicted that JM would probably find "an useful one" (Jefferson to JM, 8 May 1784).

1 The "enclosed cypher" was separated from the letter through the circumstances explained in *Papers of Madison*, I, xx. Monroe began using it in his letter of 15 Nov. 1784. Monroe inadvertently omitted a cipher for 77.

2 "Mr. Holton" was Dr. Samuel Holten (1738–1816), the conscientious delegate from Massachusetts. The disappointing attendance record made it "seem as if this were the beginning of the end of the United States in Congress Assembled" (Burnett, *The Continental Congress*, p. 613). Delegations from the required seven states did not attend until 29 Nov., when a quorum finally was present.

From Thomas Jefferson

PARIS Nov. 11. 1784.

DEAR SIR

Your letters of Aug. 20. Sep 7. & 15. I received by the last packet. That by mr Short is not yet arrived. His delay is unaccountable. I was pleased to find by the public papers (for as yet I have no other information of it) that the assembly had restrained their foreign trade to four places: I should have been more pleased had it been to one. However I trust that York & Hobbs' hole will do so little that Norfolk & Alexandria will get possession of the whole. Your letter first informs me of the exception in favor of Citizens, an exception which by the contrivance of merchants will I fear undo the whole. The popular objection which you mention that the articles passing thro' so many hands must come at a higher price to the consumer, is much like the one which might be made to a pin passing thro' the hands of so many workmen. Each being confined to a single operation will do it better & on better terms. This act of our assembly has been announced in all the gazettes of Europe with the highest commendations.[1] I am obliged to you for your information as to the prospects of the present year in our farms. It is a great satisfaction to know it, & yet it is a circumstance which few correspondents think worthy of mention. I am also much indebted for your very full observations on the navigation of the Missisipi. I had thought on the subject, & sketched the anatomy of a memorial on it which will be much aided by your communications. You mention that my name is used by some speculators in Western land jobbing as if they were acting for me as well as themselves. About the year 1776 or 1777 I consented to join mr Harvey & some others in an application for lands there: which scheme however I beleive he dropped in the threshold, for I never after heard one syllable on the subject. In 1782. I joined some gentlemen in a project to obtain some lands in the Western parts of North Carolina. But in the winter of 1782. 1783. while I was in expectation of going to Europe and that the title to Western lands might possibly come under the discussion of the ministers, I withdrew myself from this company. I am further assured that the members never prosecuted their views. These were the only occasions in which I ever took a single step for the acquisition of Western lands, & in these I retracted at the threshold. I can with truth therefore declare to you, & wish you to repeat it on every proper occasion, that no person on earth is authorized to place my name in any adventure for lands on the Western waters, that I am not engaged in any one speculation for that purpose at present, & never was engaged in any, but the two before mentioned. I am one of eight children to whom my father left his share in the loyal company; whose interests however, I never espoused, & they have long since received their quietus. Excepting these, I never was nor am now interested in one foot of land on earth, off of the waters of James river.

I shall subjoin the few books I have ventured to buy for you. I have been induced to do it by the combined circumstances of their utility & cheapness. I wish I had a catalogue of the books you would be willing to buy, because they are often to be met with on stalls very cheap, & I would get them as occasions should arise. The subscription for the Encyclopedie is still open. Whenever an opportunity offers of sending you what is published of that work (37 vols) I shall subscribe for you & send it with the other books purchased for you. Probably no opportunity will occur till the spring when I expect the packets will be removed from L'Orient to Havre. The communication between this place & l'Orient is as difficult as it is easy with Havre. From N. York packages will be readily sent to Richmond by the care for mr Neill Jamieson, a very honest refugee now living at New York but who certainly ought to be permitted to return to Norfolk.[2] Whatever money I may lay out for you here in books, or in any thing else which you may desire, may be replaced, crown for crown (without bewildering ourselves in the Exchange) in Virginia, by making paiments for the instruction or boarding of my nephews, and I wish you to be assured that this will be as perfectly convenient to me as the replacing the money here, that you may with freedom order any thing from hence of which you have occasion. If the bearer Colo Le Maire can take charge of a pamphlet on Animal magnetism, another giving an account of Robert's last voiage thro' the air,[3] & of some Phosphoretic matches, I will send them to you. These matches consist of a small wax taper, one end of which has been dipped in Phosphorus, & the whole is inclosed in a glass tube hermetically sealed. There is a little ring on the tube to shew where it is to be broken. First warm the phosphorized end (which is the furthest one from the ring) by holding it two or three seconds in your mouth, then snap it at or near the ring & draw the phosphorized end out of the tube. It blazes in the instant of it's extraction. It will be well always to decline the tube at an angle of about 45°. (the phosphorized end lowest) in order that it may kindle thoroughly. Otherwise though it blazes in the first instant it is apt to go out if held erect. These cost about 30 sous the dozen. By having them at your bedside with a candle, the latter may be lighted at any moment of the night without getting out of bed. By keeping them on your writing table, you may seal three or four letters with one of them, or light a candle if you want to seal more which in the summer is convenient. In the woods they supply the want of steel, flint & punk. Great care must be taken in extracting the taper that none of the phosphorous drops on your hand, because it is inextinguishable & will therefore burn to the bone if there be matter enough. It is said that urine will extinguish it. There is a new lamp invented here lately which with a very small consumption of oil (of olives) is thought to give a light equal to six or eight candles. The wick is hollow in the middle in the form of a hollow cylinder, & permits the air to pass up thro' it. It requires no snuffing. They make shade candlesticks of them at two guinea's price, which are excellent for reading & are much used by studious men. Colo Le Maire, whom you know is the bearer of this.[4] He comes to Virginia to obtain the 2000 acres of land given him for his services in procuring us arms, & what else he may be entitled to as having been an officer in our service. Above all things he wishes to obtain the Cincinnatus eagle, because it will procure him here the order of St. Louis, & of course a pension for life of 1000 livres. He is so extremely poor that another friend and myself furnish him money for his whole expences from here to Virginia. There I am in hopes the hospitality of the country will be a resource for him till he can convert a part of his lands advantageously into money. But as he will want some small matter of money, if it should be convenient for you to furnish him with as much as ten guineas from time to time on my account I will invest that sum in books or any thing else you may want here by way of paiment. He is honest & grateful, and you may be assured that no aid which you can give him in the forwarding his claims will be misplaced.

The lamp of war is kindled here, not to be extinguished but by torrents of blood. The firing of the Dutch on an Imperial vessel going down the Scheld, has been followed by the departure of the Imperial minister from the Hague without taking leave. Troops are in motion on both sides towards the Scheld, but probably nothing will be attempted till the spring. This court has been very silent as to the part they will act. Yet their late treaty with Holland, as well as a certainty that Holland would not have proceeded as far without an assurance of aid, furnish sufficient ground to conclude they will side actively with the republic. The king of Prussia it is beleived will do the same. He has patched up his little disputes with Holland & Dantzic. The prospect is that Holland, France, Prussia & the Porte will be engaged against the two Imperial courts. England I think will remain neuter. Their hostility towards us has attained an incredible height. Notwithstanding the daily proofs of this, they expect to keep our trade & cabotage to themselves by the virtue of their proclamation. They have no idea that we can so far act in concert as to establish retaliating measures. Their Irish affairs will puzzle them extremely. We expect every moment to hear whether their Congress took place on the 25th. Ult. Perhaps before I seal my letter I may be enabled to inform you. Should things get into confusion there, perhaps they will be more disposed to wish a friendly connection with us.

There is a dictionary of law, natural, civil & political in 13. vols 4to. published here. It is well executed, by Felice, Jaurat, De la lande & others. It supplies the diplomatic dictionary of which you saw some volumes in Philadelphia & which degenerated into a trifling thing. This work costs half a guinea a volume. If you want De Thou, I can buy it on the stalls in perfect condition, 11. vols. 4to. in French @ 6. livres a vol. Moreri is to be bought cheap on the stalls.

The inclosed papers being put into my hands by mr Grand I cannot do better than to forward them to you & ask your attention to the case should the party present himself to you.[5] I am with great sincerity Your affectionate friend & sert

TH: JEFFERSON

Address your letters À Monsr. Monsr. Jefferson ministre plenipotentiaire des etats unis de l'Amerique à Paris, Cul-de-sac Tetebout.
Books bought for you
Historia de España por Mariana. 2 vol. fol. (old) 15 livres.

Le Dictionnaire de Trevoux. 5. vols folio. in good condition 28 livres
Wicquefort de l'Ambassadeur. 2. vols. 4to. good condition 7. livres 4:
Sous
Traité de Morale. a new & good publication 12 mo.
l'Encyclopedie 37. vols. some thing above 300 livres.

8 counties only sent deputies to the Congress in Dublin. They came to
resolns on the reform of parliament &c. & adjd. to the 20th: of Jan.
recommendg. to the other counties to send deputies then.

RC (DLC). Cover missing. Docketed. The enclosures from Ferdinand Grand
are missing, but a key to their contents is to be found in Jefferson's "Summary
Journal of Letters" (Boyd, *Papers of Jefferson*, VII, 507 n.).

[1] Jefferson had seen only the port bill as first passed by the House of Delegates
on 17 June, not the statute as finally adopted on 26 June. Therefore he mentions
only four ports of entry—Norfolk, Hobbs Hole, York, and Alexandria. The statute
added Bermuda Hundred. Since all of Jefferson's lands were on "the waters of
James river," Bermuda Hundred would be of special interest to him. The *Va. Gazette and Weekly Advertiser* printed the statute on 17 July with a note that "There
was an error in the former publication of this act." No copy of the *Gazette* with
the former publication of the port bill is now available, but the House version
appeared in the *Va. Journal and Alexandria Advertiser*, 8 July 1784.
[2] Neil Jamieson was a Scottish merchant who lived at Norfolk when the Revolution began. After patriots burned his home, he moved to New York and became
an active loyalist. Jamieson claimed he lost property worth £37,100 through wartime confiscations in Virginia (Harrell, *Loyalism in Virginia*, pp. 47, 48, 97 n.).
[3] The two pamphlets are *Rapport des commissaires chargés par le roi, de l'examen
du magnétisme animal* (Paris, 1784) and *Mémoire sur les expériences aérostatiques
faites par MM. Robert frères, ingénieurs-pensionnaires du roi* (Paris, 1784).
[4] Col. Jacques Le Maire drew ten guineas from JM on Jefferson's credit, but did
not remain in the U. S. (JM to Jefferson, 22 Jan. 1786). Because his service had
been with Virginia forces, he was accepted as a member of the Society of the Cincinnati in the State of Virginia (Edgar Erskine Hume, *Sesquicentennial History and
Roster of the Society of the Cincinnati in the State of Virginia, 1783–1933* [Rich-
mond, 1934], p. 284).
[5] Ferdinand Grand, a Parisian banker, handled accounts for the Commonwealth
of Virginia and the U. S. during and after the Revolution (Boyd, *Papers of Jefferson*, III, 91–92; XI, 673–74).

Bill for Granting James Rumsey a
Patent for Ship Construction

EDITORIAL NOTE

James Rumsey (1743–1792) had been experimenting with a mechanical
pole boat when good fortune brought General Washington to his vicinity.

In September 1784 (at Bath in Berkeley County, Virginia) Washington witnessed a trial run of a model and became an enthusiast for Rumsey's invention. Since Rumsey's model gave promise of being a handmaiden to the general's favorite Potomac canal scheme, it was natural that he should give Rumsey a testimonial, and when in Richmond that fall to promote Rumsey's ideas in conversations with public men (*Pa. Gazette*, 29 Sept. 1784; Fitzpatrick, *Writings of Washington*, XXVII, 468, 480, 484). As JM explained to Jefferson, Rumsey had petitioned the General Assembly at the May 1784 session for a patent on his model but the "extravagance of his pretensions brought a ridicule upon them, and nothing was done" (JM to Jefferson, 9 Jan. 1785). With Washington as his chief promoter, the climate of opinion changed. JM apparently concerned himself with preparing legislation that would protect the invention. JM actually knew little about Rumsey's boat, which operated by the force of river current against a paddlewheel that pushed poles against the river bed—an ingenious device which steam power soon proved impracticable. But JM was interested in a means whereby inventors and authors received recognition and reward, and as Brant remarks, JM looked upon this act "as a model in its protection of the public against the evils of a monopoly" (*Madison*, II, 370).

[11] November 1784

WHEREAS it is represented to this present General Assembly that James Rumsey hath invented Boats which are constructed upon a model that will greatly facilitate navigation against the current of rapid Rivers, whereby great advantages may be derived to the Citizens of this State: And whereas the said James Rumsey hath made application for the sole and exclusive right and privilege of constructing and navigating such Boats for the term of ten years as a recompense for this invention:

BE IT THEREFORE ENACTED that the said James Rumsey his heirs, Executors and Assigns shall have the sole and exclusive right and Privilege of constructing and navigating Boats upon his model in each & every River, Creek, Bay, Inlet or Harbour within this Commonwealth for and during the said term of ten years, to be computed from the first day of January one thousand seven hundred and eighty five. If any person, other than the said James Rumsey his heirs, Executors or Assigns, shall during the term aforesaid either directly or indirectly, construct navigate, employ or use any Boat or Boats upon the model of that invented by the said James Rumsey or upon the model of any future improvement which the said Rumsey may make thereon, he or they for every Boat so constructed, navigated, employed or used, shall forfeit and pay for every such offence the sum of ⟨five hundred pounds⟩ to be recovered with costs by action of debt, to be founded on this Act, in any Court of Record ⟨one half⟩ to the use of the party who will sue for the same⟨, and the other half to the use of the said James Rumsey⟩.

PROVIDED always that the exclusive right and privilege hereby granted may, at any time during the said term of ten years, be abolished by the Legislature upon paying to the said James Rumsey his heirs, Executors or Assigns the sum of ten thousand Pounds current money *in gold or silver* ⟨of Virginia⟩:[1]

Ms (Vi). In the hand of Edmund Pendleton, Jr. Docketed by a clerk. The words within angle brackets appear to have been added, and those in italics deleted, in the Senate before final passage. The approved act is titled: "An act giving James Rumsey the exclusive right of constructing and navigating certain boats for a limited time" (Hening, *Statutes*, XI, 502).

[1] JM's authorship is indicated by his assignment to carry the engrossed bill to the Senate, after its passage by the House of Delegates on 15 Nov. (*JHDV*, Oct. 1784, p. 23). The importance of this act lay in the principle it established, not in its practical workings. As it developed, the pole boat was soon discarded for a more efficient vessel Rumsey devised using a jet propulsion principle (Brooke Hindle, *The Pursuit of Science in Revolutionary America, 1735–1789* [Chapel Hill, 1956], pp. 374–76; John W. Oliver, *History of American Technology* [New York, 1956], p. 138). Hindle noted that Rumsey "died in England without ever having run a boat at a high enough speed to be useful."

From John Francis Mercer

TRENTON Novr. 12. 84

DEAR SIR

Altho' I should have blush'd to have met you, after having so long delay'd repaying the money you kindly advanc'd me,[1] yet the sincere pleasure I felt in the expectation of again taking you by the hand effaced every other impression & my dissapointment was real when I learn'd that you had return'd to the South without my meeting you. After you left me in Congress—I was subjected to the inconvenience—I may indeed say misfortune—of committing money to the care of four different friends, whose necessities were so urgent as to make them forget mine. This added to my expences in attending an itenerant Congress, surpassing infinitely the appointment from the State, has given a very unfavorable complexion to my conduct to you. At this moment I am unable to restore the whole of the money you loan'd me & the mode I have taken of remitting you 400 Dollars (whilst I hope it will answer perfectly your purpose) discovers my inability to adopt any other. You will be so good as to shew the enclos'd order to the Treasurer & consult with him. Inform him that I only desire the money to be paid you, at the time I might draw it myself, consistently with the Law of the State. Therefore if the forms of the office require delay untill a quarter's salary has accumulated—notwithstanding this specific sum will be soon due—I would be oblig'd to you so to arrange the payment, as to comply with what is required by him. As soon as my Crops can be converted into Cash I will be punctual to pay the sum I shall still owe you.

Twelve days have expir'd since the time affix'd for the Reassembling of Congress & as yet but four states are represented—Doctor Holten alone, has appear'd from the Eastern States. This total relaxation & innatention to the Confœderal Government (not to speak of the cause, but the effect) must necessarily have an exceeding evil tendency both at home & abroad. The judicious Men who have lately return'd from Europe, all agree, that the prevalent opinion there is—that we are verging fast towards anarchy & confusion—& some of them say, they were frequently asked by men otherwise well informed, whether we had any thing like Government yet remaining among us— & in this opinion they all join, that nothing is so ardently desir'd by the British Nation & Ministry, as a renewal of the War with us—that the same old leven that work'd to such effect in 72. was still strongly fermenting at the British Court. Colo. Monroe has lately arriv'd from Canada & our North Western Frontier. He says that every thing wears the most unfavorable appearance in that Quarter. The retention of the Posts—intrigues with the Indians, & in fine every measure in that Government, indicates a settled plan, unfriendly, if not hostile to the United States.[2] From all this I am led to apprehend that if the War, which seems ready to break forth in Europe, should break out, & France becomes involv'd therein (which her late engagements with the Dutch Republic render inevitable) that Great Britain woud keep her neck out of the halter, purposely to deal with us. The lightest visions of imagination, appear as solid ground of apprehension to a suspicious mind—but really suspicion becomes a virtue in a political Character where there is a consciousness of internal Weakness & total want of resource.

In my judgement there never was a crisis, threatening an event more unfavorable to the happiness of the United States, than the present. Those repellent qualities the seeds of which are abundantly sown in the discordant manners & sentiments of the different States, have produc'd great heats & animosities in Congress now no longer under the restraint impos'd by the war—insomuch that I almost despair of seeing that body unite in those decisive, & energetic measures, requisite for the public safety & prosperity. The scanty & irregular Supply of Money to the Continental Treasury, from the feeble & disconnected efforts, of the different States, have dwindled into nothing. Several States have not yet taken up the requisitions for 84. Some after taking them up, declare they do not understand 'em, & they all conclude in just the same point—that is they pay nothing. M. Morriss tells me that the Contributions of Virginia have alone kept the wheels of Government in motion. Now notwithstanding it is much to be regretted, we must withhold too, or pay with a cautious hand—for why ruin ourselves to postpone a misfortune that must come at last, & perhaps the sooner the better. We pay greater Taxes than any people under the Sun & if neighbouring States will pay nothing the effect must be the depopulation of our Country. This evil has already made a progress of fearful extent.

I can discover no resource for Congress but to adhere strictly to the plan Recommended in April 82. & to call on those States who have pass'd the Impost to carry it immediately in execution. The refusal of Rhode Island does not change the principle on which they agreed to it, or render the measure less necessary. I believe no other plan, short of divine wisdom, & not protected by the providence of God, woud meet the unanimous concurrence of these States, & at all events the necessary delay woud be fatal to our situation—for an Years interest will be soon due in Europe & all the interest here, without a Shilling to pay. If ultimately R. I. cannot by a demand of the principal due from her & some other certain mode be induced to consent to the only alternative of Public Justice—that of providing funds for the interest—if other States should fail to carry the Law into effect—the Willing States may recant before any great injury can arise. Such are my reflections. I wish I coud see others as sober & as serious as the occasion merits but I am sorry to say that, always more anxious about where we shall sit, than what we shall do—our chief dispute now is whether we shall spend the Winter in Philadelphia or N. York. The advocates for Philadelphia are more numerous & more zealous, so that I suppose we shall revisit the State House. Wherever we go & whatever we do I shall remain yours with great esteem & sincere friendship

JOHN F. MERCER

I beg of you to remember me very particularly to Mr. Jones

RC (DLC). Cover missing. Docketed by JM. The enclosure is addressed to the state treasurer, Jacquelin Ambler, authorizing him "to pay James Madison Junr. Esqr. four hundred dollars out of my ensuing quarters salary as Delegate in Congress, when due."

[1] JM lent Mercer $600 in Oct. 1783 (*Papers of Madison*, VII, 373). Twenty years later, a portion of the balance was still unpaid (JM to Mercer, 11 Aug. 1803 [DLC]).

[2] Mercer's polarized view of the British occupation of the frontier posts was popularly held by many Virginians but JM was not among them. JM probably leaned toward the more moderate view taken by John Jay "that the King's government had a valid excuse: the waywardness of the individual states in fulfilling the peace terms concerning debts and loyalists" (Don Higginbotham, *The War of American Independence* [New York, 1971], p. 445). Monroe at least took great pains to inspect the situation at first hand, while Mercer and some other opportunists in Congress and the Virginia legislature preferred demagogically to "twist the lion's tail."

To James Monroe

RICHMOND Novr. 14. 1784.

DEAR SIR

I had intended by this post to commence our correspondence with a narrative of what has been done and is proposed to be done at present Session of the Genl As[s]embly, but by your last lettr. to Mr. Jones, I find that it is very uncertain whether this will get to Trenton before you leave it for Virga. I cannot however postpone my congratulations on your critical escape from the danger which lay in ambush for you, and your safe return to Trenton.[1] My ramble extended neither into the dangers nor gratifications of yours. It was made extremely pleasing by sundry circumstances but could have been more so I assure you Sir, if we had been cotemporarys in the route we both passed. The Indians begin to be unquiet we hear both on the N. W. & S. E. sides of the Ohio.[2] The Spaniards are charged with spurring on the latter. As means of obviating these dangers, the H of D. have resolved to authorize the Executive to Suspend the surveying of land within the unpurchasd limits—& to instruct the Delegation to urge in Congr. Treaties with the Southern Indians, and negociations with Spain touching the Mississpi. They also propose to set on foot Surveys of Potowmac & James River from their falls to their Sources. But their principal attention has been & is still occupied with a scheme proposed for a Genl. Asset. 47 have carried it agst. 32. In its present form it excludes all but Christian Sects.[3]

The Presbyterian Clergy have remonstrated agst. any narrow principles, but indirectly favor a more comprehensive establisht. I think the bottom will be enlarged & that a trial will be made of the practicability of the project. The Successor to Mr. H. is not yet appointed or nominated.[4] It is in the option of Mr. H. and I fancy he will not decline the service. There will be three vacancies in the Council, for which also no nominations have been made. Mr. C. Griffith will probably be named, & Mr. W. Nicholas. Mr. Roane is also spoken of.[5] I am Dr Sir Yrs sincerly,

J. MADISON JR.

RC (DLC). Docketed by JM. Addressed to Monroe "in Congress."

[1] Monroe had visited Fort Schuyler in the fall of 1784, as had JM, but the one journey was as hazardous as the other was peaceful. Monroe recounted his experiences in a letter to Jefferson which was probably similar to "your last lettr. to Mr. [Joseph] Jones" (Boyd, *Papers of Jefferson*, VII, 459–62).

[2] Governor Harrison wrote the speaker of the House on 18 Oct. 1784 that Indians were murdering back country settlers and a war "more dreadful than any hitherto experienced" might result. The governor added that the Indians were being encouraged "by two powerful European neighbors, who look on us with the most jealous eyes" (Executive Letter Book, pp. 402–3).

[3] In JM's text: "but Xn Sects."

[4] JM meant Governor Harrison's successor. The other "Mr. H." was of course Patrick Henry, who exercised his option on 17 Nov. JM then served on the courtesy committee appointed to notify Henry of his election (*JHDV*, Oct. 1784, p. 32).

[5] The three seats on the Council were actually filled by Joseph Jones, Spencer Roane, and Miles Selden (*JCSV*, III, 409, 448, 449). JM made a slip when he wrote "Mr. C. Griffith." He was referring to Cyrus Griffin, who was appointed chief justice of the Washington District on 5 Jan. 1785. In 1786 he was again an unsuccessful candidate for the Council.

To Richard Henry Lee

Letter not found.

ca. 14 November 1784. Lee acknowledged on 26 Nov. JM's letter from Richmond, which had arrived at Trenton on 21 Nov. The letter appears to have reported on legislative business, including the proposed general assessment bill, a revised militia law, and the postponed tax measure.

From Philip Mazzei

WILLIAMSBURGO 15 9bre 1784.

AMICO CARISSIMO,

Troppo ci vorrebbe a dirvi tutte le ragioni per cui son tuttavia in Virginia. Una è che vorrei vedere il Marchese de la Fayette prima di partire, al che m'induce non solo la mia amicizia per il medesimo, ma ancora il riguardo che devo alla mia delicatezza e al mio onore; sopra di che mi spiegai col nostro degnissimo amico E. R. Fatemi, vi prego, il favore di comunicarmi ciò che sapete di Lui e dei suoi viaggi. Sono stato ragguagliato da Mr. Prentis della vergognosa resoluzione presa da 54 &c. &c. contro 37 virtuosi Cittadini. Se quel ch'io dico nell'altra pagina credete che possa essere di qualche uso, potete facilmente farne la traduzione, correggendo ed aggiungendo, ed esporlo alla considerazione del Pubblico per mezzo delle gazzette. Avrei piacere che vi abboccaste con Mr. Blair sul modo d'impedire che la nostra Società cadesse in un sonno letargo. Reveritemi distintamente Messrs. Jones, Stewart, Marshall, Wilson Nicholas, &c. &c. Credetemi sempre, e di vero cuore, Tutto vostro.

FILIPPO MAZZEI

[Postscript]
Dopo sigillata malamente questa lettera ò ricevuto un'invito dal Genl: Nelson per pranzare da lui oggi (martedì 16. del corrente) in compagnia del nostro amabile Eroe Marchese de la Fayette, chegiunse a York iersera, dove per altro non trovò Cornwallis. Tutte le Nazioni culte ànno convenuto che il più terribil flagello del genere umano è stata la Superstizione, e che i mali resultatine sono stati gravi a proporzione del potere diretto o indiretto che ànno avuto i Ministri delle Religioni. Quando s'intese che la loro professione fù da noi messa sull'istesso piede che sono tutte le altre, l'onore e il credito che acquistammo presso i buoni e savj, in tutte le parti del Globo ove risiede Filosofia, fù maggiore di quel che ci abbia recato qualunque altra magnanima legge della nostra Repubblica. I nostri nemici e gl'invidiosi, desiderando di offuscare la nostra gloria, non seppero dir'altro se non che noi eramo allora necessitati ad abbagliare il Mondo con dimostrazioni di straordinaria saviezza e magnanimità, e che appena ottenuto l'intento e divenuti independenti, gl'intrighi le cabale e gli antichi pregiudizi avrebbero ripreso vigore, e la povera Filosofia sostenuta unicamente dalla debole base d'un forzato eroismo sarebbe precipitata. Dio non voglia che la maligna profezia seguiti ad avverarsi nella pendente controversia, susci-

tata da alcuni interessati ecclesiastici, come pur troppo è seguito in diverse altre circostanze. Non si richiedono ingegni sublimi e speculazioni profonde per concepire quanto perniciosa e ingiusta sarebbe una legge, che obligasse gl'individui a pagare qualunque benchè piccola somma per cosa, nella quale il Pubblico non à verum diritto d'ingerirsi, come vien chiaramente espresso *nel Registro dei Diritti*.* È altresì facile a prevedersi l'opposizione che potrebbe incontrare l'esecuzione di una tal legge, in varie Contee ove la mente del maggior numero degli Abitanti non è offuscata dai pregiudizi favorevoli ad una sola Setta, e quanto tremenda cosa sarebbe l'avvezzaregli uomini ad opporsi alle Leggi. Dico una sola Setta, perchè l'altre si son rette sempre, si reggono e bramano di reggersi da per se stesse senza l'interposizione della pubblica autorità. Si devono investigare i veri motivi dei più zelanti fautori della proposta Legge. Alcuni potrebbero forse temere *il credito che giornalmente acquistano*** molti ingegnosi giovani, dotati di virtuosi e nobili sentimenti, e cercare nuovi protettori al proprio nel corpo degli ecclesiastici. Amico, se scuoprite tali caratteri, smascherategli arditamente, a rischio ancora di perdere la stima popolare, la quale non può esser consolante ad un'animo retto, mentre non sia conscio d'aver fatto tutti gli sforzi possibili a favore della Patria.

* In the Bill of Rights
** La parola *credito* in quel senso significa *stima popolare*.

CONDENSED TRANSLATION

Mazzei is still in Virginia for a variety of reasons, the chief one being his desire to have a meeting with Lafayette, the reasons for which he has explained to E. R. (in a note on the envelope he adds that he has been invited by Gen. Nelson to a dinner with Lafayette). Mazzei has been informed by Mr. Prentis that a "shameful" resolution has been passed, 54 to 37, to support established religion. He is sending JM the draft of an article condemning such resolution as contrary to the Bill of Rights. It is suggested that the true aim of the supporters of the resolution is to gain the protection of the clergy to bolster their own popularity; JM is urged to unmask and resolutely combat such efforts. He should meet with Blair for the purpose of revitalizing the Constitutional Society.

RC (DLC). Addressed to JM, "in the House of Delegates [at] Richmond."

From James Monroe

DEAR SIR

You recd. I hope by the last post a small cypher from me. At fort Stanwix[1] you were necessarily acquainted with the *variance* which had taken place between the *Indian Commissioners of the U. States,* & those *of New York* as well as of the principles upon which they respectively acted & the extent to which they carried them: as I reach'd *N. York* about eight days after you had left it & *the Ind: Comm'rs* were then on the ground & have not since made a stat'ment of their final transactions there. I have nothing new to give you upon that head. The questions wh. appear to me to arise upon the subjects *of variance* are 1. whether these *Indians* are to be consider'd as members of the State of *N. York,* or whether the living simply within the bounds of a State, in the exclusion only of an European power, while they acknowlidge no obidience to its laws but hold a country over which they do not extend, nor enjoy the protection nor any of the rights of citizenship within it, is a situation wh. will even in the most qualified sense, admit their being held as members of a State? 2. whether on the other hand this is not a description of those whose manag'ment is committed by the confideration to the U S. in Congress assembled? In either event the land held by these *Indians,* having never been ceded either by *N. York* or *Massachussetts* belongs not to the *U. States;* the only point then in wh. *N. York* can be reprehensible is, for preceding by a particular [state treaty], the general *Treaty.* This must be attributed to a suspicion that there exists in *Congress* a design to injure her. The transaction will necessarily come before us, but will it not be most expedient in the present state of our affairs to form no decision thereon? I know no advantages to be deriv'd from one. If the general *treaty* hath been obstructed the injury sustain'd in that instance is now without remedy. A decision either way, will neither restore the time we have lost nor remove the impressions wh. this *variance* hath made with the *Indians* & in the *Court of G. Britain* respecting us. If the right *of Congress* hath been contraven'd shall we not derive greater injury by urging it to the reprehension of *New York* who holds herself aggriev'd in other respects than by suffering our sense of that delinquency to lay dormant? Our purchases must be made without her bounds & those *Indians* whose alliance we seek inhabit a country to which she hath no claim.

Mr. Marbois is dissatisfied with the decision of the *Court of Pennsyl-*

vania[2] in a particular affair: his own conduct in the management of that business previous to the decision, obtain'd the entire approbation of the *King of France* as he is assur'd in a letter from *the Minister* of Marine, and certainly he conducted it in as high a tone as *the Minister* the most jealous of the honor of *the King of France* cod. have done. Since that period he hath not recd. the orders of his *Court* & in the interval hath some difficulty how to act. If *Congress* go to *Philada.* he says he will be precluded from a personal attendance or communication there. I have consider'd this matter more attentively since I saw you & think that in whatever character we hold the man we cannot surrender him to the *Court of France* even if *Pensylvania* wod. accede to whatever we desir'd. That all they have a right to expect is that he be punish'd agreeably to the laws of *Pennsylva.* & that if they are not adequate, others be made for preventing the like in future, wh. might [be] effected by a recommendation from Congress. The variance wh. took place between the members of the *Committee of the States* wh. terminated in their abrupt dissolution by a secession on the part of some members, is also an affair which may come before us.[3] But had we not also better keep this affair out of sight & while we lament they could not in that instance be calm & temperate, prevail on them if possible to be so in future? But the more interesting object is the *variance* between us & *G. Britain.* Indeed the former derive their consequence principally from the weight they may have in forming her conduct with respect to us. If they are hostilely dispos'd these circumstances will tend to give them confidence. My letter to *Govr. Harrison* gave you what had taken place in *Canada.*[4] I am strongly impress'd with the hostile disposition *of* that *Court* towards us. Not only what I saw, but the information of all the American gentlemen lately from *G. B.*[5] confirm it, & particularly one of *Maryland* one of *Pennsylva.*, & *Mr. Laurens* who is now with us. The former two have lately return'd to the continent. We are certainly in no condition for *war* &, while we preserve the honor & dignity of the *U. States*, must earnestly endeavor to prevent it. If they will comply with the conditions of the late *Treaty*, as we must on our part do whatever it enjoins, our situation is as happy as we cod. expect it. The sooner we are ascertain'd upon this point the better it will be for us. We must suppose they will comply with the *Treaty* & surrender the *Western Posts* & it is therefore our business to make provision for taking possession of them in the Spring. *The Minister* whom we may order to that *Court* to obtain an answer upon this head & cultivate its good wishes toward us, will we trust inform us by the Spring that the *West:*

Posts will be given up & the troops whom we may raise for that purpose will of course be applied to the garrisoning of them. Many of the *West: Posts* I have seen & think 1200, the smallest number we shod. think of. But yet we have no Congress nor is the prospect better than when I wrote you last. All my associates are here except Grayson. I beg of you to write me weekly & give me your opinion upon these & every other subject which you think worthy of attention. A motion will certainly be made as soon as we have a Congress for its removal hence, to wh. shall we give the preference *N. York* or *Philada.* We know not whom we shall have for *Presidt. of Congs.* The *delegates* of *S. Carolina* think of *Mr. Laurens*, but if I may venture a conjecture from what I have observ'd, with respect to *Mr. Laurens's* intentions I shod. suppose his object was to attain the appointmt. to the *Court of G. Britain;* the rule heretofore adopted in the election of *President* will I think be deviated from,[6] if this shod. be the case it is not improbable *Richd. H. Lee* m[ay] be elected. I have heretofore address'd my letters to Mr. Jones to Richmond but fear from the accounts I have [of] his health he hath not left home. Is this the case? I am with great respect & esteem Dear Sir yr fnd. & servt.

JAS. MONROE

RC (DLC). Cover missing. Docketed. The italicized words are those deciphered by JM, using the code Monroe enclosed in his letter of 7 Nov.

1 Old Fort Stanwix was renamed Fort Schuyler in 1776. For JM's account of the Indian council held there in Sept. 1784 see his letter to Jefferson, 17 Oct. 1784.

2 The French chargé d'affaires, François, Marquis de Barbé-Marbois, had been publicly assaulted by a French citizen on a Philadelphia sidewalk. Marbois's assailant was fined $200 and sentenced to two years in jail, but the French diplomat was dissatisfied because he wanted the culprit turned over to French jurisdiction.

3 The Committee of the States, which was meant to serve as the de facto national government when Congress was not in session, had dissolved after New Englanders Dana and Blanchard, along with Dick of New Jersey, "simply mounted their horses and rode off toward home" on 11 Aug. The Secretary of Congress was chagrined because the semblance of a federal government had "become invisible" (Burnett, *The Continental Congress*, pp. 609–10). On 18 Oct. Governor Harrison had informed the House of Delegates of this "extraordinary proceeding" but hastened to explain the circumstance was not owing to a lack of diligence by the Virginia delegation (Executive Letter Book, p. 411).

4 Monroe's letter of 30 Oct. to Governor Harrison was sent to the House on 11 Nov. (Burnett, *Letters*, VII, 605; Executive Letter Book, pp. 421–22).

5 Monroe used the code number for "Mr. P. Henry," but JM understood the context and made the correction in his decoding.

6 The "rule heretofore adopted in the election of President" was the practice of rotating that office among the state delegations. Peyton Randolph of Virginia served two terms (1774–1775), but no delegate from Georgia, New Hampshire, North

Carolina, or Rhode Island had yet held the office. Nonetheless, Lee was elected on 30 Nov., but only after twelve ballots (*JCC*, XXVII, 649; Burnett, *Letters*, VII, 639). See also *Papers of Madison*, V, 241, 242 n. 8.

Bill Enabling the Executive to Pension Disabled Veterans, with Amendments

[16 November 1784]

WHEREAS the act of Assembly passed in the year 1782 intitled "An Act Concerning Pensioners,"[1] which has been continued by several subsequent acts will expire at the end of the present Session of Assembly, and it is expedient that the same should be further continued

BE IT THEREFORE ENACTED that the act intitled An Act "Concerning Pensioners" shall continue and be in force from and after the expiration thereof, so long as any of the persons who have, or hereafter shall receive annual allowances from this Commonwealth in Consideration of Wounds, shall continue to receive the same.

[6 December 1784]

Amendments proposed by the Committee for Courts of Justice to the Bill "for further continuing the act intitled An Act Concerning Pensioners"
Line the 5th. Strike out from the Word "thereof" to the end of the Bill and insert "for and during the Term of [three][2] years and from thence to the End of the next Session of Assembly and no longer.
To the end of the Bill add ——
AND BE IT FURTHER ENACTED that the Executive shall be and they are hereby authorized and empowered to put on the List of Pensioners with such allowances as to them shall seem just all Regular or Militia Officers and Soldiers who have been wounded or otherwise disabled in the Service of their Country upon application being made to them therefor. And whereas the said recited Act intitled An Act Concerning Pensioners directs the Courts of the several Counties within this Commonwealth to inquire into the bodily ability of all persons receiving annual Pensions from the Public and to certify to the General Assembly whether in their Opinion they ought to be continued on the Pension List
BE IT FURTHER ENACTED that the said Returns shall be made to the

Executive who are hereby authorized to continue or discontinue the said allowances as to them shall seem proper. [So much of any act or acts, as comes within the meaning of this act, is hereby repealed.]²

Ms (Vi). In a clerk's hand. Docketed: "A Bill for further continuing the act intitled 'An Act Concerning Pensioners.'" The bill as amended was printed in Hening, *Statutes*, XI, 446–47.

¹ This bill as amended was reintroduced to implement the resolution JM brought before the House on 3 Dec. 1784. For years the legislature had been bothered with special petitions from wounded veterans and their survivors who sought pensions, and although the paper work was troublesome the General Assembly had beat down previous attempts to divorce this kind of routine matter from the larger problems confronting the lawmakers. As chairman of the Committee for Courts of Justice, JM introduced a routine measure on 16 Nov. continuing the cumbersome 1782 law (Hening, *Statutes*, XI, 146). Apparently widespread dissatisfaction with the old act, which called on the county courts to certify to a veteran's disability, brought on pressure for a change that would relieve the local officials of their final responsibility and at the same time stop the flow of petitions from those veterans or their widows who for a variety of reasons were not certified for eligibility to the state Board of Auditors. Whether JM was the instigator of this reform or merely the advocate of someone else's idea is not certain, but in presenting the first (alphabetically) of over a dozen such petitions received at the Oct. 1784 session JM laid the groundwork for transferring to the governor and Council the power to approve or reject these requests. This new approach radically altered the custom of carrying trivial matters to the General Assembly and reduced the burden placed on the Committee of Claims, which at this Oct. 1784 session had studied over a dozen such petitions. JM introduced this amended bill on 6 Dec., and on 7 Dec. the House made some additions before JM carried the enacted measure to the Senate, which by 13 Dec. had also passed the bill (*JHDV*, Oct. 1784, pp. 14, 25, 59, 60, 68).
² Bracketed words were added by the Committee of the Whole before final passage.

From Richard Henry Lee

TRENTON November 20. 1784

SIR

I wish it were in my power to give you the satisfaction that I know it would afford you to be informed that Congress was assembled and proceeding well with the public business. Unfortunately, we have not yet a Congress, & altho twenty days are elapsed since the time appointed for its meeting, but 4 States have been convened. No doubt Colo. Monroe has informed his Correspondents of the intelligence he received on his Tour to Montreal; Niagara &c. that one reason assign'd for detaining the western posts from the United States was, because Virginia had not repealed her laws that impede the recovery of British debts.[1] It is sincerely to be lamented that our State should be so charged, and it is much to be wished that the Advocates for retaining those laws wd. no longer insist upon furnishing pretext for detaining from the U. S. possessions of such capital importance to the Union as these posts are. I have the honor to inclose you a copy of the treaty lately made at Fort Stanwix with the six nations.[2] It was brought here by Mr. Wolcott, who informs us that the other two Commissioners were gone to Pittsburg to hold a treaty there with the western nations—he apprehends (from the content that appeard at fort Stanwix among some Shawanese chiefs) that the commissioners will not find much difficulty in treating with the western Indians. The accounts that we daily receive of the powerful emigrations from our State to Georgia, to North & South Carolina, & from the interior parts to Kentucki, are very alarming. The causes assigned, are two—the desire of removing from heavy taxes, and the search after land. It certainly becomes our Legislature to consider this point with great attention, and to remove, or lessen the causes that effect the depopulation of the country. Do you not think Sir, that the Taxes might be considerably lessened by funding all our debts, both foreign and domestic. And then, by imposing such Taxes only as will most punctually pay the interest & sink the principal by very slow degrees and for support of the Civil list?[3] This would satisfy the public creditors, because the certainty of receiving the interest will render the principal vendible on good terms. It seems to me, that by this mode, the tax might be considerably lowerd from its present enormous height. I think that I may venture safely to say, that our Revenue, Certificate, and all other taxes, amount in the aggregate to a heavier taxation than prevails in any part of the world! Upon this circumstance, I find some British writers founding the hope of our depopulation. It surprised me a good deal that our last Assembly did not take up and adopt, for the case of our fellow Citizens, the Facilities given by Congress in their Act of the 28th of April last. By this Act (which I understand is before the Assembly) one fourth of the federal demand against us, may be discharged with Certificates of interest for money loaned the U. S. or for interest on liquidated debts of the U. S. If these certificates were by law made receivable in the Revenue tax, it would certainly & considerably facilitate the payment of that Tax.

It seems that the parliament of G. Britain was prorogued without any thing being done respecting our Trade with them, altho a Committee of the privy Council, upon the petition of the W. India planters &

Merchants for a free trade between them & the U. S. had reported an approbation of all the silly, malign commercial restraints upon our trade with their W. India islands, that are to be found in Lord Sheffields book on the Commerce of the two countries.[4]

I have the honor to be, with much esteem and regard, Sir your most humble Servant

RICHARD HENRY LEE.

[Enclosure]

[22 October 1784]

Articles of a Treaty concluded at Fort Stanwix on the 22d. day of October 1784 between Oliver Wolcott, Richard Butler, and Arthur Lee Commissioners plenepotentiary from the United States in Congress Assembled on the one part and the Sachems and Warriors of the Six Nations on the other part.

The United States of America give peace to the Senecas, Mohawks, Onondagas, & Cayugas, and receive them into their protection upon the following conditions.

Article 1st. Six Hostages shall be immediately delivered to the Commissioners by the said nations, to remain in possession of the United States till all the prisoners, white & black, which were taken by the said Senecas, Mohawks, Onondagas and Cayugas, or by any of them, in the late war, from among the people of the United States, shall be delivered up.

Art. 2d. The Oneida and Tuscarora Nations shall be secured in the possession of the Lands on which they are settled.

Art. 3d. A line shall be drawn, beginning at the mouth of a creek about four miles east of Niagara called Oyonwayea or Johnsons landing place upon the Lake named by the Indians Oswego, and by us Ontario. From thence Southerly in a direction always four miles east of the Carrying path between Lake Erie and Ontario to the mouth of Tehoseroron or Buffaloe Creek on Lake Erie. Thence South to the north boundary of the State of Pennsylvania. Thence West to the end of the said north boundary. Thence South along the west boundary of the said State to the river Ohio. The said line from the mouth of Oyonwayea to the Ohio shall be the western boundary of the Lands of the Six Nations, so that the Six Nations shall and do yield to the United States all claims to the country west of the said boundary, and then they shall be secured in the peaceful possession of the lands they inhabit

East and North of the same, reserving only Six miles square round the fort of Oswego to the United States for the support of the same.

Art. 4th. The Commissioners of the United States in consideration of the present circumstances of the Six Nations, and in execution of the humane and liberal views of the United States, upon the signing of the above articles, will order goods to be delivered to the said Six nations for their use and comfort.

RC (DLC). Cover missing. Docketed. The enclosure was docketed by Lee: "Treaty at Fort Stanwix between the United States & the six Nations October 1784."

[1] Monroe wrote a much fuller report of his tour to Jefferson on 1 Nov. than he sent JM on 15 Nov. Monroe told Jefferson: "In Canada I was informed that the commanding officer had received orders not to evacuate the posts . . . a measure said to be founded upon the supposed violation of the treaty by New York and Virginia" (Boyd, *Papers of Jefferson*, VII, 461).

[2] Lee had carefully copied the treaty that Wolcott, Richard Butler, and Arthur Lee had negotiated with the Iroquois, with JM as a witness (JM to Jefferson, 11 Oct. and 17 Oct. 1784).

[3] The idea of "funding all our debts" had been discussed in Congress since 1783, when Robert Morris was searching for ways and means of restoring public credit (Ver Steeg, *Robert Morris*, p. 172; Ferguson, *Power of the Purse*, pp. 209–10). The Grand Committee estimated the total debt was nearly $39,000,000, including principal and interest (*Papers of Madison*, VI, 436–37). Hamilton told Washington Congress was divided into two factions "—one attached to state, the other to Continental politics." The latter delegates were "strenuous advocates for funding the public debt upon solid securities," while the former were only forced into any kind of action "by the clamours of the army and other public creditors" (Syrett and Cooke, *Papers of Hamilton*, III, 318). Congress had made a stab at clearing up the financial woes of the Confederation by passing an act on 28 Apr. 1784 which, as Lee noted here, allowed states full credit on their proportional share of the debt if they paid "three-fourths of any sum . . . in actual money" and the other one-fourth in loan office certificates that could be bought at heavily discounted prices—sometimes for twelve cents on the dollar (*JCC*, XXVI, 312). A strong faction in Virginia was opposed to any funding plan until the state's claims against the U. S. related to the Northwest Territory conquest had been settled.

[4] "Lord Sheffields book" was the work by John Baker Holroyd, Earl of Sheffield, *Observations on the Commerce of the American States with Europe* . . . (London, 1783).

To James Monroe

RICHMOND [ca. 20] Novr. 1784[1]

DEAR SIR

Your favor without date was brought by thursday's post. It inclosed a Cypher for which I thank you & which I shall make use as occasion may require, though from the nature of our respective situations, its cheif value will be derived from your use of it.[2] Gel. Washington arrived here on Sunday last, and the Marquis on thursday. The latter came from Boston in a French frigate. They have both been addressed & entertained in the best manner that circumstances would admit. These attentions and the balloting for public offices have consumed the greatest part of the past week. Mr. Jones is put into the place of Mr. Short. Mr. Roan[e] and Mr. M. Selden are to go into those of Mr. M. Smith & Col. Christian who are the victims to that part of the Constitution which directs a triennial purgation of the Council. The vote is not to take effect till the Spring, but was made now in consequence of the discontinuance of the Spring Session.[3] The rejected Candidates were Col: Bland, Cys. Griffin, G. Webb, W. C. Nicholas, Mr. Brackenridge, Col: Carrington. The latter was within one vote of Mr. Selden. Col: B. Mr. N. & Mr. B. had as nearly as I recollect between 20 & 30 votes. Mr. G. & Mr. W. very few. Mr. H. Innes late Judge of the Kentucky Court is to succeed W. D. late Attorney General in that District.[4] His competitor was Mr. Stewart who was about 15 votes behind.[5] I am Dr. Sir Yrs. sincerely

J. MADISON JR.

RC (DLC). Docketed by JM. Addressed to Monroe "in Congress."

[1] On his calendar of correspondence with Monroe, JM failed to enter the date of this letter, but it obviously was written on Saturday or Sunday, when JM habitually caught up on his correspondence.

[2] Why JM alludes to Monroe's letter of 7 Nov. as undated is unexplainable. That letter enclosed the 99-word code which JM mentions in the next sentence.

[3] At its May 1784 session the General Assembly passed an act eliminating the "Spring Session" by providing for one meeting to begin "on the third Monday in October annually" (Hening, *Statutes*, XI, 388).

[4] Harry Innes was chosen to replace "W. D."—Walker Daniel—who had been killed by the Indians in Aug. 1784 (Executive Letter Book, p. 413; Abernethy, *Western Lands and the American Revolution*, p. 301).

[5] The journal does not indicate who the other nominees for the Kentucky post were, but Archibald Stuart appears to have been in contention (*JHDV*, Oct. 1784, p. 27).

From Andrew Dunscomb

COMMISSIONERS OFFICE; RICHMOND NOV: 24. 1784.

SIR,

To accomodate the late Officers of the Regular Line of this State and others on their settlements, I have to request Your influence for leave to bring in a Bill granting power to me to administer the necessary Oaths or Affirmations in the execution of my official duties.[1] With esteem and regard I am &c

ANDREW DUNSCOMB[2]

FC (Vi). A letterbook copy, addressed to JM, "In assembly."

[1] On 15 Nov. JM was appointed a member of a special committee of five directed "to inquire into the progress made by the solicitor with the continental commissioner." On 30 Dec. committee chairman Edward Carrington reported on the unsatisfactory condition in which nonexistent records and restrictive directives had placed the commissioner, and successfully moved that the Virginia delegates in Congress be instructed to procure the authority Dunscomb sought along with additional powers. The Senate concurred on the following day (*JHDV*, Oct. 1784, pp. 23, 97–98, 99).

[2] Maj. Andrew Dunscomb (ca. 1758–1802), a native New Yorker and Revolutionary veteran, succeeded Zephaniah Turner when in Aug. 1783 the latter resigned as the confederation commissioner appointed to settle accounts with Virginia. Later settling in Richmond, Dunscomb from 1792 to 1795 served successively as common councilman, alderman, auditor-treasurer, and mayor (*Va. Gazette*, 8 May 1782; Vi: "Records of the Common Hall," 2 Ms vols., I, 254, 273; II, 7; ViHi: Madge Goodrich, "Mayors of Richmond," typescript, pp. 11–12; Andrew H. Christian, Jr., *A Brief History of the Christian, Dunscomb, and Duval Families* [Richmond, 1909]).

From Richard Henry Lee

TRENTON November 26, 1784

DEAR SIR,

I received your agreeable letter the day after mine of the 28th. instant had been dispatched.[1] I thank you Sir for the very particular and satisfactory information that you have favord me with. It is certainly comfortable to know that the Legislature of our country is engaged in beneficial pursuits—for I conceive that the Gen. Assessment, and a wise digest of our militia laws are very important concerns: the one to secure our peace, and the other our morals. Refiners may weave as fine a web of reason as they please, but the experience of all times shows Religion to be the guardian of morals—and he must be a very inattentive observer in our Country, who does not see that avarice is accomplishing the destruction of religion, for want of a legal obligation to contribute something to its support. The declaration of Rights, it seems to me, rather contends against forcing modes of faith and forms of worship, than against compelling contribution for the support of religion in general. I fully agree with the presbyterians, that true freedom embraces the Mahomitan and the Gentoo as well as the Christian religion.[2] And upon this liberal ground I hope our Assembly will conduct themselves. I believe there is no doubt but that the population of our country depends eminently upon our Revenue laws, they therefore, demand intense consideration. It is natural for men to fly from oppression to ease, and whilst our taxes are extremely heavy, and North Carolina & Georgia pay little or no tax, it is not to be wonderd that so many of our people flock to these States & unfortunately they are carrying to Georgia & South Carolina the Cultivation of Tobacco. I do not mean by this, that we should suffer ill example to prevent us from honorably and punctually paying our debts. But I think that we may fairly practise here, as other Nations the most honest do—I mean, exactly to pay the interest, and slowly to sink the principal. An attempt to do the latter too suddenly will ruin, by depopulating, the country. The only mode appears to be, a funding of the whole debt, so as certainly to pay the interest, and slowly the principal. Cannot a sinking fund be brought to bear upon the latter, by throwing all overflowings of taxes into a Reservoir for gathering interest upon interest? I suppose that at all events, the facilities offerd by Congress in their Act of the 28th. of April last will be among the amendments to the Revenue law this Session.

The people have certainly sufferd much hitherto by not knowing in season what taxes are lawfully demandable from them. For want of this information, numbers are compelled to submit to the extortion and abuses of Collectors. The Treasurer used formerly to publish annually in the papers what were to be the Taxes of the year, and this practise was then very useful.[3] But at present, the dispersion of newspapers is so uncertain, that information thro that channel would reach but few. A Statement from the Treasury printed in the way of Handbills, to be put up at the Court-Houses & churches, might perhaps furnish the requisite information, & save the people from extensive abuse. I am very happy to know, for the honor of our country, that there is a probability of the impeding laws being again taken under deliberation. What I wrote to you in my last upon this subject, is a most serious consideration, and the inclosed paragraphs, taken from a late paper, will shew you how quickly the fame of our proceedings travels, and the effect likely to be produced upon our Commerce![4]

By the 5th. article of the Confederation, the annual meeting of Congress is to be on the first Monday in November, and by our Act establishing one yearly meeting of the Assembly on the third monday in October; you will see Sir, that there is very little probability of Virginia being represented in Congress for some time after its federal day of meeting. So that it becomes necessary to consider this matter.[5] I suppose that either the Assemblies time of meeting must be altered, or the Delegates for the ensuing federal year be chosen this present Session. We have not yet made a Congress but we have some reason to expect eight States on Monday next. I understand that Spain means to insist upon the exclusive navigation of the Mississippi, which will render the exploring our western waters of the greater importance.

I am dear Sir, with great esteem and regard Your most obedient and very humble Servant

RICHARD HENRY LEE

P.S. If the election of Counsellors is not over, may I be permitted to suggest what I realy believe will improve and fortify the counsels of that Board.[6] It is, that Major Gen. Gates be appointed a Member of it. He has a pretty good estate in Berkeley, is a single Man & therefore not withheld from due attendance by domestic considerations. But above all, he is a Man of great worth, solid judgement, and sound attachments to America. A propos—It is by many here suggested as a very necessary Step for Congress to take—The calling upon the States to form a Convention for the Sole purpose of revising the Confederation so far as to enable Congress to execute with more energy, effect, & vigor, the powers assigned it, than it appears by experience that they can do under the present state of things.[7] It has been observed, why do not Congress recommend the necessary alteration to the States as is proposed in the Confederation? The friends to Convention answer—It has been already done in some instances, but in vain. It is proposed to let Congress go on in the mean time as usual. I shall be glad of your opinion on this point, it being a very important one.

R. H. LEE

RC (DLC). Cover missing.

[1] JM apparently reported to Lee on the legislative session in a now-missing letter written ca. 13 Nov. 1784. Lee had in the meantime written JM on 20 Nov., which Lee incorrectly alludes to here as "mine of the 28th instant." Ballagh, *Letters of Richard Henry Lee*, II, 304, silently made the correction.

[2] Lee wrote "the Xn religion." Of course, the whole subject of a general assessment was a tender point, since Lee and JM took opposing sides on the question of an assessment to support all churches.

[3] Lee recalled the actions of both John Robinson and Robert Carter Nicholas, colonial treasurers who published tax information in the *Va. Gazette*, 12 Feb. 1762, and 21 Mar. 1771 (Purdie & Dixon and Rind editions).

[4] Lee's enclosure "from a late paper" is missing.

5 The General Assembly had tried to deal with the problem of representation in Congress at its last May 1784 session. The "act for regulating the appointment of delegates to congress" provided for the election of five delegates to the Nov. 1784 session of Congress, "three of whom, at least, shall be constantly attending to discharge the duties of their office" (Hening, *Statutes*, XI, 365–66). What Lee meant was that the legislature was habitually tardy, and that by the time it convened and appointed delegates more weeks would elapse. JM saw the problem but in his 11 Dec. 1784 letter asked Lee if the alternative, "the appointing of delegates a year before they are to serve," was a practical solution. Nonetheless, the General Assembly passed acts in its next two sessions to meet the problem through 1788, when the new federal Constitution made further action unnecessary (Hening, *Statutes*, XII, 26, 243).

6 A vacancy on the Virginia Council of State, created by William Short's resignation, had been filled by the election of Joseph Jones on 19 Nov. 1784 (*JHDV*, Oct. 1784, p. 30).

7 JM's guarded reply to Lee's suggestion for a revising convention indicates a perception that public opinion was not yet ready for drastic steps to bolster the Confederation. Lee acknowledged this widespread apathy himself in his follow-up letter to JM of 27 Dec. 1784.

From John Francis Mercer

TRENTON Novr 26th. 84

DEAR SIR

The Gentlemen from the Eastward have at length made their appearance & I expect in a day or two a Congress will be once more form'd. This commencement however has discovered so great a relaxation in the Confœderal springs that I doubt the machine will not be long kept in motion, unless great & effectual repairs are made. For my part I have no hopes but in a convocation of the States.[1] In this measure I yet see safety, it is the disposition of the people of America to place their Confœderal Government on the most respectable basis, & the patriot fire is not yet extinguish'd, but I do not know how long it will last— there will be a motion made early in the ensuing Congress for such a Convention.

I woud suggest to you a subject on which I find my Colleagues & myself concurr & indeed which we have determin'd to mention to our friends in the Legislature.[2] The recess of Congress the last year, was the first I believe since the Revolution & the situation of the members consequently new & unexpected both by themselves & the State. I must confess that I consider the with drawing the allowance during that period, as unworthy the dignity of the Government & as it is injurious to her representatives, it will in the end prove detrimental to her interest.

When Gentlemen quit home & their domestic employments—& are carried to a considerable distance from their own State—it cannot be expected that their presence for a Small interval, will be of any service to their private affairs—in fact they are by their appointments disengaged thoroughly from all pursuits but their public avocations & their style of expen[ces] cannot be temporarily suppress'd or altered for the time of this recess. I am therefore not only interestedly but politically of opinion that it woud be the wisest & most honourable conduct for the Legislatu[re] to pay us during the recess altogether. So. Carolina, make an allow[ance] by the year, nearly equal to the extent of our appointment on the supposition we charg'd for every day, & yet their Members complain of the inadequacy of the provision. Mr. Hardy & Colo. Monroe tell me they have suggested this matter to their friends. If they shoud view in the light I do the subject will be probably agitated. I know you have been so long subjected to the inconveniences of bad & insufficient pay, that I can add nothing your own reflections will not readily furnish.[3] Believe me Dr. Sir Yr. very Affectionate frie[nd] & h[umbl]e Ser.

JOHN F. MERCER

RC (DLC). Cover missing. Docketed by JM.

[1] There had been talk of "a convocation of the States" in Congress for over a year. The Massachusetts legislature had sounded the call for a national conclave to discuss "matters of common concern" in the spring of 1783. Then Mercer had opposed the idea "as a dangerous precedent" but JM had said he favored "a general Convention" if the purpose was "to strengthen the fœderal Constitution" (*Papers of Madison*, VI, 424–25, 426 n. 7).

[2] The Committee of the States had dissolved—illegally—in mid-Aug., but delegate Mercer went on a vain search for a congressional headquarters almost a month later. He went to Annapolis and "thence to Philadelphia, in search of the committee, yet found never a vestige of it" (Burnett, *The Continental Congress*, p. 610). Mercer had expected to be paid a delegate's $8.00 per diem salary despite the phantom nature of Congress. It seems obvious that the state treasurer had balked at advancing funds to Mercer on the ground that Congress had not been in session after 11 Aug. Perhaps in a missing letter JM had explained why the $400 owed him by Mercer still had not been paid (Mercer to JM, 12 Nov. 1784).

[3] JM had altogether too much knowledge of "the inconveniences of bad & insufficient pay" as a Virginia delegate from 1780 to 1783. During that time JM found the meager salary inadequate and had to draw on his father for supplementary income (*Papers of Madison*, IV, 231, 256; V, 72–73; VI, 229).

Preamble and Portion of an Extradition Bill

[26 November 1784]

WHEREAS it is the desire of the good people of this Commonwealth in all cases to manifest their reverance for the law of Nations, to cultivate amity and peace as far as may depend on them between the United States and foreign powers, and to support the dignity and energy of the fœderal Constitution:

Be it enacted by the General Assembly that if any Citizen or inhabitant of this Commonwealth shall go beyond the limits of the U. S. within the acknowledged jurisdiction of any Civilized Nation and shall within the same commit any crime for which in the judgment of the U. S. in Congress assd. the law of Nations or any Treaty between the U. S. and a foreign Nation, requires him to be surrendered to the offended Nation, and shall thereafter flee within the limits of this Commonwealth; and the Sovereign of the offended Nation shall exhibit to the U. S. in Congs. Assembd. due and satisfactory evidence of the crime, with a demand of the offender to be tried & punished where the same was committed; and the U. S. in Congs. assd. shall thereupon notify such demand to the Executive of this State, and call for the surrender of such offender, the Governor with the advice of the Council of State is hereby authorized to cause him to be apprehended and conveyed and delivered to such person or persons as the United States in Congress assembled may prescribe.[1]

Ms (Vi). In JM's hand. Four additional paragraphs were added in committees and the whole bill titled "An act punishing certain offences injurious to the tranquility of this commonwealth" (Hening, *Statutes*, XI, 471–73).

[1] JM must have written his preamble after the first extradition bill offered on 12 Nov. had been rejected by the House (JM to Monroe, 27 Nov. 1784). JM's additions were substituted for portions of an earlier text, which had been undergoing revision in the Committee of the Whole (*JHDV*, Oct. 1784, pp. 41, 42, 43). After the House approved JM's version (41 to 37), further alterations of the bill probably were made before the substitute was brought before the House on 27 Nov. Joseph Jones was heavily involved in drafting the bill and called its third reading "a fiery trial." The purpose of the bill, Jones explained, was "to prevent our people transgressing agst. the Spaniard[s] which they are disposed to do from all accounts, and to remove doubts in the Executive shod. such demand be made" (Jones to Monroe, 27 Nov. 1784 [ViW]). The final tally was 44 ayes to 43 noes. "This measure was a bitter pill for the individualistic Westerners, to whom extradition seemed an infraction of the basic right of trial by jury of the vicinage" (Nevins, *American States during and after the Revolution*, p. 344). Nevins gave Henry credit for passage of the bill, but this is unlikely since Henry had been chosen governor ten days earlier and had then left the House for a visit with his

family before taking office on 21 Dec. (Meade, *Patrick Henry*, II, 283). William C. Rives gave JM credit for the bill as "suggested and proposed by Mr. Madison" (*Life of James Madison*, I, 592).

To James Madison, Sr.

RICHD. Novr. 27. 1784

HOND. SIR

Having a moments time to drop you a line I inform you that the Bill for confirming surveys agst. subsequent entries has been negatived by a large majority, rather on the principle that it was unnecessary & retrospective, than that it was unjust in itself. On the contrary all the principal gentlemen were of opinion that it was just, but already provided for by the law.[1] Mr. Innes the late Judge of the Kentucky Court, in particular told me he thought such surveys could not be overset. You will have heard of the vote in favr. of the Genl. Assesst.[2] The bill is not yet brought in & I question whether it will, or if so, whether it will pass. This day a vote passed without a dissent for Circuit Cou[r]ts.[3] What opposition may be made to its passage I know not. I have not yet found time to do your business at the Land Office. I expected before this to have seen my brother A. & Majr. Moore. I have been a little indisposed for a few days with a bad cold which still continues, otherwise I am well. M. Joseph will tell you the price of Tobo. I think it will rise. With my regards to the family I am Dr. Sir your affect. son

J MADISON JR

RC (DLC). Cover missing. Docketed by JM.

[1] The elder Madison was probably instrumental in circulating the Orange and Culpeper County petitions which possibly JM laid before the House on 4 Nov. 1784 as protests against the injustice of the 1779 law governing land patents. The petitions called for clear instruction so that titles could be obtained on the basis of previous surveys and for ways to prevent "the collusions and illegal practices between the principal surveyors and their deputies" (*JHDV*, Oct. 1784, p. 11). The Committee on Propositions and Grievances held these requests reasonable and ordered a bill written. What apparently happened was that Harry Innes, who was elected the Kentucky district attorney, persuaded the delegates a revision was unwise. The law had indeed bedeviled absentee landowners while creating a harvest for Kentucky lawyers. For a brief explanation of the Madison family investment in Kentucky lands, see Ralph Ketcham, *James Madison: A Biography* (New York, 1971), pp. 145–46.

[2] The House of Delegates passed, 47 to 32, a resolution calling for "a moderate tax or contribution, annually, for the support of the christian religion," on Nov.

11 (*JHDV*, Oct. 1784, p. 19). JM was in the minority that opposed the proposed "General assessment" bill that was carried over to the Oct. 1785 session.

³ A resolution passed by the House of Delegates held "That for the more convenient administration of justice throughout this Commonwealth, circuit courts ought to be established" (*JHDV*, Oct. 1784, p. 43). JM was appointed chairman of the committee charged with preparing the Assize Court bill of 2 Dec. 1784, which passed despite a strong undercurrent of opposition.

To James Monroe

RICHMOND Novr. 27. 1784.

DEAR SIR

Your favor of the 15th inst: came to hand by thurday's post. Mine by the last post acknowledged your preceding one. The umbrage given to the Comsrs. of the U. S. by the negociations of N. Y. with the Indians was not altogether unknown to me, though I am less acquainted with the circumstances of it than your letter supposes.¹ The Idea which I at present have of the affair leads me to say that as far as N. Y. may claim a right of treating with Indians for the purchase of lands within her limits, she has the confederation on her side; as far as she may have exerted that right in contravention of the Genl. Treaty, or even unconfidentially with the Comisrs. of Congs. she has violated both duty & decorum. The fœderal articles give Congs. the exclusive right of *managing all affairs* with the Indians *not members* of any State, under a proviso, that the *Legislative authority*, of the State within its own limits be not violated. By Indian[s] not members of a State, must be meant those, I conceive who do not live within the body of the Society, or whose Persons or property form no objects of its laws. In the case of Indians of this description the only restraint on Congress is imposed by the *Legislative authority* of the State. If this proviso be taken in its full latitude, it must destroy the authority of Congress altogether, since no act of Congs. within the limits of a State can be conceived which will not in some way or other encroach upon the authority [of the] States. In order then to give some meaning to both parts of the sentence, as a known rule of interpretation requires, we must restrain this proviso to some particular view of the parties. What was this view? My answer is that it was to save to the States their right of preemption of lands from the Indians. My reasons are. 1. That this was the principal right formerly exerted by the Colonies with regard to the Indians. 2. that it was a right asserted by the laws as well as the proceedings of all of them, and therefore being most familiar, wd. be most likely to be in contemplation of the Parties; 3. that being of most consequence to the States individually, and least inconsistent with the general powers of Congress, it was most likely to be made a ground of Compromise. 4. it has been always said that the proviso came from the Virga. Delegates, who wd naturally be most vigilant over the territorial rights of their Constituents.[2] But whatever may be the true boundary between the authority of Congs. & that of N. Y. or however indiscreet the latter may have been, I join entirely with you in thinking that temperance on the part of the former will be the wisest policy. I concur with you equally with regard to the ignominious secession at Annapolis.[3] As Congs. are too impotent to punish such offences, the task must finally be left to the States and experience has shown in the case of Howel, that the interposition of Congs. agst. an offender instead of promoting his chastisements, may give him a significancy wch. he otherwise wd. never arrive at and may induce a State to patronize an act which of their own accord they would have punished.[4] I am sorry to find the affair of Mr. de Marb––s taking so serious a face. As the insult was comitted within the jurisdiction of Pena. I think you are right in supposing the offender could not be transferred to another jurisdiction for punishment. The proper questions therefore are 1. whether the existing law was fully put in force agst. him by Pa.? 2. whether clear provision has been made by that State agst. like contingenc[i]es? Nothing seems to be more difficult under our new Governments, than to impress on the attention of our Legislatures a due sense of those duties which spring from our relation to foreign nations. Several of us have been labouring much of late in the G. Assembly here to provide for a case with which we are every day threaten'd by the eagourness of our disorderly Citizens for Spanish plunder & Spanish blood. It has been proposed to authorize Congs. whenever satisfactory proof shall be given to them by a foreign power of such a crime being committed by our Citizens within its jurisdiction as by the law of Nations call for Surrender of the Offender, & the for[e]ign power shall actually make the demand, that the Executive may at the instance of Congs. apprehend & deliver up the offender. That there are offences of that class is clearly stated by Vattel in particular, & that the business ought to pass through Congs. is equally clear. The proposition was a few days ago rejected in Committee of the whole. To day in the report of the Comme. it has been agreed to by a small majority. This is the most material question that has agitated us during the week past.[5] The Bill for a Religious Assesst. has not been yet brought in. Mr. Henry the father of the Scheme is gone up to his

Seat for his family & will no more sit in the H. of Delegates, a circumstance very inauspicious to his offspring. An attempt will be made for circuit Courts, & Mr. Jones has it in contemplation to try whether any change has taken place in the Sentiments of the H. of D on the subject of the Treaty.[6] He will write to you by this post & I refer to him for what I may have omitted. With sincere regard & esteem I am Dr. Sir Yr. friend & servt.

J. MADISON JR.

RC (DLC). Docketed by JM. Addressed to Monroe "in Congress."

[1] Monroe assumed that JM understood the reaction of some delegates in Congress toward what appeared to them as state interference in Indian affairs. The New York commissioners assembled at old Fort Stanwix but were not able to complete their negotiations because the Mohawk chief, Brant, was convinced that the tribes should deal directly with representatives of the Confederation (Randolph C. Downes, *Council Fires on the Upper Ohio* [Pittsburgh, 1940], pp. 288–90). Some delegates in Congress considered that the New York commissioners were acting in a spirit of defiance rather than cooperation (Burnett, *Letters*, VII, 584 n. 3, 587, 613).

[2] The Articles of Confederation granted Congress "the sole and exclusive right and power" of "regulating the trade and managing all affairs with the Indians, not members of any of the states, provided that the legislative right of any state within its own limits be not infringed or violated. . . ." (Art. IX). This wording allowed the Virginia General Assembly to declare on 9 June 1779 that "the Commonwealth of Virginia has the exclusive right of a pre-emption, from the Indians, of all lands within the limits of its own chartered territory, . . . and that such exclusive right of pre-emption will, and ought to be, maintained by this Commonwealth to the utmost of its power" (*JHDV*, May 1779, p. 39). In short, Virginia was denying the claims made under any Indian treaties not sanctioned by its own laws or emissaries, and particularly the early Treaty of Fort Stanwix (3 Nov. 1768) which land speculators were still using to dispute Virginia's jurisdiction over its western lands. As JM discerned, consistency demanded that Virginia recognize the right of New York to make Indian treaties although it was an awkward situation for a nationalistic lawmaker who ordinarily was impatient with the claimants of states rights.

[3] The "ignominious secession at Annapolis" was the apparently unannounced departure of three members of the Committee of the States on 11 Aug. 1784 (Dana, Dick, and Blanchard) who left Annapolis and thereby effectively dissolved the shadow government supposed to operate between sessions of Congress (see Monroe to JM, 15 Nov. 1784). Actually, Dana had told the Massachusetts Assembly he was ill and could not stay at his post in Congress, adding, "I wish another member might come on to supply my place" (Burnett, *Letters*, VII, 566).

[4] The right of David Howell, a Rhode Island delegate, to serve as a member of Congress was challenged under the provision that no delegate was eligible to serve for "more than three years in any term of six years" (Art. V). Howell, who had earlier flouted the rules of Congress, was challenged to two duels but held on to his seat when a tired Congress decided further wrangling was useless (Burnett, *Letters*, VII, 534, 536; *Papers of Madison*, V, 372–73).

[5] With the affair involving Marbois in mind, the General Assembly had passed an extradition act on a third reading earlier in the day by a vote of 44 to 43—"a small majority" indeed (*JHDV*, Oct. 1784, p. 42).

6 Joseph Jones was the prime mover in an effort to resolve the British debt problem so that Great Britain could not use the nonpayment of old debts as an excuse for occupation of western frontier outposts in violation of the Treaty of Paris. Jones's resolutions called for installment payment of the debts and were soon discussed in the Committee of the Whole, and then became the basis of a bill which was rejected on a technicality (JM to Jefferson, 9 Jan. 1785).

From George Washington

MOUNT VERNON 28th Novr. 84.

GENTLEMEN,

After the several conversations we have had on the subject of inland navigation; and the benefits which would, probably, be derived from a commercial intercourse with the Western territory; I shall make no apology for giving you the trouble of the enclosed.[1]

It is matter of regret to me, however, that I cannot accompany them with some explanations & observations. It was intended these papers should have met me at Richmond. They missed me on the road thither — travelled back to Baltimore — returned — and were put into my hands at the moment I was setting off for Annapolis; to which place I mean to accompany the Marqs. de la Fayette on his return to New York where he expects to embark, about the middle of next month, for France.

I could not think of withholding these Papers until my return, as I shall probably accompany the Marquis from Annapolis to Baltimore. Therefore, in the order I receive[d], I send them to you. Your own judgment in this business will be the best guide — but in one word, it should seem to me, that if the public cannot take it up with efficient funds, & without those delays which might be involved by a limping conduct, it had better be placed in the hands of a corporate Company. What encouragements, and what powers, to give this Company, deserve all that consideration which I perswade myself you, Gentlemen, will bestow.

The Maryland Assembly is now sitting. If I should return in time, I will have the honor of writing to you again on this subject — in the meanwhile, if your leizure will permit, I should be glad to know your Sentimts. on, and what will be the issue of, this business. With very sincere esteem and regard I have the honor to be Gentn. Yr. Most Obedt Hble Ser

GO: WASHINGTON

P. S. As your Assembly are upon a Militia Law, I send you the thoughts of the Baron de Steuben which I found here upon my return from Richmond[2]

GW.

RC (NNC). Addressed "James Madison Esquire—or in his absence Joseph Jones Esquire At Richmond." Docketed by JM. The enclosure is missing.

[1] Washington's enclosure was undoubtedly the memorial from "sundry inhabitants" of Virginia and Maryland which JM probably laid before the House of Delegates on 4 Dec. (*JHDV*, Oct. 1784, p. 58). Washington had been in Richmond earlier in the month lobbying for legislation that would establish a state-regulated, but privately owned Potomac navigation company. JM became floor manager for the legislation after Jones was elected to the Council of State and subsequently resigned his House seat. The memorial stressed "the practicability and importance of the work" and asked for an act of incorporation with a perpetual grant of tolls to the investors (JM to Jefferson, 9 Jan. 1785). JM was ill in late Dec. and some of the burden of managing the Potomac navigation bill fell on William Grayson when efforts were made to coordinate the Maryland legislature's work into a Virginia law. For further information on the canal scheme see Alexander Crosby Brown, "America's Greatest Eighteenth Century Engineering Achievement: The Potowmack Company's Canal at Great Falls is Today's 'Magnificent Wreck,'" *Virginia Cavalcade*, XII, no. 4 (1963), 40–47; Corra Bacon-Foster, *Early Chapters in the Development of the Potomac Route to the West* (Washington, 1912), pp. 33–233; and Grace L. Nute, ed., "Washington and the Potomac: Manuscripts of the Minnesota Historical Society [1754] 1769–1796," *AHR*, XXVIII (1922–23), 497–519, 705–22.

[2] Von Steuben's missing "thoughts" may have been useful for JM since he was serving on a committee appointed 2 Nov. to revise the militia laws (*JHDV*, Oct. 1784, p. 8). The antiquated militia statute, a carry-over from colonial days, was replaced by a comprehensive act passed during this session (Hening, *Statutes*, XI, 476–94).

Bill Extending the Alien Veterans' Land Rights

[30 November 1784]

For extending the benefit of lands granted by the laws of this Commonwealth to Officers and Soldiers who have served during the late war to their representatives or devisees who may be aliens. Be it enacted that if any such alien representative or devisee shall on or before the   day of   or in case he or she be under the age of twenty one years within   after having attained such age become a citizen of this Commonwealth, he or she shall inherit or take such land in the same manner as if at the death of such officer or soldier, he or she were a Citizen of this Commonwealth; and if any such alien representative or devisee, instead of becoming a Citizen of this Commonwealth, shall chuse rather to dispose of such land, he or she is hereby authorized at any time before the   day of   or in case of infancy within   after attaining the age of twenty one years either by themselves or their attornies duly authorised therein to sell & convey the same in fee simple to any person or persons being a Citizen or Citizens of this or any other of the United States in as effectual a manner as if such alien representative or devisee were at the time of such conveyance a citizen of this Commonwealth.[1]

Ms (Vi). JM's hand. Docketed by JM: "A Bill For extending to the Representatives & devisees being aliens, of officers or Soldiers who have served during the late war, the benefit of lands granted by the laws of this Commonwealth to such officers & Soldiers." John Beckley dated the docket on 30 Nov. and noted: "Read the first Time."

[1] JM was named to the committee appointed on 29 Nov. to draft this bill. He prepared this measure overnight and presented it the following day (*JHDV*, Oct. 1784, p. 46). The bill passed its three readings, and was carried by JM to the Senate on 2 Dec. There the measure languished and finally died when "the tedious Session" ended on 7 Jan. 1785 (JM to Jefferson, 9 Jan. 1785).

From Philip Mazzei

WILLIAMSBURGO pmo: Xbre 1784

CARO E DEGNO AMICO,

La necessità non à legge. I favori che ò bisogno da voi, non posso ottenergli da altri. La lettera per Mr. Hennin deve spedirsi dall'Incaricato degli Affari di Francia nel plico della Corte, e voi sapete che ancor non conosco Mr. de Marbois. Quella per Mr. Jefferson dubito che possa andar sicura se non per il mezzo di qualche Membro del Congresso, ed io non ò familiarità bastante con veruno de quei Signori onde prendermi la libertà d'includergliela. Fatemi dunque voi, caro Amico, il favore di spedirle sabato prossimo, una a Mr. de Marbois, l'altra a qualcheduno in Congresso; e se credete proprio di francarle per delicatezza, fatelo pure, chè io vi rimborserò alla prima occasione. Ma prima vorrei che leggeste l'una e l'altra, come pure quella diretta al Mari; e se Edmond avesse tempo di leggerle anch'esso, gradirei molto che se ne dasse l'incomodo, e vi sarò obbligato se glie ne fate la proposizione. So le vostre varie, grandi, e continue occupazioni; non mi meraviglio, e non mi lagno che non mi abbiate resposto all'antecedente: ma vi prego di 2. linee ora a posta corrente, significandomi se verrete qui dopo la sessione, o se posso sperare d'incontrarvi a Mansfield, di dove passerò per andare fino a Filadelfia tra 3 settimane in circa. Addio car:mo Amico. Tutto vostro

F. MAZZEI

N. B. Abbiate la bontà di sigillare le 3. lettere prima di spedirle. [on cover of letter:] Ò veduto l'Amico a cui vi avevo pregato di mostrar le lettere.

CONDENSED TRANSLATION

Mazzei begs for JM's help in delivering three letters: one to Hennin by means of the French Chargé d'Affaires and his diplomatic pouch, one to Jefferson by the hands of a member of Congress, and the third to Mari. He asks JM to show the three letters to Edmund Randolph, but in a postscript on the cover adds that he has since shown them to Randolph himself. He would like to know if JM plans to come to Williamsburg after the current session or if he can hope to meet him at Mansfield on his way to Philadelphia in about three weeks. He hopes that JM will answer by return mail, although he still has not received an answer to his previous letter [presumably the one of 15 Nov.].

RC (DLC). Addressed to "Col: James Madison [at] Richmond."

Resolutions Providing for a Bust of Lafayette

IN THE HOUSE OF DELEGATES   the 1st. December 1784

WHEREAS it was unanimously Resolved on the 17th. day of December 1781, that a Bust of the Marquis De la Fayette, be directed to be made in Paris of the best Marble employed for such purposes with the following inscription.

"This Bust was voted on the 17th. day of December 1781 by the General Assembly of the State of Virginia, to the Honorable the Marquis De la Fayette (Major General in the service of the United States of America and late Commander in Chief of the Army of the United States in Virginia) as a lasting Monument of his merit and their gratitude;"

RESOLVED unanimously that the Governor with the advice of the Council be authorized and desired to defray the expence of carrying the said vote, into execution out of the fund allotted for the contingencies of Government; that he cause the said Bust to be presented in the name of this Commonwealth, to the City of Paris, with a request that the same may be accepted and preserved in some public place of the said City.

RESOLVED unanimously, that as a further mark of the lasting esteem of this Commonwealth for the illustrious qualities and services of the Marquis De la Fayette, the Governor with the advice of the Council be authorized and desired to cause another Bust of him with a similar Inscription to be procured by draught on the said Fund, and that the same when procured be fixed in such Public Place at the seat of Government as may hereafter be appointed for the erection of the Statue voted by the General Assembly to General Washington.[1]

Ms (Vi). In a clerk's hand.

[1] JM carried these resolutions to the Senate and apparently sent them to Lafayette on 4 Dec. Henceforth there would be action. Houdon, who was engaged to do the work, charged 1,000 crowns for the first bust and 3,000 livres for the second completed in 1787 (Boyd, *Papers of Jefferson*, XI, 560, 673). The Paris marble was destroyed during the French Revolution but the other bust is still on display in the Virginia capitol at Richmond (Brant, *Madison*, II, 336).

Bill for the Establishment of Courts of Assize

EDITORIAL NOTE

JM was chairman of the House committee for Courts of Justice, and carried a burden of work in the October 1784 session of the legislature that ordinarily would have been assigned a delegate who practiced law. However, JM's lack of formal legal training did not deter his colleagues from giving him a lawyer's work. JM's concern for this bill creating a circuit court system was not focused on its content, but rather on its secret opposition. Jefferson had proposed a court of assize, or circuit court, in the bill creating the General Court in 1776, only to have it eliminated by the ensuing session of the legislature (Boyd, *Papers of Jefferson*, I, 628–41). In recounting the course of the 1784 bill through the House, JM spoke of the measure as "nearly a transcript from the bill originally penned in 1776 by Mr. [Edmund] Pendleton," who was on the Committee of Revisors along with Jefferson and George Wythe (JM to Jefferson, 9 Jan. 1785). The term, "courts of assize," was buried deep in Anglo-French antiquity and the use of this ancient title in itself reveals something about Virginians' ideas on the conservatism of law. Perhaps the use of an old term for an innovation was adjudged necessary by Jefferson and the revisors.

JM introduced the Assize Court bill on 2 December, then pushed it through the General Assembly. The law was too drastic a change, however, and never went into effect. As JM noted nine months later, this legal reform was endangered by "the diversity of opinions" among its supporters along with the opposition of "those who mask a secret aversion to any reform under a zeal for such a one as they know will be rejected" (JM to Jefferson, 20 Aug. 1785). Operation of the courts was first postponed until 1787, then until

1788, and finally the law was repealed in 1788 without having ever been in force (Hening, *Statutes*, XII, 45, 267, 497).

One legislative hurdle for the bill, as JM later explained, was a belief held in the Senate that circuit courts ought to have "independent and complete jurisdiction," with only special appeals to higher courts. In the House of Delegates objectors claimed the assize courts furnished "but a partial relief to suitors, and might render the service of double setts of Lawyers necessary" (JM to Jefferson, 9 Jan. 1785). JM conceded certain points to opponents but held down their number by admitting that supplementary legislation would be required before the newly created courts could begin their work.

For his allies in passage of the bill, JM depended on those delegates from "the discontented extremities of the State" (JM to Jefferson, 9 Jan. 1785). Since no circuit courts then existed, disputants carried their appeals to sessions of the General Court, Court of Appeals, or High Court of Chancery—all held at the capital. This was a considerable inconvenience for most clients but no doubt some lawyers saw advantages in carrying on a practice at home and another at Richmond. Delegates who were lawyers may have feared an implicit threat to their dual practice, which in colonial times had been prohibited "to prevent frivolous suits in the general court, and trifling and vexatious appeals from the county courts" (Hening, *Statutes*, VII, 399; Hugh F. Rankin, "The General Court of Colonial Virginia," *VMHB*, LXX [1962], 142). When the court system was reconstituted after 1776, no such prohibition was retained although the jurisdiction of the General Court remained essentially as in pre-Revolutionary times. Jefferson would have liked to place the clamp back on those lawyers who, "traversing the counties seeing the clients frequently at their own courts or perhaps at their own houses must of necessity pick up all the business" and then were "permitted to come from the county courts and consume the harvest" (Boyd, *Papers of Jefferson*, II, 235). Those lawyers who suspected "that they do not possess on their abilities or knowledge sufficient to enable them to stand before judges of law" were also in the "latent opposition" (John Marshall to Charles Simms, 16 June 1784 [DLC: Simms Papers]). As John Marshall discerned matters, the greatest source of the "secret aversion" to the bill was harbored by the county justices "who are tenacious of authority [and] will not assent to any thing which may diminish their ideal dignity & put into the hands of others a power which they will not exercise themselves." Marshall also thought there was a contumacious crowd in the legislature that wanted to throw roadblocks before any plan that might "expedite & facilitate the business of recovering debts" or make it difficult to break a contract (ibid.).

The lawyers and their allies gained the last word when JM's Assize Court bill was repealed (see Hening, *Statutes*, XI, 421 n.). They not only rescinded the bill printed below but also wrote into the repeal a clause that killed Jefferson's efforts to stop legalized barratry. All laws prohibiting lawyers from practicing in both inferior and superior courts were repealed, except in cases where the attorney switched from one client to another between the lower and the appeal court (ibid., XII, 497). Even the lawyers saw there were limits to what the public would allow.

Despite all these setbacks, one eminent lawyer appreciated what JM was attempting and understood the nature of the opposition. Judge Edmund Pendleton, who had become president of the Court of Appeals, told JM he favored "the Assize scheme to any other I have heard. . . . However it is exceedingly difficult to have it well understood by [those?] not conversant in law proceedings, who have confused Ideas of different Courts which are but branches of the same Court." With many another politician, Pendleton advised JM to remember "if we can't get the very best, we must take the best we can get" (Pendleton to JM, 19 Dec. 1786 [DLC]).

[2 December 1784]

For rendering the administration of Justice more expeditious and convenient as well as less burthensome to Individuals and to the CommonWealth Be it enacted by the General Assembly that immediately after the first[1] day of January in the Year of our Lord one thousand seven hundred and eighty six the Clerk of the General Court shall make a fair transcript of the Record in each and every Suit depending in the said Court wherein an Issue is to be tried or Inquiry of damages to be made and transmit the same to the Clks of the several Assizes wherein such Suits are to be tried according to the Regulations herein after mentioned. For the tryal of Issues & Inquiry of damages on the Records so transmitted there shall in every Year be holden a Court of Assize at the Places and times following. At the city of Richmond, on the first day of April, and on the first day of October; At the city of Williamsburg, on the thirteenth day of April, and on the thirteenth day of October; At Northumberland court-house, on the first day of April, and on the first day of October; At King and Queen court house, on the twentieth day of March, and on the twentieth day of September; At Fredericksburg, on the third day of May, and on the third day of November; At Winchester, on the tenth day of April, and on the tenth day of October; At Staunton, on the first day of April, and on the first day of October; At Charlottesville, on the thirteenth day of April, and on the thirteenth day of October; At Dumfries, on the twenty third day of April, and on the twenty third day of October; At Monongalia court-house, on the first day of May, and on the twenty-fifth day of September; At Washington court-house and fort Chiswell, alternately, on the tenth day of May, and on the tenth day of October; At Suffolk, on the third day of May, and on the third day of November; at Petersburg, on the lands of Sarah Newsum, which she has ceded to the corporation of Petersburg for the purpose of erecting their public buildings, on the twenty third day of April, and on the twenty third day of October; At Brunswick court-house, on the thirteenth day of April, and on the thirteenth day of October; At Prince Edward court-house,

on the tenth day of April, and on the tenth day of October; at Bedford court-house, on the twenty third day of April, and on the twenty third day of October; and at Accomack court house, on the twenty third day of April, and on the twenty third day of October; And if any of the said several days shall happen to be Sunday then the said Courts of Assize shall respectively as the case may happen begin on the succeeding day and shall continue to sit until the Business depending before the Court shall be ended or so much thereof as can be finished before it shall be necessary for the Judges to proceed to the next Assize. In all Suits or Actions at Common Law whether real personal or mixed which shall be depending in the General Court on the said first day of January, in the Year of our Lord one thousand seven hundred and eighty six, or which shall thereafter be instituted in the said Court wherein the Venue is or shall be laid in either of the Counties of Henrico, Hanover, Chesterfield, Goochland, or Powhatan, the Issues shall be tried and the Inquiry of damages be made at the Court of Assize to be held at the city of Richmond; If the Venue is or shall be laid in either of the Counties of James city, Charles city, New-Kent, Surry, Gloucester, York, Warwick, or Elizabeth city, the Issues shall be tried and the Inquiry of damages be made in the said Court of Assize to be held at the city of Williamsburg; If the Venue is or shall be laid in either of the Counties of Richmond, Westmoreland, Lancaster, or Northumberland, the Issues shall be tried and the Inquiry of Damages made at the said Court of Assize to be held at Northumberland court-house; If the Venue is or shall be laid in either of the Counties of Essex, Middlesex, King and Queen, or King William, the Issues shall be tried and the Inquiry of damages ⟨be⟩ made at the said Court of Assize to be held at King and Queen court house; If the Venue is or shall be laid in either of the Counties of Spotsylvania, Caroline, King George, Stafford, Orange, or Culpeper, the Issues shall be tried and the Inquiry of damages ⟨be⟩ made at the said Court of Assize to be held at Fredericksburg; If the Venue is or shall be laid in either of the Counties of Frederick, Berkeley, Hampshire, or Shenandoah, the Issues shall be tried and ⟨the⟩ Inquiry of damages ⟨be⟩ made at the said Court of Assize to be held at Winchester; If the Venue is or shall be laid in either of the Counties of Augusta, Rockbridge, Rockingham, or Greenbrier, the Issues shall be tried and ⟨the⟩ Inquiry of damages ⟨be⟩ made at the said Court of Assize to be held at Staunton; If the Venue is or shall be laid in either of the Counties of Albemarle, Louisa, Fluvanna, or Amherst, the Issues
· shall be tried and ⟨the⟩ Inquiry of damages ⟨be⟩ made at the said Court

of Assize to be held at Charlottesville; If the Venue is or shall be laid
in either of the Counties of Fairfax, Fauquier, Loudoun, or Prince William, the Issues shall be tried and ⟨the⟩ Inquiry of damages ⟨be⟩ made
at the said Court of Assize to be held at Dumfries; If the Venue is or
shall be laid in either of the Counties of Harrison, Yohogania, Monongalia, or Ohio, the Issues shall be tried and ⟨the⟩ Inquiry of damages
⟨be⟩ made at the said Court of Assize to be held at Monongalia court-
house; if the Venue is or shall be laid in either of the Counties of Montgomery or Washington, the Issues shall be tried and ⟨the⟩ Inquiry ⟨of
damages be⟩ made at the said Court of Assize to be held at Washington
court-house and Fort Chiswell, alternately; If the Venue is or shall be
laid in either of the Counties of Norfolk, Isle of Wight, Princess Anne,
Nansemond, or Southampton, the Issues shall be tried and ⟨the⟩ Inquiry
of damages ⟨be⟩ made at the said Court of Assize to be held at Suffolk;
If the Venue is or shall be laid in either of the Counties of Prince
George, Sussex, Dinwiddie, or Amelia, the Issues shall be tried and
⟨the⟩ Inquiry of damages ⟨be⟩ made at the said Court of Assize to be
held at Petersburg; If the Venue is or shall be laid in either of the
Counties of Brunswick, Greensville, Lunenburg, or Mecklenburg, the
Issues shall be tried and ⟨the⟩ Inquiry of damages ⟨be⟩ made at the
said Court of Assize to be held at ⟨Brunswick court-house; if the venue
is or shall be laid in either of the counties of Prince Edward, Buckingham, Charlotte, Halifax, or Cumberland, the issues shall be tried and the
inquiry of damages be made at the said court of assize to be held at
Prince Edward court-house; if the venue is or shall be laid in either of
the counties of Bedford, Botetourt, Campbell, Pittsylvania, or Henry,
the issues shall be tried and the inquiry of damages be made at the said
court of assize to be held at Bedford court-house; if the venue is or shall
be laid in either of the counties of Accomack or Northampton, the
issues shall be tried and inquiry of damages be made at the said court
of assize to be held at Accomack court-house.⟩ To avoid improper
tryals by the management of the pl[ain]t[iff] or the Attorney for the
pl[ain]t[iff] the Venue in transitory Actions shall be laid in the County
where the Def[endan]t is arrested or where an attachment to force his
appearance is levied, but may be changed by direction of the Court
upon good Cause shewn. At some convenient time previous to the holding each Court of Assize the Judges of the General Court shall allot
and regulate among themselves the Court or Courts of Assize at which
each of them shall attend and if by sickness or other disability any one
or more of them shall be unable to attend the Governor with the Ad-

vice of Council upon Notice thereof being given to him shall and he is hereby authorized and empowered to call upon either of the Judges of the High Court of Chancery or of the Court of Admiralty to supply the place of any Judge of the General Court so disabled from performing his duty until said disability is removed and such Judge or Judges of the Court of Chancery or of the Court of Admiralty as shall be appointed by the Governor as aforesd. shall have as full and as ample power for the purposes of the Assize Court assigned to him as the Judge of the General Court whose disability he is appointed to supply and shall proceed in the same manner as the Judge of the General Court would have been bound to do if no such disability had happened. The said Judges of Assize[2] shall have full Power to try all Issues and inquire of damages by a Jury upon all Records to be transmitted to them by the Clk of the General Court and therein to determine all Questions about the legality of Evidence and other matters of Law which may arise. For which tryals they shall cause the Sheriff of the County wherein the Assize Court is to be held (who shall attend them throughout their whole Session) to empannel and return Jurors of the Bystanders qualified as the Law directs to be sworn of Juries. They shall certify under their hands and Seals upon or with each Record transmitted the verdict that shall be given therein, together with such Demurrers, exceptions to Evidence, or exceptions to the opinion of the Court as they shall be desired by either Party to certify according to the truth of the case which Verdicts and other certificates the Clks of Assize shall in convenient time before the succeeding General Court return to the Clks Office of the General Court. On the Return of the postea or certificate as aforesd. to the Clerk's office of the General Court in all such Cases where a General Verdict shall be given for either Party and there be no exceptions certified as aforesd. and where no Reasons are filed to stay Judgs within fourteen days after the Return of the Postea as aforesd. the General Court at their next succeeding Term shall enter up Judt. upon such Verdicts and an Ex[ecuti]on may issue thereupon. And in all such Cases wherein a special Verdict shall be given, exceptions certified, or Reasons filed in arrest of Judgment the Clk of the General Court shall put them on a Docket for Argument at the following General Court. The Judges of the General Court shall nevertheless for good cause shewn have power to order any Issue, or Writ of Inquiry of damages in a Suit depending before them to be tried at their own Bar. The Judges of the Court of Appeals shall and they are hereby authorized and empowered to appoint a Clk for each assize

Court who shall continue in Office during good Behavior and shall keep his office and reside in the County where the Assize Court is to be held, attend the Judges during their Settings and make due Entries and certificates of all matters and things as he shall be directed by the said Judges ⟨Courts⟩ of Assize. He shall Issue S[ub]p[oen]as for Witnesses for either Party upon the Records sent him and shall do all other things which the duty of his office may require, for which he shall be allowed such Fees as by Law shall be established and none other. The said Clk shall also prepare a Docket of all the causes so transmitted by the Clk of the General Court setting them down in the same order as they stand in the Course of the proceedings. All depositions taken in any Suit so sent to be tried at any of the Assizes shall be transmitted together with the Record. All Writs of Habeas Corpus which shall be sued out during the Session of Assize shall be returnable before the Judges of the circuit in which the Prisoner is detained. And the said Courts of Assize shall have full Power to hear & determine all Treasons Felonies Murders and other Crimes and misdemeanors which shall be brought before them for which purpose, whenever any County Court shall order a Prisoner for further tryal they ⟨or any one of the justices who sat in such court on the examination of the prisoner⟩ shall by Warrant from under ⟨his or⟩ their hands & Seals, direct the Sheriff or his deputy to remove the Prisoner and commit him to the Goal[3] of that Assize Court at which the Issues in civil Causes for the County from whence he is removed are herein directed to be tried—which warrant the sheriff is hereby directed to obey and may be furnished with Powers to impress Men for the Safeguard of such prisoners in like manner as is practiced in the removal of Criminals to the public Goal. And the Clk of the County from whence such prisoner is removed shall immediately after the Court held for his County upon the examination of such prisoner issue a Writ of Venire facias to the Sheriff of the County commanding him to summon Twelve good and lawful Men being Freeholders of the County to come before the Court of Assize where the prisoner is to be tried at its next Session and return a Pannel of their names which Freeholders or so many of them as shall appear not being challenged, together with so many other good and lawful Men of the Byestanders ⟨being freeholders of the assize district⟩ as will make up the number twelve shall be a lawful Jury for the tryal of such prisoner. If a prisoner shall desire any Witnesses to be summoned for him or her to appear on the tryal at the Assizes, the Clk of Assize shall issue Subpœnas for such Witnesses. The Keepers of the Respective Assize Goals by order of any two Justices of the same County may impress Guards for the safe keeping of all prisoners in their Custody to be paid by the Public. The Sherif[f] of each of the Counties wherein an Assize Court by this Act is directed to be held shall before every Meeting of the Assize Court in their respective Counties, summon twenty four Freeholders out of the Counties assigned to the Assize Court for the district in which they respectively reside, qualified as the Laws direct for Grand Jurors to appear at the succeeding Court of Assize—Which twenty four Men or any sixteen of them shall be a Grand Jury and shall inquire of and present all Treasons Murders Felonies or other Misdemeanors whatsoever which shall have been committed within the Jurisdiction of such assize Courts respectively. Upon any Indictment for a capital offence being found by the Grand Jury to be true agt. any person or persons the Judge ⟨court of assize,⟩ before whom the Indictment shall be found shall cause such person or persons to be immediately arraigned and tryed by a Pettet Jury summoned as herein before is directed and he she or they being found guilty to pass such judt. as the Law directs, and thereupon award execution, and if the Prisoner shall be found not guilty to acquit him or her of the Charge. Provided that on all Tryals the Prisoner shall be allowed Counsel upon Petition, and when Sentence of death shall be passed upon any Prisoner, there shall be one Calendar Month at least between Sentence and Execution. Upon the tryal of any Prisoner for any offence punishable capitally, if a bill of Exceptions or demurrer to Evidence shall be offered on behalf of the Prisoner, and a Verdict shall afterwards be found agt. him and the Judges ⟨court of assize,⟩ before whom the tryal is had shall ⟨be divided in opinion, or⟩ entertain doubts about the propriety of such exceptions or demurrers they shall direct the Sentence to ⟨or where only one judge shall attend or be present, then he shall not finally determine such exception or demurrer, but in all such cases the sentence shall, by order of such judges or judge,⟩ be suspended until the same shall be determined by the General Court before whom such demurrer or bill of exceptions shall be laid on the first day of the next succeeding Term and if the Judges of the General Court shall be of Opinion that no good Cause is shewn to the contrary execution of the Sentence shall forthwith take place in the same manner as if such Demurrer or bill of exceptions had never been offered. The Judges of the General Court may upon good cause shewn order any prisoner Committed to the Goal of a Circuit to be removed by Habeas Corpus to be tried at their Bar and in that Case a Jury shall be summoned from the Vicinage to try such offender in like manner as is directed for the summoning of a Pettit Jury to attend an Assize Court. Where the Grand Jury[4] in any Court of Assize shall present a person for an offence not capital the Judge ⟨court⟩ shall and may order the Clk to issue a Summons or other process commanding the person to appear at the next Court of Assize to answer such presentment and thereupon shall hear and determine the same as is now done upon such like occasions in the General Court. ⟨And if the grand jury shall present any person for a criminal offence, who has not before been committed or examined by a county court for the same, the court of assize shall order the clerk to issue a capias against such person, directed to all sheriffs and constables within this state, commanding them to take such person wherever found, and carry him before a magistrate of the county wherein he shall be apprehended, who shall proceed therein in the manner directed by law for examination of criminals.⟩ The Attorney General for the CommonWealth or some other to be appointed by the General Court and commissioned by the Governor to continue in office during good behaviour shall attend each of the said Assize Courts on behalf of the CommonWealth. The Goaler for the County in which an Assize Court is hereby directed to be held shall constantly attend the said Court of Assize and execute the commands of the Judge ⟨said court⟩ from time to time with regard to the duties of his office. Every person summoned as a Witness or Jury man and failing to appear may be fined by the Judge of the Assize Court to which he was summoned in the same manner as a Witness or Jury man might be fined by the General Court for such offences. And for the greater ease and convenience of Suitors the Clk of the General Court shall from time to time furnish each Clk of Assize with a sufficient number of blank Writs which may by the respective Clks of Assize be filled up and issued as they shall be required but which shall be made returnable to the Clks office of the General Court on the respective return days established by Law. And each Clk of Assize to prevent mistakes & Errors shall transmit a List of all Writs by him issued on or before the last return day in each Session of the General Court to the end that the same may be docketed and proceeded on. All and every Act or Acts of Assembly coming within the perview and meaning of this Act shall be and they are hereby repealed. This Act shall commence and be in force on the first day of May ⟨January⟩ 1786.

Ms (Vi). Docketed, with endorsements by a clerk. In John Beckley's hand, except for the portions in angle brackets, which were supplied by the various committees. The revised bill is printed in Hening, *Statutes*, XI, 421–29.

1 Dates and places were left blank in this draft of the bill, and later added to the final version of the act. A partial list of amendments to the bill is in Ms (Vi). The editors have silently included these dates and places.

2 In the final version of the bill, the words from "At some convenient time" to this point were replaced by: "Previous to the holding the courts of assize, the court of appeals shall allot and regulate among themselves the court or courts of assize, at each of which two of the judges of the said court of appeals shall attend; which two judges, or in case of failure in either through sickness or other cause to attend, the other of them . . ."

3 Beckley's spelling for "gaol."

4 Beckley wrote "in case of presentments" following "Grand Jury," but the clause was later deleted by a committee.

To James Madison, Sr.

RICHMOND Decr. 3. 1784

HON'D SIR

My last informed you that a vote had passed in favor of Circuit Courts. A bill has since been brought in and will shortly be considered.[1] The difficulty of suiting it to every palate, & the many latent objections of a selfish & private nature which will shelter themselves under some plausible objections of a public nature to which every innovation is liable render the event extremely uncertain. In the Course of this week The H. of D. have agreed to pay the British debts by annual portions for 7 years disallowing interest between the 19th. of Apl. 1775 & 3d. of March 1783, the period of hostilities.[2] It is not unlikely that the same observations above made on the Circuit Court bill may be found applicable to this Case. The bill for the Genl. Asst. was brought in yesterday. Its fate is equally uncertain. I inclose a copy of Treaty at Fort Stanwix which I rcd. by yesterdays post. The Commissrs. were proceeding to Fort Pitt to hold another Treaty.[3] No Congs. had been formed on the 20th. of Novr. nor much prospect of a speedy one. The British hold the N. Western Post yet & assign in justification the breach of the Peace in Virga. & N. York. I am much better than at the date of my last & with affct. respects to family Remain Yr. Dutiful Son

Js MADISON JR.

[P. S.] Mr. Innes is not here & I believe is gone towards Kentucky, it will be well therefore to write to him on yr. business; if he sd. appear here again I can speak to him.

RC (DLC). Docketed. Addressed, with the outer cover directing the letter to the care of "Capt. Buckner," and the postscript written on the verso.

[1] JM introduced the "Circuit Courts" or Assize bill on the preceding day. The bill was actually drafted by Edmund Pendleton as a member of the Committee of Revisors set up in 1776. The legislation became a political football, for early in 1778 the scheme passed the House of Delegates only to fail in the Senate by one vote. "Our Judiciary System is lame without it," Pendleton complained then, and the situation had since worsened (Mays, *Papers of Edmund Pendleton*, I, 247).

[2] JM crossed through the next sentence: "The bill for a Genl. Assmt. was introduced yesterday."

[3] The first conference between the congressional commissioners and the Iroquois delegation was held at old Fort Stanwix (Fort Schuyler), with JM as a witness (JM to Jefferson, 11 Oct. 1784). The congressional commissioners then headed for Pennsylvania and a similar meeting with tribesmen, but after a conference at Fort Pitt it was decided to move the treaty talks to Fort McIntosh, thirty miles downstream from Fort Pitt (Hallock F. Raup, ed., "Journal of Griffith Evans, Clerk to the Pennsylvania Commissioners at Fort Stanwix and Fort McIntosh, 1784–1785," *Pennsylvania Magazine of History and Biography*, LXV [1941], 229–30).

Bill Prohibiting Further Confiscation of British Property

[3 December 1784]

Whereas by the Definitive treaty of peace as now ratified Between the united States of America[1] and his Britannick majesty it is agreed that there shall be no future Confiscation; to the end that the same may be carried into effect within this Commonwealth Be it enacted by the General Assembly that the future Operation of the Laws concerning Escheats and forfeitures from British Subjects shall henceforth cease and determine and that no process or order of Sale shall issue nor shall the property of any British Subject be sold by virtue of any of the said Laws from and after the passing of this Act—provided always that nothing herein contained shall be Construed in any manner to affect the right, tittle or Interest of any person holding or claiming any property heretofore sold under the said Laws or particularly appropriated by any act or resolution of the General assembly, but all such rights and tittles shall be as good and valid as if this Act had never been made.

Ms (Vi). The manuscript of this legislation is not in JM's hand. His authorship is presumed by the circumstances explained below. The bill is titled: "A Bill to prevent the future operation of the Laws concerning Escheats and forfeitures from British Subjects."

[1] After the outbreak of war the property rights of British citizens were indeed cloudy until Jefferson introduced a resolution "concerning Money Due British Subjects" and the legislature passed a bill he drafted "concerning escheats and for-

feitures from British subjects" (Boyd, *Papers of Jefferson*, II, 168–72; Hening, *Statutes*, IX, 377–80; X, 66–71). The several laws provided for state-appointed custodians of sequestered British property, with all profits paid into the state treasury along with "all unpaid rents due to British subjects" (Harrell, *Loyalism in Virginia*, pp. 85–86). The escheat measure called for the legal confiscation of British property and its sale by a county escheator. The law provided that "the former owner might claim the money paid to the commonwealth for the estate," and from 1779 onward large sales were made of personal property, lands, and slaves condemned by courts of inquest (ibid., pp. 89, 95–98). As Harrell points out, a bill calling for suspension of these acts failed to pass the House of Delegates shortly after Cornwallis's defeat. Instead, an act passed late in 1781 diverted all receipts from sequestered estates to a sinking fund for military certificates, and at the May 1784 session a resolution passed which might have then led to a suspension of the "farther operation" of the escheat laws, but time ran out and nothing was done.

The matter was revived on 1 Dec. when the previous resolutions and other documents on escheats were brought before the Committee of the Whole. A drafting committee was appointed with JM as a member. This group produced the bill which was introduced on 3 Dec. and passed on 22 Dec. JM carried it to the Senate, but that body balked at approving the House version. Conferences were required before a revised bill was finally accepted by the House on 30 Dec. (*JHDV*, Oct. 1784, pp. 52, 79, 85, 92, 93, 95). The main part of the final version is in Ms (Vi), and the act is printed in Hening, *Statutes*, XI, 446.

Resolution on Pensions for Wounded Veterans

[3 December 1784]

Resolved, that it is the opinion of this committee, That the Executive ought to be authorised to put on the pension list all officers and soldiers, who have been wounded in the service of their country, and whom they may think entitled to the same, upon application being made to them therefor.[1]

Printed copy (*JHDV*, Oct. 1784, p. 53). No Ms of the resolution has been found.

[1] As chairman of the Committee for Courts of Justice, JM reported that the petition of Joseph Anderson, "praying to be put on the list of pensioners," had been considered. Instead of routinely passing on the merits of Anderson's petition, the committee recommended that this time-consuming problem should be shifted away from the legislature to the discretion of the governor and Council of State. The resolution was approved and the way cleared for the amendments incorporated in the Bill Enabling the Executive to Pension Disabled Veterans, 16 Nov. 1784. Joseph Anderson (1736– ca. 1823) had enlisted in 1779 in the 11th Virginia Regiment and subsequently "received a dangerous hurt which rendered him incapable of duty." In 1821 Anderson applied for a pension, declaring his main assets were "one Negro man aged near 70, [and] 200 acres of poor land entirely unproductive" (*Virginia Revolutionary Pension Applications*, John Frederick Dorman, comp. [15 vols.; Washington, 1958——], II, 32).

To James Monroe

Dear Sir

On Saturday last a proposition was agreed to for establishing Circuit Courts throughout this Commonwealth, and yesterday a bill for that purpose was reported.[1] On wednesday next it will undergo a discussion of the Come. of the Whole. The circumstances under which it has passed thus far seem to promise a favorable issue, but the dangers which it is yet to go thro' are formidable. They proceed from latent & interested objections which have on several former occasions proved fatal to similar attempts. The plan is pretty analagous to the Nisi prius establishmt. in England.[2] On Teusday sundry propositions were made by Mr. Jones, in favor of the 4 art. of the Treaty of peace. They passed by a large majority with blanks as to the length of time to be given for the payment of the principal and for disallowing the interest. The former was filled up with seven years, in preference of 10, 8, 6, & 5 which were contended for on different sides. The latter with the period between Apl. 19: 1775, & March. 3. 1783, in preference to the period between the first date & May 1784, the date of the exchange of Ratifications. The bill will probably pass but not I fear without some improper ingredients, & particularly some conditions relative to the N. W. Posts or the Negroes which lye without our province. The bill for the Religious Asst. was reported yesterday and will be taken up in a Come. of the Whole next week. Its friends are much disheartened at the loss of Mr. Henry.[3] Its fate is I think very uncertain. Another act[4] of the H. of D. during the prest. week is a direction to the Executive to carry into effect the vote of a Bust to the M. de la fayette, to be presented to the City of Paris, & to cause another to be procured to be set up in this Country. These resolutions are so contrived as to hide as much as possible the circumstance in the original vote of the bust being to be presented to the Marquis himself. I find by a Letter from Gl. Washington that he was on the 28th. ult: just setting out to accompany the Marquis to Annapolis & thence to Baltimore. The latter may therefore soon be expected at Trenton. He has been much caressed here as well as every where else in his Tour, and I make no doubt he will leave Congs. with equal reason to be pleased with his visit. I meant to have sent you a copy of the Resolutions touching the Busts, but have been disappointed in getting one. They were offered by Mr. Jones & agreed to unanimously, as they no doubt will also be in the Senate. Wishing you all happiness I am Dr. Sir Yrs Sincerely

J. MADISON JR.

RC (DLC). Docketed by JM. Addressed to Monroe "in Congress."

1 The Assize Court bill which JM introduced 2 Dec.

2 The "Nisi prius establishmt." which had been the model for Edmund Pendleton's original draft of the circuit court bill provided for "the trial of issues of fact before a jury and one presiding judge" (Henry C. Black, *Black's Law Dictionary* [St. Paul, 1951], p. 1197).

3 Patrick Henry's vote was lost when he was chosen governor and retired from the House of Delegates. On 24 Dec. the House, by a 45 to 38 vote, tabled the General Assessment bill until the Oct. 1785 session (*JHDV*, Oct. 1784, p. 82). JM voted for the deferment.

4 JM deleted some four or five words at the beginning of this sentence and substituted "Another act." The penmanship indicates JM made the alteration at some later time, after the return of the document.

To Lafayette

Letter not found.

4 December 1784, Richmond. Lafayette refers to this letter in the 17 December addendum to his 15 December 1784 letter to JM. The lost letter contained news of the resolution passed in the House of Delegates to have two busts of Lafayette made and placed in the Virginia capital and in Paris.

From James Monroe

TRENTON Decr. 6. 1784.

DEAR SIR,

I enclose you a paper wh. will give you a state of the representation of the States, beside wh. little else hath taken place worthy yr. attention. Mr Jay is here & will I understand accept the office of foreign affrs. upon condition Congress will establish themselves at any one place.[1] The conduct of Spn. respecting the Mississippi &ca. requires the immediate attention of Congress. The affr. is before a Committee. I think we shall leave this place & either remove to Phila. or N. York but to wh. is uncertain.[2] I am very respectfully yrs.

JAS. MONROE

RC (DLC). Cover missing. Docketed.

¹ Robert R. Livingston had resigned as Secretary for Foreign Affairs on 4 June 1783, and almost a year later Congress was still in search of a replacement. Jay was elected to the post on 7 May 1784, but he did not learn of the appointment until late July. "He was not anxious to accept it" and delayed his acceptance until assured that Congress "would sit thenceforth in New York City" and would allow Jay "the privilege of appointing his own clerks" (Samuel Flagg Bemis, ed., *The American Secretaries of State and Their Diplomacy* [10 vols.; New York, 1927–29], I, 193, 194, 200). Jay took the oath of office on 21 Dec. 1784 (Burnett, *Letters*, VII, 634 n.).

² On 24 Dec. Congress voted to adjourn until 11 Jan. and to reconvene then in New York.

From Thomas Jefferson

PARIS Dec. 8. 1784.

DEAR SIR

In mine of Nov. 11. I acknoleged the receipt of yours of Aug. 20. Sep. 7. & 15. Since that, the one of Oct. 11. by the packet has come to hand as also that of July 3. by mr Short who came in the packet, was actually in N. York when you passed through it & had waited there several days in hopes of seeing you. I thank you very much for the relation of the proceedings of assembly. It is the most grateful of all things to get those details when one is so distant from home. I like to see a disposition increasing to replenish the public coffers, & so far approve of the young stamp act.¹ But would it not be better to simplify the system of taxation rather than to spread it over such a variety of subjects & pass the money thro' so many new hands. Taxes should be proportioned to what may be annually spared by the individual. But I do not see that the sale of his land is an evidence of his ability to spare. One of my reasons for wishing to center our commerce at Norfolk was that it might bring to a point the proper subjects of taxation & reduce the army of taxgatherers almost to a single hand.² The simplest system of taxation yet adopted is that of levying on the land & the labourer. But it would be better to levy the same sums on the produce of that labour when collected in the barn of the farmer; because then if through the badness of the year he made little, he would pay little. It would be better yet to levy it only on the surplus of this produce above his own wants. It would be better too to levy it, not in his hands, but in those of the purchaser; because tho' the farmer would in fact pay it, as the purchaser must deduct it from the original price of his produce, yet the farmer would not be sensible that he paid it. This idea would no doubt meet it's difficulties & objections when it should come to be reduced to practice: yet I suspect it would be practicable & expedient. Your taxgatherers in Virginia cost as much as the whole civil list besides. What a comfort to the farmer to be allowed to supply his own wants before he should be liable to pay any thing, & then to pay only out of his surplus.

The proposition for a Convention has had the result I expected. If one could be obtained I do not know whether it would not do more harm than good. *While Mr. Henry lives* another bad constitution would be formed, & saddled for ever on us. What we have to do I think is *devo*[u]*tly* to *pray* for *his death*, in the mean time to *keep alive* the *idea* that the present is *but* an *ordinance* & to *prepar*[e] the *minds* of the *young men*. I am glad the *Episcopalians* have again shewn their teeth & fangs. The *dissenters* had almost forgotten them. I still hope something will be done for Paine. He richly deserves it; and it will give a character of littleness to our state if they suffer themselves to be restrained from the compensation due for his services by the paltry consideration that he opposed our right to the Western country. Who was there out of Virginia who did not oppose it? Place this circumstance in one scale, and the effect his writings produced in uniting us in independance in the other & say which preponderates. Have we gained more by his advocation of independance than we lost by his opposition to our territorial right? Pay him the balance only.

I look anxiously to the approaching & improving the navigation of the Patowmac & Ohio, the actual junction of that of Big-beaver & Cayahoga by a Canal; as also that of Albemarle sound & Elizabeth through the dismal.[3] These works will spread the feild of our commerce Westwardly & Southwardly beyond any thing ever yet done by man.

I once hinted to you the project of seating yourself in the neighborhood of Monticello, and my sanguine wishes made me look on your answer as not absolutely excluding the hope. Monroe is decided in settling there & is actually engaged in the endeavor to purchase. Short is the same. Would you but make it a 'partie quarree' I should beleive that life had still some happiness in store for me. Agreeable society is the first essential in constituting the happiness & of course the value of our existence: & it is a circumstance worthy great attention when we are making first our choice of a residence. Weigh well the value of this against the difference in pecuniary interest, & ask yourself which will add most to the sum of your felicity through life. I think that weighing them in this balance, your decision will be favourable to all our prayers. Looking back with fondness to the moment when I am again to be fixed in my own country, I view the prospect of this society as inestimable.

I find you thought it worth while to pass the last summer in exploring the woods of America, & I think you were right. Do you not think the men, & arts of this country would be worth another summer. You can come in April, pass the months of May, June, July, August & most of September here, & still be back to the commencement of real business in the Assembly following, which I would not have you absent from. You shall find with me a room, bed & plate, if you will do me the favor to become of the family. As you would be here only for the summer season, I think your out-fit of clothes need not cost you more than 50 guineas, & perhaps the attendance on the theatres & public entertainments with other small expences might be half a guinea or three quarters a day. Your passage backwards & forwards would I suppose be 60. or 70 guineas more. Say that the whole would be 200 guineas. You will for that have purchased the knowlege of another world. I expect Monroe will come in the Spring & return to Congress in the fall. If either this object, or the one preceding for settling you near Monticello can be at all promoted by the use of the money which the assembly have given me for my share in the revisal, make use of it freely, & be assured it can in no other way be applied so much to my gratification. The return of it may wait your perfect convenience. Should you have no occasion for it, either mr Eppes or mr Nichs. Lewis will receive it & apply it according to my general directions.

I wrote you there would be war. At that time there was no symptom which could indicate any thing else. We know of none as yet on the part either of the Emperor or Dutch. I still expect it & found my expectation on the character of the Emperor, which I collect from his public acts. These certainly shew him far above the level of common men. He would of course during the winter encourage the hopes of those who wish for peace. At present it is the general beleif here, & that even of some people who approach the men in office, that the matter will be accomodated. They found this expectation too on the character of the emperor, who they say is bizarre, & eccentric, & particularly in the dog-days. He stands in a dangerous predicament. If he sheaths the sword, he proves himself to the world a trifling personage; if he draws it, his ruin is well nigh sealed. It will not be known ultimately till the season for taking the feild. I have reason to think that before the January packet sails we shall make a short trip to England. If so, you will hear from me from thence. Both here & there I pray you to try to make me useful to you, as nothing will be more pleasing to me than to prove to you in every situation the sincere friendship I bear you. Adieu.

RC (DLC). Unsigned. Cover missing. The italicized words, unless otherwise noted, are those decoded by JM using the code first used by Jefferson on 14 Apr. 1783. Where Jefferson used a long dash, to indicate a break in thought, the editors have arbitrarily begun a new paragraph.

1 "The young stamp act" was JM's rider of 2 June 1784 on the revenue act passed at the May session of the General Assembly.

2 JM was persuaded that his 8 June 1784 Port bill would cut down on the need for customs collectors, but by the time his colleagues added their favored landings to the bill a total of five ports were authorized (Hening, *Statutes*, XI, 402).

3 A bill authorizing a canal from the Elizabeth River through the Dismal swamp had passed at the Oct. 1783 session of the General Assembly but nothing seems to have been done under its provisions. A second act, "for cutting a navigable Canal from the waters of Elizabeth River," was passed at the Oct. 1787 session but the canal was under construction from 1793 until 1822 (Alexander Crosby Brown, *The Dismal Swamp Canal* [Chesapeake, 1967], pp. 25–55).

To Richard Henry Lee

RICHMOND, December 11th, 1784.

DEAR SIR

I was, by Thursday's post, favoured with your's of the 26th of November. We had begun to despair of a Congress being made up in time for a decision on the case referred to them by the resolutions of our last session.[1] I now hope that we may yet hear from you, on that subject, before our adjournment. The bill on the resolutions in favour of the treaty of peace, mentioned in my last, is not yet reported.[2] It will, I am persuaded, need the reenforcement of an exhortation from Congress. The Glasgow merchants have authorized their agents here to compromise for the payment of their debts in four years, and a memorial will, I understand, be presented to that effect in a few days. My next will inform you of the result. The past week has been spent chiefly on the assize bill, which yesterday past the house of delegates with a very feeble opposition, and a very few dissenting voices. Its fate now depends on the senate.[3] It is pretty analogous to the nisi prius establishment of England. The number of assize courts is seventeen. A smaller number was proposed, but we thought ourselves lucky in being able to give general content by such an augmentation. The counties of Northumberland, Westmoreland, Richmond, and Lancaster, form one district; the court house of the first being the seat of the assize court. The friends of this measure here considered it as a foundation for a very important and salutary amendment of our judicial system. The bill for a general assessment has not yet undergone a discussion; the same is the case of the militia bill. The scheme for opening the navigation of the Potomac, which has been settled between the Maryland and [the Virginia] gentlemen, is before the House of Delegates, and will be favoured, as far as the objectionable amount of the tolls will admit.[4] As the concurrence of Maryland in this scheme is necessary, some difficulties will attend its progress. The difficulty of providing for a representation of this state in Congress, under the act for the annual meeting of the Assembly, has been a subject of conversation. The loss of that benefit is a serious matter; but is not the appointing of delegates a year before they are to serve, rather a singular expedient? The vacancies in the council had all been filled before the receipt of your recommendation of General Gates. I must beg the favour of you to excuse my not obeying, by this post, the last request in your letter, as to the expediency of a continental convention—having, at present, only time to add, that, with great respect and regard, I have the honour to be, Your obedient, and very humble servant,

JAMES MADISON, JUN.

Printed copy (Richard H. Lee, *Memoir of the Life of Richard Henry Lee* [2 vols.; Philadelphia, 1825], II, 218–19). The original Ms has not been found.

1 The "resolutions of our last session," passed by the House of Delegates on 19 May 1784, concerned a final settlement of the wartime accounts "subsisting between the United States and individual States" (*JHDV*, May 1784, pp. 11–12). JM had long been in pursuit of a final adjustment of the national and state claims, and was the principal author of the act of Congress of 20 Feb. 1782 which provided machinery for liquidation of accounts through 31 Dec. 1781 (*Papers of Madison*, IV, 67–68). Congress responded to the problem by providing additional commissioners for the Pennsylvania and Virginia accounts on 23 Feb. 1785 (*JCC*, XXVIII, 92). The overhanging Virginia claim, complicated by the expenses for George Rogers Clark's expeditions, was a primary reason for delay of the settlement (ibid., XXIX, 548–49; Ferguson, *Power of the Purse*, p. 216).

2 The bill "in favour of the treaty of peace" which JM mentioned in the lost letter of ca. 14 Nov. concerned the British debts owed by Virginians. Repayment was hinged, by legislative resolutions, upon Great Britain's adherence to the terms of the Treaty of Paris (*JHDV*, May 1784, p. 74; Resolutions on Private Debts Owed to British Merchants, 7–23 June 1784).

3 JM explained the temporary triumph he gained in the passage of the assize, or circuit court, bill in his 9 Jan. 1785 letter to Jefferson. The hostility of certain dele-

gates to the erection of an intermediate court between the county justices and the General Court caused one of JM's friends to bemoan that the much-needed Assize Court bill was nearly destroyed "by a set of D—— Asses" (Archibald Stuart to John Breckinridge, 26 Jan. 1786 [DLC: Breckinridge Family Papers]).

[4] The plan for navigating on the Potomac involved a conference at Annapolis between interested Maryland parties and Washington. Thomas Johnson seems to have been the chief promoter of a bill which became the model for the one the Virginia General Assembly finally accepted (*JHDV*, Oct. 1784, pp. 99, 101, 103; Hening, *Statutes*, XI, 510–25). Washington thought the toll rates excessive but urged their adoption as an attraction for private investors (Washington to Robert Morris, 1 Feb. 1785, Fitzpatrick, *Writings of Washington*, XXVIII, 48–49).

To James Monroe

RICHD. Decr. 11. 1784

DEAR SIR

Neither of the two last posts brought me a line from you. I find one in the office for Mr. Jones who is absent on a visit to King George.[1] I expect him back on Monday next. Our proceedings throughout this week have turned chiefly on the bill for assize Courts, which yesterday passed the H. of D. after a faint opposition and with very few dissenting voices. It is formed pretty much on the pattern of the English establishment. The disposition of the Senate towards the bill is not yet certainly known but is presumed to be not unfavorable. Present my compliments to Mr. Mercer. I intended to have dropped him a line by this post, but am too much abridged in time. You will be so good as to mention to him the progress of the Assize bill which if I do not forget his sentiments, will give him pleasure. With much respect I am Dr. Sir Yrs. sincerely

J. MADISON JR.

There are a number of letters in the post office here for Mr. Jefferson, from different quarters. Ought they to be sent to Europe or to His Steward?

I find that the letters of Mr. Mazzei covered to you by the last post, did not pay the postage here as I signified.[2] I sent the money for the purpose with the packet, but the Post-Master refused to take it, alledging its address to a Member of Congs. and the post went off before I could make the explanations. If you think it worth while you can settle the matter with the Post office at Trenton, & let me know the amount.

RC (DLC). Cover missing.

¹ JM and Monroe apparently had an agreement to send each other a weekly letter summarizing local news. Monroe's letter of 15 Nov. reached JM on 18 Nov. There is no record of any Monroe letters having gone astray, but Monroe seems to have assumed that a letter to his uncle, Joseph Jones, would be read by JM.

² Mazzei had sent letters to JM to be forwarded on the New York stage that left Richmond on Saturdays. JM was concerned about the cost of forwarding Mazzei's mail since the Richmond postmaster had ruled that inasmuch as the packet was addressed to a member of Congress it should pass through his office post-free (Wesley Everett Rich, *The History of the United States Post Office to the Year 1829* [Cambridge, Mass., 1924], p. 50). JM assumed that the Trenton postmaster would not be as accommodating, and he was too conscientious to use the franking privilege for his Italian friend's personal mail. James Hayes (1759–1804) was postmaster at Richmond.

To George Washington

Letter not found.

11 December 1784, Richmond. Washington had traveled to Annapolis to further his favored scheme for an interstate project to build a canal along the Potomac River. He acknowledged the arrival of this letter on 28 December. JM probably told Washington of the main business that had occupied the General Assembly since Washington's departure from Richmond ca. 20 November.

From James Monroe

TRENTON Decr. 14. 1784.

DEAR SIR

I have recd. yr. favor of the 27. of Novr. in answer to mine of the 15th. My last gave you the state of the representations here. The business of importance is still before committees or if reported not yet acted on. It seems to be the Genl. sense of Congress to appoint a minister to the Ct: of London & to give him instructions upon many subjects & particularly those wh. arise in the conduct of both parties under the treaty but whom they may appoint is incertain, indeed I fear that the difficulty of obtaining a vote for any person will obstruct this measure for a length of time. Franklin hath thro' Mr. Laurens & the Marquis of Fayatte solicited permission¹ to return home; this will no doubt be assented to as soon as taken up. An appointment must therefore be made in his place to that ct.; I think there will be little difficulty in obtaining it for Mr Jefferson, for the opinion of all the members seems

183

to concur in the propriety of it. The first question will be whether we shall or not add other ministers to those in office & annex them to the cts. of London & Madrid, or depend on those for the manag'ment of all our business in Europe.

Connecticut hath I hear authoriz'd Congress to carry into effect the impost with the assent of 12. States only. She hath also laid a duty of 5 pr. centm. upon all goods imported from a neighb[o]ring State. This affects R. Island very sensibly. The question must soon be decided whether this State will accede to this measure, or the other States recede from it for it is sd. N. York & Georgia will join in it. Have you been able to carry the point in fav[or] of the delivery of such citizens as may be guilty of the offences you describe, to the power, in whose territory & agnst, whose subjects they are committed.[2] This is certainly in strict conformity to the laws of nations but I believe not the common practice, except between those with whom particular treaties stipulate it. With us it will be beneficial as it must serve not only politic[s] but in the instance of the Indians (if the latter are comprehended in it) very humane purposes. I wish the same regulation cod. take place throughout the union but especially on the frontier next the Brit[is]h. But how are you to ascertain the fact or what evidence wod. yo[u] require of it?[3] Or do you mean it shall operate without the concurrence of the other States? I expect Mr Jones hath left Richmond before this but if he hath not be so kind as make my best respects to him as also to Mr Stewart & believe me with great respect & esteem yr. friend & servant

JAS. MONROE

RC (DLC). Cover missing. Docketed. Incorrectly calendared as being from JM to Monroe, 14 Dec. 1785, in "Letters from J. M. [to] Mr. Monroe."

[1] Monroe originally wrote "solicited the permission of Congress to return home."

[2] JM was heavily involved in the legislation providing for the extradition of western lawbreakers into the hands of Spanish authorities, as the resolutions of 3 Nov. and the act of 26 Nov. attest. As Monroe had learned from his uncle, Joseph Jones, "the policy of the [extradition] bill is to prevent our people [from] transgressing agst. the Spaniard[s,] which they are disposed to do from all accounts, and to remove doubts in the Executive shod. such demand be made" (Jones to Monroe, 27 Nov. 1784 [ViW]).

[3] The act glossed over matters of evidence and jurisdiction by saying the law applied only to citizens or inhabitants of Virginia who committed a crime "within the acknowledged jurisdiction of any civilized nation in amity with the United States" and who had become fugitives. The "offended nation" was to exhibit to the Congress "due and satisfactory evidence of the crime" with a request for surrender of the fugitive. Congress would treat this demand as tantamount to a warrant, relay it to Virginia, and leave the capture, confinement, and delivery of the fugitive in the hands of state authorities (Hening, *Statutes,* XI, 471).

From Lafayette

EDITORIAL NOTE

Lafayette arrived in New York on 4 August 1784 for a visit which lasted until 21 December 1784 when he sailed to France aboard the frigate *La Nymphe*. During his stay, he was greeted by Washington and other Virginians at Richmond on 18 November. After feastings, celebrations, and a visit to the State Assembly, the two Revolutionary heroes spent a few days at Mount Vernon and then went north, parting at Baltimore. In early December Congress was meeting in Trenton, and there Lafayette received honorary American citizenship. Arriving in New York on 15 December, Lafayette wrote to JM, who had accompanied him on a tour of the Mohawk Valley during September and October 1784 (J. Bennett Nolan, *Lafayette in America Day by Day* [Baltimore, 1934], p. 215 and passim; Richmond *Va. Gazette and Weekly Advertiser*, 20, 27 Nov. 1784).

NEWYORK December the 15th 1784

MY DEAR SIR

Before I leave this Continent, give me leave once more to Bid You Adieu, and to Assure you with the Sincerity of my Heart, that One of the Most pleasing Circumstances, not only of my Voyage, But also of my Life, Has Been to obtain as an intimate friend the Man who Before this last time, was only to me a valuable and Agreable Acquaintance. Hitherto You Had Been my friend as the World Calls it—But now I Hope you are my friend as my Heart Reckons But few men—and once for all, I wanted to tell you that I know you, esteem you, and love you with all the warmth of my regard and affection.

I Have pretty rapidly past through Mount Vernon—Annapolis—Baltimore—Philadelphia—and Trenton. There I was Happy to find delegates from every state But Mary land—and what is Better still than a Numerous Congress, I also found a very Respectable one who, I Hope, will do great deal of good. Their most Kind Reception of me, you will find in the papers. This only I will add that some Gentlemen Having proposed I Should Be Requested to continue my Services—all the House Said No American Could Harbour Any Idea that Should make it a question—and so Confi[d]entially, and affectionately it was taken up, that it Renders almost Useless Any Recommendation which However would Be Made on Occasion.[1] But as M. Jay will I Hope Accept, and as M. Jefferson will certainly Be the Minister to France, I shall Be Very Happy in my American public Business.[2]

185

Give me leave, my dear Sir, to Recommend you the three little Memorials that I laid Before the Assembly.[3] Be so Kind as to pay my Compliments to Mr. Harrison, M. Jones, and M. Henry to whom I will write from France. I Have seen Mercer who seems to Act as well in Congress as He did once in our Virginian Army. Besides His Congressional Conduct I am pleased with His future prospect of Happiness in an Union with the fair Miss Sprig. Our friend Munro is very much Beloved and Respected in Congress—and Mr. Hardy seems to me a very distinguished Young Man

I Have much Conferred with the General Upon the Pottowmack System.[4] Many people think the Navigation of the Mississipy is not an advantage—But it May Be the Excess of a very good thing Viz the oppening of your Rivers. I fancy it Has not changed your opinion— But Beg you will write me on the Subject. In the Mean while I Hope Congress will act cooly and prudently By Spain who is such a fool that allowances must Be Made.

Be so Kind, my dear Sir, as to let me often, and By every packet Hear from You. I want to Hear of Your private Concern along with your public afairs, and I Beg You will let me Know every thing that is interesting to you. I shall on my side do the same. The chevalier's[5] Best Compliments wait upon you—Adieu, Your affectionate friend

LAFAYETTE

[Postscript to Lafayette's letter of 15 December]

NEWYORK december the 17th: 1784

MY DEAR SIR

Previous to the Receipt of your letter the 4th inst I Had prepared to send you the foregoing scrawl, and am now to aknowledge your friendly communication of the Resolve which your State Have been pleased to pass.[6] I Beg you will Become an interpreter of the Gratefull sense I Have of such a favour, conferred in so particular and flattering a manner. An official communication Had Been Made of the first Resolve, to which my Answer did not Arrive, as it was in time of war. But Having Apologized through Gel Washington a long time Since, I think I Have Nothing official to do Now with propriety as the matter Stands. In Case I receive a letter, I shall of course Answer it the Best I Can.

The printer of the Irish Volunteer Journal Has Been obliged to fly for His life, and Now is in Philadelphia where He sets up a paper.[7] He lives at Mr. Sutter's [House on?] front street. I think we ought to encourage this Martyr to the cause of liberty. My Speech to the Indians Had Been printed By the French Consul at Newyork against my intention—But I Had this Matter put to Rights

Tomorrow morning I will sail. Adieu, my dear friend, God bless you, write me often and believe me for ever Yours

LAFAYETTE

Tr (owned by Oliver R. Barrett, Chicago, Illinois, 1958).

[1] The pending arrival of Lafayette in Trenton caused Congress, on 9 Dec. 1784, to appoint a special committee, consisting of John Jay and a member from each state in Congress, to greet him. Maryland delegates had yet to return from the summer recess of congressional sessions. On the tenth a proposal to present Lafayette with a standard from the Yorktown victory was made and approved. A letter from Congress to Lafayette was adopted on 11 Dec., and on 13 Dec. Jay reported the committee's reception of Lafayette and the marquis's answer (JCC, XXVII, 672–85 passim). The formal presentation by Congress took place on 11 Dec. and was reported in the New Brunswick Political Intelligencer, 4 Jan. 1785 (Nolan, Lafayette in America Day by Day, p. 238).

[2] Jay took the oath of office as Secretary for Foreign Affairs on 21 Dec. 1784 (Burnett, Letters, VII, 634 n.; VIII, 20–21 n.). Lafayette wrote Jefferson on 11 Oct. 1784 encouraging him to succeed Franklin as United States minister to France (Boyd, Papers of Jefferson, VII, 438–39).

[3] Lafayette's letter to Governor Harrison of 19 Nov. 1784 contained the memorials from Penet d'Acosta Frères et Cie, which had previously been presented for payment and laid before the Assembly, and from Coulignac and Company, on which the Assembly also acted for payment (Governor Harrison to Lafayette, 20 Nov. 1784, Executive Letter Book, pp. 431–32).

[4] Lafayette was in Washington's company from 18 Nov. to 30 Nov. Washington's interest in the Potomac River system is described in Rives, Life of Madison, I, 617–18. See also Corra Bacon-Foster, Early Chapters in the Development of the Potomac Route to the West (Washington, 1912).

[5] The Chevalier de Caraman.

[6] JM wrote the bill to have two busts of Lafayette cast, in pursuance of the Assembly's resolution of 17 Dec. 1781. See Resolutions Providing for a Bust of Lafayette, 1 Dec. 1784.

[7] "The printer" was Mathew Carey (1760–1839), who arrived in Philadelphia on 15 Nov. 1784. Prosecuted and imprisoned in Ireland for his political opinions, he came to America impoverished and almost friendless. He had, however, made some friends during his trip across the Atlantic and, through letters of introduction, met Lafayette during the latter's visit in Philadelphia. The marquis was impressed by the immigrant and gave him $400 to begin his journalism career in the U. S. (Scharf and Westcott, History of Philadelphia, III, 1976; Kenneth Wyer Rowe, Mathew Carey: A Study in American Economic Development [Baltimore, 1933], pp. 9–31).

From James Monroe

Dear Sir

Yours of the 4th. inst. I have recd. Congress are now closely engag'd in very important business. Reports upon our affairs with *G. B. Spain* & our foreign affrs. in general have been presented & alternately acted on. To adjust the points of *variance* between us & the former *Court.* It seems to be the general opinion that a *Minister* shod. be sent there, that it would tend to conciliate the disposition of either to the other, effect the settlement of those points & avert the evils wh., if things remain long in their present state, threaten both parties, that it is more honorable to both that they shod. be adjusted in one of our capitals & that we owe that respect to the elder party. We have had no official communications but those with wh. you are already possess'd on the subject. *Docr. Franklin* hath thro' *Mr. Laurens* & *Fayette* desir'd permission to return home which will of course be granted. The claim of *Spain* to the exclusive navigation of the Missisippi &ca had been presented to our view before the instructions from *Virginia* arriv'd,[1] in a note from *Marbois* covering a letter from Rondon with the extract of a letter from Don Galvez. *Mr. Marbois* assures us of the pleasure with wh. *the K. of France* will see measures taken to co[n]solidate & maintain a good understanding between *U. S.* & *Spain* altho' the letter & the extract were from people unknown to us still the manner in wh. they come entitled them to our attention,[2] I mean the contents. At the same time therefore that it was thot. necessary to make a polite return to the note it seem'd to be generally agreed that measures shod. be taken with the *Ct. of Spain* for the amicable settlement of those points; and that a *Minister* shod. also be sent there. The question then arose how shall these several negotiations be carried on & by whom, the gentn. now in office or shall others be appointed. [Laurens][3] R. R. Livingston & all those who were averse to new appointments (the affrs. with *Spain* being first before us) were for evading the question, whether new appointments shod. or not take place, & appointing *Mr. Jefferson* immediately to the *Court of Spain* in support of wh. they urg'd the particular qualification of *Mr. Jefferson* for that business. The object of the two former was readily perceiv'd. The two *Courts* of *G B* & *F* wod. then be open. The first is I believe contented with his present station, the salary of wh. will I think be rais'd & some other matters so settled as to accommodate him, but the latter wod. willingly serve the *U. S.* at either *of* those *Cts.* It was therefore in opposition to this urg'd that for the more permanent interests of the *U. States,* if we were to be represented only at two *Courts* it had better be at those of *F & G. B* than any others; that the *minister* station'd at each migh[t] make occasional trips elsewhere & return, that in the magnitude of the question & the urgency of it that of *G. Britain* was the first object before us, that the regular way was to take up the whole together; first give *Franklin* permission to return & in respect to that *Court* supply his place, that then the question wod. com[e] regularly before us, shall *Jefferson* & *Adams* transact our other busines[s] with the other *Courts* or shall we appoint others, that those who were averse to other appointments wod. derive advantage fro[m] bringing it on in this manner, for then each point wod. stand fairly on its own ground & be determin'd by its ixpedience. After very long debate it was carried that a minister shall be appointed & sent to the *Court* of *Spain* instructed & ca. The decision of the house, in the point upon wh. it turn'd was, tha[t] he shod. be appointed from the Continent, but those in office are not precluded from the vote. They are however not in nomination. R. R. Livingston, Govr. Johnson of Mary-[land] *R. H. Lee* & some others are.[1] *R. H. Lee* earnestly advocated the appointment of *Jefferson* to the *Court* of *Spain* only in my opinion to open those of *G. Britain* & *France* to himself & friends among whom are R. R. Livingston & *Arthur Lee.* He reprehends highly the opposition the other *Delegates* made to it, talks of the superior urgency of the affairs of *Spain* to us & ca. *Fayette* & *Marbois* assur'd me that *Jefferson* had been well recd. in the *Court* of *France* & that it was their wish he shod. succeed *Franklin. R. H. Lee* hath hitherto giv[en] all the opposition in his power to this appointment & will continue to do it untill opposition will be vain wh. I think will be the case. *Arthur Lee* is in the nomination for the Treasury bd. by *Mr. Gerry* & *Mr. Mercer* by a delegate from Georgia. In a late ballot Osgood had 6 votes, *Mercer,* 5 votes & *Arthur Lee* two, *Virginia* votes for *Mercer* & seem'd inclin'd to suffer *A. Lee* to retire from the publick serv[ice] in the opinion it will be advantageous to the publick. It is propos'd to recommend it to the States to invest Congress with the power to regulate the commercial intercourse of the States with other powers, without wh. it is thought impracticable to comply with our ingagements in tre[aty] or derive any advantage from them as a nation, to regulate the duties upon imports & exports, by wh. if wise regulations are adopted, we may take some share in the carr[y]ing trade by giving priviledges to our own citizens in the exp[or]tation wh. may incourage the merchants of the U. S. to imploy natives as navigators as well as the merchts of other countries to take in partnership those of the States. To enable us further to act in concert in the measures wh. may be found necessary to counteract the policy of the power[s] with whom we have not treaties of commerce: propositions to this effect are before a committee. The *regulation* & *revenue*[5] are seperated from each other, the latter will go to the States unless conceded to the U. S. for particular purposes by each particular State. As a citizen & a lawyer I am pleas'd with the regulation taking place in the judicial department. I am yrs. very sincerely

JAS. MONROE

P. S. I heartily wish we had a better cypher, as it is dangerous to trust those subjects upon wh. I wish most confidentially to correspond with you thus to chance & the curiosity of vicious or idle people. In this place I cannot procure a scribe, can you in Richmond?[6]

RC (DLC). Cover missing. Docketed. The italicized words, unless otherwise noted, are those decoded interlinearly by JM, using the code Monroe sent him 7 Nov. 1784.

[1] The "instructions from *Virginia*" concerned the resolution of 3 Nov. 1784 whereby the House of Delegates directed the state delegation in Congress to push for negotiations with Spain guaranteeing American navigation rights on the Mississippi. JM was probably instrumental in shaping this resolution. A curious counter viewpoint was expressed by Hugh Williamson of North Carolina, who thought the closing of the Mississippi would mean that "the Country joining our present Settlements will be first improved and a durable commercial and civil intercourse established" (Burnett, *Letters*, VII, 624).

[2] Marbois's note and Francesco Reudon's letter came before a committee on which Monroe served as chairman. The "polite return" was in Monroe's hand. Reudon's main point was that the Mississippi navigation cession in the Treaty of Paris of 1783 "can have no real force unless the Catholick King, my master, to whom the navigation of that river belongs, shall think proper to ratify it" (*JCC*, XXVII, 689).

[3] Monroe used "40," the code for New Hampshire. JM placed an asterisk by the code and wrote in the lower margin "* 40 probably shd. be 43—to wit Mr. Laurence."

[4] Among the nominees for the Madrid post in early 1785 was JM. Richard Dobbs Spaight nominated JM for the position on 2 Feb. but soon withdrew the nomination (PCC). The nomination is mentioned in *JCC*, XXVIII, 25 n., where the date is incorrectly inferred to be 31 Jan.

[5] These words were underlined in the text.

[6] JM eventually found a blank printed form for the enlarged code—"a scribe"—which he sent to Monroe 14 Apr. 1785.

Bill Providing Funds for a James River Canal

The distance between Norfolk and Louisville, at the Falls of the Ohio, is about 525 miles; but in the 1780s the question was not how remote the extremes of Virginia were from each other, but whether these distant points even belonged in the same empire. In tidewater Virginia there was much feeling that navigable rivers from the foothills of the Alleghenies would draw western produce to eastern ports, lessening a dependency upon the Ohio or the whims of Spaniards who controlled the Mississippi. JM had turned the matter over in his mind until convinced that trans-Allegheny Americans had to depend upon rivers flowing west and south. George Washington was typical of the other kind of Virginian, however, who wanted a network of deep river channels and canals extending into gorges that would link the transmontane region with Atlantic ports. Thus convinced, Washington traveled to Richmond in the fall of 1784 while the General Assembly was in session, the ostensible purpose of the visit being a meeting with Lafayette, but in fact the General went as a lobbyist for a Potomac canal project. With great delight, Washington reported to Lafayette on 15 February 1785 "that the exertions which you found, and left me engag'd in, to impress my Countrymen with the advantages of extending the inland navigation of our rivers, and opening free and easy communications with the Western Territory (thereby binding them to us by interest, the only knot which will hold) has not been employ'd in vain" (Fitzpatrick, *Writings of Washington*, XXVIII, 72).

Passage of bills which permitted the creation of public corporations for canal-building projects on the Potomac and James rivers was the cause of Washington's optimism, and the credit for their enactment was chiefly his. As Madison explained to Jefferson, the subject was tossed in the legislators' laps by Washington when he wrote a persuasive letter to Governor Benjamin Harrison, who in turn relayed the message to the House of Delegates with a strong endorsement. The governor's covering letter spoke of Washington's arguments as conclusive, and expressed hope that the General Assembly would move forward by "setting on foot the surveys recommended as a necessary preparatory Step to the undertaking" (ibid., XXVII, 471–80; Executive Letter Book, pp. 412–13).

With such powerful support, aided by the petitions from citizens whose signatures attested their belief in the efficacy of canals as harbingers of prosperity, the legislative course of necessary bills was sure and steady. JM was chosen as one of the floor managers for the program, and a model for the Potomac canal project was prepared and forwarded to Richmond by Washington after it had been revised and passed by the Maryland legislature (*Laws of Maryland . . . at a Session of . . . 1784* [Annapolis, 1785], chap. XXXIII). Washington had gone to Annapolis to further the scheme and although his head throbbed he reported the altered bill had passed "with only 9 dissenting voices" (Washington to JM, 28 Dec. 1784). Everybody in the Virginia legislature must have known that the Potomac bill soon to be introduced in Richmond came via Mount Vernon.

Before the model act from Maryland had reached his hands, however, JM had already introduced the bill printed below and it had gone through all the steps for enactment except Speaker Benjamin Harrison's signature. As JM told Jefferson in his letter of 9 January 1785, his bill would have financed the canal by borrowing money on a 10 percent loan guaranteed by the credit of the commonwealth "inviolably pledged for both principal and interest." The arrival of the Potomac bill from Maryland changed the whole complexion of the legislation, for the Annapolis-passed measure created a public corporation with shareholders subsidizing at least $222,222.22 in construction funds (Hening, *Statutes*, XI, 511). The House decided to drop JM's bill and use the Maryland statute (almost verbatim). Surely the appeal of a corporation with no risk of public money must have held its allurements. Thus, "it was found advisable to pass a similar one in favor of James River" and JM's energies were turned to a new channel. William Grayson handled the borrowed Potomac River bill, JM took the assignment for the James River version, and after several tries the companion bills survived a House-Senate conference committee to become law on the same day—5 January 1785. To guard against future disappointment the bills took cognizance of past failures and ordered that the work begin within a year and be finished within ten "under the penalty of entire forfeiture" (JM to Jefferson, 9 Jan. 1785). Washington, the optimist, told Robert Morris of the Potomac project and added that if he were inclined "to encounter present inconvenience for a future income, I would hazard all the money I could raise" (Fitzpatrick, *Writings of Washington*, XXVIII, 55). JM, the realist, was more cautious. "These acts are very lengthy," he wrote Jefferson, "and having passed in all the precipitancy which marks the concluding stages of a Session, abound I fear with inaccuracies."

[18 December 1784]

Whereas the opening and extending the navigation of James River will greatly enhance the value of lands lying on & near the same, as well as facilitate the communication with the Western Country, and enlarge the commerce of the State; and Whereas the state of the public revenues will not admit of advances of money for the said purpose from the public Treasury, and it may reasonably be expected that individuals whose interests will be immediately & principally promoted by such a measure will voluntarily supply the means of carrying the same into execution, in case proper opportunity & encouragement be given therefor; Be it enacted by the General Assembly &c. . that the Governour with advice of the Council of State be & he hereby is authorised to appoint   Persons as Trustees for the purpose of opening and extending the navigation of James River from tide water to   and to fill up vacancies which may happen from deaths, refusals to act, or resignations or removals out of the Commonwealth: which Trustees or any   of them shall have power to appoint by majority of voices from their own number, any one or more persons who shall be receivers of all subscriptions & payments made for the said purpose, shall each of them give bond with security in the Court of the County where he may reside with a condition that he his heirs Executors & Admtrs. shall faithfully account with the said Trustees for all monies which by virtue of his appt. may come into his hands, and that he will pay out the same on their order; and each of the said Receivers for his services herein shall be allowed such sum not exceeding   as the Trustees may judge reasonable. The Subscriptions shall be in such form as the Trustees may direct, shall oblige the subscribers to pay to the receiver the sum subscribed in three annual payments, the first payment to be become due on the   day of   shall be extended in words and not in figures, shall be under the hand & seal of the Subscriber and attended by one or more Witnesses; and so soon as the subscriptions taken by any Receiver shall amount to   pounds the same shall be recorded in the Court of the County where he may reside, and the monies therein subscribed may if not paid at the times of their becoming due, be recovered by the receivor in the name of the Trustees on motion with 10 days previous notice in the General Court, or Court of the County where the subscription shall have been recorded. All monies subscribed as above shall be & the same are hereby appropriated to the said purpose of opening & extending the said navigation, and shall in no case be applied to any other purpose whatsoever; and the said Trustees are hereby authorized to issue their orders therefor on the said Receivers & to enter into contracts with any person or persons for clearing the said river or any part thereof, cutting canals, or constructing any lock or locks, or other works which they shall judge necessary or for preserving, repairing or attending the same when cut or constructed; provided that before any such canal shall be cut or works constructed the lands thro' which or whereon the same are proposed to be executed, shall be viewed & valued by a jury in the same manner as is directed by law in cases of petitions for land to build a mill on, and shall be paid for by the said Trustees before any use shall be made of such lands.

And Be it enacted that in case the said sum of   shall have been expended without compleating the purpose for which the same was subscribed, the Trustees are hereby authorized by a Receiver or Receivers appd as aforesaid to take further subscriptions not exceeding pounds, payment thereof to be made at such times as the Trustees shall fix, and to be secured in manner aforesaid.

And Be it enacted that in case the monies subscribed in pursuance of this Act shall not on the   day of   amount to the sum of the several subscriptions shall be cancelled, and shall not be recoverable, But if the sum subscribed shall on the said of   day of amount to   in that case the same and all other sums subscribed under this act, shall bear an interest of   per Ct. to be paid annually on the   day of   And as a further security & encouragement to the Subscribers the tolls hereafter to be fixed & collected on the Said River above tide water are hereby pledged & appropriated as a fund for discharging first the interest & then the principal of their respective subscriptions.[1]

Ms (Vi). In JM's hand; docketed, "A Bill for opening and Extending the Navigation of James River." John Beckley's endorsement indicates the bill passed both houses and was headed for the speaker's table on 1 Jan. 1785, but circumstances explained in the editorial note led to its abandonment.

[1] JM was appointed chairman of a drafting committee for the James River bill on 15 Dec. and he introduced this version on 18 Dec. (*JHDV*, Oct. 1784, pp. 70, 75). It was only the speaker's signature away from becoming law by 31 Dec. Meanwhile, the Potomac bill sponsored by Washington cleared the Maryland legislature and its approach to canal building had more appeal to the delegates. As JM explained to Jefferson, his plan "was pronounced by good judges an inadequate bait for subscriptions" so that "on the arrival and acceptance of the Potowmac plan, it was found advisable to pass a similar one in favor of James River" (JM to Jefferson, 9 Jan. 1785). Unquestionably, some political logrolling that is not evident in the journal or in JM's correspondence was involved.

From Edmund Pendleton

Letter not found.

18 December 1784. The list probably kept by Peter Force (DLC: Madison Miscellany) indicates Pendleton wrote a letter from Edmundsbury on this day that was an "Appeal for the family of Philip Davis; a forger of tobacco notes." The punishment for forging tobacco notes was death (Hening, *Statutes*, IX, 516). Counterfeiting and forgery were accounted treason and under the common law the estate of the felon was forfeited to the state. The petition on behalf of "the family" was an effort to save the estate of Philip Davis for the benefit of his family. There is no surviving evidence that JM aided Davis, who, although convicted, was reprieved and his sentence was commuted to five years of public labor (*JCSV*, III, 414, 416, 419, 422; Patrick Henry to Charles Pearson, 28 Mar. 1785, Executive Letter Book, pp. 452–53).

Madison's Notes for Debates on
the General Assessment Bill

EDITORIAL NOTE

Once the Revolution began, most Virginians accepted all fundamental breaks with the past save one—the established church. Clearly it was preservation of the old, comforting traditions of the Anglican church and not the institution of established religion per se that interested many men who ordinarily had the most advanced ideas about individual rights. Thus the maintenance of even the most tenuous ties to the old formal religious past became a highly controversial matter. To men whose bent was to seek out the superficial as an answer for the complex, it was easy to assume that broken bonds with the Anglican church explained the noticeable "decline in morals during the war" (Meade, *Patrick Henry*, II, 275–78). The tide in Virginia after the peace treaty was ratified ran in a conservative direction, with religious affairs the most evident symbol of the gap between contending philosophies, and with Patrick Henry ready to champion a state-church tie. Circumstances placed JM foremost among those against a religious subsidy from the state.

The tocsin had been sounded at the May 1784 session of the General Assembly, when there had been a two-pronged effort to cling to the prewar condition vis-à-vis Anglicanism. A bill was brought forward by the conservatives for incorporating the Protestant Episcopal church, which would have given the old Anglican vestries legal title to the church buildings, parish houses, and other property. Another measure, traveling under the euphemistic name of a General Assessment bill, "would simply place Virginia in the path then followed by the three New England States least liberal in religion" (Nevins, *American States during and after the Revolution*, p. 338). JM went to Richmond in the spring of 1784 forewarned that Henry would push the bill from behind the scenes, and its adversaries hoped the issue would seem doubtful enough that Henry would not risk his popularity by championing the bill "in public" (Randolph to Jefferson, 15 May 1784, Boyd, *Papers of Jefferson*, VII, 260).

For JM and his liberal-minded friends in the legislature, the question was not whether Virginians were swearing more, drinking in excess, racing horses too avidly after Sunday church services, bearing more illegitimate children than in earlier times, or any other specific grievance—but whether the state had any right whatever to tax its citizens in support of a religious establishment. The time had not been ripe in 1776 to implement fully Article XVI of the Declaration of Rights, nor had the winds of change been strong enough in 1779, when Jefferson's bill fixing religious freedom had passed two readings and then languished in the committee pigeonhole. As sometimes happens in legislative experience, a positive law has to await the turmoil of public debate over a negative measure, until its adherents can then make their bid while the discredited bill is being swept away in little pieces. This was to be JM's experience with the General Assessment bill—although the salutary outcome was hardly foreseeable in November 1784. At the May

1784 General Assembly there had been rumblings from outlying districts where the old Anglican leaders calculated that the public good and tax-supported churches or schools were inextricably interwoven (Warwick County petition, *JHDV*, May 1784, p. 8). The Baptists, as usual, protested in the other direction, and the upshot was that an incorporating bill for the Episcopal church was introduced and carried over. As JM reported to Jefferson, the boldness of the one-time Anglicans was in itself insufficient to save the incorporating act, but it was finally saved "from a dishonorable death by the talents of Mr. Henry" (JM to Jefferson, 3 July 1784). Equally unsure of their strength on the General Assessment bill, its supporters also allowed it to be deferred until the October session.

While JM had been traveling that autumn above the Potomac, witnessing Indian powwows and chatting with old friends in Philadelphia, the advocates of a connection between church and state had been engaged in more serious pursuits. Petitions from Henry's old bailiwick in Hanover County and elsewhere seemed proof that Virginians wanted a return to the earlier custom of public support for religious bodies. JM learned one lesson from this experience and did not thereafter wait for public opinion to manifest itself casually. The advocates of a church-state tie found that the petitions, private conversations, Henry's known friendliness, and a real division among the liberals as to what was their best course—all these factors in combination meant that JM had to fight a rear-guard action at the October 1784 General Assembly session and devise stratagems to keep the liberals' loss from turning into a rout. His notes for speeches attacking the Assessment bill are not the carefully planned work needed to stop a steamroller. What his colleagues thought of such efforts was predictable—the younger progressives thought JM "display'd great Learning & Ingenuity, with all the Powers of a close reasoner" (Beverly Randolph to Monroe, 26 Nov. 1784 [DLC: Monroe Papers]). Surely Richard Henry Lee knew JM's position and probably his speeches, so Lee's remarks to JM on the debates must be read in that light. "Refiners may weave as fine a web of reason as they please, but the experience of all times shews Religion to be the guardian of morals" (26 Nov. 1784).

The battle over incorporating the Protestant Episcopal church was over by Christmas 1784, with JM voting for the revised bill, not out of conviction, but to gain time. The Christmas Eve vote to postpone a third reading of the bill "establishing a provision for the teachers of the christian religion"—the General Assessment bill in a new dress—was another bargain to gain precious months (*JHDV*, Oct. 1784, p. 82). How could public opinion in Virginia be weaned away from this reactionary measure? Where was the dream JM shared with Jefferson that was set down in the dust-covered bill for establishing religious freedom?

When such old and liberal allies as Richard Henry Lee and Edmund Pendleton thought he had overreacted to the General Assessment bill, it was time for JM to ponder. In his letter of 26 Nov. 1784 Lee assured JM that greed was destroying religion in Virginia "for want of a legal obligation to contribute something to its support," and Pendleton agreed. As Pendleton viewed the matter, the proposed bills contained nothing "which can justly alarm any other society" although he admitted "some very sagacious gentle-men, can spy designs to revive the former establishment" (Pendleton to Lee, 28 Feb. 1785, Mays, *Papers of Edmund Pendleton*, II, 474). So JM stood in the minority at the October 1784 session and was forced to bide his time, but the sentences for his "Memorial and Remonstrance against Religious As-sessments" (ca. 20 June 1785) must have been already forming in his mind.

[Outline A]

[23–24 December 1784]

Debate on Bill for Relig. Estabt proposed by Mr. Henry[1]

1. limited
2. in particular
3. What is Christianity?[2] Courts of law to Judge
4. What edition, Hebrew, Septuagint, or vulgate? What copy—what translation?
5. What books canonical, what apochryphal? the papists holding to be the former what protestants the latter, the Lutherans the latter what other protestants & papists the former
6. In What light are they to be viewed, as dictated every letter by inspiration, or the essential parts only? or the matter in generall not the words?
7. What sense the true one, for if some doctrines be essential to *Christianity*, those who reject these, whatever name they take are no *Christian* Society?
8. Is it Trinitarianism, arianism, Socinianism? Is it salvation by faith or works also—by free grace, or free will—&c &c &c—
9. What clue is to guide Judge thro' this labyrinth? When the ques-tion comes before them whether any particular Society is a Chris-tian Society?
10. Ends in what is orthodoxy, what heresy?

Ms (DLC). In JM's hand, on a halfsheet, apparently prepared for the House debate. The heading was added by JM some time later.

[1] A dramatic reconstruction of the speech is found in Brant, *Madison*, II, 344–45. Brant infers that Henry's power was so obvious that the opposition, including JM, wished to elect Henry governor and thus "get him out" of the legislature before passage of the Assessment bill. See JM to James Monroe, 14 Nov. and 27 Nov. 1784.

[2] JM used the ancient abbreviation "Xn" for Christian, and "Xnty" for Christi-anity. These have been expanded throughout.

[Outline B]

[23–24 December 1784]

I. *Rel:* not within purview of Civil Authority.
tendency of Estabg. Christianity

              1. to project of Uniformity
              2. to penal laws for supportg. it.

———

Progres[s] of Gen: Assest. proves this tendency

———

difference between estabg. & tolerating errour—

II. True question not—Is Rel: necesy.?
are Religs. Estabts. necessy. for Religion? no.
1. propensity of man to Religion.
2. Experience shews Relig: corrupted by Estabt.
3. downfal of States, mentioned by Mr. H[enry]. happened where
there was Estabts.
4. Experience gives no model of Gel. Asst?
5. Case of Pa. explained—not solitary. N. J.
See Const: of it. R. I. N. Y. D.

———

    factions greater in S. C.
6. Case of primitive Christianity.
of Reformation
of Dissenters formerly.

III. Decl: Rig[hts]. 7. Progress of Religious Liberty

IV. Policy.
1. promote emigrations from State
2. prevent [immigration] into it as *asylum*

V. Necessity of Estabts. inferred from State of Conty.

———

true causes of disease
1. War   ⎱ common to other States &
2. bad laws ⎰ produce same complts. in N. E.

3. pretext from taxes
4. State of Administration of Justice.
5. transition from old to new plan.
6. policy & hopes of friends to G. Asst.

_____

true remedies not Estabt. but being out war
1. laws cherish virtue
2. Administ: justice
3. personal example—Association for R.
4. By present vote cut off hope of G. Asst.
5. Education of youth

_____

Probable defects of Bill
    dishonor Christianity

_____

    panegyric on it on our side

_____

    Decl: Rights.[1]

Ms (DLC). Written by JM on the outer cover of a letter "Favd. by Colonel Taylor," otherwise unidentified, with a later endorsement by JM: "Debate on the Bill for Religious Assessment."

[1] Editor Hunt assumed that JM prepared these outlines (A and B) as a single document. There is nothing to substantiate this assumption and the notes in Madison, *Writings* (Hunt ed.), II, 88–89, imply a unity that probably never existed. The circumstances make it likely that JM spoke on this subject several times, but the outline he used initially is uncertain.

To James Monroe

RICHMOND Decr. 24. 1784.[1]

DEAR SIR

Your favor of the 14th. instant came to hand on thursday. A proposition was made a few days ago for this State to empower Congs. to carry into effect the imposts as soon as 12 States should make themselves parties to it. It was rejected on the following grounds 1. that it would present a disagreeable aspect of our affairs to Foreign nations. 2 that it might lead to other combinations of lesser numbers of the States. 3. that it would render R. I. an inlet for clandestine trade. 4. that it would sour her temper still further, at a crisis when her concurrence in some general & radical amendment of the Confederation may be invited by Congress. 5 that the chance is almost infinitely agst. a Union of 12 States on such new ground, and consequently the experiment would be only a fresh display of the jarring policy of the States, and afford a fresh triumph & irritation to R Island. The Act empowering Congs. to surrender Citizens of this State, to the Sovereign demanding them for certain crimes committed within his jurisdiction has passed. Congress are to Judge whether the crimes be such as according to the Law of Nations warrant such demand, as well as whether the fact be duly proven. Concurrent provision is made for punishing such offences by our own laws in case no such demand be made to or be not admitted by Congs. and legal proof can be had.[2] The latter law extends to offences agst. the Indians. As these tribes do not observe the law of Nations it was supposed neither necessary nor proper to give up Citizens to them. The Act is not suspended on the concurrence of any other State, being judged favorable to the interest of this tho' no other should follow the example, and [naturally ?] a fit branch of the fœderal prerogative. The Bill for Assize Courts has passed the Senate without any material amendment, is enrolled, and waits only to be examined by the Committee & signed by the Speakers. The Genl. Assesst. on the question for engrossing it, was yesterday carried by 44 agst. 42. Today its third reading was put off till Novr. next by 45 agst. 37 or thereabouts, and is to be printed for consideration of the people.[3] Much business is still on the table but we shall probably rise about New Years day. I am Dr Sir with sincere regard Yr. freind & Servt.

J. MADISON JR.

RC (DLC). Addressed to Monroe, "in Congress." Docketed by JM.

[1] The letter is dated "1785" but JM inserted "4" above the "5."

[2] The "concurrent provision" held that persons who committed crimes in the territory "of any christian nation or Indian tribe, in amity with the United States," would be liable to prosecution "on proof of such offence by oath of one or more credible witness or witnesses" (Hening, *Statutes*, XI, 471).

[3] The 44 to 42 vote on the proposed bill "establishing a provision for the teachers of the Christian religion" indicates the sharp division over this controversial measure. JM voted with the majority (45 to 38) in postponing action on the bill. The House voted to send twelve printed copies of the bill along with "the names of the ayes and noes" on the postponement motion, to each member of the General Assembly for distribution "in their respective counties" (*JHDV*, Oct. 1784, p. 82).

To Richard Henry Lee

Decr. 25. 1784

"In the course of the last week a proposition was made to empower Congress to collect the Impost within this State [Virginia][1] as soon as 12 States shd. unite in the Scheme. The argumts. which prevailed agst. it were the unfavorable aspect it wd. present to foreigners, the tendency of the example to inferior combinations—the field it wd. open for contraband trade—its probable affect on the temper of R. Isld. which might thwart other necessary measures requiring the unanimity of the States—the improbability of the union of 12. States on this new ground, a failure of which wd. increase the appearance of discord in their policy; and give fresh triumph & irritation to Rh. Isd.

I have not yet found leisure to scan the project of a Continental Convention with so close an eye as to have made up any observations worthy of being mentioned to you.[2] In general I hold it for a maxim that the Union of the States is essential to their safety agst. foreign danger, & internal contention; and that the perpetuity & efficacy of the present system can not be confided on. The question therefore is, in what mode & at what moment the experiment for supplying the defects ought to be made. The answer to this question can not be given without a knowledge greater than I possess of the temper & views of the different States. Virginia seems I think to have excellent dispositions towards the Confederacy, but her assent or dissent to such a proposition wd. probably depend on the chance of its having no opponent capable of rousing the prejudices & jealousies of the Assembly agst. innovations, particularly such as will derogate from their own power & importance.[3] Should a view of the other States present no objections agst. the experiment, individually I wd. wish none to be presupposed here"

FC (DLC). In JM's hand. Headed, "Extract from a letter from JM to Richd H Lee." Dockered by JM.

[1] JM's brackets.
[2] Lee had suggested in his 26 Nov. 1784 letter that there was an undercurrent of sentiment in Congress for a convention to revise the Articles of Confederation. The obstructionism of Rhode Island was forcing the delegates to consider ways and means of dropping the requirement for unanimity (Art. XIII) by the state legislatures before any alteration of the compact then holding the Union together.
[3] The chance that a revision of the Articles of Confederation would have "no opponent" in Virginia depended on the disposition, as JM well knew, of either Patrick Henry or George Mason—two powerful men whose attitude toward enlarging the powers of Congress "were not yet known" (Rives, *Life of Madison*, II, 34).

From Richard Henry Lee

DEAR SIR,

Your favor of the 11th. reached me ten days after its date and after the post had gone out for that week, so that I fear this letter will not get to Richmd. before the adjournment. The proceedings of last Assembly respecting B. debts have not yet been before Congress, because they have not arrived at this place.[1] It seems that they were deposited in Mr. Hardys Trunk which a variety of accidents have prevented him from getting brought here before the adjournment of Congress, which took place on the 24th. They have determined to make New York the place of their temporary residence, & the permanent one is to be on the banks of Delaware within 8 miles of this place, where the fœderal buildings are to be erected as soon as possible. The new Congress meets on the first Monday in Novr. annually. Now it is plain that since the meeting of our Assembly is not until late in October, and as they seldom convene until long after the stipulated time, there is no probability of Virginia being represented for a considerable time after the fœderal time appointed. North Carolina [is] in the same situation, and to avoid the inconvenience has already sent forward her choice of Delegates for 1786 to take their seats on the 2d. monday in Novr. 1785. The Confederation says, to meet *on* the 1st. Monday, yet the Credentials of most States, & ours among the number, has it *From* the 1st. Monday, which inaccuracy has caused some debates in Congress, and is fitted to exclude Members for one day, and thereby, in some instances may be productive of inconvenience—this should be alter'd in our next form. I think that the Assize law will improve much the dispensation of Justice in our Country a thing devoutly to be wished. I am very apprehensive that a war with the Southern Indians will take place. Land Speculators, & Spanish jealousy will probably force it on, before our treaty with them can take place. We have such momentous concerns with the two courts of Madrid & London, that we shall be obliged to send special Ministers to each of them, or else a war may be the consequence of neglect. Mr. Madison has been nominated for Spain, and is much approved by the Southern States.[2] The conversation concerning a Continental Convention has ceased for some time, so that perhaps it may not be revived again. The pointed manner in which Spain insists upon the exclusive navigation of Mississippi renders it of more important consequence to explore & improve the navigation of the waters running thro our States. In a few days I proceed to N. York, having given a little time for fitting a Presidents House there. The Members of Congress, except two or 3, are already departed for N. York & Philadelphia.

RC (DLC). Cover missing. Docketed by JM. Lee's complimentary closing and signature have been cut away from the third page.

[1] "The proceedings of the last Assembly respecting B[ritish]. debts" were the resolutions passed by the House of Delegates on 23 June instructing the Virginia delegates in Congress to request "a remonstrance to the British Court" against infraction of the Treaty of Paris. The delegates were further to inform Congress "that the General Assembly have no inclination to interfere with the power of making treaties with foreign nations . . . but it is conceived that a just regard to the national honor and interest of the citizens of this Commonwealth, obliges the Assembly to withhold their co-operation in the complete fulfilment of the said treaty, until the success of the aforesaid remonstrance is known, or Congress shall signify their sentiments touching the premises" (*JHDV*, May 1784, p. 74). JM had tried to soften the belligerent tone of the resolution by introducing amendments of his own, but these lacked sufficient support.

[2] Lee mistakenly inserted JM's name here but must have meant "Mr. Jefferson." Monroe had written JM nine days earlier mentioning Jefferson's nomination for the Spanish post by a group that included Lee himself (Monroe to JM, 18 Dec. 1784).

From George Washington

ANNAPOLIS 28th. Decr 1784.

DEAR SIR,

I have been favored with your letter of the 11th.

The proceedings of the Conference, and the Act & Resolutions of this Legislature consequent thereupon (herewith transmitted to the Assembly) are so full, & explanatory of the motives which governed in this business, that it is scarcely necessary for me to say any thing in addition to them; except that this State seem highly impressed with the importance of the objects wch. we have had under consideration, and are very desirous of seeing them accomplished.[1]

We have reduced most of the Tolls from what they were in the first Bill, and have added something to a few others—upon the whole, we have made them as low as we conceived from the best information before us, and such estimates as we had means to calculate upon, as they can be fixed, without hazarding the plan altogether. We made the value of the commodity the governing principle in the establishment of the Tolls; but having had an eye to some bulky articles of produce, & to the encouragement of the growth & Manufacture of some others, as well as to prevent a tedeous ennumeration of the different species of all, we departed from the genl. Rule in many instances.

The Rates of tollage as now fixed, may still appear high to some of the Southern Gentlemen, when they compare them with those on James River; but as there is no comparison in the expence & Risk of the two undertakings so neither ought there to be in the Tolls. I am fully perswaded that the Gentlemen who were appointed, and have had this matter under consideration, were actuated by no other motives than to hit (if they could do so) upon such a happy medium as would not be burthensome to indiv. or give Jealousy to the public on one hand, nor discouragement to Adventurers on the other. To secure success, and to give vigor to the undertaking, it was judged advisable for each State to contribute (upon the terms of private subscribers) to the expence of it; especially as it might have a happy influence on the Minds of the Western Settlers and it may be observed here, that only part of this money can be called for immediately, provided the work goes on—and afterwards, only in the proportion of its progression.

Though there is no obligation upon the State to adopt this (if it is inconvenient, or repugnant to their wishes) yet I should be highly pleased to hear that they had done so—(Our advantages will, most assuredly, be equal to those of Maryland and our public spirit ought not, in my opinion, to be less)—as also the Resolutions respecting the Roads of Communication—both of which, tho they look in some degree to different objects, are both very important; that by the Yohiogany (thro' Pensylvania) is particularly so for the Fur & Peltry of the Lakes, because it is the most direct Rout by which they can be transported; whilst it is exceedingly convenient to the people who inhabit the Ohio (or Alligany) above Fort Pitt—the lower part of the Monongahela—and all the Yohiogany.

Matters might perhaps have been better digested if more time had been taken, but the fear of not getting the report to Richmond before the Assembly would have risen, occasioned more hurry than accuracy— or even real dispatch. But to alter the Act now, further than to accomodate it to circumstances where it is essential, or to remedy an obvious error if any should be discovered will not do. The Bill passed this Assembly with only 9 dissenting voices—and got thro' both Houses in a day, so earnest were the members of getting it to you in time.

It is now near 12 at night, and I am writing with an Aching head, having been constantly employed in this business since the 22d. without assistance from my Colleagues—Genl. Gates having been Sick the whole time, & Colo. Blackburn not attending. But for this I would be more explicit. I am, with great esteem & regard—Dr Sir Yr. Most Obedt. Servt

Go: WASHINGTON

I am ashamed to send such a letter, but cannot give you a fairer one. GW.

RC (owned by Dr. Joseph E. Fields, Joliet, Illinois, 1958); Tr (DLC). Cover missing. Docketed by JM.

[1] The enclosures, now widely dispersed, included a holograph letter from Washington (also signed by General Gates) addressed to the General Assembly (Vi); and Washington's schedule of canal tolls, which bears JM's endorsement: "Rates of Tollage" (ICU). As JM soon explained to Jefferson, Washington was the prime mover of the Potomac canal bill and the enclosed bill from Maryland "arrived just in time for the session" (9 Jan. 1785). Washington probably sent them by an express rider, for the whole bundle was before the legislature three days later. JM apparently went through channels by turning the enclosures over to the governor, who relayed them to the Speaker of the House. Washington's report was turned over to a committee that included JM and William Grayson (*JHDV*, Oct. 1784, p. 99). Grayson introduced the Virginia version of the Maryland act, which was hurriedly "passed without opposition" (compare *Laws of Maryland . . . at the Session of . . . 1784* [Annapolis, 1785], chap. XXXIII, and Hening, *Statutes*, XI, 510–25).

Act Concerning the Appointment of Sheriffs

[28 December 1784]

Be it enacted by the General Assembly that if the *Justices of the peace* for any County within This CommonWealth shall fail to nominate persons for Sheriff according to the periods prescribed by Law every Justice so neglecting his Duty shall forfeit and pay the sum of   *pounds & more over shall be subject to be displaced by the Governor & Council.* If any person hereafter to be appointed Sheriff of any County shall fail to give Bond in   months after his appointment the Clerk of the Court shall within one month thereafter transmit to the Governor for the time being a certificate of such neglect or failure under the penalty of   pounds. If any person hereafter to be nominated Sheriff of a County shall fail to make application to the Governor for a Commission within   month after such nomination the Governor with the advice of the Council shall and may commission *any Justice of the Peace of the said County* to be Sheriff of the same.

And be it farther enacted that no under *Sheriff* shall continue in Office more than two Years.[1]

Ms (Vi). The first sentence is in JM's hand, the remainder in a clerk's. Docketed by a clerk with the title and dates of various readings.

[1] This sentence was deleted in the final version of the measure. Instead a section was added to relieve sheriffs from damage suits for failing to collect the 1783 taxes owing to "the scarcity of money and other circumstances." The amendments are on two pages accompanying the main manuscript. JM was on the drafting committee appointed 7 Dec. to prepare the bill. The legislation was introduced on 28 Dec., turned over to the Committee for Courts of Justice the next day, and finally passed 31 Dec. (*JHDV*, Oct. 1784, pp. 60, 84, 92, 96, 98; Hening, *Statutes*, XI, 463).

Resolutions Authorizing an Interstate Compact on Navigation and Jurisdiction of the Potomac

December 28th. 1784

Resolved that the Commissioners or any two of them appointed on the 28th. day of June last[1] to concert with Commissioners on the part of Maryland, regulations touching the navigation and jurisdiction of the Potowmac, be further authorized ⟨to unite⟩ with the said commissioners in representing to the State of Pennsylvania, that it is in contemplation of the ⟨said⟩ two States to promote the clearing and extending the navigation of ⟨the⟩ Potowmac from tide-water upwards as far as the same may be found practicable; to open a convenient road from the head of such navigation to the waters running into the Ohio; and to render these waters navigable as far as may be necessary & proper: that the said Work will require great expence which may not be repaid, unless a free use be secured to the said States & their Citizens, of the Waters of the Ohio and its branches, so far as the same lie within the limits of Pennsylvania: that as essential advantages will accrue from such works to a considerable portion of the said State, it is thought reasonable that the Legislature thereof should by some previous act engage that for the encouragement of the said works all articles of produce or merchandize which may be conveyed to or from either of the said two States, through either of the said rivers within the limits of Pennsylvania, to or from any place without the said limits, shall pass throughout free from all duties or tolls whatsoever, other than such tolls as may be established and be necessary for reimbursing expences incurred by the State or its Citizens in clearing, or for defraying the expence of preserving the navigation of the said rivers; And that no articles imported into the State of Pennsylvania through the channel or channels or any part thereof to be opened as aforesaid and vended or used within the said State, shall be subject to any duties or imposts other than such articles would be subject to if imported into the said State thro' any other channel whatsoever; And it is further resolved that in case a joint representation in behalf of this State and of Maryland shall be rendered by circumstances unattainable, the said Commissiers. or any two of them may of themselves make such representations on the subject ⟨to the State of Pennsylvania ,⟩ as will in such event become proper; and that in either event they report their proceedings to the next General Assembly.

Resolved that a Copy of the above Resolutions be transmitted forthwith by the Executive to the State of Maryland.

Ms, FC (Vi). In JM's hand, and later docketed by him. The FC was used for the version printed in *JHDV*, Oct. 1784, p. 91. Additions made by the General Assembly are printed here within angle brackets.

[1] The commissioners appointed exactly ten months earlier were Alexander Henderson, JM, George Mason, and Edmund Randolph. They had not met to carry out their earlier assignment, which was now considerably enlarged. An administrative blunder almost nullified the efforts made in Mar. 1785 to clarify the rights of Virginia and Maryland citizens regarding river commerce and fishing (Brant, *Madison*, II, 375–76). The Virginia commissioners—Henderson and Mason—made their report on 28 Mar. 1785 (Rutland, *Papers of George Mason*, II, 814 21), while Mason explained the circumstances and outcome of the Mount Vernon conference to JM in his letter of 9 Aug. 1785. The interstate agreement was a hopeful sign, and in one sense this meeting was the embryo of the Federal Convention of 1787.

Resolution for Opening Roads to Market Towns

[ca. 30 December 1784][1]

Whereas the opening & keeping in repair of direct roads from the different parts of this Commonth. to the several market Towns, and from one market Town to another would greatly encourage agriculture by cheapening the transportation of its productions to the places of consumption & exportation, and would in other respects contribute to the improvement of the Country by facilitating intercourse between the different parts thereof; and it is considered by the present General Assembly, that altho' the various necessary burdens which now press in on the people render a general plan for the aforesaid purpose unadvisable at this moment, yet that such a beginning ought to be made in the work as will not only produce immediate advantage to the community; but will lead to a more diffusive & compleat execution thereof: And it is the more necessary that the principal roads should be so straightened before the value of the ground to be obtained from individuals increase

Be it therefore enacted that the Governour with advice of the Council of State shall be & he hereby is authorized to cause surveys to be made in order to determine the best courses for roads, (having regard to the nature of the ground as well as to distance) from & to the following places: to wit; from

And for executing such surveys the Governor with the advice aforesaid is further authorized to appoint a proper person for each of such surveys who shall be allowed a sum not exceeding   perday during his actual employment in the service, and who may take with him so many assistants & such daily wages as the Executive shall approve. The said Surveyors shall make to the Governour the

Ms (DLC). In JM's hand and later headed by him: "1784 or 5—prepared to be introduced into the Virga. Legisl: [.]" Docketed in an unidentified hand. On the verso JM wrote notes for debates over repeal of the Episcopal Incorporation Act that took place at the Oct. 1786 session of the General Assembly.

[1] The conjectural date on this document is assigned solely by the circumstances. After the legislature began debating bills on canal construction that would favor tidewater communities (20–31 Dec. 1784), it was logical to make concessions to the counties whose marketing facilities were not based on river transportation. Directed at these circumstances, a bill aiding construction of inland roadways thus seemed most expedient, if not logical. For reasons no longer apparent, JM never presented the measure, but he did introduce Jefferson's "Bill concerning Public Roads" at the Oct. 1785 session of the General Assembly. That bill became law and by its provisions met the purposes of JM's pigeonholed proposal. See Boyd, *Papers of Jefferson*, II, 448–53. Sometime between Oct. 1784 and Dec. 1786 JM was delving into the laws of other states in search of more efficacious statutes. During this period he made a set of notes from the 1772 Pennsylvania "act for opening & keeping in repair public roads," the contents of which are in no way related to the resolution printed here despite the similarity of the opening phrases. Hunt misinterpreted JM's heading and printed the notes as a 1772 item (Madison, *Writings* [Hunt ed.], I, 13–15). On the other hand, it could be argued that JM wrote this resolution about the time of the Oct. 1786 General Assembly session. He had written Jefferson on 19 June 1786 inquiring about an alternative to "the present vicious plan" of road repairs (Boyd, *Papers of Jefferson*, IX, 661). Possibly, JM tinkered with the idea of creating a responsible board of road commissioners and intended to use this resolution as a legislative lever. If this were the case, then this resolution may have been the pending road legislation which Francis Corbin reported that JM had hoped to introduce but "he had not time to complete" (Corbin to Richard Henry Lee, 20 Jan. 1787 [ViU: Lee Family Papers]).

To George Washington

RICHMOND Jany. 1. 1785

DEAR SIR

I was yesterday honored with your favor of the 28 Ult: accompanying the Report of the Conferees &c. &c.[1] The latter have been laid before the H. of Delegates, and a Com[mitte]e app[ointe]d. to report a bill & Resolutions corresponding with those of Maryland. The only danger of miscarriage arises from the impatience of the members to depart, & the bare competency of the present numbers. By great efforts only they have been detained thus long. I am not without hopes however that the business of the Potowmac at least will be provided for before the adjournment, and some provision now depending be compleated in favor of James River. Before the rect. of your despatches a bill had been passed by the H. of D. for surveying the former as well as the latter river on a plan, which we shall endeavour by concert with the Senate, to accomodate to the provisions of Maryland.[2] A Resolution has passed both Houses instructing the Commissrs. app[ointe]d. in June last to settle with Maryd. Commissrs. the jurisdiction & navigation of the Potowmac, to join in a representation to Pena. on the subject of the Waters of the Ohio within her limits.[3] This instruction ought rather to have been committed to the late Conference; but when the Commission under which you attended it passed, I was confined to my room and it did not occur to any other member. And indeed if I had been well the haste which necessarily prevailed might have precluded me from comprehending the object within your Mission, especially as I had not previously digested any ideas on the subject nor accurately examined the text of the Confederation. It were to be wished too I think that the application to Pa. on the subject of the Road cd. have been blended with that of the Rivers. As it is it will I think be best to refer it after the example of Maryld. to the Executive. I beg you Sir to excuse the brevity which our hurry has imposed upon me. As soon as I have leisure I will endeavour to make amends for it by a fuller communication on this subject—remaining in the mean time with the most perfect esteem & sincerest regard Yr. Obedt. & humble Servt.

J. MADISON JR.

RC (DLC: Washington Papers); FC (DLC). RC docketed by Washington.

[1] After Washington wrote Governor Harrison on 10 Oct. 1784 on ways and means of building James and Potomac canals the letter had been sent to the House of Delegates to provide a kind of blueprint for creating the required public corporations (Fitzpatrick, *Writings of Washington*, XXVII, 471–80). To implement Washington's suggestions the House of Delegates appointed three Virginia "Conferees"—Washington, Horatio Gates, and Thomas Blackburn—who were to meet with Maryland appointees(*JHDV*, Oct. 1784, p. 68). A good account of Washington's activities is found in Freeman, *George Washington*, VI, 25–27. As Washington explained in his letter to JM on 28 Dec., the whole business fell on his shoul-

ders, "Genl. Gates having been Sick the whole time, & Colo. Blackburn not attending" (Washington to JM, 28 Dec. 1784). Washington relayed to Richmond the bill which had resulted from his talks with the Maryland conferees and this legislation became the model for two laws enacted by the Virginia General Assembly in its waning hours. JM's bill of 18 Dec. (which was scrapped when the Maryland measure arrived) represented the first ideas on how the canals should be financed.

[2] The survey bill, passed before Washington's dispatches arrived, was introduced on 21 Dec. but had not become law when JM received the general's 28 Dec. letter. A House-Senate conference committee had been trying to iron out differences between the two bodies on 31 Dec., when Washington's letter arrived, and on 1 Jan. 1785 JM was ordered to inform the Senate its amendments were not acceptable (*JHDV*, Oct. 1784, p. 102). This bill seems to have been allowed to die, however, for JM introduced a resolution imitative of that adopted in Maryland, which provided for a survey of the James and a link with "the nearest navigable part of the waters running into the Ohio" (ibid.).

[3] The resolution which had "passed both Houses" dealing with Potomac navigation was JM's. He introduced the resolution creating an interstate commission three days before Washington's letter arrived. JM was appointed to serve on this commission, which met at Mount Vernon in Mar. 1785, but JM did not attend its sessions. See George Mason to JM, 9 Aug. 1785.

Resolutions Appointing a Western Road Commissioner

IN THE HOUSE OF DELEGATES January the 1st 1785.

RESOLVED that Thomas Massey esquire[1] or in case of his death or failing to act through other cause, such person as shall be appointed by the Executive in his Stead, be authorized in Conjunction with the person appointed or to be appointed on the Part of Maryland, to open and keep in repair a convenient road from such part of the Waters of the Potowmack, to such part of the River Cheat—or of the River Monongalia, as on examination they shall judge most eligible; and that the sum of three thousand three hundred thirty three and one third dollars, arising from the taxes of the year 1784, out of the money subject to votes of the General Assembly, be paid by the Treasurer, on the joint order of the persons to be appointed as aforesaid, to be by them applied together with a like sum voted by the State of Maryland to the purpose aforesaid.[2]

RESOLVED that the Governor be desired to write to the State of Pensylvania, requesting permission to lay out and improve a Road through such part of the said State, as may be necessary in the best and most proper direction from fort Cumberland to the navigable Part of the River Yohogania.

Ms (Vi). In a clerk's hand, endorsed by John Beckley and Will Drew. Docketed, "Resolution's [*sic*] 1st: January 1785. appointing a Commissioner to open a Road from the Waters of the Potowmac to the Cheat River," and at the lower margin, "Mr. Madison."

¹ Thomas Massie (1748–1834) attended William and Mary and served as an officer in the Revolution, 1775–1781, including a stint as aide-de-camp to Gen. Thomas Nelson. He later settled in Nelson County (Tyler, *Encyclopedia of Virginia Biography*, II, 142).

² Washington must have been the prime mover behind this resolution, which follows the line of reasoning in his 10 Oct. 1784 letter to Governor Harrison. In that important message Washington noted that goods could be brought from Pittsburgh to Alexandria "by the Yohoghaney in 304 Miles; whereof only 31 is land transportation: And by the Monongahela and Cheat river in 300 miles; 20 only of which are land carriage" (Fitzpatrick, *Writings of Washington*, XXVII, 478). Washington had recently heard from an expert on distances and he may have shared this information about land routes with JM (Grace L. Nute, ed., "Washington and the Potomac: Manuscripts of the Minnesota Historical Society, [1754] 1769–1796, II," *AHR*, XXVIII [1922–23], 705). JM introduced the resolution and carried it to the Senate after its passage—conclusive evidence he was the author.

Resolution Authorizing Payment to Certain French Creditors

IN THE HOUSE OF DELEGATES January the 1st 1784 [1785]

RESOLVED that so much of the Petition of Savary De Valcoulon¹ agent for Messrs Coulougnac and Company merchants of France, as sets forth, that in the year one thousand seven hundred and eighty one, Mr. Peter Pennet as agent for this State in France, was furnished with goods by the said Messrs Coulougnac & C° at a very low advance to a considerable amount, for which their accounts have been liquidated and a Warrant granted the Petitioner for the Balance adjudged to be due thereon, amounting to four thousand seven hundred and eighty five pounds fourteen shillings: That when the said goods were furnished the said Pennet he drew Bills of exchange in favor of the said Coulougnac & C° for the amount of their Claim, which were returned protested, and no allowance has been made them in the said settlement by way of damages in consequence of the said Protests, and praying relief is reasonable: And for ascertaining the damages which have accrued to the said Coulougnac & C° by reason of the said protests, that two persons be appointed one to be chosen by the Petitioner and the other by the Governor on the Part of this Commonwealth, to inquire into and settle the same upon commercial principles and that their report or the report of a third person, to be chosen by them, in case of disagreement Be

binding between the Petitioner and the Commonwealth, which reports
shall be made to the Executive for a Warrant to issue for such further
to Congress to collect the Impost within this State [Virginia][1] as soon
sum as shall be stated to be due to the said Messrs Coulougnac & C°.
RESOLVED that such other part of the said Petition as prays that funds
may be provided for the immediate Payment of the said claim of
Messrs Coulougnac & C° is reasonable.

Ms (Vi). In John Beckley's hand. Docketed "Resolutions . . . Concerning the
Claim of Savary de Valcoulon," with "Mr. Madison" written in the lower margin.

[1] A petition from de Valcoulon, received by the House of Delegates on 24 Nov.,
sought adjustment of the claims of Coulignac et Cie (*JHDV*, Oct. 1784, p. 37).
The petition was committed to the standing Committee of Commerce (JM, chairman). A third resolution rejected de Valcoulon's claim for reimbursement of "expenses incurred by him in coming to America." JM carried the approved resolutions to the Senate (ibid., Oct. 1784, p. 101).

Resolutions Authorizing Surveys for
a Western Road and Canal

EDITORIAL NOTE

During the last days of the October 1784 session of the General Assembly
there was a concerned drive to answer the complaints of isolated citizens in
the western counties and the Kentucky district for better roads. Some of the
interest undoubtedly stemmed from the attention focused on canal building
by Washington's lobbying activities on behalf of the Potomac and James
canals, but JM knew too that Virginians beyond the mountains were handicapped by uncertainties over their navigational rights on the Mississippi—
a moot point that was not to be settled soon. Washington argued that roads
and canals running from the tidewater region into the Piedmont passes would
make Alexandria, Norfolk, and other cities into great depots for western
produce provided there existed a cheap means of hauling goods to and from
the areas drained by tributaries of the Ohio. The delegates must have known,
moreover, that a separatist movement was taking shape across the mountains.
At almost the moment JM was introducing this series of resolutions on western roads a group of Kentucky district citizens were meeting to discuss ways
of achieving statehood (Abernethy, *Western Lands and the American Revolution*, p. 304). Among their complaints was "a greevance" because "Merchandize brought into this District by way of Pitsburg" was doubly taxed
(Thomas P. Abernethy, ed., "Journal of the First Kentucky Convention,
Dec. 27, 1784–Jan. 5, 1785," *Journal of Southern History*, I [1935], 75). This
meant that most of the goods brought to Kentucky were even higher than
usual because of transportation costs and dual taxation—a situation that would
be somewhat relieved if roads to Virginia ports were opened. One result of
these resolutions and the Kentucky complaints was that the October 1785
session of the legislature voted to build a public highway "at least thirty feet
wide" from Greenbrier County "to the lower falls of the Great Kanawa"
(Hening, *Statutes*, XII, 73).

In the House of Delegates 1 Jany. 1785

Resolved that the Executive be authorized to appoint three persons who or any two of whom shall make an accurate examination and Survey of James river from Lynch's Ferry in Campbell County upwards of the most convenient course for a road from the highest navigable part of the said river to the nearest navigable part of the Waters running into the Ohio, and of the said Waters running into the Ohio:[1] that they report to the next General Assembly a full account of such examination & survey with an Estimate of the expence necessary for improving the navigation of the said Waters of James river & of the Western Waters, & of clearing the said road; that they be authorized to call on the Lieutenant of the County of Green Brier for a Guard of Militia, not exceeding fifty Men, in case they shall Judge such Guard to be necessary which the sd. Lieutenant is hereby ordered to furnish, and which shall be paid by the Treasurer on Order of the Executive out of the Revenue for the year 1784 subject to be appropriated by Votes of the General Assembly; that the person so appointed shall be furnished out of the said Fund with such sum, not exceeding £200, as the Executive may Judge necessary, and shall each of them be allowed for his Services the Sum of 20/. for each day he shall be employed therein.

Resolved[2] that the Executive be further authorized[3] to appoint three other Commissioners, who or any two of whom shall carefully[4] examine & fix on the most convenient course for a Canal from the Waters of Eliza. River[5] in this State, to those passing thro the State of North Carolina & report their proceedings herein with an Estimate of the expence necessary[6] for opening such Canal to the next General Assembly. And in case they shall find that the best course of such Canal will require the concurrence of the State of North Carolina in the opening thereof, they are further authorized & instructed to signify the same to the said State and to concert with any Person or persons who may be appointed on the part thereof, the most convenient & equitable plan for the execution of such Work, & to report the result to the next General Assembly. The said Commissioners shall be entitled to the same allowance, and be paid in the same manner as those to be appointed under the preceding resolution.[7]

Resolved that the same allowance to be paid in the same manner be made to Thomas Massey for the Service which he is appointed to perform in conjunction with a Commissioner appointed or to be appointed by the State of Maryland.[8]

Ms (Vi). In a clerk's hand. The draft of the second resolution is in JM's hand (Vi). Docketed by clerks. The resolutions were introduced and passed on 1 Jan. (*JHDV*, Oct. 1784, p. 102), but a clerk misdated the docket.

[1] After Washington visited Richmond and communicated his zeal for canal and road building to the legislators, he headed for Mount Vernon, no doubt leaving individual delegates pledged to work out the details of his plans. Then Washington went to Annapolis, worked his magic there, and sent the Maryland bills back to Virginia as models. One result was that several bills were written, introduced, and near final passage when Washington's dispatches arrived on 31 Dec. changing the situation. Thus the Maryland legislature's measures were generally adopted after some revision, instead of those bills prepared prior to consultation with Virginia's neighbor. For example, a bill calling for surveys of the James and Potomac rivers had been introduced on 21 Dec. and sent to a committee that included JM. A revised bill was offered on 29 Dec., passed by the House the next day, and sent to the Senate. The Senate insisted on so many amendments that the bill was finally rejected, but the business had to be carried on, and it appears that JM took the responsibility on 1 Jan. by writing and introducing these resolutions (*JHDV*, Oct. 1784, pp. 92–102). The Senate accepted JM's compromise, and JM told Jefferson the prospects were that a short road would link the James with the Kanawha and give the proposed James River canal "a great superiority over Potowmac"—a circumstance Washington had not expected (JM to Jefferson, 9 Jan. 1785). A similar optimism was expressed concerning the Elizabeth River, which flows into the Hampton Roads and did indeed become part of the Dismal Swamp canal. Completed in the nineteenth century, this canal connected Norfolk with Elizabeth City, North Carolina (Brown, *The Dismal Swamp Canal*, p. 43).

[2] The clerk's copy follows the wording in *JHDV*, Oct. 1784, p. 102. JM's copy apparently was prepared to be part of a bill and begins, "And be it further enacted." What probably happened was that JM found the time growing short and thought a resolution would pass without difficulty and accomplish the same purpose as a formal enactment. JM's Ms is headed, "at the end of the Bill add," in a clerk's hand.

[3] In JM's copy, "the Govr. with advice of Council be and he hereby is authorised."

[4] "Carely" on JM's copy and corrected by a clerk.

[5] "Elizabeth river" on JM's copy.

[6] In JM's copy, "necessary" is omitted.

[7] In JM's copy, "The said Comissioners shall be allowed for their services, such reward not exceeding   per day to each of them during the time of his actual Service, as the Governor with advice of Council shall judge reasonable, & be paid out of the same fund with the other Commissrs. to be appointed as above directed."

[8] Massey's pay was fixed in the companion resolutions on roads between the Potomac and Ohio tributaries, and passed this same day. JM carried both sets of resolutions to the Senate.

Act for Clearing and Improving the Navigation of James River

ABSTRACT

3 January 1785. JM prepared and introduced a James River canal bill on 18 Dec. 1784, but for reasons explained in the editorial note preceding that measure the bill was withdrawn after a copy of a Maryland canal law reached Richmond. "Good judges" decided JM's earlier bill provided "an inadequate bait for subscriptions," so that more liberal terms were offered to prospective investors in the revised plan (JM to Jefferson, 9 Jan. 1785). Clearly this new version was mainly the work of Washington's friends in the Maryland legislature (chiefly Thomas Johnson) and had few if any of JM's ideas in its final draft. No Ms of the bill has been found. As passed, the act provided for initial capitalization of $100,000, to be raised through the sale of 500 public shares. A toll schedule was included in the act, and the charter was to be revoked if the canal was not in operation within ten years. As JM acknowledged to Jefferson, the two canal bills were probably too detailed and "abound I fear with inaccuracies"—hence he took pains to make the circumstances clear.

Printed copy (Hening, *Statutes*, XI, 450–62).

Act Giving Canal Company Shares to General Washington

EDITORIAL NOTE

JM was ordered to prepare a bill that would give Washington shares in the budding Potomac and James river navigation companies which the legislature was then creating as entrepreneurial ventures subject to state control. When the General Assembly, after much backing and filling, decided on a way to implement plans for the two major canals, it was thought appropriate that the most influential supporter of canals, and the first citizen of the state and nation, should be rewarded for his concern. Moreover, the gift was more desirable than a pension, JM recalled, which had been "urged on the House by the indiscreet zeal" of Washington's partisans (JM to Jefferson, 9 Jan. 1785). The real point was to give Washington a stake in the enterprise without putting a strain on his financial resources, which were known to be near their limit. From such good intentions, however, came an embarrassment which Washington claimed to be the greatest "since I left the walks of public life" (Fitzpatrick, *Writings of Washington*, XXVIII, 34). Washington, a man with more wisdom than he often was given credit for, wanted to refuse the gift for several reasons, among them being a fear that public opinion would consider the shares "in the same light as a pension." After much mental anguish, while he was torn between his hopes for the canal projects and his fear of being misunderstood, Washington finally sought "the permission of the legislature to devote the fund 'to objects of a public nature.'" He intended to use the stock for "the education of poor children, particularly descendants of soldiers killed in the war" (James T. Flexner, *George Washington and the New Nation, 1783–1793* [Boston, 1970], p. 76). But after seeking JM's advice, Washington decided it would be better to divide the gift "between some *institution* which would *please the* [phil]*o-*

sophical world and some other which may be of [a] *popular cast*" (italicized words in code) (JM to Jefferson, 22 Jan. 1786). Eventually, Washington willed the Potomac shares to the proposed national university in the District of Columbia and the James River stock to the Liberty Hall Academy in Lexington, Virginia (Worthington Chauncey Ford, ed., *Wills of George Washington and His Immediate Ancestors* [Brooklyn, 1891], pp. 89–93; Brant, *Madison*, II, 369).

[4 January 1785]

Whereas the great obligations imposed by General Washington on his Country ⟨not only by his essential services in establishing its liberties, but by his patriotic attention to the means of its prosperity⟩ ought not only to be ever borne in grateful remembrance, but justly demand every token of their desire to perpetuate a ven[e]ration for his character & affection for his person. Be it enacted by the Genl. Assembly that the Treasr. be directed in addition to the subscriptions he is already authorised to make to the respective undertakings for Opening the Navigation of Potowmac & James Rivers, to subscribe to the amt. of 50 shares to the former and 100 Shares to the latter, to be paid in like manner with the subscriptions above mentioned: and that the shares so subscribed be & the same & are hereby vested in George Washington Esqr. his heirs & assigns forever in as effectual a manner as if the subscriptions had been made by himself or by his Attorney.[1]

Ms (Vi). In JM's hand, and docketed by him: "Bill For vesting in G. Washington Esqr. a certain interest in the Companies for opening & extending the Navigations of Potowmac & J. Rivers." This became the title of the act in its final form (Hening, *Statutes*, XI, 525–26). The portions within angle brackets were crossed through on Madison's draft.

[1] The first draft with its numerous errors appears to have been hastily drawn by JM. He presented it to the House on 4 Jan. 1785. It was revised and finally enacted the following day (*JHDV*, Oct. 1784, pp. 105, 107). JM then carried it to the Senate.

To James Madison, Sr.

RICHMOND Jany. 6th. 1785 Thursday

This day has put an end to our tedious Session. The principal Acts which have passed since my last, are 1. An Act remitting 1/2 of the Tax for the year 1785 within which was to have been collected that tax, and the tax of 1784 postponed into it.[1] 2. An Act amending the tax on law proceedings &c.[2] 3. An Act for clearing the navigation of Potowmac River. 4 An Act for clearing the navigation of James River. The former has passed in concurrence with a like Act of Maryland and establishes a Company for the purpose. The latter establishes a like Compy. for the like purpose. 5. An Act vesting in Genl. Washington a very handsome share in each of the Undertakings, in a form which was thought most likely to make the compliment admissible by his delicacy. The Genl. Assesst. has been put off till the next Session & is to be published in the mean time. Mr. Porter has a number of printed copies for our County. The inclosed Act for incorporating the Episcopal Church is the result of much altercation on the subject. In its original form it was wholly inadmissible. In its present form into which it has been trimmed, I assented to it with reluctance at the time, and with dissatisfaction on a review of it. There has been some error in the case too, for it was unquestionably voted in the House that *two* laymen should be deputed from each Parish to the Convention spoken of. I had taken it for granted also that the Clergy were hereafter to be elected by the Vestries, and was much surprised on examining the Act since it was printed to find that the mode in which vacant parishes are to be filled, is left to be provided for by the Convention.[3] I consider the passage of this Act however as having been so far useful as to have parried for the present the Genl. Assesst. which would otherwise have certainly been saddled upon us: & If it be unpopular among the laity it will be soon repealed, and will be a standing lesson to them of the danger of referring religious matters to the legislature. I have some business to regulate here which I have put off till the end of the Session, and have some thoughts of spending a week or two in the library of my friend the Attorney Genl. I do not wish my horses therefore to be here till Wednesday Sevennight.[4] I do not know also but I may enter into a bargain here which will require the aid of the Money in the hands of my brother A. and of the payment to be made by Mr. Cowherd at Christmas.[5] Apprize him of this that he may be ready to answer a call upon him. The inclosed letter from Judge Dandridge[6] founded on a mistake will inform you that your bond has passed into his hands. With my regards to the family I am Yr. Dutiful son

J. MADISON JR

Whoever brings down my horses must bring a Portmanteau.

RC (DLC). Cover missing. Docketed by JM. The usual salutation for the senior Madison, "Honored Sir," was omitted. JM later added "Thursday" to the date.

[1] William Ronald's committee which examined the public accounts reported on 28 Dec. 1784 that the state needed only £141,389 to meet its obligations. The next day Treasurer Jacquelin Ambler reported that £199,923 had been collected on the 1783 taxes and that the collections for the year 1784 were £22,542 ahead of disbursements. Cheered by this welcome news, the House quickly considered a tax cut before the day was over (*JHDV*, Oct. 1784, p. 94). The bill passed its third reading on 30 Dec. 1784.

[2] The "act to explain and amend the act to levy certain taxes in aid of the public revenue" made alterations on the stamp act JM had helped draft at the May 1784 session (Resolution for Schedule of Tax Rates on Documents, 2 June 1784). The revision was presented by Archibald Stuart on 1 Jan. 1785 and carried to the Senate by John Breckinridge on 4 Jan. 1785 (*JHDV*, Oct. 1784, p. 104). The 1785 revision added the Kentucky district court orders to the fee schedule and forbade the issuance of legal proceedings "unless the taxes hereby . . . imposed thereon be first paid down" (Hening, *Statutes*, XI, 438–41).

[3] As JM explained to Jefferson in his letter of 9 Jan. 1785, the delegates thought they were providing for much local autonomy by the parish vestry boards. The ambiguously worded act vested in the annual Protestant Episcopal convention authority "to regulate . . . all the religious concerns of that church" (Hening, *Statutes*, XI, 532–37). The controversial act was repealed early in 1787 (ibid., XII, 266–67).

[4] JM first wrote "Saturday sevennight," and later deleted it for "Wednesday."

[5] JM's brother Ambrose and Francis Cowherd of Orange County. Cowherd bought 281 acres from the elder Madison on 19 Aug. 1784 and a portion of the £400 purchase money must have been due 25 Dec. 1784.

[6] Bartholemew Dandridge, a judge of the Virginia General Court until his death on 18 Apr. 1785 (Tyler, *Encyclopedia of Virginia Biography*, I, 220).

From George Muter

January 6th. 1785.

SIR

I have taken the liberty of inclosing some questions, proposed by your friend Mr. Wallace: and I must request the favour of you, to put answers to them, as soon as your attention to business of more consequence, will permitt. I am with respect Sir Your Most hle Servt.

GEORGE MUTER

[Enclosure]

The following questions ⟨by Mr. Caleb Wallace⟩ are of importance & will probably be debated, when a form of Government is to be adopted.[1]

1st Whether is a representation according to numbers, or property, or in joint prop[o]r[tio]n to both, the most safe and equitable?

2d. Is a representation by Counties to be preferred; or a more equitable mode, 'though more difficult to adjust?

3d Which is to be preferred? An Annual, Triennial or Septennial rotation or succession to Executive offices? Or frequent elections without limitations in choice—or that the officers when chosen should continue during good behaviour?

4th How far may the same person be employed in the different departments of government, in an infant country, where the Council of every individual will be needed?

5th. Should there be a periodical review of the constitution of Government?

6th. Will it not be better, unalterably to fix some leading principles in the form of government, and make it consistent for the legislature to introduce such changes in lesser matters as may become expedient?

7th. Can a Census be provided, that will impartially point out the deficiencies of the constitution, and the violations that may happen?

8th. Is the belief of a God indispensable to civil Society?

9th. As Christianity is generally confessed to be highly conducive to the interests of Civil Society; may it be established by Laws, or unbelievers be subjected to Civil Incapacities?[2]

RC (DLC). Addressed by Muter. Docketed by JM. The undated enclosure is in Muter's hand.

[1] JM added the words within angle brackets at some later time.

[2] JM failed to answer these queries directly, but when Wallace wrote him directly on 12 July 1785, omitting the religious matters on question eight and nine, an answer from Montpelier was forthcoming (JM to Wallace, 23 Aug. 1785). The deference of Kentuckians to JM on matters of polity during their constitution-shaping period suggests that his reputation as a political theorist then exceeded his standing as a practical politician.

Pay Voucher as Delegate to General Assembly

7th Jany. 1785

The CommonWealth of Virginia
October session   To James Madison Dr.
1784

> To 68 days Attendance on Genl.
> Assembly as Delegate from
> Orange—a 10/.   £34...
> 150 Miles travelling—2 [lb?]. Tobo.   3...

Entered   £37...

JOHN BECKLEY. C h. D

Ms (Vi). Docketed in a clerk's hand.

To James Monroe

DEAR SIR

Yours of the 18 Ult. came to hand yesterday. The view which it gives of the operations of the Cabinet, portends I fear a revival of those intrigues & contests of ambition which have more than once distracted & dishonoured the national Councils. Foreign appointments have generally been the parents of those mischiefs, and ought for that reason, when no other reasons oppose, to be rendered as unfrequent as may be. The union between *R. H. Lee* and RRL.[1] would have been among the last of my predictions, nor can I fathom the principle on which it is founded. The policy of healing the variance between the U. S. & G. B. is no doubt obvious: but I cannot enter into the suspicions entertained of hostile designs in the latter. Her internal situation renders them extremely improbable, and the affairs of Ireland as I conceive absolutely incredible. What could she hope for or aim at? If the late war was folly, a new one for the same object would be downright phrensy. Her ill humour is the natural consequence of disappointed and disarmed ambition, and her disregard of the Treaty, may if not be justified at least be accounted for by what has passed in the U. S. Let both parties do what neither can deny its obligation to do, and the difficulty is at an end. The contest with Spain has a more dangerous root. Not only the supposed interests but the supposed rights of the parties are in direct opposition. I hope however that both parties will ponder the consequences, before they suffer amicable negociation to become abortive. The use of the Mississippi is given by Nature to our Western Country, and no power on Earth can take it from them. Whilst we assert our title to it therefore with a becoming firmness let us not forget that we can not ultimately be deprived of it, and that for the present, war is more than all things to be deprecated. Let us weigh well also the object of the price, not forgetting that the Atlantic States &c &c. . . .[2] I join in your wish that we had a better Cypher, but Richmond yields as few resources for amending ours as Trenton.[3] I have not leisure myself, and can command the assistance of no other person.

Yesterday put an end to our tedious Session, and in a manner equally singular, and unfortunate. For some time past the impatience of the Members to disperse has been repressed with the utmost difficulty. Among other expedients an order was made that the name of each

member absenting himself without leave should be advertised. On tuesday evening 7 or 8 of the members crossed to Manchester with a
view it is to be supposed of returning on wednesday morning, to
finish the remaining business which consisted only of the British debt
bill—and a bill for amending our Naval office system; bills which had
pass'd all the forms except those of being sent down (for they had
been passed) by the Senate, enrolled: examd. and signed by the
Speakers. As it happened the night of tuesday by its severity rendered the river impassable on Wednesday, or at least not safely passable.
Without the Manchester Gentlemen, there was not a house; and it
was uncertain how long their detention might be protracted. You
will judge of our situation as Wednesday was the day prefixed for the
final adjournment. Some were for considering the bills as valid, and
having them enrolled & signed; others for adjourning finally & stigmatizing the absentees, others for waiting a day longer. The latter prevailed, and on Thursday morning early we reassembled. The ice
however continued to obstruct the passage from Manchester, and
the perplexity & impatience on this side still increased. Moderation
nevertheless so far prevailed, that it was agreed to wait till yesterday
morning; when seeing little certainty of gaining the members from
the other shore, a vote of adjournment took place. A few hours after
the Sargeant at arms who was also detained at Manchester, crossed,
as I suppose his associates would have done if it had not become fruitless. In consequence of the vote for advertising, which could not be
repealed for want of a House, the names of the Absentees will I suppose be printed which will probably bring on a vindication & a contest.[4] It was unlucky that one of the two bills thus lost, should be
that which will be most likely to involve our public character. Before
this accident we had passed the bill for opening the Potowmac, and
a similar one for James River together with a third presenting to
Genl. Washington a handsome portion of shares in each of the Companies, and had taken some other measures for opening the commercial channel to the Western waters. As I shall not be in Richmond
to receive any letters which may be written hereafter you will be so
good as to address your future favors to Orange. I am Dr Sir with
sincerity Yr. friend & Sert,

                                                    J. MADISON JR.

RC (DLC). Cover missing. Docketed by JM.

¹ JM's reluctance to bother with codes is indicated by his avoidance of ciphers
although Monroe had sent JM a coding device in his 7 Nov. letter. In this entire

letter it was employed only once, for the "51" symbol (for Richard Henry Lee) in this sentence. This contradicts the assertion of Fletcher Pratt (*Secret and Urgent: The Story of Codes and Ciphers* [Indianapolis and New York, 1939], p. 155) that JM and Arthur Lee were "the only true enthusiasts" for cryptography among America's public men of the period. "RRL" was Robert R. Livingston. William C. Rives placed an asterisk after RRL and wrote at the bottom of the page: "on the appointment of Mr. Jefferson to the Court of Spain" (Madison, *Letters* [Cong. ed.], I, 120).

2 Rather than recount the details of northern delegates' willingness to trade the Mississippi rights for a preferred place for New England codfish in the Spanish market, JM used these abbreviations to make the inference.

3 "A better Cypher" than the one sent on 7 Nov. could have been found in a well-stocked printing shop. Printers sold sheets with numbered columns, otherwise blank, that permitted correspondents to devise their own codes. Apparently these sheets could not be found in the printing houses of Trenton or Richmond although one suspects JM did not tax himself in searching.

4 Rives omitted all of the second paragraph to this point in ibid., I, 121, by inserting a three-line abstract.

To Thomas Jefferson

RICHMOND Jany. 9th. 1785

DEAR SIR

My last was dated in Philada. Octr. 17. I reached this place the 14th. day after that fixed for the meeting of the Assembly and was in time for the commencement of business. Yesterday put an end to the tedious Session. According to my promise I subjoin a brief review of its most material proceedings.

| An act for the establisht of Courts of Assize. | This act was carried through the House of Delegates against much secret repugnance, but without any direct and open opposition. |

It luckily happened that the latent opposition wanted both a mouth and a head. *Mr Henry* had been previously *elected governor* and was *gone for his family*. From *his conversation since I* surmise that *his* [presen]*ce* might have *been fatal*. The act is formed precisely on the English pattern, and is nearly a transcript from the bill originally penned in 1776 by Mr. Pendleton except that writs sent blank from the Clk of Genl: Ct. are to issue in the district but retd. to Gl. Ct. In the Senate it became a consideration whether the Assize Courts ought not to be turned into so many Courts of independent and complete jurisdiction, and admitting an appeal only to the Courts of Appeals. If the fear of endangering the bill had not checked the experiment, such a proposition would probably have been sent down to the House of Delegates, where it would have been better relished by many than the Assize plan. The objections made to the latter were that as it required the issues to be made up and the judgments to be awarded in the General Court it was but a partial relief to suitors, and might render the service of double setts of Lawyers necessary. The friends of the plan thought these inconveniences as far as they were real, outweighed by the superior wisdom & uniformity of decisions incident to the plan; not to mention the difference in the frequency of appeals incident to the different places.[1] In order to leave as few handles as possible for cavil the bill omitted all the little regulations which would follow of course, and will therefore need a supplement. To give time for this provision as well as by way of collecting the mind of the public, the commencement of the law is made posterior to the next Session of Assembly. The places fixed for the Assize Courts are Northumberland Court House, Williamsbg Accomack Ct. House, Suffolk, Richmond, Petersburg, Brunswick Ct. House, King & Queen Ct. House, Prince Edwd. Ct. H. Bedford Ct. H. Montgomery & Washington Ct. Hs. alternately, Staunton, Charlottesville Fredericksbg. Dumfries, Winchester and Monongalia Ct. H. Besides the juridical advantages hoped from this innovation, we consider it as a means of reconciling to our Govt. the discontented extremities of the State.

An act for opening and extending the navigation of Potowmac river An act for do. do. of James river

The subject of clearing these great rivers was brought forward early in the Session under the auspices of General Washington, who had written an interesting private letter on it to Govr. Harrison which the latter communicated to the Genl. Assembly.[2] The conversation of the Genl. during a visit paid to Richmond in the course of the Session, still further impressed the magnitude of the object on sundry members. Shortly after his departure, a joint memorial from a number of Citizens of Va. & Maryland, interested in the Potowmac, was presented to the Assembly, stating the practicability and importance of the work; & praying for an act of incorporation, and grant of perpetual toll to the undertakers of it. A bill had been prepared at the same meeting which produced the memorial, and was transmitted to Richmond at the same time. A like memorial & bill went to Annapolis where the Legislature of Maryland were sitting. The Assembly here lent a ready ear to the project, but a difficulty arose from the height of the tolls proposed, the danger of destroying the uniformity essential in the proceedings of the two States, by altering them, and the scarcity of time for negociating with Maryland a bill satisfactory to both States. Short as the time was however, the attempt was decided on, and the negociation committed to Genl. Washington himself. Genl. Gates who happened to be in the way and Col: Blackband were associated with him.[3] The latter did not act, the two former pushed immediately to Annapolis, where the sickness of Genl. Gates threw the whole agency on Genl. Washington. By his exertions in concert with Committees of the two branches of the Legislature, an amendment of the plan was digested in a few days, passed thro' both houses in one day with nine dissenting voices only, and despatched for Richmond, where it arrived just in time for the Session. A corresponding act was immediately introduced and passed without opposition. The scheme declares that the subscribers shall be an incorporated body, that there shall be 500 Shares amounting to about 220,000 dollars, of which the States of Va. & Maryd. are each to take 50 shares, that the tolls shall be collected in three portions at the three principal falls, and with the works vest[ed] as real estate in the members of the Company, and that the works shall be begun within one year, and finished within ten years under the penalty of entire forfieture.

Previous to the receipt of the Act from Annapolis a bill on a different plan had been brought in and proceeded on for clearing James River. It proposed that subscriptions should be taken by Trustees and under their management solemnly appropriated to the object in view, that they should be regarded as a loan to the State, should bear an interest of 10 Per Ct. and should entitle the subscriber to the double of the principal remaining undischarged at the end of a moderate period; and that the tolls to be collected should stand inviolably pledged for both principal & interest. It was thought better for the public to present this exuberant harvest to the subscribers than to grant them a perpetuity in the tolls. In the case of the Potowmac which depended on another authority as well as our own, we were less at liberty to consider what wd. be best in itself. Exuberant however as the harvest appeared, it was pronounced by good judges as inadequate bait for subscriptions even from those otherwise interested in the work, and on the arrival and acceptance of the Potowmac plan, it was found advisable to pass a similar one in favor of James River. The circumstancial variations in the latter are 1. the sum to be aimed at in the first instance is 100,000 Dollars only. 2. the shares which are the same in number with those of Potowmac, are reduced to 200 dollars. each and the number of public shares raised to 100. 3. the tolls are reduced to 1/2 of the aggregate of the Potowmac tolls. 4. in the case the falls at this place where alone tolls are to be paid, shall be first opened, the Company are permited to receive the tolls immediately, and continue to do so till the lapse of ten years, within which the whole river is to be made navigable. 5. a right of pre-emption is reserved to the public on all transfers of shares. These acts are very lengthy, and having passed in all the precipitancy which marks the concluding stages of a Session, abound I fear with inaccuracies.

In addition to these acts joint resolutions have passed the Legislatures of Maryd. & Va. for clearing a road from the head of the Potowmac navigation to cheat-river or if neccssary to Monongalia, & 3333 1/3 Dollars are voted for the work by each State. Pennsylva. is also to be applied to by the Governors of the two States for leave to clear a road thro' her jurisdiction if it should be found necessary, from Potowmac to Yohogania; to which the Assembly here have added a proposition to unite with Maryland in representing to Pena. the advantages which will accrue to a part of her citizens from opening the proposed communication with the Sea and the reasonableness of her securing to those who are to be at the expence, the use of her waters, as a thoroughfare to & from the Country beyond her limits, free from all imposts & restrictions whatever, and as a channel of trade with her citizens free from greater imposts than may be levied on any other channel of importation. This Resolution did not pass till it was too late to refer it to Genl. Washington's negociations with Maryland. It now makes a part of the task alloted to the Commissrs. who are to settle with Maryd. the jurisdiction & navigation of Potowmac below tide water. By another Resolution of this State, persons are to be forthwith appd. by the Executive to survey the upper parts of Jas. river, the country thro' which a road must pass to the navigable waters of New River, and these waters down to the Ohio. I am told by a member of the Assembly who seems to be well acquainted both with the intermediate ground and with the Western waters in question, that a road of 25 or 30 miles in length will link these waters with Js. river, and will strike a branch of the former which yields a fine navigation, and falls into the main stream of the Kenhawha below the only obstructions lying in this river down to the Ohio. If these be facts James River will have a great superiority over Potowmac, the road from which to Cheat river indeed computed by Genl. Washington at 20 miles only; but he thinks the expence of making the latter navigable will require a continuation of the road to

Monongalia, which will lengthen it to 40 miles. The road to Yohogania is computed by the Genl. at 30 miles.

By another resolution Commissrs. are to be appd. to survey the ground for a canal between the waters of Elizabeth river and those of N. Carolina, and in case the best cou[r]se for such a canal shall require the concurrence of that State, to concert a joint plan and report the same to the next Session of Assembly. Besides the trade which will flow thro' this channel from N. Carolina to Norfolk the large district of Virginia watered by the Roanoak will be doubled in its value by it.

An act vesting in G. Washington a certain interest in the Companies for opening James & Potowmac rivers

The Treasurer is by this act directed to subscribe 50 Shares in the Potowmac and 100 shares in the James river Companies which shall vest in Genl. Washington & His heirs. This mode of adding some substantial to the many honorary rewards bestowed on him, was deemed least injurious to his delicacy, as well as least dangerous as a precedent. It was substituted in place of a direct pension urged on the House by the indiscreet zeal of some of his friends. Though it will not be an equivalent succour in all respects it will save the General from subscriptions which would have oppressed his finances; and if the schemes be executed within the period fixed, may yeild a revenue for some years before the term of his. At all events it will demonstrate the grateful wishes of his Country and will promote the object which he has so much at heart. The earnestness with which he espouses the undertaking is hardly to be described, and shews that a mind like his, capable of great views & which has long been occupied with them, cannot bear a vacancy; and surely he could not have chosen an occupation more worthy of succeeding to that of establishing the political rights of his Country, than the patronage of works for the extensive & lasting improvement of its natural advantages; works which will double the value of half the lands within the Commonwealth, will extend its commerces, link with its interests those of the Western States, and lessen the emigration of its Citizens, by enhancing the profitableness of situations which they now desert in search of better.

An act to discharge the people of this commonwealth from one half of the tax for the year 1775 [1785]

Our successive postponements had thrown the whole tax of 1784 on the year 1785. The remission therefore, still leaves three halves to be collected. The plentiful crops on hand both of corn & tobo. and the price of the latter which is vibrating on this river between 36/ & 40/. seem to enable the Country to bear the burden. A few more plentiful years with steadiness in our Councils will put our credit on a decent footing. The payments from this State to the Continental treasury between Apl. 83 and Novr. 84 amount to £123, 202.. 11.. 1 1/2 Va. Curry. The printed report herewith inclosed will give you a rude idea of our finances.[4]

An act giving James Rumsey the exclusive privilege of contructing & navigating certain boats for a limited time.

J. Rumsey by a memorial to the last Session represented that he had invented a mechanism, by which a boat might be worked with little labour at the rate of from 25 to 40 miles a day, against a stream running at the rate of 10 miles an hour, and prayed that di[s]closure of his invention might be purchased by the public. The apparent extravagance of his pretensions brought a ridicule upon them, and nothing was done. In the recess of the Assembly, he exemplified his machinery to General Washington and a few other gentlemen, who gave a certificate of the reality & importance of the invention, which opened the ears of the Assembly to a second memorial. The act gives a monopoly for ten years, reserving a right to abolish it at any time on paying £10,000. The inventor is soliciting similar acts from other States, and will not I suppose publish the secret till he either obtains or despairs of them.

An act for punishing certain offences injurious to the tranquility of this commonwealth.

This act authorizes the surrender of a citizen to a foreign sovereign within whose acknowledged jurisdiction the citizen shall commit a crime, of wch. satisfactory proof shall be exhibited to Congress, and for which in the judgment of Congress the laws of nations exacts such surrender. This measure was suggested by the danger of our being speedily embroiled with the nations contiguous to the U. States, particularly the Spaniards, by the licentious & predatory spirit of some of our Western people. In several instances gross outrages are said to have been already practised. The measure was warmly patronized by Mr. Henry, and most of the forensic members, and no less warmly opposed by the Speaker and some others. The opponents contended that such surrenders were unknown to the law of nations, and were interdicted by our declaration of Rights. Vattel however is express as to the case of Robbers, murderers and incendiaries. Grotius quotes various instances in which great offenders have been given up by their proper sovereigns to be punished by the offended Soverigns. Puffendorf only refers to Grotius. I have had no opportunity of consulting other authorities. With regard to the bill of rights, it was alledged to be no more or rather less violated by considering crimes committed agst. other laws as not falling under the notice of our own, and sending our Citizens to be tried where the cause of trial arose, than to try them under our own laws without a jury of the vicinage and without being confronted with their accusers or witnesses; as must be the case if they be tried at all for such offences under our own laws. And to say that such offenders Could neither be given up for punishment, nor be punished within their own Country, would amount to a licence for every aggression, and would sacrifice the peace of the whole community, to the impunity of the worst members of it. The necessity of a qualified interpretation of the bill of rights was also inferred from the law of the Confederacy which requires the surrender of our Citizens to the laws of other States, in cases of treason, felony or other high misdemeanors. The act provides however for a domestic trial in cases where a surrender may not be justified or insisted upon, and in cases of aggressions on the Indians.

An act for incorporating the Protestant Episcopal Church — This act declares the ministers & vestries who are to be trienially chosen, in each period a body corporate, enables them to hold property not exceeding the value of £800 per annum, and gives sanction to a Convention which is to be composed of the Clergy and a lay deputy from each parish, and is to regulate the affairs of the Church. It was understood by the House of Delegates that the Convention was to consist of two laymen for each clergyman, and an amendment was received for that express purpose.[5] It so happened that the insertion of the amendment did not produce that effect, and the mistake was never discovered till the bill had passed and was in print. Another circumstance still more singular is that the act is so constructed as to deprive the Vestries of the uncontrouled right of electing clergymen, unless it be referred to them by the canons of the Convention, and that this usurpation actually escaped the eye both of the friends and adversaries of the measure, both parties taking the contrary for granted throughout the whole progress of it. The former as well as the latter appear now to be dissatisfied with what has been done, and will probably concur in a revision if not a repeal of the law. Independently of those oversights the law is in various points of view exceptionable. But the necessity of some sort of incorporation for the purpose of holding & managing the property of the Church could not well be denied, nor a more harmless modification of it now obtained. A negative of the bill too would have doubled the eagerness and the pretexts for a much greater evil, a General Assessment, which there is good ground to believe was parried by this partial gratification of its warmest votaries. A Resolution for a legal provision for the "teachers of Christian Religion" had early in the Session been proposed by Mr. Henry, and in spite of all the opposition that could be mustered, carried by 47 agst. 32 votes. Many Petitions from below the blue ridge had prayed for such a law; and though several from the presbyterian laity beyond it were in a contrary Stile, the Clergy of that Sect favoured it. The other Sects Seemed to be passive. The Resolution lay some weeks before a bill was brought in, and the bill some weeks before it was called for; after the passage of the incorporating act it was taken up, and on the third reading, ordered by a small majority to be printed for consideration. The bill in its present dress proposes a tax of blank per Ct. on all taxable property for support of Teachers of the Christian Religion. Each person when he pays his tax is to name the society to which he dedicates it, and in case of refusal to do so, the tax is to be applied to the maintenance of a school in the County. As the bill stood for some time, the application in such cases was to be made by the Legislature to pious uses. In a committee of the whole it was determined by a Majority of 7 or 8 that the word "christian" should be exchanged for the word "Religious". On the report to the House the *pathetic zeal of the late governor Harrison* gained a like majority for reinstating discrimination. Should the bill ever pass into a law in its present form it may & will be easily eluded. It is chiefly obnoxious on account of its dishonorable principle and dangerous tendency.

The subject of the British debts underwent a reconsideration on the motion of Mr. Jones. Though no answer had been recd. from Congress to the Resolutions passed at the last Session, a material change had evidently taken place in the mind of the Assembly, proceeding in part from a more dispassionate view of the question, in part from the intervening exchange of the ratifications of the Treaty. *Mr Henry was out of the way.* His previous conversation I have been told, *favored the reconsideration, the speaker*, the other *champion*, at the last Session *against the treaty* was at least half *a proselight.* The proposition rejected interest during the period of blank, and left the periods of payment blank. In this form it was reced. with little opposition and by a very

great majority. After much discussion & several nice divisions the first
blank was filled up with the period between the 19 of Apl. 1775, and
the 3 of March 1783, the commencement and cessation of hostilities;
and the second with seven annual payments. Whilst the bill was depending, some proceedings of the Glascow merchants were submitted
to the H. of D. in which they signified their readiness to receive their
debts in four annual payments with immediate security, and summary
recoveries at the successive periods, and were silent as to the point of
interest. Shortly after were presented memorials from the Merchants
of this Town & Petersburg representing the advantage which a compliance with the Glascow overtures would give the foreign over the
domestic creditors.[6] Very little attention seemed to be paid by the
House to the overtures, tho' as the treaty was not to be litterally pursued, the shadow of assent from the other party was worthy of being
attended to. In the Senate the bill met with a diversity of opinions. By
a majority of one voice only an attempt to put all our domestic debts
on the same footing with British debts was lost. Whether this was sincere or a side blow at the bill I am unable to say. An attempt was next
made to put on the same footing, all those who left this Country and
joined the other side, or who remained within the British territories
for one year at any time since the 19 Apl. 1778, or who refused a tender
of paper money before Jany 1779. These discriminations were almost
unanimously disagreed to by the H. of D. The Senate insisted. The
former proposed a conference. The Senate concurred. The Conference
produced a proposition from the H. of D to which the Senate assented;
but before their assent was notified an incident happened which has left
the bill in a very singular situation. The delays attending this measure
had spun it out to the day preceding the one prefixed for a final adjournment. Several of the members went over to Manchester in the
evening, with an intention it is to be presumed of returning the next
morning. The severity of the night rendered their passage back the
next morning impossible. Without them there was no house. The impatience of the members was such as might be supposed. Some were for
stigmatizing the absentees and adjourning. The rest were some for one
thing, some for another. At length it was agreed to wait till the next
day. The next day presented the same obstructions in the river. A canoe
was sent over for enquiry by the Manchester party, but they did not
chuse to venture themselves. The impatience increased. Warm resolutions were agitated. They ended however on an agreement to wait one
day more. On the morning of the third day the prospect remained the

same. Patience could hold out no longer and an adjournment to the last day of March ensued. The question to be decided is whether a bill which had passed the House of Delegates, and been assented to by the Senate; but not sent down to the H. of D. nor enrolled, nor examined, nor signed by the two Speakers and consequently not of record, is or is not a law?[7] A bill for the better regulation of the Customs is in the same situation.

After the passage of the Bill for British debts through the H of D. a bill was introduced for liquidating the depreciated payments into the Treasury, and making the debtors liable for the deficiency. A foresight of this consequential step had shewn itself in every stage of the first bill. It was opposed by *Governor Harrison principally* and laid asleep by the refusal of the interested members to vote in the question, and the want of a quorum without them.

Among the abortive measures may be mentioned also a proposition to authorize the collection of the impost by Congress as soon as the concurrence of twelve States be should obtained. Connecticut had set the example in this project. The proposition was made by the Speaker & supported by the late Governour. It was disagreed to by a very large majority on the following grounds 1 the appearance of a schism in the confederacy which it would present to foreign eyes. 2. its tendency to combinations of smaller majorities of the States. 3 the channel it would open for smuggling; goods imported into Rhode Island in such case might not only be spread by land through the adjacent States, but if slipped into any neighbouring port might thence be carried duty-free to any part of the Associated States. 4. the greater improbability of a union of twelve States on such new ground, than of the conversion of Rhode Island to the old one. 5. the want of harmony among the other States which would be betrayed by the miscarriage of such an experiment, and the fresh triumph & obstinacy which R. I. would derive from it.

The French vice Counsul in this State has complained to the Assembly that the want of legal power over our Sheriffs, Goalers & prisons both renders his decrees nugatory, and exposes his person to insults from dissatisfied litigants.[8] The Assembly have taken no step whatever on the subject being at a loss to know what ought to be done, in compliance either with general usage, or that of France in particular. I have often wondered that the proposed convention between France and the U. S. for regulating the consular functions, has never been executed.

The delay may prove unfriendly both to their mutual harmony & their commerce.

Mr. Henry was elected successor to Mr. Harrison without competition or opposition. The victims to the article requiring a triennial removal of two Counsellors, were Merryweather Smith & General Christian.[9] Young Mr. Roane and Mr. Miles Selden, take their places. Mr. Shorts place is filled by Mr. Joseph Jones.

Nothing has passed during the Session concerning an amendment of the State Constitution. The friends of the undertaking seem to be multiplying rather than decreasing. Several Petitions from the Western side of the Blue Ridge appeared in favor of it; as did some from the Western side of the Alleghany praying for a separate Government. The latter may be considered all of them as the children of A. C.'s ambition.[10] The assize Courts and the opening of our Rivers are the best answers to them.

The Revisal has but just issued from the press. It consists of near 100 folio pages in a small type. I shall send you six copies by the first opportunity. £500 was voted at the Spring Session to each of the acting members of the Committee, but no fund having been provided for payment, no use could be made of the warrants. I drew yours however & carried them up to Orange where they now lye. A vote of this Session has provided a fund which gives them immediate value. As soon as I get home I shall send the dead warrants to Mr. Nichs Lewis who may exchange them for others and draw the money from the Treasury. Mr. Peter Carr is I hear now in Williamsburg, he did not get there so soon as I expected, but I have not heard the circumstances which delayed him. On the best enquiries I could make for a stand for his younger brother I could hear of none preferable to the Academy in Prince Edward, and accordingly recommended that in a letter to Mrs. Carr.[11] I have rcd. no answer, but am told by Mr. Underwood her neighbour that he is at school with a very proper man who has lately opened a school very convenient to Mrs. Carr. If this be the case it will be improper to remove him.

I have not yet had the pleasure of a line from you since you left Boston, nor do I know when I shall next find a subject for another to you. As soon as I do you may be assured that you shall hear from me, & that I am in the mean time with the sincerest friendship Yrs.

J. MADISON JR.

Present my respects to Miss Patsy & Mr. Short.

RC (DLC). Cover missing. Docketed by JM. "No. 6" written at top of first page. The italicized words, unless otherwise noted, are those encoded by JM in the code first used by Jefferson on 14 Apr. 1783.

[1] "By the superior wisdom & uniformity of decisions" is JM's way of contrasting the purpose of the Assize Court bill with the system it was meant to replace—the courts constituted by the county justices of the peace—where justice was meted out unevenly and oftentimes in dilatory fashion. See Charles Thomas Cullen, "St. George Tucker and Law in Virginia, 1772–1804" (University of Virginia, Ph.D. dissertation, 1971). Despite all of JM's exertions, the Assize Court Act was twice postponed and finally repealed (Hening, *Statutes*, XI, 421 n.).

[2] Governor Harrison forwarded Washington's letter of 10 Oct. 1784 along with other papers to the speaker of the House on 18 Oct. (Executive Letter Book, pp. 412–13). Harrison regarded Washington's case for canal construction as "so conclusive" he hoped the legislature would readily provide for the surveys recommended as the "necessary preparatory Step to the undertaking."

[3] "Col: Blackband" was in fact Thomas Blackburn of Prince William County, Virginia.

[4] The "printed report" JM enclosed, which is now missing, was made by the legislative committee appointed to examine the public accounts. It was reprinted from *JHDV*, Oct. 1784, pp. 85–91.

[5] The law, which JM voted for, specified that when the church held a general convention there would be "a deputation of two persons from each parish, whereof the minister shall always be one, if there be a minister in the parish, and the other person or persons shall be appointed by the vestries" (Hening, *Statutes*, XI, 536–37).

[6] Agents of "the Glasgow merchants" asked for an opportunity to present their plan for repayment of debts owed by Virginia through annual installments, but before the day was over a protest was heard from the Petersburg merchants against any preference for one set of merchants over another in the British debt settlement. Both sides were offered a chance to explain their actions "at the bar of the House" on the following Monday. But, as JM explains, the delegates lost interest in the matter the next day and rescinded the hearing (*JHDV*, Oct. 1784, pp. 74, 76).

[7] Ultimately it was held that the British debt bill had not been duly enacted, although Henry denied that the absent members had been opposed to it (Harrell, *Loyalism in Virginia*, pp. 147–48).

[8] The French vice consul in Norfolk was Martin Oster. On 19 Aug. 1784 Oster requested an order from Governor Harrison for the apprehension of two French citizens under sentence from a consular court. Harrison authorized a "precept" but Oster was unable to carry out his consular order and complained on 5, 7, and 15 Sept. that he was being subjected to public insults from his own countrymen. Oster's complaints were forwarded to the legislature by Harrison, a buck-passing gesture that left the matter unsettled (Executive Letter Book, pp. 384, 401, 404–5; J. Rives Childs, "French Consul Martin Oster Reports on Virginia, 1784–1796," *VMHB*, LXXVI [1968], 31–34).

[9] "The article requiring a triennial removal of two Counsellors" was the automatic rotation clause in the Virginia Constitution that theoretically kept any member of the Council of State from serving a continuous term of more than nine years. As JM noted, however, the article provided for the turnover of two members "at the end of every three years . . . [who shall] be ineligible for the three next years," but it was possible for a member to serve indefinitely if he retained his popularity and desired the office. Meriwether Smith and William Christian were replaced by Spencer Roane and Miles Selden, Jr., while Joseph Jones of King George County replaced William Short, who had resigned (*JHDV*, Oct. 1784, pp. 27, 30; *JCSV*, III, 409–10, 448, 449).

10 Col. Arthur Campbell's separatist designs had long been rumored at Richmond (*Papers of Madison*, IV, 126 n. 1; V, 454).

11 "The Academy in Prince Edward" was Hampden-Sydney, directed by JM's college acquaintance John Blair Smith.

To George Washington

RICHMOND Jany. 9th. 1785

DEAR SIR

I have now the pleasure of confirming the expectations hinted in my last concerning the result of the measures which have been favoured with your patronage. The Bill for opening the Potowmac has passed precisely on the model transmitted from Maryland, the last conditional clause in the latter being rendered absolute by a clause in the former which engages this State for fifty shares in the Company. Before the receipt of your despatches, some progress had been made in a bill for James River founded on different principle.[1] After the receipt of them, the bill was exchanged for one on the Potowmac principle which has passed into a law with the same rapidity & unanimity which attended the other. The circumstancial variations with respect to James River are. 1. that the Sum to be aimed at in the first instance is 100,000 Dollars, only. 2. the shares are fixed at 200 Dollars and the number of public shares at 500. 3. the tolls are reduced to one half of those granted on Potowmac. 4. in case the falls at this place, where alone tolls are to be paid shall be first opened, the Company are permitted to receive them immediately and to continue to do so until the lapse of ten years, within which period all the works are to be compleated under the same penalties as are specified in the case of the other River. 5. a pre-emption is reserved to the public on all sales and transfers of shares. We endeavoured to preserve an equal eye in this business to the interest of the two Rivers, and to regulate the dates in the two bills in such a manner as to allow the members of each Company to participate in the transactions of the other. The excessive hurry however and the length of the bills may have produced inaccuracies in these as well as in other respects.[2]

The Assembly have likewise taken several kindred measures in the form of Resolutions, of which copies are herewith inclosed.[3] No. 3 was meant to carry into effect an idea suggested in your letter to the late Governour & explained in conversations with which several members were honoured during your visit to Richmond. It had passed before the rece[i]pt of your report from Annapolis. I observed in my last that the subject of it ought to have made a part of your negociation with Maryland, and mentioned the circumstances which prevented it. I regret the omission the more, as the task devolved on Gentlemen to a notification of whose appointment and object, no answer I am informed has yet been vouchsafed to the Governour by Maryland, and whose commission it may be presumed is not altogether palatable to that State. Taking a more candid supposition, that the Silence of the latter is the effect of some miscarriage, the delay or the necessity of a separate representation to Pennsylvania, are inconveniences still to be regretted. As this goes by Col: Grayson[4] who means to pay his respects to Mount Vernon on his way to Trenton, I forbear to anticipate farther, communications which he can more fully make, and beg leave to subscribe myself with all possible respect and regard Sir Your Obedient & most humble Servt.

J. MADISON JR.

RC (ICU). Docketed by Washington, "respectg the Acts for opening the Navigation of Potom[ack] & James Rivers." Enclosures missing.

[1] The James River bill "founded on a different principle" was JM's own draft of 18 Dec. 1784, which had to be scrapped when Washington's letter and enclosures of 28 Dec. arrived in Richmond.

[2] Impatient members of the General Assembly wanted to go home and thus "the excessive hurry" to end the session caused the new Potomac and James river bills to reach the floor on 1 Jan. and become law four days later (JHDV, Oct. 1784, pp. 101, 109, 110).

[3] The missing enclosures were relayed by Washington to his Fairfax County associates, John Fitzgerald and William Harthshorne, on 18 Jan. 1785. Washington's letterbook shows that he included in his letter to the Alexandria merchants "Mr. Madisons letter enclosg. No. 1. Similar Resolutions respectg. Roads &c. No. 2. Surveying James River, & Country between that & the Western Waters. No. 3. Respecting the Jurisdiction &c. of Potomac." "No. 1" was JM's resolution of 1 Jan. 1785 authorizing surveys for a western road from Fort Cumberland "to the navigable part of the river Yohogania." "No. 2" was the James River survey authorization JM also introduced on 1 Jan., and "No. 3" carried out the "idea suggested" in Washington's letter to Governor Harrison on 10 Oct. 1784 regarding the participation of Pennsylvania in the canal-building endeavors, which JM had introduced on 28 Dec. 1784 before Washington's "report from Annapolis" arrived in Richmond (JHDV, Oct. 1784, pp. 91, 101, 102; DLC: Washington Letter Book).

[4] William Grayson (1736–1790) had been elected a delegate to Congress in June 1784 but continued to serve in the House of Delegates until the Oct. 1784 session ended. He was headed for his new duties in Trenton but decided to bypass Mount Vernon although JM's letter and the enclosures were left in safe hands. The bundle reached Washington on 17 Jan. (Weston Bristow, "William Grayson: A Study in Virginia Biography of the Eighteenth Century," Richmond College Historical Papers, II [1917], 75, 85, 117; Fitzpatrick, Writings of Washington, XXVIII, 32, 37).

Election to the American Philosophical Society

ABSTRACT

21 January 1785. JM was nominated twice by Jefferson in 1784 for membership in this society (Boyd, *Papers of Jefferson*, VI, 542, 556). He was elected to membership on this day along with Manasseh Cutler, Thomas Paine, Richard Price, Joseph Priestly, and twenty-four others (*Pa. Gazette,* 9 Feb. 1785). Correspondence concerning the honor has not been found.

To Thomas Jefferson

RICHMOND Jany. 22 1785.

DEAR SIR

I have remained here since the adjournment of the Assembly cheifly with a view of gaining from the Office of the Attorney some insight into the juridical course of practice. This has given me an opportunity of forwarding you 6 copies of the revisal with a few of the late Newspapers under the cover which incloses this.[1] They will go in a vessel belonging to Mr. Alexander the Gentleman who resides in this State as Tobo. Agent for the Farmers Genl.[2] He assures me that due care shall be taken of them. . . .

RC (DLC). Cover missing. Docketed by Jefferson and dated by JM. The lower portion of the letter has been cut away, a circumstance which led one scholar to suggest that JM was responsible for the mutilation because the lost sentences may have related to JM's unflattering view of Lafayette (Boyd, *Papers of Jefferson*, VII, 615 n.).

[1] The enclosures included a report from the Committee of Revisors which JM had been instrumental in publishing. He presented the resolution on 29 May 1784 to the General Assembly calling for publication and distribution of the report.

[2] The vessel was owned by William Alexander, who had moved to Richmond in the summer of 1784 and established a tobacco firm with international connections (Rutland, *Papers of George Mason*, I, xxx–xxxi). As an agent for the Farmers-General, Alexander consigned tobacco to the French monopoly which Virginians resented because it "stood in the way of an expanded import of American tobacco into France" (Bingham Read, "Franco-American Tobacco Diplomacy, 1784–1860," *Maryland Historical Magazine*, LI [1956], 273–75).

To John Francis Mercer

Letter not found.

24 January 1785. Mercer acknowledged on 8 February 1785 receipt of "your favor of the 24. which pursuing me by a circuitous route, did not reach this untill within a few days." In all likelihood JM reported to the Virginia congressman the legislative situation following adjournment of the October 1784 session of the General Assembly.

From George Wythe

Letter not found.

February 1785, Williamsburg. This letter informed JM that the honorary degree of Doctor of Laws had been conferred upon him by "the University of William & Mary." See JM to Wythe, 15 April 1785.

From James Monroe

N. York Feby. 1. 1785

Dear Sir

I have lately heard nothing from you nor indeed from Richmond. I shod. suspect it arose from the adjournment of the Assembly, if I did not presume, had that event taken place, I shd. been instructed to whose care I might address my letters for you in Fredericksburg or Richmond. My letters to Mr Jones have advised you of the principles upon wh. our delegation actd in the questions respecting the places of temporary & permanent residence for Congress; more explicitly perhaps than our communications to the Executive have done, altho' indeed we have been sufficiently explicit to the Executive. The comrs. for the Fœderal town are not yet elected, arising from the urgency of more important business. I am sorry I have it not in my power to inform you we had already taken measures with the *Courts of Spain* & *Great Britain* upon the subjects wh. have arose between us. The reports respecting each, have been frequently acted on, without making any decisive arrangement. That upon a letter of *Mr. Laurens* desiring permission for *Dr. Franklin* to retire hath also been before us. It contain'd a provision that a successor be appointed in his room. A division was calld for, upon wh. an amendment to the same effect was mov'd & six States agnst three were for it.[1] Thus it is upon all questions of a similar nature. Some gentn. wish to commit all our affrs. to be transacted at these several *Courts* to the two gentn. now in office, while we hold that at each *Court* a *minister* is necessary. That at the *Court* of *France* we shod. always be represented, & at that *of the U. Netherlands* untill we had pd. the publick debt or establish'd funds for it. That the nature of the business & the manner in wh. it shod. be conducted considering our situation, requires a particular *minister* at the *Court*s of *Great Britain* & *Spain* at their leasure & who might assume a tone suited to circumstances. That two *ministers* are incompetent to this business if they are to do it, at the respective *Courts* & that to attempt it elsewhere will certainly fail of success, since we have information to be depended on that the *Courts* of *Great Britain* & *Spain* dislike to treat with us elsewhere. Upon all these points we have six States & hope upon the arrival of Maryld. or Delaware, both of wh. are expected daily, to have the 7th. The comrs. of the treasury are elected, Gervais, Osgood & walter Livinston are the men. Some import communications being recd. lately from our ministers abroad, it was mov'd that they be referr'd to a committee to determine what part shod. be communicated to the States. A committee was appointed & a report made. A few days afterwards we recd. a letter from Mr. Jay containing the following paragraph "I have some reason to apprehend that I have come into the office of foreign affrs., with ideas of its duties & rights somewhat differt. from those wh. seem to be entertain'd by Congress; if that shod. prove to be the case I shall certainly think it my duty, either to execute it on the plan most agreeable to them or retire from it with as much acquiescense & respect as I accepted it with confidence in their delicacy & gratitude for the honor they did me." This was also referr'd to a committee to whom Mr Jay gave (to be ingrafted in the report) in writing the following proposition, "and that all foreign letters & papers wh. may be laid before Congress shod. *in the first instance* be restor'd to him."[2] Whether it will be the sense of the committee to make it a matter of right in the minister of foreign affrs. to advise Congress in the first instance upon the various subjects of his department & preclude themselves from a previous consideration, or will consider the offices in a different point of view, consulting him when necessary & refering or declining to refer to him, at pleasure, any of the subjects before them, is yet to be determin'd. I am very respectfully yours

JAS. MONROE

P. S. Mr. Mercer was in the nomination for the treasury but we withdrew him.

RC (DLC). Cover missing. Docketed. The italicized words, unless otherwise noted, are those encoded by Monroe in the code he sent JM on 7 Nov. 1784.

1 The six-to-three alignment that prevented action (seven states constituted a required majority) pitted Connecticut, New Jersey, New York, North Carolina, South Carolina, and Virginia against New Hampshire, Massachusetts, and Rhode Island.

2 Italicized words underlined by Monroe.

From John Francis Mercer

Dear Sir

I have your favor of the 24. which pursuing me by a circuitous route, did not reach this untill within a few days. I place value on every mark of your friendship & to convince you that public business alone was not what induc'd me to revive impressions which were strongly imprinted on my breast. I now write you from a recess, where news of private happiness can be the only subject of a[t]te[n]tion. I feel that you will participate in my pleasure when I communicate to you the accomplishment of an object, which for a long time has engross'd my attention & engag'd my wishes. I was married on the 3d. instant, to a young Lady of this place—The eldest daughter of Mr. Sprigg.[1] In a change of situation which has produc'd a revolution in many opinions my sentiments towards my friends remain unaltered. I wish & hope, to retain & improve 'em, & in whatever place I may ultimately settle, be assur'd it is much my desire to cultivate your esteem. It is more than probable I shall continue in Virginia, if I can make it tolerably agreable to my new connexion. I woud certainly prefer a Country of which I am a native, & which has been partial to the little merit I possess. You have my best wishes & be assur'd that I am most sincerely yr friend & hbl Set.

John F. Mercer

RC (DLC). Cover missing. Docketed by JM.

[1] Mercer's bride was Sophia Sprigg, daughter of Richard Sprigg of Anne Arundel County, Maryland (*Va. Journal and Alexandria Advertiser*, 24 Feb. 1785).

From Edmund Randolph

Dear sir

The inclosed letters were forwarded by the president to my care. Learning from him, that a package, in which they were covered, contained some fresh literary information, I took the liberty of opening it; especially as it was suggested, and the event shewed, that it contained two other letters, one for Mr. Page, the other for Mr. Madison himself.[1]

The executive are at last persuaded of their power to make the Beccarian experiment on the condemned; altho' the public should undergo some expense.[2] They found their opinion on the law concerning the buildings for the use of the state. An overseer, trusty and diligent, will be therefore appointed, with instructions, fitted to the views of government.

Dr. Price has published a little pamphlet, full of fervor towards America.[3] He congratulates himself on having seen the establishment of independence; and marks out some important measures to be pursued, and some ruinous errors to be avoided. Among the former he enumerates the discharge of public debts, especially to the army: to the commander however of which he recommends, that America should always remain indebted—in gratitude. He presses the necessity of extending the powers of congress, perhaps too far even for those among us, who entertain sentiments the most fœderal and of attending to education. Among the latter, he classes ecclesiastical establishments, luxury, the multiplication and unsolemn form of oaths and a mixture with foreign politics, especially for the sake of commerce. Upon the whole the composition displays friendship for mankind, a pen not confined to rigid rules or led by the dicta of others, and indeed shews Price at his political length. I borrowed it for a moment only, and cannot procure a copy for you. I am my dear friend Yrs mo: Sincerely

E. R.

RC (DLC). Cover missing. Not docketed.

[1] In JM's answer to Randolph, 10 Mar. 1785, he quoted from Jefferson's letter of 11 Nov. 1784. The other enclosures were letters from Jefferson, also dated 11 Nov., to the American Philosophical Society president, Francis Hopkinson, and to John Page (Boyd, *Papers of Jefferson*, VII, 502, 514–15).

[2] In a letter to the mayor of Richmond, 13 Jan. 1785, Governor Henry expressed dissatisfaction with the death penalty as disproportionate to crimes committed in certain cases. Since he believed that unconditional pardon was detrimental to society, he preferred the assignment of convicts to public works as an appropriate punishment, and as a deterrent to future offenders (Executive Letter Book, pp. 444–45).

[3] *Observations on the Importance of the American Revolution, and the Means of Making it a Benefit to the World* (London, 1784). Price's work was reprinted in a Boston edition of 1784.

From James Monroe

N. YORK. March 6. 1785.

DEAR SIR

The arrangment in our foreign affairs begins at length to assume some form. Upon whatever ground they were taken up for a consid-

erable time, either with respect to France, Spn. or G. B., the same difficulties arose. If it was mov'd that *Dr. Franklin* be permitted agreeable to
his request to retire home it was firmly oppos'd by *R. Island* [&] *Massachussetts*. If that a minister be appointed to *Great Britain* it was mov'd
that those instructed to form commercl. treaties be instructed &c. It was
argued on the other hand that our affairs with these courts stood on
their own ground respectively and that negotiations with each sepe-
rately & at their respective capitals wod. be more eligible & likely to
produce success. It was at length mov'd by *Mr. Howell* that a *minister*
be appointed to represent [the] *U. States* at the *Court* of *Great Britain*
and carried. Adams, R. R. Livings[ton] & Rutledge were put in nomination. It had been previously, with the ill-founded expectation of facilitating this measure, mov'd, by Mr. Pinckney "that the commns to foreign ministers unless renew'd by Congress shod. continue in force only
for three years." This was negativ'd; but being agn. renew'd by the
mover & press'd upon Congress from other quarters was at length carried. Upon several ballots Adams had 5. votes, Livingston 4. & Rutledge
2., Jersey at length voted for Adams, having previously nominated &
voted for Livingston, upon wh. Virga. & Maryld. joined in favr. of
Adams & gave him his appointmt. Mr. Smith lately an aid to the general
hath been since appointed secry. to the legation. A Mr. Trunbull of
Connecticut was his only competitor. Had this affr. come on upon the
first meeting of Congress at Trenton the event must have been the
same. 5. States, the 4. Eastern & Pena. were decidedly in favr. of Adams
in preference to any other person, Jersey was at first dispos'd to commit our for: business to Adams & Jefferson only, and wod. therefore
have voted Adams to the above *Court*. He wod. of course had the majority in Congress & the expedience of the measure wod. have superseded any difficulties with respect to the man. I suppose *Mr. Jefferson*
will shortly be appointed in the room of *Dr. Franklin* to the *Court* of
France. Carmichael writes that some person in the character of Charge'
des affrs. will shortly be sent from Spn. instructed &c. so that the affrs.
with Spn. will sleep till we hear further on the subject. I have recd.
letters from Mr. Jefferson of the 10th of Novr. & 11. of Decr. last. In
the former he considers war betwn. the Emperor & the Netherlands
with their respective associates the Empress with the Emp: & France
Prussia & the Porte with the Nether: as unavoidable. He considers the
intermediate negotiation as an act only of the Imperial Courts to enable
them to commence the campaign on better conditions; in the last he
says the genl. opinion is there will be no war but that he sees no reason

for it, except the indisposition of the Empress upon whose health the projects of the Emperor must depend. He believes that if it takes place Engld. will keep herself out of the scrape for the following reasons, 1. because she cannot borrow money to take part in it. 2. Ireland is likely to give her disturbance & 3. because her disputes with us are not settled by a full execution of the articles of the treaty and the hatred of her people towards us has arisen to such a height as to prepare their minds for a recommenc'ment of hostilities shod. their govt. find this desirable. "If the war takes place & the States have the direction of their commerce upon fœderal principles I shod. suppose, provided we settle our affrs. with *Great Britain*, it will be advantageous to us. Every divertion wh. it creates to the vessels of other power[s] from the business of commerce must form an additional demand for ours and admit us gradually into the carrying trade.["] By his last letter I find that a correspondence had taken place between our ministers & the Duke of Dorset the B. minister at Paris upon the subject of a commercial treaty. His Grace makes a previous stipulation on the part of his court "that a minister instructed &ca. by Congress repair to London." They say they are jointly authoriz'd to treat, that they have no objection that it shall be in London, from wh. I suspect they may be there at this time. The commn to Adams will perhaps find him there, but this will not give him powers singly to form a commercl. treaty.

The States of Mass: & N. York having previously agreed upon the members to constitute the Court enter'd also into a stipulation that the place of session shod. be determin'd by a majority of the States present in Congress.[1] When brought before Congress, the Delegation of Mass: propos'd Wms.burg & that of N. Yk. Wilmington. The former had 5. votes & the latter 4. Of course the decision agreeably to the covenant enter'd into by the two States was in favr. of the former. N. York was dissatisfied with the decision. Mass: mov'd that the Presdt. forward the letters to the gentn. appointed, upon wh. the displeasure of N. York was discover'd. Mr. Williamson movd "that the decision of Congress by 5. States under the agreemt. of N. Y. & Mass: under the consideration wh. requires 7. in all cases except &c was void." Whether the States of Mass: and N. Y: had independently of Congress the right of fixing the place & might chuse any intermediate plan, wh. shod. be obligatory on themselves & the Union, or whether Congress had the power of controul became the question. Whenever it came before them a decision of the main question was always evaded by those of order so that it was never taken. The two States at length agreed that whatever had been committed to the journals shod. be eras'd wh. was adm[it]ted. In this condition it remains. It is expected they will agree to some more northern position.[2] I am dear Sir very respectfully yr. frnd. & ser.

JAS. MONROE

P. S. Since the appointmt. of Adams it seems generally agreed that some person shod. be sent to the Hague, but no one is yet thought of.

RC (DLC). Cover missing. The italicized words, unless otherwise noted, are those encoded by Monroe using the code he sent JM on 7 Nov. 1784.

[1] The Articles of Confederation (Art. IX) provided for arbitration by a federal court in case of state boundary-line disputes. New York and Massachusetts proceeded to submit their differences accordingly, but a snag developed when they could not agree, as Monroe noted, upon a meeting place for the court (*JCC*, XXVIII, 19 n., 38–39). This difficulty, along with the refusal of certain judges (Monroe included) to serve on the court, prolonged the business for several years.

[2] While Congress haggled over the meeting place the states involved sent their own commissioners to Hartford, Connecticut, on 16 Dec. 1786, where an agreement was reached that gave Massachusetts "preemptive rights to two large tracts within New York's bounds, totalling about five million acres" while New York "retained all the governmental rights" over these tracts (Burnett, *Letters*, VIII, 509 n.; Nevins, *The American States during and after the Revolution*, p. 591).

To Edmund Randolph

ORANGE March 10. 1785.

MY DEAR SIR

Your favour of the 12 Ulto. came safe to hand through the conveyance of Capt. Barber together with the several articles inclosed. The letter from Mr. Jefferson speaks of the state of things on the 11th. of Novr. on the other side of the Atlantic as follows. "The lamp of war is kindled here not to be extinguished but by torrents of blood. The firing of the Dutch on an Imperial vessel going down the Scheld, has been followed by the departure of the Imperial Minister from the Hague without taking leave. Troops are in motion on both sides towards the Scheld, but probably nothing will be done till the Spring. This Court has been very silent as to the part they will act. Yet their late treaty with Holland, as well as a certainty that Holland would not have proceeded so far without assurance of aid, furnish sufficient ground to conclude they will side actively with the Republic. The King of Prussia it is believed will do the same. He has patched up his little disputes with Holland & Dantzic. The prospect is that Holland, France, Russia & the Por[te] will be engaged against the two Imperial Courts.

England I think will remain neu[tral]. Their hostility towards us has attained an incredible height. Notwithstanding this they expect to keep our trade & cabotage to themselves by the virtue of their proclamation. They have no idea that we can so far act in concert as to establish retaliating measures. Their Irish Affairs will puzzle them extremely. Should things get into confusion there perhaps they will be more disposed to wish a friendly connection with us. The Congress which met on the 25 of Ocr. consisted of deputies from 8 Counties only. They came to resolutions on the reform of Parliamt. & adjd. to the 20 of Jany. recommending to the other Counties to send deputies then."[1]

I learn from an intelligent person lately from Kentucky that the Convention there produced nothing but a statement of grievances & a claim of redress. The topic of independence was not regularly brought forward at all, and scarcely agitated without doors.[2] It is supposed that the late extension of the tax on patents which as it stood before is on the list of grievances, will turn the scale, in favor of that measure.[3]

Mr. Norton called on me about a week ago on his way to Fredg.[4] If you sd. have recd no later information from Albemarle, it may be a satisfaction to Mrs. Randolph to know that her friends in that quarter were then well—present my best respects to her & beleive me to be with the sincerest affection your friend & servt.

J. MADISON JR

RC (DLC). Docketed by Randolph and marked, "(private)." Addressed to Randolph at Richmond.

[1] The last two sentences were from a postscript Jefferson added to the 11 Nov. letter, slightly amended by JM in the copying process.

[2] The convention in Kentucky met at Danville on 27 Dec. 1784 and issued a list of "greevances" that included complaints over special taxes levied on settlers in the district (Abernethy, "Journal of the First Kentucky Convention," *Journal of Southern History*, I [1935], 67–78). JM's informant misled him, for the "topic of independence" was the gist of a resolution that held the remoteness of Richmond from the district was a burden "which can not be redressed whilst it [Kentucky] remains a part of Virginia." The convention also objected "Because . . . large Sums of Money [were] drained from the District in consequence of its connection with the Eastern part of the State," and proposed that another meeting be held in May 1785 to consider "the Expediency of the proposed Seperation."

[3] "The late extension of the tax on patents" was a levy of five shillings per hundred acres to be collected when a land title was issued on estates of more than 1,400 acres (Hening, *Statutes*, XI, 445). The tax had been approved by the Oct. 1784 session of the General Assembly and was particularly offensive to some land speculators serving at the Danville convention. JM's friend Caleb Wallace had been

present at the convention and had voted against the resolution protesting the five-shilling tax.

4 John Hatley Norton was Mrs. Randolph's brother-in-law (Mason, ed., *John Norton & Sons*, p. 518).

From Lafayette

PARIS March the 16th 1785

MY DEAR SIR

Was I to found my Hopes Upon the Letters I have from Congress, I would please my fancy with the Expectation of Wellcoming You to the European Shore—and Yet, when I Remember Your obstinate plans of life, I am affraid least my Warm Wishes Should be disappointed—in the Mean While, I will Continue writing, and By the Way Will advise You to send Your Answers By the packets Rather than By a private Vessel. Those letters I sent from Richmond are not Yet Arrived, and I do not think Any letters of the Executive, nor any Private dispatches from Virginia Have as Yet Got to Europe. The politics of this Country are not Yet perfectly Cleared Up. But I am firm in the opinion we shall Have no War at this time. The Emperor's plans Have Been Opposed by France—it Has on one side saved the dutch, whose Sacrifices, in Comparison of What threatened them Will probably Be Small. It Has on the other Kept Up the Suite in the Empire of Germany, As By its dependance Upon the protection of France and Prussia, the duke of deux ponts Has Been Emboldened to oppose Arrangements Between the Emperor and the Elector of Baviera Where By this Would Have, it is Said, given up His Electorate for the low Countries of the Austrian House. The Conditions Betwe[e]n the dutch and the Emperor are not Yet published. But I Send You a declaration of the king of France to the Emperor, Which took place When He Entered the political Field a few months Ago. Count de Vergennes Has acted, in My opinion, with a Moderation and firmness which does Him Great Honour.[1]

I am Every day pestering Governement with My prophetics Respecting the Mississipy. My favourite plan, they think, Cannot Be Accepted By Spain, who Know not How to Give up what they once Have. On My Arrival, I strongly Advised, at least, to tell the Spaniards to make for themselves New orleans a free port. I am to Have a Conference on that interesting Subject with duke de la Vauguim Who is Going Next Week to Spain as an Ambassader. I Have writen letters By post to Madrid and Cadiz, to Be intercepted and Read. I wish theyr Ministry

Were as Sensible and as well disposed as Ours is. I am told Congress Want to Send You there. Could'nt You Accept of it, only for a time, and in the Mean While make Your journey through france and italy? Kentucky, its growth, Its principles, and its inHabitants are, I find, Very little Understood in Europe, and not much so perhaps By many Europeans in America.

There is a Book of Mr. Necker Upon Finances which Has Made Great deal of Noise.[2] It Has Raised a Party Spirit, where By Both Have to an Excess Hated or Adored Him. But I only Speak of the Book, which is a Very Sensible One, and Worth Your Reading. Untill You get it, I inclose a Miniature portrait of France, Made By the Man Who of Course Knows its Ressources. Its publication may Afford Entertainement.

Cher de Caraman's Best Compliments wait Upon You, My dear Sir, and I Beg You Will Remember me to all Friends in Virginia—Mr. jefferson's Health is Recovering—But He Keeps Himself too Closely Confined. By My last letters from the General, He was in full enjoyment of a plan for the Navigation of the Pottowmack.[3] God Bless You, My dear friend, Remember me often, and for ever depend Upon the Warm Affection, and Most High Regard of Your devoted friend

LAFAYETTE

The Mercantile interest is Warmer than Ever Against the New Regulations in favour of the West india trade. They are Encouraged By the Narrow Conduct of England, and the total interruption of Commerce Betwe[e]n french and Americans, who are all flocking to Great Britain.[4]

RC (PHi). No cover or docket. Enclosure not found.

[1] In Oct. 1783, Joseph II of Austria attempted to open the Scheldt River for international navigation and thereby expand his influence in European commercial affairs. Dutch soldiers crossed into Belgium and in retaliation, imperial troops seized two Dutch forts. For a time war threatened. A conference met at Brussels in Apr. 1784. Joseph's sister, Marie Antoinette, tried to influence her husband Louis XVI, to support the imperial position, but instead Vergennes offered to mediate the problem. Joseph was forced to accept, and eventually relaxed his demand that the Scheldt be opened (Saul Padover, *The Revolutionary Emperor: Joseph the Second 1741–1790* [New York, 1933], pp. 315–30).

[2] Jacques Necker, director general of France from 1776 to 1781 and again from 1788 to 1789, described his economic theories in *Compte rendu au roi*, published in 1781.

[3] Washington's letter of 23 Dec. 1784 refers to negotiations concerning the navigation of the Potomac River. Although the general's letter of 15 Feb. 1785 is much more detailed about this subject it is unlikely that Lafayette had received this letter (Fitzpatrick, *Writings of Washington*, XXVIII, 17–18, 71–75).

⁴ Lafayette returned to France in 1782 with a whole commercial plan and used his influence in the French court to achieve its acceptance. The principal plank of his plan was that American trade should have an indefinitely privileged position in French ports. The Arrêt of Aug. 1784 provided Americans with seven ports in the West Indies and increased the list of approved imports. French commercial opinion was indignant about the new trade terms and a propaganda war in France followed. Measures later adopted to placate this interest almost totally nullified the American advantages. See Frederick L. Nussbaum, "American Tobacco and French Politics, 1783–1789," *Political Science Quarterly*, XL (1925), 497–516; and "The French Colonial Arrèt of 1784," *South Atlantic Quarterly*, XXVII (1928), 62–78; and Louis R. Gottschalk, ed., "Lafayette as Commercial Expert," *AHR*, XXXVI (1930–31), 561–70. The Arrêt had recently been published in America, in the *Pa. Packet*, 9 Mar. 1785, and the *Pa. Gazette*, 16 Mar. 1785.

From Thomas Jefferson

PARIS Mar. 18. 1785.

DEAR SIR

My last to you was dated Dec. 8. since that yours of Feb. 1. has come to hand; and I am in hopes I shall shortly receive from you the history of the last session of our assembly. I will pray you always to send your letters by the French packet which sails from N. York the 15th. of every month. I had made Neill Jamieson¹ my post master general there, who will always take care of my letters and confide them to passengers when there are any worthy of confidence. Since the removal of Congress to that place, you can chuse between N. Jamieson & our delegates there, to which you would rather address my letters. The worst conveyances you can possibly find are private hands, or merchant ships coming from Virginia directly to France. These letters either come not at all, or like the histories of antient times they detail to us events after their influence is spent.

Your *character* of the *M. Fayette* is precisely agreeable to the idea I had formed of *him*.² I take *him* to be of *unmeasured ambition* but that the *means he uses* are virtuous. *He is returned fraught* with *affection* to *America* and *disposed* to render every *possible service*. Of the cause which *separated* the *committee* of the *States* we never have had *an explicit account. Hints* and *dark sentences* from newspapers & private letterds have *excited* without *satisfying* our *cu[r]iosity*. As your *cipher* is safe pray *give me a deta[i]l* of it. The navigation of the Scheld had for a great while agitated the politics of Europe & seemed to threaten the involving it in a general war.³ All of a sudden another subject, infinitely more interesting is brought on the carpet. There is reason to beleive that the Emperor has made an exchange of territories with the Elector of Bavaria, & that while the Scheld has been the ostensible, Bavaria has been the real object of his military preparations. When the proposition was communicated to the *King of Prussia* it is said he declared qu'il mourroit le cul sur la selle rather than see it take effect. *The Dutch* it is thought would be *secretly pleased* with it. And some *think* that certain *places* said to be *reserved* by the *Emperor* on the *borders* of *France* are meant to be *given to the lat*[t]*er* for her *acquies*[c]*ence*. I am *attending* with *anxiety* to the part she will act on this occasion. I shall change my opinion of *her system* of *policy* if it be not honorable. If the Dutch escape a war, they seem still to be in danger of internal revolution. The Stadtholder & Aristocracy can carry their differences no further without an appeal to the sword. The people are on the side of the *Stadtholder*. The conduct of the *aristocracy* in pushing *their* measures to such extremity is inexplicable but on the *suppos*[i]*tion* that *France* has *promised* to *support them* which it is *thought she* was *obliged* to *do before they* would *enter into* the *late treaty*.[4] We hear nothing from England. This circumstance, with the passage of their N. F. land bill thro' the house of commons, & the sending a Consul to America (which we hear they have done) sufficiently prove a perseverance in the system of managing for us as well as for themselves in their connection with us. The administration of that country are governed by the people, & the people by their own interested wishes without calculating whether they are just or capable of being effected. Nothing will bring them to reason but physical obstruction, applied to their bodily senses. We must shew that we are capable of foregoing commerce with them, before they will be capable of consenting to an equal commerce. We have all the world besides open to supply us with gewgaws, and all the world to buy our tobacco, for in such an event England must buy it from Amsterdam, l'Orient or any other place at which we should think proper to deposit it for them. They allow our commodities to be taken from our own ports to the W. Indies in their vessels only. Let us allow their vessels to take them to no port. The transportation of our own produce is worth 750,000 £ sterl. annually, will employ 200,000 tonnage of Ships & 12,000 seamen constantly. It will be no misfortune that Gr. Br. obliges us to exclude her from a participation in this business. Our own shipping will grow fast under the exclusion, & till it is equal to the object the Dutch will supply us. The commerce with the Eng. W. I. is valuable & would be worth a sacrifice to us. But the commerce with the British dominions in Europe is a losing one & deserves no sacrifice. Our tobacco they must have from whatever place we make it's deposit, because they can get no other whose quality so well suits the habits of their people. It is not a commodity like wheat, which will not bear a double voyage. Were it so, the privilege of carrying it directly to England might be worth something. I know nothing which would act more powerfully as a sumptuary law with our people than an inhibition of commerce with England.[5] They are habituated to the luxuries of that country & will have them while they can get them. They are unacquainted with those of other countries, and therefore will not very soon bring them so far into fashion as that it shall be thought disreputable not to have them in one's house or on their table. It is to be considered how far an exemption of Ireland from this inhibition would embarrass the councils of Engld. on the one hand, and defeat the regulation itself on the other. I rather beleive it would do more harm in the latter way than good in the former. In fact a heavy aristocracy & corruption are two bridles in the mouth of the Irish which will prevent them from making any effectual efforts against their masters. We shall now *very soon call* for *decisive answers* to certain points *interesting* to the *United States* and *uncon*[n]*ected* with the *general treaty* which they have a right to *decline*. I mentioned to you in a former letter a very good dictionary of universal law called the Code d'humanité in 13. vols. 4to.[6] Meeting by chance an opportunity of buying a copy, new, & well bound for 104. livres I purchased it for you. It comes to 8 livres a volume which is a fraction over a dollar & a half, & in England costs 15/ sterl. a volume. I shall have an opportunity of sending this & what other books I have bought for you in May. But new information throws me all into doubt what to do with them. Late letters tell us you are *nominated for* the *court of Spain*.[7] I must depend on further intelligence therefore to decide whether to send them or to await your orders. I need not tell you how much I shall be pleased with such an event. Yet it has it's displeasing sides also. *I want you* in the *Virginia Assembly* and also in *Congress* yet we cannot have *you everywhere*. We must therefore be contented to have *you where you chuse*. Adieu, your'[s] affectionately

RC (DLC). Cover missing. Not signed. Docketed with an endorsement in an unknown hand, "allusion to Mr. Madison's proposed appointment abroad." The italicized words, unless otherwise noted, are those encoded by Jefferson using the code of 14 Apr. 1783.

[1] Neil Jamieson was a former Norfolk resident who had been a resident partner of a Glasgow mercantile firm. He served on the Norfolk Committee of Correspon-

dence in 1775, but later took sides with the loyalists and was forced to flee to the British lines at New York. His sequestered Virginia estate was valued at £37,100 and he later filed a claim with the commissioners adjudicating loyalists' losses. He eventually returned to Great Britain. See Wertenbaker, *Norfolk: Historic Southern Port* (1962 ed.), pp. 37, 44 and passim.

2 Jefferson's allusion is to JM's remarks concerning Lafayette in his 17 Oct. 1784 letter, not "yours of Feb. 1." Jefferson meant the Oct. message had arrived on 1 Feb. 1785 in Paris.

3 JM and Jefferson were interested in the dispute over navigational rights on the Scheldt River because the issue raised seemed pertinent to the U. S. claim for access to the Mississippi (See JM to Jefferson, 20 Aug. 1784). Joseph II tried to force the Scheldt open to world commerce by sending a loaded ship down the river "only to have it fired on and driven back by the Dutch" who controlled the river's mouth (Robert R. Palmer, *The Age of the Democratic Revolution* [2 vols.; Princeton, 1959–64], I, 345).

4 Joseph II called for opening of the Scheldt but bungled the proposition to exchange the Austrian Netherlands for his Bavarian inheritance. Vergennes blocked "the Emperor" by offering to mediate the dispute between Joseph's court and the United Provinces. Ultimately, Joseph abandoned his plan for navigation of the Scheldt (Leo Gershoy, *From Despotism to Revolution, 1763–1789* [New York, 1944], pp. 186–88).

5 Many leading public men were convinced a "sumptuary law" was needed to discourage wasteful spending by Americans. The protest of Boston citizens against the purchase of British goods was indicative of widespread discontent over resumption of prewar commercial ties with England and the subsequent purchase of "gewgaws" (*Boston Gazette*, 18 Apr., 9 May 1785).

6 Fortuné Barthélemy de Felice, ed., *Code de l'Humanité, ou la Législation universelle, naturelle, civile et politique, avec l'histoire littéraire des plus grands hommes qui ont contribué à la perfection de ce Code* (Yverdon, 1778).

7 Although JM was among those "nominated for the court of Spain" on 2 Feb. 1785, so was Jefferson, but the post was left vacant (*JCC*, XXVIII, 25 n.).

To Lafayette

ORANGE March 20th. 1785.

MY DEAR SIR

Your favour of the 15th. continued on the 17th of December came very slowly but finally safe to hand. The warm expressions of regard which it contains are extremely flattering to me, and the more so as they so entirely correspond with my own wishes for every thing which may enter into your happiness.

You have not erred in supposing me out of the number of those who have relaxed their anxiety concerning the navigation of the Mississippi.[1] If there be any who really look on the use of that river, as an object not to be sought or desired by the United States I can not but think they frame their policies on both very narrow and very delusive foundations. It is true, if the States which are to be established on the waters of the Mississippi were to be viewed in the same relation to the Atlantic States as exists between the heterogeneous and hostile Societies of Europe, it might not appear strange that a distinction or even an opposition of interests should be set up. But is it true that they can be viewed in such a relation? Will the settlements which are beginning to take place on the branches of the Mississippi, be so many distinct Societies, or only an expansion of the same Society? So many new bodies or merely the growth of the old one? Will they consist of a hostile or a foreign people, or will they not be a bone of our bones, and flesh of our flesh? Besides the confederal band, within which they will be comprehended, how much will the connection be strengthened by the ties of friendship, of marriage and consanguinity? ties which it may be remarked, will be even more numerous, between the ultramontane and the Atlantic States than between any two of the latter. But viewing this subject through the medium least favorable to my ideas, it still presents to the U. States sufficient inducements to insist on the navigation of the Mississippi. Upon this navigation depends essentially the value of that vast field of territory which is to be sold for the benefit of the common Treasury: and upon the value of this territory when settled will depend the portion of the public burdens of which the old States will be relieved by the new. Add to this the stake which a considerable proportion of those who remain in the old states will acquire in the new by adventures in land either on their own immediate account or that of their descendents.

Nature has given the use of the Mississippi to those who may settle on its waters, as she gave to the United States their independence. The impolicy of Spain may retard the former as that of G. Britain did the latter. But as G. B. could not defeat the latter, neither will Spain the former. Nature seems on all sides to be reasserting those rights which have so long been trampled on by tyranny & bigotry. Philosophy & Commerce are the auxiliaries to whom she is indebted for her triumphs. Will it be presumptuous to say that those nations will shew most wisdom as well as acquire most glory, who, instead of forcing her current into artificial channels, endeavour to ascertain its tendency & to anticipate its effects. If the United States were to become parties to the occlusion of the Mississippi they would be guilty of treason against the very laws under which they obtained & hold their national existence.

The repugnance of Spain to an amicable regulation of the use of the Mississippi, is the national offspring of a system, which every body but herself has long seen to be as destructive to her interest, as it is dishonorable to her character. An extensive desart seems to have greater charms in her eye, than a flourishing but limited empire, nay than an extensive flourishing empire. Humanity cannot suppress the wish that some of those gifts which she abuses were placed by just means, in hands that would turn them to a wiser account. What is metamorphosis² wd. the liberal policy of France work in a little time on the Island of N. Orleans? It would to her be a fund of as much real wealth, as Potosi has been of imaginary wealth to Spain. It would become the Grand Cairo of the New World.

The folly of Spain is not less displayed in the means she employs than in the ends she prefers. She is afraid of the growth and neighbourhood of the U. States because it may endanger the tranquility of her American possessions: and to obviate this danger she proposes to shut up the Mississippi. If her prudence bore any proportion to her jealousy she would see, that if the experiment were to succeed, it would double the power of the U. States to disturb her, at the same time that it provoked a disposition to exert it; she would see that the only offensive weapon which can render the U. States truly formidable to her, is a navy, and that if she could keep their inhabitants from crossing the Appalachian, she would only drive to the sea most of those swarms which would otherwise direct their course to the Western wilderness. She would reflect too that as it [is] impossible for her to destroy the power which she dreads, she ought only to consult the means of preventing a future exertion of it. What are those means? Two & two only. The first is a speedy concurrence in such a treaty with the U. S. as will produce a harmony, & remove all pretexts for interrupting it. The second, which would in fact result from the first, consists in favouring the extension of their settlements. As these become extended the members of the Confederacy must be multiplied, and along with them the Wills which are to direct the machine. And as the wills multiply, so will the chances against a dangerous union of them. We experience every day the difficulty of drawing thirteen States into the same plans. Let the number be doubled & so will the difficulty. In the multitude of our Counsellors, Spain may be told, lies her safety.

If the temper of Spain be unfriendly to the views of the U. States, they may certainly calculate on the favorable sentiments of the other powers of Europe at least of all such of them as favored our Independence. The chief advantages expected in Europe from that event center in the revolution it was to produce in the commerce between the new & old world. The commerce of the U. S. is advantageous to Europe in two respects, first by the unmanufactured produce which they export; secondly by the manufactured imports which they consume. Shut up the Mississippi and discourage the settlements on its waters and what will be the consequence? First, a greater quantity of subsistance must be raised within the antient settlemts., the culture of tobacco indigo & other articles for exportation be proportionably diminished, and their price proportionably raised on the European consumer. Secondly the hands without land at home being discouraged from seeking it where alone it could be found, must be turned in a great degree to manufacturing, our imports proportionably diminished, and a proportional loss fall on the European manufacturer. Establish the freedom of the Mississippi, and let our emigrations have free course, and how favorably for Europe will the consequence be reversed. First the culture of every article for exportation will be extended, and the price reduced in favour of her Consumers. Secondly, our people will increase without an increase of our Manufacturers, and in the same proportion will be increased the employment & profit of hers.

These consequences would affect France in common with the other commercial nations of Europe: but there are additional motives which promise the U. States her friendly wishes and offices. Not to dwell on the philanthropy which reigns in the heart of her Monarch and which has already adorned his head with a crown of laurels. He cannot be inattentive to the situation into which a controversy between his antient and new allies would throw him, nor to the use which would be made of it by his watchful adversary. Will not all his Councils then be employed to prevent this controversy? Will it not be seen that as the pretensions of the parties directly interfere, it can be prevented only by dissuasive interposition on one side or the other, that on the side of the U. S. such an interposition must from the nature of things be unavailing, or if their pretensions cd. for a moment be lulled they wd. but awake with fresh energy, and consequently that the mediating influence of France ought to be turned wholly on the side of Spain. The influence of the French Court over that of Spain is known to be great & America it is supposed to be greater than perhaps it really is. The same may be said of the intimacy of the Union between the two nations. If this influence should not be exerted, this intimacy may appear to be the cause. The United States consider Spain as the only favorite of their ally of whom they have found to be jealous, and whilst France hold[s] the first place in their affections they must at least be mortified at any appearance that the predilection may not be reciprocal.

The Mississippi has drawn me into such length that I fear you will have little patience left for any thing else. I will spare it as much as possible. I hear nothing from Congress except that Mr. Jay has accepted his appt. and that no success[o]r has yet been chosen to Dr. Franklyn. Our Legislature made a decent provision for the remittances due for 1785 from Va. to the Treasy. of the U. S. and very extensive provision for opening our inland navigation: they have passed an Act vesting in Genl. Washington a considerable interest in each of the works on Js. River & Potowmac but with an honorary rather than lucrative aspect. Whether he will accept it or not I cannot say. I meant to have sent you a copy of the Act, but have been disappointed in getting one from Richmd. They also passed an act for reforming our juridical system which promises Salutary effects, and did not pass the Act for the corrupting Religious system.[3] Whether they passed an act for paying British debts or not they do not know themselves.[4] Before the bill for that purpose had got through the last usual forms, the want of members broke up the House. It remains therefore in a situation which has no precedent, & without a precedent lawyers & legislators are as much at a loss, as a mariner without his compass. The subjects in which you interested yourself were all referred to the Executive with power to do what I hope they will do better than the Assembly.[5] I understood before I left Richmd. that you wd. receive officially from the Govr. a copy of the Resolutions which I sent you. I recd. a letter a few days ago from Mr. Mercer written in the bosom of wedlock at Mr. Spriggs; another at the same time from Monroe, who was well at New York. I have nothing to say of myself but that I have exchanged Richmond for Orange as you will have seen by the above date; that I enjoy a satisfactory share of health; that I spend the chief of my time in reading, & the chief of my reading on Law; that I shall hear with the greatest pleasure of your being far better employed, & that I am with most affect. esteem Yr. Obedt [friend?] & Sert.

                                                        J. M.

FC (DLC). Docketed by JM and others.

[1] JM obviously wrote this letter for circulation beyond Lafayette's household. In his 20 Aug. 1784 letter to Jefferson, JM gave evidence of his researches on the international use of rivers and from the circumstances he hoped Lafayette would become an advocate of full American rights to the Mississippi. As "a self-appointed representative of the United States" Lafayette used his skills as an amateur envoy to gain Spanish concessions for western settlers (Gottschalk, *Lafayette between the American and the French Revolution*, pp. 155–57). Before this letter could have reached Lafayette, he wrote Washington of a conference held with the French

ambassador to Spain "respecting the Mississipy—But the Spaniards are still obstinate, and you will have full time to oppen your navigation, which I consider as the first political, mercantile, and national plan which can now employ the United States" (Gottschalk, ed. *The Letters of Lafayette to Washington*, p. 295).

[2] JM deleted the words "miraculous transformation" and inserted "metamorphosis."

[3] Hunt omits the passage beginning, "they also passed" to "corrupting our Religious system" (Madison, *Writings* [Hunt ed.], II, 126).

[4] JM explained these strange circumstances regarding the British debt installment act in his letter to Jefferson, 9 Jan. 1785.

[5] Governor Harrison acknowledged receipt of Lafayette's letter of 19 Nov. 1784 with its enclosed petitions on behalf of French firms pressing for payment of old debts (Executive Letter Book, pp. 431–32). Lafayette had recommended these memorials to JM in his letter of 15 Dec. 1784.

To Richard Henry Lee

Letter not found.

20 March 1785. Concerns Virginia and Confederation affairs mentioned in Lee's letter of 30 May 1785.

To James Monroe

ORANGE March 21. 1785.

DEAR SIR

Your favor of the 1st day of Feby. did not come to hand till a day or two ago, having travelled on to Richmond, remained there during the absence of Mr. Jones, & on his return, been sent to me by the way of Fredg. Before I left Richmond I wrote you that the assembly had adjourned and requested that your subsequent letters might be addressed to Orange, and if I do not forget to care of Mr. Maury at Fredericksbg. This letter ought to have reached you before the date of yours. I hope it has since got to hand. I also forwarded from Richmond to your care a letter for Mr. Jefferson which I hope has not miscarried.[1] It contained a rehearsal of our last legislative politics & proceedings, which I find by his letters to me, are a material object of his curiosity. I shall be glad to know by your next, whether you have ever recd. it, that in case of miscarriage I may endeavour to supply the loss.

I do not wonder at the paragraph which you have copied from Mr. Jays letter to Congress. His feelings are such as every man must possess who is worthy of the Station which he holds. If the Office of foreign affairs be a proper one & properly filled, a reference of all foreign despatches to it in the first instance, is so obvious a course, that any other disposition of them by Congress seems to condemn their own establishment, to affront the Minister in office, and to put on him a label of caution agst. that respect & confidence of the Ministers of foreign powers, which are essential to his usefulness. I have always conceived the several ministerial departments of Congress to be provisions for aiding their Counsels as well as executing their resolutions, & that consequently whilst they retain the right of rejecting the advice which may come from either of them, they ought not to renounce the opportunity of makg use of it. The foreign department is I am sensible, in several respects the most difficult to be regulated, but I cannot think the question arising on Mr. Jay's letter is to be numbered among the difficulties. The practice of Congress during the administration of his predecessor was never fixed, & frequently improper, and I always suspected that his indifference to the plan resulted in part at least from the mortifications to which this unsteadiness subjected him.[2]

You will not be disappointed at the barrenness which is hence to mark the correspondence on my part. In the recess of the Legislature, few occurrences happen which can be interesting, and in my retired situation, few even of these fall within my knowledge. The situation of Mr. Jones will probably make his correspondence a more productive one. He has probably already mentioned to you the advances which Kentucky was said to be making towards an independent Govt. It is certain that a Convention has been held, which might have been set on foot with an eye to such an event: but I learn from an intelligent person lately from that district, that its deliberations turned altogether on the pressure of certain acts of the General Assembly, & terminated in a vote of application for redress. He supposes however that the late extension of the tax on Patents will give a successful handle to those who wish to accelerate a separation. This tax as it stood before was in the first class of their grievances.

You will I expect receive this from the hand of Mr. Burnley,[3] a young gentleman of my neighbourhood, who has passed with reputation through Mr. Wythes School & has since taken out his forensic diploma. Your civilities to him will be well placed & will confer an obligation on me. If Col. Grayson has recovered from the Gout which I hear arrested him on the moment of his intended departure, and is with you, be so kind as to make my best respects to him. I am Dear Sir with sincere regard & esteem Your obedt. friend & Servant

J. MADISON JR.

RC (DLC). Docketed by JM. Addressed to Monroe "in Congress," and "Favd. by Mr. H. Burnley" who was JM's Orange County neighbor.

¹ This was JM's letter to Jefferson of 9 Jan. 1785, which apparently was sent to Monroe unsealed, to be forwarded in a diplomatic pouch.

² Jay's predecessor was Robert R. Livingston, who held the office from 1781 to 1783, but served on an interim basis until Jay took office. Livingston's enemies said "His Office was misterious, and secret to all those, who ought to have a perfect Knowledge of all it contain'd" (Burnett, *Letters*, VII, 380).

³ Col. Hardin Burnley (1761–1809), later of Hanover County and Richmond, was a member of the Council of State and served briefly as acting governor in Dec. 1799. He was considered a rising young man in political circles after he finished his legal training under George Wythe at Williamsburg (Dicken, *Our Burnley Ancestors and Allied Families,* pp. 52–53).

To Patrick Henry

ORANGE March 25th. 1785

SIR

In compliance with your Excellency's letter of the 22 of Jany.¹ the Gentlemen to whom it was addressed excepting Mr. Grimes had a meeting yesterday for the first time, when they took the subject of it into consideration and have directed me to inform you that they recommend for County Lieutenant of Orange John Spotswood Esqr for Lieutenant Colonel Commandant, John Lee Esqr. for first Major William White Esqr. and for the other major Francis Cowherd Esqr. these being all the field offices required for the Militia of this County.²

I have the honor to be with the greatest res[pec]t. & esteem Yr. Excelly's most obt. & hble servt.

J. MADISON JR.

RC (Vi). Addressed to Governor Henry, and docketed "Orange."

¹ Governor Henry's letter concerned appointments for the Orange County militia.

² Benjamin Grymes (ca. 1750–1787) was a leading citizen and Orange County justice of the peace (Scott, *History of Orange County*, p. 71). John Spotswood (ca. 1753–1801) was a captain in the 10th Virginia Regiment who was wounded at Brandywine and later captured at Germantown. He was exchanged by the British three years later (Heitman, *Historical Register Continental*, p. 512). John Lee (1743–1802) was the son of Hancock Lee. He served as an officer in the 1st Virginia Regiment during early days of the Revolution, was a marine captain aboard the *Liberty*, and became a major with the 2d Virginia Regiment at Valley Forge. He migrated to Kentucky about 1790 and settled in Woodford County (Lee, *Lee Chronicle*, p. 355). William White (d. 1828) was commissioned for duty with the 7th Virginia Regiment in 1776, rose to the rank of captain, and was captured at Charleston, 1780. He was paroled by the British, returned to Orange County, and later received a veteran's pension (Heitman, *Historical Register Continental*, p. 587; Gwathmey, *Historical Register of Virginians*, p. 823).

From Joseph Jones

Richmond 30th. Mar: 1785.

D. Sr.

I have your favor by Col Richd. Taylor.[1] The letter for the Attorney has been delivered and he is informed when Mr Taylor will be in town. Mr Maier[2] some time past made application to the Executive, and laid before them a state of his case. Altho' it was not altogether satisfactory he had a legal demand agt. the State, yet the circumstances were in general so favourable to his Pretensions, he obtained for his present relief £150. and an assurance that his case wod. be laid before the Assembly. The other matter has not yet come forward. I will inquire into Mr. Maiers situation and if I shall find your aid necessary will apply it. On my return from King George I found a letter here from Monroe to you, which I forwarded by the way of Fredericksburg to the care of Mr. Maury, no other has since appeared. Indeed nothing very important had been decided, tho' many things of moment were depending. J. Adams is appointed Minister to Ct. London outvoting R R. Livingston and Rutledge: Adams 8 Livingston 3—Rutledg[e] 2—the first vote, Adams 6. Livingston 5.—Rutledge 2. Virga. and Maryland at first voted for L. but went over to A. finally. Jefferson it is expected will remain in France. By a letter from Short lately recd. by Mr. Nelson Jefferson was abt. to visit London wh[ethe]r merely a private trip or to meet Adams is not mentioned—but I suppose a private visit, as Adams's appointmt could not have reached him. Gadoqui is coming to America to adjust Matters respecting our boundary with Spain. G. W. is reduced to difficulties respecting his acceptance of the shares in the Companies. Inclosed you have a Copy of the act. Short writes that Berkely had postponed executing the order for the bust untill the return of the Marquis that the likeness might be taken more perfectly.[3] We have sent by way of N. York to the care of the Delegates the resol: of the last Session, and the first vessell from here will carry a duplicate.[4] The president of Congress in his letter of the last week says they have reason to think the dispute between the Emperor and the united provinces will be accommodated. He says there appears a disposition on the part of G. Britain to settle the difficulties between them and the U. States respecting the Treaty & other matt[ers,] *if by our conduct on this side [of] the water we do not prevent it.* He says also measures are taking and in great forwardness for holding a conference with the S. Tribes of Indian[s] for the purpose of accommodating matters with them. I observe by the Treaty concluded with the Nh. Tribes the Shawanese are not parties, it is said they were prevailed on [*illegible*] by British Emissar[ies] not to attend. I have this day removed to the house where Capt. Seabrooks[5] family now live and have two rooms up stair[s] such as they are and the entertaining room below. He has alrea[dy] and the rest of the family are by the 1st. May to remove for the sum[mer] into the Country, so that I am to occupy the House untill I leave Town ab. 1st. July, with the furniture in it. If you come to Town for the Court which I think you said you intended, I desire you to come here, as you can have a bed and other accommodations tho not so well as we could wish yet so as to be tolerably comfortable. yr. friend

JOS: JONES.

RC (DLC). Cover missing. Docketed. The right margin of the second page was damaged by inept mounting of the document and words thus obscured have been restored within brackets.

1 JM's letter has not been found. Col. Richard Taylor (1744–1829) had visited Kentucky before the Revolution and in the Spring of 1785 returned there as a permanent settler. Taylor served in the Kentucky legislature and was living near Louisville at the time of his death (Washington, D.C., *National Intelligencer*, 7 Feb. 1829; *Register of the Kentucky Historical Society*, XXXVI [1938], 330–39).

2 "Mr. Maier" was Col. Jacques Le Maire, whom JM had requested Jones to "watch over" (JM to Jefferson, 27 Apr. 1785).

3 William Short's missing account must have explained that the Virginia commercial agent "Berkely" (Thomas Barclay) had been instructed to have a bust of Lafayette made according to the Resolution of 1 Dec. 1784, but had postponed the arrangements with a sculptor while the marquis was on a European trip. As Jefferson later explained, however, Houdon was engaged to make a plaster model before Lafayette departed (Jefferson to Henry, 22 Aug. 1785, Boyd, *Papers of Jefferson*, VIII, 422).

4 Barclay seems to have arranged a contract for Lafayette's bust without the formality of a direct order from the Commonwealth of Virginia, but the 1 Dec. resolution "of the last Session" furnished Barclay with the authority to proceed with the business.

5 Capt. Nicholas B. Seabrook(e) (d. 1793) was master of the *Good Intent* in the state navy, 1776; an assessor of Richmond city taxes, 1783–1784; Richmond common councilman, 1783–1784; and owner of several lots on the 1788 tax rolls (ViU: Heth Papers, Return of taxable property . . . for the year 1788).

To Martha Jefferson Carr

Letter not found.

ca. 1–17 April 1785. Mentioned in Mrs. Carr's answer of 18 April. JM apparently inquired about her state of health.

To James Monroe

Dear Sir

I wrote you not long since, by a young gentleman who proposed to go as far [as] N. Y. acknowledging the rect. of your favor of Feby. 1st. I have since recd. that of March 6 which I meant to have acknowledged through the same hands. But finding that the delays which have hitherto kept back the bearer above referred to, are of uncertain continuance, & having no certain conveyance to Fredg. I embrace an opportunity of sending this to Richmond, whence it will be forwarded by Mr. Jones in the mail.

The appointment of Mr. A. to the Court of G. B. is a circumstance which does not contradict my expectations: nor can I say that it displeases me. Upon geographical considerations N. E. will always have one of the principal appointmts. and I know of no individual from that quarter, who possesses more of their confidence or would possess more of that of the other States: nor do I think him so well fitted for any Court of equal rank, as that of London. I hope it has removed all obstacles to the establishment of Mr. Jefferson at the Court of France. Will not Congress soon take up the subject of Consular arrangements?[1] I should suppose them at least of equal moment at present with some of the higher appointmts. which are likely to occupy them. Our friend Mr. Maury is waiting with a very inconvenient suspension of his other plans, the event of the offer he has made of his Services.[2] I find he considers Ireland as the Station next to be desired after that of England. He conceives & I believe very justly that the commercial intercourse between that Country & this will be very considerable, and merits our particular cultivation. I suppose from your silence on the subject that the Western Posts are still in the hands of G. B. Has the subject of the vacant lands to be disposed of, been revived?[3] What other measures are [on] foot or in contemplation for paying off the public debts? What paymts. have been made of late into the public Treasury? It is said here that Massts. is taking measures for urging R. I. into the Impost, or rendering the scheme practicable without her concurrence. Is it so? How many of the States have agreed to change the 8th. Art. of the Confederation?[4] The Legislature of this State passd a law for complying with the provisional act of Congs. for executing that article as it now stands; the operation of which confirms the necessity of changing the article. The law requires as the Act of Congs. does among other

GEORGE WASHINGTON

By Jean Antoine Houdon, commissioned in 1784 by the Virginia General Assembly to produce a statue "of the finest marble and best workmanship." The statue was not placed in the capitol at Richmond until 1796. The inscription on the pedestal was written by Madison. (Courtesy of the Virginia Department of Conservation and Economic Development.)

JAMES MONROE

Oil painting, ca. 1786, by an unknown artist. (Courtesy of the James Monroe Museum and Memorial Library, Fredericksburg.)

things a list of the Houses. If the list does not discriminate the several kinds of Houses, how can Congs. collect from it the value of the *improvements*, how do justice to all their constituents? And how can a discrimination be made in this Country, where the variety is so infinite & so unsusceptible of description. If Congs. govern themselves by number alone, this Country will certainly appeal to a more accurate mode of carrying the present rule of the Confederation into practice. The average value of the improvements in Virga. is not 1/4 perhaps not 1/10 of that of the improvements in Pena. or N. Engd. Compare this difference with the proportion between the value of Improvemts. & that of the Soil, & what an immense loss shall we be taxed with? The number of buildings will not be a less unjust rule than the number of acres, for estimating the respective abilities of the States.

The only proceeding of the late Session of Assembly which makes a noise thro' the Country is that which relates to a Genl. Assessmt. The Episcopal people are generally for it, tho' I think the zeal of some of them has cooled. The laity of the other Sects are equally unanimous on the other side. So are all the Clergy except the Presbyterian who seem as ready to set up an establishmt. which is to take them in as they were to pull down that which shut them out. I do not know a more shameful contrast than might be formed between their Memorials on the latter & former occasion.[5]

In one of your letters recd. before I left Richmond you expressed a wish for a better Cypher. Since my return to Orange I have been able to get one made out which will answer every purpose. I will either enclose it herewith or send it by the Gentleman who is already charged with a letter for you. I wish much to throw our correspondence into a more regular course. I would write regularly every week if I had a regular conveyance to Fredg. As it is I will write as often as I can find such conveyances. The business of this neighbourhood which used to go to Fredg. is in a great measure turned towards Richmd. which is too circuitous a channel. Opportunities in every direction however will be henceforward multiplied by the advance of the Season. If you are not afraid of too much loading the mail I could wish you to inclose in your letters the last N. Y. or Phila. paper. I am Dr. Sir Yrs most sincerely

J. MADISON JR.

RC (DLC). Cover missing. Docketed.

[1] Congress was faced with a dilemma on the matter of ministers and consuls to foreign stations because there was virtually no income for their maintenance. On 9 Aug. 1785 Congress asked the Secretary for Foreign Affairs to recommend "the

number of Consuls and Vice consuls necessary to be appointed by Congress," and their assignments (*JCC*, XXIX, 621). John Jay replied, in a report of 13 Oct. 1785, that consuls ought to be sent to Ireland (Dublin and Cork).

2 James Maury (1746–1840), the Fredericksburg merchant who often performed favors for JM, was appointed the U. S. consul at Liverpool in 1790 and served there until 1830.

3 Legislation providing for a continental land office to oversee the sale of western lands was then in William Grayson's hands. Grayson reported the key provisions of the ordinance of 1785 in his letter to JM of 1 May 1785.

4 "The 8th Art. of the Confederation" provided that all expenses of Congress would be met by proportional levies on the states based on land values "and the buildings and improvements thereon." JM had been consistently hostile to the provision while a delegate in Congress (*Papers of Madison*, VI, 247, 248 nn. 3 and 4; Resolutions to Strengthen Powers of Congress, 19 May 1784).

5 The Presbyterian "memorials on the latter & former occasion" were both written by JM's old friend and Princeton classmate, John Blair Smith. At the May 1784 session of the General Assembly Smith's petition called for an end to any civil interference in the affairs of any religious sect, including the use of the poor tax levies by the Episcopal vestries. At the Oct. 1784 session, however, Smith's Presbyterian petition was directed more at the Protestant Episcopal Incorporating Act than the General Assessment bill. Eckenrode excuses the seemingly inconsistent positions—which JM considered in "shameful contrast"—as the Presbyterian acceptance of the "teachers of Christian Religion" bill "as a *fait accompli*." The bill allowed taxpayers to specify the sect which would receive their levies, and Presbyterians apparently figured that half a loaf was preferable to what they then had (Eckenrode, *Separation of Church and State in Virginia*, pp. 79–91). Eckenrode calls JM's statement "strong language" and "an exaggeration" of the facts.

To James Monroe

[14 April 1785]

DEAR SIR

By an opportunity to Richd. I wrote to you 2 days ago. Havg. now one to Frebg. I inclose the Cypher then promiscd. It will probably get to hand at the same with letter via Richd. Adieu.

J. M. JR.

RC (DLC). Addressed to Monroe in Congress, "To care of [Mr. Ma]ury Esqr. Fredg." Docketed by JM, "Mr. Monroe Cypher." The date is fixed from the message JM sent Monroe on 12 Apr. 1785. Enclosure (DLC).

To George Wythe

ORANGE April 15th. 1785

SIR

I have been honoured with yours of February accompanying the Testimony which the University of William & Mary have been pleased to bestow on me.[1] A distinction which is rendered so flattering both by the characters of those from whom it is received, and of those with whom it associates me calls for acknowledgments, which I should feel greater satisfaction in expressing if I had less reason to distrust my title to it. Regarding it however as a proof that those who so worthily minister in the Temple of Science, are disposed not only to reward the merits of her illustrious Votaries, but to patronize in the humblest of them a zeal for her service I find in the sincerity of mine, an offering which they will not refuse, and which I beg you, Sir, in the most respectful manner to present to them. With great esteem and attachment I am &c

J. M.[2]

Draft (DLC). Docketed by JM.

[1] In Feb. 1785, the honorary degree of LL.D. was conferred upon JM by William and Mary College. Wythe informed JM in a missing letter that the honor had also been bestowed upon David Rittenhouse, John Page of Rosewell, Benjamin Franklin, and Edmund Randolph (*WMQ*, 2d ser., XXII [1913–14], 297–98). News of this honor was slow to reach the public, for not until 23 Apr. did the *Va. Gazette* note that JM and "Attorney-General" Randolph had "lately been presented by the University, with honorary degrees of Doctor of Laws."

[2] The initials were later added by another hand.

From Martha Jefferson Carr

April 18. 1785.

SIR

I received by your Brother your polite favour and am Sorry it is not in my power to give a more Satisfactory account of my Sons being placed at School agreeable to your Appointments.[1] My Eldest Son was taken last fall with a fever which with repeated relapses kept him Extreemly weak & low till about the first of Janry from that time till the first of April he was detained at home by the disappointments we met with in collecting the money Necessary to be advanced for his Education, he then set out for Willmsburgh with promises to Endeavour to make up his lost time. My Youngest Son has also been detained at home by Ill health till very lately, when it was my Intention to have sent him to Prince Edward but hearing that A Vacation was shortly to take place there, thought it best to postpone it till the Expiration of that, which will be some time in June; then Sir I Shall most assuredly send him. His time however has not been intirely lost as his Brother was capable of Instructing him whenever his health would admit of it. I am Extreemly Oblige to you Sir for Your kind offer of forwarding my letters to my Brother but must defer writing to him till an other Oppertunity as I am fearfull of detaining Mr Madison who is So Obligeing as to wait at goochland Court for this. With much esteem I am Sir Your very Humble Servant

M CARR

RC (DLC). Cover missing.

[1] JM's "appointments" concerned Jefferson's request that he direct the education of the late Dabney Carr's sons, Peter and Dabney, Jr. See Jefferson to JM, 8 May 1784.

From George Nicholas

CHARLOTTESVILLE April 22d. 1785.

DEAR SIR,

My brother informs me that he conversed with you on the propriety of remonstrating against certain measures of the last session of Assembly and that you seemed to think it would be best that the counties opposed to the measures should be silent. I fear this would be construed into an assent especially to the law for establishing a certain provision for the clergy: for as the Assembly only postponed the passing of it that they might know whether it was disagreeable to the people, I think they may justly conclude that all are for it who do not say to the contrary. A majority of the counties are in favor of the measure but I believe a great majority of the people against it; but if this majority should not appear by petition the fact will be denied. Another reason why all should petition is that some will certainly do it and those who support the bills will insist that those who petition are all the opposition. Would it not add greatly to the weight of the petitions if they all hold the same language? by discovering an exact uniformity of sentiment in a majority of the country it would certainly deter the majority of the Assembly from proceeding. All my expectations are from their fears and not their justice. I have been through a considerable part of the country and am well assured that it would be impossible to carry such laws into execution and that the attempt would bring about a revolution. If you think with me that it will be proper to say something to the Assembly will you commit it to paper. I wish this because, I know you are most capable of doing it properly and because it will be most likely to be generally adopted. I can get it sent to Amherst Buckingham, Albemarle, Fluvanna, Augusta, Botetourt, Rock Bridge and Rockingham and I have no doubt that Bedford and the counties southward of it will readily join in the measure. I will also send it [to] Frederick and Berkeley and if it goes from your county to Fauquier, Culpeper and Loudoun it will be adopted by the most populous part of the country.[1] I shall be glad to hear from you on this subject and am With esteem and respect Dr: Sir, Yr. obdt. servt.

G: NICHOLAS

The bill for supporting the clergy, the act for incorporating the Episcopal church and the faithful adherency to the treaty are the subjects on which the people have wish to demonstrate. It being supposed that Mr. Carter was against the latter lost him his election in this county.[2]

RC (DLC). Addressed by Nicholas. Docketed by JM, "Nicholas Geo: Apr. 22. 1785."

[1] Nicholas's argument prevailed, for JM wrote a protest against religious assessments, probably by late June. See the Memorial and Remonstrance, ca. 20 June 1785.

[2] Edward Carter represented Albemarle County in 1784 but was replaced by Joshua Fry in 1785 (Swem and Williams, *Register*, pp. 19, 21).

To Thomas Jefferson

ORANGE April 27. 1785.

DEAR SIR

I have recd. your two favors of Novr. 11 & Decr. 8. Along with the former I recd. the two pamphlets on animal magnetism & the last aeronautic expedition together with the phosphoretic matches. These articles were a great treat to my curiosity. As I had left Richmd. before they were brought thither by Col. le Maire,[1] I had no opportunity of attending myself to your wishes with regard to him; but I wrote immediately to Mr. Jones & desired him to watch over the necessities of le Maire. He wrote me for answer that the Executive tho' without regular proof of his claims were so well satisfied from circumstances of the justice of them, that they had voted him £150 for his relief till the assembly could take the whole into consideration.[2] This information has made me easy on the subject though I have not withdrawn from the hands of Mr. Jones the provisional resource. I thank you much for your attention to my literary wants. All the purchases you have made for me, are such as I should have made for myself with the same opportunities. You will oblige me by adding to them the Dictionary in 13 vol. 4°. by Felice & others, also de Thou in French. If the utility of Moreri be not superseded by some better work I should be glad to have him too.³ I am afraid if I were to attempt a catalogue of my wants I should not only trouble you beyond measure, but exceed the limits which other considerations ought to prescribe to me. I cannot however abridge the commission you were so kind as to take on yourself in a former letter, of procuring me from time to time such books as may be "either old & curious or new & useful." Under this description will fall those particularised in my former letters; to wit treatises on the antient or modern fœderal republics—on the law of Nations—and the history natural & political of the New World; to which I will add such of the Greek & Roman authors where they can be got very cheap, as are worth having and are not on the Common list of School classics. Other books which particularly occur, are the translation [French]⁴ of the Historians of the Roman Empire during its decline by——Paschals provincial letters—Don Ulloa in the Original—Lynnæus best edition Ordinances Marines—Collection of Tracts in french on the Œconomies of different nations. I forget the full title. It is much referred to by Smith on the wealth of nations. I am told a Monsr. Amelot has lately published his travels into China, which if they have any merit must be very entertaining. Of Buffon I have his original work of 31 vol. 10 vol. of Supplemt. and 16 vol. on birds. I shall be glad of the continuation as it may from time to time b[e] published. I am so pleased with the new invented lamp that I shall not grudge two guineas for one of Them. I have seen a pocket compass of somewhat larger diameter than a watch & which may be carried in the same way. It has a spring for stopping the vibration of the needle when not in use. One of these would be very convenient in case of a ramble into the Western Coun-try. In my walks for exercise or amusements, objects frequently present themselves, which it might be matter of curiosity to inspect, but which it is difficult or impossible to approach. A portable Glass would con-sequently be a source of many little gratifications. I have fancied that such an one might be fitted into a Cane without making it too heavy. On the outside of the tube might be engraved a scale of inches &c. If such a project could be executed for a few Guineas, I should be willing to submit to the price, if not, the best substitute I suppose will be a pocket telescope composed of several tubes so constructed as to slide the lesser into the greater. I should feel great remorse at troubling you with so many requests, if your kind & repeated offers did not stifle it in some measure. Your proposal for my replacing here advances for me without regard to the exchange is liable to no objection except that it will probably be too unequal in my favour. I beg that you will enable me as much as you can to keep those little matters balanced. The papers from le Grand were sent as soon as I got them to Mr. Jones with a request that he wd. make the use of them which you wished me to do.[5]

Your remarks on the tax transfers of land in a general view appear to me to be just but there were two circumstances which gave a peculiarity to the case in which our law adopted it. One was that the tax will fall much on those who are evading their quotas of other taxes by removing to Georgia & Kentucky: the other that as such transfers are more frequent among those who do not remove, in the Western than the Eastern part of the Country, it will fall heaviest where direct taxes are least collected. With regard to the tax in general on law proceedings, it cannot perhaps be justified if tried by the strict rule which proportions the quota of every man to his ability, time however will gradually in some measure equalize it, & if it be applied to the support of the Judiciary establishment, as was the ultimate view of the friends of the tax, it seems to square very well with the Theory of taxation.[6]

The people of Kentucky had lately a convention which it was expected would be the mother of a separation. I am informed they proceeded no farther than to concert an address for the Legislature on some points in which they think the laws bear unequally upon them. They will be ripe for that event at least as soon as their interest calls for it. There is no danger of a concert between them & the Counties West of the Alleghany which we mean to retain. If the latter embark in a scheme for independence it will be on their own bottom. They are more disunited in every respect from Kentucky than from Virginia.

I have not learnt with certainty whether Genl. Washington will accept or decline the shares voted him by the Assembly in the Companies for opening our rivers. If he does not chuse to take to himself any benefit from the donation, he has I think a fine opportunity at once of testifying his disinterested purposes, of shewing his respect for the Assembly, and of rendering a service to his Country. He may accept the gift so far as to apply it to the scheme of opening the rivers, & may then appropriate the revenue which it is hereafter to produce, to some patriotic establishment. I lately dropped a hint of this sort to one of his friends & was told that such an idea had been suggested to him. The private subscriptions for Potowmac I hear amount to £10,000 Sterling. I can not discover that those for James River deserve mention, or that the undertaking is pushed with any spirit. If those who are most interested in it let slip the present opportunity, their folly will probably be severely punished by the want of such another. It is said the undertaking on the Susquehannah by Maryland goes on with great spirit & expectations. I have heard nothing of Rumsey or his boats since he went into the Northern States. If his machinery for stemming the current operates on the water alone as is given out, may it not supply the great desi[de]ratum for perfecting the Balloons?[7]

I understand that Chase & Jennifer on the part of Maryland, Mason & Henderson on the part of Virginia have had a meeting on the proposition of Virga. for settling the navigation & jurisdiction of Potowmac below the falls, & have agreed to report to the two Assemblies, the establishment of a concurrent jurisdiction on that river & Chesapeak. The most amicable spirit is said to have governed the negociation.[8]

The Bill for a Genl. Assesst. has produced some fermentation below the Mountains & a violent one beyond them. The contest at the next Session on this question will be a warm & precarious one.[9] The port bill will also undergo a fiery trial. I wish the Assize Courts may not partake of the danger. The elections as far as they have come to my knowledge are likely to produce a great proportion of new members. In Albemarle young Mr. Fry has turned out Mr. Carter. The late Governor Harrison I hear has been baffled in his own County; but meant to be a candidate in Surry & in case of a rebuff there to throw another die for the borough of Norfolk. I do not know how he construes the doctrine of residence. It is *surmised* that the *machination*[s] *of Tyler who fears a rivailship for the chair* are *at the bot*[t]*om of his difficulty.*[10] *Ar. Le*[e] *is elected in Prince William. He is said* to have *paved the way by promise*[s] *to over set the port bil*[l] which is *obnoxious* to *Dumfries* and to *prevent the removal* [of][11] *the assise court* from *this town to Alexandria.*[12]

I recd. a letter from *the Marquis Fayette* dated on the *eve of his embarcation* which *has the folowing paragraph.* [*"*]*I have much confered with the General upon the potowmac system. Many people* [think][11] *the navigation of the Mississippi is not an advantage but it may be the excess of a very good thing viz., the opening of your river. I fancy it has not changed your opinion but beg you will write me on the* subject. *In the meanwhile I hope Congress will act cooly and prudently by Spain who is such a fool that allowance must be made.*["] It is *unlucky that he should have left America with* such *an idea as to the Mississippi.* It may be *of the worse consequence as it is not wholey imaginary, the* prospect of *extending the commerce of the Atlantic State*[s] *to the Western water having given birth to it.* I can not believe that *many mind*[s] *are tainted with so illiberal and short sited a policy.* I have *thought it not amiss to* [write]¹¹ *the marquis* according to the *request of his letter* and *have stated to him the motive*[s] *and obligation* which must *render* [the]¹¹ *United States inflexible* on the subject *of the Mississippi, the folly of Spain in contesting it* and *our expectation from the known influence of France over Spain and her friendly disposetion toward United States.* It is but *justice to the marquis to* [observe]¹³ that *in all our conversation* on *the Mississippi he expressd* with every *mark of sincerity a zeal for our claim* and *a pointed dislike to the national character and policy of Spain* and that if *his zeal should be found to abate* I should construe it to be the effect *of a supposed* revolution *in the sentiment of America.*¹⁴

This would have been of somewhat earlier date but I postponed it that I might be able to include some information relative to your Nephews. My last informed you that your eldest was then with Mr. Maury. I was so assured by Mr. Underwood from his neighbourhood, who I supposed could not be mistaken. I afterwards discovered that he was so, but could get no precise information till within a few days. One of my brothers being called into that part of the Country by business, I wrote to Mrs. Carr and got him to wait on her. The answer with which I have been favored imparts that "her eldest son was taken last fall with a fever which with repeated relapses kept him extremely weak & low till about the first of Jany. from which time till he was detained at home by delays in equipping him for Williamsbg. till the 1st of April, when he set out with promises to make up his lost time—that her youngest son had also been detained at him by ill health till very lately, but that he would certainly go on to the academy as soon as a vacation on hand was over, that his time had not been entirely lost as his brother was capable of instructing him whenever his health would admit." Mr. Maury's School is said to be very flourishing. Mr. Wythe & the other gentlemen of the University have examined it from time to time & published their approbation of its management. I can not speak with the same authority as to the Academy in Prince Edward. The information which I have recd. has been favorable to it. In the recommendation of these Seminaries I was much governed by the probable permanency of them, nothing being more ruinous to education than the frequent interruptions & change of Masters & methods incident to the private schools of this country.¹⁵

Our winter has been full of vicisitudes, but on the whole far from being a severe one. The Spring has been uncommonly cold & wet, and vegetation of course very backward; till within a few days during which it has been accelerated by very uncommon heat. A pocket Thermometer which stands on the second floor & the N. W. side of the House, was on the 24 inst. at 4 oClock, at 77°., on the 25. 78., on the 26. 81 1/2., to day 27. at 82. The weather during this period has been fair & the wind S. the atmosphere thick N W.—our Wheat in the ground is very unpromising throughout the Country. The price of this article on tide water is about 6/. Corn sells in this part of the Country at 10/. & under, below at 15/. and where the insect prevailed as high as 20/. It is said to have been raised by a demand for exportation. Tobo. is selling on Rappahannock at 32/. & Richmd. at 37/6. It is generally expected that it will at least get up to 40/. Some of our peaches are killed & most of our Cherries. Our Apples are as yet safe. I can not say how it is with the fruit in other parts of the Country. The mischief to the Cherries &c was done on the night of the 20. when we had a severe black frost.

I can not take my leave of you without making my acknowledgmts. for the very friendly invitation contained in your last. If I should ever visit Europe I should wish to do it less stinted in time than your plan proposes. This crisis too would be particularly inconvenient as it wd. break in upon a course of reading which if I neglect now I shall probably never resume. I have some reason also to suspect that crossing the Sea would be unfriendly to a singular disease of my constitution. The other part of your invitation has the strongest biass of my mind on its side, but my situation is as yet too dependent on circumstances to permit my embracing it absolutely. It gives me great satisfaction to find that you are looking forward to the moment which is to restore you to your native Country, though considerations of a public nature check my wishes that such an event may be expedited. Present my best respects to Mr. Short, & Miss Patsy, & accept of the affectionate regards of Dear Sir, Your sincere friend.

J. MADISON JR.

What has become of the subterraneous City discovered in Siberia?
Deaths. Thomson Mason
        Bartholemew Dandridge
        Ryland Randolph
        Peyton Randolph[16]
        Joseph Reed of Philada.

RC (DLC). Cover missing. Docketed in an unknown hand and marked "(No. 7) Copd." Italicized words were coded by JM in the code first used by Jefferson on 14 Apr. 1783. Jefferson interlinearly decoded the letter, frequently adding "s" to words which JM coded in the singular; the text printed translates JM's code with only the exceptions noted.

1 In 1779, Governor Jefferson commissioned Jacques Le Maire, a Frenchman enlisting in the Virginia Line, as a brevet lieutenant colonel of dragoons. After the war, Le Maire returned to France but held a claim against Virginia for back pay. In 1784, his petition for 2,000 acres of land and membership in the Society of Cincinnati preceded his return to America. Jefferson substantiated his claim and explained Le Maire's services in a letter to JM, 11 Nov. 1784. Jefferson's account book shows he lent Le Maire 400 francs, and gave him an order against JM for 10 guineas (Boyd, *Papers of Jefferson*, VII, 431 n.). Le Maire's claim was not settled until Jan. 1786, and by then JM had fulfilled Jefferson's request and loaned the 10 guineas to Le Maire (JM to Jefferson, 22 Jan. 1786).

2 JM's letter to Jones has not been found. Jones's reply is dated 30 Mar. 1785.

3 For de Felice's *Code de l'Humanité* see JM to Jefferson, 18 Mar. 1785, n. 6. Possibly JM wanted the sixteen volumes of Jacques Auguste de Thou's *Histoire universelle*, which was printed in French by a London publisher in 1734. De Thou (identified as *the Elder*) first published this history of his own times between 1604 and 1608. Jefferson listed Felice's title but appears to have still been searching for a copy of de Thou's work—despite an earlier assurance of its availability—when he filled JM's order that fall (Jefferson to JM, 11 Nov. 1784, 1 Sept. 1785). Louis Moréri's *Le Grand Dictionaire historique* . . . (10 vols.; Paris, 1759) was still considered as "not superseded by some better work" in 1785.

4 Bracketed by JM.

5 Along with his letter to JM, 11 Nov. 1784, Jefferson forwarded some papers from the Parisian banker, Ferdinand le Grand. The only clue to the substance of these papers is Jefferson's entry in his *Secret Journal of Letters:* "J. Madison Orange . . . . inclose to him Massieu's case recommended by Mr. Grant" (Boyd, *Papers of Jefferson*, VII, 507 n.).

6 Jefferson's remarks about taxation were included in his letter to JM, 8 Dec. 1784.

7 In his 9 Jan. 1785 letter to Jefferson, JM reported upon the passage of the act investing Washington with shares in the companies for opening the James and Potomac rivers and also the act giving the exclusive right to James Rumsey for building and operating certain boats on the Virginia rivers. These were passed during the 1784 session of the legislature (Hening, *Statutes*, XI, 502, 525). JM wrote both of these bills, which are printed under the dates of their passage, 13 Nov. 1784 and 5 Jan. 1785.

8 JM and Randolph had also been appointed by the House to serve in commercial discussions with Maryland, but a meeting was held at Mount Vernon when it was clear that a conference had to proceed without a full delegation. See Randolph to JM, 17 July 1785.

9 JM had already been at work to make certain the assessment issue would be a heated one. See George Nicholas to JM, 22 Apr. 1785.

10 For these election statistics, see JM to Monroe, 28 Apr. 1785.

11 Word not in code, probably inserted later by JM.

12 Lee's election was contested on the grounds of nonresidency, and also that he simultaneously held an office of profit in the national government. Lee's residency was upheld but the vote on his ineligibility was 80 for, 19 against, with JM voting on the losing side (*JHDV*, Oct. 1785, pp. 8, 15–17).

13 JM used the code symbol for either "do" or "la," but Jefferson in deciphering the blurred numerals chose the word "observe" which fitted JM's context.

14 Lafayette's letter of 15–17 Dec. 1784. His impression about opponents to American rights on the Mississippi may have come directly from Washington, who shared the feeling about limited American rights on the river (Freeman, *George Washington*, VI, 23–24).

15 JM received this information in a letter from Martha Jefferson Carr, dated 18 Apr. 1785.

16 The name of Peyton Randolph (1738–1784) was heavily crossed through, perhaps by someone who later recalled a better-known Peyton Randolph (who had died in 1775). JM was alluding to the decedent of 15 May 1784 (Richmond *Va. Gazette and Independent Chronicle*, 22 May 1784).

To James Monroe

ORANGE Apl. 28. 1785

DEAR SIR

I have written several letters within a little time past which were Sent to you partly by the post, partly by Mr. Burnley,¹ a young Gentleman of this County. In one of the latter I inclosed a Cypher² wch. will serve all the purposes of our future Correspondence. This covers a letter for Mr. Jefferson³ which you will be so good as to forwd. by the first packet or other equally eligible conveyance. Our Elections as far as I hear are likely to produce a great proportion of new members. In some Counties they are influenced by the Bill for a Genl. Assesst. In Culpeper Mr. Pendleton a worthy man & acceptable in his general character to the people was laid aside in consequence of his vote for the Bill, in favour of an Adversary to it.⁴ The Delegates for Albemarle are your friend Mr. W. C. Nicholas & Mr. Fry.⁵ Mr. Carter stood a poll but fell into the rear. The late Govr. Harrison I am told has been baffled in his own County, meant to be a candidate for Surry & in case of a rebuff there to throw another die for the Borough of Norfolk. I do not know how he proposes to satisfy the doctrine of residence.⁶

I hear frequent complaints of the disorders of our Coin & the wan[t o]f uniformity in the denomination of the States. Do not Congress think of a remedy for these evils? The regulation of weights & measure seem also to call for their attention. Every day will add to the difficulty of executing these works. If a *mint* be not established & a recoinage effected while the fœderal debts carry the money thro' the hands of Congress I question much whether their limited powers will ever be able to render this branch of their prerogative effectual. With regard to the regulation of weights & measures, wd. it not be highly expedient as well as honorable to the fœderal administration, to pursue the hint which has been suggested by ingenious & philosophical men, to wit, that the standard of measure sd. be first fixed by the length of a pendulum vibrating seconds at the Equator or any given latitude—& that the Standard of weight sd. be a Cubical piece of Gold or other homogeneous body of dimensions fixed by the standard of measure.[7] Such a scheme appears to be easily reducible to practice; & as it is founded on the division of time which is the same at all times & in all places & proceeds on other data which are equally so, it would not only secure a perpetual uniformity throughout the U. S. but might lead to Universal standards in these matters among nations. Next to the inconveniency of speaking different languages, is that of using different & arbitrary weights & measures. I am Dr. Sir Yr. affece. friend

J. MADISON JR.

RC (DLC). Addressed and docketed by JM.

[1] Hardin Burnley, son of Zachariah and Mary Burnley (*VMHB*, XXXVII [1929], 350).

[2] This is the "8 May 1785" code used by JM and Monroe. JM sent it in his 12 Apr. 1785 letter to Monroe, and Monroe first used it in his 8 May letter to JM.

[3] JM to Jefferson, 27 Apr. 1785.

[4] James Pendleton (1735–1793) represented Culpeper in both the House of Burgesses and the House of Delegates, was a colonel in the Revolution and high sheriff of the county (Katherine C. Gottschalk and John B. C. Nicklin, "The Pendleton Family," *VMHB*, XXXIX [1931], 283–84). Henry Fry unseated him in the 1785 election (Swem and Williams, *Register*, pp. 19, 21, 417).

[5] Wilson Cary Nicholas (1761–1820) represented Albemarle in the House of Delegates in 1784, 1785, and in the convention of 1788 to ratify the Constitution. He served in the legislature in 1789, 1790, and from 1794 to 1799, when he became a U. S. senator. From 1804 to 1807 he was collector of customs for Norfolk and Portsmouth. He was elected to the 10th and 11th Congresses as a representative, and from 1814 to 1816 he was governor of Virginia (Grigsby, *Virginia Convention of 1788*, II, 299–360). Joshua Fry (b. 1760), the son of Col. John Fry and grandson of Col. Joshua Fry, defeated Edward Carter (*WMQ*, 1st ser., X [1902], 258–59; *Magazine of Albemarle County History*, XIII [1953], 23; Swem and Williams, *Register*, p. 19).

[6] Benjamin Harrison's "own County" where John Tyler was also a resident was Charles City. He succeeded in Surry County, but the election was contested in the House on the grounds of nonresidence and he barely kept his seat by a margin of six votes (*JHDV*, Oct. 1785, pp. 12, 19, 21).

[7] Sir Isaac Newton was certainly one of the "ingenious & philosophical men" JM had in mind. It is likely that JM and Jefferson had discussed the need for uniformity in weights and measurements before the latter left for Europe. Jefferson alluded to Newton's calculation on pendulum when he drew up his observations on coinage, weights, and measures which Boyd fixes as having been drafted around Mar. 1784 (*Papers of Jefferson*, VII, 173–74). Congress took up the matter on 19 Aug. 1785, when Rufus King introduced a motion calling for a report fixing standard weights and measures by the treasury board (*JCC*, XXIX, 647 n.). Nothing concrete was accomplished, however, and the problem was still acute when the

Federal Convention met in Philadelphia. Randolph's draft, which he prepared for the Committee of Detail, contained a provision that placed the regulation of weights and measures among the specified powers of Congress (Max Farrand, ed., *The Records of the Federal Convention of 1787* [4 vols.; New Haven, 1911–37], IV, 44). For decades Congress took no official action, however, so that only the weights and measures specified by various local ordinances and state laws were reliable standards. Finally, exactly two weeks before JM died, Congress passed on 14 June 1836 a joint resolution that sanctioned the use of the existing English standard weights and measures in interstate commerce.

From William Grayson

N. YORK May 1st. 1785.

DEAR SIR.

I am afraid my silence since I came to this place has giv'n you some reason to suspect me to be impregnated with that vis inertiæ, which has been so often attributed to me.[1] The only apology I have to make, is that I wish'd to have some thing to write to you worth your acceptance. However as there would be some danger in risquing a farther delay, I shall give you what I have in the manner. The New England delegates wish to sell the Continental land, rough as it runs; what I miss in quality I will make up in quantity.

All our attentions here have been for some time turned towards the hostile preparations between the Emperor & the Dutch; as it was thought the event might have a considerable influence on the affairs of the United States. The Packet which arrived yesterday has brought different accounts of what is doing respecting this business; however I take the following to be nearly the truth of the case: That the Emperor has only made the opening the Schelde a pretext for marching his troops into the low Countries while he has been underhandedly treating with the Elector of Bavaria for an exchange of his territories in the low Countries for Bavaria: That France has not only been privy to the negotiations but has actually countenanc'd them; While no other power has entertain'd the most distant suspicions of what was going forward: That the prince de Deux Ponts presumptive heir to Bavaria, on recieving the first notice of it, made application to the King of Prussia, supposing that old Statesman would exert himself to the utmost, to prevent Bavaria from becoming part of the domains of the House of Austria. It therefore seems to be probable that all those who wish to preserve the proper ballance of power in the Germanic body will unite with the Prussian Monarch against that accession of weight to the Austrian scale. Should this confederacy take place in its fullest extent, it will be very formidable, & in all likelyhood produce a bloody contest before the matter is finally decided. War therefore seems to be as probable as ever although the ground of the contest may be altered. For my own part I cannot clearly find out from any informations wch. I have had, what have been the views of the Court of France; they seem to have departed from their antient principles in assisting the Austrian family to increase their power; 'tis true they adopted this system in the last reign, but then the French Statesmen say, that nothing done during that period ought to be quoted from their history. If the Queen of France has drawn in the Ministry to countenance the measures of her brother it is an evidence of her great influence in the Governmt. but from what appears at present, it is no proof of the criden[ce] of the public-councils as it is obvious if France keeps up large standing armies, she must neglect her marine by which she will risque her foreign possessions wheneve[r] she happens to be engaged in a war with G. B.

The Parliament has so lately sit, that little has yet transpired; the Minister is to bring forwd. a plan for a Parliamentary reform, which it is thought will require all his interest & ability to support.

The Wallachians who were so oppress'd as to be drove into a state of open resistance are on the point of being subjugated; they are in numbers about seven hundred thousand; & I heartily wish they were all *here*.

Congress are engaged in ascertaining a mode for the disposal of the Western territory; I send you the first draught as reported by the Grand Comme. also a second edition with amendments in Congress.[2] The matter is still under consideration, and other alterations will no doubt take effect. An amendment is now before the house for making the Townships 6 Ms. Sqe. & for dividing those townships by actual surveys into quarters of townships, marking at every interval of a mile (in running the external lines of the quarters,) corners for the sections of 640 acres; Then to sell every other township by sections: The reservation (instead of the four corner sections,) to be the central section of every quarter; that is to say the inside lot, whose corner is not ascertained:[3] Whether this will be carried or not I cannot tell, the Eastern people being amazingly attached to their own customs, and unreasonably anxious to have every thing regulated according to their own pleasure.

The construction of the deed of cession from Virga. has taken up four days, & at length it is agreed not to sell any land between the little Miami & Scioto untill the conditions respecting the Offs. & soldiers are complied with.[4] Some Members of Congress think they have a right to have the land laid off for the Offs. & soldiers in such manner as they please & by their own surveyors, provided they give good land & square figures: others are willing it shall be laid off in the same manner as the rest, & the Offs. & soldiers to chuse by sections. If the State insists on the right of surveying agreable to their own laws I shd. suppose that Congress could have no objection to appointing Commrs. for deciding that question as well as all others that might arise respecting the Compact.

Mr. King of Massachusetz has a resolution ready drawn which he reserves till the Ordinance is passed for preventing slavery in the new State.[5] I expect Seven States may be found liberal enough to adopt it.

Seven hundred men are voted for protecting the settlers on the frontiers, for guarding the public stores & for preventing unwarrantable intrusions on the lands of the U. S.

I inclose you a plan for altering the 9th. article of the confederation,[6] also a newspaper informing what the people of Boston are about.[7] The requisition for the present year is before Congress; one article to wit 30,000 dollars for fœderal buildings at Trenton, I objected to, & was supported by the delegates of Maryland Delawar & New Hamshire, N. Carolina was divided. Unfortunately for me the rest of the delegates for our State do not think as I do; [(]This is *entre nouz*). I shall notwithstanding do every thing in my power to frustrate the measure. We shall in all probability get it struck out of the requisition, because nine States will not vote for it; I understand however that it is intended to get seven States to vote for the sum out of the loans in Holland supposing that as a hundred thousand doll[ars] were voted at Trenton by nine States, generally, that seven can direct the particular appropriation. This matter I have not yet considered, neither do I know how it will turn out on investigation however I hope I shall find means to avoid it for the present year, & I hope by the next the Southern States will understand their interests better.

Congress have refused to let the State discount any part of the monies paid for the Western territory, out of the requisitions for the prest. year. & I believe if they don't help themselves, they will never find Congress willing to discount.[8] In the mean time they will sell the lands. A treaty is directed to be held with the Barbary States to purchase their friendship. Treaties are also to be held with the Cherokees Chickesaws &c. also with the Western Indians shortly. I am sure you are surfeited—therefore conclude with great sincerity Yr. Affect. friend & Mo. Obed. Serv.

WILLM. GRAYSON.

RC (DLC). Cover and enclosures missing. Docketed by JM over Grayson's dateline.

[1] Grayson was defending himself from the contemporary charge that he was a hypochondriac—an opinion JM shared with other Virginians. Grigsby also noted Grayson's affinity for Latin phrases, hence "vis inertiæ" (Grigsby, *Virginia Convention of 1788*, I, 202).

[2] Grayson explained the drafting of the Land Ordinance of 1785 to Washington in some detail (Burnett, *Letters*, VIII, 95–97). The amended bill finally passed Congress on 20 May 1785 (*JCC*, XXVIII, 375–81). This legislation created a national pattern for surveying and settlement, with rectilinear roads, that prevailed between the Alleghenies and the Rockies.

[3] The "reservation" was the reserved section (lot no. 16) "for the maintenance of public schools." The idea was supported throughout the debates, particularly by the New England delegates. Four other mile-square sections were reserved in each township for the use of the U. S. (Nos. 8, 11, 26, and 29). The price for the remaining thirty-one sections, to be sold to the public, was later fixed at $1.00 per acre.

[4] The 1781 "cession from Virga." of her western lands north of the Ohio reserved a tract not exceeding 150,000 acres for Virginia troops who served under George Rogers Clark. A second veterans' tract, reserved for "Virginia Troops upon Continental Establishment" in case lands south of the Ohio "prove insufficient," was "to be laid off between the Rivers Scioto and Little Miamis on the North West Side of the River Ohio" (Boyd, *Papers of Jefferson*, IV, 387).

[5] King promoted passage of a clause forbidding slavery in the Northwest Territory, but the idea originally was shaped by Jefferson in the ordinance of 1784. The antislavery section of the 1784 bill was dropped, but was later resurrected (in July 1787) to become part of the Northwest Ordinance (Burnett, *Letters*, VIII, 94, 622).

[6] The "plan for altering the 9th. article of the confederation" must have been the proposed amendment submitted to Congress on 28 Mar. by a committee headed by Monroe. The amendment would have permitted Congress to levy duties on imports and exports, a power which was denied Congress by the existing articles without the unanimous and hence impossible consent of the thirteen states (*JCC*, XVIII, 201–2).

[7] The "people of Boston" were receiving a good deal of publicity in Apr.–May 1785 because of public protests and resolutions against the importation of luxury goods from England through the agencies of British factors and merchants (*Va. Gazette*, 21 May 1785). The resulting outflow of specie was being blamed for economic distress along the New England seaboard.

[8] Virginia had claimed reimbursement from the U. S. for money spent in Clark's conquest of the Illinois country. When Congress accepted the Virginia western land cession, the U. S. agreed to repay Virginia for these expenses and a commission was formed to determine the sum involved. Meanwhile, no credit was allowed on the state's annual requisition to the national treasury. Rufus King was eager to have a sharp-eyed Yankee, Timothy Pickering, serve on the commission because he thought "the United States are in danger of being charged with a very monstrous sum to defray the expences of Genl. Clark's expedition against the Kaskaskeis" (Burnett, *Letters*, VIII, 114).

From James Monroe

Dear Sir

Your favor of the 12th. of April accompanied with the cypher I receiv'd yesterday. The appointment of Mr. Adams to the ct. of G. B.
was soon afterwards succeeded by that of Mr. Jefferson to that of
France. Their commns have been some time since forwarded & before
this they are no doubt station'd at their respective courts. The removal
of the former gave uneasiness to Mr. V[a]n. Berkell but as it was immediately resolv'd to appoint a successor, it hath probably abated.[1]
Govr. Livingston, Rutledge, & R. H. Harrison C. J. of Maryld. are in
nomination. G. B. is still possess'd of the *posts* [on][2] the *lakes nor have
we reason to suppose she means to evacuate. Of this however Mr.
Adams will inform us.* Our affair with *Spain is suspended untill the
arrival of Mr. Gardoqui. He is expected.* The affs. of *Langchamp* hath
not been acted on; for particular reasons it hath hitherto been deferr'd.
A recommendation hath been made to the States of Connecticut, N Yk.,
Jersey & Pena. to raise 700. men for the protection of the frontier settlements. It was question'd whether it were not better by requisition &
upon the Union, since it might be the commencment of an establishmt.
wh. might last for ages, & if the right of requisition existed, the effecting by other means might tend to weaken & ultimately destroy it.[3] The
delegation of Mass: at Annapolis protested agnst. this right & their state
approv'd their conduct. But as the right of requisition existed only
when exerted on the Union & it seem'd generally preferr'd to raise
them from 3. or 4. of the States most conveniently situated, it was ultimately agreed to adopt the mode of recommendation. An ordinance
regulating the mode of survey & sale of the lands ceded by Virga. hath
lately engag'd the attention of Congress—it hath not yet pass'd but as
all the points of variance seem at length accomodated, it will perhaps
in the course of the succeeding week. The original report admited of
the sale only of tracts containing 30,000 acres call'd townships; this was
adher'd to with great obstinacy by the E. men & as firmly oppos'd by
the southern. At length however the Eastern partly gave up the point
at least so far as to meet on middle ground. As it now stands it is to
be survey'd in township containing abt. 26,000 acres each, each township mark'd on the plat into lots of one mile square, and 1/2. the country sold only in townships & the other in lots. 13. surveyors are to be
appoin[t]ed for the purpose to act under the controul of the Geogra-

pher,[4] begining with the first range of townships upon the Ohio & running north to the lakes, from the termination of the line which forms
the southern boundary of the State of Pena., & so on westwd. with
each range. As soon as five ranges shall be survey'd the return will be
made to the Bd. of Treasury, who are instructed to draw for them in
the name of each State in the proportion of the requisition on each, &
transmit its portion to the loan officer in each, for sale at publick ven-
due, provided it is, nor any part, sold for less than one dolr. specie or
certificates the acre. Thus stands the ordinance at present.

Sometime since a treaty was order'd to be held with the Indians in
the southern department, to wh. commn Mr. Hawkins of No. Carolina,
Joseph Martin of Virga.[5] & some others were appointed. A treaty is
also to be held with the Indians westward at post St. Vincents or somewhere on the Wabash or Missisippi for the purpose of extinguishing
the claims to soil of the tribes who inhabit in that direction. The late
comrs. are continued in the appointment.

The interest on the loans in Holland for the last year we understand
is paid but not on those of France by the completion of a loan order'd
to be effected before the peace. No new loan is orderd nor will there
be as I conceive. A requisition is before Congress for money for the
payment of the interest on the domestic debt to the 31. of Decr. 1784 &
on the foreign to the 31. of 85. amounting to 3,000,000 of dolrs., inclusive of the current expences of Government; the monies to be applied
to the payment of the interest on the foreign debt & the expences of
govt. amounting to abt. 1,000,000 of dolrs. to be recd. in specie only &
the application to the interest on the domestic debt in certificates under
the modification of the late requisition being abt. 2 thirds. I am strongly
inclin'd to believe the wester[n] lands will absorb all the domestic debt
Eastwd.; the gentn. from that quarter think so. I am also fully persuaded that when the accts. of Virga. & No. Carolina shall be liquidated
the amount will be greater than is expected here.[6] The delay in this
business from the negligence of Mr. L. Wood prevents the operation of
these requisitions having relation to us, & when these accts. shall be
liquidated most probably ours will comprehend the greatest part of the
domestic debt. No doubt we shall be paid but we had better go on pari
passu with our neighbours to expedite the business we lately obtain'd
the addition of a 2d comr. to the State for the purpose. They are, each
to act in a district. We have had returns from but few of the States
changing the 8th. article of the confideration; several have already
adopted it. The requisition is on the principle, in that respect, of the

late one. A report sometime since pass'd Congress for appointing a committee to wait on the legislatures of R. I. New Yk. & Georgia to advise the immediate passage of the impost, but hath never been taken up. R. I. hath adopted it, with a seperate credit, for sums beyond her quota, & the appointment of her own officers. N. York hath had it before her legislature this winter & negativ'd it. I believe a bill hath been publish'd for inspection of the people in Massachussetts wh. had the objects you mention in view but that it hath not pass'd as yet into a law. Of this however in my next I will inform you. Yr. friend & servant

JAS. MONROE

RC (DLC). Cover missing. Docketed. Italicized words, unless otherwise noted, are those encoded by Monroe using the code JM sent him on 14 Apr. 1785.

[1] Adams had been serving at The Hague, and the representative of the United Provinces in New York, van Berckel, was anxious to have Adams's successor promptly appointed. Among other matters, a U. S. representative was needed to answer the queries of Dutch bankers about their American loans. William Livingston was chosen by ballot to succeed Adams on 23 June 1785 (JCC, XXVIII, 474). Livingston declined, as did the next choice, Rutledge (Burnett, Letters, VIII, 89 n.).

[2] Monroe's code number—530—called for "silver."

[3] The opposition to raising a 700-man frontier force feared they were laying the foundation for a detested standing army. Elbridge Gerry was a most outspoken opponent of a military "establishmt. wh. might last for ages." To calm these fears the troops were requisitioned from "the States most conveniently situated"—Connecticut, New Jersey, New York, and Pennsylvania (JCC, XXVIII, 247–48).

[4] The appointment of thirteen surveyors, one from each state working under "the Geographer" Thomas Hutchins, was intended to create credible informants "to the states for which they were appointed of the quality of the lands, and such other circumstances as may direct the citizens in making their purchases" (Burnett, Letters, VIII, 130–31).

[5] Gen. Joseph Martin (1740–1808) served as the Virginia negotiator with the Cherokees in 1782 (Papers of Madison, V, 62; Southern Historical Association, Publications, IV [1900], 443–44).

[6] Monroe's prophecy proved to be correct. When the Virginia claim was finally settled, the state received credit for $19,085,981 on its federal account—"the largest of any state" (Ferguson, Power of the Purse, p. 324).

From Thomas Jefferson

PARIS May 11. 1785.

DEAR SIR

Your favor of Jan. 9. came to my hands on the 13th. of April. The very full and satisfactory detail of the proceedings of assembly which it contained, gave me the highest pleasure. The value of these communications cannot be calculated at a shorter distance than the breadth of the Atlantic. Having lately made a cypher on a more convenient plan than the one we have used, I now transmit it to you by a Monsr. Doradour who goes to settle in Virginia. His family will follow him next year. Should he have occasion of your patronage I beg leave to solicit it for him. They yesterday finished printing my notes. I had 200 copies printed, but do not put them out of my own hands, except two or three copies here, & two which I shall send to America, to yourself & Colo. Monroe, if they can be ready this evening, as promised.[1] In this case you will receive one by Monsr. Doradour. I beg you to peruse it carefully because I ask your advice on it & ask nobody's else. I wish to put it into the hands of the young men at the college, as well on account of the political as physical parts.[2] But there are sentiments on some subjects which I apprehend might be displeasing to the country perhaps to the assembly or to some who lead it. I do not wish to be exposed to their censure, nor do I know how far their influence, if exerted, might effect a misapplication of law to such a publication were it made. Communicate it then in confidence to those whose judgments & information you would pay respect to: & if you think it will give no offence I will send a copy to each of the students of W. M. C. and some others to my friends & to your disposal. Otherwise I shall only send over a very few copies to particular friends in confidence & burn the rest. Answer me soon & without reserve. Do not view me as an author, & attached to what he has written. I am neither. They were at first intended only for Marbois. When I had enlarged them, I thought first of giving copies to three or four friends. I have since supposed they might set our young students into a useful train of thought, and in no event do I propose to admit them to go to the public at large. A variety of accidents have postponed my writing to you till I have no further time to continue my letter. The next packet will sail from Havre. I will then send your books & write more fully, but answer me immediately on the preceding subject. I am with much affection Dr. Sir Your friend & servt

TH: JEFFERSON

RC (DLC). Cover missing. Docketed by JM.

[1] The heavy involvement of France in American affairs prompted the secretary of the French legation in Philadelphia, François Marbois, to send a questionnaire related to the vital statistics and other particular information about each of the thirteen states to important delegates in Congress some time in 1780. Joseph Jones received the questions concerning Virginia and relayed them to Governor Thomas Jefferson. The subject matter well suited Jefferson's natural spirit of inquiry, but it took him months to gather the information, and much longer to turn the facts over in his mind and then write an answer to the queries. The result was a book

which Jefferson took to France on his diplomatic mission in 1784. Printing costs in America, along with Jefferson's fears that the manuscript might be vulnerable to attack from critics of his tenure as governor, limited Jefferson's interest in an American edition. From his Parisian vantage point, however, the American minister found his interest rekindled, and a small printed edition was not beyond his means. The volume, titled *Notes on the State of Virginia*, bore no author's name on the title page. Two hundred copies were printed in May 1785, with the erroneous date of 1782 left uncorrected by the proofreader as the publication date. The story is fully related in Jefferson, *Notes* (Peden ed.), xi–xxv.

2 JM advised Jefferson not to distribute the book to college students. He told Jefferson the *Notes* had been delivered by Comte Doradour and that both he and George Wythe believed presentation of copies to William and Mary students might be thought "an *indiscriminate gift*" (JM to Jefferson, 15 Nov. 1785).

From John Blair Smith

[ca. 16] May. 1785

Dr Sir:

I am sorry to interrupt your attention to more important objects by an appeal to you in a dispute between Carter H. Harrison Esqr. of Cumberland & myself, but as you were present at its origination, & as my character for veracity is interested in your decision, I have no doubt of your inclination to do me the justice which is in your power. All that I have to request of you at present is, to know whether you do not recollect to hear him say that "The greatest curse which heaven sent at any time into this Country, was sending Dissenters into it."[1] I am, Sir, yr. respectful hble sert.

Jno. B. Smith.

RC (DLC). Cover missing. Docketed by JM.

[1] The Reverend John Blair Smith was a Princeton classmate of JM and a pillar of Virginia Presbyterianism. Harrison, son of the former Governor Benjamin Harrison, was a leading conservative in the House of Delegates. In 1784 Harrison had introduced the bill to establish the Protestant Episcopal church in Virginia (*JHDV*, Oct. 1784, p. 65). In 1785 he called for the repeal of the 1782 manumission law (ibid., Oct. 1785, p. 110). Smith and Harrison probably quarreled on more than one occasion. Brant claimed Harrison made the statement but later denied it (Brant, *Madison*, II, 349). Eckenrode said the remark "outraged" Smith (Eckenrode, *Separation of Church and State in Virginia*, pp. 82–83). See JM's answer, 27 May 1785.

From Richard Barbour

Letter not found.

19 May 1785. Noted in the lists probably made by Peter Force (DLC: Madison Miscellany). No other reference to it has been found.

From Gabriel Royez

a Paris ce 24 May 1785

Je m'engage a fournir chez moi aussitot l'announce toutes les Livraison futures de l'Encyclopedie[1] par ordre de matieres in 4°. Dont j'ai reçu le montant des livraisons y compris la 13°. montant a la Somme de troit cent quatrevingt Livre en deduisant sur ce prix fixe par la souscription et Suivant la notte y joint un primer quarante huit livres Suivant nos convention.

ROYEZ.
Libraire quai et près les augustins.

A Monsieur James Madison
  of Orange Virginia.

ou a son ordre. Reçu la Somme De trois Cent quarante huit livres pour les 13 livraisons a pari[s] ce 24 Mai

GABRIEL ROYEZ.

RC (DLC). Cover missing.

[1] Jefferson had arranged for JM to become a subscriber to the *Encyclopédie méthodique* (Jefferson to JM, 11 Nov. 1784). Royez, a book dealer, was simply informing JM of a price change in his subscription to this work, the publication of which spanned most of JM's remaining lifetime. The 192-volume set was not completed until 1832.

To John Blair Smith

May 27. 1785.

I have before me your note requesting my information relative to a fact asserted on your part, and denied on that of Carter H. Harrison Esqr. Your own feelings will suggest to you my motives for wishing not to be made a Witness or Judge in any case where the characters of Gentlemen are concerned. Under the circumstances of the present in which I am only called on by one of the parties, & therefore might err through the want of suggestions to my memory from the other, I am persuaded you will readily excuse my declining the answer which you request.[1]

J. M.

FC (DLC). In JM's hand and docketed by him. Headed, "Copy of Answer."

[1] Brant assumed that JM's conception of gentlemanly behavior precluded involvement in this personal dispute (*Madison*, II, 349), though JM had given his opinion a year earlier in another situation (Opinion in Controversy between Joseph Jones and William Lee, 26 June 1784). Considering Harrison's prominence in the House of Delegates, another explanation of JM's circumspect conduct might relate to his conception of practical politics.

From William Grayson

NEW YORK May 28th. 1785.

DEAR SIR

I did myself the pleasure some time since of writing to you; and I expect by this time you have recieved my letter; since which nothing has happened of any consequence except the passage of the Land Ordinance & the arrival of Don Diego de Gardoqui at Philadelphia. I inclose you a copy of the Ordinance: & if it is not the best in the world, it is I am confident the best that could be procured for the present.[1] There was such a variety of interests most of them imaginary, that I am only surprised it is not more defective.

The Eastern people who before the revolution never had an idea of any quantity of Earth above a hundred acres, were for selling in large tracts of 30,000 acres while the Southern people who formerly could scarce bring their imaginations down so low as to comprehended the meaning of a hundred Acres of ground were for selling the whole territory in lots of a mile square.[2]

In this situation we remained for eight days, with great obstinacy on both sides, untill a kind of compromise took effect.

As to foreign news we are entirely uninformed: neither can [any] body here say with certainty what will be the event of the present hostile preparations in Europe.[3]

I imagine you have heard of the arrival of an American vessel at this place in four months from Canton in China laden with the commodities of that country.[4]

It seems our Countrymen were treated with as much respect as the Subjects of any other nation: i.e. the whole are looked upon by the Chinese as Barberians: & they have too much Asiactic hauteur to descend to any discrimination. Most of the mercantile people here are of opinion, this commerce can be carried on, on betters[5] from America than Europe: & that we may be able not only to supply our own wants, but to smuggle a very considerable quantity to the West Indies.[6] I could heartily wish to see the merchts. of our State engaged in this business.

Don't you think an exemption from duty on all goods imported immediately from India in Virga. bottoms to our State might have a good affect?

WILLM. GRAYSON[7]

RC (DLC). Cover and enclosure missing. Docketed by JM. The closing and original signature were clipped.

[1] The missing enclosure was the "Land Ordinance" as passed by Congress on 20 May 1785. Grayson, being a leading member of the committee appointed to draw up the ordinance, was privy to all the proposals for its makeup.

[2] The "Eastern people"—the New England delegates—were anxious to peddle the public domain before it drained population from the older states. The western settlers were hostile to the sale of "large tracts of 30,000 acres" however, as their resolution at the Kentucky convention of Dec. 1784 proved. "That to grant any Person a larger quantity of Land than he designs Bona Fide to seat himself or his Family on, is a greevance, Because it is subversive of the fundamental Principles of a free republican Government" (Abernethy, *Western Lands and the American Revolution*, p. 305).

[3] Joseph II, emperor of Austria, was trying his strength against the Dutch, but France had thus far been able to keep the peace. See Grayson to JM, 1 May 1785, and Lafayette to JM, 16 Mar. 1785.

[4] The American ship *Empress of China* reached New York from Canton on 11 May 1785 (*Pa. Gazette*, 18 May 1785).

[5] Commerce "carried on, on betters," i.e., better trading terms.

[6] Grayson first wrote, "but to smuggle in at [sic] very considerable degree to the West Indies."

[7] Grayson's name was written by an unidentified hand.

To James Monroe

ORANGE May 29. 1785

DEAR SIR

Your favor of May [8] came to hand a few days ago. It is fortunate that the variant ideas have been so easily accomodated touching the mode of surveying & selling the territorial fund. It will be equally so I think if you can dispossess the British of the Western posts, before the land office is opened. On this event and the navigation of the Mississippi will much depend the fiscal importance of the back Country to the U: States. The amount of the proposed requisition will I fear startle those to whom it will be addressed.[1] The use of certificates as a medium for discharging the interest of the home debt, is a great evil, tho' I suppose a necessary one.[2] The advantage it gives to Sharpers & Collectors,

can scarcely be described, and what is more noxious, it provokes violations of public faith, more than the weight of the Burden itself. The
1,000,000 Drs. to be paid in Specie, and the greatest part of it to be sent
abroad, will equally try the virtue of the States. If they do not flinch
however they will have the satisfaction of coming out of the trial with
more honour, though with less money.

I have lately heard that the Kentucky Delegates will be instructed to
propose to the next Session, the separation of that Country from this,
and its being handed over to Congress for admission into the Confederacy.[3] If they pursue their object through this channel, they will not
only accomplish it without difficulty, but set a useful example to other
Western Settlemts. which may chuse to be lopped off from other States.
My information as to this matter is not authentic, but such as I am inclined to believe true. I hear also that a State is actually set up in the
back Country of N. C. that it is organized, named, and has deputed
representatives to Congress.[4]

It gives me much pleasure to observe by 2 printed reports sent me
by Col. Grayson that in the latter Congs. had expunged a clause contained in the first for setting apart a district of land in each Township,
for supporting the Religion of the Majority of inhabitants. How a
regulation, so unjust in itself, so foreign to the Authority of Congs. so
hurtful to the sale of the public land, and smelling so strongly of an
antiquated Bigotry, could have received the countenance of a Commtee
is truly matter of astonishment.[5] In one view it might have been no disadvantage to this State in case the Genl. Assesst. should take place, as it
would have given a repellent quality to the new Country, in the estimation of those whom our own encroachments on Religious Liberty
would be calculated to banish to it. But the adversaries to the Assesst.
begin to think the prospect here flattering to their wishes. The printed
Bill has excited great discussion and is likely to prove the sense of the
Community to be in favor of the liberty now enjoyed. I have heard
of several Counties where the late representatives have been laid aside
for voting for the Bill, and not of a single one where the reverse has
happened. The Presbyterian Clergy too who were in general friends
to the scheme, are already in another tone, either compelled by the laity
of that sect, or alarmed at the probability of further interferences of the
Legislature, if they once begin to dictate in matters of Religion. I am
Dr. Sir Yrs. affecly.

                                                        J. Madison Jr.

The letter herewith inclosed is from Mrs. Carr, sister of Mr. Jefferson.

RC (DLC). Cover missing. Docketed by JM. Note by Monroe: "Correspondence with Mr Madison in my first mission to France."

¹ The requisition was for $3 million, payable in indents if a third was paid in specie (Ferguson, *Power of the Purse*, p. 225).

² Beginning in 1782 with Pennsylvania, the states began issuing to public creditors certificates of interest which were receivable in taxes. By thus taking over payment of the interest on the public debt the states were undermining federal control of finances and at the same time indulging in a paper money scheme. From 1784 to the end of the Confederation, Congress allowed the states to pay the part of their requisitions (meant to service the pubic debt) in indents, or certificates of interest (ibid., pp. 221–23).

³ This information was probably based upon a rumor preceding the convention held at Danville on 23 May 1785, where five resolutions were passed calling for constitutional separation, a petition to the Virginia legislature seeking a separation act, an address to the people of Kentucky, the election of delegates to another convention in July, and the holding of a convention in Aug. at Danville. At the Aug. convention (8 Aug. 1785) the petition was redrawn and George Muter (chief justice of the District Court) and Harry Innes (attorney general) were deputed to present the petition to the Virginia legislature (Lewis Collins and Richard H. Collins, *History of Kentucky* [2 vols.; Covington, Ky., 1878], I, 260–61). The petition was presented 28 Oct. 1785 (*JHDV*, Oct. 1785, p. 10). For the first Kentucky convention, see JM to Randolph, 10 Mar. 1785 and n. 2; and Abernethy, "Journal of the First Kentucky Convention," *Journal of Southern History*, I (1935), 67–78. Also, see Act Concerning Statehood for the Kentucky District, 22 Dec. 1785.

⁴ A temporary constitution for the new state of Franklin had been prepared and prefaced with a declaration of independence. At the same time the North Carolina assembly had repealed the act providing for the cession of the western territory to Congress and formed the country into a separate district of Washington within the state under the command of John Sevier. The first assembly of the self-styled state met in Mar. 1785. John Sevier was elected governor and William Cocke elected commissioner of the state of Franklin to make an appeal before the Continental Congress and to present a memorial praying admission to the Union (Williams, *History of the Lost State of Franklin* [1933 ed.], pp. 41, 43–44, 57, 65).

⁵ On 23 Apr. 1785 Congress debated the clauses in the 1785 Land Ordinance concerning the support of religion. William Ellery (R. I.) and Melancton Smith (N. Y.) led the successful assault against the appropriation of public lands for the use of religion. The question was oddly put so that the vote was taken on whether the religion clause should stand. In that way only a few noes were required to defeat the question and consequently strike the offensive phrases. Harry Ammon takes the view that by this manner, although few of the delegates favored the support of the religion clause, few had to go on record against it. Monroe seems never to have responded to JM's condemnation of the clause, nor to have explained why he and his fellow Virginia delegates chose to vote for retention of the provision (*JCC*, XXVII, 293–96; Ammon, *James Monroe*, p. 52).

To William Grayson

Letter not found.

29 May 1785. Mentioned by Grayson in his letter to JM, 27 June 1785. JM to James Monroe, 7 August 1785, notes that he had answered Grayson's letter of 1 May 1785 with suggestions concerning the revision of Article IX of the Articles of Confederation.

From Richard Henry Lee

Dear Sir,

Two days ago, and not sooner, your favor of March the 20th was deliverd to me, so that you find it has been more than two months travelling thus far. It seems to me that our Assembly were influenced more by the letter than the spirit of the Confederation. The consequence will certainly be, if our meetings are slow as usual, that Virginia will be unrepresented for some time after the federal year commences. Tho no great mischief arises from this, the appearance is not so handsome as it should be; besides that it partakes too much of that too common inattention to the great Council of the U. S. upon the wise conduct of which so much depends.

I am very happy to see by the Newspapers that the business of opening Potomac goes on so well.[1] Tis certainly an object of great consequence to extend our internal navigation. Concerning James river I have heard nothing. When I was in our Assembly it appeard to me rather to be the wish, than otherwise, that Kentucky should apply for separation. And I should suppose that if, when they found themselves compitent to the business of Self Government, they properly applied to our Assembly, no good objection could be made to a separation.[2] For they have, & will remain for a long time, if not always, more expence than profit to the rest of the country. Washington County seems to be stimulated by a troublesome person who for self aggrandisement appears willg: to dismember that part also, & join with the Revolters from N. Carolina.[3] This last seems to merit the *wise* & *firm* attention of Government & the Legislature. We have, after much debate indeed, & great waste of time, at last pass'd an Ordinance for disposing of such part of the Lands N. W of the Ohio as belongs to the U. S. & have been purchased of the Indians. If this proves agreeable to the public, it will extinguish about 10 Millions of the pub debt. And the remaining lands, going southward to the Mississippi, will nearly discharge all the domestic debt. Besides the probable prospect that we have of considerable cessions from N & S. Carolina & Georgia. This Source does indeed deserve our warmest cultivation as it seems to be almost the only one that we have for discharging our oppressive debt.[4] Dr. Franklin has leave to retire. Mr. Jefferson remains in France. And Mr. J. Adams is sent to London. If the Court of this last country is sincere, we may expect an amicable & easy settlement of existing differences between us.

The Minister (Mr. Pitt) does appear willing to be liberal in Commercial regulations, but the avaricious spirit of Commerce that is so great every where, but which in England has ever been excessive, opposes his views. And so we find it is in France, for the Marquis de La Fayette writes that the advantages already granted us are most violently exclaimed against by the Trading people of the Kingdom.[5] Mr. Gardoque (who calls himself *Plenepotentiary Charged with Affairs* is arrived at Phila. and we expect him soon here. So that we shall quickly know whether he can or will do any thing conclusive concerning the Navigation of Mississippi.[6] He reports a great scarcity of provisions at the Havannah, but yet we dont hear of the ports of that Island being opened to us for supply. It is reported that the frigate which brought him is taking in flower. The American enterprise has been well markt by a short and successful Voyage made from hence to Canton in China.[7] The Chinese were kind to our people and glad to see a new source of Commerce opened to them from a *New People*, as they called us. The Europeans there were civil but astonished at the rapidity of our movements, especially the English. I fear that our Countrymen will overdo this business. For now there appears every where a Rage for East India Voyages. So that the variety of means may defeat the Attainment of the concurrent end—A regulated & useful commerce with that part of the World. It seems very questionable now whether Congress will adjourn or not this Year—if they do, it will not be until late in August. Inattention, Sickness, and a variety of causes occasion business to go on very slowly. I . . .

RC (DLC). Cover missing. Docketed by JM. The letter is incomplete. At the bottom of the second page Lee wrote "I" as the lead-in word for the missing next page.

[1] Lee must have seen in the New York newspapers "a letter from Alexandria, in Virginia, dated May 19" which told of the meeting held at Lomax's tavern where the subscription books on the Potomac canal were opened. "It appeared that forty thousand three hundred pounds were subscribed, a sum far beyond what was requisite to incorporate the company" (reprint from a New York newspaper in *Pa. Gazette*, 1 June 1785).

[2] For JM's early thoughts on Kentucky statehood see his letters to Randolph, 10 Mar. 1785; to Jefferson, 27 Apr. 1785; to Monroe, 29 May 1785; and the reply to Lee, 7 July 1785.

[3] The "troublesome person" was Arthur Campbell, who harangued the people in Washington County, Virginia, to join with other western settlers and "declare themselves immediately independent of the States of Virginia and North Carolina" (*Cal. of Va. State Papers*, IV, 45). Williams, *The Lost State of Franklin* (1933 ed.), pp. 46–48, reprints the petition Campbell sent to Congress which was read 13 Jan. 1785. The petition asked that Congress "speedily erect the aforesaid described Territory into a free and Independent State, subject to the federal bond."

4 Lee's old-fashioned attitude toward the "oppressive" public debt was one of several inconsistencies in his political conduct. He wanted to put restraints on British trade to force concessions, but was afraid to give Congress the power to regulate trade because he feared the power of commercial interests in the North (Lee to JM, 11 Aug. 1785).

5 Lee wrote Lafayette on 11 June 1785 (Ballagh, *Letters of Richard Henry Lee,* II, 369–71).

6 Don Diego de Gardoqui's presence created a diplomatic dilemma for the plain-mannered congressmen because he was commissioned by the Spanish court as an *encargado de negocios.* Monroe reported there was some consternation because it was assumed that the Spaniard had the rank of a minister, but "to avoid giving offence we have us'd the terms us'd by his master" (Monroe to Jefferson, 15 July 1785, Boyd, *Papers of Jefferson,* VIII, 297).

7 The American ship *Empress of China* left Canton on 28 Dec. 1784 and reached New York on 11 May 1785. The successful voyage proved highly profitable and turned American merchants' attention toward the Orient as a vast and almost untapped market (*Pa. Gazette,* 18 May 1785).

From François de Barbé-Marbois

NEW YORK, may 31st. 1785.

SIR,

I have been happy in forming the acquaintance of Mr. Mazzey, & receiving at the Same time your letter dated 3d. June 1784.[1] He is now on his way to france where I know he will find many friends.[2] Mr. Jepherson one of them is generally esteemed in paris & Versailles, & I have no doubt but his appointment as a minister to our court will give great Satisfaction.

The opinion in paris is that peace will continue: The Emperor is Single on his own Side, & will probably See the necessity of altering his System.[3]

Mesmer Keeps his ground, & by what I hear from persons of respectable character I See Sufficient reasons to Doubt before pronouncing him to be a Quack.[4] With perfect esteem & respect I have the honour to be Sir, your obedt. hble. Servt.

DE MARBOIS

RC (DLC). Addressed in care of Fontaine Maury, who forwarded the letter from Fredericksburg to Orange County. Docketed by JM.

1 Not found.

2 Mazzei sailed for France on 17 June 1785 and never returned to America (Schiavo, *Philip Mazzei,* p. 159).

3 Several months earlier, Joseph II of Austria was thought to be fomenting a general war in Europe. See Lafayette to JM, 16 Mar. 1785.

4 JM wrote "Mesmer" above Barbé-Marbois's barely legible word. Franz Anton Mesmer (1734–1815) arrived in Paris during Feb. 1778, proclaiming his discovery of a superfine fluid that penetrated and surrounded all bodies. Mesmer's treatment, calling for a soaking of the human body in a fluid to produce cures for many ailments, was considered brilliant by some and quackery by others (Robert Darnton, *Mesmerism and the End of the Enlightenment in France* [Cambridge, Mass., 1968]), pp. 47–52, 71–72.

From Philip Mazzei

NEW-YORK 3. Giugno 1785

CAR. MO E DEGNO AMICO,

Le vostre lettere per Mr. Jefferson e per il Marchese le ò io, e le consegnerò in proprie mani. Io parto, ma il mio cuore resta. Tutte le mie cure paiono concentrate nel soggetto, da cui solo depende la futura libertà o schiavitù di questo almo Paese. L'America è il mio Giove, Venere la Virginia. Quando rifletto a quel che sentii nel traversar Potomack, mi vergogno della mia debolezza. Non so quel che seguirà nel perdere di vista Sandy-Hook. So bene che in qualunque luogo, e in qualsivoglia situazione non mi stancherò mai di fare i miei sforzi per la prosperità della mia cara Patria adottiva. Ma tutto sarà vano se non si mettono su cardini sani e stabili la Confederazione e i rispettivi Governi degli Stati. La nostra Società può massimamente cooperarci: il Col. Giorgio Mason, il Dr. David Stuart, il Dr. Way di Wingmilton, Mr. Elias Boudinot, Mr. de Marbois, Mr. Van-Berkle, e tutti gli altri uomini de senno, coi quali ne ò ragionato, son di questo parere. Il solo impedimento può essere la transcuratezza degli Associati. Delitto imperdonabile, perchè si manca a un sacro dovere: Vergognoso, perchè l'incomodo è quasi nulla in paragone del benefizio. Lo scusarsi del non far nulla sulla supposizione che gli altri non opreranno, è a mio giudizio un delitto, poichè tende a scoraggire altrui, e a mascherare la propria infingardaggine. Mr. Burnley, latore delle presente, mi à promesso di pregarvi a nominarlo, e di fare il suo dovere se sarà ricevuto. Il Dr. Way m'incaricò di notificare a Mr. John Page o a Mr. Andrews il suo desiderio di divenir nostro Socio. Mr. Boudinot mi disse che avrebbe scritto al nostro amico Edmond and effetto parimente di esser nominato. Mr. John Minor, il Col. Mason, e il Dr. Stuart saranno stati nominati all'adunanza dei 24. del passato, poichè ne scrissi in tempo al nostro Presidente. Mr. Monroe non à veduto la Proposizione stampata d'ordine dell Assemblea per mantenere i Ministri del Vangelo. Gli ò detto che in essa i *buoni Cristiani* confessano tacitamente di non potere obbligare i *non Cristiani*, per il che impongono loro una tassa parziale. Vi prego di mandargliela più presto che potete; l'ò pregato di scrivere su quel particolare, ed ei ne par disposto. Il Col. Innes mi obbligò, più collaforza delle sue mani che della ragione, a promettergli di scrivere sulla necessità di limitare i Porti &c. &c., ma ecco Mr. Burnley che deve partire. Addio Amico. Tutto Vostro

Filippo Mazzei.

CONDENSED TRANSLATION

Mazzei will personally deliver JM's letters to Jefferson and Lafayette. He is distressed at the prospect of departing from America, promises to continue his efforts for the prosperity of his adopted country, but fears that all will be in vain if the governments of the states and the Confederation do not rest on sound principles. To insure this all the members of the Constitutional Society must contribute their utmost. Hardin Burnley, the carrier of this letter, Dr. Way, Boudinot, John Minor, Colonel Mason, and Dr. Stuart have all applied for membership in the Society. Monroe would like to receive a copy of a proposition to support the ministers, which provides that a partial tax would be levied on non-Christians. Innes is pressing Mazzei to write a paper about harbors.

RC (DLC). Cover missing.

From Joseph Jones

Richmond 12th. June 1785

D. Sir.

Being from Town when your order[1] for the Trunk arrived was the reason it was not then sent. If an opportunity offers it shall be forwarded as you desire. In the mean time the precaution of preserving the cloaths from the moth by exposing them to the sun has been attended to and shall be repeated. I know not whether any Copy of the resolution you allude to[2] has been officially communicated to Mr. Mason. Such as Beckley copied for the Executive have been so wh[ethe]r *that* shod have been of the number I cannot tell as we are not yet favoured with the Journals by the Printer and I cannot inform myself at the Clerks office Mr. Beckley being out of Town—he will I am told return Tomorrow. If the Attorney has not sent I will contrive you the Copies you desire. I heard but have only heard that Mason and Henderson proceeded to execute the other branch of the business committed

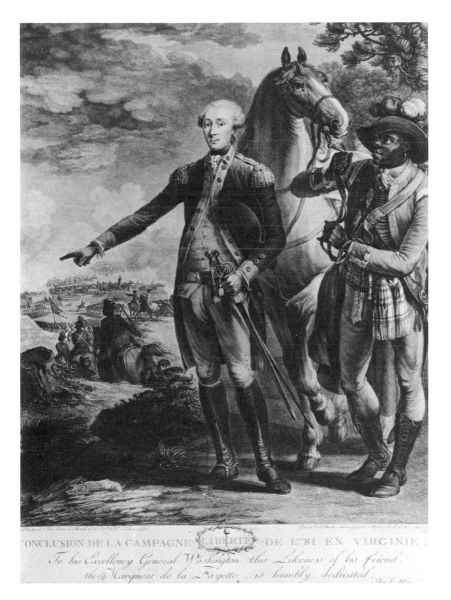

CONCLUSION DE LA CAMPAGNE LIBERTÉ DE 1781 EN VIRGINIE .

To his Excellency General Washington this Likeness of his friend
the Marquess de la Fayette , is humbly dedicated .

LAFAYETTE

From a contemporary French engraving. The black man holding the reins of the general's horse was James Lafayette, a slave who was later granted his freedom and awarded a pension by the Virginia General Assembly for his extraordinary services. (Courtesy of the Virginia Historical Society.)

PATRICK HENRY

Painting, 1815, by Thomas Sully from an earlier miniature. (Courtesy of the Colonial Williamsburg Collection.)

to the Comrs. withot. the attendance or call for attendence of the other Commrs. What they have done has not come to my knowledge. I have determined to leave Richmond the first week of the next month for King George where I shall only stay a few days and then proceed towards the Berkeley Springs to return the begining of October. I think I shall pass through Orange going or returning. At one time I had a notion of going to Rhode Island being much pressed to it by Mrs. Lightfoot near Pt. Royal whose Husband is in bad health and is advised to make a water trip to that place and his wife is determined to attend him but had I gone we were to have taken our rout by land and met him there. After some reflection I declined the northern for the western trip whr. prudently I cannot tell but my little boy must accompany me and I thought the springs on that account most proper. If I pass through Orange and you are in the County I shall certainly do myself the pleasure of seeing you. H——r——n[3] succeded in surrey where he offered after being disappointed in Chs. City. It is thought there will be a struggle for the Chair. What do you think of an alteration in the article of Confed: to vest the Congress with power to regalate Trade and collect imposts to be credited the respective States. The States having Staples will not I expect relish it, and yet the necessity of Congress possessing the power is at present apparent. Perhaps a Convention of Deputies from the several States for the purpose of forming Commercial regulations similar to the British Nav: act to be carryed into execution by Congress wod. be the most likely mode to obtain success to the measure as well as collecting the Wisdom of the States on the subject, which is unquestionably of the first importance.[4] Yr. friend & Servt

JOS: JONES.

RC (DLC). Cover addressed by Jones. Docketed by JM.

[1] JM's "order for the Trunk" has not been found.

[2] Undoubtedly either the resolution appointing Virginia commissioners to meet with Maryland commissioners to consider the jurisdiction and navigation of the Potomac River or the resolution directing the Virginia and Maryland commissioners to meet with ones from Pennsylvania to consider the same (Resolutions Appointing Virginia Members of a Potomac River Commission, 28 June 1784; or, the Resolutions Authorizing an Interstate Compact on Navigation and Jurisdiction of the Potomac, 28 Dec. 1784; Jones to JM, 23 June 1785; Randolph to JM, 17 July 1785; JM to Monroe, 28 July 1785). JM, although one of the commissioners, was never informed of the time and place of the meeting. It may have been the unfulfilled commission to meet with representatives from Pennsylvania that occasioned JM's statement to Monroe that he might have to go to Philadelphia to perform a public duty (JM to Monroe, 28 July 1785, n. 2).

³ Benjamin Harrison. John Tyler vied with Harrison for the chair of the speaker of the House and lost.

⁴ JM had spoken against a convention, similar to the one Jones was suggesting, two years earlier (*Papers of Madison*, VI, 425). Although JM disliked the plan of calling a revising convention, he had to accept the stubbornness of his legislative colleagues as a fact of life after the House of Delegates voted against relinquishing regulatory powers to Congress on 30 Nov. and 1 Dec. 1785. JM gave half-hearted support for the House of Delegates resolution of 21 Jan. 1786, which laid the groundwork for the abortive Annapolis convention, but he was pessimistic concerning the convention approach to ills of the Confederation. The call for such a convention had been sounded in New York as early as July 1782 (Syrett and Cooke, *Papers of Hamilton*, III, 110–13).

From Philip Mazzei

NEW-YORK, 15. Giugno 1785

CARISSIMO AMICO,

Il nostro comune e degno Amico Monroe vi manderà un mio scritto sulla necessità di stabilire 2. soli Porti nel nostro Stato. Il Col. Innes estorse da me la promessa di scrivere sul detto soggetto prima d' imbarcarmi, e di mandargli ciò che la Botte avrebbe prodotto. Ma siccome ei non intende questa lingua, il Col. Monroe glie ne manderà la traduzione, subito che le altre più pressanti occupazioni gli permetteranno di farla. Voi vedrete un'introduzione insulsa per i Dotti, ma che io credo utilissima per il Popolo. Son di parere che qualunque publicazione della Società dovrebbe sempre cominciare da stabilire certi dati, e poi condurre il popolo a poco a poco per la mano, come i ciechi. Vi avverto che il Col. Mason fa un'obiezione, la quale bisogna che vi prepariate a confutare. Ei dice che le città grandi tendono a corrompere la buona morale, e che conseguentemente dobbiamo evitare piuttosto che procurare di avere Emporj. Addio, son per partire. Spero che mi scriverete sotto coperta a Mr. Jefferson. Credetemi sinceramente e invariabilmente Tutto Vostro

FILIPPO MAZZEI.

CONDENSED TRANSLATION

Monroe will forward to JM a paper written by Mazzei, at the insistence of Colonel Innes, on the necessity of establishing only two harbors in the state. Colonel Mason objects even to this limited proposal, on the grounds that large cities corrupt morals, but his arguments must be refuted (so that the Port bill can become operative).

RC (DLC). Cover missing.

Memorial and Remonstrance against
Religious Assessments

EDITORIAL NOTE

The most striking element in JM's authorship of the Memorial and Remonstrance was the pains he took to keep the public ignorant of his heavy involvement in this battle over state-subsidized religion. So successful was he in maintaining anonymity that a few libraries still have a printed version with speculative attributions of the work to other public men. Although in 1786 printer Isaiah Thomas used JM's name in the title when he issued *A Memorial and Remonstrance . . . by his Excellency James Madison* (Sabin 43719), JM himself waited until 1826 to make an explicit acknowledgment of his authorship. In reply to a query from George Mason's grandson, JM recalled that Mason and George Nicholas "and some others, thought it adviseable, that a Remonstrance against the Bill should be prepared for general circulation & signature, and imposed on me the task of drawing up such a paper" (JM to George Mason [of Green Spring], 14 July 1826 [ViHi]). After forty years, the legislative undercurrents moving the General Assessment bill toward passage in 1785 had been forgotten, and the surviving documents standing alone did not tell the whole story.

The importance of formal religion in the 1780s is a concept difficult for a secularistic society to grasp. JM had a decent respect for the opinions of his peers and must have been aware of the intensity with which his Baptist and Presbyterian neighbors approached religious worship. He was also conscious of loyalties held by such patriots as Edmund Pendleton and Patrick Henry for the former established church, and of their conviction that taxes should be offered to all churches through a general assessment lest public morality languish.

Nonetheless, disestablishment was an accomplished fact, a social symptom of declining interest in organized Christianity. Church-going in Virginia had long been on the decline as communicants found more reasons for attending Sunday horse races or cock fights than for being in pews. In 1784 a foreign traveler in Richmond noted that the village had only "one small church, but [it was] spacious enough for all the pious souls of the place and the region. If the Virginians themselves did not freely and openly admit that zeal for religion, and religion generally, is now very faint among them, the fact might easily be divined from other circumstances" (Schoepf, *Travels in the Confederation*, II, 62). In the face of such realities there were still many members of the General Assembly disposed to aid the Protestant Episcopal church, and they seemed determined to carry the General Assessment bill despite widespread but inarticulate opposition from their constituents. In this confused situation the Presbyterians occupied an ambiguous position. Convinced that a religious subsidy would pass, the Hanover Presbytery first declared that "Religion as a spiritual System is not to be considered an object of human Legislation," and in the next breath made a bid to share in the proceeds of a general assessment for teachers of Christianity (ViHi: Records of the Proceedings of Hanover Presbytery from the year 1755 to the year 1786 [typed copy by George S. Wallace, 1930], pp. 326–27).

Such a compromise was anathema to JM, who had no intention of retreating from the high ground he occupied when helping fashion Article XVI of the Virginia Declaration of Rights. He had seen conservative forces in the General Assembly come within an eyelash of passing the "Bill establishing a provision for the teachers of the Christian religion" at the October 1784 session—with some sly maneuvering needed by its opponents to postpone final action on the bill and publicize its provisions in the interim. George Nicholas in neighboring Albemarle County had entreated JM to bestir himself so that apathy would not allow the bill to become law (letter to JM, 22 Apr. 1785). Surely JM discussed the matter with his neighbors, including the obstreperous Elder John Leland, a Baptist minister who loathed all forms of church-state alliances. A host of Episcopalians as well as dissenters were eager to cut all church-state ties. However, a focal point for the opposition was needed, and the usual way to protest pending legislation in the 1780s was by a petition.

Partly from pressure then, and partly from personal conviction, JM took pen in hand and wrote a cogently reasoned attack on the measure, which was popularly called a General Assessment bill. By the end of June it was ready for distribution, most likely through Nicholas and other young men in the Piedmont whom Madison could trust to keep his secret—Archibald Stuart, John Breckinridge—and the tidelands patriarch at Gunston Hall who was eager to knock the tax-subsidy props from beneath the church he attended and loved, George Mason. The Library of Congress copy of the protest is in JM's hand. No doubt he sent a copy to Mason, who was eager to see it in print. From an Alexandria press Mason broadcast copies of the Memorial and Remonstrance to friends and neighbors. Mason sent with it a covering letter which honored JM's request for anonymity. The petition, Mason explained, was "confided to me by a particular Freind, whose Name I am not at Liberty to mention" (Mason to Washington, 2 Oct. 1785, Rutland, *Papers of George Mason*, II, 830). So active was Mason in supporting JM's remonstrance that there was speculation that he was its real author (Rowland, *Life of George Mason*, II, 87).

JM's motive in seeking a cloud of anonymity over his attack on the General Assessment bill is uncertain. JM told Jefferson copies had been dispatched "thro' the *medium of confidential persons*" (italicized words in code, JM to Jefferson, 20 Aug. 1785). Eckenrode speculated that most Virginians were inclined to support the bill until the protest movement began to swell (Eckenrode, *Separation of Church and State in Virginia*, p. 95). The phalanx committed to its passage was imposing. A fortuitous circumstance was the fact that Patrick Henry was still governor and thus unable to use his oratory in the House of Delegates to overwhelm the opposition. Carter Henry Harrison, Charles Mynn Thruston, Wilson Miles Cary, John Page, and lesser lights also were convinced that religion needed bolstering. Richard Henry Lee and Edmund Pendleton were not legislators, but in Richmond their support of the General Assessment bill was certainly no secret (Mays, *Papers of Edmund Pendleton*, II, 474).

In these circumstances JM may have thought it prudent to eschew the role of rabble-rouser. There was much to be done at the October 1785 session of the legislature and JM was too good a politician to go out of his way to alienate those men whose votes or support he would need if the reforms of the court system and the whole legal code were to pass a House of Delegates fairly balanced in terms of conservative-progressive members. So it may have been prudence and expediency that caused JM to mantle his authorship of what has been called "one of the truly epoch-making documents in the history of American Church-State separation" (Anson Phelps Stokes, *Church and State in the United States* [3 vols.; New York, 1950], I, 391).

A comparison between the Memorial and Remonstrance and John Locke's "Letter on Toleration" (1685) leads to the speculation that JM had occasion to use Locke's treatise in preparing his own. Assertions of intellectual dependence are often based on slender textual coincidences, but there are a number of similarities between the views of JM and Locke toward religious ties between church and state. For example, JM speaks of the "metes and bounds" between the temporal and spiritual establishments while Locke marked "the true bounds between the church and the commonwealth" (John Locke, *Epistolia de Tolerantia: A Letter on Toleration*, Raymond Klibansky and J. W. Gough, eds. [Oxford, 1968], p. 65). JM denies to "the Civil Magistrate" any power over religion because "Religious truth" and "the means of salvation" are beyond the concerns of the state. With Locke, the whole jurisdiction of the magistrate is concerned only with "civil goods" such as life, liberty, and property and ought not "in any way to be extended to the salvation of souls" (ibid., p. 67). Indeed, Locke held that "the magistrate ought not to forbid the holding or teaching of any speculative opinions in any church, because they have no bearing on the civil rights of his subjects" (ibid., p. 121).

If this comparison of Locke and JM is strained, there is one indisputable similarity between the "Letter on Toleration" and the Memorial and Remonstrance. Neither Locke nor JM wanted their authorship revealed. A modern scholar has noted that "Locke's timid anxiety to conceal his identity was excessive"; JM sent his petition to a close circle of friends who were enjoined to secrecy (Locke, *Letter on Toleration*, p. 45; Rutland, *Papers of George Mason*, II, 830, 832). "My choice is that my name may not be associated with it," JM wrote Randolph (26 July 1785).

Whether JM gleaned his arguments from a growing number of volumes in his personal library or drew upon experience and practical politics as his guides, the result is beyond doubt. Because of his labors the campaign against the General Assessment bill had all the aspects of a well-organized endeavor. What is not generally known is that JM was not only seeking anonymity but was so circumspect that another opponent of the General Assessment bill actually had a more active following. While at least thirteen of JM's petitions were circulated (and in time bore 1,552 signatures), another (and still anonymous) petition writer found that his attack on the "Teachers of Christian Religion" measure gained more widespread support. Twenty-nine petitions, signed by 4,899 Virginians, came from the pen of this unknown opponent of a church-state tie. These petitions were based on an argument that carries beyond JM's—the General Assessment bill was not only contrary to the Virginia Declaration of Rights and to the enlightened republicanism pronounced there, but the proposed act was in conflict with "the Spirit of the Gospel." Whoever wrote this petition, which was easily the most popular of the several circulating protests, was clearly an active Christian who believed the General Assessment bill would do nothing to check "that Deism with its banefull Influence [which] is spreading itself over the state" (Vi: Westmoreland County petition).

Obviously, more Virginians were made aware of this zealous protest than JM's calmer one, and it is also notable that in Westmoreland County at least eleven women signed the remonstrance based on "the Spirit of the Gospel." Thus, while JM's role in shaping opposition to the bill is noteworthy, his protest was signed by less than one-fifth of all the protesting Virginians who were recorded as opponents of the General Assessment bill (since some 10,929 signed some kind of anti-assessment petition). About eighty petitions opposed to the General Assessment bill flowed into the legislative hopper after 27 October 1785. Some were printed, and some came in longhand, but less than one-fifth of them were based entirely on JM's work. Only eleven counties mustered enough support for the bill to send favorable petitions to Richmond. Faced with such odds, the conservatives retreated. The bill which seemed so certain of passage in November 1784 was, just a year later, allowed to die in the pigeonhole.

With the passing of time, history tended to forget the other protests of 1785–1786 and focused upon Madison's. JM himself was no longer shy about his role, and in his seventy-fifth year he remembered that chiefly because of the Memorial and Remonstrance the churchmen in the General Assembly were "entirely frustrated, and under the influence of the public sentiment thus manifested the celebrated Bill 'Establishing Religious freedom' [was] enacted into a permanent Barrier agst. future attempts on the Rights of Conscience as declared in the great Charter affixed to the Constitution of the State" (JM to George Mason [of Green Spring], 14 July 1826 [ViHi]). His latter allusion was to the benchmark Article XVI of the Virginia Declaration of Rights which had opened the door for the winds of change, toppled the established church, and left men "equally entitled to the free exercise of religion, according to the dictates of conscience." JM remembered that entering wedge with some satisfaction for (with Mason's help) he had written that, too.

[ca. 20 June 1785]

To the Honorable the General Assembly of the
Commonwealth of Virginia
A Memorial and Remonstrance

We the subscribers, citizens of the said Commonwealth, having taken into serious consideration, a Bill printed by order of the last Session of General Assembly, entitled "A Bill establishing a provision for Teachers of the Christian Religion,"[1] and conceiving that the same if finally armed with the sanctions of a law, will be a dangerous abuse of power, are bound as faithful members of a free State to remonstrate against it, and to declare the reasons by which we are determined. We remonstrate against the said Bill,

1. Because we hold it for a fundamental and undeniable truth, "that Religion or the duty which we owe to our Creator and the manner of discharging it, can be directed only by reason and conviction, not by force or violence."[2] The Religion then of every man must be left to the conviction and conscience of every man; and it is the right of every man to exercise it as these may dictate. This right is in its nature an unalienable right. It is unalienable, because the opinions of men, depending only on the evidence contemplated by their own minds cannot follow the dictates of other men: It is unalienable also, because what is here a right towards men, is a duty towards the Creator. It is the duty of every man to render to the Creator such homage and such only as he believes to be acceptable to him. This duty is precedent, both in order of time and in degree of obligation, to the claims of Civil Society. Before any man can be considered as a member of Civil Society, he must be considered as a subject of the Governour of the Universe: And if a member of Civil Society, who enters into any subordinate Association, must always do it with a reservation of his duty to the General Authority; much more must every man who becomes a member of any particular Civil Society, do it with a saving of his allegiance to the Universal Sovereign. We maintain therefore that in matters of Religion, no mans right is abridged by the institution of Civil Society and that Religion is wholly exempt from its cognizance. True it is, that no other rule exists, by which any question which may divide a Society, can be ultimately determined, but the will of the majority; but it is also true that the majority may trespass on the rights of the minority.[3]

2. Because if Religion be exempt from the authority of the Society at large, still less can it be subject to that of the Legislative Body. The latter are but the creatures and vicegerents of the former. Their jurisdiction is both derivative and limited: it is limited with regard to the co-ordinate departments, more necessarily is it limited with regard to the constituents. The preservation of a free Government requires not merely, that the metes and bounds which separate each department of power be invariably maintained; but more especially that neither of them be suffered to overleap the great Barrier which defends the rights of the people.[4] The Rulers who are guilty of such an encroachment,

exceed the commission from which they derive their authority, and are Tyrants. The People who submit to it are governed by laws made neither by themselves nor by an authority derived from them, and are slaves.

3. Because it is proper to take alarm at the first experiment on our liberties. We hold this prudent jealousy to be the first duty of Citizens, and one of the noblest characteristics of the late Revolution. The free men of America did not wait till usurped power had strengthened itself by exercise, and entangled the question in precedents. They saw all the consequences in the principle, and they avoided the consequences by denying the principle.[5] We revere this lesson too much soon to forget it. Who does not see that the same authority which can establish Christianity, in exclusion of all other Religions, may establish with the same ease any particular sect of Christians, in exclusion of all other Sects? that the same authority which can force a citizen to contribute three pence only of his property for the support of any one establishment, may force him to conform to any other establishment in all cases whatsoever?

4. Because the Bill violates that equality which ought to be the basis of every law, and which is more indispensible, in proportion as the validity or expediency of any law is more liable to be impeached. If "all men are by nature equally free and independent,"[6] all men are to be considered as entering into Society on equal conditions; as relinquishing no more, and therefore retaining no less, one than another, of their natural rights. Above all are they to be considered as retaining an *"equal* title to the free exercise of Religion according to the dictates of Conscience."[7] Whilst we assert for ourselves a freedom to embrace, to profess and to observe the Religion which we believe to be of divine origin, we cannot deny an equal freedom to those whose minds have not yet yielded to the evidence which has convinced us. If this freedom be abused, it is an offence against God, not against man: To God, therefore, not to man, must an account of it be rendered. As the Bill violates equality by subjecting some to peculiar burdens, so it violates the same principle, by granting to others peculiar exemptions. Are the Quakers and Menonists the only sects who think a compulsive support of their Religions unnecessary and unwarrantable? Can their piety alone be entrusted with the care of public worship? Ought their Religions to be endowed above all others with extraordinary privileges by which proselytes may be enticed from all others? We think too favorably of the justice and good sense of these denominations to believe that they either

covet pre-eminences over their fellow citizens or that they will be seduced by them from the common opposition to the measure.

5. Because the Bill implies either that the Civil Magistrate is a competent Judge of Religious Truth; or that he may employ Religion as an engine of Civil policy.[8] The first is an arrogant pretension falsified by the contradictory opinions of Rulers in all ages, and throughout the world: the second an unhallowed perversion of the means of salvation.

6. Because the establishment proposed by the Bill is not requisite for the support of the Christian Religion. To say that it is, is a contradiction to the Christian Religion itself, for every page of it disavows a dependence on the powers of this world: it is a contradiction to fact; for it is known that this Religion both existed and flourished, not only without the support of human laws, but in spite of every opposition from them, and not only during the period of miraculous aid, but long after it had been left to its own evidence and the ordinary care of Providence. Nay, it is a contradiction in terms; for a Religion not invented by human policy, must have pre-existed and been supported, before it was established by human policy. It is moreover to weaken in those who profess this Religion a pious confidence in its innate excellence and the patronage of its Author; and to foster in those who still reject it, a suspicion that its friends are too conscious of its fallacies to trust it to its own merits.

7. Because experience witnesseth that ecclesiastical establishments, instead of maintaining the purity and efficacy of Religion, have had a contrary operation. During almost fifteen centuries has the legal establishment of Christianity been on trial. What have been its fruits? More or less in all places, pride and indolence in the Clergy, ignorance and servility in the laity, in both, superstition, bigotry and persecution. Enquire of the Teachers of Christianity for the ages in which it appeared in its greatest lustre; those of every sect, point to the ages prior to its incorporation with Civil policy. Propose a restoration of this primitive State in which its Teachers depended on the voluntary rewards of their flocks, many of them predict its downfall. On which Side ought their testimony to have greatest weight, when for or when against their interest?

8. Because the establishment in question is not necessary for the support of Civil Government. If it be urged as necessary for the support of Civil Government only as it is a means of supporting Religion, and it be not necessary for the latter purpose, it cannot be necessary for the former. If Religion be not within the cognizance of Civil Government

how can its legal establishment be necessary to Civil Government? What influence in fact have ecclesiastical establishments had on Civil Society? In some instances they have been seen to erect a spiritual tyranny on the ruins of the Civil authority; in many instances they have been seen upholding the thrones of political tyranny: in no instance have they been seen the guardians of the liberties of the people. Rulers who wished to subvert the public liberty, may have found an established Clergy convenient auxiliaries. A just Government instituted to secure & perpetuate it needs them not. Such a Government will be best supported by protecting every Citizen in the enjoyment of his Religion with the same equal hand which protects his person and his property; by neither invading the equal rights of any Sect, nor suffering any Sect to invade those of another.

9. Because the proposed establishment is a departure from that generous policy, which, offering an Asylum to the persecuted and oppressed of every Nation and Religion, promised a lustre to our country, and an accession to the number of its citizens. What a melancholy mark is the Bill of sudden degeneracy? Instead of holding forth an Asylum to the persecuted, it is itself a signal of persecution. It degrades from the equal rank of Citizens all those whose opinions in Religion do not bend to those of the Legislative authority. Distant as it may be in its present form from the Inquisition, it differs from it only in degree. The one is the first step, the other the last in the career of intolerance. The magnanimous sufferer under this cruel scourge in foreign Regions, must view the Bill as a Beacon on our Coast, warning him to seek some other haven, where liberty and philanthrophy in their due extent, may offer a more certain repose from his Troubles.

10. Because it will have a like tendency to banish our Citizens. The allurements presented by other situations are every day thinning their number. To superadd a fresh motive to emigration by revoking the liberty which they now enjoy, would be the same species of folly which has dishonoured and depopulated flourishing kingdoms.

11. Because it will destroy that moderation and harmony which the forbearance of our laws to intermeddle with Religion has produced among its several sects. Torrents of blood have been spilt in the old world, by vain attempts of the secular arm, to extinguish Religious discord, by proscribing all difference in Religious opinion. Time has at length revealed the true remedy. Every relaxation of narrow and rigorous policy, wherever it has been tried, has been found to assuage the disease. The American Theatre has exhibited proofs that equal and com-

pleat liberty, if it does not wholly eradicate it, sufficiently destroys its malignant influence on the health and prosperity of the State.[9] If with the salutary effects of this system under our own eyes, we begin to contract the bounds of Religious freedom, we know no name that will too severely reproach our folly. At least let warning be taken at the first fruits of the threatened innovation. The very appearance of the Bill has transformed "that Christian forbearance, love and charity,"[10] which of late mutually prevailed, into animosities and jealousies, which may not soon be appeased. What mischiefs may not be dreaded, should this enemy to the public quiet be armed with the force of a law?

12. Because the policy of the Bill is adverse to the diffusion of the light of Christianity. The first wish of those who enjoy this precious gift ought to be that it may be imparted to the whole race of mankind. Compare the number of those who have as yet received it with the number still remaining under the dominion of false Religions; and how small is the former! Does the policy of the Bill tend to lessen the disproportion? No; it at once discourages those who are strangers to the light of revelation[11] from coming into the Region of it; and countenances by example the nations who continue in darkness, in shutting out those who might convey it to them. Instead of Levelling as far as possible, every obstacle to the victorious progress of Truth, the Bill with an ignoble and unchristian timidity would circumscribe it with a wall of defence against the encroachments of error.

13. Because attempts to enforce by legal sanctions, acts obnoxious to so great a proportion of Citizens, tend to enervate the laws in general, and to slacken the bands of Society. If it be difficult to execute any law which is not generally deemed necessary or salutary, what must be the case, where it is deemed invalid and dangerous? And what may be the effect of so striking an example of impotency in the Government, on its general authority?

14. Because a measure of such singular magnitude and delicacy ought not to be imposed, without the clearest evidence that it is called for by a majority of citizens, and no satisfactory method is yet proposed by which the voice of the majority in this case may be determined, or its influence secured. "The people of the respective counties are indeed requested to signify their opinion respecting the adoption of the Bill to the next Session of Assembly."[12] But the representation must be made equal, before the voice either of the Representatives or of the Counties will be that of the people. Our hope is that neither of the former will, after due consideration, espouse the dangerous principle of

the Bill. Should the event disappoint us, it will still leave us in full confidence, that a fair appeal to the latter will reverse the sentence against our liberties.

15. Because finally, "the equal right of every citizen to the free exercise of his Religion according to the dictates of conscience" is held by the same tenure with all our other rights. If we recur to its origin, it is equally the gift of nature; if we weigh its importance, it cannot be less dear to us; if we consult the "Declaration of those rights which pertain to the good people of Virginia, as the basis and foundation of Government,"[13] it is enumerated with equal solemnity, or rather studied emphasis. Either then, we must say, that the Will of the Legislature is the only measure of their authority; and that in the plenitude of this authority, they may sweep away all our fundamental rights; or, that they are bound to leave this particular right untouched and sacred: Either we must say, that they may controul the freedom of the press, may abolish the Trial by Jury, may swallow up the Executive and Judiciary Powers of the State; nay that they may despoil us of[14] our very right of suffrage, and erect themselves into an independent and hereditary Assembly or, we must say, that they have no authority to enact into law the Bill under consideration. We the Subscribers say, that the General Assembly of this Commonwealth have no such authority: And that no effort may be omitted on our part against so dangerous an usurpation, we oppose to it, this remonstrance; earnestly praying, as we are in duty bound, that the Supreme Lawgiver of the Universe, by illuminating those to whom it is addressed, may on the one hand, turn their Councils from every act which would affront his holy prerogative, or violate the trust committed to them: and on the other, guide them into every measure which may be worthy of his [blessing, may re]dound[15] to their own praise, and may establish more firmly the liberties, the prosperity and the happiness of the Commonwealth.

Ms (DLC); Ms (DLC: Breckinridge Family Papers); Broadside (Vi). JM's may have been the original draft which he then copied and sent to George Nicholas, who acknowledged its receipt on 7 July 1785. Undoubtedly a third copy was posted to George Mason. The date is fixed by circumstances. JM was concerned that his authorship of the petition not become known. He did not mention the subject in his 21 June letter to Monroe but George Nicholas, one of those who had urged JM to prepare a remonstrance, appears to have received his copy from a friend who was present at the Orange County court day on 23 June. JM's wish for anonymity led to speculation on the petition's proper date. The Breckinridge Ms is headed, "Copy of Remonstrance written by Madison, Aug 1785," in an unknown hand; and in a tribute to JM, Joseph Blau writes that the "brilliant" Memorial and Remonstrance was "written during the session of 1784–85 of the Virginia House of Delegates" (Joseph L. Blau, ed., *Cornerstones of Religious Freedom in America* [Boston, 1949], p. 71). The anonymous broadside was the most familiar form of the petition as George Mason procured a copy, had it published in Alexandria, and then widely distributed. In addition to the Mason-sponsored printing of 1785, the petition was reprinted by Isaiah Thomas in Worcester, Massachusetts, in 1786 where JM is acknowledged as the author (Sabin 43719). Nonetheless, in Mathew Carey's *American Museum . . . for the Year 1789*, pp. 120–23, the petition is printed without attribution of authorship. *Niles' Weekly Register*, XII (1817), 295–97, carried the petition as JM's, and ibid., XXX (1826), published JM's pertinent correspondence with George Mason (of Green Spring) of July 1826 and the petition, pp. 188–91 and passim. Mason told JM he had heard the Memorial and Remonstrance "attributed to yourself, as well as to others" (Mason to JM, 6 July 1826 [DLC]).

[1] This measure, introduced under the aegis of Patrick Henry at the Oct. 1784 session, had passed two readings and was close to final passage when the opposition obtained a respite by a parliamentary tactic. They pleaded the need for public consideration of the bill and were able to postpone another reading until the Oct. 1785 session (*JHDV*, Oct. 1784, p. 82).

[2] In the margin JM noted the source of this quotation—Article XVI of the Virginia Declaration of Rights of 1776. JM had a large role in the final form of the article although this section was written by George Mason (*Papers of Madison*, I, 171–75).

[3] JM's historical studies along with his experience in the legislature had convinced him of the dangers of unfettered majority rule. He pointed this out later in his friendly disagreement with Jefferson over a federal bill of rights (JM to Jefferson, 17 Oct. 1788, Madison, *Writings* [Hunt ed.], V, 272). JM reaffirmed his fear of oppression by the majority during debates at the Federal Convention (6 June 1787, James Madison, *Notes of Debates in the Federal Convention* [Athens, Ohio, 1966], p. 77). He also brought up the same point in *Federalist No. 10* (Cooke, ed., *The Federalist*, pp. 60–61).

[4] For long-range evidence of JM's tenacity on the separation of church and state "metes and bounds," see JM's annual message to Congress of 3 Dec. 1816 (James D. Richardson, ed., *A Compilation of the Messages and Papers of the Presidents, 1789–1897* [10 vols.; Washington, 1898–99], I, 580).

[5] This idea, that revolutions spring from those groaning not under oppression but in anticipation of it, was central to the argument presented in Jefferson's "Declaration of the Causes and Necessity for Taking Up Arms" of 1775. "Parliament . . . for the first time asserted a right of unbounded legislation over the colonies of America and pursuing with eagerness the newly assumed thought in the space of 10 years during which they have exercised this right have given such decisive specimens of the spirit of this new legislation as leaves no room to [doubt the] consequence of acquiescence under it" (Boyd, *Papers of Jefferson*, I, 194).

[6] JM noted in the margin that this was a quotation from Article I, Virginia Declaration of Rights.

[7] Article XVI, ibid.

[8] Locke states these ideas differently but to the same end. "The commonwealth seems to me to be a society of men constituted only for preserving and advancing their civil goods. What I call civil goods are life, liberty, bodily health and freedom from pain, and the possession of outward things, such as lands, money, furniture, and the like. It is the duty of the civil magistrate, by impartially enacted equal laws, to preserve and secure for all the people . . . these things that belong to this life. . . . The whole jurisdiction of the magistrate is concerned only with these civil goods" (*Letter on Toleration*, pp. 65–67).

[9] Surry County supporters of the General Assessment bill took the opposite view. Their petition favoring passage of the bill observed "that [the] United State[s] of

America exhibit[s] to the World the singular Instance of a free & enlighten'd Government destitute of a legal Provision for the support of Religion" (Vi: Ms, quoted in Eckenrode, *Separation of Church and State in Virginia*, p. 112).

¹⁰ JM noted in the margin, "+ Decl. Rights Art: 16."

¹¹ Changed by JM from his original "light of truth."

¹² Opponents of the General Assessment bill had staved off its enactment by passing a resolution late in the Oct. 1784 session, for which JM extracted this quotation. The ostensible purpose of the postponement was to canvass voters' attitudes toward the bill (William Taylor Thom, *The Struggle for Religious Freedom in Virginia: The Baptists* [Baltimore, 1900], pp. 75–76).

¹³ JM noted in the margin that this quotation was "Per Decl. Rights title." In fact it is a rather loose rendering of Mason's original introductory title.

¹⁴ Originally JM wrote, "nay that they can abolish."

¹⁵ Words within brackets are faded on the Ms and restored from the broadside text.

To James Monroe

ORANGE 21. June 1785.

DEAR SIR

Finding from a letter of Mr. Mazzei that you have never been furnished with a copy of the Bill for establishing the Christian Religion in this State, I now inclose one, regretting that I had taken it for granted that you must have been supplied thro' some other channel. A very warm opposition will be made to this innovation by the people of the middle and back Counties, particularly the latter. They do not scruple to declare it an alarming usurpation on their fundamental rights and that tho' the Genl. Assembly should give it the form if they will not give it the validity of a law. If there be any limitation to the power of the Legislature, particularly if this limitation is to be sought in their Declaration of Rights or Form of Government, I own the Bill appears to me to warrant this language of the people.¹

A gentleman of credit lately from Kentucky tells me that he fell in with two persons on the Ohio, who were going down the River in the character of Commissrs. from Georgia, authorized to demand from the Spanish Govr. of N. Orleans, the posts within the limits of that State, and a settlement of the boundary in general between it [and the] Spanish possessions. The Gentleman did not see their Commission, but entertains no doubt of their having one. He was informed that two others were joined in it who had taken a different route. Should there be no mistake in this case, you will no doubt be able to get a full account of the Embassy. I would willingly suppose that no State could be guilty either of so flagrant an outrage on the fœderal Constitution, or of so imprudent a mode of pursuing their claims against a foreign Nation.[2]

I observe in a late Newspaper that the commercial discontents of Boston are spreading to New York and Philada.[3] Whether they will reach Virginia or not I am unable to say. If they should, they must proceed from a different interest; from that of the planters, not that of the Merchants. The present system here is as favorable to the latter as it is ruinous to the former. Our trade was never more compleatly monopolised by G. B. when it was under the direction of the British Parliament than it is at this moment: But as our merchants are almost all connected with that Country & that only, and as we have neither ships nor seamen of our own, nor likely to have any in the present course of things, no mercantile complaints are heard. The planters are disatisfied, and with reason, but they enter little into the science of commerce, and rarely of themselves combine in defence of their interests. If any thing could rouse them to a proper view of their situation one might expect it from the contrast of the market here with that of other States. Our Staple has of late been as low as a guinea per Ct. hundred on Rappahannock, and not above 32 or 33/. on James River. The current prices in Philada. during the same period have been 44/. of this currency for tobacco of the latter inspections and in like proportion for that of the former. The prices of imports of every kind in these two markets furnish a contrast equally mortifying to us. I have not had the same information from other States northward of us, but I have little doubt that it would teach us the same lesson. Our planters cannot suffer a loss of less than 50 per Ct. on the Staple of the Country if to the direct loss in the price of the Staple be added their indirect loss in the price of what they purchase with their Staple. It is difficult notwithstanding to make them sensible of the utility of establishing a Philada.* or a Baltimore among ourselves, as one indispensible step towards relief: and the difficulty is not a little increased by the pains taken by the Merchants to prevent such a reformation, and by the opposition arising from local views. I have been told that A[rthur] L⁴[ee] *paved the way to his election in Prince William* by *promising Dumfries* that *among other* things *he would overset the Port Bill.* Mr. Jefferson writes me that the Port Bill has been published in all the Gazettes in Europe with the highest approbation every where except in G. B.[5] It would indeed be as surprising if she should be in favor of it as it is that any among

* by concentrating our Commerce at Alexandria and Norfolk, the object of the Port-Bill[6]

ourselves should be against it. I see no possibility of engaging other nations in a rivalship with her without some such regulation of our commerce. I am Dr. Sir Yrs. Affecly,

J. MADISON JR.

RC (DLC). Cover missing. Docketed by JM. Italicized words, unless otherwise noted, are those encoded by JM using the code he sent Monroe on 14 Apr. 1785.

¹ JM first wrote, "I own the Bill appears to me to justify this strong language," then altered it.

² On 5 Nov. 1784 a petition from Thomas Green in behalf of the people of Natchez was presented to the Georgia council and referred to the state assembly. The legislature took action on it in Jan. 1785, and on 3 Feb. 1785 the bill for laying out a district to be called Bourbon County was enacted. Instructions for the persons appointed justices of Bourbon County were drawn up and oaths administered to the four justices present on 8 Feb.: Thomas Green, Nicholas Long, William Davenport, and Nathaniel Christmas. Although other justices were named, these four were the only ones who took part in the negotiations with Spanish officials and seemed to have regarded themselves as special envoys. Green and Davenport went to Natchez via the Ohio and the Mississippi and must have been the two commissioners about whom JM had heard. They arrived at Natchez in June; Long and Christmas, who traveled through Indian country, arrived in Aug. They had been instructed to avoid all circumstances which might lead to conflict with Spain, to exercise their powers only in territory which Spain did not claim, or which Spain relinquished willingly to the Georgia commissioners. However, Green upon his arrival in Natchez exceeded his authority, violated his pacific instructions and demanded surrender of the district by the Spanish commander, and made threats when he was refused. Rumors spread that the commissioners were intending to use force and that George Rogers Clark was to lead an army of 2,500 Kentuckians to rout the Spaniards. Finally Gov. Miró upon orders from Capt.-General Gálvez, viceroy of New Spain, expelled the commissioners. Meanwhile Gardoqui had arrived in New York and protested to Congress the Georgians' behavior. The affair ended with Congress giving satisfaction to Gardoqui and discomfiture to the Georgians (Edmund C. Burnett, ed., "Papers relating to Bourbon County, Georgia, 1785–1786, I," *AHR*, XV [Oct. 1909], 68–69, 71–72; Arthur P. Whitaker, *The Spanish-American Frontier, 1783–1795: The Westward Movement and the Spanish Retreat in the Mississippi Valley* [Boston, 1927], pp. 55–57). A state negotiating independently with a foreign power over territorial jurisdiction was an abrogation of the Articles of Confederation, an affront to Congress, and an encroachment upon territory over which Congress had jurisdiction—all abhorrent to JM.

³ The "commercial discontents of Boston" were rumored in Virginia but had no basis in fact. Edmund Pendleton in Caroline County told of a spreading rumor that Bostonians had fired on three British ships and sunk them after their masters ignored a warning to clear the harbor (Mays, *Papers of Edmund Pendleton*, II, 482). Richard Henry Lee received Pendleton's letter in which the rumor was repeated and set the record aright. "You have been misinformed with respect to the violent proceedings at Boston," Lee wrote on 10 Oct. 1785, in a letter which Burnett thought might have been addressed to JM (*Letters*, VIII, 231 and n. 2). As Lee pointed out, both Massachusetts and New Hampshire had passed navigation acts that discriminated against foreign vessels.

⁴ Lee never fulfilled his promise, since he was removed from his seat in the House for holding "a lucrative office under Congress" (*JHDV*, Oct. 1785, pp. 16–17).

⁵ See Jefferson to JM, 11 Nov. 1784.
⁶ It appears that JM placed the asterisk by Philadelphia when he reviewed this some years later. His handwriting for the explanatory note is also of a later date.

From Joseph Jones

RICHMOND 23d. June 1785.

Dr SIR.

Mr. Beckley has at length furnished me with a copy of the resolution you lately requested might be sent to you.¹ I confide it to the care of Mr. Maury of Fredericksburg in hopes it will get safe and soon to your hands. Mr. Blair² tells me a Copy of this resolution has been transmitted to the State of Maryland but knows nothing further of the matter—perhaps the Clerk or Speaker sent one to Mr. Mason.³ It wod. seem necessary something shod. be done in it previous to the meeting of the Assembly. My determination is to be in King George by the 8th. or 10th. next month where I shall stay a few days before I set out on my trip to Berkeley. I shod. be glad to hear from you and if you mean to leave orange wch. way you bend your course. Yr. friend & Servt

JOS: JONES.

RC (DLC). Cover missing. Docketed by JM.

¹ The resolution JM sought probably was the one concerning a meeting of an interstate commission to discuss the navigation of the Potomac and related problems. See Resolutions Appointing Virginia Members of a Potomac River Commission, 28 June 1784.
² Archibald Blair, clerk of the Council of State.
³ JM did not know that George Mason and Alexander Henderson had already met with the Maryland commissioners in March 1785 until informed by Jones of the Mount Vernon conference. See Jones to JM, 12 June 1785; Mason to JM, 9 Aug. 1785.

From William Grayson

NEW YORK June 27th. 1785.

DEAR SIR.

I have recieved your favor of the 29. May acknowledging the receipt of my first letter, though making no mention of the last, which I presume has not yet come to hand.¹ Since the date thereof the affair of the treaty with the Western Indians which was decided on the 18th. March last, has been opened again & very much canvassed; the result however is that the treaty is to be held; & for the double purpose of procuring peace and for extinguishing the rights of the Indians to the territory lying between the Great Miami & the Missisippi.[2]

Accounts from Col. Harmer Commandr. at fort Mcintosh, mention that the emigration to the Country already purchased from the Indians is very considerable; that at the mouth of the Scioto there are about 500 Settlers, & at the mouth of the Miami & other parts about 1500. That he has agreable to orders dispossess'd all those who were convenient to him. Congress have directed him to move his garrison to such a point as shall be most convenient for removing all the intruders. Should his force be inadequate to the business, it is expected the troops which go down with the Commer. will be sufficient to make a general sweep.[3]

The requisition for the current year is still before Congress, and there are considerable disagreemen[t]s respecting it; it is very certain public credit ought to be supported by every nation who wishes to exist; but it is also as certain that requisitions will not support credit unless there are payments consequential thereon.

The requisition for 1784 has been illy complied with. Some of the States have not done anything & the remittances of most of them to the Continental treasury (except Virginia) has been inconsiderable.

It is therefore no mystery why those who pay least should be most anxious for new requisitions. The delegation of our State are desirous of a requisition on terms not ruinous to [i]t and despairing for the present to accomplish an exaction of past delinquencies wish only to have it so modified as that the Interest on such portions of the £750,000 (as are Continental) which our Assembly has liquidated shall be considered among the facilities as fast as they are audited & past by the Continental Commes. They also wish the expenditures of Cash or certain parts thereof annually may be admitted in the hard money portion of Virginia as paymt. pro tento.

Congress after several unsuccessful efforts have at length elected Governor Livingston for the Hague.[4]

Mr. Gardoqui chargè des affaires Plenipotentiary from the Court of Spain is at length arrived at this place; but I believe very few have seen him I understand he has been bred to the business of a Mercht. & is an agreable man; he has resided some short time in Philada. & the people from thence represent him in a favorable light.

The Commrs. appointed to make commercial treaties, have made no great progress therein; which is rather agreable to Congress than other-wise, as they begin to dislike the idea of granting the right of the most favored nation to powers whose commerce is of so little importance as not to promise any essential advantage to the U. S. The Pope without a treaty has opened Civita Vecchia, & Ancona for the commerce of America. In the same manner Leghorn & Messina are made free for us by the respective sovereigns.[5] The treaties with the Barbary States are in train, & I hope will be completed in the course of the summer, though the expence will be considerable.[6] The birth of the Duke of Normandy has been announced in due form.[7] There is no certain in-telligence respecting the Emperor & the Dutch. I remain with great sincerity Yr. Affect. frd. & Most Obed sert.

WILLM. GRAYSON

RC (DLC). Cover missing. Docketed by JM.

[1] Grayson's letters, dated 1 May 1785 and 28 May 1785, reached JM safely. JM's 29 May letter has not been found.

[2] The 18 Mar. discussion of Indian affairs centered on a proposed treaty confer-ence at Vincennes, to be scheduled for June 1785 (JCC, XXVIII, 172–73, 178–80). The various treaty negotiations were undertaken to implement the act of 15 Oct. 1783. Congress had few powers, but it was authorized to negotiate and "extinguish the Indian claims" on lands within the Northwest Territory (Walter H. Mohr, *Federal Indian Relations, 1774–1788* [Philadelphia, 1933], pp. 102–3).

[3] On 1 June 1785, Grayson was appointed to the committee appointed to consider the letter of Col. Josiah Harmar on squatters on the right bank of the Ohio. The committee report on 21 June reinforced Harmar's orders to evict "intruders from the lands of the U. S." (JCC, XXVIII, 415 n., 472).

[4] The replacement of John Adams as minister to the United Netherlands proved a difficult task for Congress. William Livingston was nominated but refused the appointment. Then John Rutledge was unanimously elected on 5 July, but he also declined the post. Frustrated, Congress did not resume its discussion until 28 Mar. 1786, when the matter again went unsolved (JCC, XXVIII, 122 and passim; XXX, 140 n., 267 n.).

[5] "Civita Vecchia" is the seaport city of Vecchiano. The pope's trade concessions were announced by his nuncio in a letter to the American Commissioners, 15 Dec. 1784 (Boyd, *Papers of Jefferson*, VII, 575–76). The Commissioners to negotiate Treaties of Amity and Commerce, including those for the duchy of Tuscany, re-ceived instructions dated 16 May 1784 from Charles Thomson (ibid., VII, 262–63). Messina, in the duchy of Naples, was made a free port to Americans through the letter of De Pio to the American Commissioners, 22 Jan. 1785 (ibid., VII, 612–14).

[6] The harassment of American shipping by the Algerine pirates was a growing concern that led to some wishful thinking by Virginians. A Richmond newspaper reported a Philadelphian "had seen a letter from Mr. Jefferson (but not officially) saying, that the Americans need be under no apprehension in future, with regard to the Barbary corsairs, as the Dey has given strict orders not to molest any of our vessels" (*Va. Gazette*, 25 June 1785).

[7] The French dauphin was born on 27 Mar. 1785. For a description of the French celebration, see C. F. Adams, ed., *Memoirs of John Quincy Adams* (12 vols.; Phila-delphia, 1874–77), I, 15–19.

Copy of a Protestant Episcopal Church Petition to the General Assembly of Virginia

EDITORIAL NOTE

Whether JM wrote the petition calling for repeal of the act incorporating the Protestant Episcopal church in Virginia or merely copied the work of another for his own personal use is a matter of speculation, with the latter circumstance appearing the most likely one. Hunt and Brant assumed that JM wrote the petition, although the former assigned a 1786 date to the document despite the internal evidence that it was produced in the fall of 1785 (Madison, *Writings* [Hunt ed.], II, 212–14). Brant attributed the petition to JM but commented upon the fact it was "couched in more violent language than he [JM] was accustomed to use" (*Madison*, II, 349, 457 n. 14). The use of "Because" as a heading for each grievance is in keeping with JM's style in his Memorial and Remonstrance, ca. 20 June 1785. However, no petition bearing the same wording is among the preserved petitions of the October 1785 session of the General Assembly (Vi), and JM's own notation of "(Copy)" makes it probable the petition was filed away, for possible use if needed. JM was not anxious to become notorious for his hostility toward subsidized religion, and in such circumstances he could have written the petition for the use of less articulate opponents of the act of incorporation which had passed at the October 1784 session—a measure which JM had voted for in a tactical move that in no way represented his true feelings toward the bill (JM to Jefferson, 9 Jan. 1785). Petitions from the Presbyterian and Baptist assemblies and from Chesterfield County had sought repeal of the incorporation act, but an effort to amend the law was aborted at the October 1785 session (*JHDV*, Oct. 1785, pp. 18, 42, 81, 85, 118, 141, 143). However, repeal of the incorporating act was delayed until the next session of the General Assembly (Thom, *Struggle for Religious Freedom in Virginia*, p. 82; Hening, *Statutes*, XII, 266).

[July ? 1785]

(Copy) To the honble. the Speaker & gentlemen the General Assembly of Virginia

We the subscribers members of the protestant Episcopal Church claim the attention of your honourable Body to our objections to the law passed at the last Session of Assembly[1] for incorporating the protestant Episcopal Church; and we remonstrate against the said law—

Because the law admits the power of the Legislative Body to interfere in matters of Religion which we think is not included in their jurisdiction.

Because the law was passed on the petition of some of the Clergy of the Protestant Episcopal Church without any application from the other members of that Church in whom the law is to operate, and we conceive it to be highly improper that the Legislature should regard as the sense of the whole Church the opinion of a few interested members who were in most instances originally imposed on the people without their consent & who were not authorised by even the smallest part of this community to make such a proposition.

Because the law constitutes the Clergy members of a Convention who are to legislate for the laity contrary to their fundamental right of Chusing their own Legislators.

Because by that law the most obnoxious & unworthy Clergyman cannot be removed from a parish except by the determination of a body,[2] one half of whom the people have no confidence in & who will always have the same interest with the minister whose conduct they are to judge of.

Because by that law power is given to the Convention to regulate matters of faith, & the obsequious Vestries are to engage to change their opinions as often as the Convention shall alter theirs.

Because a System so absurd & servile, will drive the members of the Episcopal Church over to other Sects, where there will be more consistency & liberty.

We therefore hope that the wisdom & impartiality of the present Assembly will incline them to repeal a law so pregnant with mischief & injustice.

Ms (DLC). In JM's hand. Docketed, in an unidentified hand, "Remonstrance against Act of 1784, incorporating the Episcopal Church." Another endorsement, "Conventional Scraps," has been crossed through.

[1] The "law passed at the last Session" was approved by the House of Delegates on 16 Dec. 1784 and by the Senate on 28 Dec. 1784. Thus this petition had to be framed during 1785, not 1786 as Hunt asserted (Madison, *Writings* [Hunt ed.], II, 212). Passage of the incorporating act was the "peaking out" of power for the legislative faction that favored close ties between the church and state (Hening, *Statutes*, XI, 532–37).

[2] As JM observed shortly after the incorporating bill passed, the law was so poorly worded that vestries lost their "uncontrouled right of electing Clergymen" although the legislators took "the contrary for granted throughout the whole progress of it" (JM to Jefferson, 9 Jan. 1785). Opposition to the incorporating bill was centered on this overturning of a traditional feature of the Episcopal church in Virginia (Brydon, *Virginia's Mother Church and . . . Political Conditions*, II, 353). What made the issue so vital was the fact that in 1776 the Episcopal church in Virginia had ninety-five parishes served by ninety-one clergymen, but by 1785 only seventy-two parishes still existed and thirty-four of these had no minister. Thus the filling of thirty-eight pulpits was a matter of immediate concern to the laymen (Rev. T. G. Dashiell, "History of the Church in Virginia from 1785 to the Death of Bishop Meade," *Addresses and Historical Papers . . . of the Protestant*

Episcopal Church in the Diocese of Virginia [New York, 1885], p. 62). For a view contrary to JM's see John Page's letter to Jefferson of 23 Aug. 1785, in which he declared that "Nothing but a general Assessment can prevent the State from being divided between immorality, and Enthusiastic Bigottry" (Boyd, *Papers of Jefferson*, VIII, 428).

To Richard Henry Lee

ORANGE July 7th. 1785.

DEAR SIR

Your favor of the 30th. of May came to hand yesterday only, having lain some time in Fredg. and finally reached Orange via Albemarle. I agree with you perfectly in thinking it the interest of this Country to embrace the first decent opportunity of parting with Kentucky, and to refuse firmly to part with any more of our Western settlements.[1] It seems necessary however that this first instance of a voluntary dismemberment of a State should be conducted in such a manner as to form a salutary precedent. As it will indirectly affect the whole Confederacy, Congress ought clearly to be made a party to it, either immediately, or by a proviso that the Partition-act shall not be enforced untill the actual admission of the new State into the Union. No interval whatever should be suffered between the release of our hold on that Country, and its taking on itself the obligations of a member of the federal Body. Should it be made a separate State without this precaution, it might be tempted to remain so as well with respect to the U. S. as to Virginia, by two considerations; 1. the evasion of its share of the Common debt, 2 the allurement which an exemption from taxes would prove to Citizens of States groaning under them. It is very possible that such a Course might in the end be found disadvantageous, but the charms of ambition & present interest, too often prevail against the remonstrances of sound policy. May we not also with justice insist that a reasonable Portion of the particular debt of Virginia sd. be assumed by the district which is to set up for itself?

The arrival of Mr. Guardoque will turn out I hope an auspicious step towards conciliating explanations & overtures on the subject of the Mississippi. Besides the general motives for accelerating an adjustment of this affair, the prodigious effect it would have on the sale of the back lands, renders it of peculiar importance. The same consideration presses for such arrangements with Great Britain as will give us speedy possession of the Western posts. As to the commercial arrangements which we wish from her, I see no room for sanguine expectations.[2] What could she get from us by yielding to our demands which she does not now enjoy? I can not speak with certainty as to other States, but it is apparent that the trade of this was never more compleatly monopolized when it was under the direction of her own laws than it is at this moment. Our present situation therefore verifies the doctrine held out in Deane's intercepted letters.[3] We have lost by the Revolution our trade with the West Indies, the only one which yielded us a favorable balance, without having gained new channels to compensate it.[4] What makes the British Monopoly too the more mortifying is the abuse they make of it. Not only the private planters who have resumed the practice of shipping their own Tobo. but many of our Merchants, particularly the natives of the Country who have no connections in Great Britain, have received accounts of sales which carry the most visible & shameful frauds in every article. In every point of view indeed the trade of this Country is in a deplorable Condition. A comparison of current prices here with those in the Northern States, either at this time or at any time since the peace, will shew that the loss direct on our produce & indirect on our imports, is not less than 50 Per Ct. Till very lately the price of our staple has been down at 32/ & 33/ on James River and 28/. on Rappahannock. During the same period the former was selling in Philada. and probably in other Northern ports at 44/. of our Currency & the latter in proportion; though it is clear that Tobo. in the Northern ports is intrinsically worth less than in ours; being burdened with the expence of freight from the latter to the former, & remaining at the same distance from its ultimate market. The price of Merchandize here is at least as much above as Tobo. is below the Northern Standard.

We have had from the beginning of June to the present time, very hot and very wet weather. The effect of it on upland Corn has been favorable, but much the reverse on that in the flats. It has given full opportunity to the planters to pitch their crops of Tobo. but tho' many of them have repeated this operation several times, the noxious insects still threaten to abridge the prospect.[5] Should their depredations subside, the extraordinary efforts of the Country for a crop must produce a great one. Our Wheat in this part of the Country is very indifferent. How it may be in others I cannot say, but believe the complaints are pretty general. With the highest esteem & regard I remain Dear Sir, Your Obedient & very Hble. Servt.

J. MADISON JR.

RC (ViU); FC (DLC). Lee docketed the copy he received and later drafted his letter of 11 Aug. 1785 on the bottom and verso of the second page. JM crossed through several phrases and made minor changes in the wording when he copied from his draft.

[1] In the draft, "to part with any more of our settlements beyond the Allegheny."

[2] In the draft, "I own my expectations are far from being sanguine."

[3] Former commissioner Silas Deane wrote to friends in America from a Parisian base that reunion with England was essential for the commerce of the new nation and also counseled against any reliance on France as a mercantile substitute for Great Britain. Deane's indiscretions were intercepted by British vessels and found their way into Rivington's *New-York Royal Gazette* during 1781 and 1782 (Charles Isham, "Biographical Notice of Silas Deane," *New-York Historical Society Collections*, XIX [1886], xiii).

[4] In the draft, "The revolution has robbed us of our trade with the West Indies." Undoubtedly Americans were disillusioned with the reaction of French merchants to proposals for a vigorous trade between the two former allies to replace the robust commerce between the mainland and the British West Indian colonies. The Farmers-General tobacco monopoly in France also curtailed profits for Virginia planters (F. L. Nussbaum, "American Tobacco and French Politics," *Political Science Quarterly*, XL [1925], 498–99; Bingham Duncan, "Franco-American Tobacco Diplomacy, 1784–1860," *Maryland Historical Magazine*, LI [1956], 273–301). American distress over the lost commerce with the so-called Sugar Islands was summed up in John Adams's plaintive remark that the British West Indies "can neither do without us, nor we without them" (Adams, *Works of John Adams*, VIII, 74).

[5] In the draft, "the grasshoppers & other noxious insects have been so uncommonly troublesome that in many places the prospect is likely to be much abridged."

From George Nicholas

July 7th. 1785.

DEAR SIR,

I expected to have done myself the pleasure of calling on you from the last Orange court but was disappointed in going there. I received the remonstrance[1] and had it copied for I found that any change in it must be for the worse. One hundred and fifty of our most respectable freeholders signed it in a day. I have sent copies to the counties that I mentioned in my last.[2] I am with regard and esteem Dr. Sir Yr. Obdt.

G. NICHOLAS

RC (DLC). Cover missing. Docketed by JM.

[1] In 1785, the Orange County Court met on 23 June. Thus JM's "Memorial and Remonstrance" on the General Assessment bill apparently was ready for transmittal to Nicholas then, which fixes its final preparation at sometime between 20 and 23 June.

2 Nicholas had last written JM on 22 Apr. 1785. "Memorial and Remonstrance" petitions from only six of the counties mentioned by Nicholas reached the General Assembly during the Oct. 1785 session: Albemarle, Amherst, Culpeper, Frederick, Loudoun, and Rockingham (Vi: Mss, except Rockingham, which is noted in *JHDV*, Oct. 1785, p. 6).

From James Monroe

New York July 12, 1785.

Dear Sir

I enclose a copy of the journals so far as they are printed. They contain nothing you will find respecting the requisition nor the commercial interests of the Union. The former upon the report of a committee hath been frequently before Congress of late and as often recommitted, in which state it now lies. As the principal part of the debt which in other States forms a part of the present estimate, for the payment of whose interest the requisition is in that degree made, contracted by Qr. Masters, commissaries &c. with individuals in the liquidation whereof the commissrs. of the U S. with those of each State are now engag'd was contracted in ours by State impressments and of course consider'd and provided for as a State debt, we thought it our duty to propose "that in all cases wherein claims of individuals by payment of the principal or other satisfactory compensation have been transfer'd to the States of which they are citizens, the sd. States shall be consider'd as standing in the place of the individuals and entitled to all the benefits which wod. otherwise have belong'd to them." Two thirds of the amt. requir'd will be necessary to discharge the interest upon the domestic debt, & this may be so modified in the collection as to admit certificates of interest in discount upon the liquidated debt. Our object therefore was to extend this facility to the State to obtain for her a discount of so much as she paid to her citizens of those debts due them by the U States, and thereby prevent the payment of double her proportion, for the discharge of similar debts within other states while she was exhausted by making it to her own citizens. To complete the facility to the States whose accts. were unliquidated, we also propos'd, "that for that reason and as each State suppos'd she had advancd her fœderal quota and requisitions upon a contrary principle, untill they shod. be liquidated, might be injurious to those with whom it shod. be the case, so far as they applied to the domestic debt that the requ[i]sitions might be so modified in their collection as that the States might pay in their quotas in

317

either the principal or interest of such accts. as shod. be liquidated." We presum'd the U States wod. be benefited by a State's availing itself of this facility, as it must always be the interest of the debtor to diminish the principal in preference to the interest of a debt where the engagment is not to pay interest upon interest. Lastly we propos'd "that   dolrs. shod. be deducted out of the requisition in payment of that amt. of the advances of the State for the expedition to the Kaskaskias &ca." These propositions were not recd. in the most favorable manner.[1] As to the first they said "that the assumption on the part of the State & payment to its own citizens of the debts due by the U S. were voluntary acts, that such advances therefore must be consider'd as State-advances and to be taken into consideration upon the final liquidation of State accts. when the advances of all the States and their respective quotas were ascertain'd and apportion'd. That these advances also were in discharge of specific requisitions to which the State had given its assent in a motion by her delegates when the detachment of Wayne was marching southwds." We answer'd that the failure in specific requisitions (and we would grant we had absolutely fail'd which however was not the case) was like failures in all other requisitions, that if we paid less in that than other States we had exceeded in equal degree in other instances, that these payments or failures under requisitions stood on the same ground & were to be settled on the same principles: that the resolution respecting Wayne was confin'd only to the troops under his command and untill he shod. reach the Marquis of Fayatte, or if extended to all the regular troops then in the State or during the campaign it had no connection with the Militia and State impressments for militia & regular troops; or if extended to the whole in either instance and untill the payment of the whole requisition, for the extra-advance there shod. be some consideration. In opposition to the 2d. proposition it was urg'd "that here is the estimate of the publick debt for the payment of whose interest a requisition is to be made; how can the interest be paid upon the estimate when the money necessary for it is to be applied to the discharge of the principal in some of the States." Upon the 3d. proposition we had previously taken the sense of Congress but we thought proper to bring it again to their view that we might know what they intended doing in it. They were all three committed after several days debate & the opinion of the committee being agnst them after a few days obtain a discharge. The report of the requisition will probably be brought in to day. All the States eastwd. of Pensyla. inclusive are interested in keeping up the present estimate and regulating the collection of the sums call'd for so as to pay the interest of it and of it alone. In vain it is argued that it is not founded on the true state of the domestic debt and therefore improper & oppressive. That untill the liquidation takes place it shod. be accomodated as much as possible to the convenience of the States. That it cannot be expected whilst some of the States fail altogether & present at the same time an assylum to those who fly from the duties of govt. that others will continue to harrass their citizens in making payments. I intended saying something upon the commercl. subject but have not time. Don Diego de Gardoqui hath arriv'd & been presented to Congress. He presented a letter of credence from the King & has full powers to treat upon the subject of the disputed boundary &ca yet he is stil'd Encargado de negotios, in consequence of the character of our mnstr. at Madrid. We take his stile from his letter of credence & call him Encargado de negotios[2]—He is a polite & sensible man. I have inquir'd into the report of the commissrs. of Georgia to treat with those of Spn. & find it hath arose from the application of a vain old man to the Georgia Legislature who recd. for answer "they wod. attend to it in good time" returning home under an impression his affrs. werc in a good way & gave those he conferr'd with reason to believe he was authoriz'd to treat. This the Delegates of that State suppose to be the case.[3] Yr. several letters to Mr. Jefferson I have regularly fo[r]warded in the packets as I have recd them. I am dear Sir very respectfully yr. fnd. & servt.

JAS: MONROE

P. S. What say you to a trip to the Indian Treaty to be held on the Ohio—sometime in August or Sepr. I have thoughts of it & shod. be happy in your company.[4] We might meet somewhere on the way—or perhaps you have thoughts of a trip this way—packets sail every week eastwd. to R. Islan[d] & Boston—a stage is also establish'd to lake George & the communication over lake Champlain to Montreal and Quebec easy & expeditious. Agreeable company may be found either way.

RC (DLC). Cover and enclosure missing.

[1] Monroe's motion (covering the credit to states for impressments, unsettled state accounts, and reimbursement to Virginia for the expenses of the Illinois country campaigns) was offered and debated on 22 June (JCC, XXVIII, 473–74). The practice in Virginia had been to grant individuals holding impressment vouchers a state certificate and then charge the U. S. for the sum involved, i.e., a farmer supplying the army with beef traded his quartermaster's receipt for a state bond, then the amount of the bond was to be paid Virginia by the national treasury. "Such procedure was shocking to the commissioners and to the board of treasury, but Virginia paid no attention" (Jensen, The New Nation, p. 378). Monroe brought the

319

matter before Congress again on 18 July and the issue was defeated by sectional vote—with all the northern and middle states aligned against four southern delegations (*JCC*, XXIX, 547–48).

2 Gardoqui arrived at Philadelphia 20 May 1785, whereupon he sent a letter of introduction to the President of Congress and covering letter to the Secretary of State John Jay announcing his arrival and commission as *encargado de negocios* (chargé d'affaires). On 2 July Gardoqui was formally received by Congress (*Diplomatic Correspondence of the U.S.* [1855 ed.], III, 142–43, 150–52). The orders given to Gardoqui were modeled after Floridablanca's Instruction of 29 July 1784, which allowed for the cession of St. Augustine and the modification of the boundary in the Mississippi Valley but insisted upon the exclusive right of navigation on the Mississippi. Most-favored-nation treatment was to be offered to the U. S. in Spain and the Canaries, but not in the Spanish colonies (Whitaker, *Spanish-American Frontier*, pp. 69–71).

3 The "vain old man" was Thomas Green of Natchez, who had sought the creation of Bourbon County, Georgia, in western territory also claimed by Spain. Green's summary conduct backfired when the Spanish minister protested Georgia's implicit territorial claims (JM to Monroe, 21 June 1785; Coleman, *The American Revolution in Georgia, 1763–1789*, pp. 261–64).

4 Monroe set out from New York on 25 Aug. to see the western country. He was to join Gen. Butler, one of the Indian commissioners, at Carlisle and from there they proceeded to the Ohio Valley rendezvous where the Indian treaty was to take place. By resolutions of 18 Mar., 15 June, and 29 June, Congress had directed the Indian commissioners to hold a treaty with the Indians on the western banks of the Ohio, at the rapids, or at the mouth of the Great Miami. The negotiations were to secure peace for the frontier settlements, to obtain a cession of lands as liberal and extensive as possible, and to establish a boundary line between the U. S. and the western Indian tribes. On 25 Oct. Commissioners Clark and Butler selected the mouth of the Miami as the site of the treaty, but the Indians, agitated by the British, were hesitant and suspicious (Monroe to JM, 26 Dec. 1785). Not until 31 Jan. 1786 was a treaty signed between the commissioners (Clark, Butler, and Parsons) and the Shawnees. Because of the delay and danger from the Indians, Monroe curtailed his western journey and left the commissioners at Limestone. He returned through the Kentucky settlements and the wilderness to Richmond and back to New York where he arrived 18 Dec. (Ammon, *James Monroe*, pp. 52–53; Monroe to Jefferson, 25 Aug. 1785, Boyd, *Papers of Jefferson*, VIII, 441–42; *JCC*, XXVIII, 172–73, 460–62, 487; Mohr, *Federal Indian Relations*, pp. 114–15; and Monroe to Jefferson, 19 Jan. 1786, Boyd, *Papers of Jefferson*, IX, 186–87).

From Caleb Wallace

LINCOLN COUNTY, July 12. 1785.

DEAR SIR,

Having accommodated my Family in this remote quarter of the Country, I wish to renew a correspondence which was formerly pleasing to me and I trust no[t] disagreeable to you. Since I saw you last I have removed twice, first from Charlotte to Botetourt and then from there to Kentucky; this, with some vissisitudes of fortune & health have occasioned me to neglect for a while some of the acquaintances of my youth who I shall always remember with affection. As you are yet a Stranger to the parental Tyes, I hardly know how to tell you of two fine Sons & a Daughter that are the great amusements of my leisure as well as the Objects of my most serious Cares; therefore I shall only remind you at present of the Taunts to which old Bachelors are justly exposed, and from which the best services to the public in other respects will not skreen you much longer. But I shall not say more, as I have had an intimation that you are like to be in a more honourable State e'er long. You may perhaps expect from me some interesting accounts of this Western World which I fear I shall not be able to give you. The fertility of the Soil makes it a good poor man's Country, but without peace with the Indians and an Opportunity of exporting our produce it cannot flourish. When we shall enjoy these advantages God only knows, for at present the prospects are not very flattering. A great many Horses have been lately taken and several People killed on our out Skirts, probably by runagade Indians with the Connivance if not the approbation of the Tribes to which they belong. They seem to be particularly attentive to the Passage through the Wilderness as afording them the easiest Opportunities of getting plunder. As to Trade, we have some hopes that Congress to enhance the value of the Lands on the N W side of the Ohio will endeavour to procure the quiet navigation of the Mississippi. Your Opportunities will enable you to inform me what is like to be effected in this Way. We are as harmonious amongst ourselves as can be expected of a mixture of People from various States and of various Sentiments and Manners not yet assimilated. In point of Morals, the bulk of the inhabitants are far superior to what I expected to find in any new settled Country. We have not had a single instance of Murder, and but one Criminal for Felony of any kind has yet been before the Supreme Court. I wish I could say as much to vindicate the Character of our Land-Jobbers. This Business has been attended with much villiany in other Parts. Here it is reduced to a System, and to take the advantage of the Ignorance or of the Poverty of a neighbour is almost grown into reputation; which must multiply litigation and produce aversions that will not quickly subside. Some Acts of Assembly for giving further time &c have had a happy tendency to check their designs; but the Laws for opening the Land Office and for settling and adjusting the Titles of Claimers to unpatented Lands (which passed before they were sufficiently matured and therefore liable to the imputation of defect and inconsistency) have opened a Door for this kind of speculation which cannot now be effectually shut.[1] If the Land Business was conducted with more candour & integrity the expence and attention that are requisite must for a while greatly retard all other improvements, which to me is a very mortifying consideration. Having this view of our circumstances you may be surprised to hear that a late Convention have unanimously agreed to petition the Assembly to have this District established into a State.[2] I cannot explain the prevailing Sentiments better, than by telling you We concieve the People of this District do not at present enjoy a greater portion of Liberty than an American Colony might have done a few Years ago had she been allowed a Representation in the British Parliament. We not only fear what may be done, but some Acts have already passed that are retrospective and partial in their operation; not designed to check an unforeseen evil, but for the express purpose of levying Taxes which (if they cannot be avoided) will be intolerably oppressive to this Quarter. The Act for enforcing the General Tax upon Persons & Property are not complained of because it is accounted equitable and necessary. This we must pay as far as we are able whether we remain with the old State or become a new one. The Civil List will be the only additional Expence, a considerable part of which we are now paying and the balance for a while will be more than saved out of the Taxes first alluded to. Indeed we do not consider a Tax for the Support of Government as very burthensome where the Money will presently circulate back to them that pay it; whereas were our Cash like the Widows Cruise of Oil, it would presently be drained off to the Eastern part of the State if the Connexion continues.[3] Until lately I have myself thought it would be more eligible to continue as we are a while longer; but finding that our Situation is too remote to enjoy the advantages of Government with Virginia in any tolerable degree, I have fallen in with the opinion that it is better to part in peace than to remain together in a State of Jealousy and Discontent. My greatest doubt now is that we shall lack wisdom and virtue to govern ourselves. I concieve that our Form of Government should be simple as most suitable to our infant Condition; but I also wish it to be so constructed as to admit of all the Improvements that may be needed in the most advanced periods of maturity. Some have proposed that the three Departments should at present be composed of as small numbers as can be safely trusted; that instead of a Senate, the Executive and Judiciary should sit as Advisers to the Legislative; and with the addition of two or three Commissioners from the Assembly to determine all Appeals and Impeachments. On this Subject

I confess myself a Novice, and apprehend we have few among us who are adepts in the Science of Government. For the Sake of Posterity I would willingly engage in the Study to the utmost of my ability; but I find myself constrained by the Duties of my Office to give unremitted attention to acquire that knowledge of the Law which I unhappily neglected in my Youth. For some Years past I have admired Jurisprudence as one of the most useful branches of Philosophy, and as I had Opportunity directed my reading in this Channel, but never considered the practical part of Law as a matter worthy of notice until it became my duty; which for a while will subject me to a degree of drudgery and confinement that nothing but the Necessities of the Country where I have adventured my family and possessions could induce me to undergo. Did you[r] inclination lead you into this Quarter, my prospects would brighten with regard to the management of our public Concerns. Perhaps you smile at the Idea of being politically buried in this Wilderness. As you know any event this is possible may happen.[4] Will you be so kind as to favour me with such a Form of Government as you would wish to live under when you come.[5] Providence has given you singular opportunities for maturing your judgment on the Subject, and if your leisure will permit, I know your inclination to oblige will not be wanting. Please to remember me in the most respectful manner to your worthy Parents and other Relatives. With every Sentiment of Friendship and Esteem, I am Dr Sir your most obt. Servt.

CALEB WALLACE

(turn over)

P. S. The following Questions are of importance and will probably [be] debated here when a Constitution is forming.[6]

RC (DLC). Cover addressed to JM in Orange County. Docketed by JM. The postscript was written on the outer cover.

[1] Unhappiness over the acts establishing a "Land office and for settling and adjusting the Titles . . . to unpatented Lands" was widespread, and JM had personal knowledge from his father's complaints about cloudy land titles in Kentucky. The Land Office Act of 1779 has been called "a colossal mistake" (Abernethy, *Western Lands and the American Revolution*, p. 228). Boyd indicates the flaws in the two acts (by Jefferson and Mason) resulted from changes made by the legislature which created a boon for land speculators and pettifogging lawyers (*Papers of Jefferson*, II, 134).

[2] This petition was laid before the House of Delegates on 28 Oct. 1785 and JM was selected as chairman of a special committee which recommended statehood for Kentucky (*JHDV*, Oct. 1785, pp. 10, 36, 87).

[3] "The Widows Cruise of Oil" allusion is to 1 Kings 17, where during a great drought Elijah asked a widow for bread and she replied, "I have nothing baked,

only a handful of meal in a jar, and a little oil in a cruse. . . ." Elijah assured her that God had promised them sustenance until the drought was broken. The widow believed Elijah and the "meal was not spent, neither did the cruse of oil fail. . . ."

⁴ Instead of this confusing sentence, Wallace must have meant, in colloquial terms: You may smile at the idea of being politically buried in Kentucky—but as you know, anything is possible, and stranger things have happened.

⁵ In his reply of 23 Aug. 1785, JM excused himself from offering an ideal constitution "by my Ignorance of many local circumstances" and "the want of sufficient time." Even so, JM offered enough hints on political systems to fill a seven page letter.

⁶ The questions Wallace posed were the same as those enclosed in George Muter's letter to JM, 12 Dec. 1784, except that here Wallace dropped the two queries concerning religion. JM answered Wallace's questions in his 23 Aug. 1785 reply.

From Edmund Randolph

RICHMOND July 17. 1785

MY DEAR FRIEND

By some inexplicable mystery, the inclosed letter from Mr. Jones, and my intended answer to your last epistolary favor, have still remained in my possession. Being engaged when the gentleman, who brought your friendly attention to me, I doubt whether I gave him an intelligible reply to his question, if my answer was ready.

Our apparent disobedience to the appointment of the assembly must be ascribed to the forgetfulness of our friend Henry. Genl. Washington having inquired from me the reason of our non-attendance at the time and place, marked for the conference by the government of Maryland, I immediately applied to the govr. for information, whether he had communicated the resolve of that state to the deputies. He could not recollect; but seemed anxious to avail himself of the probability of having inclosed it to you with several other public papers. Even Mason and Henderson knew nothing of the meeting; and would have been absent but for the activity and urgency of the general.¹ But I am yet disposed to believe, that the communication with Pennsylvania has been forgotten: nor can I procure satisfaction on this head.²

I dedicate to you, as the patron of the protestant Episcopal church, the inclosed journal.³ *Between friends* my experience in the last convention does not make me anxious to step forward in another. We have squeezed out a little liberality from them; but at a future day they will be harder than adament, and perhaps credulous, that they possess authority. Smith of P. Edward has waged war with the assembly, from which the act of incorporation sprang.[4] He talks judiciously, but with a temper well-roused.

I have been preparing for my journey to Frederick for some time. But my aversion to leave home, where my choicest delights, one of which is at present *incumbered,* will remain, makes me doubt of the journey. Adieu my dear Madison and believe me to be yours mo. sincerely

E. R.

RC (DLC). Cover and enclosure missing. Docketed by JM.

[1] The conference held at Mount Vernon suffered from an administrative oversight in that the instructions to notify the appointed representatives were not effectively carried out. The General Assembly resolution appointed George Mason, Alexander Henderson, Randolph, and JM. Mason claimed he learned of the appointment only by accident. The Maryland commissioners appeared in Alexandria and gathered up Mason and Henderson, both of whom lived nearby. JM and Randolph, far from the immediate scene, were uninformed of the session until after it had taken place (Rutland, *Papers of George Mason,* II, 812–14).

[2] JM wrote the resolution of 28 Dec. 1784 which invited Pennsylvania to participate in the interstate conference on "regulations touching the navigation and jurisdiction of the Potowmac" (*JHDV,* Oct. 1784, p. 91). The conference was either ignored by the Pennsylvania executive, or the careless clerk who failed to notify the Virginia commissioners also forgot to forward the invitation to Philadelphia.

[3] Randolph undoubtedly enclosed a copy of the *Journal of a Convention of the Clergy and Laity of the Protestant Episcopal Church of Virginia, Begun and Holden in the City of Richmond, Wednesday, May 18, 1785* (Richmond, 1785; Sabin 100513).

[4] John Blair Smith was president of Hampden-Sydney Academy in Prince Edward County and leading opponent of the controversial Protestant Episcopal Incorporating Act (Smith to JM, 21 June 1784; Hening, *Statutes,* XI, 532–37). Smith wrote a petition protesting the General Assessment bill which was approved by the Hanover Presbytery and sent to the General Assembly, probably on 12 Nov. 1785 (*JHDV,* Oct. 1785, p. 34). JM was critical of the Presbyterian stance, as his letter to Monroe, 12 Apr. 1785, indicated.

From John Dawson

SPRINGHILL July 20. 1785

DEAR SIR

Your goodness will excuse me, for addressing this letter to you, when you consider of what consequence it may be to me.

The General Assembly, at their Session in October last, I find, had it in contemplation to pass an Act respecting Naval Officers, by which Collectors are to be appointed to the several Districts; and altho it did not then pass for want of a sufficient number of members to make a house, I am informd that, in all probability, it will this fall.[1]

I wish to have my Name mention'd for the Collectorship of this river, & therefore have wrote to you on the occasion, well knowing of what Assistance you can be to me on the occasion, if you think proper to advocate my interest; I scarce need add, that I shall ever retain a Grateful Sense of the favour. Receive the Compliments of Mr. Jones, and accept the same from, Dear Sir, Yr. Hm: Sert

J Dawson

RC (DLC). Cover missing. Docketed by JM.

[1] A bill to amend the 1783 act "for the appointment of Naval-Officers, and ascertaining their fees" was presented at the Oct. 1784 session of the House of Delegates and although it passed three readings it apparently was never approved by the Senate (Hening, *Statutes*, XI, 258–64; *JHDV*, Oct. 1784, p. 106). JM did introduce "a bill for appointing naval officers" at the Oct. 1785 session, but it was among the many measures planned for the code revision that were not acted upon before adjournment. Dawson was elected a delegate to the General Assembly in Apr. 1786 from Spotsylvania County (Swem and Williams, *Register*, p. 25).

From George Nicholas

Sweet Springs. July 24th. [1785]

Dear Sir,

I am very unhappy to find by your letter[1] which has just now come to hand that two of mine to you have miscarried.[2] I found that no alterations could be made to the remonstrance* without injury and immediately had it copied and sent to the counties I mentioned in a former letter.[3]

One of my letters must certainly have reached you before this but for fear of accident shall desire my brother to send this on. I am with respect and esteem Dr. Sir, Yr. obdt. Servt.

G: Nicholas

RC (DLC). Cover missing. Docketed by JM and marked "Remonstrance."

[1] No letters from JM to Nicholas during 1785 have been found.

[2] The most recent surviving letters from Nicholas are dated 22 Apr. and 7 July 1785.

[3] JM placed the asterisk probably at some later time, and wrote "agst. general tax to support Christianity" at the bottom of the page.

To Edmund Randolph

MY DEAR FRIEND

Your favour of the 17th. inst: inclosing a letter from Mr. Jones and a copy of the ecclesiastical Journal, came safe to hand.[1] If I do not dislike the contents of the latter, it is because they furnish as I conceive fresh and forcible arguments against the Genl. Assessment. It may be of little consequence what tribunal is to judge of Clerical misdemesnors or how firmly the incumbent may be fastened on the parish, whilst the Vestry & people may hear & pay him or not as they like.[2] But should a legal salary be annexed to the title, this phantom of power would be substantiated into a real monster of oppression.[3] Indeed it appears to be so at present as far as the Glebes & donations extend. I had seen some prints of these proceedings before I recd. your letter, and had remarked the sprinklings of liberality to which you allude. My conjectures I believe did not err as to the quarter from which they came.

The urgency of Genl. W. in the late negociation with Maryland makes it probable I think that he will feel some chagrin at the inattention to that with Penna. which has a much nearer connection with his favorite object and was moreover suggested by himself. Shortly after the date of my last, I dropped a few lines to Col: Mason, reminding him that some report will be expected from the Commissioners by the Assembly, as well as of the real importance of the business. I have not yet recd. any answer; and begin to suspect that my letter may have miscarried. Your information leads me to doubt whether he has even been furnished with a copy of the Resolution under which he is to proceed.[4] I will write to him again and inclose one which Mr. Jones sent me.

I have a letter from the Marquis, but dated as far back as March.[5] It was accompanied with a Copy of a French Memorial to the Emperor which seems to have stifled the war in its birth; and an Extract from a late work of Mr. Neckar which has made him the idol of one party in France and the execration of the other. To avoid the trouble of transcribing, I send them as they came to me. You can peruse & return them by my brother who is the bearer of this, or by any future opportunity. The M. says he is doing all he can to forward our claim to the Mississippi; that the French Ministry understand the matter & are well disposed; but that they are apprehensive. "Spain knows not how to give up what she once has."

I had heard of the strictures on the incorporating Act, but without

being able to pick up any of the papers in which they are published.[6]
I have desired my brother to search them out if he can. Perhaps you can
refer him to the proper press & numbers.

At the instance of Col: N——l——s of A——b——le.[7] I undertook the
draught of the inclosed remonstrance agst. the Genl. Asst.*[8] Subscriptions to it are on foot I believe in sundry Counties, and will be extended
to others. My choice is that my name may not be associated with it.
I am not sure that I know precisely your ideas on this subject: But were
they more variant from mine than I take them to be, I should not be
restrained from a confidential communication.

I keep up my attention as far as I can command my time, to the
course of reading which I have of late pursued & shall continue to do so.
I am however far from being determined ever to make a professional
use of it. My wish is if possible to provide a decent & independent sub-
sistence, without encountering the difficulties which I foresee in that
line. Another of my wishes is to depend as little as possible on the labour
of slaves.[9] The difficulty of reconciling these views, has brought into
my thoughts several projects from which advantage seemed attainable.
I have in concert with a friend here, one at present on the Anvil which
we think cannot fail to yield a decent reward for our trouble. Should
we persist in it it will cost me a ride to Philada. after which it will go on
without my being ostensibly concerned. I forbear to particularize till
I can do it ore tenus. Should I take this ride, I may *possibly* continue it
into the Eastern States; Col Monroe havg given me an invitation to take
a ramble of curiosity this fall, which I have half a mind to accept, and
among other routes named this.[10] I recollect that you talked yourself of
a trip last Spring as far as Lancaster. Have you laid it aside totally? Or
will your domestic endearments forbid even the trip to Bath, from
which I promised myself the happiness of taking you by the hand in
Orange? Give my warmest respects to Mrs. R. and be assured that I
remain with sincere affection your friend

J. MADISON JR

Was the Royal assent ever given to the Act of 1769 entitled "An Act
to amend an Act, entitled an Act declaring the law concerning Extions,
& for relief of insolvent Debtors.[11]

* Copy of Remonstrance to follow this letter

RC (DLC). Cover missing. Docketed.

[1] Randolph had sent JM a copy of the printed *Journal of the Convention of the
Protestant Episcopal Church* held at Richmond in May 1785.

[2] The act incorporating the Protestant Episcopal church provided that the General Convention "shall have full power and authority, on good cause to them shewn, to remove from any parish any minister accused of unworthy behaviour, or neglecting the duties of his office" (Hening, *Statutes*, XI, 537).

[3] The bill providing state subsidies for "teachers of the Christian Religion"—popularly called the General Assessment act—had "a legal salary . . . annexed to the title" of parish ministers (Eckenrode, *Separation of Church and State in Virginia*, p. 60). The bill was published for distribution in every county and appeared in the 30 July 1785 Richmond *Va. Gazette*.

[4] JM's letter to Mason of 2 June 1785 has not been found. JM's suspicions were correct, as George Mason's letter to JM of 9 Aug. 1785 explained. The process of notifying delegates turned into a comedy of errors because of some clerical oversights.

[5] Lafayette's letter of 16 Mar. 1785.

[6] Files for the Richmond *Va. Gazette* are incomplete. The "strictures" JM mentions possibly appeared in the missing editions of 11, 18 June or 2 July.

[7] George Nicholas of Albemarle County.

[8] JM's "Memorial and Remonstrance" written in the latter part of June 1785. See also the letter from George Nicholas, 22 Apr. 1785.

[9] Brant points out that Hunt misinterpreted this comment, supposing that JM "wished to become a lawyer" to avoid dependence on slave labor (Gaillard Hunt, *Life of James Madison* [New York, 1902], p. 70; Brant, *Madison*, II, 456 n. 17).

[10] For JM's land ventures in partnership with Monroe in the Mohawk Valley, see Brant, *Madison*, II, 338–42.

[11] "An Act for the Relief of Insolvent Debtors," became English law in 1769 (*Statutes at Large* [London, 1771], X, 578–92).

From James Monroe

NEW YORK July 26. 1785.

DEAR SIR

Since my last a report proposing a change in the first paragraph of the 9th. of the articles of confideration hath been taken up & acted on two days in a committee of the whole.[1] It proposes to invest Congress with power to regulate trade externally & internally. Those in favor of it were of opinion that the exercise of this power in the hands of each State, wod. be less advantageous to its particular interests, than in those of the union, because if in the regulation of trade it was sought 1. to encourage domestic industry in any line, by a tax upon foreign, which however remote at present may hereafter be the case. 2. if to obtain reciprocity in its commercial intercourse with foreign nations, either with or without treaties. 3. if to establish a commercial interest within, in contradistinction to a foreign one, and thereby keep its councils independent of foreign influence. 4. or to raise a naval strength for the publick Safety, all these ends might be obtain'd more effectually by the exercise of the power in the hands of the Union than of each State. For unless they act in concert in every instance instead of counteracting the regulations of other powers, they will become instrumental in their hands to impede & defeat those of each other: that there was but one alternative either to act together or against each other, that the latter plan establish'd deep-rooted jealousies & enmities between them, at the same time that it wod. be unsuccessfull; greater under its operation for any length of time than they wod. have against other powers, since being more convenient & better able to frustrate each others measures, their restrictions must be more severe and pointed agnst each other than agnst other powers. That such a course tended to throw them apart & weaken the present rights of the confideracy. That their interests were nearly similar being all exporting & importing States—that it was of little consequenc[e] whether they exported the same or different materials, since the restrictions which tended to restrain exportation, wod. injure the whole, & they were all equally interested in getting their admission upon the best terms into the ports of foreign powers. That they imported nearly the same materials & of course had the same interest in that line.* On the other side it was argued 1. That it was dangerous to concentrate power since it might be turn'd to mischievous purposes; that independent of the immediate danger of intoxication in those entrusted with it, & their attempts on the govrnment, it put us more in the power of other Nations. 2. that the interests of the different parts of the Union were different from each other, & that the regulations which suited the one would not the other part. That 8. States were of a particular interest whose business it wod. be to combine to shackle & fetter the others. 3. that all attacks upon the confideration were dangerous & calculated even if they did not succeed to weaken it. These I think were the principal arguments on either side, tho' they were carried out into great extent. I think Colo. Grayson inform'd me sometime since he had transmitted to you the report otherwise I shod. now do it.[2] I wish very much your sentiments on the subject.

By the packet we are inform'd that Mr. Adams had arriv'd in London, been presented to the King & well receiv'd. The ceremonial had only taken place when his dispatches were forwarded, so that he had not proceeded to business. Mr. Gardoqui is here; Congress have authoriz'd the Secretary of foreign affrs. to treat with him upon the subject of his mission.[3] I am your friend & servant

JAS. MONROE

* That if there were different interests in every instance the restriction of every measure to 11. States the number propos'd, with the reven[ue] to each State wod. form a sufficient security.

P S. I inclose you a treatise of Mr. Mazzai in favor of the port bill in Italian.[4] I promis'd him to attempt a translation of it but really I distrust my knowledge of the language too much to attempt it provided I had leasure, which is not the case; he undertook it upon the desire of Colo. Innes for whom principally the translation is intended. By committing it to you I trust I promote his views more than I shall otherwise have it in my power to do.

RC (DLC). Cover missing. Docketed by JM, probably at a later date.

[1] Early in 1784 Congress had asked the states for the authority to regulate foreign trade for fifteen years. JM had fought unsuccessfully for Virginia's endorsement of this scheme and would lose the battle again at the Oct. 1785 Assembly session. Meanwhile, on 13 July 1785, a congressional Committee of the Whole considered Monroe's 16 Feb. report on the proposal to vest Congress with the power of regulating commerce (*JCC*, XXIX, 533). The report asked the states to amend the ninth Article of Confederation "If they wish to cement the Union." But again, factions arose and nothing came of the report except increased tension and frustration among the national-minded public men—particularly JM and Monroe (Burnett, *The Continental Congress*, pp. 634–36).

[2] See Grayson to JM, 1 May 1785.

[3] On 20 July 1785 Congress passed a resolution empowering Jay to treat with Gardoqui concerning the boundaries between the U. S. and Spanish territories under the condition that Jay communicate to Congress all propositions made relative to any compact before a final agreement. On the following day, Congress commissioned Jay to proceed in his negotiations with Gardoqui (*Diplomatic Correspondence of the U. S.* [1855 ed.], III, 154–56).

[4] The enclosure is missing. See Mazzei to JM, 13 June 1785.

To James Monroe

ORANGE July 28th. 1785

DEAR SIR

I received yesterday your favour of the 12th. inst. The date of the preceding one was early in May. From this interval and your not acknowledging some of my letters I suspect that our correspondence suffers from some fault in the post office. This has certainly been the case with letters between Col. Grayson and myself. The part of your letter which has engaged most of my attention is the postscript which invites me to a ramble this fall. I have long had it in contemplation, to seize occasions as they may arise, of traversing the Atlantic States as well as of taking a taste of the Western curiosities. A visit to the Eastern States which I have never seen formed the first article in my plan, and I had allotted to it the season which I otherwise employed last year.

A trip in to Canada would also be agreeable. With these prepossessions, you may well suppose, I read your invitation with a sufficient disposition to accept it. There are several considerations however which oblige me to hesitate. My resources do not authorize me to disregard that of the expence,[1] though this shall never be a decisive objection, but when it is an essential one: the possibility of my being called on to attend a public duty which has been imposed on me[2]—the inconveniency of sparing so much time. To these general objections particular ones occur. The time at which the Western treaty will actually be held must be extremely uncertain; great delays ought to be presupposed as happened in the last one at Fort Stanwix,[3] and a return might be obstructed by the lowness of the waters, by the want of boats at our command, or by the necessity of travelling back thro' the Wilderness via Kentucky; these circumstances compared with the time at which my attendance will be due at Richmond, seem to forbid my acceding to your first proposition. The second, to wit, a ramble towards Montreal & Quebec, is objectionable also on account of the time it would require; not to mention that the present may not be the crisis at which a Citizen of the U. States would travel with most satisfaction through that country. The Eastern ramble which is the third you suggest, has also its difficulties, though they are the least insurmountable. In the first place, your expressions leave me in doubt whether it would be agreeable to yourself or not; in the next, I should consider it as indispensable to go by land, and not by water from New York. The latter mode would not answer the purpose of a traveller; and I am not sure that the former is attainable without carrying horses from Virginia: and in the last place, it is possible as observed above, that I may be called by matters of a public nature from such a project of pleasure. Notwithstanding these difficulties, I will make some eventual arrangements, suspending a positive determination till I hear again from you, which I hope will be as early as an answer can come by the post. At all events it is not unlikely that I may be obliged to ride as far as Philada. where I should be very happy if we could meet in case your final plans should make it convenient. Besides a public undertaking which may *possibly* require such a ride, I have in conjunction with a friend here a project on the anvil, which may furnish a motive of interest. I am Dear Sir Yr. affectionate friend

J. MADISON JR.

I thank you particularly for the Journals of Congress.

RC (DLC). Cover addressed by JM. Docketed by JM at a later time. Misdated "June 28" by JM in his calendar of "Letters J. M. [to] Mr. Monroe."

[1] JM was without capital and dependent upon income from Montpelier during this period (Ketcham, *James Madison*, p. 148; JM to Jefferson, 27 Apr. 1785).

[2] JM may have thought that he would be called upon to confer with interstate commissioners at a conference on Potomac navigation. Prompted by Washington, the General Assembly passed a resolution (introduced by JM on 28 Dec. 1784) that authorized JM and other Virginia commissioners to meet with Maryland delegates and those who might be commissioned by Pennsylvania to discuss mutual matters of navigation and jurisdiction. Apparently Governor Henry had forgotten to communicate to Pennsylvania the invitation to meet with the other commissioners, as well as having failed to relate the time and place designated by Maryland to the Virginia commissioners. JM may have thought a belated meeting likely to occur once Randolph had prodded Henry's memory (*JHDV*, Oct. 1784, p. 91; Edmund Randolph to JM, 17 July 1785).

[3] See JM to Jefferson, 11 Oct. 1784.

To James Monroe

ORANGE Aug: 7th. 1785

DEAR SIR

I received the day before yesterday your favour of the 26th July. I had previously recd. the Report on the proposed change of the 9th. art: of the Confederation, transmitted by Col: Grayson, and in my answer to him offered such ideas on the subject as then occurred. I still think the probability of success or failure ought to weigh much with Congress in every recommendation to the States; of which probability Congress, in whom information from every State centers, can alone properly judge. Viewing in the abstract the question whether the power of regulating trade, to a certain degree at least, ought to be vested in Congress, it appears to me not to admit of a doubt, but that it should be decided in the affirmative. If it be necessary to regulate trade at all, it surely is necessary to lodge the power, where trade can be regulated with effect, and experience has confirmed what reason foresaw, that it can never be so regulated by the States acting in their separate capacities. They can no more exercise this power separately, than they could separately carry on war, or separately form treaties of alliance or Commerce. The nature of the thing therefore proves the former power, no less than the latter, to be within the reason of the fœderal Constitution. Much indeed is it to be wished, as I conceive, that no regulations of trade, that is to say, no restrictions or imposts whatever, were necessary. A perfect freedom is the System which would be my choice.[1] But

333

before such a system will be eligible perhaps for the U. S. they must be out of debt; before it will be attainable, all other nations must concur in it. Whilst any one of these imposes on our Vessels seamen &c in their ports, clogs from which they exempt their own, we must either retort the distinction, or renounce not merely a just profit, but our only defence against the danger which may most easily beset us. Are we not at this moment under this very alternative? The policy of G. B. (to say nothing of other nations) has shut against us the channels without which our trade with her must be a losing one; and she has consequently the triumph, as we have the chagrin, of seeing accomplished her prophetic threats, that our independence, should forfeit commercial advantages for which it would not recompence us with any new channels of trade. What is to be done? Must we remain passive victims to foreign politics; or shall we exert the lawful means which our independence has put into our hands, of extorting redress? The very question would be an affront to every Citizen who loves his Country. What then are those means? Retaliating regulations of trade only. How are these to be effectuated? only by harmony in the measures of the States. How is this harmony to be obtained? only by an acquiescence of all the States in the opinion of a reasonable majority. If Congress as they are now constituted, can not be trusted with the power of digesting and enforcing this opinion, let them be otherwise constituted: let their numbers be encreased, let them be chosen oftener, and let their period of service be short[e]ned; or if any better medium than Congress can be proposed, by which the wills of the States may be concentered, let it be substituted; or lastly let no regulation of trade adopted by Congress be in force untill it shall have been ratified by a certain proportion of the States. But let us not sacrifice the end to the means: let us not rush on certain ruin in order to avoid a possible danger. I conceive it to be of great importance that the defects of the fœderal system should be amended, not only because such amendments will make it better answer the purpose for which it was instituted, but because I apprehend danger to its very existence from a continuance of defects which expose a part if not the whole of the empire to severe distress. The suffering part, even when the minor part, can not long respect a Government which is too feeble to protect their interest; But when the suffering part come to be the major part, and they despair of seeing a protecting energy given to the General Government, from what motives is their allegiance to be any longer expected. Should G. B. persist in the machinations which distress us; and seven or eight of the States be hindered by the others from obtain-

ing relief by fœderal means, I own, I tremble at the anti-fœderal expedients into which the former may be tempted. As to the objection
against intrusting Congress with a power over trade, drawn from the
diversity of interests in the States, it may be answered. 1. that if this
objection had been listened to, no confederation could have ever taken
place among the States, 2. that if it ought now to be listened to, the
power held by Congress of forming Commercial treaties by which 9
States may indirectly dispose of the Commerce of the residue, ought
to be immediately revoked. 3 that the fact is that a case can scarcely
be imagined in which it would be the interest of any 2/3ds of the States
to oppress the remaining 1/3d. 4. that the true question is whether the
commercial interests of the States do not meet in more points than they
differ. To me it is clear that they do: and if they do there are so many
more reasons for, than against, submitting the commercial interest of
each State to the direction and care of the Majority. Put the West India
trade alone, in which the interest of every State is involved, into the
scale against all the inequalities which may result from any probable
regulation by nine States, and who will say that the latter ought to preponderate? I have heard the different interest which the Eastern States
have as Carriers pointed out as a ground of caution to the Southern
States who have no bottoms of their own agst their concurring hastily
in retaliations on G. B.[2] But will the present system of G. B. ever give
the Southern States bottoms: and if they are not their own Carriers
I shod. suppose it no mark either of folly or incivility to give our custom
to our brethren rather than to those who have not yet entitled themselves to the name of friends.

In detailing these sentiments I have nothing more in view than to
prov[e] the readiness with which I obey your requests. As far as they
are just they must have been often suggested in the discussions of Congress on the subject. I can not even give them weight by saying that
I have reason to believe they would be relished in the public Councils
of this State. From the trials of which I have been a witness I augur that
great difficulties will be encountered in every attempt to prevail on the
Legislature to part with power. The thing itself is not only unpalatable,
but the arguments which plead for it have not their full force on minds
unaccustomed to consider the interests of the State as they are interwoven with those of the Confederacy much less as they may be affected
by foreign politics whilst those wch. plead agst. it, are not only specious,
but in their nature popular: and for that reason, sure of finding patrons.[3]

335

Add to all this that the mercantile interest which has taken the lead in rousing the public attention of other States, is in this so exclusively occupied in British Commerce that what little weight they have will be most likely to fall into the opposite scale. The only circumstance which promises a favorable hearing to the meditated proposition of Congs. is that the power which it asks is to be exerted agst. G. B, and the proposition will consequently be seconded by the animosities which still prevail in a strong degree agst. her. I am My dear Sir very sincerely Yr friend & servt.

J. MADISON JR

RC (DLC). Cover missing. Docketed by JM. Marked "Regulation of Commerce."

[1] JM was well versed in free-trade doctrines, possibly from his careful reading of Adam Smith's *Wealth of Nations* (JM to Jefferson, 27 Apr. 1785). A perceptive analysis of the postwar economy is found in Gordon C. Bjork, "The Weaning of the American Economy: Independence, Market Changes, and Economic Development," *Journal of Economic History,* XXIV (1964), 541–60. Bjork pointed out that all of the problems besetting the U. S. economy (depressed prices, heavy government debt, lack of circulating medium) are classic instances of a "disorganization of traditional markets." JM, along with many other concerned public men witnessing but not comprehending the enormous change from a colony to sovereign status were too close to the scene to understand that the American economy in 1781–1785 was seeking an equilibrium "of the American price level with the world level of prices." They accordingly looked for theoretical devices that in practice would stop trade deficits and the specie drain. In time, JM's natural bent (reinforced by Adam Smith) would lead him into conflict with the public men whose early careers had been spent decrying English mercantilism but whose latter careers were devoted to erecting "a new mercantilist state on this side of the Atlantic" (Curtis P. Nettels, "British Mercantilism and the Economic Development of the Thirteen Colonies," ibid., XII [1952], 114).

[2] This latent "caution" of "the Southern States" toward a New England shipping monopoly became explicit at the Federal Convention of 1787 where JM was willing to grant the New England shippers a concession which many other Virginians believed ruinous. George Mason was among those who believed an American navigation act would permit a northern majority in Congress to oppress the so-called "Staple states." "The Southern States are the *minority* in both Houses. Is it to be expected that they will deliver themselves bound hand & foot to the Eastern States" (Madison, *Convention Notes,* pp. 549–50).

[3] JM was headed for a confrontation at the Oct. 1785 General Assembly session with the localists jealous of national legislative encroachments. Although the chief local "patron"—Patrick Henry—had been elevated to the governorship and was consequently out of the legislature, there was a coterie led by Speaker Benjamin Harrison, Carter Henry Harrison, and Meriwether Smith who were equally dedicated to preserving undiminished state sovereignty. Whether their interests were along theoretical or sectional lines is not always clear (Jackson T. Main, "Sections and Politics in Virginia, 1781–1787," *WMQ,* 3d ser., XII [1955], 105–7). The nationalists were outnumbered at the session and JM reluctantly turned to an interstate commission as a means of circumventing local obstructionism (see Resolution Authorizing a Commission to Examine Trade Regulations, 21 Jan. 1786).

From George Mason

GUNSTON-HALL, August 9th. 1785.

DEAR SIR

I shou'd have answered Your Favour of the 2d. of June,[1] long ago, had not ill Health, & the Absence of my Sons from Home, disabled me from making out the Copys of the Proceedings of the Virga. & Maryd. Commrs. which I now inclose; and upon which I wish to be favour'd with Your Sentiments.

We thought ourselves unfortunate in being deprived of your, & my Friend the Attorney's[2] Assistance, in this important Business; and nothing but absolute Necessity shou'd have induced me to enter upon it, without You; but the Maryland Gentlemen[3] wou'd have been much disgusted with a Disappoi[nt]ment, after attending, at such a Distance, in very bad Weather. We waited some Days expecting Your Arrival in Alexandria; when I received a Letter from the Attorney, upon other Business, without mentioning a Word of the Meeting, or of the Assembly's Appointment: this co[n]vinced Us that there must have been some Blunder or Neglect, in some of the public Offices, in not giving the proper Notification to the Virga. Commrs. The Maryland Gentlemen declared that Nothing had been ommitted on their Part, that they had written an official Letter to the Virga. Comrs.[4] (addressed by their Governor to the Co[mr]s of ours) proposing the Time & Place, if agreeable to them, and if not, desiring they wou'd name some other; that having recd. no Answer, they took it for granted, that the Time & Place was accepted, and attended accordingly.

So great has been the Neglect in some of our public Departments, that neither Mr. Henderson or myself had been furnished with Copys of the Assembly's Resolutions; and I shou'd not have known that I was one of the Persons appointed, had I not, by mere Accident two or three Days before the Meeting, been informed of it, by two of the Maryland Commissioners writing to Me, that they shou'd endeavour to take my House in their Way, and go with Me to Alexandria. His Excellency General Washington happened to have a Copy of the Assembly's Resolutions respecting the Application to be made to the Government of Pensylvania,[5] which He very obligingly gave Us; by which *any two* or more of the Comrs. were impowered to proceed; and it was natural for Us to conclude that these last Resolutions had pursued the Style of the former respecting the Jurisdiction of the two States; as well as that this Subject had been taken up, upon the same Principles as in the Year

337

1778;[6] when Comrs. were directed to settle the Jurisdiction of *Chesapeak Bay & the Rivers Potomack & Pokomoke;* in which Sentiments, Mr. Henderson, from what He was able to recollect of the Resolutions, concurred.

Thus disagreeably circumstanced, only two of the Virga. Commission present, & without any Copy of the Resolves upon the Principal Subject, we thought it better to proceed, than to disappoint the Maryd. Commissioners; who appeard to have brought with them the most amicable Dispositions, and express'd the greatest Desire of forming such a fair & liberal Compact, as might prove a lasting Cement of Friendship between the two States; which we were convinced, it is their mutual Interest to cultivate: We therefore, upon the particular Invitation of the General, adjourn'd to Mount Vernon, and finished the Business there. Some Time after, Mr. Henderson wrote to Mr. Beckley (Clerk of the House of Delegates) for a Copy of the Resolves; upon receiving which, we were surprized to find no mention made of *Chesapeak* or *Pokomoke River,* that our Powers were confined to *Potomack River,* and to not less than *three* of the Commissioners. I am still inclined to think that the Ommission of Chesapeake Bay & Pokomoke River was owing to Mistake, or Inadvertence, in not attending to the Resolves of 1778; and if so, it was perhaps lucky, that we had not been furnished with a Copy of the Resolves; for the Maryd. Comrs. had an express Instruction, from their Assembly, to consider the Relinquishment, on the Part of Virginia, of any Claim of laying Tolls &c, on Vessels passing thro' the Capes of Chesapeake, as a sine qua non; and if it was refused, immediately to break off all further Confurence with the Virginia Commissioners.

This blundering Business, however, will give Me the Trouble & Expence of a Journey to Richmond, next Session, to appologize for, & explain our Conduct;[7] when, if the Substance of the Compact is approved by the Assembly, I hope Forms will be dispensed with; especially as the Breach of them has been the Fault of some of their own Officers, not ours; and as I am conscious of our having been influenced by no other Motives than the Desire of promoting the public Good.

RC (DLC). Cover addressed by Mason. Docketed by JM with note: "proceedings & compact with Maryland, as to Potomack &c." Signature missing, with a marginal note in unknown hand, "cut out as an autograph for the Revd. Mr. Sprague of Massachts."

1 JM's letter of 2 June 1785 is missing.

2 The Virginia attorney general, Edmund Randolph, and JM were the other two Virginia commissioners. Never having been informed of the time and place, they failed to attend the commission meeting (Randolph to JM, 17 July 1785).

³ Samuel Chase, Daniel of St. Thomas Jenifer, and Thomas Stone were the Maryland commissioners (Mount Vernon Compact, 28 Mar. 1785, Ms [Vi]; Tr [DLC]).

⁴ It would appear that the "official Letter" must have been sent to Governor Patrick Henry, who then failed to inform the Virginia commissioners of its contents.

⁵ Washington's copy of "the Assembly's Resolutions" concerned the resolution made in the House on 28 Dec. 1784. The resolution authorized the Virginia and Maryland commissioners to meet with commissioners from Pennsylvania to consider the clearing and extending of the Potomac River and added that if a joint representation of Virginia and Maryland be unattainable, then any two of them might meet with representatives of Pennsylvania (*JHDV*, Oct. 1784, pp. 91, 99).

⁶ A resolution of 10 Dec. 1777 had authorized three Virginia commissioners to meet with the Maryland delegates and adjust the long-standing problems of maritime jurisdiction related to Chesapeake Bay, the Potomac, and the Pocomoke (*JHDV*, Oct. 1777, pp. 77–78).

⁷ Ill-health prevented Mason from making the trip to Richmond. JM took charge of the compact business in the House; so he was in on the finish of the affair even though he had missed the negotiations at Mount Vernon (Mason to JM, 7 Dec. 1785; *JHDV*, Oct. 1785, pp. 114, 117–19; Act Ratifying the Chesapeake Compact with Maryland, ca. 24–26 Dec. 1785).

From Richard Henry Lee

N. Y. Augt. 11. 1785

DEAR SIR,

Your favor of July the 7th was long coming to hand as I find my letter of the 20th May¹ was in getting to you. This joined to the uncertainty of letters ever arriving safe is a very discouraging circumstance to full & free correspondence. I have the honor of according most perfectly and entirely with your ideas for regulating our severance from Kentucky. It is unquestionably just that this district should assume her fair & full proportion of the debt created by the War because the benefit being Common so should be the expence procuring it and that this country shall be a fundamental article in the Act of parting; as well as that they shall be a component part of the Federal Union. The Contract should be Tripartite; the parties, our State, Congress, & Kentucky. Mr. Jay is commissioned to treat with Mr. Gardoque, but as yet nothing has been done.² The exclusive navn. of Miss'ipi will be earnestly contended for by Spain, who to quiet us on that head will probably grant large commercial benefits. But if we remain firm, I incline to think that the Navign. will be consented to. As yet we only know Officially that Mr. Adams has arrived in London, received his Audience & delivered his Credentials. The next packet will probably inform us of his feeling the B[ritish]. pulse & how it beats, at the subjects that he is to try them

339

upon. I think with you that there is not great room for hope of Commercial advantages from a Nation whose appetite for Commerce has ever been ravenous, and its wishes always for Monopoly. And the more especially as we have no compensation to make. I believe that we may dispose them to be reasonable, by a very careful, and considerate restraining of their Trade, in all cases where we shall not injure ourselves more than them by the restraint. But it seems to me clearly beyond doubt, that the giving Congress a power to Legislate over the Trade of the Union would be dangerous in the extreme to the 5 Southern or Staple States, whose want of ships & Seamen would expose their freightage & their produce to a most pernicious and destructive Monopoly.[3] With such a power 8 states in the Union would be stimulated by extensive interest to shut close the door of Monopoly, that by the exclusion of all Rivals whether for the purchasing our produce or freighting it, both these might be at the Mercy of our East & North. The Spirit of Commerce thro'out the world is a Spirit of Avarice and could not fail to act as above stated. What little difficulty there would be in drawing over one of the 5 to join the 8 interested States must be very discernable to those who have marked the progress of intrigues in Congres[s]. In truth it demands most careful circumspection that the Remedy be not worse than the disease, bad as the last may be. I could say much on this subject, but it is not necessary, for I am sure that your good sense reflecting calmly on the subject will sufficiently discern the danger of such an experiment. Nor do I believe it necessary, being perfectly satisfied that a well digested system of restraint being properly laid before the States by Congress would be universa[l]ly adopted by the different Assemblies. I think so, because it will be most evidently the interest of all to do so. It is true that the price of our Staple has been for some time greater at Phila. & here than in Virga. But it is as true the European price did not warrant the price at these two places as the great losses & bankruptcies of the Adventurers plainly prove. Indeed this excess of price at P. & N. Y. was occasioned by sinking Speculators, who to swim a while longer, would go any lengths to keep up appearances by making some remittance to their Creditors abroad. But this business is now chiefly over & here at present there is neither money nor inclination to purchase Tobo. The crowd of Bankrupts at P. has, I believe, nearly produced the same effect.

Draft (ViU). Written on unused portions of JM's letter to Lee, 7 July 1785.

[1] Lee's letter was dated 30 May. Burnett attributed "20 May" to a copyist's error (*Letters*, VIII, 181 n.).

² Jay's official commission was agreed upon on 21 July 1785 (*JCC*, XXIX, 567–69). The negotiations with Gardoqui "proved to be a long and fruitless" endeavor (Nettels, *The Emergence of a National Economy*, p. 68).

³ On 25 July 1785 the Committee Book of Congress recorded the referral of letters from Adams, Jefferson, and Franklin to the Secretary for Foreign Affairs (*JCC*, XXIX, 574 n.).

From James Monroe

N. YORK August 14th. 1785.

DEAR SIR

Yours of the 28th. of July I receiv'd by the last post. The rout from hence to Boston may be effected by stage in 5 days; to Lake George in the same time, thence to St. Johns in three perhaps less, to Montreal one, & thence to Quebec in two, but in the latter instance it must be posted. In either rout you will have no difficulty for the boats and stages are under good regulation. I have been in doubt for some time which to prefer, the trip to Boston or the Indian treaty (having gratified my curiosity as to Canada) & have at length given way to the circumstances which urge in favor of the latter, viz. the security & facility of travelling with the Comrs., an opportunity wh. may not offer again whereas a trip to Boston will be always equally practicable. It wod. give me pleasure to meet you in Phila. but as you delay yr. mov'ment untill you hear from me, cannot expect it, since I sit out hence on the first of Sepr. to join Genl. Butler in Carlisle. I shall return from the treaty thro' the Wilderness & see you at Richmond as you will be on the Assembly. By the first of Sepr. we expect the most important business will have been decided on ultimately, or postpon'd for the winter. The requisition will have pass'd, unless new difficulties arise. This subject hath been sifted thoroughly with the advances of the several States during the contest & their claims upon each other under them respectively. We cannot but lament that the state of our accts. agnst the union is in such a situation as to leave us totally in the dark with respect to it. We have no documents & have therefore only conjecture to build our most important measures on. Several men have been in pay for years in Richmond and yet have reason to believe they have done little. Surely the state will pursue the most efficatious measures upon this head & no longer suffer her interests in that line to be neglected.[1] Those states whose accts. are unsettled a[re] not only subjected to great disadvantages in the requisition but are cr[i]minated as avoiding it designedly for the purpose of evading the payment of what they owe to the other States, having fail'd as they presume to advance their federal quota. The contrary of this will, we suppose appear upon a settlement, why then, say they, delay it? Does it arise from our refusing any thing you ask to effect it, or the negligenc[e] of your government? The report upon the 9th. of the articles of confideration will not I believe be finally determin'd untill the winter. It will however probably be taken up merely for the Sake of investigation & to be committed to the journals for publick inspection. You have I understand a copy of & I wish much yr. sentiments on it. A navigation act by recommendation hath been propos'd in conversation & debate but not submitted to the inspection & consideration of Congress. This is the other plan & shod. not be adopted but in the ultimate decision, that it is improper the power shod. rest in Congress:[2] if this shod. be the decision it might be well to collect better information from the merchants of each State than congress now possess on the subject, indeed with or without the power, this information shod. be obtain'd or we may err in the act. If this report shod. be adopted it gives a tie to the confederacy wh. it hath not at present nor can have without it. It gives the states something to act on, the means by which they may bring abt. certain ends—without it god knows what object they have before them, or how each State will move, so as to move securely, with respect to fœderal or State objects. A report revising the *instructions to our ministers forming comm[er]cial trea[t]ies* changing the principle & substituting to that of the *right of* the *most favord nation* a simple bargain with each founded in the nature *of our intercourse with each* respectively hath been twice before Congress & postpon'd.[3] It investigates fully the impolicy of those form'd on that principle, since in the opinion of the committee, they obtain nothing from the powers not having *posesions* [in] the *west indies* wh. we may not obtain without them & embarrass us in any restrictions we may lay on the *trad*[e], of those who have, it being the only means by which we are to remove the restraints which now exist. This alterat[ion] seems to obtain the assent of Congress & will most probably be acceded to if there will be a sufficient number of States in the ensuing week. A *consulate convention* with *france* enter'd into under instructions of long standing (but from wh. the secry of f. affr. thinks there are substantial d[evi]ations) by *Dr. F*[ranklin] *for ratification* universally disapprov'd will most probably be postpon'd for the present.[4] I shall write you again before I sit out if any thing arises worthy communication. I am Dear Sir yr. friend & servant

JAS. MONROE

RC (DLC). Cover missing. Docketed. Italicized words, unless otherwise noted, were encoded by Monroe using the code first sent him by JM on 14 Apr. 1785.

¹ The original 1781 Virginia cession of its western land claims contained a provision that the state should be reimbursed for the Virginia-financed conquest of the Northwest Territory by George Rogers Clark's expedition (Abernethy, *Western Lands and the American Revolution*, pp. 244–45). In time, a commission was established to settle these claims (*Papers of Madison*, II, 72–78). The first commissioners who attempted to settle these western claims with Congress after the cession was accepted in 1781 were Thomas Marshall, William Fleming, Samuel McDowell, and Caleb Wallace. They first met on 1 Nov. 1782, and having liquidated as far as possible all accounts, prepared and submitted a report to the governor and council on 1 July 1783. By the renewed cession of 1 Mar. 1784, Virginia repeated her earlier condition that Congress fully reimburse the state for the Clark expeditions. One commissioner was to be appointed by Virginia, one by Congress, and one by the two other commissioners. Edward Carrington was the Virginia commissioner, but he resigned 19 Dec. 1785 and was replaced by William Heth. There were a series of congressional commissioners: Samuel Holden Parsons, 9 June 1785–4 Oct. 1786; Edward Fox, 5 Oct. 1786–9 Apr. 1787, who resigned because of inadequate salary; and John Pierce, appointed 11 Apr. 1787, who was the commissioner of army accounts. During Pierce's illness and absence, Heth and David Henley in 1788 came to a settlement of $500,000 to be paid to Virginia by Congress. However, a final accounting was not made until after the establishment of the national government under the Constitution (ibid., V, 229 n. 4; James, *George Rogers Clark Papers, 1781–1784*, pp. 290, 401–2, 465–66; *JHDV*, Oct. 1785, p. 99; *CVSP*, IV, 84; *JCC*, XXVIII, 442; XXXI, 737, 741; XXXII, 165–66, 171–72; Ferguson, *Power of the Purse*, pp. 216–17).

² Monroe commented to Jefferson that "a second plan hath been proposd, *a navigation act digested here* and *recommended to the States*. This hath not been presented but probably will be. One would expect in a *particular quarter of the union perfect concert in this business*, yet this is not altogether the case. The 2d. plan above attended to takes its origin *with MacHenry. The Eastern people* wish something more lasting and will of course in the first instance not agree to it. They must therefore come in with that propos'd in *the report* [on amending the ninth article]" (italicized words originally in code) (Monroe to Jefferson, 15 Aug. 1785, Boyd, *Papers of Jefferson*, VIII, 382).

³ On 4 Apr. 1785 Monroe had moved that a committee be appointed to report on and revise the instructions to ministers concerning commercial treaties. Monroe presented the report on 2 June and it was assigned to 9 June for consideration, but it does not appear in that day's, or in subsequent days' records (*JCC*, XXVIII, 229, 418–22).

⁴ On 24 June 1785 John Jay conveyed to Congress Franklin's copy of the consular convention with France. Jay's report on the proposed treaty convention, read 6 July, explicated in detail the deviations in the convention from the instructions given to the American minister. The substance of Jay's report was that the convention gave extraordinary privileges and immunities to French consuls and seemed to denigrate American sovereignty (*JCC*, XXVIII, 480; XXIX, 500–515; Monroe to Jefferson, 15 Aug. 1785, Boyd, *Papers of Jefferson*, VIII, 383 n.; Evans 19319). JM had given Washington a printed copy of Jay's report and possibly in a lost letter JM may have commented upon Jay's lawyer-like bill of particulars (see Washington to JM, 22 Oct. 1785).

To Thomas Jefferson

DEAR SIR,

Yours of the 18th. of March never reached me till the 4 inst. It came by post from N. York, which it did not leave till the 21. of July. My last was dated in April,[1] & went by Mr. Mazzei who picked it up at N. York and promised to deliver it with his own hand.

The machinations of G. B. with regard to Commerce have produced much distress and noise in the Northern States, particularly in Boston, from whence the alarm has spread to New York & Philada. Your correspondence with Congs. will no doubt have furnished you with full information on this head.[2] I only know the General fact, and that the sufferers are every where calling for such augmentation of the power of Congress as may effect relief. How far the Southern States & Virginia in particular will join in this proposition cannot be foreseen. It is easy to foresee that the circumstances which in a confined view distinguish our situation from that of our brethren, will be laid hold of by the partizans of G. B. by those who are or affect to be jealous of Congress, and those who are interested in the present course of business, to give a wrong bias to our Councils. If any thing should reconcile Virga. to the idea of giving Congress a power over her trade, it will be that this power is likely to annoy G. B. against whom the animosities of our Citizens are still strong. They seem to have less sensibility to their commercial interests; which they very little understand, and which the mercantile class here have not the same motives if they had the same capacity to lay open to the public, as that class have in the States North of us. The price of our Staple since the peace is another cause of inattention in the planters to the dark side of our commercial affairs. Should these or any other causes prevail in frustrating the scheme of the Eastern & Middle States of a general retaliation on G. B. I *tremble for the* [event].[3] A *majority* of *the states* deprived of a *regular remidy for their distresses* by *the want* of *a fœderal spirit in the minority* must *feel the* strongest *motives to some ir*regular *experiments.* The *dan*[ger] *of such a crisis* makes me surmise that the *policy of Great Britain*[4] results as much from *the hope of effecting a breach in our confederacy* as *of monopolising our trade.*

Our internal trade is taking an arrangement from which I hope good consequences. Retail stores are spreadg all over the Country, many of them carried on by native adventurers, some of them branched out from the principal Stores at the heads of navigation. The distribution of the business however into the importing & the retail departments has not yet taken place. Should the port bill be established it will I think quickly add this amendment which indeed must in a little time follow of itself. It is the more to be wished for as it is the only radical cure for credit to the consumer which continues to be given to a degree which if not checked will turn the diffusive retail of merchandize into a nusance. When the Shop keeper buys his goods of the wholesale Merchant, he must buy at so short a credit, that he can venture to give none at all.

You ask me to unriddle the *dissolution of the committee of the states at Annapolis.* I am not sure that I am myself possessed fully of the causes, *different members of Congress* having *differed in their accounts of the matter.* My conception of it is that *the abrupt departure of* some of the *Eastern delegates* which *destroyed the quorum* & which *Dana*[5] is said *to have been at the bottom of* proceeded *partly from irritations among the committee partly from dislike to the place of their session* and *partly from an impatience to get home* which prevailed over *their regard* for *their private characters* as well as *for their public duty.*

Subsequent to the date of *mine in* which I gave my idea of *Fayette* I had further opportunities of *penetrating his character.*[6] Though *his foibles did* not *disappear* all the *favorable traits* presented themselves in a *stronger light.* On *closer inspection he* certainly possesses *talents which might figure in any line.* If *he is ambitious* it is rather of the *praise* which virtue *dedicates to merit* than *of the homeage* which *fear renders to power. His disposetion is* naturally *warm and affectionate* and *his attachment to the United States* unquestionable.[7] Unless *I am grossly deceived* you will *find his zeal sincere* & *useful* whenever it can be *employed* in behalf *of the United States without opposetion* [to] *the essential interests of France.*

The opposition to the general assessment gains ground. At the *instance of some* of *its adversaries I drew up the remonstrance* herewith inclosed. It has been *sent* thro' the *medium of confidential persons in a number of the upper county*[s] and I am told will be pretty extensively signed. The presbyterian clergy have at length espoused the side of the opposition, being moved either by *a fear of their laity* or *a jealousy of the episcopalians.* The mutual hatred of these sects has been much inflamed by the late act incorporating the latter. *I am far from* being *sorry for it* as *a coalition between them* could *alone endanger our religious rights* and a tendency to *such an event had been suspected.* The fate of the Circuit Courts is uncertain. They are threatened with no small danger from the diversity of opinions entertained among the friends of some reform in that department. But the greatest danger is to be feared from those who mask a secret aversion to any reform under a zeal for such a one as they know will be rejected. The Potowmack Company are going on with very flattering prospects. Their subscriptions sometime ago amounted to upwards of four fifths of the whole sum. I have the pleasure also to find by an advertisement from the managers for James River that more than half of the sum is subscribed for that undertaking, and that the subscribers are to meet shortly for the purpose of organizing themselves & going to work. I despair of seeing the Revisal taken up at the ensuing Session.[8] The number of copies struck are so deficient (there being not above three for each County) and there has been such delay in distributing them (none of the Counties having recd. them till very lately & some probably not yet, tho' they were ready long ago) that the principal end of their being printed has been frustrated. Our fields promise very short crops both of Corn & Tobo. The latter was much injured by the Grass hopper & other insects; the former somewhat by the bug in the Southern parts of the State, but both have suffered most from dry weather which prevails at present in this part of the Country, and has generally prevailed I understand in most other parts. It seems certain that no future weather can make a great crop of either, particularly of Tobo. so great a proportion of the hills being without plants in them, & so many more with plants which must come to nothing. Notwithstandg this prospect, its price has fallen from 36/. to 32 & 30/ on James River & 28/ on Rappahannock. The scarcity of cash is one cause. *Harrison the late governor* was *elected* in *Surry* whither *he previously removed with his family. A contest* for *the chair* will *no* doubt *ensue.* Should *he fail it he* will be *for Congress.*

I have not yet recd. any of the books which you have been so kind as to pick up for me; but expect their arrival daily, as you were probably soon after the date of your last apprized that I was withdrawn from the nomination which led you to suspend the forwarding them.[9] I am invited by Col: Monroe to an option of rambles this fall, one of which is into the Eastern States. I wish much to accept so favorable an opportunity of executing the plan from which I was diverted last fall; but can not decide with certainty whether it will be practicable or not. I have in conjunction with a friend here a project of interest on the anvil which will carry me at least as far as Philada. or New York where I shall be able to take my final resolution. Adieu. Yrs. sincerely

J M Jr.

RC (DLC). Cover missing. Docketed by JM and in an unknown hand. Also headed "No. 8." Italicized words, unless otherwise noted, were encoded by JM in the code first used by Jefferson on 14 Apr. 1783. JM's deletion of some phrases leaves the suspicion that he edited this letter after it was returned to him. The enclosed Memorial and Remonstrance sent to Jefferson has not been found.

[1] JM's letter is dated 27 Apr. 1785.

[2] Despite prejudices and penalties, American commerce was returning to its prewar channels with British factors and shippers, a situation that led to unfounded rumors of ship-burnings and in fact caused Boston merchants to petition Congress in April for relief. See JM to Monroe, 21 June 1785, n. 3. John Jay wrote Jefferson on 15 June, 13 July, and 13 Aug. 1785 regarding British harassment of American trade, but he did not send Jefferson "full information" about the complex problem (*Diplomatic Correspondence of the U. S.*, I, 614–17).

[3] JM wrote the code number for "genuine," but Jefferson corrected it to "event."

[4] JM appears here to have written "is formed" and then crossed through the words.

[5] JM's opinion was based on hearsay, and he believed that Dana, Dick, and Blanchard had left the Annapolis session of the Committee of States capriciously (JM to Monroe, 27 Nov. 1784, and n. 3).

[6] In his letter to Jefferson of 17 Oct. 1784 JM had made some remarks concerning Lafayette's character.

[7] JM wrote "unquestionably."

[8] Contrast JM's pessimism here with the rather triumphant report he gave to Jefferson on the success obtained in passing a substantial portion of the revised code between 31 Oct. and 13 Dec. 1785 (JM to Jefferson, 22 Jan. 1786).

[9] Jefferson had heard that JM was nominated in Congress for the vacancy at the Spanish court. He held up a shipment of books until he was certain JM would be in Orange County rather than en route to Madrid (Jefferson to JM, 18 Mar. 1785).

From William Grayson

NEW YORK Augt. 21st. 1785.

DEAR SIR

Your favor of   [1] has come to hand; I am sorry to hear the doctrine of paper money begins to rear up it's head in our State. This subject has been so well investigated at different periods that I can hardly think any reasonable man can advocate it, unless for the purpose of advancing some object of interest; I remember in the old Government that our exchange rose to 65 P Ct.[2] This alarmed the merchants so much that the King determined to give his assent to no more paper money bills.[3] Agreable to your request I have made inquiry respecting the paper money of Pensylvany; I understand from Colo. Biddle that it is in a state of depreciation. It will however buy goods, under the inconvenience of an additional advance; almost every body says it is mighty good, yet nobody will part with ready money for it at an equal exchange. As I go through Philada. on my return to Virginia I will make

347

the most minute investigation into the matters and furnish you with the result of my inquiries in time for the meeting of our Assembly.

We have done very little since I wrote you last; the States have been so irregularly represented, that it has been impracticable to act upon any matter of consequence; the requisition is still before Congress, and I expect will pass as soon as a sufficient number of States are upon the floor. It rests however at present on principles which are not intirely advantageous to our State; although from a disposition which has lately appeared I think the State will be able to get better terms. I agree with you intirely as to the necessity of a requisition at any rate. Otherwise the public Creditors might be so clamorous, as to render the Govermnt. in some degree odious.

The Mint is still before Congress, and it is uncertain whether anything will be done in it this year. The Post Office is also under consideration, and I am apt to believe the following alteration will take effect:

To transfer the transportation of the Mail to the Stages; & to oblige all Sea Captains to deliver in their letters to the Post Office before they are admitted to an entry. The first alteration will furnish three mails a week through our State, & with much more expedition.

A Post to Canada from New York is talk'd of, also one from Alexandria to fort Pitt.[4] The change of the 9th. article of the confederation hath been the subject of debate for two days, & I expect will be taken up shortly again; there appears to be a variety of objections to the change, & I imagine the Members will not even consent to a recommendation witht. previous instructions from the legislatures.

A commission has pass'd Congress to negotiate with Mr. Gardoqui, under the direction of Congress; nothing has as yet transpired, neither can I find any idea of what will be the result. There has been no other information from Mr. Adams, except that he hath been received according to the established forms. Mr. Marbois has withdrawn the application for Lonchamp.[5]

A nephew of mine has been here & giv'n me an account of the Convention at Kentucki: from which I conclude an application will be made to our legislature to grant them independance. This matter has been the subject of conversation here, & an opinion begins to prevail that a State has no right to dismember itself witht. the previous consent of the U. S.[6] Indeed this doctrine appears to me to be founded on the nature of things, & to require no comment to support it. Should our legislature take up this opinion I presume the negotiation will be carried on through Congress, when an admission into the confederation may be stipulated at the same time the actual dismemberment takes effect. I do not know that it will be for the interest of our State to withhold independance from them although asked at an unreasonable time for themselves, yet it surely is a matter of consequence to her, that at the time they cease to be a part of Virginia, they become a part of the fœderal Union. The different States can have no other interest in this event than that of dismembering the State of Virga. of whose magnitude they are jealous. They are then gratified with a simple dismemberment witht. admitting the new State into the Confederation. Will it not therefore be proper to make the dismemberment & admission into the Union Co-existent acts & mutually dependant on each other. There seems to be another reason why this mode should be preferred; the conditions for the security of property & other matters will be more likely to be observed, if the pacta conventa are tripartite, & the U. S. as one of the dramatis personæ can be induced to guaranty them; indeed if the new State is to take upon itself the payment of any part of the public debt I should think it proper the U. S. should admit it to become debtor pro tanto & the old one exonerated in the same proportion. These are thoughts at first new, and I do not doubt but ideas on this subject much more proper have suggested themselves to your mind.

The fœderal buildings at Trenton seems rather to lose than to gain ground. A third Commissioner is wanting without whom the other two are useless & a sufficient number of States has not yet been found to appoint him. I believe the 30,000 dollars in the requisition for the construction of these buildings will not stand. Some of the Eastern States have kick'd up about the money. If it was not for fear of the imputation of instability I would as soon as No. Carolina is represented move to adjourn to Philada; perhaps this is at present the properest place at least till we can see our way clearer to the Westward.

Mr. Jay is directed to report the number of Consuls necessary & the places of destination. Some gentlemen are of opinion we may have Consuls witht. treaties. Our friend Colo. Monroe sets out in a day or two for the Indian Treaty at the mouth of the Great Miami: from thence he proceeds to Kentucki on some private business & so through the Wilderness to Virga.[7] From yr. Affect. fd. & Most Obed. Servt:

WILLM. GRAYSON

N B. I imagine you have heard the Consular Convention with France is arrived, but not yet confirmed.

RC (DLC). Cover missing.

¹ Grayson failed to check his files and sent the letter with this space still blank.

² Soltow noted that the rate fluctuated "from below 15 to over 65" percent (James H. Soltow, "The Role of Williamsburg in the Virginia Economy, 1750–1775," *WMQ*, 3d ser., XV [1958], 475).

³ In 1751 British concern over the fluctuations in American currency resulted in a statute severely limiting the use of paper money in New England (24 Geo. II c. 53, *Statutes at Large*, VII, 403–4). By 1764, southern colonies also came under statutory regulation when paper money in all American colonies was denied the status of legal tender (4 Geo. III c. 34, ibid., IX, 199 [erroneously printed under the heading of 1763]).

⁴ The report with suggestions for improving mail service from Postmaster General Ebenezer Hazard was read in Congress 12 July 1785 (*JCC*, XXIX, 525–29).

⁵ Jefferson alluded to the notorious Longchamps-Marbois imbroglio in his letter of 25 May 1784. Pennsylvania finally tried Longchamps for assaulting the French diplomat, but the international overtones of the affair caused Pennsylvania and Virginia to enact statutes covering such jurisdictional disputes.

⁶ Grayson here crossed through "in Congress assembled."

⁷ For Monroe's itinerary, see his letter to JM, 14 Aug. 1785.

To Caleb Wallace

ORANGE Augt. 23d. 1785

DR. SIR

Your favour of the 12th. of July was safely deliverd to me by Mr. Craig.¹ I accept with pleasure your propos'd exchange of Western for Eastern intelligence and though I am a stranger to parental ties can sufficiently con[c]ieve the happiness of which they are a source to congratulate you on Your possession of two fine sons & a Daughter. I do not smile at the Idea of transplanting myself into your wilderness. Such a change of my abode is not indeed probable. Yet I have no local partialities which can keep me from any place which promises the greatest real advantages but If such a removal was not even possible I should nevertheless be ready to communicate, as you desire my Ideas towards a constitution of Government for the State in embryo.² I pass over the general policy of the measure which calls for such a provision. It has been unanimously embraced by those who being most interested in it must have but consider'd it, & will I dare say be with equal unanimity acceded to by the other party which is to be consulted. I will first offer some general remarks on the Subject, & then answer your several queries.

1. *The Legislative department* ought by all means, as I think to include a Senate constituted on such principles as will give *wisdom* and steadiness to legislation. The want of these qualities is the grievance

complained of in all our republics. The want of *fidelity* in the administration of power having been the grievance felt under most Governments, and by the American States themselves under the British Government. It was natural for them to give too exclusive an attention to
this primary attribute. The Senate of Maryland with a few amendments
is a good model. Trial has I am told verified the expectations from it.
A Similar one made a part of our constitution as it was originally proposed but the inexperience & jealousy of our then Councils, rejected it
in favour of our present Senate a worse could hardly have been substituted & yet bad as it is, it is often a useful bitt in the mouth of the house
of Delegates.[3] Not a single Session passes without instances of sudden
resolutions by the latter of which they repent in time to intercede privately with the Senate for their Negative. For the other branch models
enough may be found. Care ought however to be taken against its becoming to numerous, by fixing the number which it is never to exceed.
The quorum, wages, and privileges of both branches ought also to be
fixed. A majority seems to be the natural quorum. The wages of the
members may be made payable for   years to come in the medium
value of wheat, for   years preceeding as the same shall from period
to period be rated by a respectable Jury appointed for that purpose by
the Supreme Court. The privileges of the members ought not in my
opinion to extend beyond an exemption of their persons and equipage
from arrests during the time of their actual Service. If it were possible
it would be well to define the extent of the Legislative power but the
nature of it seems in many respects to be indefinite. It is very practicable however to enumerate the essential exceptions. The Constitution
may expresly restrain them from medling with religion—from abolish-
ing Juries from taking away the Habeus corpus—from forcing a citizen
to give evidence against himself, from controuling the press, from enacting retrospective laws at least in criminal cases, from abridging the
right of suffrage, from seizing private property for public use without
paying its full Valu[e] from licensing the importation of Slaves, from
infringing the Confederation &c &c.

As a further security against fluctuating & indegested laws the Constitution of New York has provided a Council of Revision. I approve
much of such an institution & believe it is considerd by the most intelligent citizens of that state as a valuable safeguard both to public interests
& to private rights.[4] Another provision has been suggested for preserving System in Legislative proceedings which to some may appear still
better. It is that a standing commtee composed of a few select & skilful

individuals should be appointed to prepare bills on all subjects which they may judge proper to be submitted to the Legislature at their meetings & to draw bills for them during their Sessions. As an antido[te] both to the jealousy & danger of their acquiring an improper influence they might be made incapable of holding any other Office Legislative, Executive, or Judiciary. I like this Suggestion so much, that I have had thoughts of proposing it to our Assembly, who give almost as many proofs as they pass laws of their need of some such Assistance.

2 *The Executive Department* Though it claims the 2d place is not in my estimation entitled to it by its importance all the great powers which are properly executive being transferd to the Fœderal Government. I have made up no final opinion whether the first Magistrate should be chosen by the Legislature or the people at large or whether the power should be vested in one man assisted by a council or in a council of which the President shall be only primus inter pares.[5] There are examples of each in the U. States and probably advantages & disadvantages attending each. It is material I think that the number of members should be small & that their Salaries should be either unalterable by the Legislature or alterable only in such manner as will not affect any individual in place. Our Executive is the worst part of a ba[d] Constitution. The Members of it are dependant on the Legislature not only for their wages but for their reputation and therefore are not likely to withstand usurpations of that branch; they are besides too numerous and expensive, their organization vaugue & perplexed & to crown the absurdi[ty] some of the members may without any new appointment continue in Office for life contrary to one of Articles of the Declaration of Right[s.]

3d *The Judiciary Department* merits every care. Its efficacy is Demonstrated in G. Brittain where it maintains private Right against all the corruptions of the two other departments & gives a reputation to the whole Government which it is not in itself entitled to. The main points to be attended to are 1. that the Judges should hold their places during good behavior. 2. that their Salaries should be either fixed like the wages of the Representatives or not be alterable so as to affect the Individuals in Office. 3 that their Salaries be liberal. The first point is obvious: without the second the independance aimed at by the first will be Ideal only: without the 3d. the bar will be superior to the bench which destroys all security for a Systematick administration of Justice. After securing these essential points I should think it unadvisable to descend so far into detail as to bar any future Modification of this department which experience may recommend. An enumeration of the principal courts with power to the Legislature to Institute inferior Courts may suffice. The Admiralty business can never be extensive in your situation and may be refer'd to one of the other Courts. With regard to a Court of Chancery as distinct from a Court of Law, the reasons of Lord Bacon on the affirmative side outweigh in my Judgment those of Lord Kaims on the other side.[6] Yet I should think it best to leave this important question to be decided by future lights without tying the hands of the Legislature one way or the other. I consider our county courts as on a bad footing and would never myself consent to copy them into another constitution.

All the States seem to have seen the necessity of providing for Impeachments but none of them to have hit on an unexceptionable Tribunal. In some the trial is referd to the Senate in others to the Executive, in others to the Judiciary department. It has been suggested that a tribunal composed of members from each Department would be better than either and I entirely concur in their opinion. I proceed next to your queries.

1 "Whether is a representation according to number, or property, or in a joint proportion to both the most Safe? or is a representation by counties preferable to a more equitable mode that will be difficult to adjust?" Under this question may be consider'd 1. the right of Suffrage. 2 the mode of suffrage. 3 the plan of representation. As to the 1. I think the extent which ought to be given to this right a matter of great delicacy and of critical Importance. To restrain it to the landholders will in time exclude too great a proportion of citizens; to extend it to all citizens without regard to property, or even to all who possess a pittance may throw too much power into hands which will either abuse it themselves or sell it to the rich who will abuse it. I have thought it might be a good middle course to narrow this right in the choice of the least popular, & to enlarge it in that of the more popular branch of the Legislature. There is an example of this Distinction in N. Carolina if in none of the States.[7] How it operates or is relished by the people I cannot say. It would not be surprising if in the outset at least it should offend the sense of equallity which re[i]gns in a free Country. In a general vein I see no reason why the rights of property which chiefly bears the burden of Government & is so much an object of Legislation should not be respected as well as personal rights in the choice of Rulers. It must be owned indeed that property will give influence to the holder though it should give him no legal priviledges and will in generall be safe on that as well as other Accounts, expecially if the business of

Legislation be guarded with the provisions hinted at. 2 as to the mode of suffrage I lean strongly to that of the ballott, notwithstanding the objections which be against it. It appears to me to be the only radical cure for those arts of Electioneering which poison the very fountain of Liberty. The States in which the Ballott has been the Standing mode are the only instances in which elections are tolerably chaste and those arts in disgrace. If it should be thought improper to fix this mode by the constitution I should think it at least necessary to avoid any constitutional bar to a future adoption of it.*[8] 3 By the plan of representation I mean 1. the classing of the Electors 2 the proportioning of the representatives to each class. The first cannot be otherwise done than by geographical description as by Counties. The second may esily be done in the first instance either by comprizing within each county an equal number of electors; or by proportioning the number of representatives of each county to its number of electors. The dificulty arises from the disproportionate increase of electors in different Counties. There seem to be two methods only by which the representation can be equalized from time to time. The 1 is to change the bounds of the counties. The 2d to change the number of representatives allotted to them respectavely, as the former would not only be most troublesome & expensive, but would involve a variety of other adjustments. The latter method is evidently the best. Examples of a Constitutional provision for it exists in several of the States. In some it is to be executed periodically in others pro re nata. The latter seems most accurate and very practicable. I have already intimated the propriety of fixing the number of representatives which ought never to be exceeded. I should suppose 150 or even 100 might safely be made the ne plus ultra for Kentuckcy.

2 "Which is to be preferd an Anual, Trienniel, or Septennial Succession to Offices or frequent elections without limitations in choice or that the Officers when chosen should continue quamdiu se bene gesserint?" The rule ought no doubt to be different in the different Departments of power. For one part of the Legislature Annual Elections will I suppose be held indispensably though some of the ablest Statesmen & soundest Republicans in the U States are in favour of triennial. The great danger in departing from Annual elextions in this case lies in the want of some other natural term to limit the departure. For the other branch 4 or 5 Years may be the period. For neither branch does it seem necessary or proper to prohibit an indefinite reeligibility.[9] With regard to the Executive if the elections be frequent & particularly, if made as to

* The Constitutn of N York directs an experiment on this Subject.

any member of it by the people at large a reeligibility cannot I think be objected to. If they be unfrequent, a temporary or perpetual incapacitation according to the degree of unfrequency at least in the case of the first Magistrate may not be amiss. As to the Judiciary department enough has been said & as to the Subordinate officers civil & Military, nothing need be said more than that a regulation of their appointments may under a few restrictions be safely trusted to the Legislature.

3. "How far may the same person with propriety be employed in the different departments of Government in an infant Country where the counsel of every individual may be needed? ["] Temporary deviations from fundamental principles are always more or less dangerous. When the first pretext fails, those who become interested in prolonging the evil will rarely be at a loss for other pretexts. The first precedent too familiarizes the people to the irregularity, lessens their veneration for those fundamental principles, & makes them a more easy prey to Ambition & self Interest. Hence it is that abuses of every kind when once established have been so often found to perpetuate themselves. In this caution I refer cheifly to an improper mixture of the three great departments within the State. A Delegation to Congress is I conceive compatible with either.

4 "Should there be a periodical review of the Constitution? Nothing appears more eligible in theory nor has sufficient trial perhaps been yet made to condemn it in practise. Pensylvania has alone adopted the expedient. Her citizens are much divided on the subject of their constitution in general & probably on this part of it in particular I am inclind to think though am far from being certain, that it is not a favourite part even with those who are fondest of their Constitution. Another plan has been thought of which might perhaps Succeed better and would at the same time be a safeguard to the equilibrium of the constituent Departments of Government. This is that a Majority of any two of the three departments should have authority to call a plenipotentiary convention whenever they may think their constitutional powers have been Violated by the other Department or that any material part of the Constitution needs amendment. In your situation I should think [it] both imprudent & indecent not to leave a door open for at least one revision of your first Establishment; imprudent because you have neither the same resources for supporting nor the same lights for framing a good establishment now as you will have 15 or 20 Years hence; indecent because an handfull of early sett[l]ers ought not to preclude a populous Country from a choice of the Government under which they & their

Posterity are to live. Should your first Constitution be made thus temporary the objections against an intermediate union of officers will be proportionably lessen'd. Should a revision of it not be made thus necessary & certain there will be little probability of its being ever revised. Faulty as our Constitution is as well with regard to the Authority which formed it as the manner in which it is formed the Issue of an experiment has taught us the difficulty of amending it; & Although the issue might have proceeded from the unseasonableness of the time yet it may be questioned whether at any future time the greater depth to which it will have stricken its roots will not counterballance any more auspicious circumstances for overturning it.

5 & 6 "Or will it be better unalterably to fix some leading Principles in Government and make it consistant for the Legislature to introduce such changes in lessor matters as may become expedient? can censors be provided that will impartially point out differences in the Constitutions & the Violations that may happen. ["] Answers on these points may be gatherd from what has been already said.

I have been led to offer my sentiments in this loose forms rather than to attempt a delineation of such a plan of Government as would please myself not only by my Ignorance of many local circumstances & opinions which must be consulted in such a work but also by the want of sufficient time for it. At the recei[p]t of your letter I had other employment and what I now write is in the midst of preparations for a Journey of business which will carry me as far as Philadelphia at least & on which I shall set out in a day or two.

I am sorry that it is not in my power to give you some satisfactory information concerning the Mississippi. A Minister from Spain has been with Congress for some time & is authorised as I understand to treat on what ever subjects may concern the two nations. If any explanations or propositions have passed between him & the Minister of Congress, they are as yet on the list of Cabinett Secrets. As soon as any such shall be made public & come to my knowledge I shall take the first opportunity of transmitting them. Wishing you & your family all happiness I am Dr Sir Yours friend & Servant

J MADISON JR

The Constitutions of the several States were printed in a small Volume a year or two ago by order of Congs.[10] A perusal of them need not be recommended to you. Having but a single copy I cannot supply you. It is not improbable that you may be already possessed of one. The Revisall of our laws by Jefferson, Withe & Pendleton beside their Value in improving the legal code may suggest some things worthy of being attended to in framing a Constitution.

Tr (DLC). This copy in an unknown hand of the missing original Ms is headed, "To Jno. Brown (Kentucky)." The Tr is docketed by JM, "To Brown Jno." However, Gaillard Hunt saw this was an error and he made the correction in Madison, *Writings* (Hunt ed.), II, 166 n.

[1] Probably the Reverend Elijah Craig of Orange County, who seems to have visited Kentucky before he finally settled there in 1786 (*Papers of Madison*, I, 183 n. 7).

[2] George Muter's letter of 6 Jan. 1785 gave JM the first hint that the Kentucky settlers wanted his counsel.

[3] The Maryland Senate was chosen by county electors who met every five years and elected fifteen senators, nine from the western shore and six from the eastern counties. JM disliked the Virginia constitutional provision for a 24-seat Senate wherein a fourth of the members were rotated out of office annually. The plan Jefferson had proposed in 1776 created a Senate of at least 15 senators but no more than 50, who held office for six-year terms on a triennial rotation with reelection forbidden (Poore, *Federal and State Constitutions*, I, 822–23; Boyd, *Papers of Jefferson*, I, 348–49, 358–59). Surely even JM was not in favor of Jefferson's first thought on the subject—a senate elected for life (ibid., I, 341).

[4] The New York Constitution (Art. III) created a "Council of Revision" consisting of the governor, chancellor, and supreme court, which reviewed all pending legislation "about to be passed into laws." After a bill passed it was again presented to this council and a reconsideration could be ordered. Bills thus designated as "improper to the said council" became law only if passed by a two-thirds majority of both houses (Poore, *Federal and State Constitutions*, II, 1332). During the Federal Convention (21 July 1787), JM spoke out for a "Revisionary check on the Legislature" in terms similar to the New York Council (Madison, *Convention Notes*, p. 340).

[5] JM worried with this question for another two years but went to the Federal Convention convinced that a legislative body should not choose "the first Magistrate." By July 1787 he believed such a system "would agitate & divide the legislature so much that the public interest would materially suffer by it" (Farrand, ed., *Records of the Federal Convention*, II, 109).

[6] JM's belief that "the reasons of Lord Bacon . . . outweigh . . . those of Lord Kaims [Kames]" is an allusion to Bacon's separation of common law cases from equity matters ("Ordinances" in James Spedding et al., eds., *The Works of Francis Bacon* [7 vols.; London, 1857–59], VII, 401, 762). Kames, in his *Principles of Equity* (1760), commented on the English practice but favored "the union of the powers of both [common law and equity causes] in one tribunal as in the Supreme Civil Court of Scotland" (Joseph Parkes, *A History of the Court of Chancery* . . . [London, 1828], pp. 333–34).

[7] The North Carolina Constitution of 1776 allowed all taxpaying freemen "of the age of twenty-one years" who had a year's residence in the state to vote for delegates to its House of Commons. Voters for state senators were also required to own (in the county where they voted) fifty acres of land six months prior to election day (Poore, *Federal and State Constitutions*, II, 1411).

[8] JM's footnote alluded to the New York constitutional provision for printed or written ballots "after the termination of the present war" for state representatives and senators. Poore notes that a 1778 act in New York "introduced the practice of

voting by ballot for governor and lieutenant-governor only, but retained the *viva voce* method" for legislators. The constitution also provided for abolition of the ballot system if a fair trial proved it inferior to "voting *viva voce*" (ibid., II, 1333–34).

[9] JM was all too aware of Article V of the Virginia Declaration of Rights, which recommended that public officials "should, at fixed periods, be reduced to a private station." JM was no friend of this idea, which in practice had caused him to move from the Council of State to Congress and back to the House of Delegates, in the space of seven years.

[10] This compendium was printed in 1781 (Evans 17390).

From Jean August Marie Chevallié

NEW YORK the 27. Augustus 1785

Sir

Me. Chevallié merchant of Rockefort, my father embarked in 1778 in the Caracter of supercargo upon the Ship le fier Roderigue belonging to Me. Caron de Beaumarchais, and treated of the Cargo with the State of Virginia.[1] Some Contestations having been raised after wards among them, my father having manifested to Me. Caron de Beaumarchais the désire to discontinue all Connection, the latter gave him in payment of his Commission, a bill of fourty six thousand Pounds of tobacco, and a délégation of £420. Pounds hard moneys, Payable by the thrésaury of the State upon the sums that are due to him, with the intérest of these two sums from the first of July 1778 to the day of Payment.

Repeated disasters having dissipated all the hopes of tranquility wich a considérable fortune gained with infinite pain had given to my father, he resolved to send me to this continent, in order to obtain what is due to him as well by congress and the State of Virginia, as by different individuals of Philadelphia and of yorktown. Many men of Great considération espécially the Minister of the Marine, his first Secretary, the Mis. de la fayette and the Count delatoushe, knowing how little he had merited the misfortunes that oppress him, désirous to Give him a testimoney of their esteem and of their wishes, for the final arrangement of his affairs, in order to Conserve his reputation unimpaired to this day, these noblemen gave me their lettres of recommandation written with the greatest force to the french Consuls and to many members of Congress and to some men of distinction in the State of Virginia. The most flattering of them is addressed to you, Sir, by the Mis. de la fayette. I reserve to myself the honour to deliver it into your hands in about á mounth, when I intend to set out to Richmond. I shall do all that is in my power to deserve the support of your protection. It is impossible,

Sir, to express the Sentiments of Gratitude, with wich I shall be penetrated, if you put it in the power of an only Son to be useful to a father he cherishes and to justify the good opinion wich has been conceived of a young man of twenty years. With the highest respect and esteem I have the honour to be Sir Very obédient and most humble Servant

CHEVALLIÉ FILS

RC (DLC). Cover missing. Docketed by JM.

1 Pierre François Chevallié supplied goods to Virginia through a contract made by Beaumarchais with the state during the Revolutionary War years. In a letter to Benjamin Franklin concerning payment for these goods, Jefferson advised Chevallié to send a representative to the United States (Jefferson to Franklin, 1 Dec. 1784, Boyd, *Papers of Jefferson*, VII, 553–54). Chevallié's son, Jean August Marie Chevallié (1765–1838), was his father's choice to collect his claim against Virginia. The affair was eventually settled, much to the satisfaction of the Frenchmen (ibid., XI, 55). Young Chevallié settled in Richmond and, in 1790, married Sarah Magee. He speculated in western lands and became an entrepreneur with an investment in the Gallego mills. Later he married Catherine Power Lyons, daughter of Judge Peter Lyons, and their Richmond home became a social center in the capital. Chevallié remained a friend of JM's and a visit to the Chevallié home by JM and Dolley Madison in 1829 is recorded (*Richmond Portraits in an Exhibition of Makers of Richmond, 1737–1860* [Richmond, 1949], pp. 36–37).

From Jacob Read

CHAMBER OF CONGRESS
NEW YORK Monday 29th August 1785

SIR

An opinion prevails in South Carolina that the principal holders of Slaves in your State wish to divest themselves of that kind of property and that tollerable good purchases might be made on good Security being given for payments by Instalments with a regular discharge of the Interest.[1]

Under the Impression of this opinion the Honle: Mr; J: Rutledge of So. Carolina has addressed a Letter to me wishing to become engaged in any purchase I may be able to make, & to make a Joint Concern. You know his Validity & I do not mean to deceive you when I say I am possessed of a property that will fully authorize me to engage in a Considerable purchase. My present Application to you is to request you to Inform me if you know of any Such persons as may wish to Sell a gang of Hands & the Terms on which they might be had—on Receiving intelligence of the Name & Residence of the party I'd write myself to such person more particularly. Excuse the Liberty I take in troubling you on this Subject and be assured that if any occasion shall offer in which I can be at all Serviceable to you or any of your friends it will give me great pleasure to Receive your Commands.

Congress is thin & I am Sorry to say the States seem averse to do any Act that has in prospect to assert the Dignity of the federal Government. We Debate—make & hear long & often spirited Speeches but when the Moment arives for a Vote *We Adjourn* & thus the feelings of Individuals & the Welfare of the Union is trifled with.

We have not yet got through a requisition for the Expences of the Current year—our Treasury is exceedingly low. We have in short nothing Pleasing in prospect & if in a short time the States do not enable Congress to act with some Vigour & put the power of Compulsion into the hand of the Union I am free to Confess I think it almost time to give over the Force of what I cannot consider as an Official Government. We want! Greatly want!! the Assistance of your abilities & experience in Congress. I woul[d] not be thought to Derogate from the Men or abilities of the present Delegation but one cannot help drawing Comparisons betwe[en] the Language of 1780 and 1785. It will be always pleasing to me to hear of your Health & Welfare. I beg favour of a Speedy Answer[2] & am Sir With very great respect and regard Your Most Obedient & Most Humle Servant

JACOB READ

RC (DLC). Cover missing. Docketed by JM.

[1] In Apr. and May, 1785, Methodist ministers, led by bishops Francis Asbury and Thomas Coke, attempted to increase support for antislavery resolutions passed in the Methodist Conference held at Baltimore in Dec. 1784. Virginia was the focal point of these efforts. Asbury reported in his journal that he and his followers approached Washington and received his opinion opposing slavery. It was during this crusade that the Methodists drew up a petition calling for the House of Delegates to effect a general emancipation of slaves. This petition provoked considerable excitement and anger when it was considered during the 1785 session of the General Assembly (Albert Matthews, "Notes on the Proposed Abolition of Slavery in Virginia in 1785," Colonial Society of Massachusetts, *Publications*, VI [1904], 370–80). The petition against slavery was publicized long before the legislative session began, appearing in the *Va. Gazette* on 6 and 13 Aug. and again during the session on 5 Nov. 1785. This antislavery agitation clearly was conducive to the impression that slavery was on the wane in Virginia.

[2] If JM replied, his answer has not been found.

From Thomas Jefferson

PARIS Sep. 1. 1785.

DEAR SIR

My last to you was dated May 11. by Monsr. de Doradour. Since that I have received yours of Jan. 22. with 6. copies of the revisal, and that of Apr. 27. by mr Mazzei.

All is quiet here. The Emperor & Dutch are certainly agreed tho' they have not published their agreement. Most of his schemes in Germany must be postponed, if they are not prevented, by the confederacy of many of the Germanic body at the head of which is the K. of Prussia, & to which the Elector of Hanover is supposed to have acceded. The object of the league is to preserve the members of the empire in their present state. I doubt whether the jealousy entertained of this prince, & which is so fully evidenced by this league, may not defeat the election of his nephew to be king of the Romans, & thus produce an instance of breaking the lineal succession. Nothing is as yet done between him & the Turks. If any thing is produced in that quarter it will not be for this year.[1] The court of Madrid has obtained the delivery of the crew of the brig Betsy taken by the Emperor of Marocco. The Emperor had treated them kindly, new-cloathed them, & delivered them to the Spanish minister who sent them to Cadiz. This is the only American vessel ever taken by the Barbary States. The Emperor continues to give proofs of his desire to be in friendship with us, or in other words, of receiving us into the number of his tributaries. Nothing further need be feared from him. I wish the Algerines may be as easily dealt with. I fancy the peace expected between them & Spain is not likely to take place.[2] I am well informed that the late proceedings in America have produced a wonderful sensation in England in our favour. I mean the disposition which seems to be becoming general to invest Congress with the regulation of our commerce, and in the mean time the measures taken to defeat the avidity of the British government, grasping at our carrying business. I can add with truth that it was not till these symptoms appeared in America that I have been able to discover the smallest token of respect towards the United states in any part of Europe. There was an enthusiasm towards us all over Europe at the moment of the peace. The torrent of lies published unremittingly in every day's London paper first made an impression and produced a coolness. The republication of these lies in most of the papers of Europe (done probably by authority of the governments to discourage emigrations) carried them home to the belief

361

of every mind, they supposed every thing in America was anarchy, tumult, and civil war. The reception of the M. Fayette gave a check to these ideas. The late proceedings seem to be producing a decisive vibration in our favour. I think it possible that England may ply before them. It is a nation which nothing but views of interest can govern. If it produces us good there, it will here also. The defeat of the Irish propositions is also in our favor.

I have at length made up the purchase of books for you, as far as it can be done for the present. The objects which I have not yet been able to get, I shall continue to seek for. Those purchased, are packed this morning in two trunks, and you have the catalogue & prices herein inclosed.[3] The future charges of transportation shall be carried into the next bill. The amount of the present is 1154 livres 13 sous which reckoning the French crown of 6. livres at 6/8 Virginia money is £64-3. which sum you will be so good as to keep in your hands to be used occasionally in the education of my nephews when the regular resources disappoint you. To the same use I would pray you to apply twenty five guineas which I have lent the two mr Fitzhughs of Marmion, & which I have desired them to repay into your hands.[4] You will of course deduct the price of the revisals & any other articles you may have been so kind as to pay for me. Greek & Roman authors are dearer here than I believe any where in the world. No body here reads them, wherefore they are not reprinted. Don Ulloa in the original not to be found. The collection of tracts on the œconomics of different nations we cannot find; nor Amelot's travels into China. I shall send these two trunks of books to Havre there to wait a conveiance to America; for as to the fixing the packets there it is as incertain as ever. The other articles you mention shall be procured as far as they can be. Knowing that some of them would be better got in London, I commissioned mr. Short, who was going there, to get them. He is not yet returned. They will be of such a nature as that I can get some gentleman who may be going to America to take them in his portmanteau. Le Maire being now able to stand on his own legs there will be no necessity for your advancing him the money I desired if it is not already done.[5] I am anxious to hear from you on the subject of my Notes on Virginia. I have been obliged to give so many of them here that I fear their getting published. I have received an application from the Directors of the public buildings to procure them a plan for their Capitol. I shall send them one taken from the best morsel of antient architecture now remaining. It has obtained the approbation of fifteen or sixteen centuries, & is therefore preferable to any design which might be newly contrived. It will give more room, be more convenient & cost less than the plan they sent me. Pray encourage them to wait for it, & to execute it. It will be superior in beauty to any thing in America, & not inferior to any thing in the world. It is very simple. Have you a copying press? If you have not, you should get one. Mine (exclusive of paper which costs a guinea a ream) has cost me about 14. guineas. I would give ten times that sum that I had had it from the date of the stamp act. I hope you will be so good as to continue your communications both of the great & small kind which are equally useful to me. Be assured of the sincerity with which I am Dr. Sir Your friend & servt.

TH. JEFFERSON

RC (DLC); FC (DLC: Jefferson Papers). Cover missing. Docketed by JM. The enclosure is no longer with the RC, but a copy is in DLC, Jefferson Papers, and has been reproduced in Boyd, *Papers of Jefferson*, VIII, 462–64.

[1] Joseph II of Austria was attempting to widen his sphere of influence but made little headway because of French opposition. See Lafayette to JM, 16 Mar. 1785; Jefferson to JM, 18 Mar. 1785.

[2] The case of the *Betsy* had been pending since late 1784. Jefferson's prediction that the Algerines would be more difficult to deal with proved to be the case; Grayson reported to JM that the Barbary pirates had declared war against American ships (Grayson to JM, 14 Oct. 1785).

[3] JM's list of books went to Jefferson in his 27 Apr. 1785 letter. For Jefferson's enclosure, see Boyd, *Papers of Jefferson*, VIII, 462–64.

[4] Daniel and Theodorick Fitzhugh were brothers from Stafford County, Virginia.

[5] Le Maire's claim against the Commonwealth remained unsettled until Jan. 1786 (JM to Jefferson, 27 Apr. 1785, n. 1).

From Ambrose Madison

Letter not found.

9 September 1785. Mentioned in JM's letter to Ambrose dated 20 September 1785. Probably concerned property transactions and tobacco sales.

From William Grayson

NEW YORK 16th. Sepr. 1785.

DEAR SIR

I opened your letter directed to Colo. Monroe in the first instance, & forwarded the inclosed letters to France,[1] in the public Mail, as I could not hear of any private gentlemen going to whom I could with propriety intrust them.

I have recieved your letter from Philada.[2] & I heartily wish it may suit your Convenience to visit this place, as it will give me particular satisfaction to have the pleasure of seeing you. Exclusive of this I could wish to consult you on some particular matters respecting the State. The requisition is now in the last stage: it is formed on principles to suit only the Eastern & some of the middle States. There seems also to be a radical unwillingless to allow us for our assumptions, although the debt was created for Continental uses; and a proposition (where in the interest was dropped for the present) has been negatived by a considerable majority.[3] The Delegation is strongly impressed with the necessity of supporting public credit;[4] they notwithstanding as well as the Delegates of some other States, hesitate to pass the requisition in its present form. They could wish it was made conformable to the different interests of the Union, & that certain principles might be adopted to facilitate the settlement of the general account. With respect to myself I never admired the idea of facilities.[5] The word implies a payment less than the thing itself. An inundation of a kind of paper money is also to be feared; but for the sake of peace I have been willing to consent as far as one third which is more than the Southern States can ever derive any advantage from.

We have lately recieved a letter from the Governor inclosing one from Soliciter Wood furnishing a melancholy picture of the situation of the public accounts.[6] The Continental Comm. objects to every thing; says he can't proceed witht. fresh instructions & I fear it is not in our power to obtain such principles as will enable us to bring forward our Accounts. There is also a heavy party here for obliging the States to settle by a particular day, or to pay interest to those who do.

I every day discover more & more the impropriety of remaining longer at this place. It is clear to me that it has an undue influence on our proceedings. Some of the Southern States begin at length to percieve this, & I hope it will not be long before the whole will view it in the same light. My best complimts. to Mrs. House and Mrs. Trist: her arrival among her friends has given me the most sincere satisfaction. In full expectation of seeing you I remain yr. Affect. frd. & Most Obed Sert.

WILLM. GRAYSON.

5 Copies sent of the tryal.[7]
Nothing from Adams.[8]

RC (DLC). Cover missing. Docketed by JM.

[1] JM's letters to France probably included his to Jefferson dated 20 Aug. 1785. Neither the covering letter to Monroe nor those forwarded have been found.
[2] Not found.
[3] By "our assumptions" Grayson meant the military expenses of 1776–1781 which

Virginia had incurred but expected either reimbursement or credit from the national government toward annual quotas or requisitions. The New England delegates were particularly opposed to the granting of credit to Virginia for these "unauthorized expenditures," fearing "a flood of extravagant claims from Virginia (Ferguson, *The Power of the Purse*, pp. 206–7, 211; see also Monroe to JM, 12 July 1785, n. 1).

[4] The Virginia delegation fluctuated in membership during the late summer of 1785. Grayson was constant in his attendance; Monroe left in mid-Aug.; Richard Henry Lee left in early August and returned on 29 Sept. (Burnett, *Letters*, VIII, xcviii).

[5] "Facilities" or indents were certificates of interest due on the loan office domestic notes issued because the treasury had no cash. When a holder of loan office paper sought his interest due, he was issued an "indent" or "facility" in lieu of cash, and in some states these indents were accepted by state governments as tender for taxes. Congress on 28 Apr. 1784 had sanctioned this practice by allowing a state to pay up to one-fourth of its annual requisition in these "indents." The requisition finally approved at this current session on 27 Sept. 1785 permitted one-third of a state's quota to be paid "in actual money," the other portion in "facilities" (*JCC*, XXVI, 312–13; XXIX, 768).

[6] Henry's letter was delayed to include the enclosure from Leighton Wood. The governor dated his letter 12 Aug. 1785 (William Wirt Henry, *Patrick Henry: Life, Correspondence, and Speeches* [3 vols.; New York, 1891], III, 314–16) while Wood's report was dated 13 Aug. (*Cal. of Va. State Papers*, IV, 48).

[7] Grayson and Madison had been discussing the Longchamps-Marbois affair. Grayson perhaps obtained copies of Longchamps's trial report for JM.

[8] Written by Grayson in the margin.

To Ambrose Madison

PHILADA. Sepr. 20, 1785

I recd. yesterday yours of the 9 inst.[1] You will do well in hastening the exaction of a Deed from Jones, as you have now actually paid part of the purchase money. His death or a refusal of his wife to concur in a conveyance will produce much perplexity, and possibly Loss. The result of further enquiry here is more favorable than the information contained in my last. I find that Tobo. of the best quality will command 55/. Pa. Curry. that the quality alone is the object of choice, without regard to the river from which it comes—that freight may probably be had at any time, tho' it is very high as yet, not less than 25/ Pa. Cy. per Hhd. and that storage may be had at 4 or 5/. per Hhd per Month now, but it is supposed it will become cheaper. Notwithstanding these circumstances I shall be very shy of making *engagements* with persons here; such has been the frequency of unexpected failures. I am inclined to think the safest beginning will be by way of consignment which will leave us at full liberty to continue enterd or drop the plan as we may like, and will not place us in any connection with the fate of people here. A partnership will make our property in these hands liable. A consignment only leaves the property entirely ours. Wheat I am told may be sold for 8/4 per Bushel. Hemp has sold as high as 7d. per H. and the Legislature here has laid some duties which must raise it still higher, or at least favor its price. I believe I shall set off for N. Y. tomorrow or next day. On my return I shall write again unless it sd. be so near my setting out for Va as to be unnecessary. I recd. a letter yesterday from Mr. Jefferson by which I find that a packet is gone on to my father's for me under seal. Let it not be opened before my return. Adieu

RC (NN). Addressed to JM's brother "care of J. Maury, Esqr. Fredaricksbg." Unsigned. The left margin is torn, obscuring the heading.

¹ Ambrose Madison's letter of 9 Sept. 1785 has not been found.

From Thomas Jefferson

Paris Sep. 20. 1785.

Dear Sir

By mr Fitzhugh you will receive my letter of the 1'st inst. He is still here, & gives me an opportunity of again addressing you much sooner than I should have done but for the discovery of a great peice of in-attention. In that letter I send you a detail of the cost of your books, and desire you to keep the amount in your hands, as if I had forgot, that a part of it was in fact your own, as being a balance of what I had remained in your debt. I really did not attend to it in the moment of writing, & when it occurred to me, I revised my memorandum book from the time of our being in Philadelphia together, & stated our account from the beginning lest I should forget or mistake any part of it. I inclose you this state. You will always be so good as to let me know from time to time your advances for me. Correct with freedom all my proceedings for you, as in what I do I have no other desire than that of doing exactly what will be most pleasing to you.

I received this summer a letter from Messrs. Buchanan & Hay as directors of the public buildings desiring I would have drawn for them plans of sundry buildings, & in the first place of a Capitol. They fixed for their receiving this plan a day which was within one month of that on which their letter came to my hand. I engaged an Architect of capital abilities in this business. Much time was requisite, after the external form was agreed on, to make the internal distribution convenient for the three branches of government. This time was much lengthened by my avocations to other objects which I had no right to neglect. The plan however was settled. The gentlemen had sent me one which they had thought of. The one agreed on here is more convenient, more beautiful, gives more room & will not cost more than two thirds of what that would. We took for our model what is called the Maisonquarrée of Nismes, one of the most beautiful, if not the most beautiful & precious morcel of architecture left us by antiquity.[1] It was built by Caius & Lucius Caesar & repaired by Louis XIV. and has the suffrage of all the judges of architecture who have seen it as yeilding to no one of the beautiful monuments of Greece, Rome, Palmyra & Balbec which late travellers have communicated to us. It is very simple, but it is noble beyond expression, and would have done honour to our country as presenting to travellers a morsel of taste in our infancy promising much for our maturer age. I have been much mortified with information which I received two days ago from Virginia that the first brick of the Capitol would be laid within a few days. But surely the delay of this peice of a summer would have been repaid by the savings in the plan preparing here, were we to value it's other superiorities as nothing. But how is a taste in this beautiful art to be formed in our countrymen unless we avail ourselves of every occasion when public buildings are to be erected, of presenting to them models for their study & imitation? Pray try if you can effect the stopping of this work. I have written also to E. R. on the subject. The loss will be only of the laying the bricks already laid, or a part of them. The bricks themselves will do again for the interior walls, & one side wall & one end wall may remain as they will answer equally well for our plan. This loss is not to be weighed against the saving of money which will arise, against the comfort of laying out the public money for something honourable, the satisfaction of seeing an object & proof of national good taste, & the regret and mortification of erecting a monument of our barbarism which shall be loaded with execrations as long as it shall endure. The plans are in good forwardness & I hope will be ready within three or four weeks. They could not be stopped now but on paying their whole price which will be considerable. If the Undertakers are afraid to undo what they have done, encourage them to it by a recommendation from the assembly. You see I am an enthusiast on the subject of the arts. But it is an enthusiasm of which I am not ashamed, as it's object is to improve the taste of my countrymen, to increase their reputation, to reconcile to them the respect of the world & procure them it's praise.

I shall send off your books, in two trunks, to Havre within two or three days to the care of mr Limozin, American agent there. I will advise you as soon as I know by what vessel he forwards them. Adieu Your's affectionately

TH: JEFFERSON

[Enclosure]

J. Madison to Th: J Dr.

			Dollars
1783. Nov.	5.	To paid Stockdon at Princeton....................	9.133
		Dr. Wiggins.........................	2.333
		Laurence............................	4.533
	13.	to cash..................................	86.666
			102.666

Cr.

			Dollars	
Nov.	2.	By cash...........................	98.	
	12.	By do............................	4.666	102.666

Dr.

1784.

			Dollars	
Apr.	6.	To paid Dudley (by mr Maury) for a pr. spectacles............................	13.666	
		To my assumpsit to do. for a 2d. pr. spectacles.	13.666	
		To my bill on the Treasurer of Virginia for ..	407.333	
		Balance in your favour...................	68.666	503.333

Cr.

1783. Nov.	22.	By cash at Philadelphia..............	170.	
	26.	By bill on the Treasurer of Virginia (given me at Annapolis)..............	333.333	503.333

Dr.

1784. May	25.	To pd. Aitken for Blair's lectures for you	4.666	
		Balance in your favor................	77.666	82.333

Cr.

1784.	By balance as above................	68.666	
	By my omission to pay Dudley for the 2d pr of spectacles..................	13.666	82.333

1784 [1785].   J. Madison to Th: J. Dr.

		lt	s
Sep. 1. To amount of advances for books &c. as by acct. rendered this day..		1154	13
Testament politique d'Angleterre 12mo.................		2	10
Memoires de Voltaire 12mo.........................		3	0
Frederic le grand. 8vo.............................		4	0
		1164	3

RC (DLC). Cover missing. Docketed by JM: "Recd. Feby. 24. 1786." The enclosure (DLC) is mounted separately from the RC, under Jefferson to JM, 2 Aug. 1787.

[1] When Jefferson wrote of the Maison Carrée at Nîmes he had not yet seen the classic structure but was relying upon engravings and hearsay. The architect he engaged to help in the work of planning a proper capitol for Virginia was Charles Clérisseau (Boyd, *Papers of Jefferson*, IX, xxvii, 602–4).

From Caleb Wallace

LINCOLN COUNTY. Sep. 25th. 1785

DEAR SIR,

Two Days ago I received your favour of the 23. of August. Having only an Evening's leisure after attending a very Strong Session of our Court for three Weeks to answer several of my Eastern Correspondents I only intend a short Line at present. In my Letter by[1] Mr. Elijah Craig[2] I believe I omitted particularly to inform you that last December a Deputy from the Several Militia Companies in this District assembled to take under Consideration the State of the District. A Number of Grievances were then stated which cannot be redressed whilst in Connexion with Virginia; and therefore it was recommended to the People to elect another Convention to take into Consideration the propriety and Expediency of a Seperation. This Convention met in May, and unanimously resolved that a Seperation was indispensable but at the same Time it was thought expedient to recommend the election of a third finally to decide upon the Question. At this an Address to the Assembly praying for an Act of Seperation, and several Resolves expressing the Reasons on which the Prayer is founded and the Terms on which the Seperation is requested were agreed on. I must confess I am not pleased with the Splendid Dress in which they are cloathed, and wish the Substance of the Resolves had composed the Body of the Address, but hope that impropriety in form will not injure a Cause which I am anxious should be determined on the most friendly and liberal principles.[3]

George Muter and Harry Innes[4] esquires are appointed to wait on the Assembly with our Petition, who will explain our Views more to your Satisfaction than I can do by Letter. It would be presuming in me to Name these Gentlemen by Way of Recommendation; And I am perswaded you will take Pleasure in patronizing the District by which they are sent so far as our Wishes accord with your Judgment, and further

would be unreasonable for me to request. I am Dr Sir, Your friend &
Servant

CALEB WALLACE

RC (DLC). Cover missing. Docketed by JM.

¹ The version of this letter edited by James A. Pagett, "Letters of Caleb Wallace
to James Madison," Kentucky State Historical Society, *Register*, XXXV (1937),
211, replaces "by" with the word "to."

² A Virginian, the Reverend Elijah Craig migrated to Kentucky in 1786. For a
record of his career as a dissenting minister, see *Papers of James Madison*, I, 183
n. 7.

³ The December meeting resulted from a previous gathering called in Danville
by Gen. Benjamin Logan. Held on 27 Dec. 1784, the convention included representatives from the militia districts who discussed separation but felt the matter
should be determined by a civilian convention. Twenty-five delegates met on 23
May 1785. Others besides Wallace were disappointed with the resolutions passed,
and a third formal convention met on 8 Aug. 1785, adopting two resolutions stronger than the former appeal to the House of Delegates (Collins and Collins, *History
of Kentucky*, I, 21). The August address to the delegates (Vi) is printed in James
Rood Robertson, *Petitions of the Early Inhabitants of Kentucky* (Louisville, 1914),
pp. 79–82.

⁴ Muter became a district judge for Kentucky in 1785, and in 1786 was promoted
to chief justice for Kentucky. For his previous career, see *Papers of Madison*, I, 239
nn. 1 and 2.

Harry Innes became a district judge for Kentucky in 1783, and in 1785 became
attorney general for Kentucky. Both Muter and Innes were later implicated in the
Spanish schemes to gain Kentucky's independence (DLC: Innes Papers, James Wil-
kinson Correspondence).

From John Hatley Norton

WINCHESTER Octr. 1st. 1785.

DEAR SIR,

You cannot be a Stranger to the several Acts passed in our Assembly
during the late War relative to Citizens of this State & british Subjects
who had commercial Interests in this Country, as well as those who
were Partners with them in this State; & that one was enacted preventing the latter from recovering their Debts, which at this Time is un-
repealed, & another leaving them exposed to the full force of all judiciary proceedings in a[ccounts owed by them as] Debtors to Citizens of
this State.¹ This indulgence granted to the Citizens in our Case, & the
oppression fixed on the British Subject in the othe[r], you will surely
think repugnant to every principle of equity, & ought not to be coun-
tenanced in a Country which has been for so many years contending
for Liberty founded in Justice, & the Rights of Mankind, & that your

Laws shou'd not make any distinction between the Citizens of this State, & those of any other Country, as former Connections had placed them upon an equal footing as to Matters of a private nature. It is therefore to be wished that the most salutary Laws for the purpose of reforming some now in force, may have your Voice & support at the next Session of Assembly, & that a Majority of your House may second & promote your Interests & e[nd]eavours for having them enacted. In all Cases which can comprehend the true Interests of the Citizens of this State & british Subjects & those in Partnership with them res[i]d[in]g in the State, as well as the Rights of mankind in gen[eral. I think] you [as] a Man of Honour, Candour & Liberality will consider them on all Points without prejudice, & wherever you find either Defects or omissions in the Laws of our Country, you will be active in making such alterations or additions, as the Particular Cases may require; In attention to which you will do Justice to the Injured, & Honour to Yourself, being—Dr Sr Your most obedt Servt,

J. H. NORTON

(Turnover)[2]

Dr. Sr. The foregoing is Submitted to your most Serious consideration, & as all our family have been uniformly attach[ed] to the Interests of this Country, & made every exertion in their Power as to Advances of money to this State, & at a *Crisis when it was most wanted, & cou'd not have been procured from any other House in great Britain*, I should hope that the peculiarity of their present Situation [w]ill [be attended] to by the Legislature, & followed by that Degree of [I]ndulgence & generosity which have ever Characterized the inhabitants of this State— being with Respect Dr Sr Your most obedt Servt

J. H. NORTON

RC (DLC). Cover missing. The portions damaged by blotting and tears have been restored by conjectures enclosed within brackets.

[1] The Virginia legislature passed an act at the Oct. 1782 session which forbade suits by British citizens for recovery of any debt contracted before 19 Apr. 1775 (Hening, *Statutes*, XI, 176–80). Though the law was originally scheduled to expire on 1 Dec. 1783, it had been retained through a series of "stay" laws and JM had failed to win over a majority to a more liberal policy, despite his efforts at the Oct. 1784 and subsequent sessions. JM reported that continued hostility toward repayment of British debts made efforts to pass a watered-down version of a debt-recovery bill impossible (JM to Monroe, 30 Dec. 1785). This bill was finally tabled and although a bill passed in 1787 permitting recovery of debts, its enforcement was contingent upon official notice that Great Britain had reimbursed America for slaves lost during the war and had evacuated the western forts still occupied (Hening, *Statutes*, XII, 528; Andrew C. McLaughlin, "The Western Posts and British

Debts," *Annual Report of the American Historical Association for . . . 1894* [Washington, 1895], pp. 421–22). There the matter stood until the Constitution went into operation in 1789 and made legal action in federal courts possible (Harrell, *Loyalism in Virginia*, pp. 113–52; *Papers of Madison*, I, 318 n.). For Norton's postwar problems see Mason, *John Norton & Sons* (1968 ed.), pp. xxxi–xxxii, 459–81.

    ² Norton wrote a postscript on the verso of his message.

From John Hatley Norton

WINCHESTER Octr. 2d. 1785.

DEAR 'SIR,

    With this you will receive a Letter from me dated Yesterday which contains such Sentiments as wou'd naturally arise from the peculiarity of my Situation & my Brothers, in which I shou'd hope you will find nothing dictatorial or offensive. I have wrote to many of my friends on the Assembly in the same Style, who will no doubt concur in such Measures as may be conducive to the Interest of particular Individuals without injury to their own; My principle wish at pres[e]n[t is that] some favorable Clause may pass the House of Assembly preventing the Laws from operating against us in Matters of Accts., & as to Requisitions for Recovery of british Debts, good policy & prudential Motives will no doubt dictate to the Legislature when, & in what manner Individuals under the Class of british Subjects, & Natives, Partners with them, shou'd receive Payment of Debts due to them from Citizens of this State. An allowance of Interest, & Security for these Debts you will probably think but reasonable, as suppose one half the Interest.

    There is a Case at present which bears hard on some Individuals; a Transaction happens in the West Indies between two Merchts of this State. The plaintiff by accident finds an Agent for one of the Houses in this State as he came over to do some business, & takes an opporty. before he moves away of geting his Deposition. The defendt. also finds an Agent in Pennsylvania or Maryland whose deposition is absolutely necessary to confront the other, but it cannot be had because the Laws of this Country deny it to him as this Agent is out of the State. This surely is a manifest injury to the defendant, & you will think some provision shou'd be made for his Relief & all others in the same situation. I have taken the Liberty of submitting these matters to your Consideration & dont doubt your perceiving at once the glaring Hardships which must attend persons under similar Circumstances.

    Mrs. Norton & family are well & join me in Terms of the highest

Respect for you, Your father & family in Orangeburg. Dear Sir Your most obedt Servt

J. H. NORTON

RC (DLC). Cover addressed by Norton "To James Maddison esqr Member for Orange County." Docketed by JM. The word "Copy" in the lower margin was written by Norton, indicating that he took the precaution of sending the message in duplicate. Words within brackets are conjectures upon the original text, which is damaged.

To Thomas Jefferson

PHILADA. Octr. 3. 1785

DEAR SIR

In pursuance of the plan intimated in my last I came to this City about three weeks ago, from which I continued my trip to New York. I returned last night and in a day or two shall start for Virginia. Col: Monroe had left Philada. a few days before I reached it, on his way to a treaty to be held with the Indians about the end of this month on the Wabash. If a visit to the Eastern States had been his choice, short as the time would have proved, I should have made an effort to attend him. As it is I must postpone that gratification, with a purpose however of embracing it on the first convenient opportunity. Your favour of the 11 May by Monsr. Doradour inclosing your Cypher arrived in Virga. after I left it, and was sent after me to this place. Your notes which accompanied it, remained behind, and consequently I can only now say on that subject, that I shall obey your request on my return, which my call to Richmond will give me an early opportunity of doing. During my stay at New York I had several conversations with the Virga. Delegates, but with few others, on the affairs of the Confederacy. I find with much regret that there are as yet little redeemed from the confusion which has so long mortified the friends to our national honor and prosperity. Congress have kept the Vessel from sinking, but it has been by standing constantly at the pump, not by stopping the leaks which have endangered her. All their efforts for the latter purpose have been frustrated by the selfishness or perverseness of some part or other of their Constituents. The desiderata most strongly urged by our past experience & our present situation are 1. a final discrimination between such of the unauthorised expences of the States, as ought to be added to the common debt, and such as ought not. 2. a constitutional apportionment

373

of the common debt, either by a valuation of the land, or a change of the article wch. requires it. 3. a recognition by the States of the authority of Congress to enforce payment of their respective quotas. 4. a grant to Congress of an adequate power over trade. It is evident to me that the first object will never be effected in Congress, because it requires in those who are to decide it the spirit of impartial judges, whilst the spirit of those who compose Congress is rather that of advocates for the respective interests of their constituents. If this business were referred to a Commission filled by a member chosen by Congress out of each State, and sworn to impartiality, I should have hopes of seeing an end of it. The 2d. object affords less ground of hope. The execution of the 8th. art. of Confederation is generally held impracticable, and R. Island, if no other State, has put its veto on the proposed alteration of it. Until the 3d. object can be obtained the Requisitions of Congress will continue to be mere calls for voluntary contributions, which every State will be tempted to evade, by the uniform experience that those States have come off best which have done so most. The present plan of federal Government reverses the first principle of all Government. It punishes not the evil-doers, but those that do well. It may be considered I think as a fortunate circumstance for the U. S. that the use of Coercion, or such provision as would render the use of it unnecessary, might be made at little expence and perfect safety. A single frigate under the orders of Congress could make it the interest of any one of the Atlantic States to pay its just Quota. With regard to such of the Ultramontane States, as depend on the trade of the Mississippi, as small a force would have the same effect; whilst the residue trading thro' the Atlantic States might be wrought upon by means more indirect indeed, but perhaps sufficiently effectual. The fate of the 4th. object is still suspended. The Recommendations of Congs. on this subject past before your departure, have been positively complied with by few of the States I believe; but I do not learn that they have been rejected by any. A proposition has been agitated in Congress, and will I am told be revived, asking from the States a general & permanent authority to regulate trade, with a proviso that it shall in no case be exercised without the assent of *eleven* States in Congress. The Middle States favor the measure, the Eastern are Zealous for it.[1] The Southern are divided. Of the *Virginia Delegation* the *president** is an *inflexibl*[e] *adversary, Grayson unfriendly* and *Monro*[e] & *Har*[dy] *warm on the opposite side.* If the proposition should pass Congs. its fate will depend much on the re-

* R. H. Lee[2]

ception it may find in Virga. and this will depend much on the part which may be taken by a few members of the Legislature. The prospect of its being levelled agst. G. Britain will be most likely to give it popularity. In this suspence of a general provision for our commercial interests, the more suffering States are seeking relief from partial efforts which are less likely to obtain it than to drive their trade into other channels, and to kindle heart burnings on all sides. Massachussetts made the beginning. Penna. has followed with a catalogue of duties on foreign goods & tonnage, which could scarcely be enforced against the smuggler, if N. Jersey, Delaware & Maryland were to co-operate with her. The avowed object of these duties is to encourage domestic manufactures, and prevent the exportation of coin to pay for foreign. The Legislature had previously repealed the incorporation of the bank, as the cause of the latter & a great many other evils. S. Carolina I am told is deliberating on the distresses of her commerce and will probably concur in some general plan; with a proviso, no doubt against any restraint from importing slaves, of which they have received from Africa since the peace about twelve thousand. She is also deliberating on the emission of paper money, & it is expected she will legalize a suspension of Judicial proceedings which has been already effected by popular combinations. The pretext for these measures is the want of specie occasioned by the unfavorable balance of trade. Your introduction of Mr. T. Franklin has been presented to me. The arrival of his Grandfather has produced an emulation among the different parties here in doing homage to his character. He will be unanimously chosen president of the State, and will either restore to it an unexpected quiet or lose his own. It appears from his answer to some applications that he will not decline the appointment. On my journey I called at Mount Vernon & had the pleasure of finding the Genl. in perfect health. He had just returned from a trip up the Potowmac. He grows more & more sanguine, as he examines further into the practicability of opening its navigation. The subscriptions are compleated within a few shares, and the work is already begun at some of the lesser obstructions. It is overlooked by Rhumsey the inventor of the boats which I have in former letters mentioned to you. He has not yet disclosed his secret. He had of late nearly finished a boat of proper size wch. he meant to have exhibited, but the house which contained it & materials for others was consumed by fire. He assured the Genl. that the enlargement of his machinery did not lessen the prospect of utility afforded by the miniature experiments.[3] The Genl. declines the shares voted him by the assembly, but does not mean to

375

withdraw the money from the object which it is to aid, and will even appropriate the future tolls I believe to some useful public establishment if any such can be devised that will both please himself & be likely to please the State. This is accompanied by a letter from our amiable friend Mrs. Trist to Miss Patsy. She got back safe to her friends in Augst: & is well as she has generally been, but her cheerfulness seems to be rendered less uniform than it once was by the scenes of adversity through which fortune has led her. Mrs. House is well & charges me not to omit her respectful & affecte. compliments to you. I remain Dr Sir Yrs: &c.

RC (DLC). Without cover or the enclosed letter, which was from Eliza House Trist. Not signed. Docketed. JM appears to have given the letters to William Grayson for forwarding to Jefferson in Paris (Grayson to JM, 14 Oct. 1785). The italicized words, unless otherwise noted, are those encoded by JM in the code Jefferson sent him 11 May 1785.

1 JM first wrote, "The Middle States & Eastern States favor the measure," then altered it. In the preceding sentence, JM underlined "eleven."

2 JM apparently placed the asterisk and identified Lee at some later time.

3 Inventor James Rumsey claimed he had developed a paddlewheel boat which traveled upstream against the force of the current. JM had aided Rumsey in obtaining a patent after Washington saw a model and became an enthusiastic supporter of the unlikely vessel (Bill for Granting James Rumsey a Patent, 11 Nov. 1784).

From Caleb Wallace

October 8. 1785.

DEAR SIR,

By Colo. Muter I troubled you with a short Line;[1] and now have only Leisure to thank you for the Strictures on Government you were so kind as to favour me with.[2] I have yet some other Qu[e]r[i]es on the Subject which I shall reserve for another Opportunity. At present I only beg leave to observe that the Constitution of Virginia provides for the Seperation we have in View in a Way that is unprecedented. An Act of Seperation, I concieve, may direct the whole with but a little more difficulty than a Corporation is established; and so as to prevent a dangerous interval of Anarcy which must otherwise happen. The District has chosen a Convention that is to continue till next April. The Elections though voluntary were made with propriety. This Convention I concieve may be recognized and empowered to direct the Choice of another for the purpose of adopting a Form of Government and organizing it: and in the mean Time it may be provided, that all Officers civil & Military shall continue to enforce the Laws of the present Government with such exceptions as the Case may require.[3] This, or something in this Way may certainly be done with propriety. But I must confess, I find myself perplexed with real Difficulties of another Kind. Our Remote Situation and other local peculiarities excludes us from the Advantages of equal Government whilst connected with Virginia. And the Want of an Export Trade will render us incapable of defraying the Expences of a Seperate Government. The Question then is, Whether our poverty should deprive us of the Rights of Free Men, or not? If it were left to my own Decission, I believe I should advise being contented with a lesser Portion of political Advantages at present, did I not conceive that a Legislature of our own, might do much to regulate Trade or supply the Deficiency, As well as to secure our Inhabitants against the Indians who are daily despoiling us of our property and committing the most horid Murders! Or in a Word, to facilitate the Approach of more happy Days. If the Legislature should accede to the Seperation, I expect the Gentlemen from this Quarter will Solicit your Attention in preparing the Act, and I hope much from your Favour.[4]

This will be handed to you by Capt. Christopher Greenup[5] who I take the Liberty of recommending to you as a Friend I highly esteem for his Integrity and liberality of Sentiment. I have also requested him to shew you a Letter from Colo. M'Dowell and myself addressed to the Speaker of the House of Delegates on behalf of ourselves and the other Officers of this District Court.[6] From the Contents you will easily apprehend the Inconveniencies occasioned by the Inattention or Reluctance of the Assembly to provide for the Support of the Court. I shall only further observe, that after foregoing other Advantages that presented themselves to keep the Court in Existence we have great Reason to complain of the Oversight, and yet to expect a Reimbursement if the Independence of the Judges is thought to be of any Consequence to the public. True it is, that the Court has lingered in a Way greatly to the Injury of the District, but not through the Default of the Judges, but the Want of Houses and Records that could not be procured without Funds. For my own part, upon recieving my Appointment I immediately removed to the Country, and except one Trip to Botetourt to settle my Affairs, I have ever since avoided any Business that would divert my Attention from the Duties of the Office or be otherwise inconsistent, and should now avoid troubling the Legislature on the disagreeable Subject, did not Justice to the Office as well as my Family require it. If it is not too irksome to you to interest yourself in the Application, the Favour will be than[k]fully acknowledged by Dr Sir, Your most ob. Servt.

CALEB WALLACE

RC (DLC). Addressed. Carried to JM "By Capt. Greenup." Docketed by JM.

[1] See Wallace's letter to JM, 25 Sept. 1785.

[2] In his letter to JM of 12 July 1785, Wallace listed six questions about the nature of government. JM answered them in his letter of 23 Aug. 1785.

[3] After the first formal convention considering Kentucky statehood was held in Danville during Dec. 1784, the district held eight more conventions to organize its separation from Virginia. Between 8 Aug. 1785 and 26 Sept. 1786, no formal gathering is recorded in the various accounts of these conventions, but members often seemed to meet informally to discuss the progress of their goal.

[4] The first act concerning Kentucky statehood was passed by the House of Delegates in Jan. 1786. It derived from the Committee for Courts of Justice on which JM served as chairman (*JHDV*, Oct. 1785, pp. 104, 106, 127–47 passim). For the bill's progress, see the Act Concerning Statehood for the Kentucky District, 22 Dec. 1785.

[5] Christopher Greenup (1750–1818) was a Kentucky lawyer who attended the Dec. 1784 Kentucky convention. In 1785 he was appointed a district judge for Kentucky and traveled to Richmond to serve as a member of the House of Delegates at the Oct. 1785 session. After Kentucky gained her statehood, he served as one of her first two congressmen and was later governor.

[6] Samuel McDowell (1735–1817) was the father of Wallace's first wife (William H. Whitsitt, *The Life and Times of Judge Caleb Wallace* [Louisville, 1888], p. 114). He served with Wallace on the Commission for Adjudicating Western Accounts. McDowell was president of the Dec. 1784 Kentucky convention, and presided over the Kentucky Constitutional Convention (*Appleton's Cyclopedia of American Biography*, IV, 111). The Supreme Court of the District of Kentucky suffered from instability resulting from a changing membership. Leading judges were appointed but some were hesitant to leave the safety of Virginia for the frontier of Kentucky; some were tempted by the financial increases offered by other offices, and resigned; and some were killed in the Indian raids. Wallace had moved to Kentucky in Oct. 1782. When the settling of the western accounts was completed in 1783, Wallace pressed to be appointed to the court in the place of Col. William Floyd, recently killed by Indians (Whitsitt, *Life of Caleb Wallace*, pp. 106–9).

The petition submitted by McDowell and Wallace was read in the House on 23 Nov. 1785. Two acts had been passed in the 1784 sessions of the legislature in order to improve the economic situation of Kentucky judges. They were, however, not effective, as the 1785 petition stated. The legislators agreed and approved the petition, ordering the payments authorized in Oct. 1784 to be made (Hening, *Statutes*, XI, 397–98, 498–99; *JHDV*, Oct. 1785, pp. 52, 59).

From William Grayson

NEW YORK Octob. 14th. 1785.

DEAR SIR.

I have recieved your letter dated at Philada. & shall forward the inclosure to France in the manner you direct.[1] Since your departure, we have been under great anxiety for the fate of Mr. Hardy. On a party to Haerlem heights about ten days ago, he unfortunately bursted a blood vessel, and from frequent hemorrhages, has been in extreme danger till about three days ago, when matters have taken rather a more favorable turn. He has requested me to inform you of his desire to get a seat in the executive Council if practicable, as he thinks the climate of his own country will be more suitable to the situation of his health. He is the more anxious to have this done, as it is not only his own opinion but that of his Physicians, that he will never from the nature of the complaint, be proper for the bar; or indeed for any kind of violent public speaking. He desires you will do him the favor of shewing this to the Speaker & taking such measures as you may deem adviseable.[2]

Nothing new has taken effect since you left this, except that Congress have had information of war being declared by the regency of Algiers agt. these U. S. I am afraid the information is too true: however I will write you again on this subject, the moment the news is confirmed in such a manner as to admit of no doubt.

The suspicion here is that our friends the Brittish have done us this favor in order to make it indispensably necessary for us to imploy their vessels. Perhaps the Spaniards on making peace with the Algerines might wish that their arms might be turned agt. us. The Secy. for foreign affairs is for war with these pirates; but I cannot see the policy of this, & think we had better follow the scandalous example of the European powers, & make peace with them as soon as we can.[3]

Nothing has transpired from Adams, respecting the subject we were talking of, since you left this.[4]

The Report of the Secy. for foreign affairs, respecting Consuls has been recommitted, & he has made another report, principall[y] recommending the vesting the American Ministers with Consular Powers— & giving them extensive limits, where they will have deputies.[5] I shall be obliged to you to let me know as soon as you can conveniently what are your sentiments respecting the price of the Western lands: is a dollar too high all circumstances considered?

By a letter from Colo. Monroe we are informed there are not above 80 families settled on the lands of the U. S.—& these have agreed to go off when Colo. Harmer shall direct them & that the Geographer & Surveyors have left Pittsburgh to execute the Ordinance.[6] From yr. Affect. friend & Most Obed Servt.

Willm. Grayson

RC (DLC). Cover missing. Docketed by JM. The enclosures appear to have been letters from JM and Eliza House Trist to the Jefferson household in Paris.

[1] Grayson was replying to a letter from JM which has not been found. JM's enclosed letter for forwarding to France was doubtless the message to Jefferson of 3 Oct. 1785.

[2] Samuel Hardy died on 17 Oct. 1785.

³ Jay reported the Algerine declaration on 13 Oct. 1785. Speculating on the positive effects of a war on the U. S., Jay favored naval action against the pirates (*JCC*, XXIX, 833–34).

⁴ Grayson's comment on his letter of 8 Nov. 1785 makes it clear that "the subject" under discussion was the continental debt.

⁵ Jay's first and highly critical report on the French consular convention, sent to Congress in July 1785, had a wide distribution. See Washington to JM, 22 Oct. 1785. Jay's second report is dated 13 Oct. 1785. The business dragged on until Jefferson negotiated a new convention in 1788 (Burnett, *Letters*, VIII, 347 n.).

⁶ No letter from Monroe which included this information is mentioned in the *Journals*. Congress reiterated its need for funds on 27 Sept., and the delegates present regarded the sale of western lands as necessary for a reduction of the domestic debt (*JCC*, XXIX, 771). Squatters had to be moved so that the sale could proceed.

To George Washington

Letter not found.

20 October 1785. In a letter of 29 October from Washington to JM he refers to JM's "favor of the 20th." with an enclosure, which contained suggestions of a suitable form for Washington's letter to the General Assembly requesting the donation to some public institution of the Assembly's gift of canal shares to Washington.

From George Washington

Mount Vernon Oct 22nd 1785

Dear Sir

I thank you for the perusal of the enclosed reports—Mr Jay seems to have *laboured the point* respecting the Convention.¹

If any thing should occur that is interesting, & your leizure will permit it, I should be glad to hear from you on the subject.

Printed copy (Stan. V. Henkels Catalogue No. 686, 1892). Letter and enclosures not found. Listed in DLC: Madison Miscellany.

¹ JM appears either to have left several broadsides and a pamphlet on Franco-American relations and foreign affairs with Washington upon his departure from Mount Vernon on 14 Oct., or to have forwarded them to Washington in a lost letter, ca. 16 Oct. These enclosures would have included Jay's report "respecting french and american Consuls," dated 4 July 1785, which was presented to Congress on 6 July (*JCC*, XXIX, 500–515). The report was published in New York (Evans 19319), and indeed Jay's commentary seemed to have "*laboured the point* respecting the Convention." After explaining that the only question to be resolved was "whether Congress ought to ratify this Convention" on the function of consular officials, Jay discoursed at some length on the major points and found certain objectionable variations between the preliminary "Scheme" and the final "Convention." On the matter of religious worship and funerals, for example, Jay indicated

that omission of an understanding was to be regretted because Catholics worshipped freely in the U. S., "yet the protestant religion has no legal Toleration in France. This Omission therefore is a departure from the Line of Reciprocity."

From Gerard Banks

GREEN BANK. STAFFORD CY. Oct 28. 1785.

HONBLE SIR

Prompted by the good of my Country, I hope will sufficiently apologize for my addressing you on some matters of very great importance to our Country. Government at present is certainly in a very confused and unhinged situation, and no doubt calls for the deliberate efforts of a wise Legislature, which I hope is the case at this day. Yet Sir Your knowledge of mankind and things in general must point out to you that experience ever carries the most just and powerful weight; therefore the Virtuous and sensible Gentleman is ever open to conviction and well knows that he may be greatly assisted by the juditious observations of those who may be far inferior to him in point of abilities, I expect to be in Richmond the 4th. of Nov. when I shall be happy to have a conference with you on 2 or 3 Subjects, in which I am flattered you will be well pleased. I am, Honble Sir Yr. mo. obt. hble Servt

GER. BANKS[1]

P. S. The heads or out lines of one of the cases, I have lodged wth. the Honble Joseph Jones esquire.

RC (DLC). Cover addressed by Banks to JM in Richmond. On leaves of cover JM made session notes (see Notes of Debate on Commercial Regulations by Congress, 30 Nov.–1 Dec. 1785).

[1] Gerard Banks (ca. 1725–1787) resided at Green Bank near Fredericksburg. Among his children were Gerard and Henry, the latter a wealthy lawyer and merchant in Richmond. The Banks family had long been prominent in the Northern Neck (*VMHB*, XXX [1922], 67–68; Mrs. P. W. Hiden, "Adam Banks of Stafford County," *Tyler's Quarterly Historical and Genealogical Magazine*, XV [1933–34], 121–25, 236–42).

From Arthur Campbell

WASHINGTON[1] Octo. 28th. 1785

SIR

An early acquaintance, a similarity of sentiment, and the deserved estimation you have attained to, in America, encourage me to address you on a subject, that is believed to be highly interesting to the Western Inhabitants, and perhaps not less so, to the eastern parts of the State.

After various essays of the People for a separation, and the subject being agitated, both in Congress, and before the legislature, the period seems to be arrived when a last discussion and final decision are to take place; in performing this weighty task aright, it will not only call for the best exertions of the able politician, but the temper of the good man.

The fixing of proper boundaries may be the most intricate part of the business. Men may be too apt to argue, and perhaps to vote, from their own feelings, and the lights they have at the present day, without taking into consideration, either the interests or approbation of posterity. The decisions now made, ought to invite an affectionate and grateful attachment, which will be more efficacious in promoting public security, than stone walls, or military engines.

On a careful perusal of that signal Act of Congress of April 23. 1784, it must be acknowleged, there is in it, striking marks of wisdom and foresight; yet we may be permitted to doubt, whether it will beneficially apply in all cases. Natural boundaries, where they nearly coincide with artificial ones, surely should have been prefered; and why might not that amendment be made by Congress yet.[2]

From what I have learnt, no doubt it will be expected by most of the States, that Virginia will follow the example of North Carolina, and fix her limits on the highths of the Allegany; a small departure from those limits, may be found the most convenient, and in time satisfactory to all. For instance, a line extended West: from the South West corner of Maryland, to the top of great Laurel-Mountain, thence Southwardly along the top of sd. Mountain, to where it is intersected by the great Kanhawa; up said River to the confluence of little River (near Ingles Ferry), thence South to the top of the Allegany or Apalachian Mountain; thence along the highest part of the same to the North-Carolina boundary. That part of the Western Country, over the Laurel Mountain and above the Kanhawa should be added to what is expected to be the State of Washington. That below the Kanhawa, and north of the 37°. degree, until that parallel touch the top of the Laurel Mountain, and east along that Mountain to the Kanhawa, to be the State of Kentuckey. The remaining half degree to be added to the State of Frankland. This will accord with the plan of Congress. By this scheme, it is judged that three New States might have existance immediately, which would vastly increase the strength, riches, and population of the United States. Washington, with a necessary cession from Pensylvania, would soon become a firm barrier against any attempts from the Western parts of Canada. Kentuckey, and Frankland, would circulate eastwardly some of the riches of Mexico, and keep the Spaniards, the Southern and Western Indians in awe. There may be local and individual interests, that will combat this scheme; but Virginia ought to see, that it will secure her Peace, and promote her lasting prosperity.[3] The actual traveller may form the best judgment, or Commissioners sent to the spot to judge what are the most suitable boundarys; however, Mr. Hutchins Map gives a tolerable correct view of the Country.[4]

I cannot agree with the politicians, who urge, that we must ere long, have a consolidated Empire under one head, and abolish the different legislatures. Equally extravagant it appears, for one, or a few States, to erect a separate government, and dissolve the present Confederacy. Is not there much less difficulty, and far less danger, to limit the large States to a convenient, and suitable bounds; and then parcel out the Western territory, into proper divisions for free Communities, reform such of the Constitutions of the original States, as may be essentially defective and then make an effort, in good earnest, to give purity of manners, and morals, of course public virtue, a prevalence. Then may not twice thirteen States, if so many there be, unite in the closes[t] bands of amity, and reciprocal good offices, as to all national purposes, leaving to each of the Members of the Union, sovereignty and independence, as to internal legislation, and judiciary decisions.

Doctor Price, Abbe Mably, and Monsieur Turgot, hath lately said a number of good things, that ought to be attended to. I suppose we must agree with the latter, that it will take years, yet to come, to perfect our governments. When you, and I, sat in Convention in 1776, I thought the Virginia Constitution, was a specimen of consummate wisdom. I see many defects now; and it would perhaps surprize the World, if Frankland, those wild half civilized People, would produce a Form, as much superior to it, as Massachusetts is to Georgia. Divers essays ought therefore to be made, to improve the form of our government. The time may not be far distant, when we may feel the effects of external force, as well as secret intrigue to destroy it. If my intelligence from a distant Correspondent, is right; Great Britain from the moment she acknowleged our independence, set about devising means to render it of little avail. What she has already done, by introducing luxury, draining our money, impairing public credit, and destroying public spirit, may discover, that she will be systematical, in aiming at our destruction.

The foregoing hints, I have taken the liberty to transmit to you, not doubting but you will improve and make the best use of them; nor would I have used the freedom, had they not been approved, by a respectable Society in the Western Country, who aspires at the character of being real Commonwealths-Men.

I enclose a copy of some Resolves of the Frankland Assembly,[5] that may shew the necessity of the Virginia Legislature, giving some attention to the present state of this Country, and the more especially, as the County of Washington, has no legal Representatives this year.[6] Also a copy of a Petition of the Inhabitants,[7] the original was sent to Mr. Stuart, one of the Members from Botetourt, some time ago; who it is expected, will present it to the Assembly, that our business may go hand, in hand, with that of Kentucky. I am Sir, with much Esteem & Respect your most obedient Hlb. Servt.

ARTHUR CAMPBELL

RC (DLC). Addressed. Docketed by JM, and in two unidentified hands. Enclosures missing.

[1] Washington County, Virginia, Campbell's political base, when he was not urging statehood movements in Kentucky or North Carolina.

[2] The congressional resolution of 23 Apr. 1784 specified that land ceded to the Confederation "shall be divided into distinct states . . . as nearly as such cessions will admit; that is to say, by parallels of latitude, so that each State shall comprehend from north to south two degrees of latitude . . . and by meridians of longitude, one of which shall pass through the lowest point of the rapids of Ohio, and the other through the western cape of the mouth of the Great Kanhaway . . ." (JCC, XXVI, 275). This was a stumbling block to Campbell's plans for a state organized out of Washington County; so he tried to explain objections to the plan for a rational division of the western territory. Congress continued its formula for rational division in the Land Ordinance of 20 May 1785 (ibid., XXVIII, 375–81), but Campbell chose to ignore this development as he cherished dreams for a "State of Washington."

[3] By Oct. 1785 Campbell's plans to organize Washington County into an independent state were meeting stiff resistance both from local residents and the Virginia legislature. He probably wrote this letter to JM because the latter had been influential in the congressional motion for the cession of western land by Virginia, North Carolina, and Georgia. Since the motion discussed the future statehood of the ceded lands, Campbell hoped JM could provide some constitutional basis for his actions in Washington County.

Campbell had begun his program to separate Washington County from Virginia in 1782, by soliciting the opinions of its residents about the formal cession of their territory to the Confederation. By Jan. 1785 he had been successful enough in arousing support for separation that a petition for such action was presented to the Virginia Assembly. This, and the July 1785 declaration of independence by "the state of Frankland" had an effect opposite to Campbell's plans. In the Oct. 1785 session of the Virginia legislature, a strong treason act was passed. Early in 1786, Campbell was accused of treasonous behavior, and depositions were taken showing that Campbell was more interested in increasing his landholdings than in preserving and promoting the freedom of the county residents. After new depositions were taken, Campbell was called before a board of commissioners and deprived of his office as county judge. His efforts to build support across his county were not, however, forgotten, and he was reinstated as judge at the request of the county court. In 1787 he was elected to the House of Delegates, and continued his career in spite of the blemish of separation activities (Lillian Stuart Butt, "The Political Career of Arthur Campbell," unpublished M.S. thesis, University of Virginia, 1934, pp. 15–47).

4 Thomas Hutchins prepared a map for *A Topographical Description of Virginia, Pennsylvania, Maryland and North Carolina* . . . (London, 1778), and traveled extensively through the west, keeping journals and drawing maps. In 1785 he was Geographer of the United States (*JCC*, XXVII, 291).

5 Two Franklin resolves were passed by the second general assembly held at Jonesborough on 1 Aug. 1785. The first concerned what were considered illegal confiscations of land; the second, the establishment of "a lasting and permanent union as well with North Carolina as the rest of the States on the continent." These resolutions were formally submitted to the North Carolina Assembly (Williams, *History of the Lost State of Franklin* [1933 ed.], pp. 90–91).

6 Campbell's cryptic remark goes against the facts. Andrew Kincannon and William Russell represented Washington County in the 1785 session of the House of Delegates (Swem and Williams, *Register*, p. 22). The House found no illegality in their election (*JHDV*, Oct. 1785, p. 74).

7 At the Oct. 1785 session the only petition from Washington County read in the House concerned the division of Lincoln County into three districts; the division affected the boundary of Washington County (ibid., Oct. 1785, p. 63). Campbell may allude to a separatist petition which Archibald Stuart of Botetourt County prudently seems to have ignored.

From Thomas Jefferson

FONTAINEBLEAU Oct. 28. 1785.

DEAR SIR

Seven o'clock, and retired to my fireside, I have determined to enter into conversation with you; this is a village of about 5000 inhabitants, when the court is not here and 20,000 when they are, occupying a valley thro' which runs a brook, and on each side of it a ridge of small mountains most of which are naked rock.[1] The king comes here, in the fall always, to hunt. His court attend him, as do also the foreign diplomatic corps. But as this is not indispensably required, & my finances do not admit the expence of a continued residence here, I propose to come occasionally to attend the king's levees, returning again to Paris, distant 40 miles. This being the first trip, I set out yesterday morning to take a view of the place. For this purpose I shaped my course towards the highest of the mountains in sight, to the top of which was about a league. As soon as I had got clear of the town I fell in with a poor woman walking at the same rate with myself & going the same course.

Wishing to know the condition of the labouring poor I entered into conversation with her, which I began by enquiries for the path which would lead me into the mountain; & thence proceeded to enquiries into her vocation, condition & circumstance. She told me she was a day labourer, at 8. sous or 4 d. sterling the day; that she had two children to maintain, & to pay a rent of 30 livres for her house (which would consume the hire of 75 days) that often she could get no emploiment, and of course was without bread. As we had walked together near a mile & she had so far served me as a guide, I gave her, on parting, 24 sous. She burst into tears of a gratitude which I could perceive was unfeigned, because she was unable to utter a word. She had probably never before received so great an aid. This little attendrissement, with the solitude of my walk led me into a train of reflections on that unequal division of property which occasions the numberless instances of wretchedness which I had observed in this country & is to be observed all over Europe. The property of this country is absolutely concentered in a very few hands, having revenues of from half a million of guineas a year downwards. These employ the flower of the country as servants, some of them having as many as 200 domestics, not labouring. They employ also a great number of manufacturers, & tradesmen, & lastly the class of labouring husbandmen. But after all these comes the most numerous of all the classes, that is, the poor who cannot find work. I asked myself what could be the reason that so many should be permitted to beg who are willing to work, in a country where there is a very considerable proportion of uncultivated lands? These lands are kept idle mostly for the sake of game. It should seem then that it must be because of the enormous wealth of the proprietors which places them above attention to the increase of their revenues by permitting these lands to be laboured. I am conscious that an equal division of property is impracticable. But the consequences of this enormous inequality producing so much misery to the bulk of mankind, legislators cannot invent too many devices for subdividing property, only taking care to let their subdivisions go hand in hand with the natural affections of the human mind.[2] The descent of property of every kind therefore to all the children, or to all the brothers & sisters, or other relations in equal degree is a politic measure, and a practicable one. Another means of silently lessening the inequality of property is to exempt all from taxation below a certain point, & to tax the higher portions of property in geometrical progression as they rise. Whenever there is in any country, uncultivated lands and unemployed poor, it is clear that the laws of property have been so far extended as to violate natural right. The earth is given as a common stock for man to labour & live on. If, for the encouragement of industry we allow it to be appropriated, we must take care that other employment be furnished to those excluded from the appropriation. If we do not the fundamental right to labour the earth returns to the unemployed. It is too soon yet in our country to say that every man who can not find employment but who can find uncultivated land, shall be at liberty to cultivate it, paying a moderate rent. But it is not too soon to provide by every possible means that as few as possible shall be without a little portion of land. The small landholders are the most precious part of a state.

The next object which struck my attention in my walk was the deer with which the wood abounded. They were of the kind called Cerfs and are certainly of the same species with ours. They are blackish indeed under the belly, & not white as ours, & they are more of the chesnut red. But these are such small differences as would be sure to happen in two races from the same stock, breeding separately a number of ages. Their hares are totally different from the animal we call by that name: but their rabbet is almost exactly like him. The only difference is in their manners; the land on which I walked for sometime being absolutely reduced to a honeycomb by their burrowing. I think there is no instance of ours burrowing. After descending the hill again I saw a man cutting fern. I went to him under pretence of asking the shortest road to the town, & afterwards asked for what use he was cutting fern. He told me that this part of the country furnished a great deal of fruit to Paris. That when packed in straw it acquired an ill taste, but that dry fern preserved it perfectly without communicating any taste at all. I treasured this observation for the preservation of my apples on my return to my own country. They have no apple here to compare with our Newtown pipping. They have nothing which deserves the name of a peach; there being not sun enough to ripen the plumbpeach & the best of their soft peaches being like our autumn peaches. Their cherries & strawberries are fair, but I think less flavoured. Their plumbs I think are better; so also the gooseberries, and the pears infinitely beyond any thing we possess. They have no grape better than our sweet-water. But they have a succession of as good from very early in the summer till frost. I am tomorrow to go to mr Malsherbes (an uncle of the Chevalr. Luzerne's) about 7. leagues from hence, who is the most curious man in France as to his trees. He is making for me a collection of the vines from which the Burgundy, Champagne, Bourdeaux, Frontignac, and other the most valuable wines of this country are made. Another gentleman is collecting for me the best eating grapes, including what we call the raisin. I propose also to endeavor to colonise their hare, rabbet, red & grey partridge, pheasants of different kinds, & some other birds. But I find that I am wandering beyond the limits of my walk & will therefore bid you Adieu. Yours affectionately

TH: JEFFERSON

RC (DLC); FC (DLC: Jefferson Papers). Cover missing. Docketed.

1 Jefferson was unsure about the size of Fontainebleau, at a time when American politicians were in a quandary about locating their own national capital—should it be in a village or near a large commercial city? The entourage following Louis XVI along with "its dependants created a town of sixty thousand inhabitants" (James M. Thompson, *The French Revolution* [New York, 1945], p. 16).

2 Perhaps Jefferson's real meaning is better conveyed by this emended version: "But, the consequences of this enormous inequality! It produces so much misery to the bulk of mankind that legislators cannot invent too many devices subdividing property...."

From George Washington

MOUNT VERNON 29th. Octor. 1785

MY DR SIR,

Receive my thanks for your obliging favor of the 20th.[1]—with its enclosure—of the latter I now avail myself in a letter to the Governor, for the General Assembly.[2] Your delicate sensibility deserves my particular acknowledgements: both your requests are complied with—the first, by congeniality of sentiment; the second because I would fulfil your desire.

Conceiving it would be better to suggest a wish, than to propose an absolute condition of acceptance, I have so expressed myself to the Assembly and shall be obliged to you, not only for information of the result but (if there is an acquiesence on the part of the Country) for your sentiments respecting the appropriations—from what may be said upon the occasion, you will learn what would be most pleasing, & of the greatest utility to the Public.

By Colo. Henry Lee I sent you the Reports of the Secretary for Foreign affairs on the Consular Department.[3] I hope you have received them. With every sentiment of esteem & regard I am Dr. Sir &c. &c.

GEO: WASHINGTON

FC (DLC: Washington Papers).

1 JM's letter of 20 Oct. has not been found. In it JM apparently alluded to Washington's sensitivity regarding the General Assembly's gift of canal shares in the Oct.

1784 session. Washington wanted to convey the shares to some public foundation, and JM became the liaison between Mount Vernon and Richmond on the matter (JM to Jefferson, 3 Oct. 1785; Amendments to the Act Conveying Canal Shares to George Washington, 16 Nov. 1785).

[2] JM probably had suggested that Washington avoid an outright refusal of the shares but appropriate their proceeds to some objects of public good. Washington's "letter to the Governor" (Henry) of 29 Oct. carries this intention (Fitzpatrick, *Writings of Washington*, XXVIII, 303–4).

[3] Jay submitted a report "respecting the number of Consuls necessary to be appointed and for what foreign Ports" on 19 Sept. 1785 (*JCC*, XXIX, 722–24). The report was printed in broadside form a short time later (Evans 19320).

The General Assembly Session of October 1785

EDITORIAL NOTE

The Virginia legislative session of 1785 was a complicated interplay of power politics and constitutional issues. Even before the delegates and senators met in Richmond, the people were excited by the issues which would be discussed. Petitions concerning slavery and emancipation raised tempers on a subject which would long occupy the General Assembly. The attempt to gain state funds to support "teachers of the Christian religion" drew voluble response from supporters and opponents. Closely tied to the above measure was Jefferson's bill for the establishment of religious freedom, which was one of the major components of the Revised State Code of Laws. The code revision was an old issue revived during this session. Another subject of debate was the Assize Court bill to systematize the administration of justice.

The separation of Kentucky from its mother state, Virginia, was acknowledged as imminent, but the issue was broadened by Virginia's own problems in dealing with the central government. The Confederation had not proved an effective instrument of government, and two measures were considered to strengthen congressional powers. A resolution recommending national control of trade excited many tempers, while the proposal to appoint delegates to a convention at Annapolis alarmed advocates of state sovereignty who were opposed to "the idea of bracing the federal system" (JM to Monroe, 22 Jan. 1786).

JM played a major role in the politics that surrounded the debates on these issues. The brief dispute over receiving the general emancipation petitions disheartened JM, but he did not give in to any kind of emotional commentary and simply reported an outrageous motion to throw antislavery petitions under the clerk's table rather than to place them on it.

The bill for religious freedom was of course Jefferson's, but when he left for France he urged JM to see to its passage. JM became deeply involved in the debate over the role of religion in Virginia's society when he wrote anonymously a long remonstrance against the proposed General Assessment bill. This issue was also laden with emotionalism, and JM sought to present a rational argument against this measure limiting religious freedom. The threat of such restrictions had created discontent, particularly among the dissenters, and their opposition necessarily bred discord and disharmony in the state.

JM's idealism did not allow him to ignore the realities of politics. He knew well that his stand against the General Assessment bill, as on other issues, would evoke the criticism of the conservatives. This group could exert a powerful influence through effective leaders. Governor Patrick Henry, growing increasingly conservative, still exercised a decisive influence over the Assembly and was a known supporter of the Episcopal church in Virginia as well as a patron of the General Assessment bill. Benjamin Harrison, the House speaker, also opposed JM on these issues. The Harrison family, like the Lees, tended to be more conservative when it came to maintaining institutions associated with the stability of society, and viewed both slavery ·and a state-supported church as keystones to the Virginia social structure.

JM relied on a number of liberal allies who usually viewed issues in the same light as he himself did. Thomas Mathews, Andrew Kincannon, Francis Corbin, Archibald Stuart, and others repeatedly voted on his side. In an overview of the session, however, neither coherent political parties nor lasting factions controlled Virginia politics. Issues and personalities created flimsy coalitions which could not be depended upon in the next contest. JM sought to establish his ideal, a government based on logic and rational principles, but he was realistic enough to know that political maneuvering was an integral part of Virginia's political process. Compromise was not excluded because the ultimate principle could probably be gained only after a series of political struggles; intransigence on one issue, however, might reduce JM's own political effectiveness and severely limit his opportunities to improve the instruments of government.

The influence of Enlightenment thought is evident in the course JM pursued in the 1785 session. An intent to bring order and reason into his state's government became manifest in his efforts to forward passage of the Revised Code and amendments in the Assize Court and Port bills. JM presented 118 bills in the Revised Code early in the session in the hope of completing the long-unfinished business. The legislature slowly progressed through the bills until conservative, pragmatic Virginians balked at Jefferson's bill on crimes and punishments, which was based on enlightened Beccarian principles. Refusing to accept the liberal and humanitarian experiment in penal reform, the legislators debated and delayed, jeopardizing the whole legal experiment. Finally in mid-December the Committee of the Whole discharged the bill from further consideration. With little time left, JM decided to postpone the majority of the bills in favor of trying to pass the most important, among them the bill for religious freedom. Although JM ultimately guided forty-three of the revisors' bills through the legislature, he was disappointed in not passing the entire Revised Code during this session. He feared that breaking it into parts would weaken the reform as a whole.

The payment of British debts, also, continued as an unresolved problem despite JM's efforts to gain passage of a bill similar to the one offered in the October 1784 session calling upon Virginians to honor their prewar financial obligations. He saw that this was essential to the success of the new republican experiment for Virginia, and also as a means of establishing respect and credit abroad. In hope of improving the image and effectiveness of the Confederation, JM advocated a resolution giving Congress power to regulate foreign trade. He wished indirectly to improve the finances of the Confederation by writing into the resolution the power of Congress to collect duties on imports, the income to be deposited in the national treasury. Upon its failing to pass, various localist measures were advocated to give Virginia a broader control over trade. JM gladly saw them dropped from consideration and replaced on the last day of the session by a resolution to appoint commissioners to meet with representatives from other states to consider the condition of interstate trade and some feasible means of creating a uniform commercial system for the United States. JM thought that the several states would benefit far more by unified action than by acting alone. Although not enthusiastic over the prospects of the coming convention, JM thought such an attempt to bolster the weakening Confederation preferable to inaction.

JM's concern over the impotence of the Confederation undoubtedly affected his position on state policy. He favored a legal, constitutional separation of Kentucky from Virginia, effective only after Kentucky applied to Congress and was accepted into the Union as an independent state, and he wrote into the bill an amendment requiring Kentucky to follow this procedure. The act thus implicitly asserted the free authority of Congress over the Union. In writing the bill to ratify a Virginia-Maryland compact on the regulation of Chesapeake Bay and the Potomac River, JM included recognition of Congress's authority over interstate treaties by requiring congressional approval of the agreement.

As a state legislator JM was always aware of the need for political maneuvering to gain the passage of bills. But his cognizance of such realities did not divert him from his principles. He supported Kentucky's petition for separation as just and reasonable, demonstrating that he was more than a politician simply using power to win contests. He could rise above self-interest and state politics to assert the rights of men suffering from an inequitable distribution of power between the established East and the struggling West. His goal was rational administration and equal justice. JM saw the means to these ends strengthened by better political and economic organization, a federal union maintaining a workable balance of power with state sovereignty, and a republican nation extending its ideals westward.

Appendix A of this volume carries a full listing of legislation which JM introduced or carried to the Senate but probably did not draft.

Bills for a Revised State Code of Laws

EDITORIAL NOTE

A revision of the Virginia code of laws was already overdue when the colony forsook its royal allegiance in 1776. Changing circumstances made it necessary to enact new laws in the transition from colony to commonwealth while retaining the bedrock of English common law. JM was barely on the legislative scene and no lawyer, but he was more than an interested spectator as Jefferson attempted to direct the process. What Jefferson had in mind was no mere collection of laws already in force but a complete revision of old statutes and the enactment of new ones necessary to eliminate all vestiges of monarchism and substitute republican tenets. To press the matter Jefferson refused a diplomatic appointment, a decision "largely determined by his zeal to remake the legal structure of the commonwealth" (Boyd, *Papers of Jefferson*, II, 306). But as Jefferson found, his impatience made few converts among legislative colleagues, although they voted for his bill creating a committee of revisors on 26 October 1776. One result of this measure was the joint election of a committee of revisors by the General Assembly, with Jefferson as the de facto chairman (*JHDV*, Oct. 1776, p. 41). Expediency left the old laws in force, for all practical purposes, and only those antiquated laws which special situations demanded were repealed or replaced by new legislation. The result was a breakdown for Jefferson's original plan of swift revision. By 1779 most of the work had been done by the three lawyer-committeemen (Jefferson, Pendleton, and Wythe), but Speaker Benjamin Harrison, no friend to sudden reform, took his time about distributing copies of the committee report. The committee plan was still in a pigeonhole five years later when JM, at Jefferson's urging, resurrected the ambitious scheme at the May 1784 session of the General Assembly, and talked the legislature into printing the revisors' report for public distribution (*JHDV*, May 1784, p. 27).

Apparently prodded by a promise to Jefferson made before they parted company—one headed toward Paris and the other toward Orange County—JM kept the legal reform movement alive. His admirer, Archibald Stuart, probably overstated the situation when he reported on JM's legislative adroitness. JM, Stuart wrote, "has by means perfectly constitutional become almost a Dictator. . . . His influence alone has overcome the impatience of the house & carried them half thro the Revis[e]d Code" (Stuart to John Breckinridge, 7 Dec. 1785 [DLC: Breckinridge Family Papers]). Because of JM's preliminary work on the printed revisors' report and the appropriation for the revisors' fees, after small doses the House of Delegates was ready (in JM's judgment) for the main medicine. Since the idea of a general revision had first been broached in 1776, a number of bills had been lifted from the revisors' hopper and passed into law because of urgent problems, but on 31 October 1785 JM took the long-delayed step of introducing 118 separate bills that remained from the 126 in Jefferson's original scheme (*JHDV*, Oct. 1785, pp. 12–14; Boyd, *Papers of Jefferson*, II, 305–33). The objects of the laws were broad, ranging from the relatively unimportant act "concerning seamen" to the far-reaching statute "for establishing religious freedom." By this time, JM was in an advantageous position to carry the business forward, for as chairman of the Committee for Courts of Justice he reported them to the House of Delegates and guided both the committee deliberation and the general debate. His selection for this key assignment—in view of JM's regard for the law as an avocation rather than his means of livelihood—could not have been a capricious decision. Instead, JM's selection as chairman reflected an assumption that JM was learned in the law although not a lawyer. No man in the legislature was better qualified to work for the legal reformation necessary to blend the colonial past with the newly wrought republican frame of government.

As JM explained to Jefferson on 22 January 1786, the legislators were not unanimous on their zeal for change. After some preliminary skirmishing, the House of Delegates agreed to spend three sessions each week debating the revision. Progress was made until the bill "for proportioning crimes and punishments in cases heretofore capital" was under discussion. Age-old fears were aroused by this bill, which Jefferson had written after much research and with a reformer's view that crimes were not deterred "at all by capital punishment"—a statement of principle not overly apparent in the bill itself (Malone, *Jefferson the Virginian*, pp. 269–72; Ford, *Writings of Jefferson*, I, 60). The impact of the Enlightenment, particularly Beccaria's *Tratto dei Delitti e delle Pene* (1764), with its strictures on the futility of torture and execution, remained as an ideal. Then, as now, there was much disagreement over the possibilities that a drastic change in the treatment of criminals would be effective. JM lived to recall the debate with misgivings, for in retrospect he concluded "the Revisors were unfortunately misled into some of the specious errors of Beccaria, then in the Zenith of his fame as a philosophical Legislator." The smooth course of the revising calendar was checked, with more than half of the business still untouched (JM to Monroe, 17 Dec. 1785). Thereafter, the House was in no mood to go further; so as JM sensed the situation he deemed it unwise to press for a longer session and undoubtedly greater obstructionism from "the adversaries of the Code." Thirty-six bills were adopted, and all but two of those remaining were postponed until the next legislative session. On the whole, JM believed the work had been readily accepted in its main parts, and if Speaker Benjamin Harrison had been a friend to the reform instead of its enemy, a great deal more might have been accomplished. JM took some solace from the fact that the mood of the House still allowed him to bring forward Jefferson's bill on religious freedom which would have been delayed for at least another year. The reaction to arch-conservative efforts to keep a semblance of the old official Anglican connection intact had "all the effect that could have been wished," JM told Jefferson; so the opportunity was exploited and the bill "establishing religious freedom" was coaxed through the General Assembly despite some haggling over the preamble.

The first stride had carried Virginia some distance toward an exemplary civil and criminal code that would have an impact in other states. The tendency of other legislatures, particularly in North Carolina, was to follow Virginia's lead. There was one joker in the deck. The bills enacted were not to become law until 1 January 1787, a delaying device used so that the entire work could be finished at the October 1786 session, whereupon the whole revision would take effect at the same time. Few of the bills left dangling at the adjournment in January 1786 survived the legislative ordeal, however. The enthusiasm for reform was about spent by late 1785, and a year later JM was too concerned over national survival to place himself again into a situation where local concerns were all-important. Thus despite the effort and expectations, the major share of the Revised Code never was enacted into law. In retrospect the work upon which Jefferson had "exacted perhaps the most severe of his public labours," produced much public discussion but accounted for far less change in the Virginia code than the leaders of 1776 anticipated (JM to Samuel Harris Smith, 4 Nov. 1826 [DLC]). Jefferson himself was disappointed, and before JM's yeoman service had brought some results the principal author of the revision suggested that it "digests only the British statutes and our own acts" and held that its only merit was "that it may remove from our book shelves about twenty folio volumes of statutes" (Boyd, *Papers of Jefferson*, VIII, 632). JM would have considered his friend's judgment too harsh. As JM well knew, part of the value of reform movements lay in the legislative mood they helped create.

[31 October 1785]

A bill, "to arrange the counties into Senatorial districts."

A bill, "concerning election of members of the General Assembly."

A bill, "empowering one of the Privy Council to officiate in certain cases as Lieutenant Governor."

A bill, "empowering the Governor, with the advice of the Privy Council, to lay embargoes."

A bill, "for regulating and disciplining the militia."[1]

A bill, "making provisions against invasions and insurrections."

A bill, "for the annual appointment of delegates to Congress, and of a member for the committee of the States."[2]

A bill, "establishing a Board of Auditors."[3]

A bill, "concerning the public treasurer."

A bill, "for appointing naval officers."

A bill, "for the appointment of clerks to the Governor and Council."

A bill, "concerning seamen."

A bill, "for establishing cross posts."

A bill, "directing the course of descents."

A bill, "concerning wills, the distribution of intestates' estates and the duty of executors and administrators."

A bill, "for regulating conveyances."

A bill, "securing the rights derived from grants to aliens."[4]

A bill, "concerning escheats."

A bill, "to prevent frauds and perjuries."

A bill, "of mortmain."

A bill, "concerning the dower and jointures of widows."

A bill, "for the preservation of the estates of idiots and lunatics."

A bill, "providing that wrongful alienations of land shall be void so far as they be wrongful."

A bill, "for levying county rates."

A bill, "for the support of the poor."[5]

A bill, "for ascertaining the salaries and fees of certain officers."

A bill, "declaring bills of credit to be equal to gold and silver coin of the same denominations."

A bill, *"to prevent the circulation of private bank notes."*

A bill, *"to prevent losses by pirates, enemies and others, on the high seas."*

A bill, "for the preservation of vessels wrecked or in distress, and of their crews and cargoes."

A bill, *"concerning estrays."*

A bill, *"for the restitution of stolen goods."*

A bill, *"for preventing infection of the horned cattle."*

A bill, *"for improving the breed of horses."*

A bill, "for preservation of deer."

A bill, "for preventing frauds by the dealers in flour, beef, pork, tar, pitch and turpentine."

A bill, *"for licensing and regulating taverns."*

A bill, *"concerning public roads."*

A bill, "for establishing public ferries."[6]

A bill, *"concerning milldams and other obstructions of water courses."*

A bill, *"for unlading ballast and burial of dead bodies from on board ships."*

A bill, "concerning public store houses."

A bill, *"concerning slaves."*[7]

A bill, *"concerning servants."*

A bill, *"for apprehending and securing runaways."*

A bill, *"declaring what persons shall be deemed mulattoes."*

A bill, "declaring who shall be deemed citizens of this Commonwealth."

A bill, *"concerning aliens."*

A bill, *"declaring that none shall be condemned without trial, and that justice shall not be sold or deferred."*

A bill, *"directing what prisoners shall be let to bail."*

A bill, "directing the mode of giving out and prosecuting writs of habeas corpus."[8]

A bill, *"concerning guardians, infants, masters and apprentices."*

A bill, *"to enable guardians and committees to perform certain acts for the benefit of those who are under their care."*

A bill, *"for the restraint, maintenance and cure of persons not sound in mind."*

A bill, "for registering births and deaths."

A bill, "for proportioning crimes and punishments in cases heretofore capital."[9]

A bill, "punishing persons guilty of certain forgeries."

A bill, "concerning treasons, felonies and other offences committed out of the jurisdiction of this Commonwealth."

A bill, "concerning truces, safe conducts, passports, licences and letters of marque."

A bill, "for the employment, government and support of malefactors condemned to labor for the Commonwealth."

A bill, "to encourage the apprehenders of horse stealers."

A bilt, "for preserving the privileges of ambassadors."

A bill, "for the suppression and punishment of riots, routs and unlawful assemblies."

A bill, "forbidding and punishing affrays."

A bill, "against conspirators."

A bill, "against conveying or taking pretended titles."

A bill, "for punishing bribery and extortion."

A bill, "prescribing the punishment of those who sell unwholesome meat or drink."

A bill, "to prevent the spreading of the smallpox."

A bill, "for compelling vessels and persons coming, and goods brought from infected places, to perform quarantine."

A bill, "for the more general diffusion of knowledge."

A bill, "for amending the constitution of the college of William and Mary, and establishing more certain revenues for its support."

A bill, "for establishing a public library."

A bill, "for establishing religious freedom."

A bill, "for saving the property of the church heretofore by law established."

A bill "for punishing disturbers of religious worship and sabbath breakers."

A bill, "for appointing days of public fasting and thanksgiving."

A bill, "annulling marriages prohibited by the Livitical law, and appointing the mode of solemnizing lawful marriages."

A bill, "against usury."

A bill, "to prevent gaming."

A bill, "to prevent forestalling, regrating, engrossing and sales by auction."

A bill, "constituting the high court of chancery."

A bill, "constituting the general court."

A bill, "constituting the court of admiralty."

A bill, "constituting the court of appeals."

A bill, "for constituting courts martial."

A bill, "constituting justices of the peace and county courts."

A bill, "concerning sheriffs."

A bill, "for licensing counsel, attornies at law, and proctors."

A bill, "prescribing the oaths of fidelity, and the oaths of certain public officers."

A bill, "to prevent the sale of public offices."

A bill, "directing the method of proceeding upon impeachments."

A bill, "for regulating proceedings in courts of equity."

A bill, "for regulating proceedings in courts of common law."

A bill, "directing the method of proceeding against and trying free persons charged with certain crimes."

A bill, "directing the method of trying slaves charged with treason or felony."

A bill, "for reforming the method of proceeding in writs of right."

A bill, "concerning partitions and joint rights and obligations."

A bill, "for the speedy determination of suits wherein foreigners are parties."

A bill, "for the speedy recovery of money due from certain persons to the public."

A bill, "for recovering demands of small value in a summary way."

A bill, "providing that actions popular, prosecuted by collusion, shall be no bar to those which be pursued with good faith."

A bill, "for preventing vexatious and malicious prosecutions, and moderating amercements."

A bill, "providing a mean[s] to help and speed poor persons in their suits."

A bill, "providing that an infant may sue by his next friend."

A bill, "declaring when the death of persons absenting themselves, shall be presumed."

A bill, "prescribing a method of protecting inland bills of exchange, and allowing assignees of obligations to bring actions thereupon in their own names."

A bill, "for limitation of actions."

A bill, "for granting attachments against the estates of debtors removing privately, or absconding."

A bill, "concerning inquests."

A bill, "permitting those who will not take oaths, to be otherwise qualified."

A bill, "for regulating the commencement of the year, and the computation of time."

A bill, "allowing a bill of exceptions to be sealed."

A bill, "for enforcing performance of awards made by rule of court."

A bill, "concerning executions."

A bill, "concerning rents and distresses."

A bill, "providing remedy and punishment in cases of forcible entries and detainers."

A bill, "for repealing certain acts of Parliament and of General Assembly."

Printed copy (*JHDV*, Oct. 1785, pp. 12–14). Titles in italics were enacted into law at this session. JM was serving as an agent of legislative reform and wrote none of these bills, which were drafted by the Committee of Revisors in 1776–1779. JM took 118 of the original 126 bills, omitting only those which had been wartime measures and were no longer needed, or had been repealed by post-1779 legislation (Boyd, *Papers of Jefferson*, II, 322–24).

[1] The militia bill passed at the Oct. 1784 session had many flaws. One result of these imperfections was the presentation of petitions from Amherst and Washington counties calling for outright repeal of that act at this session. The House ordered the petitioners' grievances incorporated in a new militia bill (*JHDV*, Oct. 1785, pp. 34, 85–86). After debate in the Committee of the Whole, this bill was amended and joined with JM's next offering on "invasions and insurrections." The surviving version was "An act to amend and reduce into one act, the several laws for regulating and disciplining the militia, and guarding against invasions and insurrections" (Hening, *Statutes*, XII, 9–24).

[2] This is not the original bill which Jefferson drafted, although the older title was retained. A revision of the 1779 act was passed at the May 1784 session (ibid., XI, 365–66). As it turned out, that act needed some clarification so that Virginia would have a delegation in Congress for the session scheduled to begin 7 Nov. 1785 (ibid., XII, 26–27; Boyd, *Papers of Jefferson*, II, 367–70).

[3] This bill was superseded by another measure "for the reform of certain public Boards," which was first introduced by Thomas Underwood on 1 Dec. 1785 as a bill to amend the "act for establishing a board of auditors for publick accounts" passed in 1778.

[4] JM had tried to secure the property titles of heirs of aliens who served in the Revolution, but his bill of 30 Nov. 1784 was sidetracked, as was this measure.

[5] A committee headed by Carter Braxton was ordered on 27 Oct. 1785 to prepare a bill "to provide for the poor of the respective parishes in this Commonwealth" (*JHDV*, Oct. 1785, p. 9). When Braxton's committee considered the revisors' bill it borrowed only a few portions, causing Jefferson to comment later that this bill "passd. with great alterns." (Boyd, *Papers of Jefferson*, II, 423 n.). Dropped by the committee was a provision for a superintendent of the poor who was prohibited from whipping an indigent person "with more stripes than ten, at one time, or for one offence" (ibid., II, 420).

[6] The General Assembly passed another act at this session "for establishing new ferries" instead of this bill, which contained a comprehensive listing of all crossings with statutory fees or tolls.

7 For an example of the changing legislative climate between 1779 and 1785, compare the final version (Hening, *Statutes*, XII, 182–83) with Jefferson's draft (Boyd, *Papers of Jefferson*, II, 470–72). The bill that finally passed on 9 Dec. 1785 reiterated a provision in the 1778 ban on slave importations which exempted slaveowners moving into Virginia from the prohibition (Hening, *Statutes*, IX, 471–72).

8 JM's motive in offering this bill, which was so similar to the 1784 act of the same title, is not clear, inasmuch as other revisors' bills previously enacted were ordinarily passed over. Perhaps because of the redundancy, JM's fellow legislators prevented this bill from reaching a final vote.

9 After passing thirty-five of the revisors' bills, the House of Delegates balked on this measure. JM reported that this bill was "assailed on all sides. Mr. Mercer has proclaimed unceasing hostility against it" (JM to Monroe, 9 Dec. 1785). The basis for Mercer's assault is not known, thus precluding a judgment as to whether the penalties were too light or too severe for the opposition's views on criminal justice. However, JM later reported the bill failed again (at the 1786 session) by a single vote, owing to the "rage agst. Horse stealers," who were sentenced to three years at hard labor in the original bill (JM to Jefferson, 15 Feb. 1787 [DLC]). Thus it is possible JM's colleagues in both 1785 and 1786 thought three years' confinement insufficient punishment for a felony that was considered one of the worst crimes in a saddle-oriented society where "a horse must be mounted, if only to fetch a prise of snuff from across the way" (Schoepf, *Travels in the Confederation*, II, 65).

Act for Establishing Religious Freedom

[31 October 1785][1]

I. Whereas Almighty God hath created the mind free; that all attempts to influence it by temporal punishments or burthens, or by civil incapacitations, tend only to beget habits of hypocrisy and meanness, and are a departure from the plan of the Holy author of our religion,[2] who being Lord both of body and mind, yet chose not to propagate it by coercions on either, as was in his Almighty power to do; that the impious presumption of legislators and rulers, civil as well as ecclesiastical, who being themselves but fallible and uninspired men, have assumed dominion over the faith of others, setting up their own opinions and modes of thinking as the only true and infallible, and as such endeavouring to impose them on others, hath established and maintained false religions over the greatest part of the world, and through all time; that to compel a man to furnish contributions of money for the propagation of opinions which he disbelieves, is sinful and tyrannical; that even the forcing him to support this or that teacher of his own religious persuasion, is depriving him of the comfortable liberty of giving his contributions to the particular pastor, whose morals he would make his pattern, and whose powers he feels most persuasive to righteousness, and is withdrawing from the ministry those temporary rewards, which proceeding from an approbation of their personal conduct, are an additional incitement to earnest and unremitting labours for the instruction of mankind; that our civil rights have no dependence on our religious opinions, any more than our opinions in physics or geometry; that therefore the proscribing any citizen as unworthy the public confidence by laying upon him an incapacity of being called to offices of trust and emolument, unless he profess or renounce this or that religious opinion, is depriving him injuriously of those privileges and advantages to which in common with his fellow-citizens he has a natural right; that it tends only to corrupt the principles of that religion it is meant to encourage, by bribing with a monopoly of wor[l]dly honours and emoluments, those who will externally profess and conform to it; that though indeed these are criminal who do not withstand such temptation, yet neither are those innocent who lay the bait in their way; that to suffer the civil magistrate to intrude his powers into the field of opinion, and to restrain the profession or propagation of principles on supposition of their ill tendency, is a dangerous fallacy, which at once destroys all religious liberty, because he being of course judge of that tendency will make his opinions the rule of judgment; and approve or condemn the sentiments of others only as they shall square with or differ from his own; that it is time enough for the rightful purposes of civil government, for its officers to interfere when principles break out into overt acts against peace and good order; and finally, that truth is great and will prevail if left to herself, that she is the proper and sufficient antagonist to error, and has nothing to fear from the conflict, unless by human interposition disarmed of her natural weapons, free argument and debate, errors ceasing to be dangerous when it is permitted freely to contradict them:

II. *Be it enacted by the General Assembly,* That no man shall be compelled to frequent or support any religious worship, place, or ministry whatsoever, nor shall be enforced restrained, molested, or burthened in his body or goods, nor shall otherwise suffer on account of his religious opinions or belief; but that all men shall be free to profess, and by argument to maintain, their opinion in matters of religion, and that the same shall in no wise diminish, enlarge, or affect their civil capacities.

III. And though we well know that this assembly elected by the people for the ordinary purposes of legislation only, have no power to restrain the acts of succeeding assemblies, constituted with powers equal to our own, and that therefore to declare this act to be irrevocable would be of no effect in law; yet we are free to declare, and do declare, that the rights hereby asserted are of the natural rights of mankind, and that if any act shall be hereafter passed to repeal the present, or to narrow its operation such act will be an infringement of natural right.

Printed copy (Hening, *Statutes*, XII, 84–86). No Ms copy has been found. Jefferson drew up the bill in 1777 as part of the Revised Code of Virginia laws. The earliest printed copy is a broadside printed in Williamsburg in 1779. The *Report of the Committee of Revisors Appointed by the General Assembly in Virginia in MDCCLXXVI* (Richmond, 1784) contained the same text except for slight variations in punctuation and spelling. These texts are the closest to Jefferson's original. The act above is an amended version of these; however, what is generally accepted as "The Act for Establishing Religious Freedom" is a hybridized version written by Jefferson himself in 1786. For a detailed consideration of the various texts, see Boyd, *Papers of Jefferson*, II, 547–52.

1 JM introduced this bill along with 117 others for the Revised Code in the House on 31 Oct. 1785. The bills were read twice and referred to a Committee of the Whole House. This bill was considered by a Committee of the Whole on 15 Dec., when an unidentified amendment was proposed and passed on the following day. A second amendment, which would have struck out the preamble and replaced it with a statement from the Virginia Declaration of Rights, was defeated on the same day with JM voting against it. The bill passed on 17 Dec. Alexander White carried it to the Senate. On 29 Dec. the Senate reported the bill back with an amendment, which the House took under consideration. JM voted with the majority against the amendment. On 9 Jan. 1786 the Senate reported back requesting a joint conference on the amendment. The House appointed JM, Zachariah Johnston and Innes to manage the business on the part of the House. The conference was held 12 Jan. On 13 Jan. the House agreed to the amendments and added its own changes. The House passed these amendments and ordered JM to notify the Senate on 16 Jan. The Senate reported the enrolled bill back, and the speaker signed the act on 19 Jan. 1786 (*JHDV*, Oct. 1785, pp. 95–96, 115 and passim). Thus while adoption of the whole Revised Code was not achieved during the session (after thirty-six had been enacted, most of the remaining bills were postponed to the 1786 session)—the House decided that a few bills were of particular importance. Of these, the bill for religious freedom was the only one enacted into law, as JM "presided as midwife at its legislative birth" (Malone, *Jefferson the Virginian*, p. 279). The enacting clauses remained unaltered, but Jefferson's philosophical preamble met opposition in both Houses. The amendment replacing the preamble with a statement from the Declaration of Rights was defeated in the House and then revived by the Senate. JM headed the House delegation to the joint conference to work out the differences. He dismissed the Senate's objections as "frivolous" but saw to it that the House sent up the bill with several alterations to meet the Senate's objections. The Senate returned further amendments which JM thought best to accept and not run further risk since "they did not affect the substance though they somewhat defaced the composition," and it was growing late in the session (JM to Jefferson, 22 Jan. 1786). By the deletion of some of the more sweeping statements about the supremacy of reason, the broad base on which Jefferson founded the bill was somewhat diminished (Boyd, *Papers of Jefferson*, II, 549–52). Nevertheless JM presumed that the enactment had "in this country extinguished for ever the ambitious hope of making laws for the human mind" (JM to Jefferson, 22 Jan. 1786) while Jefferson expressed his satisfaction at seeing "the standard of reason at length erected" (Jefferson to JM, 16 Dec. 1786 [DLC]).

[2] JM and Jefferson undoubtedly discussed this bill some years after its passage, for Jefferson in his "Autobiography" mentions the debate over the preamble and says that the effort was made to alter this phrase to read, "a departure from the plan of Jesus Christ, the holy author of our religion" (Ford, *Writings of Jefferson*, I, 62). Jefferson held that in defeating the proposed change the legislators "meant to comprehend, within the mantle of it's protection, the Jew and the Gentile, the Christian and Mahometan, the Hindoo, and infidel of every denomination."

From William Grayson

NEW YORK Nov. 8th. 1785.

DEAR SIR

The President being this moment about to set out for Virginia obliges me to be very short at present.[1] We have no authentic advices from Europe respecting the Algerine War, although the Papers speak of several captures of american vessels.[2] Nothing new from Mr. Adams respecting the debts. I will again look at his letters, & give you the necessary information in confidence. You will then judge for yourself as to the expediency or inexpediency of a certain measure.[3]

I shall at all events stay here till next Munday in order to collect some documents which are necessary for the State, & will write you again before I leave this. Mr. Hancock is talked of by the Southern States for President, though I suppose if Governor Nash or Paca were to come forward, they would change their tone.[4]

Since you left this We have had a considerable flurry respecting a motion brought forward by Massachusetz & Virginia respecting the dismemberment of States: The motion is on the journals.[5]

Contracts for the transportation of the Mail are made: two mails a week throughout America, for six months & three mails a week for the six other months—to begin in Jany. next. From yr. Affect. frd. & Most Obed Sert

WILLM. GRAYSON

RC (DLC). Cover missing. Docketed by JM.

[1] Richard Henry Lee was elected President of Congress 30 Nov. 1784. His term technically expired on 7 Nov. 1785, hence the speculation concerning Hancock as Lee's successor.

[2] On both 31 Oct. and 3 Nov. 1785, the *N. Y. Packet* published letters reporting Algerine atrocities against foreign ships. The 3 Nov. issue specifically dealt with the capture of two American ships.

[3] The House of Delegates was about to consider a bill on the problem of British debts and this is doubtless the "certain measure" Grayson had in mind.

[4] Governors Abner Nash of North Carolina and William Paca of Maryland. Nash was elected a delegate to the 1786 session and traveled to New York, but

because of illness, never took his seat. Paca was not elected to serve (Burnett, *Letters*, VIII, xciii, lxxxvi–lxxxvii).

[5] The motion appears in *JCC*, XXIX, 810. It opposed dismemberment of the original states for the formation of governments independent of the Confederation. After several delays, the matter was tabled without further action (ibid., pp. 811–12). The purpose of the motion was to rebuff the separatist movements in frontier areas. Governor Henry wrote Speaker Benjamin Harrison on 17 Oct. 1785 expressing concern over "the Assumption of sovereign power by the Western Inhabitants of No. Carolina" which "exposes our Citizens to the contagion of their example" (Executive Letter Book, pp. 483–84).

To George Washington

RICHMOND Novr. 11. 1785

DEAR SIR

I recd. your favor of the 29th. ulto. on thursday. That by Col. Lee had been previously delivered. Your letter for the Assembly was laid before them yesterday.[1] I have reason to believe that it was received with every sentiment which could correspond with yours. Nothing passed from which any conjecture could be formed as to the objects which would be most pleasing for the appropriation of the fund. The disposition is I am persuaded much stronger to acquiesce in your choice whatever it may be, than to lead or anticipate it: and I see no inconveniency in your taking time for a choice that will please yourself.[2] The letter was referred to a Committee which will no doubt make such report as will give effect to your wishes.

Our Session commenced very inauspiciously with a contest for the Chair which was followed by a rigid scrutiny into Mr. Harrison's election in his County. He gained the Chair by a majority of 6 votes and retained his seat by a majority of still fewer. His residence was the point on which the latter question turned. Doctr. Lee's election was questioned on a similar point and was also established; but it was held to be vitiated by his acceptance of a lucrative post under the United States.[3] The House have engaged with some alacrity in the consideration of the Revised Code prepared by Mr. Jefferson Mr. Pendleton and Mr. Wythe. The present temper promises an adoption of it in substance. The greatest danger arises from its length compared with the patience of the members. If it is persisted in it must exclude several matters which are of moment, but I hope only for the present Assembly. The pulse of the H. of D. was felt on thursday with regard to a general manumission by a petition presented on that subject. It was rejected without dissent but not without an avowed patronage of its principle by sundry respectable

403

members. A motion was made to throw it under the table, which was treated with as much indignation on one side, as the petition itself was on the other. There are several petitions before the House against any step towards freeing the slaves, and even praying for a repeal of the law which licences particular manumissions.[4] The Merchants of several of our Towns have made representations on the distresses of our commerce, which have raised the question whether relief shall be attempted by a reference to Congs. or by measures within our own Compass. On a pretty full discussion it was determined by a Large majority that the power over trade ought to be vested in Congress, under certain qualifications. If the qualifications suggested & no others should be annexed, I think they will not be subversive of the principle tho' they will no doubt lessen its utility. The Speaker Mr. M. Smith & Mr. Braxton are the champions against Congress. Mr. Thruston & Mr. White have since come in, and I fancy I may set down both as auxiliaries. They are however not a little puzzled by the difficulty of substituting any practicable regulations within ourselves. Mr. Braxton proposed two that did not much aid his side of the question; the 1. was that all British vessels from the W. Indies should be excluded from our ports—the 2. that no Merchant should carry on trade here untill he sd. have been a resident years. Unless some plan freer from objection can be devised for this State, its patrons will be reduced clearly to the dilemma of acceding to a general one, or leaving our trade under all its present embarrassments. There has been some little skirmishing on the ground of public faith, which leads me to hope that its friends have less to fear than was surmised. The Assize & Port Bills have not yet been awakened. The Senate will make a House today for the first time. With the greatest respect & regard I have the honor to be Dr. Sir, Yr. Obedt. & very Hble Servt.

J. MADISON JR.

P. S. Inclosed herewith are two reports from the Commssrs for examining the head of James River &c. and the ground between the waters of Elizabeth River & N. Carolina—also a sensible pamphlet said to be written by St. George Tucker[5] of this State.

RC (DLC: Washington Papers); FC (DLC). Cover and enclosures missing. Docketed by Washington.

[1] Washington's letter to Governor Henry of 29 Oct. 1785 (Fitzpatrick, *Writings of Washington*, XXVIII, 303–4). Washington followed JM's (and others') advice by declining ownership of the canal company shares and allocating them to philanthropic purposes.

² The act repealing the gift set no time limit on Washington's decision but instead appropriated the shares "and profits hereafter accruing therefrom . . . to such objects of a public nature, in such manner" as Washington "by deed during his life, or by his last will and testament, shall direct" (Hening, *Statutes*, XII, 44). See Freeman, *Washington*, VI, 28–29.

³ Arthur Lee's election to the House of Delegates as a Prince William County representative was upheld by his peers, but they did an about-face when Lee's right to serve in the legislature, and also to hold office as a U. S. treasury commissioner, was challenged. Thereupon, the House decided Lee had to vacate his seat. JM voted for Lee's retention of the seat, a maneuver perhaps made expedient because of Lee's family connections (*JHDV*, Oct. 1785, pp. 15–17). After Lee left the General Assembly he served in the department of finance until 1789, when the treasury board was dissolved (R. H. Lee, *Life of Arthur Lee*, I, 172–73).

⁴ The petition for emancipation of the slaves was drawn up by a group of Methodists under the leadership of Francis Asbury and Thomas Coke in early May 1785. It "was given to every Preacher, intreating the General Assembly of *Virginia*, to pass a Law for the immediate or gradual emancipation of all the Slaves. It is to be signed by all the Freeholders we can procure, and those I believe will not be few" (Matthews, "Notes on the Proposed Abolition of Slavery in Virginia in 1785," Colonial Society of Massachusetts, *Publications*, VI [1904], 371, 375–76; Thomas Coke, *Extracts of the Journals of the Rev. Dr. Coke's Three Visits to America* [London, 1790], p. 39). Notice of the petition was published in the *Va. Gazette*, 6, 13 Aug., 5 Nov. 1785. Presented and read to the House on 8 Nov. 1785, it was rejected "*nemine contra dicente*" 10 Nov. On the same day petitions against a general emancipation from Amelia, Brunswick, Halifax, and Pittsylvania were presented. On 29 Nov. petitions for repeal of the 1781 law allowing personal manumission were presented from Lunenburg and Halifax counties. Carter Henry Harrison on 14 Dec. reported from the Committee of Propositions and Grievances on the Halifax petitions, resolving that the repeal of the act to authorize the manumission of slaves is reasonable. A parliamentary struggle ensued in which a motion was made to strike out "is reasonable" and insert "be rejected." The House was divided 50 ayes to 50 noes, and the motion lost when Speaker Benjamin Harrison voted no. The main question was then put to the House and passed by a vote of 52 to 51. In both instances, JM voted against repealing the act. The Committee of Propositions and Grievances was then ordered to prepare and bring in a bill, which was rejected on 24 Dec. A special committee ordered to bring in a bill to amend the act authorizing manumission was presented and rejected on 17 Jan. 1786 (*JHDV*, Oct. 1785, pp. 27, 30, 31, 65, 91–92, 110, 145). See also JM to Ambrose Madison, 15 Dec. 1785, for JM's opinion of the significance of the controversy, and JM to Jefferson, 22 Jan. 1786, for JM's report on the slavery issue during the session.

⁵ Most likely *Reflections on the Policy and Necessity of encouraging the Commerce of the Citizens of the United States of America, and of granting them exclusive Privileges of Trade* (Richmond, 1785). The pamphlet is attributed to Tucker by both Evans (19214, 20036) and Sabin (97381).

From James Madison, Sr.

Letter not found.

ca. 12–14 November 1785. Mentioned by JM in his 18 November answer to his father, and carried from Orange by Captain Barbour. The elder Madison had inquired about "Turpin in the land office," and requested copies of some journals. Tobacco prices also were discussed.

Debates and Resolutions Related to the Regulation of Commerce by Congress, Including a Call for a Convention at Annapolis, November 1785–January 1786

EDITORIAL NOTE

History is replete with ironies and surely one occurring fairly early in JM's development as a public man concerns the Annapolis convention of 1786. Often cited as a seedling for the full-grown Federal Convention of 1787 where JM was thrust into the national prominence he maintained for the next three decades, the documents and letters emanating from the October 1785 session of the Virginia General Assembly show that Madison was consistently lukewarm to the convention approach as a remedy for the ills of the national government. As JM's views of the national crisis of 1783–1786 developed, he became convinced that the only stable foundation for the national government was a steady, permanent revenue. Ways and means of procuring that income, the lack of which was a daily embarrassment to the Confederation, was of much greater interest to JM in 1784–1785 than expedient measures that promised only temporary solutions to the basic problem.

Shortly before the October 1785 session of the Virginia General Assembly convened, JM visited New York and Philadelphia and there held conversations with others who shared his great concern over a permanent source of income for the Confederation. In a letter to Jefferson, JM dismissed several proposals as impracticable and revealed a willingness to use force as a way of coercing such recalcitrant states as Rhode Island into a viable federal bond. JM's letter indicated his preference for a revision in the Articles of Confederation that would give Congress the power to regulate trade and at the same time provide a system of duty collections that would pour vital cash into a federal treasury notorious for its emptiness (JM to Jefferson, 3 Oct. 1785). At the earlier sessions of the Virginia legislature JM had tried to bend his colleagues into a more flexible attitude toward national commercial regulation, but at the May and October 1784 sessions the opposition of Patrick Henry and Richard Henry Lee made such gestures futile. Congress had reopened the issue again in the spring of 1785 by asking the states to revise the ninth Article of Confederation so that the interstate squabbles over imports and exports, the prohibitive features of foreign trade regulations (particularly those affecting the West Indies market), and the creation of a national income source could all be handled in the same solution.

JM had returned to Richmond convinced from his northern trip that Virginia could be the keystone to a whole plan of national commercial regulation. He expected the other states would look, as they so often did, to Virginia for a cue to their own conduct. Thus when the October 1785 session opened, JM's foremost concern was the passage of resolutions approving an alteration of the Articles of Confederation that would permit Congress to regulate America's international trade. Fortunately, Henry was now governor and not able to use his forensic skills to impede the legislation intended to show other states that Virginia was willing to hand its commercial regulatory powers over to Congress. The discouraging fact, outside of the local politics apparent in Richmond, was that all thirteen states would have to approve the change. Still, JM thought a revision of Article IX was preferable to the calling of a convention to discuss the needed reforms. He had spoken against conventions when New York proposed the idea in 1782 and was no more interested when Massachusetts brought the same approach forward in 1785.

The documents which follow show Madison's unwavering determination to strike the problem at its root. Had the resolutions of 14 November passed, they would have been used as coercive ammunition for legislators in the seaboard states who were mindful of their shipping and mercantile interests and would have shown the confidence of a southern state in the federal government, which was not then apparent. For as a state dependent upon outsiders for ships to carry her tobacco to foreign ports and bring her goods back from them, Virginians well knew they would be in a position to be damaged by federal regulations if they were drawn for the benefit of the New England shipowners and not for the national good. Richard Henry Lee had counseled against the "Intrigue and coalition" of the New England carriers who "might fix a ruinous Monopoly upon the trade & productions of the [southern] Staple States" (Lee to John Jay, 11 Sept. 1785, Ballagh, *Letters of Lee*, II, 389). On the other hand, JM was a rarity in southern politics—a public man willing to trust the national legislature to do the right thing for the whole country, not for a single section. His colleagues were in no mood for such magnanimity, as the votes of 30 November and 1 December proved. In some despair, JM finally joined with the opposition to vote down the resolution that would have limited the national regulatory power to a fixed period of somewhere between thirteen and twenty-five years. He believed the power had to be unlimited for it to be effective. Otherwise, the same difficulties would be encountered all over again, and a time limit made the resolution unpalatable to JM. When those legislators who were more inclined to compromise suggested that an interstate convention might provide ideas on ways to keep the Confederation from tottering, JM was not an enthusiastic supporter for the implementing resolution of 21 January 1786 even though he was aware of the drafter's intentions. The slight attention JM initially paid to the resolution, which created the Annapolis convention by calling on other states to join in the endeavor, is indicated by his reports of the incident to Jefferson and Monroe (22 Jan. 1786). He alluded to the resolution as having been proposed by John Tyler at the eleventh hour when adjournment was minutes away and when it was apparent that all the declamation of the session on trade regulation had "produced nothing."

So JM thought the notion of meeting in Annapolis a poorly baked half-loaf. His hopes in January 1786 still rested in some kind of miraculous event that would bring such diverse men as the Rhode Islanders and Georgians into an agreement and save the Union from perishing because of pecuniary malnutrition. Keeping the United States solvent while her citizens battled for world markets seemed as great a challenge as George III's armies had furnished.

Over a year before the plan for a general overhaul of the Confederation gained ground JM labored to replace parts of the cumbersome federal machinery. Early in the October 1785 session the House of Delegates appointed a special committee to prepare an authorization for the Virginia delegates in Congress to support more flexible commercial regulations. Long an advocate of expanded national legislation in this field, JM served on the committee which made a report on 14 November (*JHDV*, Oct. 1785, p. 36). The record tells nothing of the acrimony touched off by the resulting resolution although most of the delegates apparently liked the sections that would create obstructions for British shippers. On the other hand, they were afraid to endorse the whole resolution because it might entail the surrender of some power to the Confederation. This dilemma was by now an old story for JM, who readily discerned the strength of the opposition and knew that only deft handling could guide the entire set of propositions through to passage (Resolution Calling for the Regulation of Commerce by Congress, 14 Nov. 1785). Except for the popular section that favored a navigation act to retaliate against Great Britain for its postwar discrimination against American shipping—chiefly to the British West Indies—the resolution was too controversial for it to pass easily. A 5 percent import duty and a prohibition on interstate duties were old propositions that had partisans in the pro-Confederation ranks and enemies among the state-oriented delegates. The five-faceted resolution finally came to the Committee of the Whole on 30 November where only three sections emerged intact from the prior debate. The 5 percent impost was dropped, and with its departure JM lost interest in the business. He voted for an amendment to the resolutions that would have extended congressional authority over foreign commerce beyond a thirteen-year limitation (provided the extension carried by a two-thirds majority in Congress). This amendment lost, 28 to 79, on a complex split of votes that proved JM's powers of persuasion had limitations when confronted by entrenched politicians jealous of any surrender of state powers to Congress. If JM ever needed proof that the Confederation was doomed because of the countervailing influence of parochial politics, the outcome here provided it. Probably with some pique, JM then joined a majority that voted to reconsider the emasculated resolution on 1 December. This vote (with the localists) can only be explained by JM's conclusion that the thirteen-year limitation "so far destroyed its value" that supporters of the measure chose "to do nothing [rather] than to adopt it in that form" (JM to Jefferson, 22 Jan. 1786). As JM explained, much of the opposition was sectional in character, so that a suspicion spread that a navigation act (confining shipping to American bottoms) would permit New England shippers to abuse their advantage if given a virtual monopoly of American ocean-borne commerce. The resolution was tabled, but in the final hours of the session two developments indicated the hopes and fears of the delegates. The resolution was still on the table when a bill passed on 21 January "to impose additional tonnage [fees] on British vessels," and at the same time a crack was left in the door for those who wanted a national approach to commercial regulations (*JHDV*, Oct. 1785, pp. 153–54; Hening, *Statutes*, XII, 32). A resolution, which JM credited to John Tyler, provided impetus for a national conference "to examine the relative situations and trade" of the several states. This was a halting step on the road to the Federal Convention of 1787. The first turn would take the nationalists to Annapolis.

This is a hindsight view, of course. In January 1786, JM was not certain that conventions would solve the problems burdening the Confederation. Left to his own devices, JM preferred "to trust to further experience" and hope the Confederation could right itself by adequate reforms rather than to cast about for "a temporary measure which may stand in the way of a permanent one" (JM to Washington, 9 Dec. 1785).

Draft of Resolutions on Foreign Trade

[ca. 12 November 1785]

1. Resd. that to vest Congs. with authority to regulate the foreign trade of the U. S. wd. add energy & dignity to the federal Govt.[1]
2. Resd. that the unrestrained exercise of the powers possessed by each State over its own commerce may be productive of discord among the parties to the Union; and that Congs. ought to be vested with authority to regulate the same in certain cases.
3. Resd. that in regulating the foreign trade of U. S. Congs. ought to enjoy the right
   1. of prohibiting vessels belonging to any foreign nation from entering into any of the ports of the U. S. such prohibition being Uniform through[ou]t the same: and
   2. of imposing duties on the vessels, produce or manufactures of foreign nations, & collecting them in such manner, as to Congs. may seem best; to be appropriated to the establishmt. & support of a marine, & to this purpose alone; unless   States in Congress assd. shall concur, on principles of extreme necessity, in any other appropriation. But Congs. shall notwithstanding, have power to grant drawbacks, & shall not change the application of those duties wch. may arise from their recommendations concerning imposts on imported goods.
4. Resd. that no State ought to be at liberty to impose duties on any goods ware or merchandizes imported by land or water from any other State; but each State ought to be free to prohibit altogether the importation from any other State, of any particular species or de-

scription of goods wares or merchandizes, which are at the same time prohibited to be imported from all other places whatsoever.[2]

5. Resd. that to every act of Congs. done in pursuance of the foregoing authorities, and prohibiting foreign vessels, or imposing duties on Cargoes the assent of three fourths[3] of the States in Congs shall be necessary; but the power of appropriating to the marine in the first instance shall be exercised with the assent of nine States.

6. Resd. that no Act of Congs. done in pursuance of the foregoing authorities, shall be in force longer than   years, unless continued by 3/4 of the confederated States within one year immediately preceding the expiration of the said period.[4]

Ms (DLC). Undated. In JM's hand. This draft was later dated in an unknown hand "[Sept., 1786]" with a note attached: "date uncertain—supposed about the time of Convention at Annapolis." Brant, however, correctly surmised that the draft is erroneously dated and that it is an early draft of the resolutions instructing the Virginia delegates in Congress to propose that the states "authorise" the regulation of commerce of the Confederation (see Resolution Calling for the Regulation of Commerce, 14 Nov. 1785). Brant points out that the draft contains the four resolves which remained in the final measure (nos. 3–6) (Brant, *Madison*, II, 379–80).

[1] JM was appointed to the committee on 7 Nov. charged with drafting resolutions authorizing the Virginia delegates in Congress to seek greater flexibility in commercial regulation (*JHDV*, Oct. 1785, p. 25). JM wrote this draft, which probably served as starting point in the committee discussions and was particularly acceptable on such points as a discriminatory navigation act and the prohibition of tariffs on interstate imports.

[2] JM's purpose in allowing states to prohibit certain interstate importations must have been written with the slave trade in mind. Since 1778 Virginia had prohibited the importation of slaves and had made exception only in extraordinary circumstances (Hening, *Statutes*, IX, 471–72; X, 307–8).

[3] In committee the required number of assenting states was reduced from nine to eight.

[4] JM considered the renewal clause an integral part of the whole plan. When it was rejected during debates in the Committee of the Whole, JM lost patience with his opponents and joined them in a vote tabling the whole resolution (JM to Jefferson, 22 Jan. 1786).

From William Grayson

NEW YORK Nov. 14th. 1785.

DEAR SIR

On inquiring at the Office for F. A.[1] I find it is uncustomary to give copies unless by special direction of Congress, a circumstance I did not advert to, when I was writing to you last. I shall therefore give you the best information in my power from memory. Mr. A. says that a

Commee. of merchts. from Glasgow waited on him in London & told him their business was to lay the affair of the debts before parliament; that he dissuaded them from taking this step, as he was apprehensive it might be productive of disagreable consequences; by holding out the idea of a speedy accomodation of all subjects of dispute. That he had some conversation with Lord Caermarthen on the subject of the debts among other things.

That his Lordship mentioned to him the bill for opening the Courts of justice, and that the same he had understood had been lost by the accidental circumstance of a frost. That his Lordship objected to the loss of interest which was to be incurred by that bill, & farther apprehended great losses to the Brittish merchants by the emigrations to Kentucki. That with respect to the interest Mr. Adams had urged, the calamities of war, the sufferings of the debtors & the infraction of the treaty in other instances on their parts; & that as to the injuries apprehended from the emigrations to Kentucki he concieved they were groundless, as few persons Went to that country who did not greatly better their situations; & as there was a regular administration of justice in those quarters, such removals were undoubtedly of advantage.

That upon the whole interest & policy dictated to them to act with moderation, & give time to the distressed debtors to make payment, that the loss of the negroes carried off, & the product of their labor, as well as the want of the fur trade arising from the posts being withheld were real & heavy grievances on the debtors & furnished strong reasons against a rigorous exaction of claims. This I think is the substance of what Mr. A. has remarked, to the best of my memory; from his subsequent correspondence, it does not appear to me to be probable that any thing will be done very speedily, in this or any other business. Mr. Adams thinks nothing will touch them but restraints laid on their trade by Congress: At the same he insinuates that such restraints may eventually produce hostilities.[2] Upon the whole it is difficult to determine whether the bill alluded to ought to pass this session or not, I was in great hopes it would have been in my power to have giv'n you better information before this but the last letters mention nothing about the matter.[3]

By last Post the delegation wrote to the Governor giving their reasons for not assenting to the requisition; their design was only that the will of the State might not be fettered by their acts. If the State for the sake of preserving public credit should think it expedient to pass a legislative act complying with the requisition I then beg leave to submit to your consideration the propriety of purchasing in different parts of the Continent as many certificates of interest, as that when added to the interest due the citizens of the State on liquidated certificates may be equal to two thirds of their proportion of the same, having in contemplation at the same time the one fourth of the requisition of 1784 which remains yet to be satisfyed as far as it relates to facilities. This mode I should think would be preferable to that of laying an interest tax on the Citizens for the full two thirds of the States proportion, as thereby a competition would be raised & the interest of course obtained on worse terms than if the purchase was conducted as far as relates to the deficiency by State agents. With respect to the interest due the Citizens of the State, perhaps an interest tax pro tanto may be an eligible mode. Some of the delegates have it in contemplation [to] recommend to their States to purchase principal, which may be now had at 2/8 in the pound without charging for the back interest;[4] however I do not concieve this to be the interest of our State. Her claim agt. the Continent for the Western expedition must be soon allowed, is a credit in some shape or another. It is beside expected the sales of the Western lands will very soon greatly diminish the domestic debt; of course the demands on our State will be lessened according to such diminution.

I am sorry to inform you that the Surveyors from the back Country have returned without doing any thing more than merely making a beginning. They have alledged in excuse the advanced season of the year, & the unsettled situation of Indian affairs. The Eastern Surveyors Who have returned this Way, speak of the country in the highest style, & talk of nothing but forming confederacies, purchasing townships, & settling the country à la mode New England. Indeed from every appearance it is plain to me, the influx into that country from the Eastern States & the State of N. Jersey will be beyond the most sanguine expectation. The Consular arrangement has been before Congress since you left this; & nothing was done except that of vesting the Ministers and chargè des affaires at foreign Courts with the powers of Consuls general. The ballance remains for the new Congress.[5]

Yesterday the English & French packets both arrived, but do not understand they have brought any news of consequence. Indeed their contents have not yet got abroad.[6] From Yr. Affect. fd. & Most Obed Servt.

WILLM. GRAYSON.

N. B. the part of this letter which relates to a certain subject is entirely confidential.

RC (DLC). Cover missing. Docketed by JM.

¹ John Jay's office as Secretary for Foreign Affairs.

² Grayson summarized Adams's letters to Jay during the summer of 1785. The comments concerning Anglo-American trade and negotiations about the British debts versus the western posts problem were made in Adams's letters of 6 and 17 June, those about hostilities, in Adams's letter of 6 Aug. (*Diplomatic Correspondence of the U. S.*, II, 371 and passim).

³ JM and Grayson had discussed the British debt problem and possible forms for a Virginia law covering the matter (Grayson to JM, 8 Nov. 1785).

⁴ JM sat on the committee which determined Virginia's action regarding Confederation requisitions. The ultimate decision was to combine the use of "facility notes" and the exchange of paper for specie in order to pay the state's share of the public debt (*JHDV*, Oct. 1785, pp. 71, 77–78, 88).

⁵ On 13 Oct. 1785, Jay reported in Congress his suggestions for appropriate consular arrangements with other nations. The matter was to be considered on 17 Oct., but was postponed until 24 Oct. when a report was given. Motions were made but no action was taken, and the matter reassigned to Jay in order that he study consuls' salaries and the customs rates of other countries. Discussion on the subject was not resumed until 1786 (*JCC*, XXIX, 831–33 and passim).

⁶ The British packet *Halifax* and the French packet *Courier de New York* arrived in New York harbor on 12 and 13 Nov. (*N. Y. Packet*, 14 Nov. 1785). Important communications about relations between the U. S. and European nations were brought by at least one of these ships as Jay made reference to them in his letter to Congress of 18 Nov. 1785 (Burnett, *Letters*, VIII, 256 n.). See also Grayson's letter to JM, 22 Nov. 1785.

Resolution Calling for the Regulation of Commerce by Congress

[14 November 1785]¹

Whereas, the relative situation of the United States has been found on trial, to require uniformity in their commercial regulations, as the only effectual policy for obtaining in the ports of foreign nations, a stipulation of privileges, reciprocal to those enjoyed by the subjects of such nations in the ports of the United States; for preventing animosities, which cannot fail to arise among the several States from the interference of partial and separate regulations; ⟨and for deriving from commerce, such aids to the public revenue as it ought to contribute;⟩ and whereas, such uniformity can be best concerted and carried into effect by the federal councils, which, having been instituted for the purpose of managing the interests of the States, in cases which cannot so well be provided for, by measures individually pursued, ought to be invested with authority in this case, as being within the reason and policy of their institution;

Resolved, That the delegates representing this Commonwealth in Congress, be instructed to propose in Congress, a recommendation to the States in Union, to authorise that assembly to regulate their trade, and to collect a revenue therefrom, on the following principles, and under the following qualifications:

1st. That the United States in Congress assembled, be authorised to prohibit vessels belonging to any[2] nation, which has no commercial treaty with the United States, from entering any of the ports thereof, or to impose any duties on such vessels and their cargoes which may be judged necessary: all such prohibitions and duties to be uniform throughout the United States, and the proceeds of the latter to be carried into the treasury of the State within which they shall accrue.

⟨ 2d. That over and above any duties which may be so laid, the United States in Congress assembled, be authorised to collect in manner prescribed by an act "to provide certain and adequate funds for the payment of this State's quota of the debts contracted by the United States," an impost not exceeding five per centum ad valorem on all goods, wares and merchandizes whatsoever, imported into the United States from any foreign ports; such impost to be uniform as aforesaid, and to be carried to the treasury of the United States.⟩

3d. That no State be at liberty to impose duties on any goods, wares or merchandizes, imported by land or by water from any other State, but may altogether prohibit the importation from any other State of any particular species or description of goods, wares or merchandize, of which the importation is at the same time prohibited from all other places whatsoever.

4th. That no act of Congress that may be authorised, as hereby proposed, shall be entered into by less than two thirds of the confederated States, nor be in force longer than [twenty-five] years,[3] ⟨unless continued by a like proportion of votes within one year immediately preceding the expiration of the said period, or be revived in like manner after the expiration thereof; nor shall any impost whatsoever, be collected by virtue of the authority proposed in the second article, after the year 17   .⟩

Printed copy (*JHDV*, Oct. 1785, p. 36). No Ms copy has been found. Clauses in angle brackets were deleted by amendments from the final version of the bill.

[1] On 7 Nov. Prentis reported out of the Committee of the Whole a resolution that an act ought to pass authorizing Virginia delegates in Congress to support measures for a general regulation of commerce. JM was appointed a member to a special committee ordered to write a bill. On 11 Nov. the committee was discharged

from drawing up a bill and ordered to prepare a resolution to give instructions to the delegates. The instructions were reported and read to the House by Prentis on 14 Nov. (*JHDV*, Oct. 1785, pp. 25, 32, 36). The authorship of the resolution is debatable. That JM was a foremost advocate of strengthening the national confederation, and that he considered federal regulation of commerce essential, is beyond doubt. His promotion and support of the bill are not in doubt. However, the textual history of the resolution is not so clear. It seems likely that JM at least strongly influenced the form and substance of the resolution if he did not actually write it himself. See Boyd, *Papers of Jefferson*, IX, 204–6 n., for a detailed consideration of the resolution. The resolution bears the mark of JM's reasoning in his speech to the House on commercial regulations (Notes for Debate on Commercial Regulations, 30 Nov.–1 Dec. 1785) and in his draft of resolutions on foreign trade (Draft of Resolutions on Foreign Trade [ca. 12 Nov. 1785]). See Rives, *Life of Madison*, II, 53–54; Brant, *Madison*, II, 379–80.

2 "Foreign" was inserted after "any" in final version of the bill.

3 On 30 Nov. Alexander White reported and read to the Committee of the Whole an amended version of the resolution in which "twenty five" had been amended to thirteen years. The length of time had originally been left blank. The resolution was passed and ordered to the Senate on that day, but the order was rescinded on the following day. JM voted with the majority on reconsidering the resolution. It was then amended and finally tabled by the House (*JHDV*, Oct. 1785, pp. 66–67) where it remained until the end of the session. JM wrote to Jefferson that the friends of the resolution preferred to take no further action since the limitation to thirteen years destroyed its value. Immediately after the miscarriage of the resolution, Tyler proposed a resolution calling for a general meeting of commissioners from the states to consider a federal plan for regulating commerce (JM to Jefferson, 22 Jan. 1786). Action on this last day of the session thus led to the Annapolis convention.

To Thomas Jefferson

RICHMOND Novr. 15. 1785:

DEAR SIR

I acknowledged from Philada. your favor of the 11 of May. On my return to Orange I found the copy of your Notes brought along with it by Mr. Doradour.[1] I have looked them over carefully myself & consulted several judicious friends in confidence. We are all sensible that the *fre[e]dom of your strictures* on some *particular measures* and *opinions* will displease *their respective abettors*. But we equally concur in thinking that this consideration ought not to be weighed against the *utility of your plan*. We think both the facts and remarks which you have assembled too *valuable* not to be made known, at least to those for whom *you destine* them, and speak of them to *one another* in *terms which* I must *not repeat to you*. Mr. Wythe suggested that it might be better to put the number you may allot to the University into the library, rather than to distribute them among the Students. In the latter case the Stock will be immediately exhausted. In the former[2] the dis-

415

cretion of the professors will make it serve the Students as they successively come in. Perhaps too an *indiscriminate gift*[3] might offend *some narrow minded parents*. Mr. Wythe desired me to present you with his most friendly regards. He mentioned the difficulty he experiences in using his pen as an apology for not giving these assurances himself. I postpone my acct. of the Assembly till I can make it more satisfactory, observing only that we are at work on the Revisal, and I am not without hopes of seeing it pass this Session with as few alterations as could be expected. Some are made unavoidable by a change of circumstances. The greatest danger is to be apprehended from the impatience which a certain lapse of time always produces. Mr. W. Maury informs me that Master P. Carr has read at Williamsbg. Horace—Some of Tully's select orations—Greek Testament, Aesops fables in Greek—ten books of Homer—and is now beginning Xenophon, Juvenal & Livy. He has been also employed in the French. Your other Nephew is at Hampden Sidney. I have no particular acct. of him.

RC (DLC). Cover missing. Not signed. Docketed. Italicized words, unless otherwise noted, were encoded by JM in the code Jefferson sent him 11 May 1785.

[1] Jefferson had sent JM a copy of his privately printed *Notes on the State of Virginia* (Paris, 1785) in the care of the Comte de Doradour, a French émigré who planned to settle in Virginia.

[2] The succeeding eight words were inserted here by JM instead of "it will," which was deleted.

[3] Underlined in Ms.

From the Reverend James Madison

WILLIAMG. NOVR. 15. 1785.

DEAR COL.

As several Matters will probably be agitated this Session in wh. the Interests of our University may be deeply concerned, I have wish'd to give you some Information respecting them, & then as a Friend to Science I am sure we shall have a powerful Advocate in our Favour.

The 1st. is involved in the Dismemberment of the State. The Seperation of Kentucky may take Place, without an express Reserve of the Fees due to the College from that Country.[1] If this Matter be pass'd over in Silence, it is possible, the Surveyors might find some Plea to refuse Payment. The Debt is of Importance to the College. Would it not then be prudent to give us a securing Clause in the Act of Seperation wh. may probably be pass'd? The 2d. is of much less Importance, because it is scarce possible that the House will attend to it. The Tenants upon our Lands have grown restive.[2] They intend to petition the Assembly, I am told, for a Destruction of the Coll. Rights, & to vest in them a Fee simple Estate.[3] However unreasonable the Demand may be, yet it will be well for us to have a Friend at Court, & therefore I have mentioned their Intentions to you. Besides that General Petition of the College Tenants, the Holders of the Lands near James Town, lately given to the College, mean also to present a Petition, in Order to have their former Leases, which we consider as illegal, confirmed to them. The Atty. gave it as his opinion that they were illegal. The Object of this Petition then must be, supposing his Opinion to be well founded, to obtain from the Assembly, the Confirmation of what was originally illegal. This last Petition however, will probably attract a general Attention. But I thought it adviseable to mention particularly the first Matter, as an entire Silence of the Act for a Seperation, might be construed by the opposite Party even as a Ground for a Refusal of Payment, or might be considered as a sufft. Plea of Justification in the new Govt. to appropriate those Fees to their own interior purposes, especially as in some of their Resolves respecting their Greivances, the Payment of such Fees to this Coll. is enumerated as one.[4] If we can get no more after the Seperation, wh. is reasonable eno' perhaps, yet let us have what is due prior to the Seperation. But wd. it not be possible to secure all the Fees due for surveying officers Lands even after the Seperation, the Survey having already commenced? I leave this however to your own better Judgt.

When shall we have the Happiness to see you here. I had hopes the fœderal Court might be some Inducement to bring you down.[5] If it shd still sit, & at a Time your Absence can be spared, perhaps you may be induced to visit us. Whatever may be the Cause of transferring you to this Place, we shall esteem it a fortunate one. My Wife desires to be particularly remembered as well as Dr Cole.[6] Yr. Friend

J MADISON

RC (DLC). Cover missing.

[1] The 1779 act "for establishing a Land office" provided that all county surveyors receive a certificate of competency from "the president and professors of William and Mary college" (Hening, *Statutes*, X, 53). The college was to receive "one sixth part of the legal fees which shall be received by such surveyor" and this subvention became a major source of revenue for William and Mary. An act passed at the Oct. 1783 session of the General Assembly had added surveys of military bounty lands to the sources of income (ibid., XI, 310). Despite the Reverend James

Madison's plea, the committee drafting the act of separation for the Kentucky district passed over the provision although surveys made through 1 Sept. 1788 were to be subject to the 1779 law.

2 After the seat of government was moved from Williamsburg to Richmond, title in the public lands in the old capital was conveyed to the college by an act passed at the May 1784 session of the General Assembly (Hening, *Statutes*, XI, 406). These included "the lands commonly called the palace lands," a tract in Williamsburg "commonly called the Vineyard," certain public lands near Jamestown, "together with all the lots and houses in the said city which are the property of this commonwealth." The college president and faculty were empowered to sell or use the lands "in any manner they shall judge best for the interest and advantage of the said university" (ibid.; *The History of the College of William and Mary from Its Foundation, 1693, to 1870* [Baltimore, 1870], p. 46).

3 The *JHDV* of the Oct. 1785 session does not mention a petition from the tenants of the college lands.

4 At the Danville convention held in Dec. 1784 the delegates passed a bill of complaints that included: "Resolved that the one sixth part of all Surveyors Fees arising within this District, appropriated to the support of the University of William & Mary, and not to the Transilvania Seminary[,] is a greevance [*sic*]" (Abernethy, "Journal of the First Kentucky Convention," *Journal of Southern History,* I [1935], 73).

5 The "fœderal court" was a board of arbitration set up by Congress in 1784–1785 to adjudicate a territorial dispute between Massachusetts and New York. The appointed judges were to meet at Williamsburg for their deliberations, but delays ensued and the scheduled meeting was not held there (*JCC*, XXIX, 865).

6 Probably Dr. Walter King Cole (d. 1794), who was educated at William and Mary, served as a surgeon in the Virginia navy during the Revolution, and petitioned the General Assembly for compensation because of slaves and lands confiscated during the war (*JHDV*, Oct. 1785, p. 53; Wyndam B. Blanton, *Medicine in Virginia in the Eighteenth Century*, [Richmond, 1931], pp. 75, 387–88).

Act Securing the Copyright for Authors

[16 November 1785]

I. *BE it enacted by the General Assembly*, That the author of any book or pamphlet already printed,[1] being a citizen of any one of the United States, who has not transferred to any other person or persons the copy or copies of such book, or pamphlet, share, or shares thereof, his heirs and assigns, or the person or persons who have purchased or acquired such copy or copies, share or shares, in order to print or reprint the same, his heirs and assigns shall have the exclusive right of printing and re-printing such book or pamphlet, within this commonwealth, for the term of twenty-one years,[2] to be computed from the first publication thereof; and that the author of any book or pamphlet already composed and not printed or published, or that shall hereafter be composed, being a citizen, as aforesaid, his heirs and assigns shall have the exclusive right of printing and re-printing such book or pamphlet, within this commonwealth, for the like term of twenty-one years, to be computed from the first publication thereof. And if any person or persons whatsoever, shall print, re-print, or cause to be printed or re-printed, within this commonwealth, any such book or pamphlet; or shall import into this commonwealth, from any foreign kingdom or state, any printed or re-printed copies of such book or pamphlet, without the consent of the author or proprietor thereof first obtained in writing, signed in presence of two credible witnesses at least; or who, knowing the same to be so printed, re-printed, or imported, without such consent first had and obtained, shall publish, sell, or expose to sale, or cause to be published, sold, or exposed to sale, any copy or copies of any such book or pamphlet; the person or persons offending herein, shall forfeit to the party injured, double the value of all the copies so printed, re-printed, or imported; or so published, sold, or exposed to sale; to be recovered at the suit of such party, in any court of record within this commonwealth.

II. *Provided nevertheless,* That no person shall be entitled to the benefit of this act, until he shall have registered the title of such book or pamphlet with the clerk of the council, and procured a certificate of such registry from the said clerk; which certificate the clerk is hereby required to give, taking only three shillings for his trouble.

Printed copy (Hening, *Statutes,* XII, 30–31).

[1] JM was entreated by Noah Webster in 1784 to introduce this bill (see Webster to JM, 5 July 1784). Webster was conducting a one-man campaign for state copyright laws because of the lack of national legislation. He visited Richmond in Nov. 1785 and recorded in his diary a conversation with JM on 11 Nov. (NN: Webster Diary). No manuscript of the bill JM introduced has been found, but since he offered the measure on 16 Nov. and carried it to the Senate on 18 Nov., his authorship is beyond doubt (*JHDV,* Oct. 1785, pp. 40, 43).

[2] The twenty-one-year term of the copyright was generous when compared with the fourteen years granted in most of the states, but Massachusetts, New Hampshire, and Rhode Island copyrights were also for twenty-one years. The last of the original thirteen states to enact a copyright statute was New York in 1786 (Lyman Ray Patterson, *Copyright in Historical Perspective* [Nashville, Tenn., 1968], pp. 183–87). JM remained aware of the cumbersome burden placed on authors and inventors when he compiled a list of federal responsibilities at the Federal Convention which included the power "To secure to literary authors their copy rights for a limited time" (Madison, *Convention Notes,* p. 477). JM also noted the problem in *Federalist No. 43.* The federal Constitution contained a copyright clause, of course, and a federal copyright statute was enacted in 1790—but JM's direct involvement in both instances is a matter of conjecture.

Amendments to the Act Conveying Canal Shares to George Washington

[16 November 1785]

I. WHEREAS by an act, intituled "An act for vesting in George Washington, esq. a certain interest in the companies established for opening and extending the navigation of James and Potowmack rivers,"[1] and reciting, "that whereas it is the desire of the representatives of this commonwealth to embrace every suitable occasion of testifying their sense of the unexampled merits of George Washington, esq. towards his country; and it is their wish in particular, that those great works for its improvement, which, both as springing from the liberty which he has been so instrumental in establishing, and as encouraged by his patronage, will be durable monuments of his glory, may be made monuments also of the gratitude of his country:" It is enacted, "that the treasurer be directed in addition to the subscriptions he is already authorized to make to the respective undertakings for opening the navigations of Potowmack and James rivers, to subscribe to the amount of fifty shares to the former and one hundred shares to the latter, to be paid in like manner with the subscriptions above mentioned; and that the shares so subscribed be and the same are hereby vested in George Washington, esq. his heirs and assigns forever, in as effectual a manner as if the subscriptions had been made by himself or by his attorney." And whereas, the said George Washington, esq. in his letter addressed to the governor,[2] which has been laid before the general assembly, hath expressed his sentiments thereupon, in the words following, to wit:—"Your excellency having been pleased to transmit me a copy of the act appropriating to my benefit certain shares in the companies for opening the navigation of James and Potowmack rivers, I take the liberty of returning to the general assembly, through your hands, the profound and grateful acknowledgments, inspired by so signal a mark of their beneficient intentions towards me. I beg you, sir, to assure them, that I am filled on this occasion with every sentiment which can flow from a heart warm with love for my country—sensible to every token of its approbation and affection; and solicitous to testify, in every instance, a respectful submission to its wishes: With these sentiments in my bosom, I need not dwell on the anxiety I feel, in being obliged, in this instance, to decline a favour, which is rendered no less flattering by the manner in which it is conveyed, than it is affectionate in itself. In explaining this obligation, I pass over a comparison of my endeavours in the public service with the many honourable testimonies of approbation which have already so far over-rated and over-paid them; reciting one consideration only, which supersedes the necessity of recurring to every other. When I was first called to the station with which I was honoured during the late conflict for our liberties—to the diffidence which I had so many reasons to feel in accepting it, I thought it my duty to join to a firm resolution to shut my hand against every pecuniary recompence; to this resolution I have invariably adhered—from this resolution (if I had the inclination) I do not consider myself at liberty to depart. Whilst I repeat, therefore, my fervent acknowledgments to the legislature for their very kind sentiments and intentions in my favour, and at the same time beg them to be persuaded, that a remembrance of this singular proof of their goodness towards me, will never cease to cherish returns of the warmest affection and gratitude, I must pray, that their act, so far as it has for its object my personal emolument, may not have its effect: But if it should please the general assembly to permit me to turn the destination of the fund vested in me, from my private emoluments, to objects of a public nature, it will be my study in selecting these, to prove the sincerity of my gratitude for the honour conferred on me, by preferring such as may appear most subservient to the enlightened and patriotic views of the legislature." And whereas the desire of the general assembly to mark by the provision above mentioned, their sense of the illustrious merits of the said George Washington, esq. at the same time that it is strengthened by this fresh and endearing proof of his title to the gratitude of his country, is superseded by their respect for his disinterested wishes and patriotic views:

II. *Be it enacted*, That the said recited act, so far as it vests in George Washington, esq. and his heirs, the shares therein directed to be subscribed in his name, shall be, and the same is hereby repealed.

III. *And be it further enacted*, That the said shares with the tolls and profits hereafter accruing therefrom, shall stand appropriated to such objects of a public nature, in such manner, and under such distributions, as the said George Washington, esq. by deed during his life, or by his last will and testament, shall direct and appoint.

Printed copy (Hening, *Statutes*, XII, 42–44). No Ms copy has been found. The bill as enacted was titled "An act to amend the act intituled An act for vesting in George Washington, esq. a certain interest in the companies established for opening and extending the navigation of James and Potowmack rivers."

[1] JM wrote the original bill vesting Washington with the canal shares, which was introduced on 4 Jan. 1785. JM preferred this gift as a more suitable means of

expressing Virginia's gratitude to the general than conferring a pension. However, even the grant of canal shares touched Washington's sensibility, and he declined to accept them for himself. Instead he requested that the shares be held in trust for the benefit of the public. Before he wrote the letter to the governor, he discussed the matter with JM at Mount Vernon in Sept. 1785 (JM to Jefferson, 3 Oct. 1785). JM apparently sent Washington recommendations which Washington embodied in his letter to the governor for the General Assembly. Washington further requested from JM information of the result and JM's sentiment respecting a proper appropriation of the funds (Washington to JM, 29 Oct. 1785). The bill was easily passed, and JM suggested that the fund be divided between an institution of "*the* [phil]*osophical world*" and "some other . . . of [a] *popular cast*" (italics in code, JM to Jefferson, 22 Jan. 1786). Washington dropped his idea of establishing two charity schools and dedicated the Potomac shares to the establishment of a university in the District of Columbia and the James River shares to Liberty Hall Academy, later to become Washington and Lee University (Washington to Jefferson, 26 Sept. 1785, Boyd, *Papers of Jefferson*, VIII, 556; Brant, *Madison*, II, 369).

² The letter from Washington was referred to the House from the governor and committed to a special committee of which JM was a member and Tyler chairman on 11 Nov. Tyler reported to the House on 15 Nov. that new legislation should be enacted changing the destination of the canal shares vested in Washington, and on the following day Tyler presented the bill. The House heard the third reading, passed the bill, and ordered Tyler to carry it to the Senate on 18 Nov. The speaker of the House signed the act 7 Jan. 1786.

To James Madison, Sr.

RICHD. NOVR. 18: 1785

HOND SIR

I rcd. yrs. by Capt. Barbour who I hope will enquire as to Turpin in the land office. I wish you rather to confide such business to friends coming here who can be relied on than to refer it to me. I am so little Master of my time, and the Office is removed so far out of the way that I cannot be relied on. I will endeavor to get the Journals for you soon. The price of Tobo. forbids the sale of your Hhd. The Assembly have made some progress in the Revisal, and I hope will go thro' it. Public Credt. seems to have more friends and paper Money more Adversaries than I had expected. Delegates to Congs. for 1786. R. H. Lee, Wm. Grayson Js. Monroe, H. Lee Jr. Edwd. Carrington. Councilor Carter Braxton. Yr. affe. Son

J. MADISON JR.

RC (DLC). Cover missing. Docketed by JM's father. JM later added, "Madison Js. Novr. 18. 1785."

From William Grayson

New York. Nov. 22nd. 1785.

Dear Sir,

I wrote you by the last Post, since which other letters have arrived from the gentleman therein mentioned.[1] They came by the last packett; and one is dated as late as the 15th. of September last. In it however there is no mention of the Algerine War. Mr. Jefferson has also wrote by the french packett, but his letter is of an old date. There has been a conference with Mr. Pitt.

That gentleman thinks the war could make no change in the nature of the debts due by or to the citizens or subjects of either country; that the interest is as much due as principal; that the Brittish lawyers hold this opinion. In answer Mr. A. observes the lawyers in America hold a very different opinion respecting the War, and that no jury from New Hamshire to Georgia would allow interest during the war. That the war put an end to all laws and government, consequently to all contracts made under those laws. That it is a maxim of law that a personal right or obligation once destroyed is lost forever: that the treaty & new laws were necessary for the restoration of the contracts or obligations; that the contracts could not be said to have had any existence during the War. Mr. Pitt replied, that if these were the ideas in America, it was necessary there should be some new stipulation respecting the subject.

With respect to the negroes he acknowledged that this was so clear a case, as that satisfaction ought to be made therefor, as soon as the number carried off could be made appear. To this Mr. A. replied, that Colo. Smith who had transacted the business with Sir Guy Carleton could evince it by documents then ready to be produced. He acknowledged also with respect to Mr. A's. construction of the Armistice there could be no great difficulty: that with reguard to the Posts it was so connected with other matters as not to be decided on singly. As to the commercial treaty there seems to have been a great difference of sentiment; Mr. A. is of opinion that nothing will be done shortly. Mr. Pitt however has promised that during the recess of parliament he will turn his thoughts to those subjects. Mr. A. thinks that the reason why the Elector of Hanover came into the Confederation agt. the Emperor was to preserve peace, in Europe, on *our accounts*. I need not observe he is a strong advocate for *restrictions* on their *commerce*. I have been detained here longer than I expected, waiting to forward some documents which I concieved might be of advantage to our State; & which I have had more difficulty in procuring than I at first expected.

I have by this post sent the aggregate amounts in specie value of the advances to each State; by which it will appear that our State has had but little comparatively.[2] The Union in fact owe her a million of dollars & upwards on this account provided she has made equal exertions in other respects; that is to say she has recieved a million less than her fœderal proportion. It is said however that no advantage can be immediately derived from this circumstance, as it is contended that the interest on all these sums is suspended till the final settlement of accounts by the resolution of the 3rd. of June 1784. This same resolution then holds out an additional temptation for prolongating the settlement. Rhode Island has had a million of dollars; is it likely then to suppose the wishes for the arrival of a period when she is to account? The same observation will apply to those who are similarly circumstanced. It will be difficult then when Virginia meets with embarrassments to get them removed by Congress.[3]

Virginia has a demand (in opposing Lord Dunmore) of £400,000 Virga. money incurred from Sepr. 1775 to December 1776: which I do not know is supported by any resolution of Congress. It is true she has the same reason to have it allowed as Massachuzetz.[4] Besides there are resolutions of Congress which direct assistance which assistance Congress says shall be paid: however it is said here that all this goes for nothing. This subject of our public accounts deserves great consideration. I hope you will [con]sider this letter as confidential & remain Yr. Affect. friend & Most Obedt. Servt.

WILLM. GRAYSON

RC (DLC). Addressed and franked by Grayson. Docketed by JM.

[1] "The gentleman" correspondent was John Adams, then the U. S. minister to Great Britain. The issue facing Adams which was a concern of JM's was the interest on British debts owed by Americans since 1775.

[2] See Grayson's letter to Patrick Henry, 22 Nov. 1785 (Burnett, *Letters*, VIII, 257–58).

[3] The debt problem caused tensions resulting in sectional disagreements. Southerners contended that they bore more than their share of the debt while the North profited from congressional decisions on its repayment (Ferguson, *The Power of the Purse*, pp. 183, 335–36).

[4] Virginians took arms against their royal governor, Lord Dunmore, in 1775 and 1776. Norfolk was heavily damaged in the effort, which finally resulted in the expulsion of Dunmore and his supporters (Wertenbaker, *Norfolk: Historic Southern Port* [1962 ed.], pp. 52–68). The destruction of Norfolk was as severe, in Grayson's mind, as the British actions had been for Boston.

From William Grayson

Dear Sir.

I am very busy preparing to decamp for Virginia. Of course I shall not lay you under the trouble of reading a long letter from me this Post. There is one thing very singular in Adam's correspondence. He is always pressing the necessity of commercial restrictions; says no treaty can be had without them, and yet he decidedly acknowledges, that in the *prosecution* of this *commercial war* there is every reason to suppose we shall incur a *real war;* for says he nothing but the opinion they have of our *strength* & their *weakness* prevents it at present: for the nation is against us. There are still pro's & Con's here respecting the Algerine war: & not a word from Europe officially. The new Congress have chos'n Hancock Presidt. and Doct. Ramsay Chairman until his arrival. The business immediately before them is whether Temple shall be recieved as Consul Genl. from G. Brittain. I presume it will be decided ultimately in the affirmative as Congress have passed a resolution that Ministers & Chargès des Affaires at foreign courts shall be Consuls general ex Officio. Temple has come out in great State, & has taken the best house in the City.[1]

The inconvenience which Members of Congress have experienced here this last year from living at common boarding houses, & mixing with the landlady her Aunts cousins & acquaintances & with all other sorts of company has been complained of loudly. We have not, I confess suffered in this way, though we have purchased the exemption at a dear rate to our purses; we have had a house though a small one, & yet that same house has went deep into our allowances, so that our dignity has almost eat up our finances. I understand some of the States mean to relieve their delegates from the weight of this inconvenience by establishing a kind of State house at the expence of such State. Although I cannot help admiring the idea of doing something yet I think the plan of jumbling all together whether grave or gay, married or single, like Falstaff in the buck baskett, heel to point, altogether improper.[2] I should rather suppose (if the legislature gets into a merry mood,) that it would be better to allow each delegate a certain sum of money, provided he disburses the same in House rent: it is also supposed hard that a Member of Congress when he goes home to see his family should be put upon stoppages. I should hope no person would be appointed but would conscientiously discharge his duty to the State to the best of his judgment. I remain Yr. Affect. fd. & Most Obed Servt.

WILLM. GRAYSON.

You will please to consider what relates to Adams as altogether confidential.

The affair of the negroes which has made so much noise in our house is rather trifling.[3]

Negroes carried off from N. Y.

Men	1,386
Women	954
Children	657
Total	2,997.

RC (DLC). Cover missing. Docketed by JM.

[1] John Temple (1732–1798), a native of Massachusetts, had served the crown in a variety of colonial offices before 1771, then moved to England and was surveyor general of customs there from 1771 to 1774. He returned to his homeland and tried to regain his American residency in 1778. Denied permission to stay in the U. S., he returned to England. He served as British consul general in the U. S. from 1785 until his death (*Papers of Madison*, V, 3–5).

[2] The allusion is to Falstaff's hiding place in Shakespeare's *Merry Wives of Windsor*, Act III, scene v (George van Santvoord, ed. [New Haven, 1922], pp. 70–71):

"By the Lord, a buck-basket! rammed me in with foul shirts and smocks, socks, foul stockings, greasy napkins. . . . In the circumference of a peck, hilt to point, heel to head . . . it was a miracle to 'scape suffocation."

[3] Washington appointed commissioners of embarkation in 1783 who supervised the British withdrawal from New York. Washington kept the information on Negroes who had embarked until Congress requested it and sent a messenger to Mount Vernon, fearful of trusting such a valuable compilation to the ordinary post. The exaggerated idea that slaves by the tens of thousands had been whisked away was demolished when Washington turned the commissioners' report over to Congress (Burnett, *Letters*, VIII, 103; John C. Fitzpatrick, *The Diaries of George Washington, 1748–1799* [4 vols.; Boston, 1925], II, 411–12). Still the matter remained a seething issue in Virginia, and in 1791 the state legislature passed a resolution protesting the British refusal to compensate Americans for the lost slaves (Washington to Henry Lee, 7 Dec. 1791, Fitzpatrick, *Writings of Washington*, XXXI, 441).

From Benjamin Waller

WILLIAMSBURG Novr. 28th. 1785

SIR;

Colo. Richard Cary, on his return from Richmond delivered me a friendly Hint from Mr. Matthews; but whether from the Councillor or

Delegate, of that name,[1] he did not say, nor indeed did I ask; so that I am at a Loss which of them to thank. The Purport was, that Umbrage was taken at my not attending the Court of Appeals at Richmond. Presuming on a former half-Year's acquaintance, I venture to address you on the Subject, instead of writing, at Random, to either of the above Gentlemen. True it is, Sir, that I have not attended that Court; and sorry I am that the Default of so insignificant a Member should give Offence. It is a fact; that my appointment to the two Offices I have been honoured with by the General Assembly, were conferred merely through their own Grace and Favor, without Solicitation: that then, and at all other times, I expressed a Compliance to serve in any Station they thought proper; provided it might be performed down here; but that I could not travel any Distance from home in my old Age. During my Seat in Council, the two Sessions of the Court of Appeals held here, and at every Court of Admiralty, I never absented myself from Duty a Day, not even an hour. Until lately the Court of Appeals hath dispatched little business, but not for Want of Members. I own it is my Duty to attend, however useless; but now advanced in my 70th: Year, subject to the natural Infirmities incident thereto, and thereby chiefly confined at home; can I, my good Sir, with any Pretence to Prudence, quit Quiet & Retirement (almost the only remaining Comforts) to launch into Noise, a Crowd, and a new World, (for few of my Cotemporaries are left) and possibly be exposed to Ridicule and Contempt? Whether the World be tired of us, or We of the World, or both possibly mutually weary of each other, Tempus abire est, We must either decently yield to Succession, or be shouldered out.

When by an Act, in 1779, the Courts were removed to Richmond, I should have resigned; had not the next Session of Assembly fixed the Admiralty Court here. When, after fleeing from Leslie & Arnold twice, I found I must fall under the Power of Lord Cornwallis, and expected to be paroled, or carried into Captivity, that this Disability might not be detrimental, I wrote a Letter of Resignation to the Governor, and sent it to Major Day[2] for a Conveyance; but he, scarcely escaping himself, left the Letter behind him. After the Enemy had quitted the Town, and I had, by a lucky accident, escaped a Parole, hearing of the Letter, I sent for and destroyed it. For, having been severely pillaged by the Enemy; a little by others; and grievously by the Paper Money, and the advantages taken under the Laws relating to it, I was obliged to take this Step to pay taxes and subsist.

During the War, the Admiralty Court did much Business, and decided more Property than any Court in the State; the Commonwealth's Share of the Condemnations, I am persuaded, did then fully defray the Judges Salaries. Since the Peace Matters are changed. As soon as the Assise Courts were established, I resolved to resign, if alive, at the Commencement of the Act: accordingly the inclosed have been written, but kept back 'til a proper Season. A Quarter's Salary will be due to me at their Date; but if, contrary to the modern Custom, a Month's Wages extraordinary should be thought too much, at dismissing a greyheaded Servant, be pleased to alter the Date. The good natured manner of merry Charles, his discharging Lord Chancellor Shaftsbury, hath never been impeached. Ignorant to whom the Resignation should be directed; out of Session I know to the Governor; but whether to one or both of the Speakers, during the Session, is to me doubtful. Be so kind, Sr. when the time is arrived, to seal and deliver one or both of them on my behalf; and pardon all this Trouble.[3] I trust your Humanity will do this, and oblige, Sr., Yr. mo: obt. Servt.

BEN WALLER

RC (DLC). Letter and cover in a clerk's hand. Franked by Waller. Docketed by JM. Enclosure of Waller's letter of resignation to Speaker of House of Delegates, 2 Dec. 1785 (Vi).

[1] Col. Richard Cary was an Admiralty Court judge. Councillor Matthews was Sampson Matthews of Augusta County (JCSV, III, 2 and passim; "Virginia Legislative Papers," VMHB, XV [1907–8], 14; see Papers of Madison, V, 265 n. 9); Delegate Mathews was Thomas Mathews (1742–1812) of Norfolk borough (Swem and Williams, Register, p. 22; DAR Patriot Index [Washington, 1966], p. 444; Cal. of Va. State Papers, X, 119–20).

[2] Maj. Benjamin Day (1753–1821) took oath at Williamsburg 9 Jan. 1781 as assistant in the Adjutant General's Office. He later served as the Fredericksburg mayor (Gwathmey, Historical Register of Virginians, p. 214; S. J. Quinn, The History of the City of Fredericksburg, Virginia [Richmond, 1908], pp. 194–95, 220, 336).

[3] Waller's letter of resignation was received and held in abeyance on 5 Dec. John Tyler was elected judge of the Court of Admiralty to replace him 20 Dec. 1785 (JHDV, Oct. 1785, pp. 71, 100). Although the three judges of the Court of Admiralty were not commissioned as jurists on the Court of Appeals, however, they took the oath of office and served on the appeals bench (Hening, Statutes, X, 90).

From George Washington

MOUNT VERNON Novr. 30th. 1785.

MY DEAR SIR,

Receive my thanks for your obliging communications of the 11th. I hear with much pleasure that the assembly are engaged, seriously, in the consideration of the Revised Laws. A short & simple code, in my opinion, tho' I have the sentiments of some of the Gentlemen of the long Robe against me, would be productive of happy consequences, and redound to the honor of this or any Country which shall adopt such.[1]

I hope the resolutions which were published for the consideration of the House, respecting the reference to Congress for the regulation of a Commercial system will have passed.[2] The proposition in my opinion is so self evident that I confess I am at a loss to discover wherein lyes the weight of the objection to the measure. We are either a United people, or we are not. If the former, let us, in all matters of general concern act as a nation, which have national objects to promote, and a national character to support. If we are not, let us no longer act a farce by pretending to it. For whilst we are playing a dble game, or playing a game between the two we never shall be consistent or respectable—but *may* be the dupes of some powers and, most *assuredly*, the contempt of all.[3] In any case it behoves us to provide good Militia Laws, and look well to the execution of them—but, if we mean by our conduct that the States shall act independently of each other it becomes *indispensably* necessary—for therein will consist our strength and respectab[il]ity in the Union.

It is much to be wished that public faith may be held inviolate. Painful is it even in thought that attempts should be made to weaken the bands of it. It is a dangerous experiment—once slacken the reins and the power is lost—and it is questionable with me whether the advocates of the measure foresee all the consequences of it. It is an old adage that honesty is the best policy—this applies to public as well as private life—to States as well as individuals. I hope the Port and Assize Bills no longer sleep but are awakened to a happy establishment. The first with some alterations, would in my judgment be productive of great good to this Country—without it, the Trade thereof I conceive will ever labor & languish. With respect to the Second if it institutes a speedier Administration of Justice it is equally desirable.

It gives me great pleasure to hear that our assembly were in a way of adopting a mode for establishing the Cut betwn. Elizabeth River & Pasquotank which was likely to meet the approbation of the State of No. Carolina. It appears to me that no Country in the Universe is better calculated to derive benefits from inland Navigation than this is—and certain I am, that the conveniences to the Citizens individually, and the sources of wealth to the Country generally, which will be opened thereby will be found to exceed the most sanguine imagination. The Mind can scarcely take in at one view all the benefits which will result therefrom. The saving in draught Cattle, preservation of Roads &ca. &ca. will be felt most interestingly. This business only wants a beginning. Rappahanock, Shannondoah, Roanoke, and the branches of York River will soon perceive the advantages which water transportation (in ways hardly thought of at first) have over that of Land and will extend Navigation to almost every Mans door.

From the complexion of the debates in the Pensylvania[4] it should seem as if that Legislature intended their assent to the proposition from the States of Virginia & Maryland (respecting a Road to the Yohiogany[)] should be conditional of permission given to open a Communication between the Chesapeak & Delaware by way of the Rivers Elk & Christeen—which I am sure will never be obtained if the Baltimore interest can give it effectual opposition.

The Directors of the Potomack Company have sent to the Delegates of this County to be laid before the Assembly a Petition (which sets forth the Reasons) for relief in the depth of the Canals which it may be found necessary to open at the great & little Falls of the River. As public œconomy and private interest equally prompt the measure and no possible disadvantage that we can see will attend granting the prayer of it, we flatter ourselves no opposition will be given to it.

To save trouble to expedite the business, and to secure uniformity without delay, or an intercourse between the Assemblies on so trivial a matter we have taken the liberty of sending the draught of a Bill to Members of both Assemblies, which if approved will be found exactly similar. With the highest esteem and regard, I am Dr. Sir yr. Obed. & Affecte Hbl Ser

Go: Washington

RC (NjP); FC (DLC: Washington Papers). Cover missing. RC in Washington's hand, FC in clerk's hand.

[1] In FC, "a code so short plain & simple" follows "adopt."

[2] The resolution of 14 Nov. concerning commercial regulations, "published for the consideration of the House," had been printed by James Hayes for public distribution (Evans 19352).

[3] Whether the RC was underlined by Washington or by some other hand is unclear.

[4] "Pennsylvania Assembly" in FC.

Notes for Debate on Commercial Regulations by Congress

[30 November–1 December 1785]

⟨1784–5 Notes of Speech⟩

Genl. Regns. necessary ⟨thro: the States⟩
1. Counteract foreign plans
2. encourage Ships & Seamen
3. _____ manufactures
4. revenue
5. frugality — articles of luxury easily smuggled
6. embargoes in war. Delaware

———

necessary to prevent animosity.
    contention: France
    & smuggling   Mass: & Cnt.
                   N. Y. & N. J.
                   Penna.
                   Irish propositions

———

necessary to Justice — N. Carola.
    & Policy —   W. Country

———

necessary, as within reason of Constiton.
    power of War
              Peace
              Alliance
              Ambassrs.
              Treaties of Commerce especially
              which already (1) comprise
              2. or require it (3) State [illegible] treaty

———

Safe. 1. with regd. to liberties of States
    (1) control over Congs. (2) Greece
    Swiss (3) Dutch. (4) peculia[r]
    situation of U. S.

2. with regd. to Virga.
  (1) Tobo. (2.) Ships (3.) coast trade lo[c]al

_____

  (4) 5. S. States — Cont. & N. J

_____

Necessary to preserve a Confederation.
  (1) decline of Congs. (2) inadequacy to end
  (3) G. B. aims to break the Union, as to monopoly of Trad[e]
  Consequences of breaking or dissolving Union.
    1. appeal to Sword
    2. Standg. armies
    3. perpetual Debts
    4. Sport of foreign politic[s]
    5. glorious prospect of Revolution if
       blasted
power May be qualified
  1. duties on *Ships* & cargoes confined to Nations not in
     treaty.
  2. limited to 5 per Ct. on all for union
     treasy.
  3. enumerated luxuries taxed for State treasy.
       or prohibited
  4. restrain States from regulating so as to
     oppress each other but may *prohibit*
  5. 2/3 of Congs. regd. & no act
     to be in force more than 15 years
  Mr. Braxton ideas
     Speakers do. French sd.
     H. Lees — do. Rum
     Ronald — manufacturers

_____

     Fedl. Town.
     Navigation Act
     Jealousy of Eastern States

     Ms (DLC). Written by JM on verso of Gerard Banks's letter of 28 Oct. 1785.
Hunt printed a later, slightly expanded version found on the verso of JM's notes
for a speech on paper money, ca. 31 Oct. 1786 (DLC) (see Madison, *Writings*, II,
194–96). Used by JM during a hasty preparation for the House debates on 30 Nov.
and 1 Dec. of resolutions granting Congress power to regulate international trade
and collect a 5 percent ad valorem duty (*JHDV*, Oct. 1785, pp. 66–67). JM appears
to have added the heading and several other words much later, as noted here within
angle brackets.

To Ambrose Madison

Decr. 1. 1785.

DR. BROTHER

As I write by Mr. Porter[1] to my father I shall not repeat the news from the Assembly. I have nothing from Philada. later than my last which I sent by Mr. William Walker[2] with a letter for you from the back Country put into my hands by Col. John Campbell.[3] Tobo. does not command more than four dollars cash or 28/. part goods. If an oppy. offers and you can send me some fresh butter either from your own Dairy or purchased in the neighborhood, I shall be glad of it, as I lodge with Mr. Jones & breakfast at home. Some good hams from my fathers Meat House will also be acceptable as we prefer dining at home: Perhaps a waggon can be engaged to take these articles. My last suggested the propriety of your going on with the plan settled between us.[4] Nothing can be done I suppose this fall: but we should be ready for the Spring. I hope Sawney is by this time fixed at Edmundson's old place. Kentucky applied for a separation early in the Session. Her representatives seem to cool on that point. The H. of Delegates have passed a bill for repealing the 5/. on patents, and probably other measures will pass having a like tendency to satisfy them. My opinion is that a separation ought to be forwarded by the Assembly as far as decency will permit. Yrs. afly.

J. M. JR.

RC (NN). Cover addressed in JM's hand to "Mr. Ambrose Madison Orange favd. by Mr. Porter."

[1] Charles Porter, the other delegate from Orange (*Papers of Madison*, I, 193 n.).

[2] William Walker, the delegate from James City County.

[3] Col. John Campbell (d. 1808) moved to the Falls of the Ohio (Louisville) after the Revolution and became the keeper of public stores and magistrate for Jefferson County. He participated in the separatist movement and was active in early Kentucky politics. Campbell County is named for him. See Eckenrode, "List of the Revolutionary Soldiers of Virginia," *Eighth Annual Report of the . . . Virginia State Library, 1910–1911*, p. 81; *JCSV*, III, 361–62, 450, 491–92.

[4] For "the plan settled between us," see JM to Ambrose Madison, 20 Sept. 1785.

To James Madison, Sr.

Letter not found.

ca. 1 December 1785. Mentioned in JM's 1 December 1785 letter to his brother Ambrose. Contained news about the activities of the Assembly.

From George Mason

DEAR SIR

I have had such frequent Fits of the Convulsive Cholic, complicated with the Gout in the Stomach, since You was here, that I dare not undertake a Journey to Richmond; and therefore, after putting it off as long as I well cou'd, in Hopes of recovering such Health as wou'd permit me to present the Compact with the State of Maryland, in person, I have now inclosed it in a Letter to the Speaker.[1] I incurred a small Expence of £3. 16. 9. in waiting three or four Days in Alexandria for the Maryland Commissioners; which the Assembly may repay me, if they please; otherwise I am very well satisfyed without it. I also incurred an Expence equal to about £5 Specie, attending the Committee upon the Revisal of the Laws in Fredericksburg, and about double that Sum in Wmsburg., at different times, after the Sessions of Assembly ended, in collecting Evidence, & cross examining witnesses between the Commonwealth & Colo. Richd. Henderson, in the Cause which I was directed to manage by a Vote of both Houses;[2] but I never made any Particular Account [of] it. I must entreat You, if You find it necessary, to make my Apology to the Assembly for having rather exceeded our Authority. I gave You the Reasons, in a former Letter,[3] soon after the Meeting of the Commissioners; but least You shou'd not recollect them, I will repeat them.

"Neither Mr. Henderson,[4] nor myself, had been furnished with Copys of the Assembly's Resolutions; and I shou'd not have known that I was one of the Persons appointed, had I not by mere Accident, two or three Days before the Meeting, been informed of it, by a Letter from two of the Maryland Commissioners. His Excellency General Washington happened to have a copy of the Assembly's Resolutions, respecting the Application to the Government of Pensylvania; which He very obligingly gave Us; by which *any two* or more of the Commissioners were empowerd to proceed; & it was natural for Us to conclude, that these last Resolutions, in the Number of Commissioners empower'd to act, had pursued the Style of the former, respecting the Jurisdiction of the two States, as well as that this Subject had been taken up upon the same Principles, as in the Year 1778; when Commissioners were directed to settle the Jurisdiction of *Chesapeake Bay & the Rivers Potomack & Pokomoke;* in which Sentiments, Mr. Henderson, from what He was able to recollect of the Resolutions, concurred. Thus disagreeably circumstanced, only two of the Virginia Commissioners present, & without any Copy of the Resolves upon the principal Subject, we thought it better to proceed, than to disappoint the Maryland Commissioners, who appeared to have brought with them the most amicable Dispositions, & expressed the greatest Desire of forming such a fair & liberal Compact, as might prove a lasting Cement of Friendship between the two States; which we were convinced it is their mutual Interest to cultivate; We therefore, upon the particular Invitation of the General, adjourned to Mount Vernon, & finished the Business there. Some time after, Mr. Henderson wrote to Mr. Beckley (Clerk of the House of Delegates) for a copy of the Resolves, upon receiving which, we were surprized to find no mention made of *Chesapeake Bay or Pokomoke River*, that our Powers were confined to *Potomack River*, and to not less than *three* of the Commissioners. I am still inclined to think that the Omission of Chesapeake Bay and Pokomoke River was oweing to Mistake, or Inadvertence, in not attending to the Resolves of 1778; and if so, it was perhaps lucky, that We had not been furnished with a Copy of the Resolves; for the Maryland Commissioners had it in express Instruction from their Assembly, to consider the Relinquishment, on the Part of Virginia, of any Claim of laying Tolls &c. on Vessels passing thro' the Capes of Chesapeake, as a Sine qua non, and if it was refused, immediately to break off all further Conferrence with the Virginia Commissioners. However, if the Substance of the Compact is approved by the Assembly, I hope Forms will be dispensed with; especially as the Breach of them has been the Fault of some of their own Officers, not ours; and as I am conscious of having been influenced by no other Motives than the Desire of promoting the public Good."[5]

My Paper draws to an End, & leaves Me only Room to beg Your Attention to the inclosed Memorandum, to express my Desire of hearing from You on the Subject of the Compact, & such other public Matters as You may have time to communicate, as soon as Convenience will permit; and to assure You that I am, with the most sincere Esteem & Regard, Dr. Sir Your affecte Friend & obdt. Sevt.

G MASON

RC (DLC). Cover missing. Docketed by JM. The enclosure is Mason's transcript of "The Compact between Maryland and Virginia Relating to the Jurisdiction and Navigation of the Potomac and Pokomoke Rivers" of 28 Mar. 1785 (Rutland, *Papers of George Mason*, II, 816–21). The General Assembly ratified the agreement in Dec. 1785–Jan. 1786, when JM acted as a manager for the confirming legislation (*JHDV*, Oct. 1785, pp. 90, 114, 117, 128).

¹ The Speaker laid the letter before the House on 13 Dec. 1785, when it was read and ordered to be referred to the Committee of Commerce (*JHDV*, Oct. 1785, p. 90). Carter Braxton presented a bill on 26 Dec. "to approve, confirm and ratify the compact" made at the Mount Vernon convention. The bill became law after JM carried the amended version to the Senate on 30 Dec. (ibid., pp. 113, 119).

² Col. Richard Henderson (1735–1785) was a speculator in western lands who pressed for recognition from Virginia for his negotiation of the Watauga purchase of Cherokee lands in Kentucky in 1775. Jefferson and Mason were appointed a committee of two in 1778 to hear and report on Henderson's and the Indiana company's land claims (Rutland, *Papers of George Mason*, I, lx, 273 n., 425 n., 451 n.).

³ See Mason to JM, 9 Aug. 1785.

⁴ Alexander Henderson, the other Virginia commissioner who attended the Mount Vernon convention.

⁵ Mason's quotation marks encompass long passages from his 9 Aug. letter to JM.

To James Monroe

RICHMD. Decr. 9. 1785

DEAR SIR

Supposing that you will be at New York by the time this reaches it I drop a few lines for the post of today. Mr. Jones tells me he informed You that a substitute had been brought forward to the commercial propositions which you left on the carpet.¹ The subject has not since been called up. If any change has taken place, in the mind of the House, it has not been unfavorable to the idea of confiding to Congress a power over trade. I am far from thinking however that a perpetual power can be made palatable at this time. It is more probable that the other idea of a Convention of Commissrs*² from the States for deliberating on the state of commerce and the degree of power which ought to be lodged in Congress, will be attempted.³ Should it fail in the House, it is possible that a revival of the printed propositions with an extension of their term to twenty five years, will be thought on by those who contend that something of a general nature ought to be done. My own opinion is unaltered. The propositions for a State effort have passed and a bill is orderd in, but the passage of the bill will be a work of difficulty & uncertainty; many having acquiesced in the preliminary stages who will strenuously oppose the measure in its last stages. No decisive vote has been yet taken on the Assize bill. I conceive it to be in some danger, but that the chance is in its favour. The case of the British debts will be introduced in a day or two. We have got through more than half of the Revisal. The Criminal bill has been assaile[d] on all sides. Mr. Mercer

* to Annapolis.

436

has proclaim'd unceasing hostility against it. Some alterations have been made, & others probably will be made, but I think the main principle of it will finally triumph over all opposition.[4] I had hoped that this Session wd. have finished the code, but a vote agst. postponing the further consideration of it till the next, was carried by so small a Majority that I perceive it will be necessary to contend for nothing more than a few of the more important bills, leaving the residue of them for another year. My proposed amendment[5] to the report on the Memorial of Kentucky, was agreed to in a Committee of the whole without alteration, and with very few dissents. It lies on the table for the ratification of the House. The members from that district have become extremely cold on the subject of an immediate separation.[6] The half tax is postponed till March & the Sepr. tax bill Novr. next. Not a word has passed in the House as to a paper emission. I wish to hear from you on your arrival at N. Y. and to receive in particular whatever you may be at liberty to disclose with regard to the Treaty of peace, &c. with G. B. Mr. Jones wishes you to accept this as on his acct. as well as mine. He sent C. Griffins order on the bank by the last post and hopes you red. it at Fredg. Col. Grayson will no doubt have left you. I have omitted for some time writing to him on a supposition that I should be too late. I am Dr. Sir Yrs. Affecly.

J. MADISON JR.

RC (DLC). Cover missing. Docketed by JM.

[1] Monroe intended to set off from New York 1 Sept. 1785 for the Indian treaty conference on the Ohio and then to return thence through Virginia to New York. He changed his date of departure to 25 Aug., by which time his two propositions to vest in the national government the power to regulate commerce and to pass a federal navigation act had been introduced and were still under consideration in Congress (Monroe to Jefferson, 15 and 25 Aug. 1785, Boyd, *Papers of Jefferson*, VIII, 381–83, 441–42).

[2] JM inserted the asterisk and marginal note at a later time.

[3] After all other efforts to shore up the powers of Congress in international trade failed, John Tyler's resolution calling for a delegation to the Annapolis convention passed on 21 Jan. 1786.

[4] A bill "for proportioning crimes and punishments in cases heretofore capital" was part of the Revised Code. Despite JM's optimism, the Committee of the Whole was discharged 15 Dec. from further proceeding on the bill (*JHDV*, Oct. 1785, p. 94).

[5] JM wanted the separation of Kentucky to hinge on the assent of a local convention and Congress in order to prevent the western district from falling into a state of anarchy. See Act Concerning Statehood for the Kentucky District, 22 Dec. 1785.

[6] The ambivalence of certain Kentucky public men was noted by John Brown the following spring. Defense of the Ohio frontier was the most worrisome prob-

lem Kentuckians faced, Brown observed. "However, Our Western Politicians are much divided in Opinion, as to the Propriety of a Seperation & at present it is a very doubtful matter" (Brown to John Breckinridge, 20 May 1786 [DLC: Breckinridge Family Papers]).

To George Washington

RICHMOND Decr. 9. 1785

DEAR SIR

Your favour of the 30. Novr. was received a few days ago. This would have followed much earlier the one which yours acknowledges had I not wished it to contain some final information relative to the commercial propositions. The discussion of them has consumed much time, and though the absolute necessity of some such general system prevailed over all the efforts of its adversaries in the first instance, the stratagem of limiting its duration to a short term has ultimately disappointed our hopes. I think it better to trust to further experience and even distress, for an adequate remedy, than to try a temporary measure which may stand in the way of a permanent one, and must confirm that transatlantic policy which is founded on our supposed distrust of Congress and of one another.[1] Those whose opposition in this case did not spring from illiberal animosities towards the Northern States,[2] seem to have been frightened on one side at the idea of a perpetual & irrevocable grant of power, and on the other flattered with a hope, that a temporary grant might be renewed from time to time, if its utility should be confirmed by the experiment. But we have already granted perpetual & irrevocable powers of a much more extensive nature than those now proposed and for reasons not stronger than the reasons which urge the latter. And as to the hope of renewal, it is the most visionary one that perhaps ever deluded men of sense.[3] Nothing but the peculiarity of our circumstances could ever have produced those sacrifices of sovereignty on which the fœderal Government now rests. If they had been temporary, and the expiration of the term required a renewal at this crisis, pressing as the crisis is, and recent as is our experience of the value of the confederacy, sure I am that it would be impossible to revive it. What room have we then to hope that the expiration of temporary grants of commercial powers would always find a unanimous disposition in the States, to follow their own example. It ought to be remembered too that besides the caprice, jealousy, and diversity of opinions, which will be certain obstacles in our way, the policy of foreign nations may hereafter imitate that of the Macedonian Prince who effected his purposes against the Grecian confederacy by gaining over a few of the leading men in the smaller members of it. Add to the whole, that the difficulty now found in obtaining a unanimous concurrence of the States in any measure whatever, must continually increase with every increase of their number and perhaps in a greater ratio, as the Ultramontane States may either have or suppose they have a less similitude of interests to the Atlantic States than these have to one another. The propositions however have not yet received the final vote of the House, having lain on the table for sometime as a report from the Commee. of the whole. The question was suspended in order to consider a proposition which had for its object a Meeting of Politico-Commercial Commissrs from all the States for the purpose of digesting and reporting the requisite augmentation of the power of Congress over trade.[4] What the event will be cannot be foreseen. The friends to the original propositions are I am told rather increasing, but I despair of a majority in any event for a longer term than 25 years for their duration. The other scheme will have fewer enemies and may perhaps be carried. It seems naturally to grow out of the proposed appointment of Commssrs for Virga. & Maryd, concerted at Mount Vernon for keeping up harmony in the commercial regulations of the two States. Maryd has ratified the Report, but has invited into the plan Delaware and Penna. who will naturally pay the same compliment to their neighbours &c. &c. Besides these general propositions on the subject of trade, it has been proposed that some intermediate measures should be taken by ourselves, and a sort of navigation act will I am apprehensive be attempted. It is backed by the mercantile interest of most of our towns except Alexandria which alone seems to have liberality or light on the subject. It was refused even to suspend the measure on the concurrence of Maryland or N. Carolina. This folly however can not one would think, brave the ruin which it threatens to our Merchts. as well as people at large, when a final vote comes to be given.

We have got thro' a great part of the Revisal, and might by this time have been at the end of it had the time wasted in disputing whether it could be finished at this Session been spent in forwarding the work. As it is, we must content ourselves with passing a few more of the important bills, leaving the residue for our successors of the next year. As none of the bills passed are to be in force till Jan. 1787, and the residue unpassed will probably be least disputable in their nature, this expedient tho' little eligible, is not inadmissible. Our public credit has had a severe attack and a narrow escape.[5] As a compromise it has been necessary to set forward the half tax till March, and the whole tax of Sepr. next till Novr. ensuing. The latter postponement was meant to give the planters more time to deal with the Mercht[s] in the sale of their Tobo., and is made a permanent regulation. The Assize bill is now depending. It has many enemies and its fate is precarious. My hopes how[ever] prevail over my apprehensions. The fate of the Port bill is more precarious. The failure of an interview between our Commssrs and Commssrs on the part of N. Carolina has embarrassed the projected Canal between the Waters of the two States. If N. C. were entirely well disposed the passing an Act suspended on & referred to her legislature would be sufficient, and this course must, I suppose be tried, tho' previous negociation would have promised more certain success. Kentucky has made a formal application for independen[ce.] Her memorial has been considered, and the terms of separation fixed by a Come. of the whole. The substance of them is that all *private* rights & interests derived from the laws of Virginia shall be secured that the unlocated lands shall be applied to the objects to which the laws of Va. have appropriated them—that nonresidents shall be subjected to no higher taxes than residents—that the Ohio shall be a common high way for Citizens of the U. S. and the jurisdiction of Kentucky & Virga. as far as the remaing. territory of the latter will lie thereon, be concurrent only with the new States on the opposite Shore—that the proposed State shall take its due share of our State debts —and that the separation shall not take place unless these terms shall be approved by a Convention to be held to decide the question, nor untill Congs. shall assent thereto, and fix the terms of their admission into the Union. The limits of the proposed State are to be the same with the present limits of the district. The apparent coolness of the Representatives of Kentucky as to a separation since these terms have been defined indicates that they had some views which will not be favored by them. They disliked much to be hung up on the will of Congs. I am Dr. Sir with highest esteem and unfeigned regard. Yr. obedt. & hble Servt.

J. MADISON, JR.

RC (DLC: Washington Papers); FC (DLC). Cover missing. RC docketed by Washington. FC docketed.

1 The resolution instructing the Virginia delegates to support proposals that Congress regulate commerce, with a thirteen-year time limit, was passed 30 Nov. 1785. On the following day the vote was rescinded and the resolution tabled. JM voted for retracting passage of the resolution. There was a small group of men who had voted with JM the day before on an amendment (defeated) providing for the continuation of authority to Congress after the time limit who the next day voted

against JM and the recall. These apparently were the "deluded men of sense." Among them were Zachariah Johnston, Archibald Stuart, William Thornton, Thomas Mathews, Richard Lee, and John Tyler (*JHDV*, Oct. 1785, pp. 66–67; see Resolution Calling for the Regulation of Commerce by Congress, 14 Nov. 1785).

[2] For further details on the "illiberal animosities towards the Northern States," see JM to Monroe, 30 Dec. 1785.

[3] The dim "hope of renewal" caused JM to decide ultimately the whole proposition was unsound, and explains his vote with the opposition to table the entire resolution (JM to Jefferson, 22 Jan. 1786).

[4] The proposed meeting of commercial commissioners was revived and passed on the last day of the session—21 Jan. 1786. JM was a patron of the measure though apparently not its principal author.

[5] A bill to postpone collection of the 1785 revenue tax was defeated on 21 Nov. in the House of Delegates by a 50–48 vote. Of course JM voted against the bill, which would have further reduced state income (already cut in half by an act of the Oct. 1784 session [Hening, *Statutes*, XI, 540–43]).

Resolutions on Kentucky Statehood

[12 December 1785]

. . .

Fifth,—That the use and navigation of the river Ohio, so far as the territory of the proposed State, or the territory which shall remain within the limits of this Commonwealth, lies thereon, shall be free and common to the citizens of the United States, the respective jurisdictions of this Commonwealth, and of the proposed State over the river as aforesaid; shall be concurrent only with the States which may possess the opposite shore of the said river.[1]

Sixth,—That a time ought to be appointed for the free male inhabitants of the said district to elect a Convention with power to approve or disapprove of a separation on the conditions above mentioned; which Convention, in case they approve thereof, shall and may name a day on which the authority of this Commonwealth over the district aforesaid, under the exceptions aforesaid, shall cease and determine forever: *It being nevertheless, always understood and provided,* that previous thereto, the assent of the United States in Congress to such separation, their release of this Commonwealth from so much of its Federal obligations as arise from the said district being part thereof, and the fixing the terms on which the proposed State shall be admitted into the Confederacy, shall be obtained and declared.

Printed copy (*JHDV*, Oct. 1785, p. 88). No Ms of the resolutions has been found.

[1] JM served as chairman of a special committee which was formed to consider the Kentucky petition for statehood presented on 28 Oct. (Vi; *JHDV*, Oct. 1785,

pp. 10, 36). The committee report, carried before the House of Delegates by Mann Page, recommended that the movement toward statehood proceed, provided that all property rights of Virginians in the proposed state be unquestioned and that the new state assume its share of the national debt. When the amended resolutions came out of the Committee of the Whole, these additional provisions had been tacked on to the first report. JM spoke of his "proposed amendment" but did not go into particulars, so that Brant assumed that a single additional amendment was involved—specifically the sixth—whereby "the partition act should not take effect until the new state had been admitted into the Union" by Congress (Brant, *Madison*, II, 372). JM may have limited his proposal to this nationalistic resolution, but his views on free navigation of international riverways make it equally possible that he was the originator of that section. In short, his reference to a single amendment "to the report on the Memorial of Kentucky" obscures the precise nature of JM's addition to the Committee of the Whole report (JM to Monroe, 9 Dec. 1785).

To James Madison, Sr.

Letter not found.

ca. 13 December 1785. Mentioned in JM's letter to his brother, Ambrose, 15 December 1785. In the letter to his father, 24 December 1785, JM wrote that the previous letter had concerned the miscarriage of the Assize Court bill.

To Ambrose Madison

RICHMOND Decr. 15 — 1785

DR. BROR.

I wrote to my father a day or two ago[1] by Col: Burnley[2] to which I refer. The principal step since taken by the H. of Delegates has been the rejection of a bill on which the Assize scheme depended. The majority consisted of 63 agst, 49.[3] Yesterday the vote of the Speaker decided in the affirmative a resolution to repeal the Act which permits Masters to free their slaves. I hope the bill which must follow on the subject may be less successful. Many who concurred in the Resolution will probably be content finally with some amendment of the law in favor of Creditors.[4] Should it prove otherwise this retrograde step with regard to an emancipation will not only dishonor us extremely but hasten the event which is dreaded[5] by stimulating the efforts of the friends to it. The residue of the Revisal from No. 65 will be put off, except the Religious Bill and a few others. Leave was given yesterday for a bill in favor of British Creditors, but not without proofs that it will be opposed in every stage of its progress thro' the House. The price of

Tobo. is not much if at all changed. I have nothing to add to my last on that subject which signified my wishes for your going on with your purpose. The low price is the effect of the dearth of money more than of the price in Europe. I inclose a letter from Mr. Smith which you will communicate to brother F. & Capt: Walker, and let them know that I will apply according to its request any remittances to my hands. I have recd. from Capt. W. £4. 10 which will lessen so much his balance. Adieu

J. M. JR.

Inform Col: F. Taylor that I have got from Dunscomb a written memorandum of the reasons which hinder him from taking cognizance of Col. Ts. acct. and that I found it would be in vain to present his Memorial to the House.

RC (NN). Addressed by JM. Docketed by Ambrose Madison.

1 Letter not found.

2 Zachariah Burnley (*Papers of Madison*, I, 148 n. 2, 315, 316 n. 1).

3 JM had introduced the bill amending the Assize Court Act that he had brought forward at the Oct. 1784 session as a judicial reform (Bill for the Establishment of Courts of Assize, 2 Dec. 1784). A manuscript of this amending measure has not been found. JM introduced the bill on 26 Nov.; it was amended by the Committee of the Whole on 12 Dec. and defeated on 13 Dec. (*JHDV*, Oct. 1785, pp. 89–90). Carter Henry Harrison and Meriwether Smith were among the opponents of JM's bill, which entrenched local politicians had consistently opposed. "You have also heard of the fate of the Assize Bill," Archibald Stuart observed, "by which the work of an Age I may almost say was destroyed by a set of D—— Asses" (Stuart to John Breckinridge, 26 Jan. 1786 [DLC: Breckinridge Family Papers]).

4 Brant interprets this to mean that the contest over manumission was economic, not social. Theoretically, creditors of owners who freed their slaves would suffer financial loss, since manumission was tantamount to liquidation of a capital asset (Brant, *Madison*, II, 361). However, many of the leading social conservatives of the Harrison coalition voted for repeal of the act. It seems unlikely that concern for creditors in a planter-dominated, pro-debtor legislature was the main motivation behind the attempted repeal. For whatever reasons, the bill to amend the act allowing manumission was rejected without recorded vote on 17 Jan. 1786 (*JHDV*, Oct. 1785, p. 145).

5 "The event which is dreaded," i.e., a general emancipation of slaves. Neither JM nor Jefferson thought this the proper time to forward the cause of emancipation. Jefferson, in commenting on the failure of the Virginia legislature to pass emancipation, said that there were men enough of virtue and talent in the General Assembly to sponsor such an act—"But they saw that the moment for doing it with success was not yet arrived." Further, an unsuccessful attempt "would only rivet still closer the chains of bondage, and retard the moment of delivery to this oppressed description of men" (Jefferson to Jean Nicolas Démeunier, 26 June 1786, Boyd, *Papers of Jefferson*, X, 62–64). Closer to the political realities in Virginia than Jefferson, JM perceived the complexity of the whole slavery problem. JM's fears regarding emancipation are elucidated in his note to William Thornton in 1788 on Negro colonization. He viewed the removal of freed Negroes from America as a

necessity upon which the fate of the emancipation cause depended. For the happiness and well-being of both society and Negroes, the latter must be wholly incorporated into the former. And this JM viewed as impossible because of white prejudice based on color. Meanwhile the insidious presence of freedmen inhibited masters from freeing more of their slaves and made the continuance of existing manumission laws precarious (Gaillard Hunt, "William Thornton and Negro Colonization," American Antiquarian Society, *Proceedings*, new ser., XXX [1920], 51–52; Winthrop D. Jordan, *White over Black: American Attitudes toward the Negro, 1550–1812* [Chapel Hill, 1968], pp. 552–53).

Act Giving Executive the Power to Deal with Aliens

[15 December 1785][1]

BE it enacted by the General Assembly, That it shall and may be lawful for the governor, with the advice of the council of state, to apprehend and secure, or cause to be apprehended and secured, or compelled to depart this commonwealth, all suspicious persons, being the subjects of any foreign power or state,[2] who shall have made a declaration of war, or actually commenced hostilities against the said states, or from whom the United States in congress, shall apprehend hostile designs against the said states; provided information thereof shall have been previously received by the executive from congress: And that in all such cases, the governor, with the advice of the council of state, shall, and he is hereby empowered, to send for the person and papers of any foreigner within this state, in order to obtain such information as he may judge necessary. All sheriffs and jailers shall receive such suspicious persons whom, by warrant from the governor they shall be commanded to receive, and them in their prisons or custody detain, or transport out of the commonwealth, as by such warrant they may be commanded. And all others the good citizens of this commonwealth, shall be aiding and assisting in apprehending, securing or transporting any such suspicious person, when commanded by warrant or proclamation of the governor, or required by the sheriff or jailer to whose custody such suspicious persons may have been committed. Every person acting under the authority aforesaid, shall be indemnified from all suits to be commenced or prosecuted for any action or thing done by virtue thereof, and may plead the general issue, and give this act in evidence: Saving always to the merchants of any foreign state, betwixt whom the United States of America war shall have arisen, and to their families, agents, and servants, found in this commonwealth at the beginning of the war, the privileges allowed by law.

Printed copy, "An act giving powers to the governor and council in certain cases" (Hening, *Statutes*, XII, 47–48). No Ms copy has been found.

1 Alexander White reported, and the House passed, a resolve that an act ought to pass giving the governor and council power in certain cases on 29 Nov. White presented the bill on 1 Dec. The following day it was committed to a committee with JM appointed chairman. JM reported amendments to the bill 15 Dec., and it was passed 16 Dec. Prentis was ordered to carry it to the Senate (*JHDV*, Oct. 1785, p. 64 and passim). The first draft of the bill should be attributed to White, but the bill in its final form was the work of JM. Brant attributes it to him. He says that JM drafted it without enthusiasm as chairman of Courts of Justice (Brant, *Madison*, II, 360).

2 The bill was occasioned by the arrival of several Algerines in Virginia, who, having no apparent object, were suspected of an unfriendly one. The governor and council called the Algerines before them, but found themselves powerless to act (JM to Jefferson, 22 Jan. 1786; *JCSV*, III, 487–88, 495–96). The Assembly consequently was asked for an exclusion law. As redrafted by JM the governor's power to act was made contingent upon receiving notice from Congress that the U. S. was at war or threatened with war. Brant claimed that JM thus twisted Henry's xenophobia "into a recognition of the primary jurisdiction of Congress over aliens, and gave them implied immunity from molestation in the absence of congressional action" (*Madison*, II, 360).

To James Monroe

RICHMOND Decr. 17—1785

DEAR SIR

Since my last by the preceding post the fate of the Assize laws has been determined by a negative in the H. of Delegates on the Bill on which its execution depended. The majority consisted of 63 agst. 49. A reform of the County Courts is the substitute proposed by the adversaries of the Assize, and if it can be put into any rational shape, will be received by the other side as auxiliary to the Assize plan which may be resumed at another Session.[1] It is surmised that the Senate will not part with this plan in any event, and as the law passed at the last Session, unless repealed or suspended, stops the proceedings of the Genl. Court after the 1st. day of Jany. a bill must be sent to the Senate which will give them an opportunity of proposing some amendment which may revive the question at the present Session.[2] Our progress in the Revisal has been stopped by the waste of time produced by the inveterate and prolix opposition of its adversaries & the approach of Christmas. The Bill proportioning crimes & punishments was the one at which we stuck after wading thro' the most difficult parts of it.[3] A few subsequent bills however were excepted from the postponement. Among these was the Bill for establishing Religious freedom, which has got thro' the H. of

Delegates without alteration, though not without warm opposition. Mr. Mercer & Mr. Corbin were the principal combatants against it. Mr. Jones is well. With sincerity I am Yr. affe. friend

                                                                J. MADISON JR.

RC (DLC). Cover addressed by JM. Docketed by JM and by several unknown hands. Misdated 17 Dec. 1784 in calendar of "Letters from J. M. [to] Mr. Monroe."

[1] The Assize bill providing for a circuit court system passed at the Oct. 1784 session but was not to become operative until 1 Jan. 1786. "Adversaries of the Assize" feared a lessening of their control over local political matters and kept the advocates of legal reform at bay through substitute bills and other devices until a suspension act was passed in 1786, and a total repeal in 1787 (Hening, *Statutes*, XI, 421 n.).

[2] This letter is printed, from the words "Our progress . . ." to the end of the text, under the date 17 Dec. 1784, in Madison, *Letters* (Cong. ed.), I, 114.

[3] The discipline JM tried to maintain in the House of Delegates finally broke when his opponents took advantage of uneasiness over bill 64 on Jefferson's original catalogue of 126 revised statutes. JM undertook the burden of guiding the Revised Code through the General Assembly, beginning on 31 Oct. Among the important bills passed before the tacticians stopped further action were the act regulating elections for the General Assembly and a law covering the troublesome problem of wills and intestate estates (Hening, *Statutes*, XII, 120–29, 140–54). JM's power crested about one week after the admiring delegate from Botetourt County, Archibald Stuart, reported JM was in complete control of the House. "Can you suppose it possible that Madison should shine with more than usual splendor [in] this Assembly. It is sir not only possible but a fact. He has astonished mankind & has by means perfectly constitutional become almost a Dictator upon all subjects that the House have not so far prejudged as to shut their Ears from Reason & armed their minds from Conviction. His influence alone has hitherto overcome the impatience of the house & carried them half thro the Revisd. Code altho motions are daily made to leave the ballance of the Business to another assembly" (Stuart to John Breckinridge, 7 Dec. 1785 [DLC: Breckinridge Family Papers]). On 15 Dec. the House voted to end its labors on the rest of the code and JM's influence rapidly declined. A somewhat bitter Stuart later observed (after he had been found ineligible for his seat) that the House of Delegates "was upon the whole the most Stupid navish & designing Assembly that ever sat in this or I believe in any other Country —& as . . . [a] proof of this I need urge no other Argument with you but that Madison after the three first weeks lost all weight in the House, & the general Observation was that, those who had a favorite scheme ought to get Madison to oppose it, by which means it would certainly be carried" (Stuart to Breckinridge, 26 Jan. 1786 [ibid.]).

From James Monroe

                                                    NEW YORK Decr. 19. 1785.

DEAR SIR

I arriv'd last night & found only six States present. Mr. Hancock we hear is on the road & will be with us in a few days. He accepts the chair.

The conduct of the legislature, in complying with the requisition of Congress,[1] in the opinion of all here, does the highest honor to the State, and at the same time that it evinces a regard for publick justice & a mind superior to little resentments, gives an additional assurance of the strength & permanence of the fœderal government. We earnestly wish to have the result of the deliberations of the house upon the commercl. propositions. I find the most enlighten'd members here fully impress'd with the expedience of puting an end to the dismemberment of the old States—doubtful of the propriety of admiting a single new one into the confideracy—& well inclin'd to a revision of the compact between the U. S. & Virga. respecting the division of the country beyond the Ohio.[2] Mr. Jones sd. he wod. visit Fredricksburg before Christmas. I will write him by the next post. I hop[e] you are both well—& am very sincerely your friend & servant

JAS. MONROE

RC (DLC). Cover missing. Docketed.

[1] Virginia was one of the few southern states attempting to comply with the requisition system (Nevins, *American States during and after the Revolution*, pp. 477–78). JM served on a special committee of the House of Delegates which reported on 8 Dec. 1785 that the state had paid $160,982 in specie on its 1784 requisition and was entitled to an additional credit "of 53,660 dollars paper" (*JHDV*, Oct. 1785, p. 77). By a resolution of 8 Dec. the state treasurer was directed to pay the remainder of the 1784 requisition in paper "facility notes" totaling $32,186.

[2] Virginia had ceded title to its western lands (the Kentucky district and certain military warrant tracts above the Ohio excepted) early in 1781, but certain delegates had questioned whether the cession had strings attached (*Papers of Madison*, VI, 471–72).

Bill Providing for Installment Payments on British Debts

[19 December 1785]

Whereas by the 4th art: of the Definitive Treaty of peace between the U. S. of America & G. B. it was stipulated among other things by the contracting parties, "that Creditors on either side shall meet with no lawful impediment to the recovery of the full value in sterling money of all bona fide debts heretofore contracted". Be it therefore enacted by the Genl. Assembly that so much of all Acts of Assembly and ordinances of Convention made since the 19th. day of April 1775, as disable British subjects from prosecuting for the recovery of debts due from the Citizens of this Commonwlth, shall be and the same are hereby re-pealed:[1] and that from and after the passing of this act, the said British subjects may sue and implead the Citizens of this Commonwlth in like manner as if such disabling acts or ordinances had never passed. Pro-vided always, that in consideration of the almost total suspension of Commerce and the depredations of the Enemy during the late war, which render an immediate discharge of the whole of the said debts im-practicable, the same so far as they become due before the day of the date of the provisional articles of peace, may be discharged by   equal payments; the first of which shall be demandable on the day of   in the year   and the remaining payments successively on the same day in the   years next following: But no interest on any debt due to any British subject from any Citizen of this Comonwlth shall be allowed for any intermediate time between the 19th. day of April 1775 and the 3d. day of March 1783, which intermediate time shall be considered in law as one day only in all matters depending between the said British Creditors and Citizens of this Commonwealth.

And whereas in many instances the Agents or Factors for British Mer-chants who remained here during the late war may have settled the Accounts of such Merchants with their debtors since the 19th day of April 1775, and taken bonds or [ot]her specialties therefor in specie in their own *or such Merchants* names, for the principal sum [d]ue, or for the Principal and interest together, whereby it may appear that such bonds or specialties were due to Citizens of this Commonwealth. Be it enacted that all Bonds, or other Specialties given to Citizens or others for any debt or debts due to British subjects since the said 19th day of April 1775 and prior to the   day of   shall be considered as British Debts [and] shall be recoverable as such only, and shall carry no interest during the period between the 19th day of April 1775 and the 3d. day of March 1783.

And be it further enacted that any of the said British debts which have been adjusted since the said 3d. day of March 1783, and bonds and other specialties given therefor, shall be discharged by way of the in-stalments aforesaid, notwithstanding their subsequent date to the said 3d. day of March 1783 and if any part of the specialty so given shall be for interest allowed between the 19th. day of April 1775, and the 3d. day of March 1783, the same so far as it shall be for such interest shall be and is hereby declared null and void.

And be it further enacted that if the Creditor is put to his Action at law for any balance due to him, execution on the Jdgt. when obtained shall issue for such proportion only of the same as shall have accrued at the time of rendering the Jdgt. according to the periods of payment heretofore established; and execution for the residue may issue annually until the whole shall be discharged, without any further proceedings on the said Jdgt.: provided always that the person agst. whom such Jdgt. shall be obtained shall in open Court with one or more sufficient sureties enter into recognizance for payment of such Jdgt. in the proportions and at the times prescribed by this Act: and in default thereof execution may issue for the full amount of such Jdgt. against the person or Estate of such debtor.

And be it further enacted that no Citizen of this Commonwlth who has been a resident within the same since the   day of   and who was a partner with any British Merchant or Merchts. shall be compelled to pay the debts due by such Copartnership otherwise than by instalments as is by this act directed in case of debts due to British subjects from Citizens of this Comonwlth. except for such part or share of such copartnership as may be held by such Citizen, for which he shall remain liable as other Citizens are, and shall also be entitled to recoveries in all respects equally with his fellow Citizens so far as the share held by him shall extend in debts due to such copartnerships.

Provided always and be it further enacted that in case the U S. in Congress shall at any time judge that the execution of this Act, ought for national purposes to be suspended, and shall signify the same it shall and may be lawful for the Governor with advice of the Council of State, by proclamation to suspend the operation of this Act until the next ensuing General Assembly.[2]

Ms (Vi). In JM's hand and docketed by him, "A Bill to enable British subjects to recover their debts from Citizens of this Commonwealth." Endorsed by clerks, with an annotation, facing a bracket symbol, "Madison, Stuart, A. White, Corbin, Thruston, Zane."

[1] JM and Joseph Jones were leaders of the faction in Richmond that believed a state could not act contrary to the pledged honor of the U. S. No doubt JM acted in concert with Jones at the May 1784 session of the General Assembly, when resolutions acknowledging the debts to British merchants and a proposal for installment payments were rejected (Resolutions on Private Debts Owed to British Merchants, 7–23 June 1784). When Jones moved to the Council of State the burden of leadership toward some kind of compromise fell on JM. Whatever his feelings regarding the justice of the anti-debt viewpoint in Virginia, he saw that with Henry still out of the legislature the chance of revising the bill (which had been sidetracked a year earlier) were much improved. "The shadow of assent" from those delegates usually under Henry's thumb emboldened JM and his following; so they brought out this bill on 19 Dec., and after vigorous debate it was left on the table (*JHDV*, Oct. 1785, p. 115). Then the old prejudices and vested interests came to the surface again,

and as JM reported to Jefferson, friends of the measure "thought it best to let it sleep" (22 Jan. 1786). The matter was still unsettled in 1787 and became an issue in the ratification contest in Virginia (Harrell, *Loyalism in Virginia*, pp. 156–57; Jackson Turner Main, *The Antifederalists: Critics of the Constitution, 1781–1788* [Chapel Hill, 1961], p. 229).

2 The strongest argument of the faction against debt repayment was that the infraction of the peace treaty was not one-sided. They continually insisted that no debts should be repaid until the British withdrew from the Northwest Territory posts they still occupied. This feeling was so intense that an act passed the General Assembly in 1787 suspending compliance with the 1783 treaty "until the governor with the advice of council shall by his proclamation, notify to this state, that Great Britain hath delivered up to the United States the posts therein now occupied by British troops" (Hening, *Statutes*, XII, 528).

Act Concerning Statehood for the Kentucky District

[22 December 1785]1

I. WHEREAS it is represented to be the desire of the good people inhabiting the district known by the name of the Kentucky district, that the same should be separated from this commonwealth whereof it is a part, and be formed into an independent member of the American confederacy, and it is judged by the general assembly that such a partition of the commonwealth is rendered expedient by the remoteness of the more fertile, which must be the more populous part of the said district, and by the interjacent natural impediments to a convenient and regular communication therewith.

II. *Be it enacted by the General Assembly,* That in the month of August next, on the respective court days of the counties within the said district; and at the respective places of holding courts therein, representatives to continue in appointment for one year, and to compose a convention with the powers, and for the purposes hereinafter mentioned, shall be elected by the free male inhabitants of each county in like manner as delegates to the general assembly have been elected within the said district, in the proportions following: In the county of Jefferson shall be elected five representatives, in the county of Nelson five representatives, in the county of Fayette five representatives, in the county of Bourbon five representatives, in the county of Lincoln five representatives, in the county of Madison five representatives, and in the county of Mercer five representatives. That full opportunity may be given to the good people, of exercising their right of suffrage on an occasion so interesting to them, each of the officers holding such elections, shall continue the same from day to day, passing over Sunday, for five days, including the first day, shall cause this act to be read on each day, immediately preceding the opening of the election, at the door of the court-house, or other convenient place, and shall fix up two copies at least of this act in the most public situations at the place of election, twenty days before the commencement thereof. Each of the said officers shall deliver to each person duly elected a representative a certificate of his election, and shall moreover transmit a general return to the clerk of the supreme court of the district, to be by him laid before the convention: For every neglect of any of the duties hereby enjoined on such officer, he shall forfeit one hundred pounds, to be recovered by action of debt, by any person suing for the same. The said convention shall be held at Danville, on the fourth Monday of September, and as soon as two thirds of the representatives shall be convened, they shall and may proceed, after choosing a president and other proper officers, and settling the proper rules of proceeding, to consider, and by a majority of voices, to determine, whether it be expedient for, and be the will of the good people of the said district, that the same be erected into an independent state, on the terms and conditions following:

First. That the boundary between the proposed state and Virginia, shall remain the same as at present separates the district from the residue of the commonwealth.

Second. That the proposed state shall take upon itself a just proportion of the public debt of this commonwealth.

Third. That all private rights and interests in lands within the said district, derived from the laws of Virginia, prior to such separation, shall remain valid and secure under the laws of the proposed state, and shall be determined by the laws now existing in this state.

Fourth. That the lands within the proposed state of non-resident proprietors, shall not in any case be taxed higher than the lands of residents at any time prior to the admission of the proposed state to a vote by its delegates in congress, where such non-residents reside out of the United States; nor at any time either before or after such admission, where such non-residents reside within this commonwealth, within which this stipulation shall be reciprocal; or where such non-residents reside within any other of the United States, which shall declare the same to be reciprocal within its limits; nor shall a neglect of cultivation or improvement of any land within either the proposed state, or this commonwealth, belonging to non-residents, citizens of the other, subject such non-residents to forfeiture or other penalty, within the term of six years after the admission of the said state into the fœderal union.

Fifth. That no grant of land, nor land warrant to be issued by the proposed state, shall interfere with any warrant heretofore issued from the land-office of Virginia, which shall be located on land within the said district now liable thereto, on or before the first day of September, one thousand seven hundred and eighty-eight.

Sixth. That the unlocated lands within the said district, which stand appropriated by the laws of this commonwealth to individuals or descriptions of individuals, for military or other services, shall be exempt from the disposition of the proposed state, and shall remain subject to be disposed of by the commonwealth of Virginia, according to such appropriation, until the first day of September, one thousand seven hundred and eighty-eight, and no longer; and thereafter the residue of all lands remaining within the limits of the said district, shall be subject to the disposition of the proposed state.

Seventh. That the use and navigation of the river Ohio, so far as the territory of the proposed state, or the territory which shall remain within the limits of this commonwealth lies thereon, shall be free and common to citizens of the United States; and the respective jurisdictions of this commonwealth, and of the proposed state, on the river as aforesaid, shall be concurrent only with the states which may possess the opposite shores of the said river.

Eighth. That in case any complaint or dispute shall at any time arise between the commonwealth of Virginia and the said district, after it shall be an independent state, concerning the meaning or execution of the foregoing articles, the same shall be determined by six commissioners, of whom two shall be chosen by each of the parties, and the remainder by the commissioners so first appointed.

III. *And be it further enacted,* That if the said convention shall approve of an erection of the said district into an independent state, on the foregoing terms and conditions, they shall and may proceed to fix a day posterior to the first day of September, one thousand seven hundred and eighty-seven, on which the authority of this commonwealth, and of its laws, under the exceptions aforesaid, shall cease and determine for ever, over the proposed state, and the said articles become a solemn compact, mutually binding on the parties, and unalterable by either without the consent of the other.

Provided however, That prior to the first day of June, one thousand seven hundred and eighty-seven, the United States in congress shall assent to the erection of the said district into an independant state, shall release this commonwealth from all its fœderal obligations arising from

452

the said district, as being part thereof; and shall agree that the proposed state shall immediately after the day to be fixed as aforesaid, posterior to the first day of September, one thousand seven hundred and eighty-seven, or at some convenient time future thereto, be admitted into the fœderal union.[2] And to the end that no period of anarchy may happen to the good people of the proposed state, it is to be understood that the said convention shall have authority to take the necessary provisional measures for the election and meeting of a convention at some time prior to the day fixed for the determination of the authority of this commonwealth, and of its laws over the said district, and posterior to the first day of June, one thousand seven hundred and eighty-seven, aforesaid, with full power and authority to frame and establish a fundamental constitution of government for the proposed state,[3] and to declare what laws shall be in force therein, until the same shall be abrogated or altered by the legislative authority acting under the constitution, so to be framed and established.

IV. This act shall be transmitted by the executive to the delegates representing this commonwealth in congress, who are hereby instructed to use their endeavors to obtain from congress a speedy act, to the effect above specified.

Printed copy (Hening, *Statutes*, XII, 37–40). The Ms has not been found.

[1] Petitioned by a Kentucky convention for independence, the General Assembly responded with the act that provided the needed impetus for statehood, although the formal severance was delayed until 1792. After a Committee of the Whole studied the situation, a special committee was chosen on 14 Nov. 1785, with JM as chairman (*JHDV*, Oct. 1785, pp. 10, 36). On 12 Dec. the Committee for Courts of Justice (JM, chairman) was ordered to bring in a bill, which Mann Page introduced. After some amending, the bill passed the House on 6 Jan. 1786, when James Garrard of Fayette County carried it to the Senate. Francis Corbin carried the recommitted bill back to the Senate after further emendation. In such circumstances, the principal authorship of the bill cannot be ascertained with any certainty, but JM's relationship with the Kentucky separatists and his chairmanship of the several committees justifies a presumption that he contributed substantially to preparation of the bill. Undoubtedly, the act is the product of several minds, for it is hardly likely that JM would have had the temerity to write a bill by himself wherein one of the new counties would bear his name.

[2] Delays in settling jurisdiction over public lands and the transition from the Confederation under Congress to the newly erected federal government strained the patience of Kentuckians. "The assertion may be safely ventured," wrote a local historian a half-century later, "that no sober political critic of the present day can believe, that any community in these States, would now be so trifled with and tantalized, as the people of this district were, for eight years, in obtaining a separate municipal existence" (Mann Butler, *A History of the Commonwealth of Kentucky* [Louisville, 1834], p. 169).

[3] JM had been solicited for his ideas on "a fundamental constitution" for Kentucky. His advice went to Caleb Wallace, 23 Aug. 1785.

To James Madison, Sr.

RICHMOND Decr. 24. 1785.

My last informed you of the miscarriage of the Assize scheme. It has been followed with an attempt to reform the County Courts, which will probably end in the appointment of four months in which the Courts shall be confined to Docket business & compelled to dispatch it. A Bill is depending for the payment of British debts, nearly on the model of that which fell thro' last year. It is extremely grating and will be rejected unless the prospect of an accomodation with G. B. on the subject of the Posts & the Negroes, or the apprehensions of being saddled with worse terms by delay, should overcome the disinclination. The port bill has not been yet taken up. It will be severely attacked. We have a variety of orders of the day which will consume time, and other bills are to be brought in. Of course the end of the Session is remote, unless impatience should produce the same effect as a conclusion of the business. The petition of the little fork has been just rejected, by a general vote. I have not yet disposed of your Tobo. The price has not latterly exceeded I believe four dollars, and I am told to day that 20/. is talked of. I have never yet had it in my power to make the enquiries at the land office, or to get out your patents. Capt Barbour[1] tells me he has been there and could not get the information relative to Turpin[2] without a knowledge of some dates which you have not mentioned to him or to me. If you have any unliquidated claims agst. the U. S. that can be settled by the Commissrs. before the 1st. day of Jany., or loan office certificates issued from the Cont. Office here, the interest up to Decr. 1782 will be paid at the Treasy. in specie. Let this circumstance be known if you please, tho' I suppose it will be too late. It may be of the less consequence, as such warrants for interest will in future be receivable in Taxes. The Quitrents for the Northern Neck are abolished by a bill which is gone up to the Senate. The Bill for establishing Religious freedom passed the H. of Delegates as it stands in the Revised Code. The Senate have disagreed to the preamble and substituted the last article of the Declaration of Rights. Which house is to recede, is uncertain. Both are much attached to their respective ideas. Capt: Barbour tells me Payne has engaged his brother Js. B. to pay the money due to you.[3] I wish you could let Majr. Moore[4] have about £18 of it, the amount of his interest on the certificate obtained from Dunscomb by Mr. Hubbard Taylor[5] & left with me. Let me know whether such an arrangement will be practicable. Be kind eno' also to let Capt Walker

& my brother F. know that I am called on for their balances to the Steward of Hampden Sidney by a man here who has an order on me for them. Present my regards to the family, and believe me to be your Affece. Son

J. MADISON JR.

RC (DLC). Addressed and docketed in JM's hand. Without salutation; endorsed in an unknown hand, "Richd. Lee." The cover is filled over with JM's ledger accounts.

[1] Philip Pendleton Barbour (*Papers of Madison*, I, 148 n. 2).

[2] Probably Dr. Philip Turpin, who owned considerable real property in Richmond (*Papers of Madison*, VII, 232–33).

[3] John C. Payne, JM's future brother-in-law and "Js. B"—James Barbour. The Barbours were neighbors of the Madison family (*Papers of Madison*, I, 32 n. 106, 148 n. 2).

[4] Maj. William Moore (*Papers of Madison*, I, 148 n. 2).

[5] Hubbard Taylor (1760–1845) of Caroline and son of Col. James Taylor of Midway. He moved to Fayette, later Clarke County, Kentucky, in 1790 ("Genealogy," *VMHB*, IX [1901 2], 196; XXIX [1921], 372).

To James Monroe

RICHMOND Decr. 24. 1785

Dear Sir

The proceedings of the Assembly since my last dated this day week have related 1. to the Bill for establishing Religious freedom in the Revisal. 2. a Bill concerning British debts 3. a Bill concerning the Proprietary interest in the Northern Neck. 4. for reforming the County Courts. The first employed the H. of Delegates several days; The preamble being the principal subject of contention. It at length passed without alteration. The Senate I am told have exchanged after equal altercation. The preamble of the revisal for the last clause in the Declaration of Rights; an exchange wch. was proposed in the H. of D. and negatived by a Considerable Majority. I do not learn that they have made or will make any other alteration. The Bill for the payment of British debts is nearly a transcript of that which went thro' the two Houses last year, except that it leaves the periods of instalment blank and gives the Creditor an opportunity of taking immediate execution for the whole debt if the debtor refuses to give security for complying with the instalments. The Bill was near being put off to the next Session on the second reading. A majority were for it, but having got inadvertently into a hobble, from the manner in which the question was put, the result was that Monday next[1] should be appointed for its consideration. The arrival

& sentiments of Col: Grayson will be favorable to some provision on the subject. A clause is annexed to the Bill authorizing the Executive to suspend its operation in case Congs. shall signify the policy of so doing. The general cry is that the Treaty ought not to be executed here until the posts are surrendered, and an attempt will be made to suspend the operation of the Bill on that event or at least on the event of a positive declaration from Congs. that it ought to be put in force. The last mode will probably be fixed on, notwithstanding its departure from the regular course of proceedings, and the embarrassment in which it may place Congress. The bill for reforming the County Courts proposes to select five Justices, who are to sit quarterly, be paid scantily, and to possess the Civil Jurisdiction of the County Courts, and the Criminal jurisdiction of the Genl. Court under certain restrictions. It is meant as a substitute for the Assize system, to all the objections against which it is liable, without possessing its advantages. It is uncertain whether it will pass at all, or what form it will finally take. I am inclined to think it will be thrown out. The Bill relating to the N. Neck passed the H. of D. yesterday. It removes the records into the Land Office, here, assimilates locations of surplus land to the general plan, and abolishes the Quitrent. It was suggested that the latter point was of a judiciary nature, that it involved questions of fact, of law, and of the Treaty of peace, and that the Representatives of the late proprietor ought at least to be previously heard according to the request of their agent.[2] Very little attention was paid to these considerations, and the bill passed *almost* unanimously. With sincere affection I am Your friend & Servt.

J. MADISON JR.

RC (DLC). Addressed by JM. Docketed.

[1] See JM to Monroe, 30 Dec. 1785, for the subsequent fate of the bill.

[2] The great Northern Neck proprietor Thomas, 6th Lord Fairfax died in 1781, leaving a 5/6 interest in the proprietary to the 7th Lord, Robert Fairfax and the other 1/6 to Denny Martin (Fairfax), his eldest nephew. By a 1779 act all Virginia property belonging to British subjects became vested in the Commonwealth of Virginia. A 1782 act presumed that the lands of the neutral Lord Fairfax, upon his death, had "descended upon alien enemies"; therefore all past due, as well as future, quitrents were to be sequestered and paid into Virginia's public treasury (Hening, *Statutes*, XI, 128–29). His executors, Thomas Bryan Martin and Gabriel Jones, considered this unjust, and in May 1783 successfully sought a change in the sequestering act (ibid., XI, 289). Otherwise, the sequestration continued. In 1784 Denny Martin Fairfax came over to Virginia from England to claim his remaining rights. His arrival raised questions concerning the unappropriated lands and uncollected quitrents. A petition of Bryan Fairfax, attorney-in-fact for Robert, Lord Fairfax, and Denny Fairfax, was presented to the House on 9 Dec. 1785, denying that by the principle of antenati and the law of nations the Fairfax heirs could be deprived of

their income. The petition was referred to a Committee of the Whole the same day, but later withdrawn and referred to a special committee on Northern Neck records 16 Dec. It was to this petition that JM alluded (Stuart E. Brown, Jr., *Virginia Baron: The Story of Thomas 6th Lord Fairfax* [Berryville, Va., 1965], pp. 187, 190–91, 197–99; *JHDV*, Oct. 1785, pp. 82, 95, 136).

Act Ratifying the Chesapeake Compact with Maryland

[ca. 24–26 December 1785][1]

I. WHEREAS, at a meeting of the commissioners appointed by the general assembly of the state of Maryland and Virginia, to wit: Daniel of St. Thomas Jenifer, Thomas Stone, and Samuel Chase, esquires, on the part of the state of Maryland, and George Mason and Alexander Henderson, esquires, on the part of the state of Virginia, at Mount-Vernon, in Virginia, on the 28th day of March, in the year one thousand seven hundred and eighty-five, the following compact was mutually agreed to by the said commissioners:

First. The commonwealth of Virginia disclaims all right to impose any toll, duty, or charge, prohibition or restraint, on any vessel whatever sailing through the capes of Chesapeake bay to the state of Maryland, or from the said state through the said capes outward bound; and agrees that the waters of Chesapeake bay, and the river Pocomoke, within the limits of Virginia, be forever considered as a common highway, free for the use and navigation of any vessel belonging to the said state of Maryland, or any of its citizens, or carrying on any commerce to or from the said state, or with any of its citizens; and that every such vessel inward or outward bound, may freely enter any of the rivers within the commonwealth of Virginia as a harbour, or for safety against an enemy, without the payment of port duties, or any other charge; and also, that the before mentioned parts of Chesapeake bay, and Pocomoke river, be free for the navigation of vessels from one part of the state of Maryland to another.

Second. The state of Maryland agrees that any vessel belonging to the commonwealth of Virginia, or any of its citizens, or carrying on commerce to or from the said commonwealth, or with any of its citizens, may freely enter any of the rivers of the said state of Maryland as a harbour, or for safety against an enemy, without the payment of any port duty, or other charge.

Third. Vessels of war, the property of either state, shall not be subject to the payment of any port duty or other charge.

Fourth. Vessels not exceeding forty feet keel, nor fifty tons burthen, the property of any citizen of Virginia or Maryland, or of citizens of both states, trading from one state to the other only, and having on board only the produce of the said states, may enter and trade in any part of either state, with a permit from the naval-officer of the district from which such vessel departs with her cargo, and shall be subject to no port charges.

Fifth. All merchant vessels (except such as are described in the fourth article) navigating the river Potowmack, shall enter and clear at some naval office on the said river, in one or both states, according to the laws of the state in which the entry shall be made. And where any vessel shall make an entry in both states, such vessel shall be subject to tonnage in each state only in proportion to the commodities carried to, or taken from, such state.

Sixth. The river Potowmack shall be considered as a common highway, for the purpose of navigation and commerce to the citizens of Virginia, and Maryland, and of the United States, and to all other persons in amity with the said states, trading to or from Virginia or Maryland.

Seventh. The citizens of each state respectively shall have full property in the shores of Potowmack river adjoining their lands, with all emoluments and advantages thereunto belonging, and the privilege of making and carrying out wharves and other improvements, so as not to obstruct or injure the navigation of the river; but the right of fishing in the river shall be common to, and equally enjoyed by the citizens of both states. *Provided,* That such common right be not exercised by the citizens of the one state, to the hindrance or disturbance of the fisheries on the shores of the other state; and that the citizens of neither state shall have a right to fish with nets or seines on the shores of the other.

Eighth. All laws and regulations which may be necessary for the preservation of fish, or for the performance of quarantine, in the river Potowmack, or for preserving and keeping open the channel and navigation thereof, or of the river Pocomoke, within the limits of Virginia, by preventing the throwing out ballast, or giving any other obstruction thereto, shall be made with the mutual consent and approbation of both states.

Ninth. Light houses, beacons, buoys, or other necessary signals, shall be erected, fixed, and maintained upon Chesapeake bay, between the sea and the mouths of the rivers Potowmack and Pocomoke, and upon the river Potowmack, at the expence of both states. If upon Potowmack river, at the joint and equal charge of both states; and if upon the before mentioned part of Chesapeake bay, Virginia shall defray five parts, and Maryland three parts of such expence; and if this proportion shall in future times be found unequal, the same shall be corrected. And for ascertaining the proper places, mode, and plans for erecting and fixing light houses, buoys, beacons and other signals, as aforesaid, both states shall upon the application of either to the other, appoint an equal number of commissioners, not less than three nor more than five from each state, to meet at such times and places as the said commissioners or a major part of them, shall judge fit, to fix upon the proper places, mode, and plans for erecting and fixing such light houses, beacons, or other signals, and report the same, with an estimate of the expence, to the legislatures of both states, for their approbation.

Tenth. All piracies, crimes or offences committed on that part of Chesapeake bay which lies within the limits of Virginia, or that part of the said bay where the line of division from the south point of Potowmack river (now called Smith's Point) to Watkins's Point, near the mouth of Pocomoke river, may be doubtful; and on that part of Pocomoke river, within the limits of Virginia, or where the line of division between the two states upon the said river, is doubtful, by any persons not citizens of the commonwealth of Virginia, against the citizens of Maryland, shall be tried in the court of the state of Maryland which hath legal cognizance of such offence. And all piracies, crimes, and offences committed on the before mentioned parts of Chesapeake bay and Pocomoke river, by any persons not citizens of Maryland, against any citizen of Virginia, shall be tried in the court of the commonwealth of Virginia which hath legal cognizance of such offence. All piracies, crimes, and offences committed on the said parts of Chesapeake bay and Pocomoke river, by persons not citizens of either state, against persons not citizens of either state, shall be tried in the court of the commonwealth of Virginia having legal cognizance of such offences: And all piracies, crimes, and offences committed on the said parts of Chesapeake bay and Pocomoke river, by any citizen of the commonwealth of Virginia, or of the state of Maryland, either against the other, shall be tried in the court of that state of which the offender is a citizen. The jurisdiction of each state over the river Potowmack, shall be exercised in the same manner as is prescribed for the before mentioned parts of Chesapeake bay and Pocomoke river, in every respect, except in the case of piracies, crimes, and offences committed by persons not citizens of either state, upon persons not citizens of either state, in which case the offenders shall be tried by the court of the state to which they shall first be brought. And if the inhabitants of either state shall commit any violence, injury, or tresspass, to or upon the property or lands of the other, adjacent to the said bay or rivers, or to any person upon such lands, upon proof of due notice to the offender to appear and answer, any court of record, or civil magistrate of the state where the offence shall have been committed, having jurisdiction thereof, may enter the appearance of such person, and proceed to trial and judgment, in the same manner, as if legal process had been served on such offender; and such judgment shall be valid and effectual against the person and property of such offender, both in the state where the offence shall have been committed, and also in the state where the said offender may reside, and execution may be issued by the court, or magistrate, giving such judgment, in the same manner as upon judgments given in other cases; or upon a transcript of such judgment, properly authenticated, being produced to any court; or magistrate, of the state where such offender may reside, having jurisdiction within the state, or county where the offender may reside, in cases of a similar nature, such court, or magistrate, shall order execution to issue upon such authenticated judgment in the same manner, and to the same extent, as if the judgment had been given by the court, or magistrate, to which such transcript shall be exhibited.

Eleventh. Any vessel entering into any port on the river Potowmack, may be libelled, or attached for debt, by process from the state in which such vessel entered. And if the commercial regulations of either state shall be violated by any person carrying on commerce in Potowmack or Pocomoke rivers, the vessel owned or commanded by the person so offending, and the property on board, may be seized, by process from the state whose laws are offended, in order for trial. And if any person shall fly from justice, in a civil or criminal case, or shall attempt to defraud creditors by removing his property, such person, or any property so removed, may be taken on any part of Chesapeake bay, or the rivers aforesaid, by process of the state from which such person shall fly, or property be removed; and process from the state of Virginia may be served on any part of the said rivers, upon any person, or property of any person not a citizen of Maryland, indebted to any citizen of Virginia, or charged with injury having been by him committed; and process from the state of Maryland may be served on any part of the said rivers, upon any person, or property of any person, not a citizen of Virginia, indebted to a citizen of Maryland, or charged with injury by him committed. And in all cases of trial in pursuance of the jurisdiction settled by this compact, citizens of either state shall attend as witnesses in the other, upon a summons from any court, or magistrate, having jurisdiction, being served by a proper officer of the county where such citizen shall reside.

Twelfth. The citizens of either state having lands in the other, shall have full liberty to transport to their own state, the produce of such lands, or to remove their effects, free from any duty, tax, or charge whatsoever, for the liberty to remove such produce or effects.

Thirteenth. These articles shall be laid before the legislatures of Virginia and Maryland, and their approbation being obtained, shall be confirmed and ratified by a law of each state, never to be repealed, or altered, by either, without the consent of the other.

II. And whereas this general assembly are of opinion that the said compact is made on just and mutual principles for the true interest of both governments, and the same having been confirmed by the general assembly of the state of Maryland: *Be it therefore enacted*, That the said compact is hereby approved, confirmed, and ratified by the general assembly of Virginia, and that every article, clause, matter and thing therein contained, shall be obligatory on this state and the citizens thereof, and shall be forever faithfully and inviolably observed and kept by this government and all its citizens, according to the true intent and meaning of the said compact; and the faith and honour of this state is hereby solemnly pledged and engaged to the general assembly of the state of Maryland, and the government and citizens thereof, that this law shall never be repealed, or altered, by the legislature of this commonwealth, without the consent of the state of Maryland.

Printed copy (Hening, *Statutes*, XII, 50–55). A Ms of the bill has not been found. The full title is, "An act to approve, confirm, and ratify the compact made by certain commissioners appointed by the general assembly of the state of Maryland and commissioners appointed by this commonwealth."

[1] The date when a bill bearing this designation was first read in the House of Delegates is uncertain, but on 27 Dec. JM was appointed chairman of a special committee appointed to revise legislation then before the House (*JHDV*, Oct. 1785, p. 114). The compact grew out of the proceedings of the Mount Vernon convention of Mar. 1785, which JM was supposed to attend but did not because of a communications breakdown. He learned of the conference from a Virginia commissioner's report (George Mason to JM, 9 Aug. 1785). Probably JM offered the initial legislation a few days before the second reading on 27 Dec. and on 29 Dec. he presented a revised version, which was amended and passed the same day. After final passage of the bill, JM then carried the measure to the Senate (*JHDV*, Oct. 1785, pp. 118–19). The Maryland General Assembly also ratified the proceedings and the cooperative spirit thus evidenced was an encouraging factor in passage of the Resolution Authorizing a Commission to Examine Trade Regulations, 21 Jan. 1786.

From James Madison, Sr.

Letter not found.

24 December 1785. Mentioned by JM in his answer of 27 December. His father apparently raised a question about the petition for a final settlement of the Harry Beverley estate.

From James Monroe

New York Decr. 26 — 1785.

Dear Sir

Your favor of the 9th. reach'd me a few days since. Mine by the last post advis'd you of my arrival here; still I am with out a colleague and the representation of the States, the same. I am perfectly satisfied that the more fully the subject is investigated, and the better the interests of the States severally are understood, the more obvious will appear the necessity of commiting to the U S. permanently the power of regulating their trade. Whether it will be expedient to accept it for a limited time only it is difficult to determine. If it is expedient for a day, while the States bear the relation they now do to each other & to other powers, or rather while they adjoin each other & are bounded by the ocean, it will still be so. Whether then will it be expedient to avail ourselves of the present disposition so far only as to try an experiment, the success of wh., as such, must depend upon a variety of circumstances, or to delay any remedy untill under the pressure of the present difficulties it may be made complete? As an experiment in what light will it be conceiv'd & how treated by foreign powers. Will they not all wish to defeat it and of course avoid those stipulations in our favor wh. may hereafter furnish arguments for its renewal. We may with propriety also take into the consideration the diversity of interest wh. will arise in the admission of western States into the confideracy. In a govt. also so fluctuating there will never be energy, or calculation on it either at home or abroad, everything will be in a state of incertainty. The states severally will be at a loss how to act under it (in thier respective delegations); they will fear to take those decisive measures with respect to other powers, wh. might be necessary, least their vigorous operation, may prevent its renewal — but whether these or any other considerations, may be of sufficient weight to induce us to seek only a permanent change, is what I have not absolutely determin'd on. I beg of you to give me your sentiments thereon as well as of the course you think

I may with propriety take here, provided the State shod. confide it only for a limited time.

Some dispatches have lately been recd. from *Adams*. They are as we expected they wd. be. *Pit*[t] admits that the *removal of the negroes* is a *violation of the* [treaty.] Th[at] when the *number* is *ascertaind* they must *pay for them*. That they will take up the subject of *the posts* with that of the *debts*. Yet he says that the *whol*[e] *nation* are *host*[ile] *to us* — that they will give us no *commercial treaty*, that they have sent *out Sir J Johnson*[1] for *Canada* with *entrentching to*[o]*ls* &ca. This is the amt. of what we have, nor can I well determine how you shod. act under it. If it be practicable to carry into effect, a complete co[m]plyance on our part, let their conduct be as it may, I shod. not hesit[ate] to adopt it. But if this is not the case, I cannot well conceive the [ad]vantage of a partial complyance, or the paymt. by instalment, [as] hath been here-tofore propos'd. If they mean to quarrell, their grou[nd] for it will be equally justifiable, in that instance, as in an absolu[te] failure. And if the end we seek, is to be obtain'd by further neg[o]tiation, or by bargain of one for the other, by this measure we lose the consideration we shod. have to give for it. In all the measures of this country toward us we perceive not only the utmost vigilance & attention to their own interest in opposition to ours, but a disposition to seek opportunities to injure us. They restrict us most severely in commerce, give land, & provision to our fishermen to settle within their bounds, and we have too much reason to suspect that they encourage the Algerines to attack us. In this situation to whom may we look for assistance even agnst these pirates. The monopoly of the trade of the medeteranean is in the hands of France, Britain & the Netherlands; will they or either of them, give up this advantage, for our convenience for nothing. Is it not strange in this situation that we shod. be disputing whether we shall act together or cement & strengthen the Union.

There hath been a newspaper controversy here between Mr. Jay & Mr. Littlepage of our State, upon some subject of a private nature between them. As I have not read their publications I am unacquainted with the merit of either party.[2] It is however to be lamented that Mr. Jay enter'd into a controversy of this kind, since his character is too well establish'd to be call'd in question upon any unimportant or trivial occasion. Be so kind as [to] give no intimation to anyone except, Mr. Jones, of the contents of what I have wrote you in cypher. I am Dear Sir your friend & servant

JAS. MONROE.

P S. Is the revenue law in any respect chang'd — are the facilities of other States admissible in payment of taxes — or rather is it accomodated to all the purposes of the requisition? Our ministers are taking measures with the regencies of Algiers &ca. It is sd. that Mr. Consul Barclay, a Mr. Lambe & Majr. Franks are sent to these different powers for this purpose, but the latter I think is not confirm'd by an official communication.[3]

RC (DLC). Cover missing. Docketed. Italicized words, unless otherwise noted, were encoded by Monroe using the code JM sent him on 14 Apr. 1785.

[1] Sir John Johnson (1742–1830), son of Sir William Johnson, was commissioned a lieutenant-colonel in Canada and during the Revolution led mixed forces of Indians and British in raids on the Mohawk Valley. By a commission of 14 Mar. 1782 he became "Superintendent General and Inspector General of the Six Nations Indians and those in the Province of Quebec." He exercised an important influence in Indian affairs and was active in relief measures on behalf of Loyalists. On 18 Nov. 1785 he made a speech to the Six Nations encouraging them to assert their territorial rights against American encroachments (*DAB*, X, 103–4; Mohr, *Federal Indian Relations, 1774–1788*, pp. 114–15).

[2] Lewis Littlepage came to Jay in Madrid in 1780, placed by his uncle Benjamin Lewis under Jay's guidance while the young man remained in Europe. He soon fell into dissolute company of which Jay disapproved and yet Jay continued to give him financial support. Littlepage demonstrated his disdain by challenging Jay to a duel in Paris in 1783. When back in New York, Jay attempted to collect the sizable amount owed him by his protégé. Thereupon, Littlepage launched a series of defamatory letters against Jay in the local newspapers to which Jay replied in kind (Frank Monaghan, *John Jay: Defender of Liberty against Kings & Peoples* ... [New York and Indianapolis, 1935], pp. 159–61).

[3] Barclay and John Lamb were commissioned in early Oct. 1785 and given instructions by Adams and Jefferson. Barclay, accompanied by Maj. Franks as his secretary, went to Morocco in 1786 and successfully negotiated a treaty, especially concerning neutral rights and the exchange of prisoners. Lamb's assignment to Algiers turned out a more difficult one and he a less able negotiator. The dey Mohammed demanded exorbitant ransoms for American prisoners, and Lamb, instead of returning to the U. S. to confer with Congress, retreated to Spain, pleaded ill-health, and finally resigned his commission in mid-1786 (Boyd, *Papers of Jefferson*, VIII, 473–74, 526, 610–24; X, 149; Gardner W. Allen, *Our Navy and the Barbary Corsairs* [Hamden, Conn., 1965], pp. 28–30). For Barclay's and Franks's careers see *Papers of Madison*, IV, 291 n. 20, 450 n. 14.

To James Madison, Sr.

RICHMOND Decr. 27. 1785

HOND SIR

Mr. Js. Davis has just handed your favor of the 24. inst. It is too late to revise the proceedings relative to the Trustees of Beverley. The Act authorises the Commssrs who are to settle your accounts to make a reasonable allowance for your trouble.[1] I cannot get a copy of the Act without paying the £10. Capt. P. Barbour will inform you of Dean's answer to his application. He carried a letter from me giving you an acct. of the latest proceedings of the Assembly.[2] Nothing of consequence has been done since. It is uncertain when we shall rise. If an opportunity should offer, I shall be glad of the fresh butter at all events. I am with best regards to the family Yr: affe. Son.

J. Madison Jr.

RC (DLC). Cover addressed by JM, partly written over with ledger accounts in unknown hand dated "Jany. 2d. 1786."

[1] The elder Madison and George Taylor petitioned the Assembly for the appointment of examiners of their accounts dating beyond 1765 (Vi: Petition of Taylor & Madison, 15 Nov. 1785). The House referred the petition to JM's Committee for Courts of Justice, which reported a bill on 1 Dec. that was finally passed on 3 Dec., when Joseph Prentis carried it to the Senate (*JIIDV*, Oct. 1785, pp. 38, 53–54 and passim; Hening, *Statutes*, XII, 219). The business began at the Oct. 1765 session of the House of Burgesses (ibid., VIII, 166–68).

[2] See JM to JM, Sr., 24 Dec. 1785.

To James Monroe

Richmond Decr. 30. 1785

Dear Sir,

The past week has been rendered important by nothing but some discussions on the subject of British debts. The bill brought in varied from that which miscarried last year 1. by adding provision in favor of the Creditor for *securing* payment at the dates of the instalments 2 by annexing a clause empowering the Executive to suspend the operation of the Act in case Congress should notify their wish to that effect. Great difficulty was found in drawing the House into Commte on the subject. It was at length effected on Wednesday. The changes made in the Bill by the Committee are 1. striking out the clause saving the Creditors from the act of limitation which makes the whole a scene of Mockery—2. striking out the provision for securities—3 converting the clause author[iz]ing Congs. to direct a Suspension of the Act, into a clause suspending it, untill Congs. should notify to the Executive that G. B. had complied with the Treaty on her part, *or that they were satisfied with the steps taken by her for evacuating the posts, paying for Negroes*

465

and for a full compliance with the Treaty. The sentence underlined was prepared as an amendment to the amendment and admitted by a very small majority only. 4. exonerating the public from responsibility for the payments into the Treasury by British debtors, beyond the real value of the liquidated paper. Since these proceedings of the Committee of the whole, the subject has slept on the table, no one having called for the report. Being convinced myself that nothing can be now done that will not extremely dishonor us, and embarrass Congs. my wish is that the report may not be called for at all.[1] In the course of the debates no pains were spared, to disparage the Treaty by insinuations agst. Congs., the Eastern States, and the negociators of the Treaty, particularly J. Adams. These insinuations & artifices explain perhaps one of the motives from which the augmen[ta]tion of the fœderal powers & respectability have been opposed. The Reform of the County Courts has dwindled into directions for going thro' the docket quarterly, under the same penalties as now oblige them to do their business monthly. The experiment has demonstrated the impracticability of rendering these Courts fit instruments of Justice; and if it had preceded the Assize Question would I think have ensured its success.[2] Some wish to renew this question in a varied form, or at least under a varied title; but the Session is too near its period for such an attempt. When it will end I know not. The business depending wd. employ the House till March. A system of navigation and Commercial regulations, for this State alone, is before us and comprizes matter for a Month's debate. The Compact with Maryd. has been ratified. It was proposed to submit it to Congs. for their sanction, as being within the word *Treaty* used in the Confederation.[3] This was oppd. It was then attempted to transmit it to our Delegates to be by them simply laid before Congs. Even this was negatived by a large Majority. I can add no more without risking the opportunity by the post, except that I remain yr. affec. friend

Js Madison Jr.

RC (DLC). Addressed to Monroe "in Congress." Docketed by JM.

[1] The report was not called for and the bill died with the end of the session. JM wrote to Jefferson that the several amendments had rendered the bill so inadequate that its patrons thought it best to let it sleep (JM to Jefferson, 22 Jan. 1786).

[2] There was an attempt to permit the Courts of Assize Act to go into effect on 1 Jan. 1786, as the law provided, but opponents of this reform measure (which JM had introduced at the Oct. 1784 session) were more anxious for an outright repeal. Archibald Stuart thought the bill "for reforming the county courts" was a ploy to weaken support for the Courts of Assize law. The county court bill was ordered

prepared after a supplemental Assize Court bill was defeated on 13 Dec. by a 49–63 vote, with JM voting "aye." The county court bill was introduced on 19 Dec. and passed the third reading on 28 Dec. "I believe upon a supposition that the County Court system might be amended, by which means many in the House hoped for the sum of 15/ *pr Diem* which was proposed to be levied off the littigants & paid to the setting magistrates. When this Eutopian scheme fell thro a Majority Could not be procured to repeal the old Law" (Stuart to John Breckinridge, 26 Jan. 1786 [DLC: Breckinridge Family Papers]). The Senate appears to have balked at this heavy expense and the House received the amended county court bill back on 4 Jan., passing it without any *per diem* provisions (Hening, *Statutes*, XII, 32–36). On the preceding day JM had introduced a bill to keep the Assize Court Act alive. In its new mode, the bill "to suspend the operation of the act . . . for the establishment of Courts of Assize" passed a third reading on 5 Jan. 1786 (*JHDV*, Oct. 1785, p. 129). After JM left the General Assembly the Assize Court bill was again suspended in 1787, and finally repealed on 5 Jan. 1788 (Hening, *Statutes*, XII, 497). Supporters of the assize, or circuit, courts, were convinced their opponents were more interested in holding on to power in their local courts (where many legislators also served as presiding county justices) than in judicial reform. Stuart noted that in Augusta County "there are now about seven hundred Causes On the Docket" (Stuart to John Breckinridge, 26 Jan. 1786 [DLC: Breckinridge Family Papers]).

[3] The House journal is silent on this sparring contest between the localists and delegates of JM's bent, who might have used the Mount Vernon compact as a test case under the sixth article of Confederation: "No two or more states shall enter into any treaty, confederation or alliance whatever between them, without the consent of the United States in Congress assembled, specifying accurately the purposes for which the same is to be entered into, and how long it shall continue." Presumably, JM led the nationalists in this losing battle.

Notes on Charters of Incorporation

EDITORIAL NOTE

Neither the time, place, nor exact topic of these notes can be fixed with certainty. JM apparently jotted down the main ideas of two acquaintances, possibly Edmund Randolph and John Marshall, and in all likelihood at the time when a repeal of the act incorporating the Protestant Episcopal church was under consideration by the House of Delegates. If JM made these notes after hearing an informal discussion of the legal points involved, he may have wanted to keep a record of the main points brought forth by two respected lawyers concerning the alleged favoritism of the General Assembly toward the Protestant Episcopal church. John Marshall was not a delegate to the General Assembly at either the 1785 or 1786 sessions, but it seems reasonable to assume that JM valued his ideas on the subject, which arose in January 1786 when an effort was made in the legislature to amend the incorporation act passed at the October 1784 session. JM might have taken the notes for his own reference for the matter was sure to come up again, and did at the next session when the earlier act was repealed (*JHDV*, Oct. 1785, pp. 141, 143; Hening, *Statutes*, XII, 266–67).

[January 1786?]

Mr R

Original policy of corporations

———

necessity in large Cities from 1. [licen]tiousness[1]
   of Crowded people
   2. Commercial Cities where [many?] of different nations

———

Repeal of Charter never conl 1: collective Charter
rights same as individual patent right
   2. example of Maryld. & Pen[nsylvania]
   3. difference between giving & receiving
   4. Recognition of Chart: by Constn.
   5. comparison of case to Right of Suff[rage]
   6. Tyranical acts of G. B. & Ch [. . .]
   7. suspension of Charter of N. Y. & Mas[s.] by Parliamt.
   8. disfranchisement of [. . .] & [. . .] Gr[. . .] not precedents because
      all rig[hts] perhaps then in dissolution
   9. power of parlt. on this head referd. by Blackstone its omnipotence
  10. Bank of England Chart: not perpetu[al] lest Parlt. be precluded
  11. Cases of River Companies
  12. Case of W & M. — as respectg their lan[ds]
  13. Assembly may abridg Salary of Judge, but not take away of
  14. Bill dissolves corporation. Consequences: 1. Property reverts 2. dbt
      cannot be paid. 3. Renewal not of itself adequate

———

Mr Marshall

Has Assembly the power?
   1. Nature of Charter that gives property either in visible things or in
      Righ[ts] or privileges valuable.
   2. action may be brot vs. & by Corporation
   3. attempt vs individl of Corporation wd be same & wd. alarm
   4. vested Right of any sort cannot be touched.
   5. Laws of incorpn. distinct from general laws & not like them repeal-
      able: being compacts between two parties.
   6. examples. 1. case of freehold granted to individual 2. Citizenship
      granted to Mr. Fa[y]ette[2] 3 Charter to Rumsey
   7. Irrevocable [. . .] for party [interested in?] corporation

8. 1. Art. of bill [of] Rights. There are certain rights not alienable. note. people of Norfolk the to[ries?] by [...] vs. Corporation [...]

9. Marq. Becca. laws are to be general, & not to affect—to In[di]vidual only such power not being given in[formation?] of power—

10. If sense of people, Legislature may interpose—sense not yet expressed by majority.

Ms (DLC). In JM's hand, on the verso of his Resolution for Opening Roads to Market Towns, ca. 30 Dec. 1784.

[1] This and other words or portions of words within brackets are conjectural readings of what appears to be a hasty jotting down of the speaker's main ideas. Illegible words are noted by an ellipsis.
[2] This allusion is to the act conferring citizenship on Lafayette, which was offered and passed at the Oct. 1785 session (on 1 Nov. 1785). Thus the notes would have been taken down some time after that legislation was enacted, but presumably before the session ended on 21 Jan. 1786.

Resolution for Printing and Distributing Session Laws

[18 January 1786]

Resolved, That so soon as the copies of the laws allotted to the several counties, other than the counties in Kentucky, shall be printed, the same be distributed under the order of the Executive, by expresses, who shall be paid out of the contingent fund.[1]

Printed Copy (*JHDV*, Oct. 1785, pp. 146–47).

[1] JM proposed this resolution and was ordered to carry the approved measure to the Senate. The resolution reflects JM's anxiety to have a general distribution of the statutes which included the thirty-six bills passed as part of the revised code presented 31 Oct. 1785. He had complained to Jefferson about the deficient number of copies and delay in distribution of the revisors' report (JM to Jefferson, 20 Aug. 1785).

To Ambrose Madison

RICHMOND Jany. 21. 1786

DR. BROTHER

The Assembly will rise this evening. Have my horses sent if you please as early as you can. If any fresh butter has been procured or should be on hand & Anthony can bring it, I shall be glad of it, not immediately on my own acct. but as it will enable me to return Civilities which can not be so well discharged any other way. Yr. letter by Col. Burnley never came to hand, nor have I rec'd. any acct. from you since early in the Session.[1] The price of Tobo. continues at abt. 24/. I have a late letter from Philada. which informs me it remains there much as it has done for a considerable time past. There can not possibly be risk in taking it here at the current price, or at its rise within a reasonable period. FitzPatrick is to carry to my fathers 2 Trunks of books lately recd. from Havre de Grace and a box with a few others and some of my Cloathes.[2] I purpose to make up his load with salt. If there sd. be any appearance of wet on the box or Trunks it will be proper to open them. Yrs.

J. MADISON JR.

RC (NN: Ford Collection). Addressed by JM. A note on the cover in Ambrose Madison's hand reads: "There is a Pott of Butter weighg abt. 12 lb. for Anthony if he can carry it. Majr Lee desires you would give Fitzpatrick a note to him for payment for bringing up the things from Richmond."

[1] Ambrose Madison's letter to JM has not been found.

[2] Thomas Fitzpatrick had helped the Madison family exchange letters and transport packages on previous occasions (*Papers of Madison*, VI, 4 n. 1). The trunks contained books sent to JM by Jefferson (JM to Jefferson, 22 Jan. 1786).

Resolution Authorizing a Commission to Examine Trade Regulations

EDITORIAL NOTE

This resolution which paved the way for the Annapolis convention of 1786 was not written by JM even though circumstantial evidence and speculating historians have given him the credit. The summary of evidence on authorship of the resolution in Boyd, *Papers of Jefferson*, IX, 206–8, presents a logical case. Despite JM's claim, made in 1804, that he introduced the resolution, Boyd's argument concludes that John Tyler wrote it after an effort to transfer some of the state regulatory powers over commerce to Congress had stagnated in the House of Delegates (JM to Noah Webster, 12 Oct. 1804 [DLC]). JM himself attributed the resolution of 21 January, introduced and passed on the last day of the session, to Tyler, when the fact was not then twenty-four hours old (JM to Jefferson, 22 Jan. 1786). Indeed, JM was not convinced the plan to convene the several states for a commercial conference was a good one, and he suspected it was being patronized by half-hearted localists. He thought it would "probably miscarry" but considered it "better than nothing." Still, the resolution had the effect of informing the country that lassitude had not overcome its political machinery. News of the convention call was printed in the *Pa. Packet* on 7 Feb. 1786 and spread by other newspapers. The reaction in most state legislatures proved more favorable than JM had supposed possible. Thus by the next summer, he became more optimistic when eight states had appointed deputies as a result of Governor Henry's circular invitation. Clearly by this time JM realized that the stakes were higher than mere achievement of interstate harmony. "Gentlemen both within & without Congs. wish to make this Meeting subservient to a plenipotentiary Convention for amending the Confederation," he wrote Jefferson (1? Aug. 1786 [DLC]).

IN THE HOUSE OF DELEGATES. January 21st 1786

RESOLVED that Edmund Randolph, James Madison jr., Walter Jones, St George Tucker, Meriwether Smith ⟨David Ross, William Ronald & George Mason⟩ Esqrs be appointed Commissioners, who, or any three ⟨five⟩ of whom shall meet such Commissioners as may be appointed by the other States in the Union at a time and place to be agreed on, to take into Consideration the Trade of the United States to examine the relative situations and trade of the said States, to consider how far an uniform System in their Commercial regulations may be necessary to their common Interest and their permanent Harmony, and to report to the several States such an act relative to this great Object as, when unanimously ratified by them will enable the United States in Congress assembled effectually to provide for the same. That the said Commissioners shall immediately transmit to the several states Copies of the preceeding resolution with a circular Letter requesting their Concurrence therein, and proposing a time and place for the meeting aforesaid.[1]

Ms (Vi); Ms (DNA: PCC). The Vi Ms is in a clerk's hand and is endorsed by the House and Senate clerks. Docketed, "Reso. for appointing Commissioners to meet Commissioners to take under their Consideration the Trade of the United States." The docket indicates copies were made for Walter Jones and George Mason "& sent by H Lee." The DNA Ms is the official notice signed by Governor Henry and forwarded to the secretary of the Continental Congress. Portions in angle brackets were additions or changes made in the Senate before final passage.

[1] "A time and place for the meeting" was set by the convening states after the Virginia commissioners took the initiative and picked Annapolis as the site and set "the first monday in Sepr. for the time of holding the Convention" (JM to Jefferson, 18 Mar. 1786). JM did not attend this caucus, which was held in Richmond by a quorum of the commissioners after JM had departed for Orange County following the legislative session adjournment.

To John Francis Mercer

Letter not found.

ca. 21 January 1786. Acknowledged by Mercer in his letter to JM, 28 March 1786. It apparently contained a commentary on the October 1785 session of the House of Delegates.

To Thomas Jefferson

RICHMOND Jan. 22d. 1786

DEAR SIR

My last dated Novr 15 from this place answered yours of May 11th. on the subject of your printed notes. I have since had opportunities of consulting other friends on the plan you propose, who concur in the result of the consultations which I transmitted you. Mr. Wythe's idea seems to be generally approved, that the copies destined for the University should be dealt out by the discretion of the Professors, rather than indiscriminately and at once put into the hands of the students, which, other objections apart, would at once exhaust the Stock.[1] A vessel from Havre de Grace brought me a few days ago two Trunks of Books, but without letter or catalogue attending them. I have forwarded them to Orange without exam[in]ing much into the contents, lest I should miss a conveyance which is very precarious at this season, and be deprived of the amusement they promise me for the residue of the winter.

Our Assembly last night closed a Session of 97 days, during the whole of which except the first seven, I have shared in the confinement. It opened with a very warm struggle for the chair between Mr. Harrison & Mr. Tyler which ended in the victory of the former by a majority of 6 votes. This victory was shortly afterwards nearly frustrated by an impeachment of his election in the County of Surry. Having failed in his native County of Charles City, he abdicated his residence there, removed into the County of Surry where he had an Estate, took every step which the interval would admit, to constitute himself an inhabitant, and was in consequence elected a representative. A charge of non residence was nevertheless brought against him, decided agst. him in the Com[m]ittee of privileges by the casting voice of the Chairman, and reversed in the House by a very small majority. The election of Docr. Lee was attacked on two grounds. 1st. of non-residence, 2dly. of holding a lucrative office under Congs. On the 1st. he was acquitted,

472

on the 2d. expelled, by a large majority. The revised Code was brought forward pretty early in the Session. It was first referred to Come. of Cts. of Justice to report such of the bills as were not of a temporary nature, and on their report committed to Comtee of the whole. Some difficulties were raised as to the proper mode of proceeding, and some opposition made to the work itself. These however being surmounted, and three days in each week appropriated to the task, we went on slowly but successfully, till we arrived at the bill concerning crimes and punishments. Here the adversaries of the code exerted their whole force, which being abetted by the impatience of its friends in an advanced stage of the Session, so far prevailed that the prosecution of the work was postponed till the next Session.[2] The operation of the bills passed is suspended untill the beginning of 1787, so that if the code sd. be resumed by the next Assembly and finished early in the Session, the whole system may commence at once. I found it more popular in the Assembly than I had formed any idea of, and though it was considered by paragraphs and carried through all the customary forms, it might have been finished at one Session with great ease, if the time spent on motions to put it off and other dilatory artifices, had been employed on its merits. The [adversaries][3] *were* the *speaker, Thruston* and *Mercer* who *came late in the session, into a vacan*[cy] *left by* the *death* [of] *Col: Brent* [of] *Stafford,* and *contributed principally to the mischieved.* The titles in the inclosed List will point out to you such of the bills as were adopted from the Revisal. The alterations which they underwent are too numerous to be specified, but have not materially viciated the work. The bills passed over were either temporary ones, such as being not essential as parts of the System, may be adopted at any time and were likely to impede it at this, or such as have been rendered unnecessary by Acts passed since the epoch at which the revisal was prepared. After the completion of the work at this Session was despaired of it was proposed and decided that a few of the bills following the bill concerning crimes and punishments should be taken up as of peculiar importance.[4] The only one of these which was pursued into an Act is the Bill concerning Religious freedom. The steps taken throughout the Country to defeat the Genl. Assessment, had produced all the effect that could have been wished. The table was loaded with petitions & remonstrances from all parts against the interposition of the Legislature in matters of Religion. A General convention of the Presbyterian church prayed expressly that the bill in the Revisal might be passed into a law, as the best safeguard short of a constitutional one, for their religious rights. The bill was carried thro' the H of Delegates, without alteration. The Senate objected to the preamble, and sent down a proposed substitution of the 16th. art: of the Declaration of Rights. The H. of D. disagreed. The Senate insisted and asked a Conference. Their objections were frivolous indeed.[5] In order to remove them as they were understood by the Managers of the H. of D. The preamble was sent up again from the H. of D. with one or two verbal alterations. As an amendment to these the Senate sent down a few others; which as they did not affect the substance though they somewhat defaced the composition, it was thought better to agree to than to run further risks, especially as it was getting late in the Session and the House growing thin. The enacting clauses past without a single alteration, and I flatter myself have in this Country extinguished for ever the ambitious hope of making laws for the human mind.

Acts not included in the Revisal

For the naturalization of the Marquis de la fayette.	This was brought forward by Col: Henry Lee Jr. and passed without opposition. It recites his merits towards this Country and constitutes him a Citizen of it.
To amend the Act vesting in Genl. Washington certain shares in the River Companies	The donation presented to Genl. W. embarrass[ed] him much. On one side he disliked the appearance of slighting the bounty of his Country and of an ostentatious

disinterestedness. On the other an acceptance of reward in any shape was irreconcileable with the law he had imposed on himself. His answer to the Assembly declined in the most affectionate terms the emolument allotted to himself, but intimated his willingness to accept it so far as to dedicate it to some public and patriotic use. This Act recites the original act & his answer, and appropriates the future revenue from the shares to such public objects as he shall appoint. *He has been pleased to ask my* ideas with regard to the *most proper objects. I suggest in* general only, *a part[i]tion of the fund* between some *institution* which would *please the* [phil]*osophical world* and some other which may be of [a] *popular cast.* If your knowledge of the *several institutions, in France* or *else where*, should suggest *models, or hints, I could wish for your ideas* on the *case which is* no less *concerns the good of the common* wealth than *the character of its most illustrious citizen.*

474

An Act empowering the Governor & Council to grant conditional pardons in certain case[s].

Some of the malefactors consigned by the Executive to labour, brought the legality of such pardons before the late Court of Appeals who adjudged them to be void. This Act gives the Executive a power in such cases for one year. It passed before the bill in the revisal on this subject was taken up, and was urged against the necessity of passing it at this Session. The expiration of this Act at the next Session will become an argument on the other side.

An Act giving powers to the Governor & Council in certain cases.

This Act empowers the Executive to confine or send away suspicious aliens, on notice from Congs. that their sovereigns have declared or commenced hostilities agst. U. S. or that the latter have declared War agst such sovereigns. It was occasioned by the arrival of two or three Algerines here, who having no apparent object were suspected of an unfriendly one. The Executive caused them to be brought before them, but found themselves unarmed with power to proceed. These adventurers have since gone off.

Act for safe keeping land papers of the Northern Neck.

Abolishes the quitrent, and removes the papers to the Registers office.

Act for reforming County Courts.

Requires them to clear their dockets quarterly. It amounts to nothing, and is cheifly the result of efforts to render Courts of Assize unnecessary.[6]

Act to suspend the operation of the Act establishing Courts of Assize.

The latter Act passed at last Session required sundry supplemental regulations to fit it for operation. An Attempt to provide these which involved the merits of the innovation drew forth the united exertions of its adversaries. On the question on the supplemental bill they prevailed by 63 votes agst. 49. The best that could be done in this situation was to suspend instead of repealing the original act, which will give another chance to our successors for introducing the proposed reform. The various interests opposed to it, will never be conquered without considerable difficulty.

Resolution proposing a general meeting of Commssrs from the States to consider and recommend a fœderal plan for regulating Commerce, and appointg as Commssrs from Va. Ed. Randolph, Js. Madison Jr., Walter Jones, St. G. Tucker M. Smith, G. Mason, & David Ross who are to communicate the proposal & suggest time & places for meeting.

The necessity of harmony in the comercial regulations of the States has been rendered every day more apparent. The local efforts to counteract the policy of G. B. instead of succeeding have in every instance recoiled more or less on the States which ventured on the trial. Notwithstanding these lessons, The Merchts. of this State except those of Alexandria and a few of the more intelligent individuals elsewhere, were so far carried away by their jealousies of the Northern Marine, as to wish for a navigation Act confined to this State alone. In opposition to those narrow ideas the printed propositions herewith enclosed was made. As printed it went into a Comme. of the whole.[7] The alterations of the pen shew the state in which it came out. Its object was to give Congs. such direct power only as would not alarm, but to limit that of the States in such manner as wd. indirectly require a conformity to the plans of Congs. The renunciation of the right of laying duties on imports from other States, would amount to a prohibition of duties on imports from foreign Countries, unless similar duties existed in other States. This idea was favored by the discord produced between several States by rival and adverse regulations. The evil had proceeded so far between Connecticut & Massts. that the former laid heavier duties on imports from the latter than from G. B. of which the latter sent a letter of complaint to the Executive here and I suppose to the other Executives. Without some such self-denying compact it will, I conceive be impossible to preserve harmony among the contiguous States. In the Committee of the whole the proposition was combated at first on its general merits. This ground was however soon changed for that of its perpetual duration, which was reduced first to 25 years, and then to 13 years. *Its adversaries* were the *Speaker, Thruston and Corbin. They* were *bitter and illiberal against Congress* & the *Northern States,* beyond *example. Thruston* considered it as problematical, whether it would not be better to *encourage the British than the Eastern marine. Braxton* and *Smith* were in the same *sentiment*[s] but *absent at* this *crisis of the question.* The limitation of the plan to 13 years so far destroyed its value in the judgment of its friends that they chose rather, to do nothing than to adopt it in that form. The report accordingly remained on the table uncalled for to the end of the Session. And on the last day the resolution above quoted was substituted. It had been proposed by Mr. Tyler immediately after the miscarriage of the printed proposition, but was left on the table till it was found that Several propositions for regulating our trade without regard to other States produced nothing. In this extremity The resolution was generally acceded to, not without the *opposition however of Corbin and Smith*. The Commsrs. *first name*[d] *were the Attorne*[y] *Doctr. Jones* and *myself*. In the House of D. *Tucker* and *Smith were added and* In the Senate *Mason, Ros*[s] *and Ronald.* The *last does not undertake.*

The port bill was attacked and nearly defeated.[8] An amendatory bill was passed with difficulty thro' the H. of D. and rejected in the Senate. The original one will take effect before the next Session, but will probably be repealed then. It would have been repealed at this, if its adversaries had known their strength in time and exerted it with Judgment.

A Bill was brought in for paying British debts but was rendered so inadequate to its object by alterations inserted by a Committee of the whole that the patrons of it thought it best to let it sleep.

Several petitions (from Methodists cheifly) appeared in favor of a gradual abolition of slavery, and several from another quarter for a repeal of the law which licences private manumissions. The former were not thrown under the table, but were treated with all the indignity short of it. A proposition for bringing in a Bill conformably to the latter, was decided in the affirmative by the casting voice of the Speaker, but the bill was thrown out on the first reading by a considerable majority.

A considerable itch for paper money discovered itself, though no overt attempt was made. The partizens of the measure, among whom Mr. M. S. may be considered as the most zealous, *flatter themselves,* and *I fear upon too good ground* that it will be *among the measures of the next session.*[9] The unfavorable balance of trade and the substitution of facilities in the taxes *will have* [dis]*missed the little specie remaining among us* and strengthened the common *argument for a paper medium.*

Act for postponing the tax of the present year and admitting facilities in payment.	This tax was to have been collected in Sepr. last, and had been in part actually collected in specie. Notwithstanding this and the distress of public credit, an effort was

made to remit the tax altogether. *The party was headed by Braxton who was courting an appointment into the council.* On the question for a third reading the affirmative was carried by 52 agst. 42. On the final question, a vigorous effort on the negative side with a reinforcement of a few new members, threw the bill out. The oratory however was not obtained, without subscribing to a postponement instead of remission, and the admission of facilities instead of Specie.[10] The postponement too extends not only to the tax which was under collection, and which will not now come in till May, but to the tax of Sepr. next which will not now be in the Treasury till the beginning of next year. The wisdom of seven Sessions will be unable to repair the mischiefs of this single Act.

Act concerning the erection of Kentucky into an independent State. This was prayed for by a Memorial from a Convention held in Kentucky, and passed without opposition. It contains stipulations in favor of territorial rights held under the laws of Virga. and suspends the actual separation on the decision of a Convention authorized to meet for that purpose, and on the assent of Congress. The boundary of the proposed State is to remain the same as the present boundary of the district.

Act to amend the Militia law. At the last Session of 1784. an act passed displacing all the Militia officers, and providing for the appointmt. of experienced men. In most counties it was carried into execution, and generally much to the advantage of the Militia. In consequence of a few petitions agst. the law as a breach of the Constitution, This act reverses all proceedings under it, and reinstates the old officers.[11]

Act to extend the operation of the Escheat law to the Northern Neck. From the peculiar situation of that district the Escheat law was not originally extended to it. Its extension at this time was occasioned by a bill brought in by Mr. Mercer for seizing & selling the deeded land of the late lord Fairfax on the ground of its being devized to aliens, leaving them at liberty indeed to assert their pretensions before the Court of Appeals. As the bill however stated the law & the fact, and excluded the ordinary inquest, in the face of pretensions set up even by a Citizen (Martin)[12] to whom it is said the reversion is given by the Will; it was opposed as exerting at least a legislative interference in and improper influence on the Judiciary question. It was proposed to substitute the present act as an amendmt. to the bill, in a Committee of the whole which was disagreed to. The bill being of a popular cast went thro' the H. of D. by a great majority. In the Senate it was rejected by a greater one, if not unanimously. The extension of the escheat law was in consequence taken up and passed.

"Act for punishing certain offences."	To wit, attempts to dismember the State without the consent of the Legislature. It is pointed agst. the faction headed by A. C.[13] in the County of Washington.
Act for amending the appropriating Act.	Complies with the requisition of Congs. for the present year, to wit 1786. It directs 512,000 dollars the quota of this State, to be paid

before May next the time fixed by Congress, *although it is known* that the *postponement* of the *taxes renders the payment of a shilling impossible.* Our payments last year *gained us a little reputation.* Our conduct *this must stamp us with ignominy.*

Act for regulating the Salaries of the Civil list.	Reduces that of the Govr. from £1000 to £800 & the others some at a greater and some at a less proportion.
Act for disposing of waste lands on Eastern waters.	Meant cheifly to affect vacant land in Northern Neck, erroneously conceived to be in great quantity and of great value. The

price is fixed at £25 Per Hundred Acres at wch. not an acre will be sold.

An Act imposing addl. tonnage on British vessels . . .	amounting in the whole to 5/. per ton—

Nothing has been yet done with N. C. towards opening a Canal thro' the Dismal [Swamp]. The powers given to Commssrs on our part are renewed, and some negociation will be brought about if possible. A certain interest in that State is suspected of being disinclined to promote the object, notwithstanding its manifest importance to the community at large. On Potowmack they have been at work some time. On this river they have about eighty hands ready to break ground, and have engaged a man to plan for them. I fear there is a want of skill for the undertaking that threatens a waste of labour and a discouragement to the interprize. I do not learn that any measures have been taken to procure from Europe the aid which ought be purchased at any price, and which might I should suppose be purchased at a moderate one.

I had an opportunity a few days ago of knowing that Mrs. Carr and her family, as well as your little daughter, were well. I am apprehensive that some impediments still detained your younger nephew from his destination. Peter has been in Williamsburg, and I am told by Mr. Maury that his progress is satisfactory. He has read under him Horace—some of Cicero's Orations—Greek testament—Æsop's fables in Greek—ten books of Homer's Illiad & is now beginning Xenophon, Juvenal & Livy. He has also given some attention to French.

I have paid to le Maire ten guineas. He will set out in about three weeks I am told for France. Mr. Jones has promised to collect & forward by him all such papers as are in print and will explain the situation of our affairs to you. Among these will be the most important acts of the Session, & the Journal as far as it will be printed.

Mr. Wm. Hay's in sinking a well on the declivity of the Hill above the proposed seat of the Capitol and nearly in a line from the Capitol to Belvidere, found about seventy feet below the surface, several large bones apparently belong[in]g to a fish not less than the Shark, and what is more singular, several fragments of potters ware in the stile of the Indians. Before he reached these curiosities he passed thro' about fifty feet of soft blue clay. I have not seen these articles, having but just heard of them, & been too closely engaged; but have My information from the most unexceptionable witnesses who have. I am told by Genl. Russel,[14] of Washington County, that in sinking a Salt-well, in that County he fell in with the hip bone of the incognitum, the socket of which was about 8 inches diameter. It was very soft in the subterraneous State, but seemed to undergo a petrifaction on being exposed to the air. Adieu affectly—

Promotions.   Edwd. Carrington & H. Lee Jr. added to R. H. Lee, Js. Monroe, and Wm. Grayson, in the delegation to Congress.
Carter Braxton to the Council
Jno. Tyler to Court of Admiralty in room of B. Waller resd.

prices current. Tobo. 23/. on James River and proporti[on]ally elsewhere.

Wheat 5/ to 6/. per Bushel

Corn 15/ to 20/ per Barrel

Pork 28/ to 30/. per Ct.

RC (DLC). No cover. Not signed. Enclosures missing. Italicized words, unless otherwise noted, are those encoded by JM using the code Jefferson sent him 11 May 1785.

1 JM was advising Jefferson against his proposed distribution of copies of the *Notes on the State of Virginia* to the William and Mary student body.

2 The Revised Code remained half finished. At the Oct. 1786 session JM's aide Thomas Mathews reintroduced the remaining bills and guided twenty-three into law. The residue fell victim to indifference and apathy, since JM's return to Congress left a power vacuum in the House of Delegates that was filled by Patrick Henry. Henry was no particular friend of reform and by inclination tended to react negatively to any proposition from either JM or his coadjutor Jefferson. See Boyd, *Papers of Jefferson*, II, 322–24.

3 The code numbers and Jefferson's interlinear deciphering read "authors" but later JM corrected his error and wrote "adversaries" above it.

4 John Francis Mercer, whose conduct chagrined Jefferson in Congress, seized on the bill "concerning crimes and punishments" and found himself leading a determined band in the opposition (JM to Monroe, 9 Dec. 1785). Later, JM reported the same bill was again defeated, owing to a "rage agst. Horse stealers" (JM to Jefferson, 15 Feb. 1787 [DLC]).

5 For reasons not now clear, a group in the House that included John Francis Mercer, Francis Corbin, Carter Henry Harrison, and Speaker Benjamin Harrison tried to emasculate the preamble Jefferson wrote for the bill establishing freedom of religion as it first appeared in 1779. JM does not spell out their desired changes, but Jefferson later reported that efforts were made to insert the words "Jesus Christ" ahead of the phrase—"the holy author of our religion." They definitely tried to drop the whole of Jefferson's preamble and insert instead the gist of Article XVI of the Virginia Declaration of Rights. As the other leading petition against the General Assessment bill indicated, "Deism with its baneful Influence is spreading itself over the State" (Vi: Westmoreland County petition [2 Nov. 1785]). The substitute motions were beaten back in the House on 16 Dec. (38 ayes, 66 noes) and again on 29 Dec. (35 ayes, 56 noes), but several of Jefferson's appeals that smacked of a deistic philosophy were dropped in Committee of the Whole deliberations (Boyd, *Papers of Jefferson*, II, 545–46).

6 JM still hoped that he could keep alive the bill for the circuit, or assize courts which had passed at the Oct. 1784 session. Opponents of the bill who feared a diminution of their local authority apparently worked for this so-called reform bill that made a pretense at clearing up crowded dockets. If the county courts kept litigation from piling up, then the need for a circuit court (to reduce the backlog of cases) would diminish. Besides the entrenched county justices, some lawyers were ambivalent about the heavy dockets. JM's friend, Archibald Stuart, favored the Assize Court bill but gleefully reported that in Augusta County the prospect was for a lawyer's paradise. Augusta "is the best Courtt ever I attended there are now about seven hundred Causes On the Docket & there are no Attys but Nicholas and Bowyer" (Stuart to John Breckinridge, 26 Jan. 1786 [DLC: Breckinridge Family Papers]).

⁷ The public printer was ordered to prepare 200 copies of the four resolutions offered by Joseph Prentis on 14 Nov. 1785 to the Committee of the Whole (*JHDV*, Oct. 1785, pp. 36–37). JM undoubtedly sent the broadside, a copy of which Julian Boyd found at the New York Public Library (Evans 19352) of the 14 Nov. resolution calling for the regulation of commerce by Congress. These dealt with the key issues of vesting in Congress a power to regulate commerce and the imposition of a federal 5 percent import duty. As JM explained, he grew petulant as the localists prevailed, and ultimately he voted to kill the resolution on commercial powers because of the thirteen-year limit imposed by the House majority.

⁸ The so-called Port bill was JM's measure of 8 June 1784 restricting foreign vessels to certain Virginia ports. Opposition to the law was spreading in the tidewater but it was not repealed "in the next Session," as JM expected. However, it was drastically amended at the Oct. 1787 session (Hening, *Statutes*, XII, 434–38).

⁹ Petitions from Brunswick and Campbell counties would be offered at the Oct. 1786 session calling for a new emission of paper currency, but the majority (including JM) was unimpressed (JM to Jefferson, 4 Dec. 1786 [DLC]; *JHDV*, Oct. 1786, pp. 15–16). "M. S." was Meriwether Smith, whose attachment to a paper-money act was notorious. JM's notes for a speech made against the proposed paper-money bill were probably used in the 1 Nov. 1786 debates (Madison, *Writings* [Hunt ed.], II, 279–81).

¹⁰ The "facilities" were "facility notes," a kind of paper money that might be heavily discounted but still was preferable to no circulating medium at all. By whatever name, the tobacco notes circulating in the period also filled the functions of specie and in Virginia may have been colloquially called "facilities" (Mathews, *Dictionary of Americanisms*, p. 575; Hening, *Statutes*, XII, 259).

¹¹ The ancient militia laws were revised by the act of the Oct. 1784 General Assembly which broadened the base of a county's defense force. But petitions from Amherst and Washington counties attacked the constitutionality of the law, and a new bill was brought in to meet this objection. JM served on the committee that prepared the first law but seems to have avoided involvement in this revision, which passed the House on 5 Jan. 1786 (*JHDV*, Oct. 1785, p. 129).

¹² Thomas Bryan Martin (1731–1798) was the executor of Lord Fairfax's will. The question of whether Fairfax's holdings had become the property of enemy aliens arose because of his death in 1781. The matter was not finally settled until the U. S. Supreme Court upheld Fairfax's division of his estate according to his will.

¹³ Some time later, when the letter was returned to him, JM by a notation identified A. C. as "Arthur Cambel."

¹⁴ Brig.-Gen. William Russell (d. 1793) served as colonel of the 13th Virginia Regiment, was captured at Charleston, exchanged, and breveted a brigadier-general in Nov. 1783 (Heitman, *Historical Register Continental*, p. 478).

To James Monroe

RICHMOND Jany. 22d. 1786

DEAR SIR

Your favors of the 19th. Decr. and 7th. Jany.¹ came both to hand by yesterdays mail. The Assembly adjourned last night after a Session of 97 days. If its importance were to be measured by the list of the laws which it has produced, all preceding Legislative merit would be eclipsed, the number in this instance amounting to 114 or 115. If we recur to the proper criterion no Session has perhaps afforded less ground for applause. Not a single member seems to be pleased with a review of what has passed. I was too hasty in informing you that an amendment of the Port bill had passed.[2] I was led into the error by the mistake of some who told me it had passed the Senate when it had only been agreed to in a Committee of the Senate. Instead of passing it they sent down a repeal of the old port bill by way of amendment. This was disagreed to by the H. of D. as indirectly originating. The Senate adhered & the bill was lost. An attempt was then made by the adversaries of the port measure to suspend its operation till the end of the next Session. This also was negatived so that the old bill is left as it stood without alteration. Defective as it is particularly in putting Citizens of other States on the footing of foreigners, and destitute as it is of proper concomitant provisions, it was judg'd best to hold it fast and trust to a succeeding Assembly for amendments. The Navigation System for the State after having been prepared at great length by Mr. G. Baker was procrastinated in a very singular manner, and finally died away of itself, without any thing being done, except a short act passed yesterday in great hurry imposing a tonnage of 5/. on the vessels of foreigners not having treated with the U. S.[3] This failure of local measures in the commercial line, instead of reviving the original propositions for a general plan, revived that of Mr. Tyler for the appointment of Commsrs to meet Comsrs from the other States on the subject of general regulations.[4] It went through by a very great majority, being opposed only by Mr. M. Smith and Mr. Corbin. The expedient is no doubt liable to objections and will probably miscarry. I think however it is better than nothing, and as a recommendation of additional powers to Congress is within the purview of the Commission it may possibly lead to better consequences than at first occur. The Commssrs first named were the Attorney Doctr. W. Jones of the Senate and myself. The importunity of Mr. Page[5] procured the addition of St. George Tucker who is sensible, fœderal and skilled in Commerce; to whom was added on the motion of I know not whom Mr. M. Smith who is at least exceptionable in the second quality having made unceasing war during the Session agst. the idea of bracing the federal system. In the Senate a further addition was made of Col. Mason Mr. D. Ross and Mr. Ronald. The name of the latter was struck out at his desire. The others stand. It is not unlikely that this multitude of associates will stifle the thing in its birth. By some it was probably meant to do so. I am glad to find that Virginia has merit where you are, and should be more so if I saw greater reason for it. The bill which is considered at N. Y. as a compliance with the requisitions of Congs. is more so in appearance than reality. It will bring no specie into the Treasy. and but little Continental paper. Another act has since passed which professes to comply more regularly with the demand of Congs. but this will fail as to *specie*, and as to *punctuality*. It will probably procure the indents called for, and fulfils the views of Congs. in making those of other States receivable into our Treasy. Among the Acts passed since my last I must not omit an economical revision of the Civil list.[6] The saving will amount to 5 or 6000 pounds. The Govr was reduced by H. of D. to £800, to which the Senate objected. Which receded I really forget. The Council to £2000—the Attorney to £200, Register from £1100 to £800—Auditors & Solicitor from £4 to 300, Speaker of H. of D. to 40/. per day including daily pay as a member—& of Senate to 20/. &c—Delegates to Congs. to 6 dollars per day. The Act however is not to commence till November next. I mentioned in my last the propriety of addressing your future letters to Orange. Adieu Yrs. Affecly

J. MADISON JR

RC (DLC). Cover missing. Docketed by JM.

1 The 7 Jan. 1785 letter has not been found.

2 JM wrote the Port bill which had passed at the May 1784 session and was well aware of opposition fostered by the smaller seaport communities that were excluded from foreign trade by that measure. The chief opponent of the bill was George Mason, who eventually wrote a stinging attack on the law, but rumors of Mason's carrying the battle in 1785 to Richmond proved unfounded. Instead, a weaker opposition appeared in the form of a petition from Lancaster, Northumberland, and adjacent tidewater counties seeking amendment of the bill. The Committee on Commerce was ordered to bring in a bill amending the act JM wrote, and on 11 Jan. 1786 this measure narrowly passed the House by a 50 to 46 vote, with JM voting for it (*JHDV*, Oct. 1785, p. 137). But the bill then became bogged down in a conference committee and the impasse continued until the session adjourned.

3 What happened was that the delegates realized they had come to the end of the session without passing any kind of retaliatory act against the discriminatory provisions of British edicts on the West Indian trade. The result was a hastily contrived bill which was presented late in the final day of the session, passed three hurried readings, and went to the Senate where an immediate concurrence was obtained for "An act to impose additional tonnage on British vessels" (Hening, *Statutes*, XII, 32). The law imposed an additional five-shillings-per-ton levy on British ships coming into Virginia ports.

4 See the Resolution Authorizing a Commission to Examine Trade Regulations, 21 Jan. 1786.

5 John Page of Gloucester.

6 "An act for regulating and fixing the salaries of the officers of civil government" (Hening, *Statutes*, XII, 48–49). See *JHDV*, Oct. 1785, pp. 55, 68, 69, and passim. The bill was enacted 21 Jan. 1786 (*JHDV*, Oct. 1785, pp. 153–54).

Pay Voucher as Delegate to the General Assembly

[28 January 1786]

Comwlth of Virga. to Js. Madison Jr.   Orange

Novr. Session.

To Attendance as Delegate		
to 21. Jany. 21. 1786. inclusive 89 days		£44.10
To travelling to & from Richmond 150 Miles		3 —

£47.10

Entered

J Beckley C. h. d.

Ms (Vi). Docketed by John Beckley.

From Samuel House

Letter not found.

ca. 1–8 February 1786. Mentioned in JM to Eliza Trist, 14 March 1786, and probably contained a dismal report by House on his sister's health.

To James Monroe

Letter not found.

4 February 1786. Recorded in "Letters from J. M. [to] Mr. Monroe" (DLC) as "unimportant."

From Thomas Jefferson

Paris Feb. 8. 1786.

Dear Sir

My last letters have been of the 1st. & 20th. of Sep. and the 28th. of Oct. yours unacknoleged, are of Aug. 20. Oct. 3. & Nov. 15. I take this the first safe opportunity of inclosing you the bills of lading for your books, & two others for your name sake of Williamsburgh & for the attorney which I will pray you to forward. I thank you for the communication of the remonstrance against the assessment.[1] Mazzei who is now in Holland promised me to have it published in the Leyden gazette.

485

It will do us great honour. I wish it may be as much approved by our assembly as by the wisest part of Europe. I have heard with great pleasure that our assembly have come to the resolution of giving the regulation of their commerce to the federal head.[2] I will venture to assert that there is not one of it's opposers who, placed on this ground, would not see the wisdom of this measure. The politics of Europe render it indispensably necessary that with respect to every thing external we be one nation only, firmly hooped together. Interior government is what each state should keep to itself. If it could be seen in Europe that all our states could be brought to concur in what the Virginia assembly has done, it would produce a total revolution in their opinion of us, and respect for us, and it should ever be held in mind that insult & war are the consequences of a want of respectability in the national character. As long as the states exercise separately those acts of power which respect foreign nations, so long will there continue to be irregularities committing by some one or other of them which will constantly keep us on an ill footing with foreign nations.

I thank you for your information as to my Notes. The copies I have remaining shall be sent over to be given to some of my friends and to select subjects in the college. I have been unfortunate here with this trifle. I gave out a few copies only, & to confidential persons, writing in every copy a restraint against it's publication. Among others I gave a copy to mr Williamos. He died. I immediately took every precaution I could to recover this copy. But by some means or other a book seller had got hold of it. He had employed a hireling translator and was about publishing it in the most injurious form possible. An Abbé Morellet, a man of letters here to whom I had given a copy, got notice of this. He had translated some passages for a particular purpose: and he compounded with the bookseller to translate & give him the whole, on his declining the first publication. I found it necessary to confirm this, and it will be published in French, still mutilated however in it's freest parts. I am now at a loss what to do as to England. Every thing, good or bad, is thought worth publishing there; and I apprehend a translation back from the French and publication there. I rather believe it will be most eligible to let the original come out in that country, but am not yet decided.

I have purchased little for you in the book way since I sent the catalogue of my former purchases. I wish first to have your answer to that, and your information what parts of those purchases went out of your plan. You can easily say buy more of this kind, less of that &c. My wish is to conform myself to yours. I can get for you the original Paris edition in folio of the Encyclopedie for 620 livres, 35. vols; a good edn. in 39. vols. 4to. for 380 lt and a good one in 39. vols 8vo. for 280 lt. The new one will be superior in far the greater number of articles, but not in all, and the possession of the ancient one has more over the advantage of supplying present use. I have bought one for myself, but wait your orders as to you. I remember your purchase of a watch in Philadelphia. If she should not have proved good, you can probably sell her. In that case I can get for you here, one made as perfect as human art can make it for about 24. louis. I have had such a one made by the best & most faithful hand in Paris. She has a second hand, but no repeating, no day of the month, nor other useless thing to impede and injure the movements which are necessary. For 12. louis more you can have in the same cover, but on the backside, & absolutely unconnected with the movements of the watch, a pedometer which shall render you an exact account of the distances you walk. Your pleasure hereon shall be awaited.

Houdon is returned. He called on me the other day to remonstrate against the inscription proposed for genl. W's statue.[3] He says it is too long to be put on the pedestal. I told him I was not at liberty to permit any alteration, but I would represent his objection to a friend who could judge of it's validity, and whether a change could be authorized. This has been the subject of conversations here, and various devices & inscriptions have been suggested. The one which has appeared best to me may be translated as follows. 'Behold, Reader, the form of George Washington. For his worth, ask History: that will tell it, when this stone shall have yeilded to the decays of time. His country erects this monument: Houdon makes it.' This for one side. on the 2d. represent the evacuation of Boston with the motto 'hostibus primum fugatis.' On the 3d. the capture of the Hessians with 'hostibus iterum devictis.' On the 4th. the surrender of York, with 'hostibus ultimum debellatis.' This is seising the three most brilliant actions of his military life. By giving out here a wish of receiving mottos for this statue, we might have thousands offered, of which still better might be chosen. The artist made the same objection of *length* to the inscription for the bust of the M. de la fayette. An alteration of that might come in time still, if an alteration was wished. However I am not certain that it is desireable in either case. The state of Georgia has given 20,000 acres of land to the Count d'Estaing. This gift is considered here as very honourable to him, and it has gratified him much.

I am persuaded that a gift of lands by the state of Virginia to the Marquis de la fayette would give a good opinion here of our character, and would reflect honour on the Marquis. Nor am I sure that the day will not come when it might be an useful asylum to him. The time of life at which he visited America was too well adapted to receive good & lasting impressions to permit him ever to accomodate himself to the principles of monarchical government; and it will need all his own prudence & that of his friends to make this country a safe residence for him. How glorious, how comfortable in reflection will it be to have prepared a refuge for him in case of a reverse. In the mean time he could settle it with tenants from the freest part of this country, Bretagny. I have never suggested the smallest idea of this kind to him: because the execution of it should convey the first notice. If the state has not a right to give him lands with their own officers, they could buy up at cheap prices the shares of others. I am not certain however whether in the public or private opinion, a similar gift to Count Rochambeau could be dispensed with. If the state could give to both, it would be better: but in any event I think they should to the Marquis. C. Rochambeau too has really deserved more attention than he has received. Why not set up his bust, that of Gates, Greene, Franklin in your new Capitol? À propos of the Capitol, do my dear friend exert yourself to get the plan begun on set aside, & that adopted which was drawn here.[4] It was taken from a model which has been the admiration of 16 centuries, which has been the object of as many pilgrimages as the tomb of Mahomet; which will give unrivalled honour to our State, and furnish a model whereon to form the taste of our young men. It will cost much less too than the one begun, because it does not cover one half the Area. Ask if you please, a sight of my letter of Jan. 26. to messrs Buchanan & Hay, which will spare me the repeating it's substance here.

Every thing is quiet in Europe. I recollect but one new invention in the arts which is worth mentioning. It is a mixture of the arts of engraving & printing, rendering both cheaper. Write or draw any thing on a plate of brass with the ink of the inventor, and in half an hour he gives you engraved copies of it so perfectly like the original that they could not be suspected to be copies. His types for printing a whole page are all in one solid peice. An author therefore only prints a few copies of his work from time to time as they are called for, this saves the loss of printing more copies than may possibly be sold, and prevents an edition from being over exhausted. I am with a lively esteem Dear Sir your sincere friend & servant

TH: JEFFERSON

P. S. Could you procure and send me an hundred or two nuts of the Paccan? They would enable me to oblige some characters here whom I should be much gratified to oblige. They should come packed in sand. The seeds of the sugar maple too would be a great present.

RC (DLC); FC (DLC: Jefferson Papers). Docketed in an unknown hand. Enclosure not found.

¹ JM had enclosed his Memorial and Remonstrance (ca. 20 June 1785) in his letter to Jefferson, 20 Aug. 1785.

² Jefferson's source lacked knowledge of the reversal of the vote several days following passage of the resolution favoring federal regulation of commerce by Congress. The resolution came out of the Committee of the Whole on 28 Nov., passed on 30 Nov., and the vote rescinded on 1 Dec. See Resolution Calling for the Regulation of Commerce by Congress, 14 Nov. 1785.

³ JM wrote the inscription presented to the House of Delegates on 22 June 1784. Although there was much discussion concerning the tribute to Washington, this official inscription was affixed, over Houdon's protest, to the bust (Boyd, *Papers of Jefferson*, IX, 270–71 n.).

⁴ Jefferson's design for the state capitol had been sent to Dr. James Currie and was based on the Maison Carrée at Nîmes (Jefferson to JM, 1 Sept. 1785; Jefferson to Dr. Currie, 28 Jan. 1786, Boyd, *Papers of Jefferson*, IX, 240). This design was used in constructing the building finished in 1792, to which wings were added in 1906 and 1964 (*A Hornbook of Virginia History* [Richmond, 1965], p. 55).

From Thomas Jefferson

Paris Feb. 9. 1786

DEAR SIR

In my letter of yesterday I forgot to inclose one I have received on the subject of a debt due to mr Paradise,¹ and I wish the present letter may reach the bearer of that in time to go by the same conveiance. The inclosed from Doctor Bancroft will explain itself. I add my solicitations to his, not to ask any thing to be done for mr Paradise inconsistent with the justice due to others, but that every thing may be done for him which justice will permit. Your assistance in this either by yourself or by interesting such other person in it as may be more in the way to forward it will oblige Dear Sir Your friend & servant

TH: JEFFERSON

RC (DLC). Addressed and franked by Jefferson. On the visor of the cover, "L'Orient March 5th. 1786 forwarded by Sir your most obedt. Servant Z: Loreil-he." Docketed. The enclosure was Edward Bancroft's letter to Jefferson, 18 Nov. 1785 (Boyd, *Papers of Jefferson*, IX, 40–41).

¹ John Paradise (1743–1795) was born in Greece of British-Greek parents. He attended Oxford and in 1769 married Lucy Ludwell of Virginia, an heiress to the fortune of Philip Ludwell III (d. 1767). Their extravagant mode of living led them into heavy debt, which occasioned Bancroft's letter to Jefferson. Lucy Paradise's inheritance was confiscated during the war but later released after the Treaty of Paris was signed. Bancroft appealed to Jefferson to aid Paradise in recovering "what is due to him from the State of Virginia" (ibid, IX, 41; Archibald B. Shepperson, *John Paradise and Lucy Ludwell of London and Williamsburg* [Richmond, 1942], pp. 182–85).

From James Monroe

NEW YORK Feby. 9. 1786.

DEAR SIR

I have recd. yours of the day subsequent to the adjournment of the assembly. Since my last the subject of the impost has been taken up; a report made on it some time last year was recommitted & a report being brought in to the following effect viz: that it be earnestly recommended to the States of New York & Georgia, the only States who have fail'd in some degree or other to comply with the recommendation of the 18th. of April 1783., to take it into their immediate Consideration, especially that part wh. respects the impost, & to comply with the same —stating Further that the plans authoriz'd by the confideration have fail'd or are highly inexpedient, viz: requisitions, loans, or emissions of paper bills of credit. It implies a relinquishment of the supplementary funds, and admits the necessity of a further reference to the States & especially R I. to extend their powers upon that subject so as to come up to the recommendation—being taken up it was delay'd & protracted by its advocates, particularly Mr. Pinckney & ultimately (there being but 7. States present for it) postpon'd to take up a motion of his own, to the same effect, but in different language; this is now under consideration & will probably pass to day.¹ This subject hath imploy[ed] Congress for several days, so that nothing else hath been before them since the arrival of Mr. Lee.²

I have confer'd with Mr. Scott upon the subject of his lands upon the Mohawk river.³ I enclose you a draft of a patent in wh. he owns an undivided right to about 8000 acres. He wishes to sell — his terms are, in short payments, by wh. he means abt. one third immediately & the other two thirds in annual payments 20/. New York currency. I have heard that similar land may be obtain'd still cheaper, even of the same tract but of this I am not yet ascertain'd. I believe it will make no difference as to the quantity in the price. He has he says given orders to his agents to dispose of none untill I hear from you. If you are inclin'd to purchase & can spare the time I think you had better come here since perhaps you wod. be able to make a better bargain than any of yr. friends; he says he will have the land divided & sell if you prefer tracts ascertain'd; but I understand this wod. in case you had yr. election, raise a few shillings the price. If you shod. decli[ne] coming I need not inform you that you may command to any purpose you may please any service I can render you. In this instance you had better associate with me Colo. Grayson who will probably be here in a few days. Yi. affey.

JAS. MONROE

RC (DLC); Tr (NN: Monroe Papers). Franked and addressed by Monroe to JM "near Fredricksburg." Docketed in an unknown hand. Enclosure missing. The right margin of the Ms is obscured by mounting, and brackets enclose portions of words taken from the transcript.

1 On 3 Jan. 1786 the report of the Secretary of Congress, dated 4 Jan. 1786, was given on the number of states that had complied in whole or in part with the recommended Revenue System of 18 Apr. 1783. On 3 Feb. chairman Monroe made the report of the committee appointed to consider what measures Congress ought to take in pursuance of the recommendations then made to the several states. It was recommended that New York and Georgia consider and comply with the 18 Apr. 1783 proposal of a federal impost. No action was taken 9 Feb. (JCC, XXX, 7–11, 44–49).

2 Henry Lee presented his credentials on 1 Feb. 1786 (ibid., XXX, 36).

3 The tract was originally patented by Lt. John Scott in 1722, to which his son added eleven hundred acres in 1725 (Ruth L. Higgins, Expansion in New York with Especial Reference to the Eighteenth Century [Columbus, 1931], pp. 61, 66). This was the beginning of JM's speculative venture in the Mohawk Valley. He had been considering such a scheme at least since Oct. 1785 when he had discussed it with Washington at Mount Vernon. His interest in the Mohawk River region had been stimulated by his journey to the Indian treaty at old Fort Stanwix (Rome, N.Y.) in the late summer and early autumn of 1784 and spurred on by his financial need and desire to be free of dependence upon a farming income. At the same time, JM's lack of capital hindered him from immediately going forward with the venture (Brant, Madison, II, 336, 339; JM to Edmund Randolph, 26 July 1785; JM to Monroe, 24 Feb. 1786).

From Eliza House Trist

Letter not found.

9 February 1786. Contained news of Mrs. Trist's state of health and her proposed trip through various states. Mentioned in JM's response of 14 March 1786.

From James Monroe

DEAR SIR

In my last I mention'd to you, the subject of the impost was reviv'd & that a report of a Committee had given place to a motion of Mr. Pinckney, the latter being still before the house. The report, and motion with a report from the Bd. of treasury to the same effect have since been committed, in which State the business now lies. I inclose you a paper containing the report.[1] It is doubted whether in any event this State will adopt it. Those members elected in opposition to such as were turn'd out, for their opposition to the measure, have I hear imbib'd their sentiments & act under them. They are it is said possess'd to great amount (I mean the leaders of the party) of publick securities, and doubtful of their payment by federal exertion, seem inclin'd to pursue the course Pena. latterly did & provide for it, by establishing State funds.[2] The more extensive the funds of the State, & the more fully they exclude the citizens of other States & foreigners from such provision, the better of course for the party. I am sincerely yr. friend & servant

JAS. MONROE

If you visit this place shortly I will present you to a young lady who will be adopted a citizen of Virga. in the course of this week.[3]

RC (DLC). Cover missing. Docketed in an unknown hand. The enclosure has not been found.

[1] The report from the Board of Treasury was presented on 8 Feb. See Monroe to JM, 9 Feb. 1786.

[2] Pennsylvania began issuing certificates of interest in 1783 and in 1786 began assuming continental securities and issuing state securities in their place. New York followed Pennsylvania's example in Feb. 1786. All the continental debt paper was to be exchanged for state notes. Both state schemes appeared to involve speculative interests. With Congress unable to pay its debts, public creditors derived greater benefits when their securities were incorporated into state schemes for debt redemption (Ferguson, *Power of the Purse*, pp. 221–22, 228–32).

[3] Monroe's oblique allusion is to his fiancée, Elizabeth Kortright, daughter of Laurence Kortright, a New York merchant who specialized in the West Indian trade. She and Monroe were married on 16 Feb. 1786 (Ammon, *James Monroe*, p. 61).

To Edmund Randolph

Letter not found.

ca. 14 February 1786. Mentioned in JM to Jefferson, 18 March 1786, where JM noted the arrival of a letter written by the Attorney General "dated prior to his receipt of mine." Apparently JM wrote Randolph some time in the middle of February concerning Jefferson's plea that work on the state capitol should be suspended until his set of plans could be completed and sent to Virginia (Jefferson to JM, 20 Sept. 1785).

From Henry Lee

NEW YORK 16h. Feby. [1786]

MY DEAR SIR

By way of introduction of a correspondence, with a character I love & respect so sincerely, I enclose a report passed yesterday by Congress, the only material business done lately & which proves the dreadful situation of our fœderal government.[1] The report speaks so fully on the subject that I withhold remarks which might [my?] solicitude for the public gives birth to.

We have received some advices from our agent in Madeira which afford some ground to hope success will attend our negotiations with the Barbary powers tho when you consider the enmity which certainly prevails in the British cabinet towards us, their influence with those pirates and our scanty purse, I profess my fears preponderate.[2] Indian affairs do not wear a promising countenance—an additional evil to our many evils, if the spring should open with a war with the savages.

Only eight states are represented. Grayson joined us two days ago, & Monroe becomes Benedict this evening.[3] My best wishes attend you, farewel my friend. Yours truely,

H. LEE JUNR

RC (DLC). Cover missing. Docketed by JM. Enclosure not found.

[1] On 15 Feb. 1786, Congress approved the report of a committee delegated to consider the "System of General Revenue" recommended by Congress on 18 Apr. 1783 (*JCC*, XXX, 70–76).

[2] John Pintard, U. S. commercial agent in Madeira, wrote to Jay on 5 and 12 Dec. 1785. Jay forwarded these letters to Congress who returned them for a report which Jay rendered on 19 May 1786 (ibid., XXX, 76 n.).

[3] Monroe was about to lose his bachelor's status—hence Lee jested with bachelor JM by alluding to their traitorous companion as a "Benedict."

From James Monroe

Letter not found.

16 February 1786. In this letter, mentioned in JM's letter of 19 March 1786 to Monroe, Monroe proposed a joint purchase of land in the Mohawk Valley from one Taylor. In the letter he also discussed the possibilities of reforming the Confederation and the inadequate powers of the Virginia commissioners if a convention were to undertake such a reform.

To James Monroe

ORANGE Feby. 24th. 1786

DEAR SIR

Your favor of the 9th. Feby. is just handed to me. Having but a moment to answer it I confine myself to the Paragraph relating to Mr. Scotts proposition.[1] I thank you most sincerely for the attention you have given to my request on that matter. My opinion is not changed with regard to the policy of some such speculation, and I shall revolve well your communications. The difficulty however of commanding money at present even under prospects which in other situations might have been confided in, and the possibility of more eligible dispositions of any resources I may have, are lessons of caution which I must not disregard. It is incumbent on me therefore, whatever latent views I may retain, not to authorize in Mr. Scott any reliance on me which may retard or prevent other negociatiations [sic]. Of this you will be kind enough to apprize him, that he may untie the hands of his Agents if he thinks proper. I shall write again by the first opportunity, which I hope will urge brevity less than the present, remaining in the meantime Yr. affect. friend

J. MADISON JR.

RC (DLC). Addressed by JM to Monroe "in Congress." Docketed by JM.

[1] "Mr. Scotts proposition" was a land speculation involving 8,000 acres in the Mohawk Valley. Monroe had explained the terms in his letter of 9 Feb. 1785.

From Edmund Randolph

RICHMOND March 1 1786.

MY DEAR SIR

I am much indebted to you for Bayle and the Confessional. I delivered the treatises on air, with the history of their journey from hence to Orange, to Dr. Currie.[1] He put them into the hands of McClurg who reports in strong terms of approbation the work of Scheele, as being most learned in Chymistry.

494

The circular letters have been dispatched, with an authentication of our commercial Character from the governor. But I forwarded them without troubling him with that charge.[2]

I presume, you have received letters from Mr. J. If not, I mention from one of the 20th. of Sepr. to me, the celebrity of the code de l'humanitès; the tranquil State of Europe; except that G. B. seems not to be calmed in her resentment vs America—the strenuous naval equipments of France, as if in actual war. He has caused a very handsome plan to be prepared for our Capitol: which has not yet arrived, but will surely come in time for our purpose.

Of the three new departments in the auditors office, Mr. Pendleton has the first, Mr. Randolph the second, and Mr. Starke the last, which is temporary.[3] The general Opinion declares, that Mr. H—y will resign before the last reappointment take[s] place, under the constitution. I disbelieve it, because he seems to have made no preparation for a retreat, and nothing has been uttered by himself, as far as I have heard.

I ought to have informed you that Annapolis is the place, and the first monday in Sepr. the time for our convention. That city was preferred, as being most central, and farther removed from the suspicion, which Phila. or N. York might have excited, of congressional or mercantile influence. I am my dear friend yrs affely.

                                                                    E. R.

RC (DLC). Addressed by Randolph. Docketed by JM. The right margin is frayed, and so certain portions are restored within brackets.

[1] Dr. James Currie (1745–1807) was a prominent Richmond physician and businessman. Born in Scotland and educated at Edinburgh's famous medical school, he emigrated to America and was an ardent patriot in 1776, when a kinsman of the same name and profession adhered to the royal cause. Dr. Currie was a friend of Jefferson's and was involved in the construction of the state capitol. His home was at the corner of Tenth and Broad Streets in Richmond (Blanton, *Medicine in Virginia in the Eighteenth Century*, pp. 335–36).

[2] The commissioners appointed by the General Assembly were assigned the task of informing the other states of their mission, which was to discuss with other state delegates the nation's commercial problems (*JHDV*, Oct. 1785, p. 153). This duty must have been completed soon after JM departed from Richmond (JM to Jefferson, 18 Mar. 1786).

[3] The increasing complexity of government caused revisions in the commonwealth's small bureaucracy. The auditor's office was revised by an act agreed to on 10 Jan. 1786 (*JHDV*, Oct. 1785, p. 136; Hening, *Statutes*, XII, 106–9). J. Pendleton, Bolling Stark, and H. Randolph had feared their appointments to that office would suffer from the revision and pleaded with the governor that he maintain their services (*Cal. of Va. State Papers*, IV, 80, 83, and passim).

From Daniel Carroll

DEAR SIR,

Our General Assembly adjournd this day after a Session of 4 Months. The proposition from yr. Assembly, for a meeting of Commissioners, from all the States, to adjust a general commercial System, reach'd us not long before the conclusion of the Session.[1] Our House of Delegates propos'd Commissioners for that purpose. The measure appear'd to the Senate, tho' undoubtedly adopted by yr. Assembly with the best intentions, to have a tendency to weaken the authority of Congress, on which the *Union*, & consequently the Liberty, & Safety of all the States depend. We had just receiv'd the Act of Congress of the 15 of Feby last, by which it appears that Body relyes *solely* on the States complying with their Act of the 10th of Apl. 1783. I am afraid the Idea of Commsrs. meeting from all the States, on the regulation of Trade, will retard the Act of Congress from being carry'd into execution, if not entirely distroy it. The reluctant States are very willing to lay hold of anything which will procrastinate that measure. There are many other considerations, which I need not suggest to you. I shall only observe, that sound policy, if not the Spirit of the Confederation dictates, that all matters of a general tendency, shou'd be in the representative Body of the whole, or under its authority.

Our Assembly have granted the 5 P Cent compleatly, on 12 States complying including Maryland—& have granted 10/ on every £100 property for 25 years for their proportion of the internal fund riquir'd.

It gave me pleasure to hear from Col. Mercer that you enjoy'd yr. health & I request you will believe me to be Dear Sr. with great esteem, Yr affte & Obt Servt

DANL. CARROLL

PS If you shoud favour me with a few lines direct to me at George Town by post.

RC (DLC). Cover missing. Docketed by JM.

[1] The "proposition" from the Virginia General Assembly was the resolution of 21 Jan. 1786 calling for a conference of all the states to consider strengthened commercial regulations. Without being explicit, Carroll explained the lukewarmness of the upper chamber in Maryland toward the convention call. Indeed, that body rejected the proposal, which meant that the convened delegates met in Annapolis without any representation from Maryland itself. JM probably shared some of Car-

roll's reservations, which Burnett did not take into account when he wrote of JM's lack of enthusiasm for the forthcoming meeting. "It seems rather a remarkable state of affairs that Madison should have deemed it politically unwise to intimate ... that his wishes in promoting the Annapolis Convention extended farther from a commercial reform" (Burnett, *The Continental Congress*, p. 666). Burnett's hindsight caused him to assume that JM was pushing for vigorous action by the convention, an assumption that flies in the face of JM's guarded statements of 22 Jan. 1786 to Jefferson and Monroe regarding the proposed convention. JM's recollection that he moved circumspectly at this time to avoid raising "the suspicion of a bias in favor" of the convention was made forty years later (JM to Noah Webster, 10 Mar. 1826, Madison, *Writings* [Hunt ed.], IX, 246–47). After thinking about the matter for seven weeks, JM's view was more benign, as he told Monroe "on the whole I cannot disapprove of the experiment" (JM to Monroe, 14 Mar. 1786).

To James Monroe

ORANGE March 14th. 1786.

DEAR SIR

I acknowledged some time since your favor of the 9th. of Feby. inclosing the plot and proposition from young Mr. Scott. I have only now to repeat on that subject that I wish him to place no expectation on one that may divert him from other negociations. If I find that my resources will make it worth while to renew the matter on my part, I will trouble you to obtain further explanations, unless I should determine to make a trip myself. Indeed I should not think of closing any bargain in such a case without either examining the land myself, or making use of the examination of others. My private opinion is that the vacant land in that part of America opens the surest field of speculation of any in the U.S. Its quality is excellent, its communication with the Sea is almost, and in time will be altogether, by water alone.[1] This channel too, as running thro' our own jurisdiction, is free from the uncertainties incident to the Western navigation, and what removes every doubt of the value of land in that quarter is that land in the same situation and of the same soil, bears now & has long borne a high price. You I suppose have no view of turning any part of your speculations that way. If you had even so far as to meditate a visit to that region, it would have great weight with me. It wd. have decisive weight as to a trip myself. How do you propose to dispose of yourself during the Summer? I have just recd. a few lines from the attorney[2] which inform me that it has been agreed by the meeting of the deputies for a Continental Convention, to propose Annapolis as the place & the first monday in Sepr. for the time of its assembling, and that a circular letter has been dispatched to that effect. What is thought of this measure where you are and what probability is there that it will be generally acceded to by the States? I am far from entertaining sanguine expectations from it, and am sensible that it may be viewed in one objectionable light. Yet on the whole I cannot disapprove of the experiment. Something it is agreed is necessary to be done, towards the commerce at least of the U.S., and if anything can be done, it seem[s] as likely to result from the proposed Convention, and more likely to result f[rom] the present crisis, than from any other mode or time. If nothing can be done we may at least expect a full discovery as to that matter from the experiment, and such a peice of knowledge will be worth the trouble and expence of obtaining it. I have a letter from Mr. Jefferson of the 20th. of Sepr. but he says nothing to me which you have not probably recd. more fully either from your private or public communication with him. I am Dr Sir very sincerely Yr. Affe. friend,

JS. MADISON JR.

RC (DLC). Cover addressed and docketed by JM. Portions within brackets are obscured by an archivist's mounting.

[1] The New York back country lured speculators from throughout the eastern seaboard and even aroused the interest of capitalists in Europe. In particular the vast tracts of land north and west of Fort Stanwix offered the greatest attraction. The New York legislature disposed of the public lands in large lots at nominal prices, upon which land jobbers capitalized (David M. Ellis et al., *A History of New York State* [rev. ed.; Ithaca, 1967], pp. 150–51).

[2] Edmund Randolph to JM, 1 Mar. 1786.

To Eliza House Trist

March 14th. 1786

Your favor of the 9th. of February[1] has been several weeks in my pocket, and has for the same space kept me impatient for an opportunity to tell you how much pleasure it gave me. I construe your vein of pleasantry into a proof of your returning health, and am therefore doubly entertained with it. I wish I could exhibit in another Coat that would furnish you [with] a similar topic. I do not like however your talking of your Doctor as if he were still in your service. I had flattered myself that you had long since been sufficiently restored to dismiss him. Your brother's letter[2] which is of earlier date than yours first created doubts on that head, and if yours had not so soon followed would have left very unfavorable impressions. I hope the mild season which is approaching will bring all the healing influences which you promise yourself from it, whether you continue to breathe your native air, or execute your purpose of trying a change of it. Were I to judge from the travels you have projected, I should suppose you meant rather to try the strength of your constitution, than to repair its defects. A trip to the Antient dominion has indeed an air of moderation and of a pursuit of health; but one from thence to New London and thence to Har[t]ford seems more likely to break down a good constitution than to reestablish an infirm one. I recd. two letters from Mr. Jefferson at the same time that yours came to hand.[3] They came I find by the two young gentlemen who were the bearers of his & Miss Patsy's to you. The written and verbal information you must have recd. leaves me nothing to add from mine. I am extremely sorry at the circumstance you mention of his being obliged notwithstanding his frugality, to intrench on his private resources. It is the more to be lamented, as it will probably circumscribe the collection of philosophical treasures which his return will import into his native Country. His portrait of the French character is of itself a proof of the spirit with which he eyes Europe. He has never [written] in full to me on that subject, and I am therefore particularly obliged to you for the extract. Perhaps some of the traits in the picture, as coming from his political situation are unfit for indiscriminate communication, and I shall accordingly use reserve in that respect. I have this moment a line from Mr. Randolph which informs me that it has been agreed to propose to the other States Annapolis as the fittest place for holding the meditated Convention.[4] This event therefore as far as the opportunity of seeing some of your Southern friends depended on it will disappoint you. Mrs Randolph will be no less disappointed. She expressed great satisfaction in the hop[e] of making her accompanying Mr. R. subservient to an interview with you. The time fixed for the meeting at Annapolis is the first monday in Sepr. I am personally glad that it is put off to so late a day, as it will lengthen the period during which I shall be master of my time. Present my best compliments to Mrs. House & Miss Polly. Browse I hope also maintains his title to them by diligence & proficiency in his studies.[5] What classics is he reading & has he begun French yet? With my sincerest wishes for your happiness I remain Your friend & servt.

J. MADISON JR.

RC (Blumhaven Library and Gallery, Philadelphia). Cover missing. No docket. Portions within brackets obscured by blotting or fading.

1 Mrs. Trist's letter has not been found.
2 Samuel House's letter has not been found.
3 Jefferson to JM, dated 1 and 20 Sept. 1785.
4 Randolph's letter of 1 Mar. 1786.
5 Hore Browse Trist, Jr., Mrs. Trist's son named after his uncle.

To Caleb Wallace

Letter not found.

15 March 1786. Printed copy of Memorial and Remonstrance enclosed. Mentioned in Wallace's letter of 30 September 1786 to JM (DLC).

To Thomas Jefferson

VIRGA. ORANGE March 18th. 1786

DEAR SIR

Your two favours of the 1 & 20 Sepr. under the same cover by Mr. Fitzhugh did not come to hand till the 24th ult: and of course till it was too late for any Legislative interposition with regard to the Capitol. I have written to the Attorney on the subject. A letter which I have from him dated prior to his receipt of mine takes notice of the plan you had promised and makes no doubt that it will arrive in time for the purpose of the Commissioners.¹ I do not gather from his expressions however that he was aware of the change which will become necessary in the foundation already laid; a change which will not be submitted to without reluctance for two reasons. 1. the appearance of caprice to which it may expose the Commissioners. 2 which is the material one, the danger of retarding the work till the next Session of Assembly can interpose a vote for its suspension, and possibly for a removal to Williamsburg. This danger is not altogether imaginary.² Not a Session had passed since I became a member without one or other or both of these attempts. At the late Session, a suspension was moved by the Williamsburg Interest, which was within a few votes of being agreed to. It is a great object therefore with the Richmond Interest to get the building so far advanced before the fall as to put an end to such experiments. The circumstances which will weigh in the other scale, and which it is to be hoped will preponderate, are, the fear of being reproached with sacrificing public considerations to a local policy, and a hope that the substitution of a more œconomical plan, may better reconcile the Assembly to a prosecution of the Undertaking.

Since I have been at home I have had leisure to review the literary cargo for which I am so much indebted to your friendship. The collection is perfectly to my mind. I must trouble you only to get two little mistakes rectified. The number of Vol. in the Encyclopedie correspondends with your list, but a duplicate has been packed up of Tom. 1. 1ere. partie of Histoire Naturelle Quadrupedes, premiere livraison, and there is left out the 2d. part of the same Tom. which as appears by the Avis to the 1st. livraison makes the 1st. Tome of Histoire des Oiseaux, as well as by the Histoire des oiseaux sent, which begins with Tom. II. 1re partie, and with the letter F. From the Avis to the sixth livraison I infer that the vol. omitted made part of the 5me. livraison. The duplicate vol. seems to have been a good deal handled, and possibly belongs to your own Sett. Shall I keep it in my hands or send it back? The other mistake is an omission of the 4th. vol. of D'Albon sur l'interêt de plusierrs nations &c. The binding of the three vols. which are come is distinguished from that of most of the other books by the circumstance of the figure on the back numbering the vols. being on a black instead of a red ground. The authors name above is on a red ground. I mention these circumstances that the binder may supply the omitted vol. in proper uniform. I annex a State of our account balanced. I had an opportunity a few days after your letters were recd. of remitting the balance to the hands of Mrs. Carr with a request that it might be made use of as you direct to prevent a loss of time to her sons from occasional disappointments in the stated funds. I have not yet heard from the Mr. Fitzhughs on the subject of your advance to them. The advance to Le Maire had been made a considerable time before I received your countermanding instructions.[3] I have no copying press, but must postpone that conveniency to other wants which will absorb my little resources. I am fully apprized of the value of this machine and mean to get one when I can better afford it, and may have more use for it. I am led to think it wd. be a very œconomical acquisition to all our public offices which are obliged to furnish copies of papers belonging to them.

A Quorum of the deputies appointed by the Assembly for a Commercial Convention had a meeting at Richmond shortly after I left it, and the Attorney tells me, it has been agreed to propose Annapolis for the place, and the first monday in Sepr. for the time of holding the Convention. It was thought prudent to avoid the neighbourhood of Congress, and the large Commercial towns, in order to disarm the adversaries to the object, of insinuations of influence from either of these quarters. I have not heard what opinion is entertained of this project at New York, nor what reception it has found in any of the States. If it should come to nothing, it will I fear confirm G. B. and all the world in the belief that we are not to be respected, nor apprehended as a nation in matters of Commerce. The States are every day giving proofs that separate regulations are more likely to set them by the ears, than to attain the common object. When Massts. set on foot a retaliation of the policy of G. B. Connecticut declared her ports free. N. Jersey served N. York in the same way. And Delaware I am told has lately followed the example in opposition to the commercial plans of Penna. A miscarriage of this attempt to unite the States in some effectual plan, will have another effect of a serious nature. It will dissipate every prospect of drawing a steady revenue from our imposts either directly into the federal treasury, or indirectly thro' the treasuries of the Commercial States; and of consequence the former must depend for supplies solely on annual requisitions, and the latter on direct Taxes drawn from the property of the Country. That these dependencies are in an alarming degree fallacious is put by experience out of all question. The payments from the States under the calls of Congress have in no year borne any proportion to the public wants. During the last year, that is from Novr. 1784 to Novr 1785, the aggregate payments, as stated to the late Assembly fell short of 400,000 dollrs. a sum neither equal to the interest due on the foreign debts, nor even to the current expences of the federal Government. The greatest part of this sum too went from Virga. which will not supply a single shilling the present year. Another unhappy effect of a continuance of the present anarchy of our commerce, will be a continuance of the unfavorable balance on it, which by draining us of our metals furnishes pretexts for the pernicious substitution of paper money, for indulgences to debtors, for postponements of taxes. In fact most of our political evils may be traced up to our commercial ones, as most of our moral may to our political. The lessons which the mercantile interest of Europe have received from late experience will probably check their propensity to credit us beyond our resources, and so far the evil of an unfavorable balance will correct itself. But the Merchants of G. B. if no others will continue to credit us at least as far as our remittances can be strained, and that is far enough to perpetuate our difficulties unless the luxurious propensity of our own people can be otherwise checked. This view of our situation presents the proposed Convention as a remedial experiment which ought to command every assent; but if it be a just view it is one which assuredly will not be taken by all even of those whose intentions are good. I consider the event therefore as extremely uncertain, or rather, considering that the States must first agree to the proposition for sending deputies—that these must agree in a plan to be sent back to the States, and that these again must agree unanimously in a ratification of it. I almost despair of success. It is necessary however that something should be tried & if this be not the best possible expedient, it is the best that could possibly be carried thro' the Legislature here. And if the present crisis cannot effect unanimity, from what future concurrences of circurrences [circumstances?] is it to be expected? Two considerations particularly remonstrate against delay. One is the danger of having the same *game played on our confederacy* by which *Philip* [man]*aged that of* the *Grecian state. I saw during the late assembly* of the *influence of* the *desperate circumstances of indi-*[vi]*du*[al]*s on their public conduct* to *admonish me of* the *possibility of finding in the council of some one of the states fit instru*[ments] *of foreign machinations.* The other consideration is the probability of an early *increase* of the *confederated states which more* than *proportion*[ally] *impede measures which require unanimity* as the *new members may bring sentiment*[s] and *interests les*[s] *congenial with those of* the *Atlantic states than those of the latter are one with another.*

The price of our Staple is down at 22/ at Richmond. One argument for putting off the taxes was that as it would relieve the planters from the necessity of selling & would enable them to make a better bargain with the purchasers. The price has notwithstanding been falling ever since. How far the event may have proceeded from a change in the Market of Europe I know not. That it has in part proceeded from the practice of remitting and postponing the taxes may I think be fairly deduced. The scarcity of money must of necessity sink the price of every article. And the relaxation in collecting the taxes, increases this scarcity by diverting the money from the public Treasury to the shops of merchandize. In the former case it would return into circulation. In the latter it goes out of the Country to balance the increased consumption. A vigorous and steady collection of taxes would make the money necessary here and would therefore be a mean[s] of keeping it here. In our situation it would have the salutary operation of a sumptuary law. The price of Indian Corn in this part of the Country which produced the best crops, is not higher than 2 dollrs. per barrl. It would have been much higher but for the peculiar mildness of the winter, December and Jany. scarcely reminded us that it was winter. February, though temperate was less unseasonable. Our deepest snow, (about 7 inches) was in the present month. I observe the tops of the blue ridge still marked with its remains. My last was dated Jan. 22. and contained a narrative of the proceedings of the Assembly. I shall write you again as soon as a subject & opportunity occur, remaining in the mean time Yr. Affecte. friend,

Dr. to T. J.

	livrs.	Sols
1785 Sepr. 1 To amt. of books &c.................	1164——	3

Credt.

	drs.	livrs.	sols
By balance stated by T. J. 77-2/3.................		407——15	
By advance to lemaire 10 Gu[i]n[ea]s............		234	
	drs.		
By do. for 6 Copies of Revisal at 2 1/2.............		81	
		722——15	
*By £25 Va. Cy. remitted to Mrs. C...............		441—— 8	
		1164—— 3	

* £25 I discover exceeds the sum extended a few livres which may be carried into the next acct. if it be thought worth while.

RC (DLC). Cover missing. Not signed. Docketed by JM and several unidentified hands. Italicized words, unless otherwise noted, are those encoded by JM in the code Jefferson sent him 11 May 1785. Brackets indicate miscoding and letters omitted by JM.

1 Randolph wrote JM on 1 Mar. 1786. JM's letter to the attorney general has not been found.

2 Williamsburg residents made common cause with their peninsula neighbors in arguing that the capital removal in 1780 had been a mistake. "The inhabitants of this town and of all lower Virginia desire greatly that the seat of government should be brought back thither, and are doing all they can to bring it about; and chiefly because they fear that besides the great loss they have already suffered they may have to pay taxes for erecting at Richmond the new public buildings necessary in future," a Williamsburg visitor observed (Schoepf, *Travels in the Confederation*, II, 81).

3 Jacques Le Maire, a wartime purchasing agent for the Commonwealth of Virginia, had been breveted a lieutenant colonel. He laid his claim for unpaid balances before the governor and Council early in 1785 and received a partial payment of £150. See JM to Jefferson, 27 Apr. 1785.

To James Monroe

ORANGE 19th. March 1786

DEAR SIR

I am just favored with yours of the 11 & 16. of Feby.[1] A newspaper since the date of the latter has verified to me your inauguration into the mysteries of Wedlock, of which you dropped a previous hint in the former. You will accept my sincerest congratulations on this event, with every wish for the happiness it promises. I join you cheerfully in the purchase from Taylor,[2] as preferable to taking it wholly to myself. The only circumstance I regret is that the first payment will rest with you alone if the conveyance should be accelerated. A few months will elapse inevitably before I shall be able to place on the spot my half of the sum, but the day shall be shortened as much as possible. I accede also fully to your idea of extending the purchase in that quarter. Perhaps we may be able to go beyond the thousand acres you have taken into view. But ought we not to explore the ground before we venture too far? Proximity of situation is but presumptive evidence of the quality of soil. The value of land depends on a variety of little circumstances which can only be judged of from inspection, and a knowledge of which gives a seller an undue advantage over an uninformed buyer. Can we not about the last of May or June take a turn into that district. I am in a manner determined on it myself. It will separate you but for a moment from New York, and may give us lights of great consequence. I have a project in my head, which if it hits your idea and can be effectuated may render such an excursion of decisive value to us.[3] I reserve it for oral communication.

"The Question of policy" you say "is whether it will be better to correct the vices of the Confederation, by recommendation gradually as it moves along, or by a Convention. If the latter should be determined on, the powers of the Virga. Commssrs are inadequate."[4] If all on whom the correction of these vices depends were well informed and well disposed, the mode would be of little moment. But as we have both ignorance and iniquity to control, we must defeat the designs of the latter by humouring the prejudices of the former. The efforts for bringing about a correction thro' the medium of Congress have miscarried. Let a Convention then be tried. If it succeeds in the first instance, it can be repeated as other defects force themselves on the public attention, and as the public mind becomes prepared for further remedies. The Assembly here would refer nothing to Congress. They would have revolted equally against a plenipotentiary commission to their deputies for the Convention. The option therefore lay between doing what was done and doing nothing. Whether a right choice was made time only can prove. I am not in general an advocate for temporizing or partial remedies. But a rigor in this respect, if pushed too far may hazard every thing. If the present paroxism of our affairs be totally neglected our case may become desperate. If any thing comes of the Convention it will probably be of a permanent not a temporary nature, which I think will be a great point. The mind feels a peculiar complacency, in seeing a good thing done when it is not subject to the trouble & uncertainty of doing it over again. The Commission is to be sure not filled to every man's mind. The History of it may be a subject for some future tête atête. You will be kind enough to forward the letter for Mr. Jefferson[5] and to be assured that I am with the sincerest affection Yr friend & Servt.

Js. MADISON JR

RC (DLC). Cover addressed. Docketed by JM.

[1] Monroe's letter of 16 Feb. 1786 has not been found.

[2] Probably John Taylor, later a prominent Albany speculator, who bought up land confiscated by the commissioners of forfeitures during the 1780s (David Maldwyn Ellis, *Landlords and Farmers in the Hudson-Mohawk Region, 1790–1850* [Ithaca, 1946], pp. 45, 128). Monroe and JM bought almost 1,000 acres for $1.50 an acre near the mouth of Oriskany Creek in upstate New York (Ketcham, *James Madison*, pp. 146–47).

[3] JM's project was to borrow a greater sum of money through Jefferson's private credit in France and make a large speculation in land in the Mohawk region on behalf of Jefferson, Monroe, and himself (JM to Jefferson, 12 Aug. 1786, Boyd, *Papers of Jefferson*, X, 234–36).

[4] This quotation must have been taken from the missing 16 Feb. letter from Monroe.

[5] JM to Jefferson, 18 Mar. 1786.

From James Monroe

NEW YORK March 19th. 1786.

DEAR SIR

I enclose you a copy of Mr. Jay's publication of the correspondence between him & Mr. Littlepage revis'd and corrected. It may furnish some matter of entertainment.[1] Jersey having taken into consideration the late requisition, the house of delegates resolv'd that having enter'd into the confederation upon terms highly disadvantageous to that State from the necessity of publick affrs. at the time, & a confidence that those points in which they were aggriev'd wod. be remedied & finding this was not the case & a compact founded in such unequal principles likely, by this acquiescence to be fetter'd on them, they wod. not therefore comply with the same untill their grievances were redress'd; in the course of their reasoning they mention the failure of some States to comply with the impost & seem to rest themselves on that ground in such a manner as to intimate that if they shod. comply their objections wod. be nearly remov'd. This resolution being brought before Congress gave great uneasiness. It is to be observ'd that here is no express act of the Legislature but merely the negative of a proposition to comply with the requisition in the branch with whom it shod. originate. They therefor[e] are in a less direct opposition to the confederation than if it were the act of the legislature—but being in a high degree reprehensible Congress resolv'd that a committee be appointed to attend the legislature & endeavor to prevail on them to rescind the resolution & acce[de] to the measure. The Committee were, Pinckney, G[or]ham & Grayson; they left us immediately & have n[ot] since return'd.[2] We have in the papers an act st[ated] to be of R. I. passing the impost in the full latitud[e] recommended by Congress. It is believ'd to be the case—in that event this State (New York) will most probably p[ass] it also. It is also sd. that Georgia hath p[assed] it. A report urging in very pointed terms a com[pli]ance with the recommendation for changing a[s] therein propos'd the 8th. of the articles of confeder-[a]tion is before Congress.[3] It will most probably pass altho' some gentn. in the Eastern States wod. willing[ly] throw it aside. The better dispos'd & better inform'd are aware of the impolicy of an opposition to it even if injurious to those States (wh. is not admitted) while they seek a more important alteration in the extension of the powers of Congress in the regula[ti]on of trade. You will before this have heard that I have it in my power to make you acquainted with a Lady of this State adopted of Virga.[4] I am sincerely yr. friend & servt.

JAS. MONROE

RC (DLC). Cover and enclosure missing. Docketed. Words within brackets restore the portion on the right margin damaged by careless mounting.

[1] The teapot-tempestuous controversy between Jay and Lewis Littlepage appeared in the New York *Daily Advertiser* between 6 and 12 Dec. 1785. By 7 Jan. 1786 editor Francis Childs had the correspondence in pamphlet form. It created a minor sensation at home and left a poor impression of American diplomats abroad (Davis, *The King's Chevalier*, pp. 122–25; Monroe to JM, 26 Dec. 1785; *Letters, Being the Whole of the Correspondence Between The Hon. John Jay, Esquire, and Mr. Lewis Littlepage. A Young Man whom Mr. Jay, when in Spain Patronized and took into his Family* [New York, 1786], Evans 19735).

[2] On 6 Mar. Congress learned of the New Jersey legislature's resolution not to meet the 27 Sept. 1785 requisition and referred it to a committee which reported the following day. Congress sent a committee (Charles Pinckney, Nathaniel Gorham, and William Grayson) to persuade the New Jersey legislature toward a more tractable course (*JCC*, XXX, 95–97).

3 On 27 Feb. Dane moved that a committee of five (Dane, Grayson, Mitchell, Monroe, and Kean) be appointed to examine the extent of the states' compliance with the alteration of Article VIII as recommended by Congress on 18 Apr. 1783. The committee was to consider and report upon what measures Congress might adopt for carrying into effect a federal rule for apportioning federal taxes on the several states. On 8 Mar. the committee reported (*JCC*, XXX, 85, 102–8).

4 Monroe's recently acquired bride, Elizabeth Kortright Monroe.

From William Grayson

New York March 22nd. 1786.

Dr Sir.

I should have done myself the pleasure of writing to you sooner, but really nothing occurr'd here of sufficient consequence to communicate. Congress from the small number of States that have come forward have remained in a kind of political torpor. They have of course taken no active steps, till lately that they have addressed the States on the subject of commerce. They were not long since a good deal alarmed at the conduct of sister Jersey. The House of delegates of that State in a moody fit declared that they would not only not comply with the requisition of 1785, but with no other requisition, until the 5 ℞ Ct. Impost was adopted. The State by this Act having declared Independance, Congress thought it was a matter that merited some attention. They therefore ordered a Comme. to go to Trenton & expostulate with the House on the impropriety of their conduct. The Comme. was heard, and the House were so complaisant as to rescind the resolution but they have passed no legislative act in affirmance of the requisition, & I very much doubt whether they will.[1] It may however have this effect, that other States will not be deterred (by her conduct in an absolute refusal) from passing the requisition. There is at present a greater prospect of the Impost than has been ever known; Georgia & Rhode Island have come into the measure, & it remains only with N. York to give her consent to make it productive. The Legislature is now sitting and deliberating on this subject but I doubt extremely whether the result will be favorable.

Our foreign affairs are very little altered one way or other since I had the pleasure of seeing you. Mr. Adams has done nothing with the Brittish Ministry; & Mr. Jay has done very little more with Mr. Gardoqui. The Commrs. in Europe have dispatched Mr. Barclay, Mr. Franks, Mr. Lamb & Mr. Randal[l] to negotiate with the Barbary powers & We understand that Mr. Barclay has actually arrived at the Court of the Emperor of Morocco. I am very apprehensive that no good will come of all this. These potentates are the most greedy & rapacious in the whole world, & yet we offer nothing worth their acceptance. In addition to this it is shrewdly to be suspected that the Maritime powers will underhandedly counteract all our measures. They cannot but be pleased to see American vessels (in addition to the dearness of labor) tottering under the accumulated pressure of Corsair insurance. Some people are seriously of opinion that we should turn Algerines ourselves; they must surely be out of their senses. However not more so, than some others who thought it for the interest of the U. S. to keep constantly at war with them. This latter sentimt. which proceeds from our Secy. of foreign affairs comes fully up to the idea of fighting for nothing & finding ourselves.

There has been a great contest in Jersey for the Argent papier; but though it went triumphantly through the lower house, it was lost in the Council, 8 to 5. Some of the Members who were adverse to it, have been burn't in effigy, in particular Colo. Ogden at, or near, Elizabeth town. The old Governor was drawn up to the stake but pardoned, on account of his having been the first magistrate. This same Jersey bill was one of the most iniquitous things I ever saw in my life; the money was a tender; if it was refused, the debt was suspended for 12. years, in the mean time the act of limitation ran of course, which in effect destroyed it.[2] Jersey has not been singular in her attempts at cheating. In this place a bill is depending, of the same purport as that of Jersey, & which it is probable will pass, although it is violently opposed by the upright & respectable part of the Commy.[3] The Antients were surely men of more candor than We are. They contended openly for an abolition of debts in so many words, while we strive as hard for the same thing under the decent & specious pretense of a circulating medium. Montesquieu was not wrong when he said the democratical might be as tyrannical as the despotic; for where is there a greater act of despotism than that of issuing paper to depreciate for the purpose of paying debts on easy terms. If Lord Effingham is right that an act agt. the Constitution is void, surely paper money with a tender annexed to it is void, for it is not an attack upon property,[4] the security of which is made a fundamental in every State in the Union. There has been some serious thoughts in the minds of some of the Members of Congress to recommend to the States the meeting of a general Convention, to consider of an alteration of the Confœderation, & there is a motion to this effect

now under consideration. It is contended that the present Confederation is utterly inefficient, and that if it remains much longer in its'
present State of imbecillity we shall be one of the most contemptible
Nations on the face of the Earth: for my own part I have not yet made
up my mind on the subject. I am doubtful whether it is not better to
bear those ills we have than fly to others that we know not of. I am
however in no doubt about the weakness of the fœderal Government;
if it was weaker notwithstanding, it would answer if the States had
power as in the United Netherlands the fœderal Governmt. is weak but
the Individual States are strong. It is no wonder our Government should
not work well, being formed on the Dutch model where circumstances
are so materially different. Your friend Colo. Monro has taken to himself a Wife out of the house of Kortright. Mr. King is to be married
in a few days to Miss Alsop. Mr. Gerry is already Married to Miss
Thomson. Mr. Houston is to be married to Miss Mary Bayard. Many
more maneuvres are going forwd. among the members of Congress
which seems to portend a conjunction copulative. In short I think we
have got into Calypso's Island. I heartily wish you were here: as I have
a great desire to see you figure in the character of a married man.

I tryed to get you the book respecting canals, but all were sold but
one, which at Genl. Washingtons desire I sent to him. All I could do
was to imploy the book seller to import some this will be done with all
convenient speed. Out of the importation I have engaged 5. Copies:
two for you, two for myself & one for the Potowmack people. I remain
with the greatest friendship Yr. Most Obed Serv

WILLM. GRAYSON

RC (DLC). Cover missing. Docketed by JM.

1 The New Jersey resolution declining payment of the congressional requisition
assessed 27 Sept. 1785 was read in Congress on 6 Mar. 1786. Grayson was chairman
of the committee considering this action, and on 7 Mar. a three-man delegation,
headed by Charles Pinckney and including Grayson, was appointed to visit the state
legislature and to request their reconsideration of the resolution. On 22 Mar. Pinckney reported that the New Jersey legislature had rescinded their opposition to the
requisition but passed no measures for complying with its assessment (JCC, XXX,
95–97, 122). The whole affair was something of a farce since not a single state complied with the 1785 requisition (Ferguson, Power of the Purse, p. 224).

2 Grayson was critical of New Jersey emissions of paper money, but in fact the
paper currency of that state emitted between 1709 and 1786 was faithfully and punctually redeemed. For a discussion of New Jersey finances, see Richard A. Lester,
"Currency Issues to Overcome Depressions in Delaware, New Jersey, New York
and Maryland, 1715–37," Journal of Political Economy, XLVII (1939), 199. William
Livingston was "the old Governor."

3 In 1786, New York approved an emission of £200,000 to establish funds for a land bank and partially to repay interest due on previous loans (Nettels, *Emergence of a National Economy*, p. 83). The issue was so successful, Nettels observed, "the paper often passed at par."

4 From the context Grayson's mind was ahead of his pen. He obviously meant to ask rhetorically, "Is it not an attack upon property?"

From John Francis Mercer

MARLBRO. Mar 28, 1786

DEAR SIR

I return'd yesterday on my way to the General Court from Maryland where I had the pleasure of receiving your favor from Richmond. The sequel of proceedings which you enumerated by no means coincided with my opinions, but that does not make them less right. I have enclosed you a statement of my political doctrines, which from what I recollect will hardly meet with your approbation.[1] I have dispersed them throughout the County I represented, in order to make them acquainted with my Sentiments, & to give them an opportunity of expressing their concurrence or disaprobation the next Election. I have not yet determined with myself whether I shall serve any longer perhaps my County will determine for me—whether they reject me or not will not occasion one moments concern.[2] I shall have left a record of my Opinions with them, that will at least present them in as fair a veiw as they merit I would not wish to be calumniated—but my Ambition becomes every day more limited—it is now only to be thought a Good Man, or only to think so myself. A[3] man cannot be well contracted to a narrower Circle. I really wish well to America & in general & to this State particularly—few circumstances coud give me more pleasure than to see these Governments answer the ends that were expected—but my doubts go far beyond my hopes. The confœderal Government was always an object of derision rather than anything else with me—its like a Mans attempting to walk with both legs cut off. All our Executives are one water mixed with water—wishy washy Stuff. A british Gentleman travelling with 3,000 a year or any rich Citizen among ourselves will command more respect than the whole Muster of Governmental fry put together. Can such Men have confidence enough to carry the laws into Execution agt. a powerful Citizen or a Combination of them. In Maryland it was try'd the other day & it exactly cost £2000 their Currency to be acquitted of a very black murder, committed by a very vicious man too, but who happened to have powerful Connexions. If the whole Governments coud be amalgamated & made into a tolerabl[y] good one, I confess it woud be very satisfactory to me. Coud I see a chance of this I shoud not begrudge spend-[ing] a year or two more in a very thankless mode of life. I shall be over into this part of the World with my family in the Month of Ma[y.] I shall be really happy to see you here before you go to Maryland & it woud not be out of your way in many respects. Adeiu & believe me to be a very sincere friend & Sert.

JOHN F MERCER

RC (DLC). Cover missing. Docketed by JM. Enclosure not found.

[1] As JM and Mercer had taken opposite sides on key issues during the Oct. 1785 General Assembly, it is possible JM's lost letter (of ca. 21 Jan. 1786) alluded to such pending matters as the criminal punishment, Assize Court, and Port bills. See JM to Monroe, 9 Dec. 1785, and the commentary on Mercer's "mischief" in JM to Jefferson, 22 Jan. 1786.

[2] Mercer represented Stafford County in the 1785 House but did not serve in 1786 (Swem and Williams, *Register*, pp. 22, 25).

[3] Mercer wrote "I," but obviously meant "A."

APPENDIX A

Legislation Introduced by Madison, 1784–1786

The preserved legislative documents JM wrote while serving in the Virginia House of Delegates from May 1784 to January 1786 are printed in the regular sections of this work. Several exceptions to the rules of authorship are also carried in the main portion because of strong circumstantial evidence, usually when JM both introduced a bill and was then directed to carry the approved legislation forward to the Senate—a courtesy ordinarily extended to the author of a measure. There were other bills and resolutions which JM introduced but seems to have been connected with only in an official capacity, such as chairman of either the Committee on Commerce or the Committee for Courts of Justice. These matters do not fall within the editorial guidelines for documents deserving full textual treatment. Accordingly, the legislation listed below was introduced by JM but no Ms in his handwriting has been found, and neither circumstances nor external evidence led the editors to conclude that JM was concerned with their preparation, floor support, or final enactment.

May 1784 session

25 May   Resolution recommending the establishment of a lumber inspection office at Norfolk and Portsmouth

October 1784 session

6 Nov.   Resolution recommending the continuance of the commodity inspection laws

6 Nov.   Resolution recommending renewal of the 1781 paper-money act

6 Nov.   Resolution favoring a lapsing of the wartime act for taking a census and determining the extent of taxable lands

6 Nov.   Resolution recommending renewal of the pension act of 1782

11 Nov. Bill amending the act "for giving further time to enter certificates for settlement rights, and for locating warrants upon pre-emption rights"

16 Nov. Bill for renewing the paper-money act

16 Nov. Bill for renewing the pension act of 1782

18 Nov. Resolution creating a welcoming committee for Lafayette

25 Nov. Resolution concerning the estate of Stephen Yancey

27 Nov. Resolution favoring a bill to create circuit courts

3 Dec.   Resolution authorizing the executive to place wounded veterans on the pension list

18 Dec. Bill concerning the estate of Stephen Yancey

18 Dec. Bill for incorporating the Society of the Cincinnati

22 Dec. Resolution referring the petition of John Conrad to the governor and council

23 Dec. Amendments to a bill repealing parts of an act establishing the town of Louisville

24 Dec. Act providing arms and ammunition for the defense of the Commonwealth

October 1785 session

28 Oct. Resolution recommending continuance of the 1781 act for adjusting claims for property impressed for public service

28 Oct. Resolution recommending continuance of the 1784 act concerning certificates for settlement rights

28 Oct. Resolution recommending discontinuance of the 1781 paper-money act

31 Oct. Bill for continuing the act adjusting claims for property impressed for public service

31 Oct. Bill for continuing the act concerning certificates for settlement rights

31 Oct. One hundred seventeen [eighteen] of the printed bills contained in the Revised Code (see Bills for a Revised State Code of Laws, 31 Oct. 1785)

9 Nov. Bill amending the acts concerning the appointments of sheriffs

9 Nov. Resolution rejecting the petition of Burditt Ashton

14 Nov. Bill amending the act regulating the appointment of delegates to Congress

22 Nov. Bill reviving the act regulating and collecting certain officers' fees

26 Nov. Bill amending the act for the establishment of Courts of Assize

3 Jan. Bill suspending operation of the act for the establishment of Courts of Assize

APPENDIX B

Meteorological Journal for Orange County, Virginia, in Madison's Hand

1–18 April, 9 July–22 August 1784
10 February–28 August 1785
2 February–31 March 1786

EDITORIAL NOTE

The spring following the unusually severe winter of 1783–1784 seemed a propitious time to begin collecting information on the vagaries of weather in the Virginia Piedmont. JM and other members of the Madison family eagerly took on the task which must have grown out of the conversations JM held with Jefferson at Philadelphia when the two congressmen were able to place legislative concerns aside. Moreover, JM and Jefferson were both members of the American Philosophical Society, which was then in search of meteorological information on the great winter storms of 1779–1780 (Hindle, *Pursuit of Science in Revolutionary America*, p. 348). A discourse on Buffon probably had also whetted their intellectual appetites, and they were particularly intrigued by the Frenchman's idea that solar energy was not the sole source of planetary heat. Jefferson appears to have misinterpreted Buffon's theories to JM, but he was ardent if not accurate, and determined to convince his fellow Virginians they could do something about the weather besides talk about it—they could record it.

Jefferson kept a personal weather record from 1776 through 1820 and at one time hoped that by collecting information from various points in Virginia he might develop a meteorological map with charts on wind directions and air temperatures for the state (Edwin T. Martin, *Thomas Jefferson: Scientist* [New York, 1952], pp. 134, 141–42). In 1784 he first enlisted the Reverend James Madison of Williamsburg in the projected accumulation of meteorological information, then appealed to JM to join the endeavor as the Piedmont recorder. The clergyman procured a thermometer and set about the business, but both James Madisons found barometers in short supply. JM began his recordings after he received Jefferson's suggestion that was tantamount to an order. "It will be an amusement to you and may become useful," Jefferson ventured (16 Mar. 1784) Jefferson's explicitness made a refusal to keep the journal unthinkable, and so on 1 April 1784 JM launched the business despite the lack of a device for recording the barometric pressure. The endeavor was amateurish, but not exacting, and it seems certain that James Madison, Sr., and perhaps one or two of JM's brothers were interested in the daily ritual to the point that they became involved. Jefferson's spark ignited their interest at a time when it was commonly thought that comparative meteorological records might be helpful in combating epidemics, aid in the selection of planting seasons, and also determine if human settlements and the blows of civilization affected climate (Raymond Phineas Stearns, *Science in the British Colonies of America* [Urbana, Ill., 1970], pp. 595–96).

The motives were there, but the mechanisms were not. No barometer was procured during 1784; so JM's entries remained meager and based mainly on visual observations. The entries from 1 April 1784 to 18 April 1784 are in his hand-printing. His father (or brothers) then resumed the record on 10 May and kept entries through 7 July. On 8 July JM resumed his record-keeping, but occasional entries (such as the observation on birds of 15 July) are not in his hand. After JM departed on his northern trip (ca. 23 Aug. 1784) the family kept records until 10 February 1785, when JM was back at the Orange County homestead. His entries then carry forward to 28 August 1785—the departure date for another northern excursion—and JM did not resume the weather-watcher's role at Montpelier until 2 February 1786. JM's entries then carried down to 25 June, when he was called away by official duties. The remaining entries for 1786–1789 are in other hands. The final page of the first notebook contains a list of French authors and several specific titles. This list was probably made near the outset of the period when Jefferson was acting as JM's book-buying agent in Paris between 1785 and 1788. The second notebook begins with a 1 January 1789 entry and ends 26 April 1793, but only the entries of 17 June–19 August 1792 and 13–26 April 1793 are in JM's hand. Clearly the journal-keeping had long since become a family endeavor, kept more for the pleasure of the keeping than for the usefulness of the information. Other notebooks belonging in the set, for the period 1793 to 1796, are owned by the Presbyterian Historical Society of Philadelphia. The entries printed below are typical and cover the longest sustained period of JM's personal involvement.

1784	Thermr. sun rise	Baromr. sun rise	Wind sun rise	Weather sun rise	Thermr. 4 oC P.M.	Baromr. 4 oC P.M.	Wind 4 oC P.M.	Weather 4 oC P.M.	Shooting or falling of leaves of trees: flowers, other remarkable plants	Appearance or disappearance of birds &c.	Miscellanea
April 1			W if any	sky muddy			N.E. if any	sky muddy		Wild geese flying N.ward	
2			N.E.	cloudy			N.E.	ground covered with snow and snowing with rain			
3			N.E.	rainy			N.E.	clear, tops of bl[ue]: ridge covered with snow			
4			S.W.	clear			N.E.	clear			
5			S W	clear			S.	clear			
6			S.	clear			W.	flying clouds	Garden peas first up. Blue Hyacinths blossom		
7			W	clear. ground sprinkled with snow. bl: ridge covered			W.	clear			
8			S.W.	clear. snow on bl. ridge disappears			N.W.	clear	White do. blossom		
9			S.	cloudy			N.E.	sky muddy, air thick	Jonquils blossom		

April 10	N.E.	rainy, trees covered with sleet	S.W.	cloudy & damp but no rain sleet still on trees	
11	S.W.	thick fog	N.W.	clear	Daffidils blossom.
12	N.	clear	W.	clear	
13	S.W. if any	air thick, sky muddy	S.	air thick & smokey	Hickories on tops of S.W. Mountains begin to bud
14	S.	cloudy & moist	W.	cloudy with light showers	
15	W.	flying clouds	N.W.	clear	
16	S.W.	clear, except muddy to westward	N.W.	clear	Peach-trees begin to blossom
17	N.	clear	N.	clear	Cherry trees begin to blossom
18	N	clear	N E	sky muddy	
[no entries 19 April–9 May] N.E.					
May 10	S.W.	Cloudy	S.W.	Thunder cloud to the W. but no Rain	Forwd. Peas Podded
11	S.W.	Fair		Fair	
12	North-wdy.	Fair & Hot		Fair & very Hot	6 Weeks' Pease Blossom

1784	Thermr. sun rise	Baromr. sun rise	Wind sun rise	Weather sun rise	Thermr. 4 oC P.M.	Baromr. 4 oC P.M.	Wind 4 oC P.M.	Weather 4 oC P.M.	Shooting or falling of leaves of trees: flowers, other remarkable plants	Appearance or disapearance of birds &c.	Miscellanea
May 13			N.	Fair & Hot				Cloudy all day	Dble rows forwd. Pease, come up		
14				Fair & cool				Fair	Winsor Beans blossom		
15				Fair & pleasant				Thunder & Rain & hard wind			
16			E.	Fair			E.	Hard Thunder & much Rain			
17			E.	Cloudy & foggy			E.NE	Cloudy & misty			
18			E.	Cloudy & misty.			E.	Misty &c			
19			E	Rain			S W.	Clouds dispersing			
20			S.W.	Fog & cloudy towards the G. Mountains			S.	Fair & pleasant			
21			Southerly	Fair, Cool			N. NE	Fair & pleasant			

Date	Wind	Weather	Wind	Weather	Observations	
May 22	N.	Fair		Clouds gathering up.		
23	E.	Rainy & misty	E by N	Cloudy & Misty	Strawberrys gathered Duke Cherrys eatable	Purple in the Shade, 12 O,Clock Bells & Sweet Wns. in Blossom.
24	E	Hard Rain	S.	clear	Forward Pease first gathered.	
25	S.E.	Foggy	S.W.	Thunder cloud at West		
26	S E	Cloudy & a little Rain	N E	Thunder cloud & Showery		
27	S W.	Flying clouds	Northy.	Clear		
28	S Wy.	Clear.	N	Clear		
29	S.W.	Clear & pleasant	N W	Clear & Windy		
30	S W	Clear	N E	Clear.		
31	S W.	Clear	S W.	Clear.		
June 1	W by S	Clear.	S W.	Cloudy to the West	Dble rows of forwd. Peas begin to blossom	
2	S W.	Sky muddy	N. E.	Violent Gust. Wind shifted from W. to N. & N.E		Horseearflies began to be plenty

1784	Thermr. sun rise	Baromr. sun rise	Wind sun rise	Weather sun rise	Thermr. 4 oC P.M.	Baromr. 4 oC P.M.	Wind 4 oC P.M.	Weather 4 oC P.M.	Shooting or falling of leaves of trees: flowers, other remarkable plants	Appearance or disapearance of birds &c.	Miscellanea
June 3			N E	Sky muddy			WSW	Sky muddy		Light flies appear'd	
4			WSW	Clear & cool							
5			W.	Clear			SW. vering to S.				
6			W.	Flying Clouds			S W.	Hard Rain & wind			
7			N E by N.	Flying Clouds			N.	Clear & pleasant			
8			N.	Cloudy, to the West & Mountains			N E	Cloudy	Windsor Beans first drest		
9			N E.	Cloudy & misty			S W.	Cloud to the W. & N.W. & Rain at night			
10			N E.	Clear but band of clouds towards blue ridge			N E	Clear			
11			Westerly.	Cloudy.			S W. by W.	Smoaky			

June					
12	W.	Cloudy.		Cloudy wth. some Thunder little rain	
13	S W	small Rain	N E	Clouds rising	
14	N E.	Cool & Fair. Clouds to the E.			
15	S Easterly.	Cloudy.	E.	Cool after small Rain	
16	S E.	Fog. at G. Mount. & very cool.		Clear & cool	
17	Southerly	Clear & cool		Clear & cool	
18	Southerly.	Clear & cool.		Clear	
19		Smokey.		Smokey & Hot	
20		Do. & Hot.	S W	Clcud to the W.	
21	S by W.	Sky Muddy	S W.	smokey Clear, hot & dry	
22	S W	Cloudy	S E.	Cloudy.	
23	S W	Foggy	S at 5 o'Clock.	Clcud to the West & Thunr.	
24		very hot	S.	very Hot & dry	
25	S W	Clear & very hot	N	Clear & very hot & dry	
26	S W	Clear & very hot	S.	Clouds & Thunder & Hot	Young Martin's begin to fly

1784	Thermr. sun rise	Baromr. sun rise	Wind sun rise	Weather sun rise	Thermr. 4 oC P.M.	Baromr. 4 oC P.M.	Wind 4 oC P.M.	Weather 4 oC P.M.	Shooting or falling of leaves of trees: flowers, other remarkable plants	Appearance or disappearance of birds &c.	Miscellanea
June 27			S W	Clear & hot			N E	Thunder clouds			
28			N E	Cloudy & cool			N.	Clear & pleasant			
29			E	Fog towds. the mounts.			S E	Clear & cool			
30			S W.	very cloudy.			N E	Rain.			
July 1			N E	Cloudy.				Clear			
2			S W	Flying Clouds.				Cloudy			
3			S W	Clear			N W	Rain. Clouds Rise N			
4			N E	Cloudy			S W	Clear			
5			S W	Fog rising			N W.	some Clouds after hard Rains & wind			
6			N.	Clear & cool			changes from N.E to SW	clear & cool			
7			S. W	clear & cool			S.W.	clear & cool			
8			S. W	clear				clear			
9			N. E	clear			S.W.	clear & cool			
10			N. E.	clear			N.E.	cloudy & misty			
11			N. E.	cloudy after rainy night			N.E.	very cloudy			
12			N. E.	cloudy			S.	cloudy			

Date	Wind	Weather	Wind	Weather	Notes
July 13	S.W. by W.	cloudy	S.	flying clouds	Sawyers, or Cherry-dorries first heard
14	S	foggy	S.W.	clear	
15	S. W.	clear	S.W.	clear	
16	S.	somewhat cloudy	S.	cloud gathering in West & N. West 6 oClock shower of rain	
17	N.	somewhat cloudy	N.E.	clear	
18	N. W.	clear	N.E.	clear	
19	N. E.	cloudy. 8 oCl: rainy	S. S.W.	rainy all day	
20	S. W.	clearing after much rain	S.W.	clear	
21	S. W.	clear	S.W.	clear	
22	S. W.	clear	S.W.	clear	
23	S. W.	somewhat cloudy	S. W.	light shower	
24	E	damp & foggy	S. W.	clear after shower to W bearing away to N.E	
25	S. W.	somewhat cloudy	S. W.	pretty clear	
26	S. W.	cloudy 7 oC. beging to rain	S. S.E.	clear	

1784	Thermr. sun rise	Baromr. sun rise	Wind sun rise	Weather sun rise	Thermr. 4 oC P.M.	Baromr. 4 oC P.M.	Wind 4 oC P.M.	Weather 4 oC P.M.	Shooting or falling of leaves of trees: flowers, other remarkable plants	Appearance or disappearance of birds &c.	Miscellanea
[July] 27			S. W. W	clear			N. W.	clear			
28				clear				clear 8 oC. shower			
29			N. E.	somewhat cloudy			N. E.	somewhat cloudy			
30			N. E.	cloudy ½ after 2 oC. rains			S. S.W.	cloudy after light shower			
31			S. E.	cloudy			S.	cloudy with sprinkling of rain			
Augst. 1			S	cloudy			S. S.W.	clear			
2			S	cloudy			N. W.	black cloud S.E.			
3			S. W.	little Foggy			S. S.W.	clear after cloud gone from W to S.E.			
4			S. W.	clear			S. S.W.	clear. 6 oC. small shower of rain			
5			N E	cloudy			N. E.	no clouds but thick atmosphere			
6			N E	clear			N. E.	clear			

Augst. 7	N.E by E	clear	S.	somewhat cloudy
8	S.	air thick	S SE.	air thick
9	S. S.E.	cloudy 8 oC. showry	N E	clouds beginni[n]g to break in N after considerable rain
10	W	foggy W.ward	N. E	clear
11	N. E	somewhat cloudy	S. W	clear
12	S SE	cloudy 8 oC. light rain	S. SW	cloudy after light rain since 8 oC.
13	SW by W	drisley	S	clear except bank of cloud W & N W
14	SE by E	clear except some fog	S. W	clear
Sunday 15	S.	clear. very hot	S. S.W.	clear extremely hot
16	S. W.	clear very hot	S.	cloud rising N.W. 5 oC. shower of rain extremely hot
17	S SW.	thick fog very hot	S. W.	clear extremely hot

1784	Thermr. sun rise	Baromr. sun rise	Wind sun rise	Weather sun rise	Thermr. 4 oC P.M.	Baromr. 4 oC P.M.	Wind 4 oC P.M.	Weather 4 oC P.M.	Shooting or falling of leaves of trees: flowers, other remarkable plants	Appearance or disappearance of birds &c.	Miscellanea
[August] 18			S. W	somewhat cloudy 2 oC. cloud passing N.eastwardly, very hot			N E	heavy cloud N E with approaching rain from 4 to 6 oC. successive thunder showers extremely hot			
19			S W	cloudy. from 12 to 1 oC rain hot			N.	clear. air cooler			
20			S. E.	clear			N E.	clear			
21			N. E	somewhat cloudy			S W	clear			
22			S. W.	raining very moderately			S W	cloudy without rain since 10 oC A.M.			

1785	Ther: s.rise	Wind do.	Weather sunrise	Thermr. 4 oC. p.m.	Wind do.	Weather 4 oC. P.M.	Shooting or falling of leaves of trees: flowers, other remarkable plants	Appearance or disappearance of birds &c.	Miscellanea
Febr. 10	49 ½	SW	fair	56 ½	S	Sky somewhat muddy			
11	49 ½	NE by E	cloudy	55	E	somewhat cloudy			
12	46.	S.W.	cloudy & beginning to snow	46	W	fair and the ground naked			
13	40.	N.E.	broken clouds in NW.	43	W	fair			
14	37	NE by E	fair except bank of cloud N.W.	40	N	fair			
15	35 ½	SW	somewhat cloudy	42.	S	fair			
16	41.	S	Atmosphere thick	54	S	somewhat cloudy, atmosphere very thick			
17	44	NE	fair	48	E	fair			
18	38 ½	E.	somewhat cloudy	45	E	fair except somewhat cloudy NW			
19	43	S.E	somewhat cloudy	48	E	fair			
20	44	SSW	cloudy NW	52	S	somewhat cloudy			
21	44 ½	SW	fair	49	NW	fair and very windy			
22	42	S.E	fair	46	E	fair			
23	40	S.	fair	47	NE	fair			
24	48	NE	snow & rain, the latter freezing on the trees	46	SW	fair, very little snow or rain having fallen			
25	41	NW.	wind clouds	42	N	fair			
26	35	SW	fair	38	N	cloudy, snowing on Great Mountains			

1785	Ther: s.rise	Wind do.	Weather sunrise	Thermr. 4 oC. P.M.	Wind do.	Weather 4 oC. P.M.	Shooting or falling of leaves of trees: flowers, other remarkable plants	Appearance or disappearance of birds &c.	Miscellanea
27	34	N	fair	41	N	fair			
28	34	N	fair	43	W	sky somewhat muddy			
March 1	38	NE	somewhat cloudy	46 ½	E.	somewhat cloudy			
2	40	N.	fair, ground thinly covered with snow during night	40	N.	cloudy, snow gone			
3	38	SW	fair	44	S	fair			
4	42	S	cloudy	47	S	cloudy			
5	46	S	thick fogg	55 ½	SW	fair		Wild geese flying Northward	
6	50	S.W.	bank of cloud NW.	56	S	sky somewhat muddy			
7	51 ½	NE	cloudy	57	NE	cloudy NW			
8	46	NE	cloudy & beging to rain, light[nin]g SW.	45	N.E.	wet, rain freezing on trees			
9	42	N	cloudy, trees & covered with sleet	48	W	fair & windy			
10	38	SW	fair	39 ½	W	fair & windy			
11	32	NW	fair	41	W	fair			
12	37	S	fair	46	SW	fair			Garden peas first sown
13	44	S.	cloudy & moist	50	NW	moderate rain			
14	46	NE	rainy	52	S.W	fair, windy			
15	38	W	fair	41	W	fair, windy			

Date	Temp	Wind	Weather	Temp	Wind	Weather	Notes
March 16	*32	NE.	fair, windy. *Therm. at 21° in S.W porch	35 ½	N	fair windy	
17	30	SW	fair	41	S	fair	
18	40	S.	cloudy	42	S.W.	cloudy	
19	41 ½	NE	rainy	42 ½	NE	mixture of light rain & snow	Crow black birds first observed
20	42	E	clouds getting high & thin	46	SE	cloudy mixture of rain & snow beginning to fall	
21	41	S	ground sprinkled with snow, cloudy & foggy	44	N	cloudy	
22	44	SW	foggy	51 ½	NW	fair & windy	
23	42	SW	fair	50	N	fair	
24	44	E	fair	43	SW	snowing	
25	42	SW	cloudy ground sprinkled with rain	48	NE	cloudy	
26	43	E	cloudy	44	E	cloudy 6 oC. ground covered with snow & still snowing	
27	41	NE	cloudy ground thinly covered with snow	48	NW	fair, snow gone	
28	42	SW	fair	58	S.	fair	Martins appear.
29	52	E	cloudy	53	NE	light rain	Windsor beans first sown
30	58	S.W	clouds breaking away after very rainy night	59	SW	fair & windy after 2 shewers with violent wind from S.W. one at 10 oC. other at ½ past 1	

1785	Ther: sun-rise	Wind sun-rise	Weather sunrise	Thermr. 4 oC. P.M.	Wind do.	Weather 4 oC. P.M.	Shooting or falling of leaves of trees: flowers, other remarkable plants	Appearance or disappearance of birds &c.	Miscellanea
31	52	S.W.	fair	59	from W to NW	flying clouds, extremely blustering	daffidil begins to blossom		
Apl. 1	50	E.	fair	58 ½	N	fair			
2	48	NE	cloudy 8 oC. rain, 2 oC. rain & Hail	46	S.W.	snowing, ground nearly covered ¾ after 4. clearing			
3	38	S.W	clear. Blue ridge covered with snow	44	from W to NW	flying Clouds Wind blustering, shower of snow on blue ridge			
4	40	S.W.	fair	44 ½	W	flying clouds, strong wind	White & blue Hyacinths or march pinks begin to blossom		
5	44	N	fair	53	N	fair			
6	48	E	fair	52	E	cloudy			
7	47	E	cloudy	47 ½	NE	very light rain since 8 oC			
8	48	E	fair	50	W	flying clouds	Jonquil begins to blossom		
9	46	SW	fair	50	W	broken clouds			
10	48	SW.	fair	56	NW	fair			
11	52	SSW	fair	66	W	fair	{Peach trees begin to blossom & Asparagus to shoot		

Date	Temp	Wind	Weather	Temp	Wind	Weather	Plants	Notes
Aprl. 12	62	N.NE	fair	65	E	fair. Atmosphere thick NW	Garden peas first up—	WhipperWill first heard.
13	57	SE.	fair, atmosphere thick NW	64	N	fair. Atmosphere thick NW		
14	51	NE	somewhat cloudy	52	SE	sky muddy		
15	48	SW	atmosphere very thick parculy. NW	53	N.E	fair atmosphere thick NW		
16	44	E	fair. large white frost wch. killed some of for-warded cherries	55	E	fair	Mulberry budding Plum Tree be-ging. to leaf.	
17	45	SW	somewhat cloudy. atmosphere thick	59 ½	S.W	atmosphere thick NW sky some-what cloudy	Cherry Tree be-gins to blossom.	
18	59	S.W	Atmosphere thick & somewhat cloudy	67 ½	SW	somewhat cloudy		
19	59	NE	rainy	55	NE	rainy. Sun sets clear	Peach trees in full blossom Hickory buds opening on tops of mountains	
20	46	W	fair, ground thinly Frozen ½ after 8 dash of snow	46	N	somewhat cloudy		
21	42 ½	SW.	fair, black frost ¾ Inch high in garden. ice in branches, cherries in part killed, & some peaches	55	SW.	fair. Daffidil blossoms killed. Jonquil do. touched by fr[ost]	Poplars leafing, Mulberry Buds openg.	
22	48	S.W.	fair	65	S.	fair		Asparagus at dinner.

1785	Ther: sunrise	Wind sunrise	Weather sunrise	Thermr. 4 oC. P.M.	Wind do.	Weather 4 oC. P.M.	Shooting or falling of leaves of trees: flowers, other remarkable plants	Appearance or disappearance of birds &c.	Miscellanea
23	58	S	fair, atmosphere thick N.W.	69	S	fair, atmosphere thick NW	Gooseberry bushes in blossom		
24	65	S.	fair, sky muddy NW	77	S	fair, atmosphere thick NW	Cherry trees & plum tree in full blossom		
25	64	E	fair	78	S	fair, atmosphere thick NW			
26	71	S	fair, atmosphere thick NW	81 ½	S	fair, atmosphere thick NW	peach blossoms falling		
27	72	S.	fair atmosphere thick NW	82	S.	fair, atmosphere thick NW			
28	70	S	fair atmosphere thick NW	82	S	fair, atmosphere thick NW	tulip in blossom		
29	72	S.	Cloudy	78		cloudy, light shower with some thunder	Cherry blossoms falling		
30	69	NE	fair	68	NW	somewhat cloudy			
May 1	56	SE	fair	63	N	fair			
2	56	NE	somewhat cloudy	60	E	cloudy			
3	54		raing. moderately	55 ½	NE	raining still moderately			
4	55	NE	still raining 8 oCl. fair	62	N	fair			
5	58	NNE	somewhat cloudy & moist	65	S	showery	Garden peas begin to blossom about 14 inches high		

May 6	60	N.NW	cloudy & foggy	66	NE.	clouded Horison NW. ½ after 6 oC. thunder clouds NE & S.E.	
7	59	N	fair	65	N	fair	
8	58	NW	fair	66 ½	N	fair	
9	62	E	fair	69 ½	W	fair	Narsissus firs: in blossom
10	62	SW	fair	65	SE	somewhat Cloudy	Piony's blowing, Primrose b ow-ing / Monthly honeysuckle blowing
11	59	NE	raining	61	NE	still raining	Snowdrop in blossom [now?]
12	60	NW	thick fog	66	S.	fair	Woodbine in blossom
13	60	SW	sky muddy	69	SSW	fair	
14	62	SW	fair	64	N	showery	
15	60	SW	fair	65	S by W	cloudy	
16	63	SW	somewhat cloudy	68	N.	somewhat cloudy	
17	61	NNE	fair	66	E	somewhat cloudy	Locusts in blos-som
18	61	S	fair	72	SW b[y] W	somewhat cloudy	
19	66	NE	rainy	70	N	fair	
20	62	W	fair	70	SSW	somewhat cloudy	
21	67	E	fair	70	W	thunder cloud NNE	
22	67	SW	cloudy & damp 7 oC. raining	66	NE	still raining, a great deal hav-ing fallen	Strawberries be-ginning to redden
23	63	NNE	cloudy & foggy	67	SW by W	nearly fair	

1785	Ther: sunrise	Wind sunrise	Weather sunrise	Thermr. 4 oC. P.M.	Wind do.	Weather 4 oC. P.M.	Shooting or falling of leaves of trees: flowers, other remarkable plants	Appearance or disappearance of birds &c.	Miscellanea
24	63	SSW	clouds breaking after much rain during the night	68 ½	NWW	fair	Cherries beginning to redden		
25	63	SW	fair	70	SW	fair	Damask rose blossoms		
26	63	N	fair	68	W	fair			
27	60	SW	fair	65	N	fair			
28	58	SW	fair	64	NNE	scattered & moist clouds	Strawberries beginning to be ripe		
29	58	SW b[y] W	fair	68	SW	fair		Cherry birds appear. Horse-ear flies first observed	
30	62	SSW	fair	72	E	sky somewhat muddy showery	Garden peas first at dinner		
31	67	E	cloudy, from 6 oC: light rain	67	NE	showery	Cherries begin to be ripe		
June 1	64	SW	fair	76 ½	SW b[y] S	fair			
2	68	SW by W	fair	80 ½	S	fair 8 oCl. light light shower of rain			
3	74 ½	NE	fair	80 ½	W by S	thunder shower passing from NW to NE 5 oC heavy show[er]		Cherry birds disappear	
4	73	SW	foggy ½ after 2 oC. thunder shower	76	W	fair 9 oC. thunder shower			

[June]							
5	72	SSW	fair	82	SSW	fair, except some appearance of thunder cloud forming W.	
6	76	NNE	somewhat cloudy	81 ½	E	somewhat cloudy still very thick & somewhat misty	
7	74	E	very thick & dripping rain	72 ½	E	still thick, some rain havg. fallen	
8	67 ½	NE	still thick, considerable rain havg. fallen	67	NE	rain having fallen since morning	
9	64	NE	still thick	69	ESE	cloucs dispersing, 6 oC. cloudy & misty	
10	67	NE	still very thick & foggy	74	NE	some watery clouds	
11	71	NNE	thick fog	80	WSW	fair, except a distant thunder cloud NNE. 4h. 40 m. hard [thunder?] between 7 & 9 oC. 2 powerful rains with much lightening from NW & N.	a red & white double pink full blown
12	73	SW	somewhat cloudy	80	W	fair 8 oC. small shower of rain	
13	72 ½	SW	fair	82	SSW	fair	Lilly first blown also Hollyhock
14	76	NNE	somewhat cloudy	86	NE	fair 6H. 30m. light shower. much thunder but not [illegible]	

535

1785	Ther: sunrise	Wind sunrise	Weather sunrise	Thermr. 4 oC. P.M.	Wind do.	Weather 4 oC. P.M.	Shooting or falling of leaves of trees: flowers, other remarkable plants	Appearance or disappearance of birds &c.	Miscellanea
[June] 15	75	SW	fair	*86 ½	S	fair. *in the passage below 86°			
16	**78	SSW	fair	86	S	fair			
17	80	SW	fair	86	WSW	fair 6 oC. moderate shower of rain from WSW			
18	76	SW b[y] W	somewhat cloudy	84 ½	NNE	fair			
19	78	NNE	fair	86 ½	WSW	fair			
20	78	SSW	fair	88 ½	SSW	fair			
21	78	NE	somewhat cloudy	85	SW	thunder cloud in WSW & a very slight shower of rain			
22	77	SW	fair, between 2 & 3 oC. P.M. shower of rain from thunder clouds NW of great extent	77 ½	NE	somewhat cloudy			
23	76	W	somewhat cloudy. between 2 & 3 oC. shower of rain moderate	82	E	fair, between 10 & 4 oC. P.M. heavy rain			
24	74	N.E	thick & misty. 8 oC. beging. to rain	73	NE	still thick & raining moderately with intermissions			

** window up during this month

536

Date	Temp	Wind	Weather	Temp	Wind	Weather	Remarks
June 25	72	NE	still thick & misty, 9 oC. A.M. fair	77	NNE	fair	
26	74	SSW	somewhat foggy	83	SE	fair	
27	77	N	cloudy & damp	79	NNE	fair	
28	67	NNE	fair	74	E	fair	
29	66	SW	fair	78	W	fair	
30	70	W	fair	79 ½	SSW	fair	
July 1	73	SW	fair	82	WSW	fair	Harvest of Wheat begun
2	74	SW	fair	84	SSW	fair	
3	75	SW	fair	82	W	moderate shower	
4				83	NE	shower in the night	
5	78	SW	fair	80	S	showery	From 8 to 9 oC. P.M. lightng. almost without intermission without thunder just above horison E.
6	77	S	foggy	86 ½	NW	moderate shower	
7	78	W	fair	86	SW	fair	
8	79 ½	SW	somewhat cloudy	86	NE	fair	Cimblings first at table
9	79 ½	SE	fair, between 1 & 2 oC. P.M. light shower	80 ½	N	somewhat cloudy	Cucumbers first at table
10	74	N	somewhat cloudy	81.	ESE	fair	
11	75	SSW	somewhat cloudy	85	SSW	fair	
12	72	N	fair	75 ½	NNE	fair	
13	72	W	fair	78	W by S	somewhat cloudy	
14	72 ½	WSW	somewhat cloudy	80	E	fair	

1785	Ther: sunrise	Wind sunrise	Weather sunrise	Thermr. 4 oC. p.m.	Wind do.	Weather 4 oC. P.M.	Shooting or falling of leaves of trees: flowers, other remarkable plants	Appearance or disappearance of birds &c.	Miscellanea
[July] 15	72 ½	S	somewhat cloudy 7 oC. A.M. dash of rain	73	NE	fine shower from NE			
16	72	W	foggy	80	SSW	fair			
17	72	SW	somewhat cloudy	79	SSW	fair			Appearance of [Sawyers?] first noted
18	72 ½	NW	cloudy	78	NNE	fair			
19	67 ½	N	fair	78	SSW	fair			
20	72	S	somewhat cloudy	70	SSW	dash of rain			
21	73	SW	cloudy	79	WSW	small thunder cloud WSW bearing S.			
22	75	SW	fair, between 2 & 3 oC. thunder shower from NW	79	W	fair			
23	75	SW	fair	79	SW	fair			
24	72	E	fair	78	SW	fair			
25	71	N	somewhat cloudy	77	SW	fair			
26	74	SW	cloudy ½ after 5 oC. beging. to rain moderately	76	E	breaking away after a moderate rain, 5 oC. shower of rain			Tobacco re-planted
27	73	SSW	thick fog	84 ½	N	somewhat cloudy			
28	76	SSW	fair	84 ½	S	somewhat cloudy			
29	75	NW	fair	78 ½	NW	somewhat cloudy, 5 oC small shower			

Date	Temp	Wind	Weather	Temp	Wind	Weather
30	66 ½	NW	fair	75	NE	fair
31	67	E	fair	77	SW	fair
Aug: 1.	69 ½	SW	fair	80	W by S	fair
2	72	SSW	fair	86	S	fair, ½ of 7 oCl. fine shower
3	76	SW	somewhat cloudy	80	NE	thundershower passing SE.wardly
4	71	NE	somewhat cloudy	78	N.	fair
5	71 ½	SE	cloudy	76	SE	cloudy
6	74	SW	cloudy, ½ past 3 oC. PM. thunder cloud passing SEwardly	82 ½	N	fair
7	75	W by S	fair	76 ½	NW	fair
8	62	N	fair	74 ½	NE	fair
9	64	N	fair	77 ½	SSE	fair
10	67	SW	fair	83 ½	SW	fair
11	73	NW	fair	83 ½	SW	fair
12	71 ½	[E?]	fair	82	S	sky muddy
13	75	S	fair	87	S	fair
14	76	SE	NW horison muddy	80	NE	somewhat cloudy
15	74	N	fair	82	E by N	fair
16	77	E	somewhat cloudy & air moist	82 ½	SE	fair
17	78	SW	foggy & cloudy	87	S.S.W.	fair, except NW horison darkish
18	79	S	fair	88	SW	thunder clouds towards NNE & SSW

1785		Ther: sunrise	Wind sunrise	Weather sunrise	Thermr. 4 oC. p.m.	Wind do.	Weather 4 oC. P.M.	Shooting or falling of leaves of trees: flowers, other remarkable plants	Appearance or disappearance of birds &c.	Miscellanea
Augt.	19	78	SE	cloudy	79 ½	E	somewhat cloudy			saw at Mr. Thoms. Scotts in Culpeper 44 young snakes sweezed out of large snake called the Water Macooson. They were from 5 to nine inches long, but expired in a few minutes after being in the air.
	20	74	NE	foggy	82	E	fair			
	21	74	SW.	foggy	79½	SE	somewhat cloudy dripping rain from 7 oC. AM			
	22	77	SSW	cloudy, between 3 & 4 oC. A.M. small shower of rain	75	SSW				
	23	73	NE	very cloudy & damp (from 8 to 9 oC. A.M. moderate rain[)]	72	NE	cloudy			
	24	70	N	fair	76	E	fair			
	25	69	SW	fair	80	SW	fair			
	26	69	NE	fair	70	SSW	fair			
	27	72	SW	somewhat cloudy	81	SW	fair			
	28	74	SW	cloudy & damp after very rainy night	75	NE	very black cloud to the North			

Date	Temp	Wind	Observation	Temp	Wind	Observation
2	38	E	somewhat cloudy	50	S	fair
3	38	SW	somewhat cloudy	48	E	cloudy 6 oC. beginning to snow
4	43	NE	cloudy	45 ½	NE	cloudy & small mixture of snow & rain falling
5	44	NE	ground thinly covered with snow & snowing	47	NW	fair
6	40	W	ground covered in spots only G. Mount. covd.			
7	44	SW	fair	58	SSW	fair
8	52	SE	somewhat cloudy	53 ½	SW	somewhat cloudy
9	48	SW	fair	55	S.W.	fair
10	49	SW	fair, atmosphere somewhat thick		SW	fair, very warm
11	49	NE	cloudy, ½ after 12 oC. begins to snow	49	NE	continues to snow
12	40	N	clouds breaking snow 4 inches deep	44	NE by E	cloudy
13	39	SE	cloudy	42	SSE	cloudy, snowing NWestwardly. 7 oC. begins to snow
14	40	NE	snowing 8 oC. Clouds breaking, fall of snow 5 inch	47	W	fair
15	40	E	cloudy	45	S	cloudy & damp 7 oC. snowing
16	40	NE	broken clouds, fall of snow 2 ½ inches	50	SW by W	fair

1786		Thermr. sun-rise	Wind sun-rise	Weather sunrise	Thermr. oC. P.M.	Wind do.	Weather 4 oC. P.M.	Shooting or falling of leaves of trees: flowers, other remarkable plants	Appearance or disappearance of birds &c.	Miscellanea
Feby:	17	44	S	somewhat cloudy	53	S	fair			
	18	52	SW	somewhat cloudy	59	SW	cloudy & moist			
	19	46	NE	somewhat cloudy	48	E	clouding up, 8 oC snowing			
	20	44	SE	rainy, ground nearly covered with mixture of snow & sleet	46	SW	cloudy & misty, snow gone			
	21	41	NW	fair	47	N	fair			
	22	43	W	cloudy	47	W	cloudy			
	23	41	NE	snowing	46	NE	still snowing, melting in part as it falls			
	24	39	NW	fair, Snow 1 ½ inches deep.	42	NW	fair, snow nearly gone			
	25	32*	SW	fair* in open air Thermr. at 21°	42	SW	sky muddy			
	26	36	W	fair	45	SW	sky muddy			
	27	41	SW	somewhat cloudy	48	NW	fair & windy			
	28	38	N	fair	44	SW	cloudy			
March.	1	42	SE	foggy, ground dashed with snow during the night	52	E	somewhat cloudy			
	2	44	NE	snowing	45	NE	still snowing			
	3	37	W	cloudy, snow 7 inches deep	37	N	broken clouds with showers of snow on the Blue Ridge			

March 4	31	W	fair	39	N	somewhat cloudy		
5	35	N	fair	42	NE	cloudy		
6	39	NE	cloudy	44	NNE	somewhat cloudy after 4 to 6 oC. shower of snow		
7	41	NW	fair	44	NW	somewhat cloudy		
8	43	SW	somewhat cloudy, 12 oC. small dash of snow	46	SW	somewhat cloudy		
9	40	NW	fair	45	W	fair, windy		
10	38	NW	fair	47	W	fair		
11	40	NE	fair	50	NE	fair		
12	44	W	fair	52	NE	cloudy		
13	48	NE	somewhat cloudy	53	E	cloudy		
14	45	E	sky muddy	50	E	cloudy		(14) 6 weeks peas, forward do. & Windsor beans [own]
15	47	NE	rainy	49	NE	still rainy		
16	48	SW	fair	67	W	fair		
17	52	SW	somewhat cloudy	56	W	cloudy & moist.		
18	50	NE	fair	55	N	fair		
19	48	SW	fair	53	E	cloudy		(19) Crow black birds first observed
20	46	NE	cloudy	48	NE	showery	Pionies shooting	
21	48	N	fair	58	NW	fair windy		(21) Martins appear
22	51	NW	fair	59	SW	somewhat cloudy	White Hyacinth blossoming	
23	44	W	fair		NW	blusdering & moist flying clouds		remarkable aurora borealis

1786	Thermr. sun–rise	Wind sun–rise	Weather sunrise	Thermr. 4 oC. P.M.	Wind do.	Weather 4 oC. P.M.	Shooting or falling of leaves of trees: flowers, other remarkable plants	Appearance or disappearance of birds &c.	Miscellanea
[March] 24	47	NW	fair	57	WSW	fair	Blue Hyacinth blossoming Peach trees blossoming in high situations		
25	52	SW	fair	70	SW	fair, smokey	Jonquils blossoming		
26	58	SW	very smokey	70 ½	SW	very smokey			
27	58	NE	cloudy, ground moist from shower in night	50	W	flying clouds, with showers of snow on blue ridge			
28	45	SW	fair	55	SW	fair	Cherry trees blossoming		
29	50	S	cloudy	60	S	sky muddy NW	Garden peas coming up		
30	60	S:	cloudy & moist	64	SE	somewhat cloudy	Daffadil blossoming		
31	62	NE	cloudy & foggy	57	E	very light rain			

Ms notebook (PPAmP). The Ms is kept in a slipcase volume labeled "Meteorological Journal of James Madison, 1784–1793." The first page of the notebook carries an unidentified writer's explanation: "Amer Philos Socy Meteorological Journal MS of Jas Madison at his plantation 1783–88 recd. 1839." Entries from 10 May to 7 July 1784 were kept by other members of the family. Insignificant changes in wording, spelling, and punctuation in the column headings have been disregarded.

INDEX

The Papers of James Madison

DESIGNED BY JOHN B. GOETZ
COMPOSED BY THE UNIVERSITY OF CHICAGO PRESS
IN LINOTYPE JANSON WITH DISPLAY LINES IN
MONOTYPE JANSON AND CASLON OLD STYLE
PRINTED BY THE UNIVERSITY OF CHICAGO PRESS
ON WARREN'S UNIVERSITY TEXT, A PAPER WATERMARKED
WITH JAMES MADISON'S SIGNATURE AND MADE EXPRESSLY
FOR THE VOLUMES OF THIS SET
PLATES PRINTED BY MERIDEN GRAVURE COMPANY
BOUND BY A. C. ENGDAHL IN COLUMBIA BAYSIDE LINEN